CHEAP SLEEP GUIDE TO

KATIE WOOD was born and educ
read Communications then English at university.
freelance journalist before specializing in travel in 1981. Since then
she has written some 28 guidebooks on topics ranging from family
holidays to the environmental and social impacts of tourism. Her
books have been universally praised for their practical, down-to-
earth approach and the quality of her research.

A fellow of the Royal Geographical Society, Katie continues to
write freelance for various publications, including the *Scotsman*, and
is Travel Correspondent for Scottish Television – a position which
takes her all over the world. She is also BBC Scotland's regular
resident expert for the radio show 'Travel Time'.

She currently lives in Perthshire, Scotland with her husband and
two children.

CHEAP SLEEP GUIDE TO EUROPE 1995

Katie Wood

Researcher: Neil Curtis

📖 HarperCollins*Publishers*

HarperCollins
An Imprint of HarperCollinsPublishers,
77–85 Fulham Palace Road,
Hammersmith, London W6 8JB

9 8 7 6 5 4 3 2 1

Copyright © Katie Wood 1992, 1993, 1994, 1995

The Author asserts the moral right to
be identified as the author of this work

A catalogue record for this book is
available from the British Library

ISBN 0 00 638379 3

Set in Meridien by
Rowland Phototypesetting Limited
Bury St Edmunds, Suffolk

Printed in Great Britain by
HarperCollinsManufacturing Glasgow

CONTENTS

INTRODUCTION

The single most difficult thing when travelling round Europe on a budget is to find a clean, safe and comfortable place to lay your head come nightfall. Whether you're Inter-Railing, hitching, cycling, bussing or driving round the continent, unless you want to follow a strict timetable and book beds ahead (and you can rarely book the real budget ones anyway), your main headache is going to be getting accommodation sorted out.

In the main cities and resorts in high season, you'll soon begin to feel as if you're back in the school nativity play again – the Mary and Joseph 'no room at the inn' syndrome really gets to you after a while, as you trail round the streets looking for a suitable pension, hostel or campsite. It's not much to ask, you grumble to anyone who'll listen, a bed for under £10 a night, preferably nearer £5. But the trouble these days is that so many people are 'doing Europe' using the same guidebooks, that supply never meets the demand. Or does it? Well, there actually *are* enough places, it's all a matter of knowing where to look. In your home town, you could probably find beds for £5–8 without a problem. But that's because you would *know* where to look, whereas a tourist in your town would never find it so simple. And that's the position, a stranger, that you will be in many times in Europe.

This book can be your guide to the 'inside knowledge' that a local has. I've stayed in more than my fair share of dives, from a house of ill-repute in Casablanca (not a lot of sleep that night!) to what turned out to be a hippy commune in Denmark (you thought no one said 'far-out, man' any longer?). Neither were experiences I'd repeat, but as the wrinklies say, 'If I'd known then what I know now . . .' So as I slap on the vitamin E cream, you might as well have the benefit of my good and bad experiences now.

This guide is written as a reaction to the literally hundreds of letters I receive each year from readers of my *Europe by Train* guide. You asked for more accommodation suggestions – well, now you've got them, in a book dedicated exclusively to this subject. And as I've listed so many, it should spread *Cheap Sleep* readers more thinly and at least give each of you a chance of getting that pack off your back and putting your feet up, after a long day's travelling. I know, after a couple of hours searching, in true biblical style, you'd even settle for a stable.

This guide covers all types of cheap accommodation: pensions; hostels; campsites; sleep-ins; student hostels; campus accommodation; private accommodation with families; and, if all else fails, 'safe' places to sleep rough. The recommendations will obviously vary in quality and price, but they are all the cheapest around in that country — it's just a fact that a 'cheap sleep' in Norway will cost you three times what it will in Turkey.

In terms of hierarchy and which type of accommodation suits who, basically, **hotels**, **pensions** and **B&Bs** are usually the most expensive, but they are also one of the most comfortable options. About the same price, and an excellent way of finding out more about the locals, is to stay with them direct: **private accommodation** is generally arranged through Tourist Offices. Effectively you become a paying guest, mixing with the family and getting the opportunity to ask all the questions about their lifestyle and culture that you otherwise might not have had the chance to. Private and HI **hostels** are pretty much on a par in terms of price. If a private hostel is offering rates half that of the local HI, it's generally because standards are extremely low.

Sleep-Ins and **YMCA/YWCA Interpoints** are fairly recent developments. Very reasonably priced, and an excellent way to meet other travellers, the only problem is that they're limited to certain locations in Europe. **Camping** is fine if you're the outdoor type and are experienced in pitching a tent and cooking over a camping stove. Official camping is obviously more regimented than 'freelance' camping, but as the latter is illegal in some countries (I state which in the guide), the choice is often made for you. Always clean up after yourself and seek permission from the landowner, wherever you are. Using **student halls of residence** is a good way to get round Europe. It's cheap, they're well equipped, and you meet other travellers. Tourist Offices have details.

If you come across a place suggested in this guide that has dropped standards, upped prices or is definitely not worth recommending any longer, please drop me a line and let me know. Likewise, if you find a little gem, pass on the info so we can all benefit. Particularly in Eastern Europe, where the demand for cheap beds now exceeds supply ten times over, we could all do with other travellers' hints and help.

However you do it, wherever you get to, I sincerely hope this much-requested guide will help you.

KATIE WOOD
Perthshire, Scotland
December 1994

AUSTRIA (Österreich)

Despite being widely regarded as one of the most expensive countries to visit, accommodation prices in Austria are reasonable, especially when the quality of the places to stay is taken into account. The standard of all types of accommodation in Austria is high, with impeccable levels of cleanliness almost guaranteed. With only a few exceptions, finding moderately priced accommodation on arrival is relatively easy in most places throughout the year. As the student hostels and HI hostels do not open until July, late June can be a particularly bad time for those looking for inexpensive accommodation in the cities. Finding somewhere cheap to stay in Vienna can be tricky at any time of the year, while Salzburg becomes very crowded during its summer festival (late July–August). However, as there are reasonably cheap rooms available in the cities, and plenty of hostel beds, you can save yourself frustration on arrival (and probably money as well) by taking the trouble to book ahead. If you have not booked in advance, it might be advisable to take a tent, even if only for use in emergencies.

Hotels are graded from one star up to five stars. In general, hotel prices are higher in the cities (especially Vienna) and in the Alpine resorts, so unless you are travelling extensively, hotels are likely to be beyond your budget in most places you visit. Away from the main tourist towns and resorts, a double in a one-star hotel generally costs from 400AS upwards per person (£24; $36), but in the more popular tourist areas prices for a similar room start around 700AS p.p. (£42; $63). As hoteliers try to fill their rooms outside the peak-season months of July to August, prices may be reduced: in May, June and September by 15–25%, and by up to 40% for the rest of the year. **Pensions**, seasonal hotels and *Gästhauser* are cheaper than hotels. These are graded from one star up to four stars, with a two-star pension being the rough equivalent of a one-star hotel. Outside Vienna, prices for doubles are normally under 400AS (£24; $36). Unfortunately, these tend to fill up quickly during the busy periods.

Private rooms and **Gästhauser** can be booked through some Tourist Offices, or through private organizations which control a number of rooms. Alternatively, simply approach the owner of any house or farmhouse displaying a sign saying '*Zimmer frei*', or showing a stylized white bed on a green background. In the cities and resorts expect to pay from 300–400AS (£18–24; $27–36) for doubles. Elsewhere, 150–200AS for a single (£9–12; $13.50–18.00), 200–350AS (£12–21; $18.00–31.50) for doubles is the normal price range. Travellers staying only one night may be liable to a small surcharge. The overnight price usually includes a continental breakfast.

At some **farms** it is possible to rent apartments. Most sleep from three to five people, but occasionally larger apartments are available. Assuming you fill all the bed space, you can expect to pay from 150–200AS each per night (£9–12; $13.50–18.00) in the summer. During the winter months prices rise slightly, adding perhaps another 20AS (£1.20; $1.80) per night to the bill. The minimum length of stay permissible in farm accommodation seems to vary between regions. In the Tyrol it is only possible to pre-book for a week at a time, but in other areas stays of one night seem quite acceptable. If there is a train station nearby, farm accommodation can make a good base for exploring the surrounding area.

There are about a hundred **HI hostels** spread over the country, covering all the main places of interest. Many are only open for the period between April/May and September/October, while some open only during July and August. Providing there is space, stays of longer than three days are allowed. The large city hostels can be very institutional, but in the rural areas hostels can be a bit more easygoing, although the 10 p.m. curfew will probably be strictly enforced. In city hostels there is usually a midnight curfew. In general, prices vary from 140–190AS (£8.40–11.40; $12.50–17.00), usually with breakfast. Higher prices are sometimes charged at the large city hostels, which seek to attract groups by providing a range of facilities that may be of little interest to the budget traveller. As a result, they tend to be monopolized by these groups. It is advisable to have an HI card. While some hostels may let you stay for a 25AS surcharge (£1.50; $2.25), the hostels in Vienna are for members only, as is the main hostel in Innsbruck.

You will also find a few **independent hostels** in the main towns. These are mainly seasonal (May/June to September/October). Unfortunately, curfews are usually just as restrictive as those of their HI counterparts. Prices for dormitory accommodation are similar to the HI hostels, but some of the independent hostels also offer singles and doubles, with prices ranging from 130–220AS (£7.80–13.20; $11.70–19.80) per person. Similar prices are charged for accommodation in the various **student residences** that are let out for periods between July and September. Some are run by students themselves, and a much more relaxed atmosphere usually prevails in these establishments.

It is easy to recommend **camping** in Austria, as the campsites are among the best in Europe. Charges at the 450 sites are reasonable, given that they are immaculately maintained and have all the necessary facilities. Pitching a tent costs 50–150AS (£3–9; $4.50–13.50) and there is a similar fee per occupant. The International Camping Carnet is not obligatory, but holders qualify for reductions at most sites. All the main towns have at least one campsite, and there are plenty of sites in the countryside. Except in Vienna and Linz, the city sites are all within walking distance of the centre. One site in Vienna stays open all year round, but elsewhere even the city sites only open for a period between Easter/May and September/October.

Freelance camping is allowed, but you must first obtain the consent of the local *Bürgermeister*, or the landowner. Avoid lighting fires in or around woodland. Camping rough is a useful option for those planning to do a bit of walking along the excellent network of hiking trails. Be sure to have a good quality sleeping bag, as it gets very cold at night. For anyone planning to hike extensively in the Alps, there are about seven hundred mountain huts, with 25,000 sleeping places (beds, or mattresses on the floor to put your sleeping bag on). Even if all the places are filled, it is unlikely that you will be turned away. All the huts have at least rudimentary kitchen facilities, and many serve meals. Joining one of the clubs might save you money in the long run. The largest is the Österreichischer Alpenverein, which offers its members discounts of 30–60% on the normal overnight prices of 60–180AS (£3.60–10.80; $5.40–16.20), plus reduced prices on various cable-car trips and organized outings. Membership costs about 300AS (£18; $27) for under 26s, 400AS (£24; $36) otherwise. If you are going hiking in the east of the country, it might be better to get in touch with the Österreichischer Touristenklub.

Note: The Austrian telephone network is being converted to a digital system, so numbers may change without notice. Check with the local tourist office if listed numbers are incorrect.

ADDRESSES

Austrian National Tourist Office	30 Saint George Street, London, W1R 0AL (tel. 0171 629 0461)
Austrian YHA Österreichische Jugendherbergsverband	Schottenring 28, 1010 Wien (tel. 0222 533 5353) List from the Austrian National Tourist Office.
Camping Österreichischer Camping Club	Johannesgasse 20, 1010 Wien. List from the Austrian National Tourist Office.

Farm accommodation   Various regional lists available from the
                      Austrian National Tourist Office.

Mountain huts   Österreichischer Alpenverein,
                      Wilhelm-Greil-straße 15, Innsbruck
                      6020 (tel. 05222 584107).
                      Austrian Alpine Club, Getreidemarkt 3,
                      1060 Wien (tel. 0222 563 8673). The UK
                      branch is at Longcroft House, Fretherne
                      Road, Welwyn Garden City, Herts.,
                      AL8 6PQ (tel. 01707 324835).
                      Österreichischer Touristenklub (ÖTK),
                      1 Backerstraße 16, Wien
                      (tel. 0222 523844).

Graz (tel. code 0316)

TOURIST OFFICE
Grazer Tourismus, Herrengasse 16, A-8010 Graz (tel. 835241). A
10–15 minute walk from the train station. Go right from the
station, left along Annenstraße, straight through Südtirolerplatz
and over the River Mur. Murgasse leads into the Hauptplatz, from
which you go right after about 250m. Alternatively, take tram 3
from Europaplatz to the right of the train station.

HOTELS
Cheapest doubles around 290AS (£17.40; $26)

Frühstuckspension Kugerl-Lukas, Waagner-Biro-Straße 8 (tel.
52590). Go right from Graz Hbf, right through the underpass,
then right again. A few minutes' walk.
Gasthof Dorrer, Steinberstraße 41 (tel. 52647). Well out from the
centre, in the north-western part of the city.

Cheapest doubles around 440AS (£26.40; $39.60)

Gasthof Schmid Greiner, Grabenstraße 64 (tel. 681482). A 15–20
minute walk from Graz Hbf. Go down Keplerstraße, across the
river and straight on until you see Grabenstraße on the left.
Gasthof Dokterbauer, Krottendorferstraße 91 (tel. 284235). In
Graz-West, far from the town centre.
Gasthof Saringer, Gaisbergweg 7 (tel. 53514). In the north-west of
the city, well out from the centre.

Cheapest doubles around 470AS (£28.20; $42.30)

Gasthof Kokol, Thalstraße 3 (tel. 53329). In Graz-Nord, far from
the centre.
Gasthof Kehlberghof, Kehlbergstraße 83 (tel. 284125). In Graz-
West, far from the city centre.

PRIVATE ROOMS
Rooms around 130AS (£7.80; $11.70) per person

Geiger, Waltendorfer Hauptstraße 199a, Waltendorf (tel. 464160).
tram 3 from Graz Hbf to Krenngasse.
Puchleitner, Kainbach 155, Ries (tel. 301 6685). From the crossroads right of Graz Hbf take tram 7 heading down Annenstraße
to the terminus in St Leonhard.

Cheapest rooms around 160AS (£9.60; $14.40) per person

Prugger, Riesstraße 96c, Ries (tel. 378642). Same direction as Puchleitner above. Walk up Riesstraße from the tram terminus.
Stampfl, Muhl 27, Stattegg (tel. 691956). From Hauptplatz (see
Tourist Office above) take tram 4 or 5 to Andritz.
Sagmeister, Purgleitnerstraße 17, Jakomini (tel. 440225). Local
train to Graz Ostbahnhof, or tram 6 from Graz Hbf to the junction
of Munzgrabenstraße and Moserhofgasse. Purgleitnerstraße is
parallel to the right of Brucknerstraße, which runs off Munzgrabenstraße.

Cheapest rooms around 180AS (£10.80; $16.20) per person

Maier, Zinsdorfgasse 16, Geidorf (tel. 348353). Bus 31 to Zinsen-
dorfgasse, or bus 63 to Universität.
Hofer, Richard Wagnerstraße 13 (tel. 383408). Bus 31 to
Kreuzgasse.

Rooms around 200AS (£12; $18) per person

Weinzettl, Drosselweg 7 (tel. 432752). Tram 3 from Graz Hbf to
Krenngasse.

HI HOSTEL
Idlhofgasse 74 (tel. 914876). 110AS (£6.60; $9.90) in 8-bedded
dorms, 170AS (£10.20; $15.30) in 4-bedded rooms. Five minutes'
walk from the train station. On leaving the station turn right along

Bahnhofgurtel, left up Josef-Huber-Gasse, then right into Idlhofgasse.

CAMPING

Graz-Nord (tel. 627622). Open May—Sept. From the crossroads to the right of Graz Hbf take tram 7 heading down Eggenberger-straße to the terminus on Burenstraße in Baiersdorf. Go down Burgenlandstraße, and straight on until you see the camping area.

Central, Graz-Strassgang (tel. 281831). Open April—Oct. From Hauptplatz (see **Tourist Office** above) take tram 4 or 5 to the junction of Theodor-Körner-Straße and Robert-Stolz-Gasse. Go to the right up Stolz-Gasse. The campsite is on the other side of Grabenstraße, a short walk to the right.

Innsbruck (tel. code 0512)

TOURIST OFFICES

Tourismusverband Innsbruck-Igls, Burggraben 3, 6021 Innsbruck. Contact this office in advance for information. On arrival, you can book accommodation or obtain information at Innsbruck Information at the same address (tel. 5356). Open daily 8 a.m.–7 p.m. Another branch operates at the main train station (Innsbruck Hbf) (tel. 583766). Open daily 9 a.m.–10 p.m. If you are arriving by car or motorbike, there are offices providing information and accommodation services on all the main routes into Innsbruck. The commission for booking rooms at any of the offices above is 25AS (£1.50; $2.25).

HOTELS

Prices quoted are per person. However, solo travellers can usually expect a supplement to be added to these prices.
Cheapest prices 190–225AS (£11.40–13.50; $17–20.25)

Ferrarihof, Brennerstraße 8 (tel. 580968). Tram 1 to the Bergisel terminus or a 15-minute walk from Innsbruck Hbf.

Glockenhaus, Weiherburggasse 3 (tel. 286515).

Laurin, Gumppstraße 19 (tel. 41104). Tram 3 from Innsbruck Hbf to Gumppstraße, or a 10-minute walk, left off Amraserstraße shortly after crossing the Sill.

Paula, Weiherburggasse 35 (tel. 292262).

Rimml, Harterhofweg 82 (tel. 284726). Far from the centre, off the main road to Seefeld in the suburb of Kranebitten. Bus LK to Kranebitten.

Engl, Innstraße 22 (tel. 283112). On the opposite bank of the river to the Old Town.

Innbrücke, Innstraße 1 (tel. 281934).

Cheapest prices 230–250AS (£13.80–15; $20.70–22.50)

Gartenhotel Putzker, Layrstraße 2 (tel. 281912). Bus F to Fischnalerstraße (across Fürstenweg from Layrstraße) or a 15–20-minute walk from Innsbruck Hbf. Near the St Anne column go down Anichstraße, and then follow Blasius-Hueber-Straße across the Inn. Turn left along Fürstenweg, and then right at Layrstraße.

Goldenes Brünnl, St Nikolaus-Gasse 1 (tel. 283519). Bus K to Innstraße, or a 15-minute walk from Innsbruck Hbf. Cross the river by the Innbrücke and head right along Innstraße until you see St Nicholas-Gasse on the left.

Ölberg, Höhenstraße 52 (tel. 286125). A long walk from the station in the hills above the suburb of Hotting. Bus N to Ölberg from Innsbruck Hbf.

Innrain, Innrain 38 (tel. 588981). A 10-minute walk from Innsbruck Hbf. Follow Marktgraben to the start of Innrain.

Lisbeth, Dr Glatz-Straße 24 (tel. 41107). Bus S or K to Dr Glatz-Straße then left down the street from the way the bus was travelling. Or take tram 3 to the Dr Glatz-Straße stop on Amraserstraße (the tram stop is slightly further away). A 15–20-minute walk from Innsbruck Hbf: right off Amraserstraße, or left off Burgenlandstraße.

Bergisel, Bergisel 2 (tel. 581912). A three-star hotel with only a few rooms at these prices. A 15-minute walk from Innsbruck Hbf or tram 1 to the Bergisel terminus.

Bistro, Pradlerstraße 2 (tel. 46319). Bus R to Pradlerstraße or a 10-minute walk from Innsbruck Hbf. Left off Amraserstraße down Defreggerstraße shortly after crossing the Sill, then left along Pradlerstraße.

Goldener Winkel, Reichenauer Straße 16 (tel. 46368). Bus R to Pradlerstraße, or a 12-minute walk from Innsbruck Hbf.

Eckenried, Mühlan-Eckenried 9 (tel. 267319).

Cheapest prices around 260–290AS (£15.25–17.40; $22.80–26)

Hotel-Pension Binder, Dr Glatz-Straße 20 (tel. 42236). See Lisbeth (above) for directions.

Riese Haymon, Haymongasse 4 (tel. 589837). About 12 minutes' walk from Innsbruck Hbf. At the junction of Südbahnstraße and Leopoldstraße, Rotes Gassl is diagonally opposite. Haymongasse is left off Rotes Gassl.

Heis, Dorfgasse 9 (tel. 285345). Bus A to Daxgasse, then a short walk up that street into Dorfgasse, or a 20-minute walk from Innsbruck Hbf. Cross the Inn by the Innbrücke, head away from the river up Höttingergasse, left at the top of the street, and then right at Dorfgasse.

Menghini, Beda-Weber-Gasse 29 (tel. 41243). Bus S or K to Dr Glatz-Straße. Follow the street right from the direction the bus was travelling, right along Kaufmannstraße, then first left into Beda-Weber-Gasse. A 20-minute walk from Innsbruck Hbf: left off Südbahnstraße along Karmelitengasse, left over the Olympiabrücke and straight on to Burgenlandstraße, then right down Wetterherrenweg, before going left at Beda-Weber-Gasse.

Neuhauser, Exlgasse 49 (tel. 284185). Bus B to Exlgasse from Innsbruck Hbf, bus F to Angergasse then a short walk back to Exlgasse. A long way from Innsbruck Hbf, but only a few minutes' walk from the Höttinger Bahnhof.

Stoi, Salurner Straße 7 (tel. 585434). A few minutes' walk from Innsbruck Hbf. The street leads away from the station at the left hand end of Südtiroler Platz. You will probably have to book at least two weeks in advance though.

Oberrauch, Leopoldstraße 35 (tel. 587881). Just over five minutes' walk from the station. Head off Südbahnstraße down Mentlgasse on to Leopoldstraße, then a short walk right.

PRIVATE ROOMS
Cheapest prices around 140AS (£8.40; $12.60) per person

Elisabeth Mayr, Pradler Saggen 3 (tel. 449243). Bus R to Paulus-kirche, or a 15−20 minute-walk from the station. At the end of König-Laurin-Straße turn right along Dreiheiligenstraße, across the Sill then left along Kärnterstraße beside the river. Pradler Saggen is in from the river, just beyond Prinz-Eugen-Straße.

Cheapest prices around 150−170AS (£9−10.20; $13.50−15.30) per person

Anna Hueber, Oberkoflerweg 16 (tel 267655). Open July−Oct. Bus C, D or E to Anton-Rauch-Strasse, or a 25-minute walk from Innsbruck Hbf. Over the Mühlauer Brucke, up Anton-Rauch-Strasse, and then left at Oberkoflerweg.

Agnes Lechthaler, Luigenstraße 39 (tel. 439103). Near Schloß

Amras. Bus K to Amras, or a 30-minute walk from Innsbruck Hbf. Right off Amraser Seestraße down Geyrstraße into Luigenstraße.

Hermine Rofner, Plonergasse 10 (tel. 437935). Open June—Sept. Bus S or K to Dr Glatz-Straße. Walk down the street to the right of the direction the bus was travelling, left at Kaufmannstraße then left almost immediately into Plonergasse. A 20-minute walk from Innsbruck Hbf. Follow directions for Hotel Menghini to Wetterherrenweg but turn left along Kaufmannstraße and then right at Plonergasse.

Friederike Aschaber, Pradler Saggen 5 (tel. 430384). Open July—Sept.

Josef Löffler, Purnhofweg 25 (tel. 205241).

Cheapest prices around 175—190AS (£10.50—11.40; $15.75—17) per person

NMJosefine Egger, Gumppstraße 57 (tel. 416075). A 10—15-minute walk from Innsbruck Hbf, left off Amraserstraße shortly after crossing the Sill, or tram 3 to Gumppstraße.

Anny Gastl, Prinz-Eugen-Straße 81 (tel. 447962). Bus R to Pauluskirche or about 20 minutes' walk from Innsbruck Hbf. Follow Reichenauerstraße until you see Prinz-Eugen-Straße on the left.

Trude Mader, Schloßstraße 10 (tel. 428504). Near Schloß Ambras. Tram 3 to the Amras terminus or a half-hour walk from Innsbruck Hbf.

Maria Rauschgatt, Karwendelstraße 6 (tel. 571410). Bus C or W to Karwendelstraße or a 20-minute walk from Innsbruck Hbf. At the junction of Südbahnstraße and Leopoldstraße cross over and take Anton-Melzer-Straße into Egger-Lienz-Straße from which you turn left down Fritz-Pregl-Straße into Karwendelstraße.

Ida Jende, Vögelebich 44 (tel. 277205). Open Dec.—Oct.

STUDENT RESIDENCES

Technikerhaus, Fischnalerstraße 26 (tel. 282110). Open July—Aug. Prices start around 228AS (£28.80; $43.20). Bus B to Technikerheim or a 20-minute walk from Innsbruck Hbf. Near the St Anne column take Anichstraße. Follow Blasius-Hueber-Straße across the Inn then turn left on Prandtauer Ufer along the river. Go right at Hutterweg then left along Santifallerstraße into Fischnalerstraße.

Internationales Studentenhaus, Rechengasse 7 (tel. 59477). Open JulySept. Prices start around 240AS (£14.40; $21.60). Follow directions for Technikerhaus to Blasius-Hueber-Straße, turn left along Innrain, then right at Rechengasse.

HI HOSTELS

Jugendherberge Innsbruck, Reichenauerstraße 147 (tel. 346179/ 180). Open all year. From 10 July–31 Aug. a temporary hostel operates at the same address in a student dormitory. Both charge around 160AS (£9.60; $14.40) for the first night, 130AS (£7.80; $11.70) per night thereafter. The overnight price includes breakfast and bed linen. Open to HI members only. Bus O or R to Campingplatz-Jugendherberge from Innsbruck Hbf or a 20-minute walk.

Torsten-Arneus-Schwedenhaus, Rennweg 17b (tel. 585814). Open July–Aug. Curfew 10 p.m. Members only. 100AS (£6; $9). Breakfast and sheets cost extra. Bus C to Handelsakademie from Innsbruck Hbf or a 15–20-minute walk.

Jugendherberge St Nikolaus & Glockenhaus, Innstraße 95 (tel. 286515). Open year round. Doubles and quads around 150AS (£9; $13.50) per person. Dormitory accommodation 130AS (£7.80; $11.70). Bus K to Schmelzergasse, or a 15–20-minute walk from Innsbruck Hbf.

Volkshaus Innsbruck, Radetzkystraße 47 (tel. 466682). Open all year. 100AS (£6; $9) without breakfast. Bus O or R to Radetzkystraße or a 15–20-minute walk from Innsbruck Hbf. Left off Reichenauerstraße.

PRIVATE HOSTELS

Jugendzentrum St Paulus, Reichenauerstraße 72 (tel. 44291). Open mid-June–mid-Aug. Curfew 10 p.m. Dorms 90AS (£5.40; $8) without breakfast. Bus R to Pauluskirche or about 15 minutes' walk from Innsbruck Hbf. See Jugendherberge HI hostel above for directions.

MK-Jugendzentrum, Sillgasse 8a (tel. 571311). Open July–mid-Sept. Curfew 11 p.m. 150AS (£9; $13.50) for B&B in dorms. Price falls by about a quarter after the first night. A 5-minute walk from Innsbruck Hbf, right of Museumstraße.

CAMPING

Innsbruck Kranebitten, Kranebitter Allee 214 (tel. 284180). Open Apr.–Oct. Far from the centre in the suburb of Kranebitten, just off the main road to Seefeld. Bus LK to Kranebitten.

Kitzbühel (tel. code 05356)

TOURIST OFFICE
Tourismusverband, Hinterstadt 18, 6370 Kitzbühel (tel. 2155/
2272). Open Mon.–Sat. 8.30 a.m.–7.30 p.m., Sun. 9 a.m.–5 p.m.
(off-season: 8.30 a.m.–12 p.m. and 3–6 p.m.). The Tourist Office
charges no commission for finding rooms. Just outside the door is
a free telephone you can use to make reservations for local accommodation. From Kitzbühel Hbf go straight down Bahnhofstraße,
left along Josef-Pirchl-Straße and then right at Hinterstadt. From
the other train station, Hahnenkamm, walk down Josef-Herold-
Straße into Vorderstadt, go left, then left again into Hinterstadt. Of
the two train stations, Hahnenkamm is the closest to the town
centre but not all trains stop at the station. Arriving from Innsbruck
or Wörgl the train reaches Hahnenkamm before Kitzbühel Hbf;
coming from Salzburg the train reaches Kitzbühel Hbf first.

ACCOMMODATION
The prices quoted below are for the summer high season (July–
Aug.) and are based on two people sharing a room. Supplements
for single rooms are shown where applicable. All prices below are
only valid for stays of three days and upwards. The vast majority
of the establishments listed below are either in the town centre or
on the fringes of the town (exceptions are noted). As the town is
small you will have no trouble getting to accommodation just outside on foot. Try to reserve these accommodation suggestions in
advance as their location ensures their popularity. Even if you cannot find a bed in one of these places you should still be able to find
accommodation relatively easily outside the winter season, as there
are literally thousands of rooms available in and around Kitzbühel,
though you will either have to pay higher prices to stay in the
town itself or stay a fair distance outside the town if you want
similarly priced accommodation.

PENSIONS
Cheapest price for B&B around 130AS (£7.80; $11.70) per person

Schmidinger, Ehrenbachgasse 13 (tel. 3134).

Cheapest price for B&B around 160AS (£9.60; $14.40) per person

Astlingerhof, Bichlnweg 11 (tel. 2775). Single supplement 30AS

(£1.80; $2.70). Out from the centre, off Jochbergerstraße (main road to Aurach and Jochberg).

Jodlhof, Aschbachweg 17 (tel. 3004). Just outside the town, near the hospital (Krankenhaus).

Hörl, Josef-Pirchl-Straße 60 (tel. 3144). Single supplement 20AS (£1.20; $1.80). See **Tourist Office** above.

Cheapest price for B&B around 170AS (£10.20; $15.30) per person

Eugenie, Pulverturmweg 3 (tel. 2820).

Reiwag, Josef-Pirchl-Straße 54 (tel. 2601). Single supplement 25AS (£1.50; $2.25). See **Tourist Office** above.

Cheapest price for B&B around 180AS (£10.80; $16.20) per person

Arnika, St Johannerstraße 31a (tel. 2338). Single supplement 20AS (£1.20; $1.80). Out from the town on the road to St Johanne. An easy walk from Kitzbühel Hbf. Turn right at the end of Bahnhofstraße.

Erlenhof, Burgstallstraße 27 (tel.2828). Just outside the town in Ecking. Single supplement 15AS (£0.90; $1.35).

Cheapest price for B&B around 190AS (£11.40; $17) per person

Karlberger, Hahnenkammstraße 9 (tel. 4003). Just outside the town in Ecking, near the Schischule Total.

Hebenstreit, Jodlfeld 1 (tel. 3022). Single supplement 50AS (£3; $4.50). Just outside the town, near the junction of Unterleitenweg and Aschbachweg.

Maria Hilde, Faistenbergerweg 3 (tel. 3130). Single supplement 20AS (£1.20; $1.80).

Cheapest price for B&B around 200–220AS (£12–13.20; $18–19.80) per person

Caroline, Schulgasse 7 (tel. 2274/71971). Off Josef-Herold-Straße. See **Tourist Office** above.

Entstraßer, Jochbergerstraße 93 (tel. 4884). Single supplement 20AS (£1.20; $1.80). Out from the town on the road to Aurach and Jochberg.

Christl, Webergasse 21 (tel. 2145). Single supplement 50AS (£3; $4.50).

Neuhaus, Franz-Reisch-Straße 23 (tel. 2200). Single supplement 30AS (£1.80; $2.70).

PRIVATE ROOMS
Cheapest price around 130AS (£7.80; $11.70) per person

Haus Wibmer, Webergasse 6 (tel. 3950). Single supplement 20AS
(£1.20; $1.80).

Cheapest price around 140AS (£8.40; $12.60) per person

Haus Gasteiger, Pfarrau 16 (tel. 2148). Just outside the town.
Haus Schmiedl, Im Gries 15 (tel. 2748). Single supplement 10AS
(£0.60; $0.90).

Cheapest price around 160AS (£9.60; $14.40) per person

Haus Koller, Knappengasse 16 (tel. 3165).
Wetti Schmidinger, Ehrenbachgasse 13 (tel. 3134). Single sup-
plement 20AS (£1.20; $1.80).
Haus Reiter, Hornweg 24 (tel. 53542).

Cheapest price around 170AS (£10.20; $15.30) per person

Restaurant Glockenspiel, Hinterstadt 13 (2nd floor) (tel. 2516).
Marienheim, Hornweg 8 (tel. 2092). Single supplement 20AS
(£1.20; $1.80).

Cheapest price around 180AS (£10.80; $16.20) per person

Haus Gantschnigg, Kirchgasse 25 (tel. 4358). Single supplement
30AS (£1.90; $2.70).
Haus Hain, Ehrenbachgasse 20 (tel. 2546).
Landhaus Resch, Alfons-Petzold-Weg 2a (tel. 41652).
Haus Haggenmuller, Josef-Herold-Straße 3 (tel. 4610/2709). See
Tourist Office above.

Cheapest price around 190–200AS (£11.40–12; $17–18) per person

Anna-Maria Hechenberger, Webergasse 3 (tel. 2487).
Gästehaus Reiter, Hammerschmiedstraße 5b (tel. 3124).
Haus Kasparek, Ehrenbachgasse 15 (tel. 4219). Single supplement
30AS (£1.80; $2.70).

FARMHOUSE ACCOMMODATION
Cheapest price around 150AS (£9; $13.50) per person

Eckinghof, Schwarzseestraße 5 (tel. 53263). Single supplement 20AS (£1.20; $1.80). Just outside the town in Ecking.

Cheapest price around 160AS (£9.60; $14.40) per person

Reiterhof, Malernweg 14 (tel. 4209). Single supplement 10AS (£0.60; $0.90). Just outside the town on the road to Högl.

HI HOSTEL
Oberndorf 64, Niederstraßeerhof (tel. 05352−3651).

CAMPING
Schwarzsee, Reitherstraße (tel. 2806/4479). 80AS (£4.80; $7.20), plus 65−72AS (£3.90; $5.85) per person and 6AS (£0.36; $0.55) per day. Open all year round. As the name suggests, the site is near the Schwarzsee, a fair distance from the town centre. The site is an easy walk from the Schwarzsee train station.

Salzburg (tel. code 0662)

TOURIST OFFICES
Fremdenverkehrsbetriebe der Stadt Salzburg, Auersperg Straße 7, A-5020 Salzburg (tel. 88987−0). Head office of the city tourist board. Contact this office for information in advance. The tourist board run six information centres in the city. A list of hotels and a list of private rooms are available from these offices.

Information Mozartplatz, Mozartplatz 5 (tel. 847568). In the centre of the Old Town. Open Mon.−Sat. 9 a.m.−6 p.m.; Sun. (Easter−Oct., Christmas only) 9 a.m.−8 p.m.

Information Hauptbahnhof (tel. 871712/873638). In the train station (platform 10). Open daily 8.30 a.m.−8 p.m. all year round.

Information Salzburg-Mitte, Münchner Bundesstraße 1 (tel. 432228/433110). Open daily Easter−Oct. (closed Sundays during winter). For traffic arriving from Munich.

Information Salzburg-Süd, Park & Ride Parkplatz, Alpenstraße (tel. 20966). Open daily Easter−Oct. (closed Sundays during winter). For traffic arriving from Carinthia and Steiermark.

Information Salzburg-Nord, Autobahnstation Kasern (tel. 663220).
Open Apr.–Oct. for traffic arriving from Vienna and Linz.

Information Salzburg-West, Flughafen, Innsbrucker Bundesstraße
95 (BP filling station) (tel. 852451). Open Apr.–Oct. Serves the
airport, and traffic arriving from Innsbruck.

BASIC DIRECTIONS

Salzburg Hbf and the bus station are right next to each other. From
the stations Rainerstraße heads down to Mirbellplatz, another
important bus terminal. Continuing straight on down Dreifaltig-
keitsgasse you arrive at the junction with Linzer Gasse just before
the Staatsbrücke crosses over the River Salzach. Crossing the bridge
and heading left along the riverside you can turn right at the next
bridge (Mozartsteg) into Mozartplatz. The walk from the train
station to Mirbellplatz takes about ten minutes, from the station to
the Salzach about fifteen minutes, and from the station to
Mozartplatz about twenty minutes. Buses 1, 2, 5, 6, 51 and 55 all
run from Salzburg Hbf to the Staatsbrücke, buses 5, 51 and 55
continue on to Mozartsteg.

FINDING ACCOMMODATION

Despite the fact that the city often seems very crowded during the
day you can usually find suitable accommodation without too
much trouble, as many people visit the city as part of a coach tour
and do not spend the night in Salzburg. However, accommodation
can be very difficult to find during the city's summer festival (late
July–Aug.). All the hostels fill rapidly at this time. Unless you
have a tent you may have to spend around 200AS (£12; $18) on
a private room (assuming there are any available), or even more
on a hotel. Prices in some hotels fall slightly outside the peak season
(May–Oct.).

HOTELS

Cheapest doubles around 340AS (£20.40; $30.60)

Junger Fuchs, Linzer Gasse 54 (tel. (875496). Singles start around
200AS (£12; $18). Prices fall slightly off-season. Left off Mir-
bellplatz at Schrannengasse, then right down Wolf-Dietrich-
Straße into Linzer Gasse, or a bus to the Staatsbrücke and walk
up Linzer Gasse.

Cheapest doubles around 380AS (£22.80; $34.20)

Sandwirt, Lastenstraße 6a (tel. 874351). Take the rear exit from the train station on to Lastenstraße and head right. A few minutes' walk.

Cheapest doubles around 400–420AS (£24–25.20; $36–37.80)

Noisternig, Innsbrucker Bundesstraße 57 (tel. 827646). Singles start at the same price. Bus 77 from Salzburg Hbf runs along the street, stopping 300m from the hotel. Buses 1 and 2 run around the town before stopping near the Post Office on Maxglaner Hauptstraße. Continue in the direction the bus was going and then turn left at Innsbrucker Bundesstraße, about 150m away.

Elisabeth, Vogelweiderstraße 52 (tel. 871664). Take the rear exit from the train station on to Lastenstraße, left, then sharp right at Weiserhofstraße, then left along Breitenfelderstraße into Vogelweiderstraße. Just under 10 minutes' walk. Bus 15 runs to the town centre from Vogelweiderstraße.

Merian, Merianstraße 40 (tel. 874006–11). Take the rear exit from the train station on to Lastenstraße, head right, then left down Merianstraße. About 8 minutes' walk. Bus 15 runs from the stop on Bayerhamerstraße to the town centre.

Hämmerle, Innsbrucker Bundesstraße 57a (tel. 827647). Singles start at 240AS (£14.40; $21.60). See Hotel Noisternig, above, for directions.

Haus Wartenberg, Riedenburgerstraße 2 (tel. 844284). Bus 1 or 2 from Salzburg Hbf to the stop on Neutorstraße after passing Leopoldskronstraße on the left. Then a 300m walk, on along Neutorstraße, right at Bayernstraße, then right again.

Cheapest doubles around 440–450AS (£26.40–27; $39.60–40.50)

Winkler, Linzer Bundesstraße 92 (tel. 660924). Singles start at 200AS (£12; $18). Near the terminal for bus 29 on Linzer Bundesstraße. The bus runs from Mirbellplatz, not Salzburg Hbf.

Hinterbrühl, Schanzlgasse 12 (tel. 846798). Buses 5 and 55 stop at the end of Schanzlgasse shortly after crossing the Salzach by the Nonntaler Brücke.

Wastlwirt, Rochusgasse 15 (tel. 845483). Singles start around 300AS (£18; $27). Bus 27 from Mirbellplatz runs along Rochusgasse, stopping about 300m past the hotel.

Cheapest doubles around 460AS (£27.60; $41.40)

Samhof, Negrellistraße 19 (tel. (874622). Singles start around 230AS (£13.80; $20.70). Bus 33 from Salzburg Hbf stops by the junction of Samstraße, Negrellisstraße and Maxstraße. The hotel is a short walk away.

Cheapest doubles around 480–490AS (£28.80–29.40; $43–44)

Bergland, Rupertgasse 15 (tel. 872318/874005). About 15 minutes' walk from the train station. Rupertgasse is left of Bayerhamer-straße (see Jugendherberge Glockengasse HI hostel below for directions). A 10–15-minute-walk from the centre.

Teufl-Überfuhr, Franz-Hinterholzer-Kai 38 (tel. 621213). Bus 51 from Salzburg Hbf to the first stop on Alpenstraße (after the bus passes Aspergasse on the right), then a 5-minute walk, on along Alpenstraße, left down Falstauergasse to the Salzach, then right along Franz-Hinterholzer-Kai.

Edelweiß, Kendlerstraße 57 (tel. 824883). Bus 27 from Mirbellplatz stops almost outside the hotel.

Cheapest doubles around 500–525AS (£30–31.50; $45–47.25)

Wallner, Aiglhofstraße 15 (tel. 845023). Bus 29 from Mirbell-platz runs along the street, stopping about 200m beyond the hotel.

Itzlinger Hof, Itzlinger Hauptstraße 11 (tel. 51210). About 8-minutes' walk from Salzburg Hbf. Follow Kaiserschützenstraße away from the station, right down Fanny-von-Lehnert-Straße to the end, left, then right at Itzlinger Hauptstraße. Bus 51 runs along the street to the town centre.

Lilienhof, Siezenheimer Straße 62 (tel. (433630). Take bus 77 from Salzburg Hbf to Innsbrucker Bundesstraße, then change to bus 80 which runs down Otto-von-Lilienthal-Straße. The hotel is on the corner of the junction with Siezenheimer Straße, a short walk from the bus stop.

Wegscheider, Thumeggerstraße 4 (tel. 820385). Singles around 250AS (£15; $22.50). Bus 5 from Salzburg Hbf or bus 15 from Mirbellplatz to the first stop on Berchtesgadenerstraße, then a short walk. Thumeggerstraße is off Neukomgasse.

Dietmann, Ignaz-Harrer-Straße 13 (tel. 431364). Prices fall slightly off-season. Bus 77 from Salzburg Hbf runs along the street but the hotel is only 10 minutes' walk from the station. Head left down Rainerstraße, then right at St Julien Straße which runs into Ignaz-Harrer-Straße.

Junior, Innsbrucker Bundesstraße 49 (tel. 827648). See Hotel Noisternig, above, for directions.

Ganshof, Ganshofstraße 13 (tel. 846628). Bus 27 from Mirbellplatz to the first stop on the street, then a short walk in the direction the bus was going.

Billroth, Billrothstraße 10—18 (tel. 620596). Bus 51 from Salzburg Hbf to the stop on Alpenstraße just past the junction with Billrothstraße. Under 5 minutes' walk from the bus stop.

Helmhof, Kirchengasse 29 (tel. 433079). Bus 29 from Mirbellplatz to the stop after Münchener Bundesstraße crosses the motorway. Down to the end of Fischergasse, then left down Lieferinger Hauptstraße, over the motorway and right at Kirchengasse.

Erna, Galsbergstraße 43 (tel. 641415). In Parsch, east of the city centre.

Cheapest doubles around 540—550AS (£32.40—33; $48.60—49.50)

Salzburg International Hotel, Moosstraße 106 (tel. 824617/ 824618). Price is for doubles with a shower/bath. Bus 15 from Mirbellplatz to Moosstraße, then change to bus 60. Bus 60 stops almost at the door of the hotel.

Zur Post, Maxglaner Hauptstraße 45 (tel. 832339). Buses 1 and 2 from Salzburg Hbf run along the street stopping a short distance beyond the hotel.

Romerwirt, Nonntaler Hauptstraße 47 (tel. 843391/829423). Bus 5 from Salzburg Hbf to the first stop on Nonntaler Hauptstraße, just along the street from the hotel.

Noppinger, Maxglaner Hauptstraße 29 (tel. 846235). See Zur Post, above, for directions. Close to the bus stop.

Überfuhr, Ignaz-Rieder-Kai 43 (tel. 623010). Bus 5 from Salzburg Hbf to Mozartsteg then bus 49 along Aignerstraße to the stop at the junction with Überfuhrstraße, followed by a short walk, down Überfuhrstraße to the Salzach, then right.

PRIVATE ROOMS
Prices for private rooms start around 200AS (£12; $18) per person. Prices are set according to the location of the house, and the facilities available in the room. All the owners below offer basic rooms with the use of the shower/bath in the house.

Maria Bamberger, Gerhart-Hauptmann-Straße 10 (tel. 842 9653/ 821474). Doubles and triples. Bus 5 from Salzburg Hbf.

Josefa Fagerer, Moosstraße 68d (tel. 824978). Singles and doubles. Bus 15 from Mirbellplatz along Moosstraße until the stop just around the corner on Firmianstraße. Then a few minutes' walk, back on to Moosstraße, then left.

Helga Bankhammer, Moosstraße 77 (tel. 830067). Doubles only. See Josefa Fagerer, above, for directions. A 5-minute walk from the bus stop.

Elfriede Feichtner, Hildebrandtgasse 17 (tel. 22814). Singles only. Open July–Sept. Bus 51 from Salzburg Hbf.

Georg Gandolf, Moosstraße 170 (tel. 842 8485/826364). Doubles and triples. Bus 15 from Mirbellplatz to the start of Moosstraße, then change to bus 60.

Adele Gellner, Samergasse 10a (tel. 798833). Open July–Aug. Doubles only. Bus 15 from Mirbellplatz.

Hilda Hollbacher, Lieferinger Hauptstraße 101 (tel. 356283). Open June–Sept. Singles and doubles. See Hotel Helmhof, above, for directions.

Anna Sommerauer, Moosstraße 100 (tel. 824877). Singles only. See Georg Gandolf, above, for directions.

Maria Schweiger, Gerhart-Hauptmann-Straße 9 (tel. 841 9785/820824). Open June–Aug. Doubles only. Bus 5 from Salzburg Hbf.

Maria Langwieder, Törringstraße 41 (tel. 433129). Singles, doubles and triples. Bus 29 from Mirbellplatz.

Elisabeth Mayerhofer, Moosstraße 68c (tel. 842 8394). See Josefa Fagerer, above, for directions.

Theresia Nussbaumer, Moosstraße 164 (tel. 830229). Singles, doubles and triples. See Georg Gandolf, above, for directions.

Karoline Oberholzner, Gerhart-Hauptmann-Straße 38 (tel. 842 9630/821465). Bus 5 from Salzburg Hbf.

HI HOSTELS

Jugendgästehaus Salzburg, Josef-Preis-Allee 18 (tel. 842 6700/846857). Midnight curfew. Dorms 160AS (£9.60; $14.40). Quads 195AS (£11.70; $17.55) per person. Doubles 225AS (£13.50; $20.25) per person. With breakfast. Very popular with school groups. Advance reservations by letter advised. Otherwise arrive between 7 a.m. and 9 a.m., or as soon as possible after 11 a.m., when the reception re-opens. Bus 5 or 51 to Justizgebäude (the first stop on Petersbrunnstraße after crossing the river), then a 5-minute walk on along Petersbrunnstraße, then left down Josef-Preis-Allee.

Jugendherberge Aigen, Aigner Straße 34 (tel. 23248). B&B in dorms 125AS (£7.50; $11.25). Bus 5 from Salzburg Hbf to Mozartsteg, then bus 49 along Aignerstraße. The bus stops about 350m beyond the hostel.

Jugendherberge Glockengasse, Glockengasse 8 (tel. 876241). Open Apr.–mid-Oct. Midnight curfew. B&B in dorms 105AS (£6.30;

$9.45). Cooking facilities available. A 15-minute walk from Salzburg Hbf, 10 minutes' walk from the town centre. From the station head left down Rainerstraße, left through the underpass into Gabelsbergerstraße. Straight on into Bayernhamerstraße, right down Bayernhamerstraße until it joins Schallmooser Hauptstraße. The small alley across the street leads into Glockengasse. Bus 29 runs from Schallmooser Hauptstraße to the town centre.

Jugendherberge Eduard-Heinrich-Haus, Eduard-Heinrich-Straße 2 (tel. 25976). B&B in dorms 125AS (£7.50; $11.25). Bus 51 from Salzburg Hbf to the third stop on Alpenstraße, at the junction with Hans-Sperl-Straße and Egger-Lienz-Gasse. About 6 minutes' walk from the bus stop, down Egger-Lienz-Gasse, right at Henri-Dunant-Straße, and then left.

Jugendherberge Haunspergstraße, Haunspergstraße 27 (tel. 875030). Curfew 11 p.m. Open 4 July–31 Aug. B&B in dorms 130AS (£7.80; $11.70). A 5-minute walk from Salzburg Hbf. Left a short distance from the station, then right along Porschestraße, right again at Elisabethstraße, then left at Stauffenstraße into Haunspergstraße.

St Elisabeth, Plainstraße 83 (tel. 50728). Open 11 July–31 Aug. B&B in dorms 125AS (£7.50; $11.25). A 5-minute walk from the train station. Take Kaiserschützenstraße heading away from Salzburg Hbf, on down Jahnstraße, then right.

Salzburg-Walserfeld, Schulstraße 18 (tel. 851377). Open 1 July–25 Aug. B&B in dorms 120AS (£7.20; $10.80). 11 p.m. curfew. Bus 77 from Salzburg Hbf.

HOSTEL
International Youth Hostel, Paracelsusstraße 9 (tel. 879649). Dorms 110AS (£6.60; $9.90), double rooms 150AS (£9; $13.50). Very noisy, and extremely popular with Americans. A short walk from the Hauptbahnhof.

CAMPING
Stadt-Camping, Bayerhamerstraße 14a (tel. (871169). Open May–Sept. 60AS (£3.60; $5.40) per person, (tent included). About 700m from the rear exit of Salzburg Hbf. See Hotel Merian, above, for directions. Right at Bayerhamerstraße.

Schloß Aigen, Weberbartlweg 20 (tel. 22079/272243). Open May–Sept. 50AS (£3; $4.50) per tent, 40AS (£2.40; $3.60) per person. Bus 5 from Salzburg Hbf to Mozartsteg, then bus 49 along Aignerstraße to the stop Glaserstraße. From the stop, a 10-minute walk along Glaserstraße, then left up Weberbartlweg. The closest train station is Bahnhof Aigen, on Aigenerstraße, a 20-minute walk from the campsite.

Gnigl (Ost), Parscher Straße 4 (tel. 644143/644144). Open mid-May—mid-Sept. 20AS (£1.20; $1.80) per tent, 30AS (£1.80; $2.70) per person. Bus 29 from Mirbellplatz along Linzer Bundesstraße to the stop near the junction with Parscherstraße (after the bus crosses over the railway) then a 200m walk. Bus 27 from Mirbellplatz to the first stop on Eichstraße (again over the railway) is 400m from the site.

Stadtblick, Rauchenbichlerstraße 21 (tel. 50652). Open Apr.—Oct. 40AS (£2.40; $3.60) per tent, 60—65AS (£3.60—3.90; $5.40—5.85) per person. Bus 51 from Salzburg Hbf to the stop on Kirchenstraße by the junction with Rauchenbichlerstraße, then a 5-minute walk to the site.

'Nord-Sam', Samstraße 22a (tel. 660494/660611). Open Apr.—Sept. 60—80AS (£3.60—4.80; $5.40—7.20) per tent, 35—50AS (£2.10—3; $3.15—4.50) per person. Bus 33 from Salzburg Hbf to the first stop after Samstraße passes under the railway lines.

ASK, Flughafen (West), Karolingerstraße 4 (tel. 845602). Open mid-May—mid-Sept. 30AS (£1.80; $2.70) per tent, 45AS (£2.70; $4) per person. About 10-minutes' walk from the airport, right off Innsbrucker Bundesstraße. Bus 77 from the train station stops by the junction of Innsbrucker Bundesstraße and Karolingerstraße, leaving a short walk to the site.

Kasern (Jägerwirt), Carl-Zuckmayer-Straße 26 (tel. 50576). Open Apr.—Sept. 20AS (£1.20; $1.80) per tent, 55AS (£3.30; $5) per person.

HI HOSTEL NEARBY

Traunerstraße 22, Traunstein (tel. 861 4742). Open only to visitors aged 26 and under. DM15 (£6.40; $9.60). In Germany, on the line from Munich to Salzburg. About 40 minutes from Salzburg by local train. If you are leaving Munich in the late afternoon during the summer you might want to consider staying here, then getting into Salzburg early next morning.

Vienna (Wien) (tel. code 0222)

TOURIST OFFICES

Wiener Fremdenverkehrsamt, Obere Augartenstraße 40, 1025 Wien (tel. 21114). Contact this office if you want to obtain information in advance. On arrival, information and room-finding services are available at eight tourist offices throughout the city.

Kärntnerstraße 38 (tel. 513 8852). Open daily 9 a.m.–7 p.m. U-Bahn lines U1, U2 and U4: Karlsplatz/Ober.

Westbahnhof. Open daily 6.15 a.m.–11 p.m.

Südbahnhof. Open daily 6.30 a.m.–10 p.m.

Flughafen Wien-Schwechat. In the airport arrivals hall. Open daily June–Sept. 8.30 a.m.–11 p.m.; Oct.–May 8.30 a.m.–10 p.m.

Reichsbrücke landing stage. If arriving by boat go to the DDSG information counter. Open Apr.–Oct. 7 a.m.–6 p.m.

Autobahn A1 (west motorway). At the Wien-Auhof services. Open Apr.–Oct. 8 a.m.–10 p.m.; Nov. 9 a.m.–7 p.m., Dec.–Mar. 10 a.m.–6 p.m. For traffic from Innsbruck, Salzburg, Prague and České Budějovice (via Linz) and Germany.

Autobahn A2 (south motorway). Exit: Zentrum, Triester Straße. Open July–Sept. 8 a.m.–10 p.m.; Mar.–June and Oct. 9 a.m.– 7 p.m. For traffic arriving from Graz, Klagenfurt, Llubljana and Italy.

Florisdorfer Brücke/Donauinsel. Open late Mar.–Sept. 9 a.m.– 7 p.m. For traffic arriving from Brno, Moravia and from Prague (via Moravia).

VIENNA'S STATIONS
The vast majority of people travelling to Vienna by train arrive at one of the two main stations, either the Westbahnhof, or the Südbahnhof. Any train passing through Salzburg, Innsbruck, Switzerland, or what was formerly West Germany arrives at the Westbahnhof. Trains from Budapest and Romania going on to these places stop at the Westbahnhof. Of the two daily trains running from Budapest to Vienna, one (via Gyor) goes to the Westbahnhof, the other (via Sopron) goes to the Südbahnhof. Trains from Graz, Klagenfurt, Poland, Brno, Bratislava, Italy, Greece, Sofia, Belgrade and Zagreb stop at the Südbahnhof, as do trains from Budapest continuing on to any of these destinations. The only other railway station you are likely to arrive at is Franz-Josefs Bahnhof. This station receives international trains from Berlin, Leipzig, Dresden, Prague and Česke Budějovice, as well as local services from Krems-an-der-Donau. Wien-Nord and Wien-Mitte deal with local commuter trains only, but Wien-Mitte is the main bus station and the city air terminal.

FINDING ACCOMMODATION IN SUMMER
Finding a cheap bed can be a problem during the summer months. Late June is particularly bad. By this time, large numbers of inde-

pendent travellers are arriving in town but the extra bed space created by the conversion of student accommodation into temporary hotels and hostels is available only from July to September. It is advisable to reserve accommodation in writing well in advance of your date of arrival throughout the summer. Failing this, try to phone ahead at least twenty-four hours in advance.

HOTELS AND PENSIONS

A continental breakfast is included in the overnight price at all the hotels below, unless indicated otherwise. At a few hotels a buffet breakfast is provided.

Cheapest doubles around 400AS (£24; $36)

Rosen-Hotel Europahaus, Linzerstraße 429 (tel. 922538). A student residence run as a hotel during the summer vacation (1 July–30 Sept). Tram 52 from the Mariahilferstraße stop by the Westbahnhof runs along Linzerstraße.

Cheapest doubles around 450AS (£27; $40.50)

Don Bosco, Hagenmüllergasse 33 (tel. 71184/711555). Tram 18 from the Westbahnhof or Südbahnhof dir: Stadionbrücke to L.-Koessler Platz near the Donaukanal. Open 1 July–30 Sept.

Cyrus, Laxenburgerstraße 14 (tel. 604 4288/602 2578). Singles start at the same price. Near the Südbahnhof.

Auhof, Auhofstraße 205 (tel. 888 5289). Without breakfast. Far out in the west of the city.

Jägerwald, Karl Bekehrtystraße 66 (tel. 946266). Singles start around 230AS (£13.80; $20.70). Out in the western suburbs.

Auer, Lazarettgasse 3 (tel. 432121). U6: Alserstraße.

Cheapest doubles around 480AS (£28.80; $43)

Matauschek, Breitenseerstraße 14 (tel. 982532). Schnellbahn: Breitensee (change at Penzing).

Reimer, Kirchengasse 18 (tel. 523 6162). A 10–15-minute walk from the Westbahnhof, left off Mariahilferstraße as you walk towards the centre.

Esterhazy, Nelkengasse 3 (tel. 587 5159). Without breakfast. A 10-minute walk from the Westbahnhof.

Goldenes Einhorn, Am Hundsturm 5 (tel. 554755). Without breakfast. A 15-minute walk from the Westbahnhof. Walk right around Margaretengürtel and Gumpendorfergürtel to the U-Bahn station.

Cheapest doubles around 500AS (£30; $45)

Auersperg, Auerspergstraße 9 (tel. 432 5490/512 7493). Buffet breakfast. U2: Lerchenfelderstraße. Open 1 July–30 Sept.

Falstaff, Müllnergasse 5 (tel. 349127/349186). U4: Rossauer Lane.

Hargita, Andreasgasse 1 (tel. 526 1928/526 28564). Without breakfast. A 5–10-minute walk from the Westbahnhof.

Quisisana, Windmühlgasse 6 (tel. 587 3341). Windmühlgasse runs between Mariahilferstraße and Gumpendorferstraße.

Kagranerhof, Wagramerstraße 141 (tel. 231187). U1: Zentrum Kagran. Cross Czernetzplatz into Wagramerstraße.

Praterstern, Mayergasse 6 (tel. 240123). Without breakfast. Near Wien-Nord station. Schnellbahn/U1: Praterstern (Wien-Nord).

Cheapest doubles around 540AS (£33; $49.50)

Alsergrund, Alserstraße 33 (tel. 433 2317/512 7493). U6: Alserstraße, or from the Westbahnhof tram 5 to Alserstraße.

Kreiner, Hadersdorf Hauptstraße 31 (tel. 971131). Out in the western suburb of Hadersdorf. Schnellbahn: Hadersdorf Weidlingau.

Stadt Bamberg, Mariahilferstraße 167 (tel. 837608). A short walk from the Westbahnhof.

Auge Gottes, Nussdorferstraße 75 (tel. 342585). A student residence run as a hotel during the summer vacation (1 July–30 Sept.).

Cheapest doubles around 560AS (£34; $51)

Wild, Langegasse 10 (tel. 435174). U2: Lerchenfelderstraße. A short walk up Lerchenfelderstraße, then right.

Baltic, Skodagasse 15 (tel. 420173). Tram 5 from the Westbahnhof or Franz-Josefs Bhf to Skodagasse.

Caroline, Gudrunstraße 138 (tel. 604 8070). U1: Keplerplatz. The hotel is about 500m from the U-Bahn stop, across Laxenburgerstraße.

Fünfhaus, Sperrgasse 12 (tel. 892 3545). A 5-minute walk from the Westbahnhof to the junction of Hernalsergurtel and Alserstraße.

Strandhotel Alte Donau, Wagramerstraße 51 (tel. 236730). U1: Alte Donau.

Kraml, Brauergasse 5 (tel. 587 8588). U4: Pilgramgasse.

Stalehner, Ranftlgasse 11 (tel. 408 2505). U6: Alserstraße, or tram 8.

Stasta, Lehmanngasse 11 (tel. 865 9788).
Adlon, Hofenedergasse 4 (tel. 266788). Near Wien-Nord.
Kugel, Siebensterngasse 43 (tel. 933355). U2: Volkstheater.
Pani, Erlaerstraße 37 (tel. 667 1697). Schnellbahn: Liesing, then
bus 64A or 66A along Erlaerstraße.

PRIVATE ROOMS AND APARTMENTS
Private rooms and apartments are only rarely available through
Tourist Offices. Apply instead to:

Mitwohnzentrale, Laudongasse 7 (tel. 402 6061). Open Mon.–Fri.
10 a.m.–2 p.m. and 3–6 p.m. This private accommodation
agency finds rooms and apartments for those staying at least
three days. Room prices start at 200AS (£12; $18) per day, while
apartments cost from 600AS (£36; $54) per day. On top of the
cost of your accommodation the agency levies a commission,
which varies according to the length of your stay. Tram 5 from
Franz-Josefs Bhf to Laudongasse.

ÖKISTA, Türkenstraße 6 (tel. 401480). Open Mon.–Fri. 8.30 a.m.–
5 p.m. KISTA (the student travel agency) find slightly cheaper
rooms than Mitwohnzentrale, and charge no commission for
doing so. U2: Schottentor. From Maria Theresien-Straße a short
walk along Wahringerstraße or Liechtensteinstraße takes you
into Türkenstraße.

Österreichisches Verkehrsbüro, Friedrichstraße 7, 1043 Wien (tel.
588000). Write or phone in advance for information.

Reisebüro Hippesroither, Zschokkegasse 91, 1220 Wien (tel. 210
6551). Write or phone in advance for information.

Hedwig Gally, Arnsteingasse 25/10 (tel. 812 9073/830 4244). Not
far from the Westbahnhof. Prices for doubles start around 380AS
(£22.80; $34.20).

Irmgard Lauria, Kaiserstraße 77, Apartment 8 (tel. 934152). About
220AS (£13.20; $19.80) per person in quads with cooking facili-
ties. Dorms cost around 180AS (£10.80; $16.20). A 5–10-minute
walk from the Westbahnhof. Go diagonally left across Europa
Platz, down Stollgasse into Kaiserstraße.

HI HOSTELS
Expect to pay 130–150AS (£7.80–9; $11.70–13.50) for B&B

Jugendgästehaus Wien-Brigittenau, Friedrich-Engelsplatz 24 (tel.
33282940/3300598). Curfew 12.30 a.m. 170AS (£10.20;
$15.30). U1 U4 to Schwedenplatz, then tram N to Florisdorfer
Brücke Friedrich-Engelsplatz.

Myrthengasse, Myrthengasse 7/Neustiftgasse 85 (tel. 523 6316/ 9429). Curfew 12.30 a.m. 170AS (£10.20; $15.30). U6 to Burggasse, bus 48A to Neubaug. Walk back a short distance then right. Fifteen minutes on foot from the centre and the Westbahnhof.

Jugendgästehaus Hütteldorf-Hacking, Schloßbergasse 8 (tel. 877 0263). Curfew 11.45 p.m. 170AS (£10.20; $15.30). Schnellbahn from Westbahnhof to Hütteldorf (last train 10.15 p.m.) or U4 to the same stop.

Schloßherberge am Wilhelminenberg, Savoyenstraße 2 (tel. 458503). Curfew midnight. 200AS (£12; $18). U6 to Thaliastraße (or tram 5 from the Westbahnhof). Then bus 46B or 146B from here to the hostel.

Ruthensteiner, Robert Hamerlinggasse 24 (tel. 893 4202/2796). 24-hr reception. Singles 230AS (£13.80; $20.70), doubles 390AS (£23.40; $35); triples 500AS (£30; $45). Dorms 140AS (£8.40; $12.60). Five-minute walk from the Westbahnhof.

Turmherberge 'Don Bosco', Lechnerstraße 12 (tel. 713 1494). Open 1 Mar.–30 Nov. 11.30 p.m. curfew. Roman Catholic-run hostel in an old church bell tower. Very cheap. Bed only 65AS (£3.90; $5.85). Over the years this hotel has sometimes enforced a men-only policy, sometimes not. Women should ring ahead before heading out to the hostel.

HOSTELS/UNIVERSITY DORMS

Hostel Zöhrer, Skodagasse 26 (tel. 430730). Open all year. Cooking facilities. B&B 170AS (£10.20; $15.30). Off Alserstraße (U6: Alserstraße). Tram 5 from the Westbahnhof or Franz-Josefs Bhf to Skodagasse.

Kolpingfamilie Wien-Meidling, Bendlgasse 10–12 (tel. 835487). Open all year. Cooking facilities. Bed only 110–170AS (£6.60–10.20; $9.90–15.30). Breakfast and dinner available. U6: Niederhofstraße.

YMCA Inter-Rail Point, Kenyongasse 25 (tel. 936304). Open mid-July–mid-Aug. Slightly cheaper than the main HI hostels. Reluctant to take phone reservations. Ring to check that it is open in 1995. A 5–10-minute walk from the Westbahnhof.

Believe-It-Or-Not, Myrthengasse 10 (tel. 5264658/964658). 190AS (£11.40; $17). See directions for the HI Hostel in Myrthengasse.

Gästehaus Pfeilheim, Pfeilgasse 4–6 (tel. 431661/422534). Open July–Sept. Singles 240AS (£14.40; $21.60), doubles 400AS (£24; $36). From the Westbahnhof and Franz-Josefs Bhf tram 5 to Thaliastraße/ Lerchenfelderstraße.

Gästehaus Rudolfinum, Mayerhofgasse 3 (tel. 505 5384). Open

July—Sept. Singles 240AS (£14.40; $21.60), doubles 400AS (£24; $36). U1: Taubstummengasse. Mayerhofgasse is off Favoritenstraße on the right as you walk towards the Südbahnhof. A 10-minute walk from the Südbahnhof.

Porzellaneum der Wiener Universität, Porzellangasse 30 (tel. 347282). Singles and doubles around 170AS (£10.20; $15.30) per person. About 10% extra for one-night stays. A 5-minute walk from Franz-Josefs Bhf. Porzellangasse begins at J.-Tandler-Platz on Alserbachstraße by the station.

Katholisches Studentenhaus, Peter-Jordan-Straße 29 (tel. 349264). Singles and doubles around 165AS (£10; $15) per person. Tram 38 from the Westbahnhof to Hardtgasse. From the Südbahnhof tram D to Schottentor (U2: Schottentor) to join tram 38.

Katholisches Studentenhaus, Zaunschertgasse 4 (tel. 382197). An affiliate of the dormitory above. Doubles only.

CAMPING
Expect to pay around 55AS (£3.30; $5) per tent and per person

Aktiv Camping Neue Donau, Am Kleehaufel (tel. 220 9310). Open late Apr.—Sept. Near the Praterbrücke, 6km from the centre. U1: Kaisermühlen, then bus 91A to the site, or Schnellbahn: Lobau (from the Südbahnhof), followed by a 500m walk to the campsite.

Wien-Süd, Breitenfurterstraße 269 (tel. 865 9218). Open July—Aug. Six kilometres from the centre. U6: Philadelphiabrücke, then bus 62A, or Schnellbahn: Atzgersdorf Mauer, then an easy walk or bus 66A to the site.

Wien-West I, Hüttelbergstraße 40 (tel. 941449). Open 15 July—15 Sept. Six kilometres from the centre. Schnellbahn (from Westbahnhof) or U4 to Hutteldorf, then bus 152 to the site.

Wien-West II, Huttelbergstraße 80 (tel. 942314). Open all year. 4-bed bungalows available, 100AS (£6; $9; DM14,40) p.p. Just up the road from Wien-West I.

Schwimmbad Camping Rodaun, An der Au 2 (tel. 884154). Open 17 March—16 Nov. About 10km from the town centre. U4 to Hietzing (tram 58 from the Westbhf.) then tram 60 to the end.

Schloß Laxenburg, Munchendorferstraße, Laxenburg (tel. 02236 71333). Open late Mar.—early Oct. Sixteen kilometres from the centre, in the grounds of an old Habsburg hunting lodge. Until 9.40 p.m. you can catch a bus from Wien-Mitte to the site.

SLEEPING OUT

Although not really recommended, the Prater Park is the most obvious. Schnellbahn/U1: Praterstern (Wien-Nord), or Schnellbahn: Stadtlauer Brücke Lusthaus at the other end of the park.

THE BALTIC REPUBLICS

The combination of the rich and diverse cultures and histories of the three Baltic states, and the tangible atmosphere of their newly won independence makes this a fascinating time to visit the region. Moreover, in recent years it has become progressively easier to visit the states of the Baltic region. The only potential visa complication is that the principal overnight train service from Poland to Lithuania (which forms the main approach to the Baltic region for travellers exploring Europe by train) crosses Byelorussian territory, and it is necessary to purchase a transit visa in hard currency on the way ($30 or DM50 for a one-way transit visa). A rail link exists (via Suwalki in Poland and Šeštokai in Lithuania) which avoids Byelorus, but this is far less convenient and requires at least two changes of trains.

All three countries now have their own currencies, although only the Estonian kroon (Kr) is firmly established as a hard currency. The Latvian lat (LS) and the Lithuanian lita (LT) were both introduced in 1993, and you may still find that hotels and hostels require payment in US dollars or Deutschmarks. In Estonia you should be able to get by with local currency, although it's as well to be alert to the possibility that Western currency may be demanded and to carry a comfortable supply of dollars just in case.

Although the role of Intourist, the former state tourism organization of the USSR, is now much reduced in the Baltics, it's still possible to book and pay for accommodation in advance through their London office. For accommodation in Estonia, there's nothing to stop you contacting a hotel directly, making a reservation, and paying in Kroons when you arrive; indeed, this may prove to be cheaper than using Intourist's services. There are a number of 'Western' travel companies with experience of organizing both set tours and independent travel in the region; addresses are given at the end of this introduction.

Overnight trains between Tallinn, Riga, Vilnius and Warsaw offer 4-berth couchettes, and the price of rail travel is so low that couchette accommodation for the night is a cost-cutting alternative to staying in a hotel or hostel, though the advantages are slightly offset by the limited number of services. You should reserve your place in advance wherever possible. Prices of just a few dollars (paid in the local currency) are typical for an overnight trip (Vilnius to Riga costs approximately $1 (£0.65); Riga to Tallinn about $3 (£2)), though prices are more expensive if you are *arriving* in Vilnius *from* Warsaw, for example. A small supplementary charge for bedding is normally payable on the train (in the currency of the country that you are leaving), so keep this in mind when changing currency back into dollars or Deutschmarks prior to leaving a country.

Many of the **hotels** previously made available to foreign visitors by Intourist are now adapting (in various ways) to the challenges of the free market. Some have gone out of business altogether, others have been converted to hostel-type accommodation (as described below), thereby entering the list of possibilities available to the budget traveller. Those bought out by foreign management have generally moved upmarket, and thus out of the range of those seeking cheap sleep. Those that have not attempted to adapt to Western tastes should be relatively affordable.

Travellers who have spent time in Eastern Europe will be familiar with the concept of local people congregating in train stations to offer **private rooms** to recently arrived backpackers. This phenomenon has yet to emerge in the Baltic republics, but more locals will probably open their doors once visitors from the West begin to arrive in greater numbers. Agencies offering this kind of accommodation are springing up in the principal cities.

Only Estonia has a network of **hostels** organized across the country on familiar HI lines (see Estonia section). Some of the hostels listed in the sections for the individual countries display the familiar HI tree-and-hut symbol, even though no they have no affiliation with the HI. This subtle deception doesn't necessarily mean that the accommodation offered is below the standard you would normally expect from this symbol; indeed, the independently managed hostels have some of the most comfortable accommodation available.

Camping is not as widespread in the Baltic republics as elsewhere in Europe, and organized networks do not yet exist. Published information on the authorized sites is scarce. Contact the sites listed directly for more information.

Tourist information in the form familiar to Western travellers is still in its formative stages in the Baltic republics; Tallinn leads the way with its impressive information office right in the heart of the Old Town. More sources of information are bound to appear as the need increases. Travellers using the more expensive hotels will have access to lobby service desks which supply local information. You may also care to contact the respective embassies in your own country (addresses below) for general information. The accommodation agencies and tour organizers listed in the sections for each town will provide information, and you should also make use of travel companies with specialist expertise in the region. Information on trains and buses (both within individual countries and for international journeys) is available at the stations themselves, but long queues are almost inevitable, and you should be prepared to negotiate the language barrier (Russian, or sometimes German, is likely to be of more use than English). The *Thomas Cook European Timetable* can be an invaluable asset, particularly for the planning of overnight journeys, but even the most up-to-date edition won't necessarily correspond to the times displayed in the stations.

One of the best sources of current information on the Baltic republics in English is *The Baltic Independent*, published weekly in Tallinn and distributed throughout the region. It provides a comprehensive overview of news from all three republics, ranging from general interest articles to in-depth economic and political analysis. It is available for 2Kr in Estonia, or contact AS *The Baltic Independent*, PO Box 45, Pärnu maantee 67a, EE0090 Tallinn (tel. 68 30 73 (subscriptions)/68 12 69/68 12 65; fax 68 23 31/44 14 83). A note of caution: overseas subscriptions are expensive.

ADDRESSES
(See also addresses for individual countries)
Baltic Accommodation and Travel Service Ltd. (BATS), Väinä-möisenkatu 23 A 13, 00100 Helsinki, Finland (tel./fax Helsinki 496585 – except in Summer, when you should contact the 'Maria' hostel in Tallinn). This company manages a varying list of accommodation throughout the Baltic region; contact them directly for their most up-to-date list of hostels and similarly priced accommodation.

● Travel agents/Tour operators
The following companies deal with some or all of the Baltic republics. Contact them directly for full details of the services that they can provide.

Progressive Tours	12 Porchester Place, London W2 2BS (tel. 0171 262 1676).
Amber Travel	10 Victoria Terrace, Royal Leamington Spa CV31 3AB (tel. 01926 431134; fax 01926 431040).
Swan Hellenic	77 New Oxford Street, London W61A 1PP (tel. 0171 831 1616).
Martin Randall Travel	10 Barley Mow Passage, London W4 4PH (tel. 0181 994 6477).
Regent Holidays	15 John Street, Bristol BS1 2HR (tel. 01272 211711).
Intourist Travel Ltd.	Intourist House, 219 Marsh Wall London E14 9FJ (tel. 0171 538 8600 [general enquiries]; 0171 538 5965 [independent travel]; fax 0171 538 5967).

Travelines	18 Station Parade, London W5 3LD (tel. 0181 993 7201).
Instone Travel	83 Whitechapel High Street, London E1 7QX (tel. 0171 247 3434).
Canterbury Travel	248 Streatfield Road, Harrow HA3 9BY (tel. 0181 206 0411; fax 0181 206 0427).
Gunnel Travel Service Ltd.	Hayling Cottage, Stratford St Mary, Colchester CO7 6JW (tel. 01206 322352).
Schnieder Reisen GmbH	Harkortstraße 121, 2000 Hamburg 50, Germany (tel. 380 20 60; fax 38 89 65). Organizes tours and produces useful brochure.

Estonia (Eesti)

USEFUL ADDRESSES

Eesti Puhkemajade Organisatsioon (Estonian Youth Hostels Association; HI-affiliated), Liivalaia 2, EE0001 Tallinn (tel. 63 45 99/ fax 44 10 96). The Estonian network of youth hostels is unique in the Baltic region, and as well as their hostels in Tallinn and Tartu there are several others throughout the country, located in varying types of accommodation. Room sizes vary from single rooms to more familiar dormitory accommodation. There are no age limits. Advance reservations are advisable. HI members receive a discount (supposedly 25%, according to the above office, although it is only 15% in Tartu, for example). Full details are given in the booklet available from the above address, which can be obtained on request.

Estonian Embassy: 16 Hyde Park Gate, London SW7 5DG (tel. 071 589 3428; fax 071 589 3430).

Tallinn (tel. 0142)

TOURIST OFFICE

Tallinn City Tourist Office, Raekoja plats 18, Tallinn EE0001. Recently opened, and conveniently located on the main town square. Open Mon.–Fri. 9 a.m.–5 p.m.; weekends 10 a.m.–3 p.m. Some English spoken. Make use of their knowledge of the local accommodation situation, particularly with respect to current prices.

ACCOMMODATION AGENCIES

Eutour Ltd, Travel Agency, Sakala 11c, EE0001 Tallinn (tel. 68 16 44; fax. 68 18 93). This company organizes tours for foreign tourists, and also offers an accommodation-finding service in Tallinn. The following prices apply for different types of accommodation (prices per person, per night): camping, 60–100Kr; motel, 100–120Kr; hotel, 100–130Kr; private flats in the centre (breakfast included), 120–140Kr; private flats in a new suburb, 100–130Kr. (Operating from an address formerly used by the Baltic Accommodation and Travel Service.)

BASIC DIRECTIONS

The heart of Tallinn is the Old Town, which consists of Toompea (the Castle Hill) and the area to the east of this, which is still largely contained within the old town walls and has Raekoja plats (Town Hall Square) at its centre. The area south and south-east of the Old Town forms the focus of the 'New' Town. The train station is north-west of Toompea, just outside the Old Town; the local bus station is just next to the train station, and the long-distance station is at Lastekodu 46, about 1.5km south-east of the Old Town. The majority of the accommodation and eating possibilities in Tallinn are concentrated in the Old Town or immediately around it, or in the area immediately south of this, centred on Pärnu maantee.

HOTELS

All prices shown are per person (prices offered by Intourist are in brackets):

Annara, Elektroni 8, EE0013 Tallinn (tel. 52 87 13).

Burmani Willa, Kadaka tee 62, EE0108 Tallinn (tel. 53 22 60; fax 53 20 85).

Kelluka, Kelluka tee 11, EE0020 Tallinn (tel. 23 88 11; fax 23 73 98).

Kullervo, Tedre 27/29, EE0013 Tallinn (tel. 52 72 12/55 75 53; fax 52 72 12).

Külaliste Maja, Tatari 56/58, EE0001 Tallinn (tel. 68 21 72) (guest house).

Palace, Vabaduse väljak 3, EE0001 Tallinn (tel. 44 47 61; fax 44 30 98).

Rummu, Rummu t. 3, EE0019 Tallinn (Motel) (tel. 23 91 29).

Stroomi, Tšaikovski 11, EE0003 Tallinn (tel. 49 52 19).

Tallinn, Toompuiestee 27, EE0031 Tallinn (tel. 60 43 40).

Maardu, Veeru t. 6, EE0030 Tallinn (tel. 23 04 78).

EMI, Sütiste tee 21, EE0108 Tallinn (tel. 52 16 11/52 73 62). 40Kr.

Ranna (Intourist: singles £14; doubles £20).

Pääsu, Sõpruse pst. 182, EE0034 Tallinn (tel. 52 00 34) (Intourist: singles from £14; doubles from £32).

Vitamiin, Narva maantee 7, EE0102 Tallinn (tel. 43 85 85). 200Kr (Intourist: singles from £19; doubles from £32).

Pirita, Regati pst. 1, EE0019 Tallinn (tel. 23 85 98; fax 23 74 33) (Intourist: singles from £23; doubles from £33).

Kungla, Kreutzwaldi 23, EE0104 Tallinn (tel. 42 70 40/42 14 60). 250Kr (Intourist: singles from £24; doubles from £29).

Mihkli, Endla 23, EE0001 Tallinn (tel. 45 37 04/45 17 67). 330Kr.

Peoleo, Pärnu mnt. 555, EE3054 Tallinn (tel. 55 65 66/77 16 01; fax 77 14 63) (motel) (Intourist: singles from £39; doubles from £52).

Olümpia, Liivalaia 33, EE0105 Tallinn (tel. 60 26 00) (Intourist: singles from £42; doubles from £52).

Viru, Viru väljak 4, EE0104 Tallinn (tel. 65 03 00; fax 44 43 71) (Intourist: singles from £47; doubles from £60).

PENSIONS

'Maria', Roosikrantsi 10 A-8 (3rd floor) (tel. 66 63 04). Double rooms $30 (£20), bed in 4-bed room $10 (£6.75). Prices include bedlinen, breakfast and shower. Operated by BATS (see introduction to chapter). The Old Town is within easy walking distance. Open May–September (advance booking essential). Reservations can be made by tel./fax to Helsinki 49 65 85 outside the summer period.

Peedu pansionaat, Võrse 22, EE0034 Tallinn (tel. 52 86 09). 250Kr.

PRIVATE ROOMS/FURNISHED FLATS

Contact the Tallinn City Tourist Office (see above) for details of private accommodation, or agencies who can organize this for you.

HOSTELS

Eesti Puhkemajad, 'Agnes', Narva maantee 7, EE0001 Tallinn (tel. 43 88 70). 1-, 2- and 3-bedded rooms available, with toilet/shower facilities shared between 3–4 rooms. Prices 80–180Kr, including bedlinen (bed in a 2-bed room 94Kr. Friendly staff, with some English spoken. The Old Town is within easy walking distance and it's a 20–25 minute walk from the railway station.

Eesti Puhkemajad, Kuramaa 15, EE0036 Tallinn (tel. 32 77 81). 1-,

2- and 3-bedded rooms, with shared toilet/shower/kitchen for 3 rooms. Prices 70–90Kr, including bedlinen.

Tallinna Pedagoogika-Ülikool (Tallinn Pedagogical University), International Relations Dept, Narva maantee 25 (tel. 42 20 88; fax 42 53 39). On the same road as the 'Agnes' hostel, but further out. Contact them well in advance of your trip to check availability of rooms in their student hostel.

CAMPING

Aegna, Aegna saar, Tallinn (tel. 23 86 26). Open from May–Aug. Cabins available.

Kalev, Kloostrimetsa tee 56 A, EE0019 Tallinn (tel. 23 86 86/23 91 91). Open from June–Oct. Cottage for two persons: 80Kr.

Leevike, EE3054 Tallinn (tel. 55 65 25). Cabins available. About 1.5km from Tallinn by the Pärnu road.

Tartu (tel. 01434)

TOURIST OFFICE

There is a small tourist office in Küütri, on the left-hand side as you walk towards the Ülikooli end. They should be able to advise on the current accommodation situation.

HOTELS

Park-Hotell, Vallikraavi 23, EE2400 Tartu (tel. 31 745/33 663).

Taru, Rebase 9, EE2400 Tartu (tel. 73 700; fax 74 095) (Intourist: singles from £44; doubles from £57).

Pro, Tuglase 13, EE2400 Tartu (tel. 61 853; fax 31 481) (Intourist: singles from £23; doubles from £33).

Remark, Tähe 94, EE2400 Tartu (tel. 76 911).

Salimo, Kopli 1, EE2400 Tartu (tel. 70 888).

PRIVATE ROOMS

Contact the tourist office mentioned above to see if they have any details of accommodation agencies.

HOSTELS

Eesti Puhkemajad, Soola 3, EE2400 Tartu (tel. 33041). 1-, 2- and 3-bedded rooms, with toilet/basin en suite. Shower and sauna facilities available. 100–280Kr, including bedlinen and a full breakfast (single room 100Kr, with a reduction of 15Kr if you have an HI card). Within easy walking distance of the town centre and main sites, one minute from the bus station.

Tartu Ülikooli Üliõpilaskond (Student Union of Tartu University), Ülikooli 20–305, 202 400 Tartu (tel. 35331; fax 35440). Contact in advance for details and prices of the hostel accommodation that they have available.

CAMPING
Contact the tourist office mentioned above to see if they have any details of campsites.

Latvia (Latvija)

Latvian Embassy: Consular Offices, 72 Queensborough Terrace, London W2 3SP (tel. 0171 727 1698; fax 0171 221 9740).

Riga (Rīga) (tel. 0132)

TOURIST OFFICE
There is currently no tourist office in Riga.

ACCOMMODATION AGENCIES
Contact these agencies well in advance to obtain up-to-date information on the services they provide.

Latvijas Tūristu Klubs, Skārņu iela 22 (tel. 212377). Can provide accommodation in Riga, Kaunas and Ventspils.

'Patricia', Elizabetes iela 22–24 (tel. 284868). Provides a tourist information and accommodation service.

Pavadonis, Elizabetes iela 45–47, Riga LV 1050 (tel. 322 402). This travel agent can organize accommodation for foreign tourists.

BASIC DIRECTIONS
Most of the accommodation and eating opportunities are concentrated in the bustling Old Town, located on the east bank of the Daugava. The train and bus stations are immediately to the southeast of the Old Town. To the north-east of the Old Town are a series of gardens and boulevards. The main street is Kaļķu iela,

which splits the Old Town in two, and is continuous with October Bridge (which crosses the Daugava) and Brīvības bulvāris, which cuts across the ring of boulevards and parks, leading out to the north-east of the city. The Old Town is a maze of winding streets and lanes, making by foot the best way to get around the heart of Riga.

HOTELS

Baltija, Raiņa bulvāris 33 (tel. 227461). Only Russian spoken. Very cheap, and you can pay in lats: 8 LS.

Plavnieki, Salnas iela 26 (tel. 137040).

Zemgale, Valdeķu iela 66 (tel. 622714).

Aurora, Marijas iela 5 (tel. 224479). Opposite the train station. 37—56LS. Basic facilities only.

Viktorija, Čaka iela 55 (tel. 272305). Doubles $25 (£16.50).

Sports, Gogoļa iela 5 (tel. 226780). Doubles from $5 (£3.50). Very handy for the train station.

Tūrists, Slokas iela 1 (tel. 615455). Doubles $18 (£12). No English spoken.

Saulīte, Merķeļa iela 12 (tel. 224546). 15—33LS, or $20 (£13.50) for Western tourists! Handy for train station; no English or German spoken.

Latvija, Elizabetes iela 55 (Intourist: singles from $24 (£36); doubles from $66 (£44)).

Rīga, Aspazijas bulvāris 22 (tel. 216700). $50—70 (£33.50—46.50). Ex-Intourist hotel, in good location.

Ridzene, Endrupa iela 1 (tel. 324433).

Caravel, Katrīnas Dambis 25 (tel. 329876).

HOSTELS

Latvijas Universitātes Tūristu Klubs (Tourism Club of University of Latvia), Raiņa bulvāris 19, Riga LV 1586 (tel. 223114; fax 371 8820113) run two hostels. They can also help organize local trips, and will supply general information both for Riga and Latvia. Some English and German spoken. Contact LUTK in advance to book a bed at either of their two hostels (located in student accommodation):

Bastejs, Basteja bulvāris 10. Single room DM30 (£12.50; $18.75), double room (toilet and shower in room) DM50 (£21; $31.50); bed in 2- or 3-bed room (toilet and shower on corridor) DM15 ((£6.25; $9.25).

Argo, Burtnieku iela 1a (20 minutes from the centre). Bed in 2- or 3-bed room DM7 (£3; $4.50).

Hotel Laine, Skolas iela 11, Riga LV 1010 (tel. 287658/288816; fax 287658). $7 (£4.50) for a single room; a bed in a 2-bed room costs $6 (£4), in a 3-bed room $5 (£3.50), in a 4-bed room $4 (£2.50). 'Luxury' double/single for $22/19 (£14.50/12.50). Bedlinen included. English spoken. Old Riga is within easy walking distance; approximately 10−15 minute walk from the train and bus stations. The same management operate another hostel at Biešu iela, on the west bank of the Daugava: a bed in 2-bed apartment (including toilet, shower, kitchen) costs $6 (£4) (whole apartment for one person: $10 (£6.75)). 'Luxury' double/single $16/14 (£10.50/9.50).

BATS, Grēcinieku iela 28. This hostel has operated in the past, though only opening during the summer. Contact well in advance to confirm that it is open for 1995 and to find out prices. Superb location in the heart of the Old Town, a moment's walk from the river.

YMCA Interpoint, Kalnciema iela 10−12 (tel. 332131). Open 7 a.m.−12 a.m. Located 500m from the station. This hostel has operated in previous years, but during July and August only. Check well in advance to make sure that it is operating in 1995. You may find it easier to confirm details with Interpoint European Coordination, National Council of YMCAs of Ireland, St George's Building, 37−41 High Street, Belfast BT1 2AB, Northern Ireland (tel. 327757; fax 438809)

CAMPING

Try asking at LUTK (see Hostels) for details of any sites that are open.

Lithuania (Lietuva)

Lithuanian Embassy: 17 Essex Villas, London W8 7BP (tel. 0171 938 2481; fax 0171 938 3329).

Lithuanian Youth Hostels: Kouno 1-A No. 407, Vilnius (tel. 3702 63 52 44).

Kaunas

TOURIST OFFICE
At present there is no tourist information office in Kaunas.

HOTELS
Neris, Donelaicio gatvė 27 (tel. 20 38 63).
Nemunas, Laisvės alėja 88 (tel. 22 31 02).
Lietuva, Daukanto gatvė 21 (tel. 20 59 92). There is a branch of
    this hotel at Laisvės alėja 35 (tel. 22 17 91).
Baltija, Vytauto prospektas 71 (tel. 22 36 39).
Njaris, (Intourist: singles £42, doubles £37)

PRIVATE ACCOMMODATION
Your best bet is to hang around the station looking lost. Those
locals with rooms will find you. Haggle and agree a price on the
spot. You could ask for information at the Tourist Information
Office, but they're not too keen to help with private rooms.

HOSTEL
BATS hostel, Prancūzų gatvė 59, 3000 Kaunas. $10 (£6.75) for a
bed in a 3-bed apartment (with toilet, shower, kitchen and bal-
cony). Not an ideal location, 15 minutes walk from the train station
in the opposite direction to the town centre.

Vilnius (tel. 0122)

TOURIST OFFICE
At present there is no tourist information office in Vilnius, but try
the Lithuanian Youth Hostels office (see above).

ACCOMMODATION AGENCIES
Norwegian information office, Didžioji gatvė 13 (Postal address:
    Post Box 324-APS-3, LT-2300 Vilnius) (tel. 22 41 40; fax 22 12
    55). Will arrange rooms for $15–20 (£10.00–13.50) per night.
Nakvynė Hotel Travel Service, Kauno 8 (tel. 63 77 32/63 48 23).
    Offers 'family accommodation' in Vilnius: 'houses with all con-
    veniences'. Contact in advance to find out the prices for their
    services.

FINDING ACCOMMODATION

A useful publication to have when organizing your trip is *Vilnius in Your Pocket*, which is published five times a year. It is available for 2.5LT in Vilnius, or write to PO Box 52, 2000 Vilnius-C (tel. 22 29 76; fax 22 29 82). This comprehensive listing of what is going on in the city includes an accommodation section that may include late additions for the summer season.

BASIC DIRECTIONS

The most prominent feature of central Vilnius is Castle Hill, on the south-west corner of which is Katedros aikštė (Cathedral Square). South from here is the Old Town, the main artery of which is Pilies gatvė/Didžioji gatvė. The train and bus stations are south of the Old Town. Gedimino Prospektas, the main thoroughfare of the New Town, runs west from Castle Hill.

HOTELS

The following should have rooms available for under $3 (£2). The security in these hotels may be somewhat suspect, and you shouldn't expect service geared towards tourists:

Karininkų Namų, Pamėnkalnio 13 (tel. 61 84 46).

Pažanga, Saulėtekio 39a (tel. 76 44 83/76 38 96). Situated in a former dormitory for foreign students. Reservations required.

Sportas, Bistryčios 13 (tel. 74 89 53/74 89 46/74 89 58).

Žvaigždė, Pylimo 63 (tel. 61 96 26). Dormitory rooms for 4–6 persons.

Prices in the following hotels start at around $15 (£10)

Gintaras, Sodų 14 (tel. 63 44 96, reservations 62 41 57). Gloomy but cheap; close to train station.

Vilnius, Gedimino prospektas 20/1 (tel. 62 41 57 (Mon.–Fri.)/62 36 65 (Sat.–Sun.)). Singles $17 (£11.50), doubles $30 (£20), triples $42 (£28).

Silelis, Blindžių 17 (tel. 35 16 64, reservations 35 13 05). Singles $17 (£11.50), doubles $34 (£22.50), triples $45 ($30).

Trinapolis, Verkių 66 (tel. 77 87 35; fax 77 49 33). Singles $25 (£16.50), doubles $20 (£13.50) per person, triples $15 (£10) per person. In the outskirts.

Litimpex, Verkių 37 (tel. 35 58 66; fax 35 43 53). Singles $20 (£13.50), doubles $35 (£23.50). In a northern suburb, with transport to town provided.

Skrydis (Airport), Rodūnės kelias 2 (tel. 66 94 67/66 94 62/63 52 63). Singles $24 (£16), doubles $38 (£25.50).

Astorija, Didžioji 35/2 (tel. 62 99 14, reservations 22 40 31; fax 22 00 97). Singles from $29 (£19.50), doubles from $40 (£26.50).

Taffotel, Saltoniškių 56 (tel. 35 11 36, reservations 35 40 13). Singles $30 (£20), doubles $55 (£36.50).

Žalgiris, Šeimyniškių 21a (tel. 35 34 28, reservations 35 20 78; fax 35 39 33). Singles from $35 (£23.50), doubles from $80 (£53.50).

Žaliasis Tiltas. Two locations: Vilniaus 2/30 (tel. 61 54 60); Gedimino prospektas 12 (tel. 61 54 50, reservations tel./fax 22 17 16). Singles $40 (£26.50), doubles $60 (£40).

Zebis, Sibiro 6 (tel. 69 07 07; fax 69 08 90). Singles from $40 (£26.50).

Turistas, Ukmergės 14 (tel. 73 31 06; fax 35 31 61). Singles $50 (£33.50), doubles $70 (£46.50).

PENSIONS

Nakuyné, Kaumo 8 (tel. 63 77 32/43 48 23).

Vingriai, Vingrių 23–2 (tel. 22 29 50). Singles $35 (£23.50).

HOSTELS

BATS Backpackers Hostel, Geležinio vilko 27 (tel. 66 16 92/66 76 80; advance booking by fax: 22 29 56). $14 (£9.50) per person. Take trolleybus 15 or 16 from the bus/train station, to the 5th stop ('Kaunas'); then a short walk two blocks north.

Lithuanian Alternative Youth Hostels (tel. 44 51 40/75 66 50). Summer only; summer camps in Vingis Park. $5 (£3.50) per night.

Lithuanian Youth Hostels, Filaretų 17 (tel. 26 06 06). Bus 34 from the train station. No curfew. Beds from $6 (£4).

VUSA, Student Representation of Vilnius University, Universiteto 3, Vilnius 2734 (tel. 61 79 20/61 44 14; fax 61 34 73). Hostel accommodation available, with kitchen facilities. Contact VUSA directly prior to your arrival in Vilnius to make a booking and confirm their current prices.

BED & BREAKFAST

Litinterp, Vokiečių 10–15 (tel. 61 20 40; fax 22 29 82). Bed and breakfast accommodation in the Old Town. Singles $15 (£10), doubles $25 (£16.50).

Grybas, Aušros Vartų 3 (tel. 22 24 16). Singles $60 (£40), doubles $90 (£60) (2 rooms). English spoken. In the old town, near the station.

CAMPING

Rytų Kempingas, Mūrininkų gvy., 4020 Rukainiai (25km east of Vilnius, on the main road to Minsk) (tel. 54 42 87; fax 22 01 72). Small summer lodgings for 3—4 people, or you can pitch your tent.

Contact BATS (see introduction to this chapter) for details of campsites they manage in the Vilnius/Trakai region.

Camping away from managed sites is prohibited in Vilnius, but permitted in the countryside.

BELGIUM (België/Belgique)

On the whole, Belgium poses no serious problems for the budget traveller but, unless you can afford to stay in hotels all the time, you will have to stay in different types of accommodation as you travel around since some of the main places of interest lack hostels and/or campsites. However, as Belgium is a small country with a very efficient rail network, those with railpasses have the option of choosing one or two bases and visiting other places on daytrips; e.g. from Ghent or Bruges you can easily visit all of Flanders, from Namur all of Wallonia.

Unlike in neighbouring France, there are no really cheap **hotel** rooms in Belgium. You will do well to find a double for under 1100BF (£22; $33) in the main towns, where the cheapest hotels normally charge around 1200BF (£24; $36) for doubles. Considering the number of other possibilities open to budget travellers in Belgium, it is unlikely you will ever have to take a hotel room unless you want to, but if you do have to spend a night or two in a cheap hotel you should have little cause for complaint about the standard of cleanliness or comfort.

Hostelling is a cheap and, usually, convenient way of seeing the country. With the exception of Ghent, Leuven, Lier and Ieper, all the main towns of interest have a hostel. Ghent has been devoid of hostels since its HI hostel closed in the mid-1980s. The HI hostel in Liège closed around the same time, but luckily travellers have the option of the excellent Tilff-Liège HI hostel on the outskirts of the city, just a short train trip away. Elsewhere, problems are only likely to arise around Easter and during the period July–August, when it can be difficult to find a hostel bed in Brussels, Bruges and Ostend.

There are two HI-affiliated hostel associations in Belgium. The Flemish Association operates around twenty hostels; its Walloon counterpart half that number. The normal overnight charge is 300–350BF (£6–7; $9.00–10.50), which includes breakfast. The exceptions are the Flemish YHA-operated hostels in Bruges and Ostend, and the hostels of both associations in Brussels, where prices range from 350–650BF (£7–13; $10.50–19.50). Where space is available most hostels admit non-members on the payment of a 100BF (£2; $3) supplement. Curfews are normally 11 p.m. but the hostels in the cities tend to stay open later.

As well as HI hostels, Antwerp, Bruges and Brussels offer a number of independent hostels. Generally free of the organized groups who head for the main HI hostels, the prices and standards of the independent hostels tend to be on a par with those of the official establishments, while curfews are normally more relaxed. In the larger cities you may also find 'Sleep-Ins' with dormitory accommodation as cheap as 250BF (£5; $7.50). Wallonia is littered with *gîtes d'étapes* which can provide very cheap lodgings in places not served by hostels. An organization called 'Friends of Nature' (Natuurvrienden/Amis de la Nature) also operates a network of hostels throughout the country. Ask the local Tourist Office for details of any such hostels in the locality.

Despite there being over 500 **campsites** in this small country, camping is not an ideal way to see Belgium unless you have a railpass or a car. Sites are heavily concentrated in the rural parts of Wallonia and along the Flemish coast, and the rest of the country is more sparsely served. Major tourist attractions such as Ieper, Kortrijk, Mechelen, Leuven, Lier and Diest all lack campsites, though a short rail trip will invariably find you one in a neighbouring town. Visitors to Liège should head for the site at Tilff, just outside the city. Sites range in quality, and are priced accordingly. Compared to other western European countries, camping in Belgium is very cheap. Prices for a solo traveller can be as low as 60BF (£1.25; $2) per night, but 100–150BF (£2–3; $3.00–4.50) is more normal. However, prices at some of the coastal sites can be as high as 250BF (£5; $7.50) per night.

You should only end up on the street by design, or unforeseen disaster. If you do, vagrancy charges can only be pressed if you are penniless. Late arrivals hoping to sleep in train station waiting rooms should note that only Ostend station stays open all night. The rest close for anything between two to five hours. If you are desperate, your best chance to avoid being thrown on to the street in the early hours is to try the little waiting rooms on the platforms (there are none in Antwerpen Centraal, but you can try Antwerpen-Berchem).

ADDRESSES

Belgian Tourist Office	Premier House, 2 Gayton Road, Harrow, Middlesex, HA1 2XU (tel. 0181 427 6760).
Flemish YHA	Vlaamse Jeugdherbergcentrale, Van Stralenstraat 40, B-2060 Antwerpen (tel. 0323 27218).
Walloon YHA	Centrale Wallone des Auberges de la Jeunesse, rue van Oost 52, B-1030 Bruxelles (tel. 02 215 3100).
Gîtes d'étapes	Gîte d'étape du CBTJ, rue Montoyer 31/8,

B-1040 Bruxelles (tel. 02 512 5417).
Étapes de la Route, rue Traversière 9,
B-1030 Bruxelles (tel. 02 218 6025).

Friends of Nature   Natuurvrienden (Flanders)
(tel. 03 36 18 62).
Amis de la Nature (Wallonia)
(tel. 041 52 28 75).

Camping   Map available from the Belgian Tourist
Office.

Antwerp (Antwerpen) (tel. code 03)

TOURIST OFFICE
Dienst voor Toerisme, Grote Markt 15, B-2000 1 Antwerpen (tel. 232 0103). Open Mon.–Sat. 9 a.m.–6 p.m., Sundays and public holidays 9 a.m.–5 p.m. Town plan 20BF (£0.40; $0.60). Hotel lists and free hotel reservations.

BASIC DIRECTIONS
Paris–Amsterdam trains stop at Antwerpen-Berchem from which you can catch a connecting train to the main station at Antwerpen-Centraal. The main exit of Antwerpen-Centraal is on Koningin Astridplein, a 15–20-minute walk from the Cathedral of Our Lady and the Grote Markt in the heart of the old city.

HOTELS
Cheapest doubles around 950BF (£19; $28.50)

Vredehof, De Keyzerhoeve 14 (tel. 568 9900). Singles around 650BF (£13; $19.50). Far out from the centre (27km) in the suburb of Antwerpen-Zandvliet.

Cheapest doubles around 1600BF (£32; $48)

Billard Palace, Koningin Astridplein 40 (tel. 233 4455). On the left-hand side of the square as you emerge from Antwerpen-Centraal.
Rubenshof, Amerikalei 115–117 (tel. 237 0789). About 25–30 minutes' walk from the main train station, close to the Fine Arts Museum (Kon. Museum voor Schone Kunsten). Walk down De

Keyserlei, then turn left at the junction with Frankrijklei and keep going. Tram 12, or bus 23.

Cheapest doubles around 1700BF (£34; $51)

Monico, Koningin Astridplein 34 (tel. 225 0093).

Cheapest doubles around 2000BF (£40; $60)

Anwerpia, Steenhouwersvest 55 (tel. 226 5760). Singles available at 1500BF (£30; $45). Breakfast included.

HI HOSTEL
Op-Sinjoorke, Eric Sasselaan 2 (tel. 238 0273). Midnight curfew. B&B in dorms around 335BF (£6.70; $10) for HI members. From Central Station bus 27 to Camille Huysmanslaan. From there the hostel is signposted. Alternatively, tram 2 dir. Hoboken to the Bouwcentrum stop.

HOSTELS
New International Youth Hotel, Provinciestraat 256 (tel. 230 0522). Curfew 11 p.m. Singles 790BF (£15.80; $23.70), doubles around 570BF (£11.40; $16) per person, triples 550BF (£10; $15) per person, quads 500BF (£9.60; $14.40) per person. Tram 11 from Antwerpen-Centraal, or a 10-minute walk.

Boomerang, Volkstraat 58 (tel. 238 4782). B&B in dorms around 400BF (£8; $12). Small rooms are slightly cheaper than at the New International Youth Home. Near the Kon. Museum voor Schone Kunsten. From Antwerpen-Centraal take bus 23.

Square Sleep-Inn, Bolivarplaats 1 (tel. 237 3748). One to four-bedded rooms. Singles are about 550BF (£11; $16.50).

Scoutel-VVKSM, Stoomstraat 3–7 (tel. 226 4606). Five minutes from Antwerpen-Centraal.

International Seamen's House, Falconrui 21 (tel. 232 1609). Compared to the other hostels singles are cheap, doubles more expensive.

CAMPING
Both of the following municipal sites charge the same, about 50BF (£1; $1.50) per person and per tent, and are open 1 Apr.–30 Sept.

De Molen, Thonetlaan, St Annastrand (tel. 219 6090). Across the River Schelde from the city centre.

Vogelzang, Vogelzanglaan (behind the Bouwcentrum) (tel. 238

5717). Tram 2 dir. Hoboken from Central Station takes you to the Bouwcentrum.

Bruges (Brugge) (tel. code 050)

TOURIST OFFICES
Dienst voor Toerisme, Burg 11, B-8000 Brugge (tel. 44 86 86). Apr.–Sept. open Mon.–Fri. 9.30 a.m.–6.30 p.m., weekends 10 a.m.–12 p.m. and 2–6.30 p.m.; Oct.–Mar. open Mon.–Fri. 9.30 a.m.–12.45 p.m., and 2–5.45 p.m., Sat. 10 a.m.–12.45 p.m. and 2–5.45 p.m. Accommodation service. Excellent map of the city with the sights and suggested walking tours 20BF (£0.40; $0.60). The branch office in the train station has a restricted range of information but also offers an accommodation service. Mar.–Oct. open 2.45–9 p.m.; Nov.–Feb. open 1.45–8 p.m.

BASIC DIRECTIONS
Bruges' train station is a 15–20 minute-walk from the city centre. After crossing Stationsplein in front of the station, the main road leading away to the left passes the equestrian statue of King Albert I, before arriving at the wide expanse of 't Zand. From the right hand side of the square, Zuidzandstraat runs past Sint-Salvators Kerk into Steenstraat, which leads in turn to the Markt. From the far left corner of the Markt, Philipstockstraat leads into Burg. As you enter this square the Town Hall is on your right-hand side. Across the square is the former palace of the 'Brugse Vrije', now the seat of the Tourist Office.

Going straight across the road from the left-hand side of Stationsplein takes you into Oostmeers. Heading right from Stationsplein round the main road takes you up past the coach park to the junction with the road to Lille (Rijsel) and Kortrijk. Going right from this junction is Baron Ruzettelaan. Heading left along Katelijnestraat and continuing straight ahead takes you past the end of Heilige-Geeststraat into Simon Stevinplein. Crossing the square and turning right takes you down Steenstraat into the Markt.

HOTELS
Cheapest doubles around 1120BF (£22.50; $33.75)

De Royal, 't Zand 5 (tel. 34 32 84).

Cheapest doubles around 1220BF (£24.40; $36.60)

't Keizerhof, Oostmeers 126 (tel. 33 87 28).
Ensor, Speelmansrei 10 (tel. 34 25 89).

Cheapest doubles around 1260BF (£25.20; $37.80)

't Speelmanshuys, 't Zand 3 (tel. 33 95 52).

Cheapest doubles around 1320BF (£26.40; $39.50)

Leopold, 't Zand 26 (tel. 33 51 29).
Central, Markt 30 (tel. 33 18 05).
De Gulden Kogge, Damse Vaart Zuid 12, Damme (tel. 35 42 17).
    Damme is a picturesque and historic village about 6km from
    Bruges. Buses run to Damme from the train station in Bruges.

Cheapest doubles around 1380BF (£27.50; $41.25)

Imperial, Dweerstraat 24 (tel. 33 90 14). Dweerstraat runs left off
    Zuidzandstraat.
Rembrandt-Rubens, Walplein 38 (tel. 33 64 39). From Oostmeers
    turn right along Zonnekemeers into Walplein or turn left off
    Katelijnestraat down Walstraat into the square.
Jacobs, Baliestraat 1 (tel. 33 98 31). A 10-minute walk from the
    Markt, by St Giles' Church (Sint-Gillis-Kerk).
Het Geestelijk Hof, Heilige Geeststraat 2 (tel. 34 25 94). From
    Zuidzandstraat go right around Sint-Salvators-Kerk to the start
    of Heilige Geeststraat.

Cheapest doubles around 1480BF (£29.60; $44.40)

Gasthof De Krakele, St Pieterskaai 63 (tel. 31 56 43).

Cheapest doubles around 1540BF (£31; $46.50)

Singe d'Or, 't Zand 18 (tel. 33 48 48).
De Pauw, St Gilliskerkhof 8 (tel. 33 71 18). By St Giles' church. A
    10-minute walk from the Markt.

Cheapest doubles around 1650BF (£33; $49.50)

Le Panier d'Or, Markt 28 (tel. 34 32 34).

Cordoeanier, Cordoeanierstraat 16—18 (tel. 33 90 51). Off Philipstockstraat.
Graaf Van Vlaanderen, 't Zand 19 (tel. 33 31 50).

BED & BREAKFAST
Cheapest doubles around 1250BF (£25; $37.50)

K. & A. Dieltjens-Debruyne, St Walburgastraat 14 (tel. 33 42 94).
Well located, about 5 minutes' walk from the Markt.
José Claerhout, St Pieterskaai 66 (tel. 31 32 46).

Cheapest doubles around 1350BF (£27; $40.50)

Catherine Nijssen, Moerstraat 50 (tel. 34 31 71).
Robert Van Nevel, Carmersstraat 13 (tel. 34 68 60). 16th-century
loft in a peaceful old quarter less than 10 minutes from the
Markt.

HI HOSTEL
Baron Ruzettelaan 143 (tel. 35 26 79). B&B in dorms around 375BF
(£7.50; $11.25). Quads with showers around 475BF (£9.50;
$14.25) per person. Non-members pay a supplement of around
100BF (£2; $3) if space is available. Excellent for an HI hostel. The
bar serves cheap beer from 6 p.m.–midnight. Reserve in advance.
A 20-minute walk from the train station or the centre, or bus 2 to
Steenbrugge.

HOSTELS
All the hostels advertise in the train station. Some will pick you up
if you give them a phone call. See the adverts for details. Prices for
dorms at all the hostels are roughly the same as at the HI hostel.
All the hostels include breakfast in the overnight price.

Kilroy's Garden, Singel 12 (tel. 38 93 82). The most recently
opened. Only a few minutes' walk from the station. Also offers
two-, three-and four-bed rooms.
Bruno's Passage, Dweerstraat 26 (tel. 34 02 32). Dorms from
around 350—420BF (£7.00—8.50; $10.50—12.75) depending on
the size of the dorm. Dweerstraat runs left off Zuidzandstraat
Snuffel Travellers' Inn, Ezelstraat 49 (tel. 33 31 33). Doubles around
500BF (£10; $15) per person. Dorms around 375BF (£7.50;
$11.25). From the Markt follow Sint-Jakobsstraat which runs
into Ezelstraat. Bus 3, 8, 9 or 13 from the train station.
Bauhaus International Youth Hotel, Langestraat 135—37 (tel. 34 10

93). Mixed dorms around 340BF (£6.80; $10.20), singles around
600BF (£12; $18), doubles around 500BF (£10; $15) per person,
triples around 420BF (£8.50; $12.75) per person, quads around
380BF (£7.60; $11.40) per person.

CAMPING
St Michiel, Tillegemstraat 55 (tel. 059 80 68 24 or Bruges 38 08
19). Open all year. Around 120BF (£2.40; $3.60) per tent, 100BF
(£2; $3) per person. In the Sint-Michiels area of the city. Bus 7
from the train station.
Memling, Veltemweg 109 (tel. 35 58 45). Open Mar.–Dec. Around
85BF (£1.75; $2.60) per tent and per person. The smaller of the
two sites, in the Sint-Kruis area of the city. There is a large
supermarket nearby.

Brussels (Brussel/Bruxelles) (tel. code 02)

TOURIST OFFICES
TIB, Hôtel de Ville, Grand Place (tel. 513 8940). June–Sept.
open daily 9 a.m.–6 p.m.; Oct.–May same hours, but Mon.–
Sat. only. The office sells the useful *Brussels Guide & Map* 50BF
(£1; $1.50). Free hotel reservations and information on public
transport.
National Tourist Office, rue du Marché-aux-Herbes 63 (tel. 504
0390). June–Sept. open daily 9 a.m.–7 p.m.; Apr.–May and
Oct. 9 a.m.–6 p.m. daily; Nov.–Mar. open Mon.–Sat. 9 a.m.–
6 p.m., Sun. 1–5 p.m. Information on the whole of the country.
The office makes hotel reservations in Brussels.
Tourist Information, Zaventem International Airport. Accommodation service and information on public transport.
Acotra, rue de la Madeleine 51 (tel. 512 8607/512 5540). Youth
tourism office. Good source of information on cheap accommodation for young travellers. Acotra also has an office at the
airport.
BTR, blvd Anspach 111, B-1000 Brussels (tel. 513 7484). For
advance reservation of hotels.

STREET SIGNS
Historically Brussels is a Flemish city, but the majority of its inhabitants today (around 70%) are French speakers. It is only in comparatively recent times that the city was declared bilingual, and

street names given in their Flemish as well as French forms. The section below uses a mixture of Flemish and French street names. Hopefully the directions given will get you right to where you want to go, but do not worry about approaching someone if you get lost. The people of Brussels are generally friendly and few Flemish speakers will object to you using the French version of a street name (or vice versa).

ARRIVING IN BRUSSELS

There are three main train stations of interest to tourists: Gare du Nord, Gare du Midi and Gare Centrale. The latter is most convenient for the sights and for the Tourist Offices, but not all through-trains stop at this station. There are frequent connections from Gare du Nord and Gare du Midi to Gare Centrale, so it is no problem if your train does not stop at Gare Centrale. There is a half-hourly train service between Zaventem International Airport and Gare Centrale and Gare du Nord until 11.45 p.m. (a 20-minute trip, free with railpasses).

Running along the front of Gare Centrale is the busy Keizerinlaan. Towards the left hand end of this road, rue de l'Infante Isabella runs away from the station. Follow this street down past the Chapel of Mary Magdalene and continue straight ahead, passing the restaurants to arrive at the start of rue Marché-aux-Herbes, just beyond the entrance to the Galeries Royales St Hubert on your right. Continuing down this street takes you to the National Tourist Office. Turning left takes you into Grand Place. TIB is located in the Town Hall on the opposite side of the square.

The two main coach companies operating from the UK both drop passengers a short distance from the Grand Place. Hoverspeed coaches stop at pl. de la Bourse, from which Boterstraat leads into Grand Place. Eurolines stop a little further away at pl. de Brouckere. From this square follow Anspachlaan to pl. de la Bourse, then turn left along Beurstraat down the side of the Stock Exchange to the start of Boterstraat.

HOTELS
Cheapest doubles around 1050–1100BF (£21–22; $31.50–33.00)

Bosquet, rue Bosquet 70 (tel. 538 5230). Basic, but price includes breakfast. A 10–15-minute walk from Gare du Midi or 5 minutes' walk from Metro: Place Louise.
New Galaxy, rue du Progrès 7A (tel. 219 4776). Rue du Progrès runs between Gare du Nord and the Rogier metro stop (about 500m separates the two). Leave Gare du Nord by the side exit

on to pl. du Nord, or head left from the main exit around the station.

Osborne, 67 rue Bosquet (tel. 537 9251). See Bosquet, above, for directions from Gare du Midi. From the Place Louise metro station walk down av. Louise then turn right along rue Jourdan into rue Bosquet.

Cheapest doubles around 1200BF (£24; $36)

Jamar, blvd Jamar 11 (tel. 522 0104). Near Gare du Midi.

La Potinière, Fr. Jos. Navezstraat 165 (tel. 2152 030). A 10–15-minute walk from Gare du Nord.

Cheapest doubles around 1250–1350BF (£25–27; $37.50–40.50)

De France, Jamarlaan 21 (tel. 522 7935). About 300m from Gare du Midi. From the station walk down av. Paul Henri Spaak to pl. Bara. Jamarlaan is off to the right.

Les Bluets, Berckmansstraat 124 (tel. 534 3983). Follow the directions for Bosquet, above. Berckmannstraat is right off Jasparlaan coming from Gare du Midi, the second street on the left after rue Bosquet walking from pl. Louise.

International, rue Royale 344 (tel. 217 3344). All rooms have a shower. About 500m from the Botanique metro station; only a little further away from Gare du Nord.

Albert, rue Royale Sainte-Marie 27–29 (tel. 217 9391).

Pacific, rue Antoine Dansaert 57 (tel. 511 8459).

Cheapest doubles around 1400–1500BF (£28–30; $42–45)

Lloyd George, av. Lloyd George 12 (tel. 648 3072).

Sabina, rue du Nord 78 (tel. 218 2637). About 200m from the Madou metro station.

Paris, blvd Poincarré 80 (tel. 527 0920). Near Gare du Midi.

Elysée, rue de la Montagne 4 (tel. 511 9682). Good central location. Rue de la Montagne runs uphill from the start of rue Marché-aux-Herbes near the Galeries Royales St Hubert.

Cheapest doubles around 1600–1650BF (£32–33; $48.00–49.50)

Plasky, E. Plaskylaan 212 (tel. 733 7530). Bus 63 from the Madou metro station.

Madou, rue du Congrès 45 (tel. 218 8375). Near the Madou metro stop. From pl. Madou cross pl. Surlet de Chokier and walk down rue du Congrès.

Gascogne, Adolphe Maxlaan 137 (tel. 217 6962). Closed August. About 600m from Gare du Nord, a few minutes' walk from the Rogier metro station.

Grande-Clôche, pl. Rouppe 10−12 (tel. 512 6140). A few minutes' walk from the Anneessens metro station; about 750m from Gare du Midi.

't Zilveren Tasje, rue du Congrès 48 (tel. 217 3274). See the Madou above for directions.

Barry, pl. Anneessens 25 (tel. 511 2795).

Eperonniers, rue des Eperonniers 1 (tel. 513 5366).

Duke of Windsor, Capouilletstraat 4 (tel. 539 1819).

Cheapest doubles around 1740−1900BF (£35−38; $52.50−57.00)

De Boeck's, rue Veydt 40 (tel. 537 4033).

Windsor, pl. Rouppe 13 (tel. 511 2014).

Rembrandt, rue de la Concorde 42 (tel. 512 7139).

Cheapest doubles around 2000−2200BF (£40−44; $60−66)

George V, 't Kintstraat 23 (tel. 513 5093). About 600m from the Anneessens metro stop or a 10−15-minute walk from Gare du Midi.

Opera, rue Grétry 53 (tel. 219 4343).

HI HOSTELS

'Breugel' (Flemish YHA), Heilige Geeststraat 2 (tel. 511 0436). Open 7−10 a.m., 2 p.m.−12 a.m. B&B in dorms around 380BF (£7.60; $11.40). Singles 650BF (£13; $19.50), doubles 510BF (£10.20; $15.30) per person, quads 425BF (£8.50; $12.75) per person. A 5-minute walk from Gare Centrale.

Centre Jacques Brel (Walloon YHA), rue de la Sablonnière 30 (tel. 218 0187). Curfew 1 a.m. B&B in dorms around 380BF (£7.60; $11.40). Singles 620BF (£12.40; $18.60), doubles 510BF (£10.20; $15.30) per person, triples and quads 425BF (£8.50; $12.75) per person. A 10-minute walk from Gare du Nord; about 400m from the Botanique metro station.

'Jean Nihon' (Walloon YHA), rue de l'Eléphant 4 (tel. 410 3858). Same prices as the other Walloon YHA hostel. Metro: Zwarte Vijvers (slightly closer) or Graaf Van Vlaanderen. Under 10 minutes' walk from both. From Graaf Van Vlaanderen follow St Mariastraat across Graaf Van Vlaanderenstraat into Briefdragerstraat. Turn left along Schoolstraat, across Gentse Steenweg and on down Paalstraat. At the fork in the road rue de l'Eléphant is to the right. From Zwarte Vijvers follow Gentse Steenweg until you see Paalstraat on your right. Going this way you should pass Ostendstraat on the right a short distance from the metro station; if not you are going the wrong way.

HOSTELS

CHAB, rue Traversière 8 (tel. 217 0158). Curfew 2 a.m. Large co-ed rooms with mattresses on floor around 290BF (£5.80; $8.70). Beds in small dorms around 350BF (£7; $10.50). Singles 590BF (£11.80; $17.70), doubles 490BF (£9.80; $14.70) per person; triples and quads 410BF (£8.20; $12.30) per person. Overnight price includes breakfast. Bus 61 from the Gare du Nord to rue Traversière, or a 10-minute walk.

Sleep Well, rue de la Blanchisserie 27 (tel. 218 5050). Curfew 1 a.m. Dorms around 295BF (£5.90; $8.85). Singles 495BF (£9.90; $14.85), doubles 425BF (£8.50; $12.75) per person, four- to six-bed rooms 375BF (£7.50; $11.25) per person. In July and August only, places are available in very large dorms for around 250BF (£5; $7.50). Overnight prices include breakfast. Those whose passport includes the number 27 get a 25% discount on the overnight price. Due to move next door to rue de Damier 22, when it will become 'Brusswell'.

Centre International Etudiants Tiers-Monde, rue de Parme 26 (tel. 537 8961). A 10-minute walk from Gare du Midi, slightly closer to the Place Louise metro station.

Maison Internationale, chaussée de Waure 205 (tel. 648 9787). Bus 37 or 38 from Gare Centrale, or train to Gare du Quartier Leopold. Also offers camping in summer.

Foyer International Protestant 'David Livingstone', av. Coghen 119 (tel. 343 3089).

Entraide Educative et Sociale, pl. Loix 20 (tel. 537 9642).

CAMPING

Unless you pitch your tent at the Maison Internationale (see the Hostels section above) you are going to have to do a fair bit of commuting to one of the sites in the suburbs.

Beersel, Steenweg op Ukkel 75, Beersel (tel. 331 0561/378 1977). Open all year. Basic, but very cheap. Around 100BF (£2; $3) for a solo traveller. From Nord-Bourse tram 55, then bus UH. The most convenient site if you are arriving from Paris, Mons and Charleroi on the E10/A7.

Paul Rosmant, Warandeberg 52, Wezembeek-Oppem (tel. 782

1009). Open Apr.–Sept. Around 85BF (£1.70; $2.60) per tent and per person, plus a municipality tax of 30BF (£0.60; $0.90). Metro to Kraainem, then change to bus 30 to pl. St Pierre. Just off the Brussels ring road. The most convenient site if you are arriving by road from Leuven, Liège or Germany.

Veldkant, Veldkantstraat, Grimbergen (tel. 269 2597). Open Apr.–Oct. 120BF (£2.40; $3.60) per tent, 90BF (£1.80; $2.70) per person. Bus G from Gare du Nord to the end of the line, then a 10-minute walk. The easiest site to get to if you are arriving by road from Antwerp.

Ghent (Gent) (tel. code 091)

TOURIST OFFICES
Dienst voor Toerisme, Predikherenlei 2, B-9000 Gent – use this address for enquiries in advance of your visit. On arrival contact Info-Toerisme in the Stadhuis (Town Hall) on Botermarkt (tel. 224 1555). Open Easter–early Nov. daily, 9.30 a.m.–6.30 p.m.; at other times of the year the office closes at 4.30 p.m.

HOTELS
Cheapest doubles 1010BF (£20.20; $30.30)

Formule 1, Vliegtwglaan 21 (tel. 51 63 10). Bus 70 from Gent-Dampoort and Gent-St Pieters. Breakfast 120BF (£2.40; $3.60).

Cheapest doubles around 1600BF (£32; $48), triples around 1850BF (£37; $55.50) as indicated

Flandria, Barrestraat 3 (tel. 223 0626). Doubles 1300–1600BF (£26–32; $39–48), triples 1800–2200BF (£36–44; $54–66). Good central location, a few minutes' walk from the Stadhuis.

Adoma, Sint-Denijslaan 203 (tel. 222 6550). A 5-minute walk from Gent-St Pieters, going left from the rear exit. Doubles 1640BF (£33; $49.50), triples 2260BF (£45.20; $67.80).

Castel, Kon. Maria Hendrikaplein 8 (tel. 220 2354). Doubles and triples.

Trianon, Sint-Denijslaan 203 (tel. 221 3944). Doubles with showers 1550BF (£31; $46.50). Head right from the rear exit of Gent-St Pieters.

B&B
Around 450BF (£9; $13.50) per person

Peter Klingele, Voorhoutkaai 6. No telephone. Good location on the Leie, near Gent-Dampoort. Follow the directions for M. & L. Laquiere-Seydlitz, below.

Doubles around 1125BF (£22.50; $33.75) per person

Joost Van Damme-Deltour, Drabstraat 28 (tel. 225 5568).
Riet Dhooge, Aannemersstraat 76 (tel. 228 1939).
Vincent Ronse, Plotersgracht 12 (tel. 225 6604)

Singles around 620BF (£12.40; $18.60)

Christin De Muynck, Blekersdijk 46 (tel. 224 3294). Good location near Gent-Dampoort. Follow Dampoortstraat or Hagelandkaai towards the Leie. At the bridge, turn right down Ham, then left on to Blekersdijk.

Doubles around 1450BF (£29; $43.50)

May Howard, Leeuwstraat 17 (tel. 225 1688). Good central location.

Doubles around 1550BF (£31; $46.50)

M. & L. Laquiere-Seydlitz, Gebroeders Van Eyckstraat 50 (tel. 223 4530). Well located, a 5-minute walk from the town centre. From Gent-Dampoort walk past the end of the dock and take Schoolkaai (across the inlet of the Leie from Hagelandkaai), left along the waterfront down Voorhuitkaai, then over the bridge and straight on into Gebroeders Van Eyckstraat.

UNIVERSITY ACCOMMODATION
From mid-July to late September single rooms are available in the university's four halls of residence for around 500BF (£10; $15), including breakfast and the use of showers. The halls are open round the clock. Contact Vermeylen Hall, Stalhof 6, B-9000 Gent (tel. 222 0911). You can try telephoning the other halls themselves: Fabiola (tel. 222 6091); Boudewijn, Harelbekestraat 70 (tel. 222 9721); Astrid, Krijgslaan 250 (tel. 222 9081).

CAMPING
Blaarmeersen, Zuiderlaan 12 (tel. 221 5399). Open March–
  mid-Oct. 110BF (£2.20; $3.30) per tent, 100BF (£2; $3) per
  person. From Gent-St Pieters station a 20-minute walk, or bus
  51, 52 or 53 to Europaburg, then bus 38.
Witte Berken, Pontstraat 4, 903 Drongen (tel. 222 0550). Just outside Ghent. Open July–Aug. 65BF (£1.30; $2) per tent and per
  person. Caravans for hire.

HI HOSTELS
The first youth hostel listed is in Ghent itself, the other three are
in surrounding towns; railpass holders who are stuck for a bed may
have to travel to one of the latter:

De Draeke, Sint-Widostraat (tel. 233 7050). 335BF (£6.70; $10)
  per person in three-, four- and six-person rooms. Price includes
  breakfast. Bed linen 120BF (£2.40; $3.60).
De Valk, Mellestraat 18A, B-9270 Laarne (tel. 30 03 67/30 60 50).
  230BF (£4.40; $6.60) per person in 2–5-person rooms. Bed linen
  120BF (£2.30; $3.45).
Kampstraat 59 (Recreatiedomein 'De Gavers'), Geraardsbergen (tel.
  054 41 61 89). Geraardsbergen is roughly 32km from Ghent,
  served by frequent local trains. The hostel is 5 minutes' walk
  from Schendeleke station.
Passionistenlaan 1A, Kortrijk (tel. 056 20 14 42). Ten minutes from
  the train station. Kortrijk is about 56km from Ghent, with
  frequent InterCity trains leaving from Gent-St Pieters and Gent-
  Dampoort.

Liège (tel. code 041)

TOURIST OFFICES
Office du Tourisme de la Ville de Liège, En Féronstrée 92 (tel. 21
92 21). Open Mon.–Fri. 10 a.m.–5 p.m.; Sat. 10 a.m.–4 p.m., Sun.
10 a.m.–2 p.m. City plans, and advice on accommodation possibilities. Close to the Musée d'Art Wallon, along from the Town Hall
on pl. du Marché.
  Branch offices are located at Gare des Guillemins (tel. 52 44 19)
and blvd de la Sauvenière 77. Same services as the main office on
En Féronstrée.

HOTELS
The city's cheaper hotels are located around Gare des Guillemins. Rue des Guillemins is the street running left from the station down to pl. des Guillemins. The red light district is along to the right of Gare des Guillemins, but the area around the station is quite safe to walk around in.

Cheapest singles around 650BF (£13; $19.50), cheapest doubles around 950BF (£19; $28.50)

Les Nations, rue des Guillemins 139 (tel. 52 44 34).

Cheapest singles around 1020BF (£20.40; $30.60), cheapest doubles around 1200BF (£24; $36)

Du Midi, pl. des Guillemins 1 (tel. 52 20 04).

Cheapest singles around 850BF (£17; $25.50), cheapest doubles around 1270BF (£25.40; $38)

Le Berger, rue des Urbanistes 10 (tel. 23 00 80).

Cheapest singles around 950BF (£19; $28.50), cheapest doubles around 1380BF (£27.60; $41.50)

Metropole, rue des Guillemins 141 (tel. 52 42 93).

Cheapest doubles around 1650BF (£33; $49.50)

De La Couronne, pl. des Guillemins 11 (tel. 52 21 68/54 16 69).

HI HOSTEL
Rue Blandot 4, Tilff (tel. 88 21 00). 310BF (£6.20; $9.30) per person, including breakfast. Bed linen 120BF (£2.40; $3.60). This excellent hostel is only 500m from the train station in Tilff, 5km from Liège (frequent train services).

FOYER
Foyer International des Etudiants, rue du Vertbois 29 (tel. 23 28 85). Three-night minimum stay. 200BF (£4; $6) in dorms. The foyer is of poor quality. By the Eglise St-Jacques, off blvd d'Avroy between the Charlemagne statue and the start of blvd de la Sauvenière.

CAMPING

Camping Club de Sainval, Chemin du Halage, Tilff (tel. 26 71 04). Around 50BF (£1; $1.50) per tent and per person. Tilff is 5km from Liège (frequent train services).

Camping du S.I., rue du Chera, Tilff (tel. 88 12 86/88 16 30). 50BF (£1; $1.50) per tent, 40BF (£0.85; $1.30) per person.

Camping de l'Allée Verte, Allée Verte 25, Vise (tel. 79 32 04). Around 30BF (£0.60; $0.90) per tent and per person. Vise is about 24km from Liège. On the train line to/from Maastricht (frequent service).

BULGARIA

When travelling in Bulgaria you will find that the reception you will receive from people working in the tourist industry will vary dramatically. In some cases, you will find people who will do their utmost to help you to find suitably priced accommodation, and who will provide you with any other available information to help you enjoy your stay. Sadly, there is currently a dearth in tourist information (particularly town plans showing the places of interest), and in cheap accommodation, so it is often the case that staff in the tourist industry simply cannot help you, no matter how much they might like to.

Unfortunately, it is just not possible to say with any certainty where you might have trouble finding cheap accommodation and where you should not. In many popular destinations (such as Sofia, Plovdiv and Veliko Târnovo) the supply of cheap lodgings just manages to satisfy demand at most times of the year, while in others (such as Varna and the Black Sea resorts) the increase in the number of tourists has swamped the existing accommodation possibilities. While the supply of budget accommodation is rising throughout the country the number of visitors continues to rise also. As ongoing strife in Yugoslavia continues to make Bulgaria an attractive option for reaching Greece overland, there is likely to be dramatically increased pressure on accommodation possibilities in obvious stopover points such as Sofia, Plovdiv and Veliko Târnovo.

Budget travellers will probably be interested in only the one- and two-star **hotel** categories (the only difference is that rooms in one-star hotels do not have a private bath). Prices in one-star hotels are usually around £10.25 ($15) for a single, £4–6 ($6–9) for a double. Comparable rooms in a two-star hotel cost £13.75 ($20.50) and £6–12 ($9–18) respectively. Hotel accommodation is now more difficult to find than it was during the days of state control because of the increased number of visitors, and finding a hotel room on arrival can pose problems throughout much of the year. One-star hotels in popular towns still tend to be filled with groups of East European holidaymakers, so you still have a better chance of finding a room in a two-star hotel. Because of language difficulties, it is always better to approach hotels in person if you arrive after the Tourist Office has closed, rather than contacting them by telephone. If you are told upfront that there are no rooms available this is likely to be true and not, as is often the case in neighbouring Romania, a ploy to get you to offer a bribe.

Arranging lodgings in the home of a Bulgarian family is both a cheaper and a more interesting option than staying in a hotel. **Private rooms** can be booked through Balkantourist and, in some cases, through other organizations such as ORBITA (the student travel organization). In Sofia, doubles cost about £4.50–5.75 ($6.75–8.50) per person, with the cheaper rooms generally being located out in the suburbs. As the public transport system in Sofia is cheap and reasonably efficient, it is practicable to stay in the suburbs if you cannot find a room in the centre. Outside the capital, doubles in popular destinations like Plovdiv and Veliko Târnovo rarely cost more than £5 ($7.50) per person. In the countryside, rooms can cost as little as £2.50 ($3.75) per person, though it can be very difficult to find rooms in rural areas. One occasional draw-back to booking rooms through an agency in the past has been the existence of a minimum stay requirement: particularly along the Black Sea coast, where a minimum stay of three to five days was required in some towns. In more popular towns, it is not unusual to be approached by touts offering private rooms during the peak season. The rooms on offer are often of lower quality than those offered by accommodation agencies, but they may be your only hope of getting a cheap bed. Touts are well aware of the local lodging situation, so there is not a great deal of room for haggling over their initial asking price, which at the very height of the season can be on a par with rooms booked through a local agency.

The student travel organization ORBITA controls a network of hotels and **youth hostels**. In the past, ORBITA youth hostels admitted Westerners by prior reservation only. While groups of five or more were sometimes allowed to book hostels on arrival in Sofia, others had to book months in advance. Nowadays, the situation is that while ORBITA still prefers dealing with groups, and while it is still almost impossible to find a space at an ORBITA hostel on arrival, their staff are more likely to admit you to a hostel if there is space available. Realistically, only during university summer vacations, mid-July until mid-September, do independent travellers have a slim chance of finding a place in student accommodation. If you are lucky enough to do so, you can expect to pay around £1.50 ($2.25) for a bed.

The Bulgarian Tourist Union, which is affiliated to the HI, also operates a chain of hostels, around 60 of which are listed in the HI handbook. Facilities are little more than basic, and the hostels are often located far from the centre of town, but at around £1.50 ($2.25) for a bed the price is fine. Once again, these should be booked well in advance as they are popular with visiting groups. However, as the staff at these hostels were traditionally more accommodating to Western visitors stuck for a bed than their counterparts in hotels, or in the ORBITA hostels, it might be worthwhile making a personal enquiry at any hostel you come across.

Camping is both a cheap way to see the country and an ideal way to meet young East European travellers. Charges are around £1.50 ($2.25) per tent, with a similar fee per occupant. Moreover, taking a tent normally provides insurance against having to pay out for a hotel room if you cannot find a hostel bed or a private room, as virtually all the main tourist destinations have a campsite in or around town (city sites are often located on the outskirts). With the exception of sites along the Black Sea coast which become very crowded in summer, finding a place to pitch your tent is generally straightforward. The Bulgarian National Tourist Office in London/your capital city may be able to provide you with a map of the 120 campsites Western visitors were once restricted to (at the time of writing, the London office was very short of information). This map covers all the places you are likely to visit, and contains details of site facilities and opening periods (normally May—mid-Oct. inclusive). At most of these sites comfortable chalet accommodation is available to let. A chalet sleeping two normally costs in the region of £1—2 ($1.50—3.00) per night. **Freelance camping** and **sleeping rough** are both illegal and steep fines are usually imposed on those apprehended. However, in recent years the police have been turning a blind eye to people sleeping rough in some of the Black Sea resorts during the peak season, possibly because they are well aware of the dire shortage of accommodation possibilities in that area.

Hikers and climbers should contact the Bulgarian Tourist Union for permission to use the network of **mountain chalets** (*hizha*) they operate, and to make the necessary reservations. The standard of accommodation in *hizha* varies tremendously from those with only the bare essentials to those which seem like hotels.

TOURIST INFORMATION
As the quality of tourist information available locally to visitors is poor, it is advisable to purchase a good guidebook before setting off on holiday. At the time of writing, this is easier said than done, though hopefully the situation will have improved by 1995. Some of the guidebooks which covered the old Eastern Bloc are good sources of information on the main sights to see, but the information on accommodation in these books is now obsolete.

ADDRESSES
Bulgarian National   18 Princes Street, London, W1R 7RE
  Tourist Office   (tel. 0171 499 6988).

Hotels	Balkantourist, Knyaz Dondukov 37, Sofia (tel. 88 44 30).
Private rooms	See Balkantourist above.
Hostels	ORBITA, (Student Travel Office), bul. Alexander Stamboliiski 45a, Sofia (tel. 88 48 01).
	ORBITA, bul. Vitosha 4, Sofia (tel. 831659).
	Bulgarian Tourist Union, Zentralrat, bul. Tolbuchin 18, Sofia (tel. 87 94 05).
Mountain huts	Bulgarian Tourist Union. Address above.

Plovdiv (tel. code 032)

TOURIST OFFICE
Puldin Tour, bul. Bulgaria 34 (tel. 55 38 48). Open daily 8 a.m.–9 p.m. The office is close to the fairgrounds, across the River Marica from the town centre. From the railway station take bus 1 or 7 to the stop after crossing the river, or take tram 102 to the ninth stop. The office is one block along bul. Bulgaria from the tram stop.

HOTELS
Bulgaria, ul. Patriarch Evtimii (tel. 22 60 64). Two-star hotel. Singles £14.25 ($21), doubles £23.50 ($35.25). Follow Vasil Kolarov from Central Square and then go right.
Leipzig, bul. Ruski 70 (tel. 23 22 50). Two-star hotel. Similar prices to the Bulgaria. Ruski is the main street which runs away from the train station. The Leipzig is four blocks along the street.

Enquire at Puldin Tour about rooms in the centrally located Republica (Knyaz Aleksandâr 39, tel. 22 21 33) and any other hotels that may be cheaper than the two above. In the past, the doors of the city's cheapest hotels have been closed to Western guests, but the situation may now have altered.

PRIVATE ROOMS
Available from Puldin Tour. Normally prices are around £5 ($7.50) for a double, but prices rise during the Plovdiv Fair (last two weeks of Sept.) to around £8 ($12).

CAMPING

Trakiya. Open Apr.–Nov. Twin-bedded bungalows around £5.75 ($8.50). Four kilometres from the centre on the road to Sofia (an extension of bul. Bulgaria), by the Gorski Kat restaurant. Take bus 4 or 18 to the last stop, from which the site is a 10-minute walk along the main road.

Maritsa. Open Apr.–Nov. Bungalows available. Five kilometres further out than the Trakia site.

Chaya. Open mid-Apr.–mid-Oct. Bungalows available. Fifteen kilometres east of Plovdiv, just off the highway to Istanbul.

Sofia (tel. code 02)

TOURIST OFFICES

For information, currency exchange, and to book private rooms, contact one of the several Balkantourist offices in the city, or the small branch at Sofia airport.

Knyaz Dondukov 37 (tel. 88 06 55). Open daily 8 a.m.–9 p.m. Take tram 1, 7 or 15 from the train station to pl. Sveta Nedelya.

Bul. Alexander Stambolijska 27 (tel. 87 29 67/88 52 56). Open summer 7 a.m.–10 p.m.; out of season 8 a.m.–9 p.m.

Bul. Vitosa 1 (tel. 43331). Open daily 8 a.m.–8 p.m.

Pirin Travel Agency, bul. Alexander Stambolijska 30 (tel. 97 05 79) act as agent for HI hostels. Their helpful staff can also give information about the city.

HOTELS

In recent years the amount of hotel accommodation available to Western visitors has been increased as non-Balkantourist hotels which were previously debarred from admitting Westerners now admit anyone. Nevertheless, there are still no real bargains to be found in the centrally located hotels. Singles in the hotels below normally cost around £10–15 ($15–22.50), doubles around £20–26 ($30–39). Book hotel rooms through Balkantourist.

Zdravec, Knyaginya Mariya Luiza (tel. 83 39 49). Tram 1, 7 or 15 from the train station along Knyaginya Mariya Luiza.

Edelvais, Knyaginya Mariya Luiza (tel. 83 54 31).

Sredna Gora, Knyaginya Mariya Luiza 60 (tel. 83 53 11).

Bulgaria, bul. Tsar Osvoboditel 4 (tel. 87 19 77). Where Knyaz Dondukov goes left from pl. Sveta Nedelya (see Tourist Offices) bul. Tsar Osvoboditel heads right.

Serdika, bul. Yanko Sakâzor 2 (tel. 44 34 11). Bus 13, 213 or 285 from the train station to the junction of Slivnica and Volgograd. Walk down Volgograd (or take trolleybus 1) until you see bul. Yanko Sakâzor, the second major road on the left.

Pliska, bul. Trakiya 87 (tel. 71281). Out from the city centre but easily reached from the train station. Buses 13 and 213 from the station run along Trakiya. You will know you are on Trakiya when you see the stadium and the large Park Na Svobodata on the right.

Slaviya, ul. Sofiiski Geroi 2 (tel. 52 55 51). Just outside the centre, easily reached on public transport. Tram 13 from the train station runs down bul. Hristo Botev before turning right along General Totleben into 9 Septemvri. Sofiiski is to the left near the start of 9 Septemvri.

Sevastopol, ul. Rakovski 116 (tel. 87 59 41). One of the cheaper hotels. Prices at the bottom of the ranges quoted above. Centrally located. To the right of Knyaz Dondukov (see Tourist Offices) is Tsar Osvoboditel which crosses Rakovski.

Hemus, bul. Cherni Vrâh 31 (tel. 66 14 15). Prices at the top of the ranges quoted but a very clean, pleasant hotel. Breakfast included. Tram 9 from the train station runs along Cherni Vrâh.

Preslav, ul. Traiditsa 3 (tel. 87 65 86).

Gorna Banya, Oural 1 (tel. 57 00 86).

Kopitoto (tel. 57 50 51). Far from the centre in the foothills of Mount Vitosha. From the train station take tram 6, 9 or 13 along Hristo Botev to pl. Dimitar Blagoev, change to tram 5 to the terminus, and then again to bus 62.

Iskâr, ul. Iskâr 9 (tel. 83 58 11). B&B in singles £6.25 ($9.50). Very cheap, if not especially pleasant. Communal showers and bathrooms. Walking down Dondukov (see Tourist Offices) from pl. Sveta Nedelya, ul. Iskâr is parallel one block to the left.

PRIVATE ROOMS

Private rooms arranged through an official agency are the best accommodation option open to travellers in Sofia. Balkantourist at Knyaz Dondukov will arrange centrally located doubles for around £8 ($12). The rooms offered by touts at the train station are frequently of poor quality and/or far from the centre, and probably only to be considered if you are desperate. The Markela bureau, bul. Knyaginay Mariya Luiza 17, has rooms for £2 ($3) a night.

HI HOSTELS

There are five hostels in the vicinity of Sofia, and all can be conveniently booked from the Pirin Travel Agency, bul. Alexander Stambolijska 30 (tel. 87 05 79/88 10 79). Turn left off Vitosa close to pl. Sveta Nedelya and it is opposite the Orbita offices.

Tourist, Komplex 'Krasma polyana' (tel. 88 10 79). Situated 8km from the railway station; take tram 4 or 11.
Aleko (tel. 88 10 79), in the Vitosha Mountain National Park, about 20km from central Sofia. Take bus 66.
Belite Brezi, also in the Vitosha Park (tel. 88 10 79). Bus 61 or 62.
Planinarska Pessen. As above. Bus 61 or 261.
Planinetz. Also in the Vitosha Park (tel. 57 31 39).

HOSTEL

ORBITA Student Hostel, Anton Ivanov 76 (tel. 65 29 52). ISIC card required. Tram 9 from the train station to the junction of Georgi Trajkov and Anton Ivanov (also tram 2 from the city centre). Do not expect to find a place here during the peak season. The ORBITA head office is at Stamboliiski 45 (tel. 80 18 12).

CAMPING

The two most convenient sites are both about 9.5km out from the centre. Both offer bungalows for hire:

Cherniya Kos. (tel. 57 11 29). Open May–Oct. Twin-bedded bungalows £9.25 ($14). Off the road to Pernik, by the foot of Mount Vitosa. From the train station take tram 6, 9 or 13 along Hristo Bonev to pl. Dimitar Blagoev, then take tram 5 to its terminus, then bus 58 or 59.
Vranya (tel. 78 12 13). Open all year round. Off the E80 to Plovdiv. Bus 213 from the train station, then change to bus 5.

There are another two sites about 16km out from the city centre:

Bankya (tel. 983 2509). Open May–Sept. Off the E80 on the way to Belgrade.
Lebed (tel. 77 30 45). Open May–Oct. Chalets only. £9.25 ($14) for two-bed chalets. Off the road to Samokov.

Varna (tel. code 052)

TOURIST OFFICES
Balkantourist has three offices in the city and can book private rooms for you:

Opposite the train station (tel. 22 56 30). Open daily 8 a.m.–6 p.m.
ul. Musala 3 (tel. 22 55 24). Near Hotel Musala. Open daily 8 a.m.–
  6 p.m.
Bul. Knjaz Boris I 73 (tel. 22 55 09). Open weekdays 9 a.m.–
  5 p.m.

Pirin Travel, near Hotel Musala, can also give information and advice, as well as booking tickets and tours: Kabakciev 13 (tel. 22 27 10).

HOTELS
Musala, ul. Musala 1 (tel. 223925). The cheapest hotel in the town. Singles around £8 ($12), doubles around £11.50 ($17.25). Beside the Tourist Office.
Orbita, bul. Tsar Osroboditel 25 (tel. 225162). Doubles around £17 ($25.50).
Odessa, bul. Primorski 4 (tel. 228381). Doubles around £17 ($25.50).

PRIVATE ROOMS
Available from Balkantourist. £6 ($9). Generally located in or around the town centre. Terziiski, at ul. Sheinova 8, also has rooms.

CAMPING
Galata. Open mid-June–mid-Sept., during which time it is frequently filled to capacity. There are bungalows, but you will have to be very fortunate to get one of them. Bus 17 from bul. Botev to Galata.

SLEEPING ROUGH
Given the vastly increased numbers visiting Varna in recent years there is simply not enough accommodation to go round during the summer. Perhaps it is in recognition of this fact that the local police have been tolerant of people sleeping rough, despite its being illegal.

The park by the railway station has become a popular place for sleeping out. For safety's sake, you can deposit your pack at the left-luggage (*garderob*) opposite the station (open 5.30 a.m.– 10.30 p.m.).

Veliko Târnovo (tel. code 062)

TOURIST OFFICE
Balkantourist, inside the Etâr Hotel, off Hristo Botev (tel. 28165). Open daily 10 a.m.–noon and 3–8 p.m. Town maps and brochures, as well as private accommodation from £6 ($9).

HOTELS
Stadium, Todor Balina 14 (tel. 20324). Doubles from £4 ($6). Bus 7 or 11 from the centre.
Etâr (tel. 26851). Doubles from £12 ($18). Off Hristo Botev.
Yantra, pl. Velchova Zavera 1 (tel. 20391). Doubles around £17 ($25.50). In the old town, off Dimitar Blagoev.
Orbita, Hristo Botev 15. Cheap but frequently filled to capacity, especially during the summer.
Motel Sveta Gora (tel. 20472). Cheap rooms. See the Sveta Gora campsite for directions.

PRIVATE ROOMS
Available from Balkantourist. The office has a fair supply of rooms in the old town, but these can go quickly at the height of the tourist season.

HI HOSTELS
The Pirin Travel Agency at ul. Dimitar Blagoev 79 (tel. 20373) will make reservations in local hostels for HI members. The most convenient is the excellent hostel operating in the Hotel Edelvais at the same address as Pirin.

CAMPING
Sveta Gora. Open June–Oct. Bungalows available. About 2.5km west of the town, by the Motel Sveta Gora, in the Sveta Gora Park. Ask for directions from the terminus of buses 4, 12 or 13 (infrequent services) which you can catch at the bus or train stations.

Bolyarski stan (tel. 40094). Open all year round. Also with bungalows. Three kilometres west of the town. From the theatre on Vasil Levski (see Tourist Offices) take bus 11 to the junction of the main roads to Sofia and Varna.

CROATIA (Hrvatska)

After some very difficult years, Croatia's tourist industry is currently struggling back to its feet. Restoration of buildings and monuments is continuing in the ancient city of Dubrovnik, Hydrofoil links with the Italian coasts are starting again, and package companies are tentatively offering holidays to resorts like Split and Porec. However, things are still far from stable, and prices especially are liable to change without much notice. The new national currency, the Croatian Dinar (Hrd) is not a hard, convertible currency, so prices are usually quoted in dollars or deutschmarks.

Independent travellers should be wary of travelling anywhere other than Zagreb or the main holiday resorts on the coast. The capital has been largely unaffected by the war, apart from the large numbers of UN vehicles and personnel everywhere. In the countryside, however, poorly trained and ill-disciplined police and soldiers can act unpredictably, and sleeping rough would be extremely unwise. Many campsites and tourist hotels have been taken over as refugee centres, and the aid community has snapped up much of the remaining accommodation. Locals often assume that all foreigners are highly paid UN staff and adjust prices accordingly. The information which follows is given in the hope that the situation continues to improve in 1995.

Hotels are likely to prove an expensive option for the independent traveller in the summer months but can fall to bargain levels in off-peak periods. A C-class hotel can cost as little as £10 ($15) for a double room, but will double in price in July and August. **Private rooms** tend to be a cheaper option. These are classified by the Tourist Offices as Category I (doubles from around £9.30; $14), Category II (£7.30; $11) and Category III (£5.30; $8). Prices will vary between different towns, and are often higher in July and August.

There are seven **HI hostels** in Croatia which offer dormitory beds from around £4 ($6), but these tend to fill up quickly. There's also a more informal network of **independent hostels** and **student residences** (summer only) which cost roughly the same. The situation with Croatia's **campsites** is rather different; many have closed as a result of the war and others now operate as refugee camps. Before setting off for one of the sites listed below be sure to ring ahead and check that it is indeed still open.

Lastly, **sleeping rough** is not really an option in Croatia. Police tour the beaches in the tourist resorts, and at best you are liable to be fined if caught.

ADDRESSES

Phoenix Holidays (for the Croatian National Tourist Office)	INA House, 210 Shepherds Bush Rd, London, W6 7NL (tel. 0171 371 6600)
Croatian Embassy	18/21 Jermyn Street, London SW1Y 6HP (tel. 0171 434 2946).
Atlas Travel Agency	Pile 1, 5000 Dubrovnik (tel. 42 22 22).

Dubrovnik (tel. code 050)

In the peak season (July to September) what hotels are left will be expensive. Even C-class hotels such as the Stadion and the Dubravka charge around £14.50 ($21.75) per person at this time. Prices at hotels are lower in May and June, but only if you are travelling in April or October are there more than a handful of hotels with affordable rooms.

TOURIST OFFICE
Dubrovnik Tourist Office, C. Zuzorić 1/11 (tel. 26304).

HOTELS
PEAK SEASON:

Gruž, Gruška obala 25 (tel. 24777). Half-board £15.25 ($23) per person.

MAY AND JUNE:
Expect to pay around £14 ($21) p.p. for doubles

Dubravka (tel. 26284).
Stadion (tel. 23449).

APRIL AND OCTOBER:
Expect to pay around £12 ($18) p.p. for doubles

Neptun (B class) (tel. 23755).
Sumratin (B), I.L. Ribara 27 (tel. 24722).
Jadran (B) (tel. 23322/23276).
Bellevue (B), P. Čingrije 7 (tel. 25077).
Adriatic (B) (tel. 24144).
Lapad (B), Lapadska obala 37 (tel. 23473).

Dubravka and Stadion. Tel. nos as above.
Gruž. At this time of year half-board here costs around £8 ($12) p.p.

PRIVATE ROOMS

Private rooms can be booked at various offices in town. In July and August prices per person in doubles are: Category I £8.50–12.00 ($13–18); Category II £7.20–9.60 ($10.75–14.50); Category III £5.70–7.20 ($8.50–10.75). At other times prices are: Category I £7.20–9.60 ($10.75–14.50); Category II £5.70–7.20 ($8.50–10.75); Category III £4.35–5.70 ($6.50–8.50).

Atlas, Pile 1 (tel. 27333).
Dalmacijaturist, M. Pracata 7 (tel. 29367/24077/24078).
Dubrovnikturist, Put Republike 5 (tel. 32108/29679).
Generalturist, F. Supila 29 (tel. 235 5456).
Kvarner-Express, Grucka obala 69 (tel. 22772).
Putnik, F. Supila 7 (tel. 26650/26651/26398).
Razvitakturist, U Pilama 2 (tel. 26677/26111).
Unisturist, Masarykov put 9 (tel. 25594).
Sunturist, F. Supila 8 (tel. 24965/23843).
Turisticki Informativni centar, P. Miličevića 1 (tel. 263545/23746).

HI HOSTEL

YH Dubrovnik, Vinka Sagrastena 3 (tel. 23241). Open 15 Apr.–15 Oct. 1 a.m. curfew. Around £6 ($9). A 10-minute walk from the bus station.

HOSTEL

International Youth and Student Center Dvorac Rašica, Ivanska 14 (tel. 23841/23241). Bus 2 or 4 from the bus station of ferry terminal, or walk up Od Batale on to Ivanska. Open July–Oct. Advance reservation essential July and Aug. Contact Ferijalni Savez, Mose Pijade 12/1, PO Box 374, 11000 Beograd, or Yugotours-Narom.

CAMPING

Solitudo (tel. 20770). Open 1 Apr.–31 Oct. Roughly 3km west of the bus station. Bus 6 from the Old Town, or from near the bus station. £2.65 ($4) per tent, £4 ($6) p.p.

There is another site in Kupari, about 8km out of Dubrovnik, accessible by bus 10 (tel. 48 60 20). Open 15 Apr.–15 Oct. £1.50 ($2.25) per tent, £2 ($3) p.p.

SLEEPING ROUGH
There is virtually no chance of you getting away with sleeping on the beach as the police make regular patrols. You can take a chance and bed down in the terraced park overlooking the sea below Marsala Tita, but if you are caught you can expect a steep fine. If you really are stuck, head for the campsites: even if you have to pay the price for one person and a tent, it is far better than being fined.

Split (tel. code 058)

HOTELS
Hotels in Split are very expensive: for example, the D-class Central (tel. 41132) charges £17.35 ($26) p.p. for doubles with showers during the peak season of June to September. At other times prices fall to around £14 ($21) p.p. The Slavija (tel. 47053) has doubles which are slightly more expensive, but these rooms lack private showers.

PRIVATE ROOMS
Let by the Tourist Office: OOUR Turist biro, Titova obala 12 (tel. 42142). In July and Aug. prices p.p. in doubles are: Category I £9.65–11.50 ($14.50–17.25), Category II £8.35 ($12.50), Category III £6.85 ($10.25). At other times: Category I £7.65–9.15 ($11.50–13.75), Category II £6.35 ($9.50), Category III £5.35 ($8).

HOSTEL
Studencki Dom, Maleśina 66 (tel. 55 17 74). B&B in triples £6.35 ($9.50) p.p. Close to Proleterskin Brigada. Reached by bus 18 from the open-air market.

CAMPING
Trstenik, Put Trstenika (tel. 52 19 71). Open 1 May–1 Oct. Has been closed, but may reopen in 1995.

SLEEPING ROUGH
Probably your best chance of remaining undetected is to bed down deep in the woods of Marjan Park. The risk is yours.

Zagreb (tel. code 041)

TOURIST OFFICE
Tourist Information Centre, Trg bana Josipa Jelačića 11 (tel. 27 25 30).

HOTELS
Cheapest doubles around £16.65 ($25) p.p.

Park (tel. 23 34 22).
Jadran (tel. 41 46 00).
Tomislavov Dom (tel. 48 04 44).
Šumski Dvor (tel. 27 58 92/27 21 95).

PRIVATE ROOMS
Expect to pay £8–12 ($12–18) p.p. in doubles

Evistas, Tomislavov trg 19 (tel. 42 05 67).
Di-Prom, Trnsko 25 (tel. 52 36 17).
Staza, Heinzelova 3 (tel. 21 30 82).
Turističko društvo Novi Zagreb, Trnsko 15e (tel. 52 15 23).

HI HOSTEL
Omladinski Hotel, Petrijnska 77 (tel. 43 49 64). Dorms around £5 ($7.50), doubles and triples around £12.65 ($19) p.p. Turn right on leaving the station, walk one block and you will see Petrijnska on your left. Fills quickly.

INDEPENDENT HOSTEL
Studentski Centar, Savska 25 (tel. 27 46 74). Dorms £7 ($10.50) mid-July–Sept. From Trg Republike tram 14 to the junction of Vodnikova and Savska.

CAMPING
Plitvice, Zagreb/Lučko (tel. 52 22 30/52 98 82). Closed in 1994, but worth checking. About 10km from town, on the road to Maribor.

CZECH REPUBLIC (České)

The present position in the Czech Republic is that there is a general shortage of cheap accommodation possibilities in the peak season of July and August (late May to early September in Prague), though a steady improvement seems likely in the next few years. The situation in the major tourist destinations is nowhere near as dire as in 1990–91, though it can still be very difficult to find a cheap bed in the high season. In the smaller towns, the situation is hard to gauge. Happily, more visitors are finding their way out from the usual tourist destinations to the exquisite small towns. However, a growth in accommodation possibilities tends to follow an influx, so if the town has become reasonably well visited, tourists can toil to find accommodation in peak season. On the other hand, there are many smaller towns (particularly in north Bohemia) where you will have no trouble at all finding cheap accommodation at any time of year.

Hotels are divided into five categories from five-star luxury hotels to budget, 'no frills' one-star accommodation. In most towns, the lower three grades are now within the reach of the budget traveller. Even in some popular tourist destinations there are doubles available for as little as £10 ($15). As might be expected, prices are higher in Prague, where it is difficult to find a double room for under £15 ($22.50). More likely, you will have to pay £20–30 ($30–45) if you want a double room in the capital. Hotel bills often have to be settled in hard currency (Deutschmarks/US dollars are preferred), with traveller's cheques sometimes refused.

Throughout the Czech Republic, it is possible to stay in the homes of local people. Prices for **private rooms** booked through agencies are no longer officially fixed, with the result that they have risen, and rooms are not the bargain they were a couple of years ago. Now you can expect to pay around £10 ($15) for a single in Prague, around £6 ($9) elsewhere. However, private rooms are the most widely available budget option. With the obvious potential for new agencies in this field there are now alternatives to dealing with Čedok or Pragotur, the only organizations that let private rooms when the industry was state-controlled. Nevertheless, because of the number of rooms they control, Pragotur are still the best to deal with in the capital, with Čedok predominant in the country as a whole (České Budějovice is one notable exception). Some rooms in the cities can be far from the centre, but as public transport systems in the cities are cheap and efficient, distance should not deter you, providing the room on offer is well served by public transport. Whichever agency you deal with, the accessibility of the room should be one of your prime considerations. Unfortunately, beggars cannot be choosers. In a busy office you can expect to be asked to step out of the queue if you refuse a room, as the agencies know there are plenty of people who will be glad to accept it.

The asking price for private rooms offered by individuals will not be too dissimilar to those you will pay at one of the local agencies (although breakfast is usually included in private offers). However, whereas the standard of rooms booked through an agency is reasonably uniform, the quality of privately offered rooms varies dramatically. You might be lucky and get a perfectly acceptable room with a decent location but, especially in Prague, many are situated in the centre of the vast housing schemes on the outskirts of town and can be difficult to reach by public transport. In peak season, your room for manoeuvre as regards price and location can be severely constrained by the sheer numbers of those looking for accommodation. If you are stuck, you can always stay one night, and then get into town early next morning to look for something better. If you do take up a private offer, take care of your valuables.

Hostelling probably offers the best value for money out of all the accommodation possibilites, but finding a hostel bed is not easy. There are roughly 50 hostels listed in the HI handbook. These are operated by CKM (the student travel organization). Prices range from £2.50–5.50 ($3.75–8.25) – usually towards the lower end of the scale. The few permanent hostels are a great bargain. Standards are excellent as these are in fact CKM hotels which offer discounts of 70–80% to HI members and students. However, not only do they have to be booked several months in advance if you plan to arrive during the peak season, but a quick comparison of the hostel list with a guidebook will tell you that apart from Prague, the spa towns of Mariánské Lázně and Karlovy Vary, and Banská Bystrica, the places of major interest lack permanent hostels. Many of the temporary hostels listed in the HI handbook (including the four hostels in Brno) are converted student dormitories, which open only during July and August. If you are travelling at that time of year it is always worth contacting the local CKM office, as they control the letting of rooms in student dormitories in many towns not mentioned in the HI handbook. Rooms in student dorms generally cost around £2.50–3.50 ($3.75–5.25).

In recent years, there has been a growth in the number of independent hostels, particularly in Prague. Again, the vast majority of these are in converted student dormitories, operating only in July and August. The established tourist agencies (Čedok, CKM, Pragotur) may not be a fruitful source of information on independent hostels, either because they are genuinely unaware of new hostels, or because they are intent on selling you accommodation they control. Ask other travellers about hostelling possibilities, and keep your eyes open for hostels advertised at bus and train stations.

Most small towns have very basic dormitory hostels known as *turistická ubytovna*, where a bunk bed costs around £1 ($1.50). Facilities seldom extend to anything more than toilets and cold showers. These hostels are meant primarily for workers living away from home, or for groups of workers on holiday, but it is most unlikely you will be turned away if there is room at the hostel. Unfortunately, many such hostels open only when they have a group booking. Nevertheless, it is worth enquiring about *turistická ubytovna* at the local Čedok or CKM offices, as they sometimes offer the only hostel accommodation available in town.

If you are travelling between May and September/mid-October, **camping** is a great way to see the country very cheaply (few sites remain open outside these months). *Camping Czechoslovakia* (from Čedok) lists around 250 sites, graded A, AB and B, with details of opening times and facilities available, and has a map showing their locations. Prices for a solo traveller are about £1.50–2.50 ($2.25–3.75) per night, but, as Čedok warns, 'don't expect luxury'. Sites are usually clean, but at the B-class sites outside showers are the norm. Very occasionally in peak season, you might have a little trouble finding a space, but even then only at the sites in Prague and Bratislava (and perhaps at weekends in České Budějovice, Tbor, Mariánské Lázně and Karlovy Vary). At the vast majority of the sites listed in *Camping Czechoslovakia* it is possible to rent two- or four-bed chalets (*chata*). The standard of chalets varies from site to site: while some are quite cramped, others are spacious and very comfortable. At some sites you may be required to pay for all the beds in the chalet, even if they are not all occupied. Expect to pay between £2–4 ($3–6) per person in a fully occupied chalet.

Most, but not all, of the main places of interest have a convenient campsite listed in *Camping Czechoslovakia*. However, there are a host of other primitive sites, known in Czech as *tbořiště*. Facilities at these sites are spartan: you may have to wash in the river nearby, and may prefer to use the woods to the site's toilets. On the plus side, these sites are exceptionally cheap at around £1 ($1.50) per night for a solo traveller. Again, few of these sites remain open outside the months of May to September. In the past, these were aimed at East European holidaymakers, and were not advertised to Westerners. Indeed, the official agencies were loath even to admit their existence. Nowadays, local Čedok offices are more likely to be forthcoming about tbořiště in the vicinity, though it is always worth asking locals if Čedok officials say there are none. Alternatively, the book *Ubytovani CSR* lists all the hotels, hostels and campsites in the Czech Republic (in Czech, but easy to follow), while the 1:100,000 tourist map of the country shows the location of all campsites in both the Czech and Slovak Republics.

If you are stuck for a bed, but have an Inter-Rail, Eurail or BIJ ticket, you can always catch a night train (see overnight-train suggestions below). One of the best ways to arrive in Brno reasonably early in the morning is to take an overnight train from Prague to Bratislava, or vice versa, and then catch the early train to Brno. Travelling overnight from Bratislava to Prague can allow you to catch early morning connections to Tabor, Olomouc, Pilsen, Cheb and the spa towns. Even leaving Prague to head out into east and central Slovakia can show you interesting towns such as Bardejor, Presov, Banska Bystrica and Banska Stiavnica.

TOURIST INFORMATION
At the time of writing, few cities had tourist offices organized along Western lines. In most towns, the information that is available is distributed by accommodation agencies such as Čedok or CKM. In very few towns can you pick up a small plan showing the main sites of interest (even the information distributed in Prague is poor). If you are heading for the Czech Republic or Slovakia, it is best to buy a good guidebook before setting off on holiday. When you arrive, bookshops in the main cities should have English versions of *Czechoslovakia*, published by Ctibor Rybár, a useful guide to the country (you can enquire as to whether Čedok in London are still selling copies of this book in 1995). One useful item which you can pick up at some Čedok offices is a list of altered street names. As many of the maps on sale in the country do not yet show current street names, finding your way around can be a confusing matter.

ADDRESSES
Čedok Tours & Holidays 49 Southwark Street, London SE1 1RU (tel. 0171 378 6009).

Youth hostels CKM Club of Young Travellers, Žitná 12, 121 05 Praha 2.
Travel Section and Secretariat: CKM, Malostranské nbřež 1, 11 00 Praha 1—Mal Strana (tel. 02 53 88 58).
1—Mal Strana (tel. 02 53 88 58).

Overnight-train suggestions (check times locally, or with the Thomas Cook timetable):

Praha Hlav. Nad.	23.17	Bratislava	05.35
Praha Hlav. Nad.	00.15	Bratislava	05.16 (continues to Budapest)
Praha Holešovice	22.38	Bratislava	04.55

Early morning connection to Brno:

Bratislava	05.50	Brno	07.20
Bratislava	22.50	Praha Holešovice	05.08
Bratislava	23.50	Praha Hlav. Nad.	05.45
Bratislava	00.35	Praha Hlav. Nad.	06.03

Early morning connections from Prague:

Praha Holešovice	05.57	Brno	09.19		
Praha Hlav. Nad.	06.30	Karlovy Vary	10.07		
Praha Hlav. Nad.	07.49	Tabor	09.45	České Budějovice	11.01
Praha Hlav. Nad.	07.50	Plzen	09.28	Domazlice	10.34
Praha Hlav. Nad.	08.47	Plzen	10.37	Mariánské Lázně	11.58	Cheb	12.32
Praha Holešovice	20.27	Kosice	05.46		
Praha Hlav. Nad.	00.00	Kosice	09.53		
Kosice	20.10	Praha Holešovice	05.32		
Kosice	20.38	Praha Hlav. Nad.	06.31		
Kosice	00.20	Olomouc	06.52	Praha Hlav. Nad.	10.05
Kosice	16.55	Karlovy Vary	07.50	Cheb	09.02
Bratislava	23.00	Kosice	05.25		
Bratislava	00.20	Kosice	07.07		
Kosice	23.10	Bratislava	05.44		
Kosice	23.55	Bratislava	06.27		

Brno (tel. code 05)

TOURIST INFORMATION
Čedok, across the street from the main train station, sell maps of the city for around £0.30 ($0.45).

ACCOMMODATION AGENCIES
CKM, Česká 11 (tel. 23641). Open Mon.–Fri. 10 a.m.–12 p.m. and 2–5 p.m.; Sat. 10 a.m.–12 p.m. CKM operate hostels in converted student dorms from 1 July–31 Aug. The office is a 15-minute walk from the main train station. Cross the road and head down Masarykova into náměstí Svobody. Keep going straight on along the left-hand side of the square into Česká.

Čedok, Divadelní 3 (tel. 23179). Open Mon.–Fri. 9 a.m.–6 p.m., Sat. 9 a.m.–12 p.m. Information and reservations for hotels and hostels available. A 10-minute walk from the main train station. Head right until you come to Benešova. Go along the left-hand side of the street.

ARRIVING IN BRNO
Most trains arrive at Brno Hlavní nádraží (main train station) on the fringe of the Old Town. Some night trains only stop at Brno Královo Pole on the outskirts of the city. Unless you arrive here on a Sunday morning, you rarely have to wait more than 20 minutes for a connecting train to Hlavní nádraží. The main bus station is located a few blocks behind the main train station.

HOTELS
Kozák, Horova 30 (tel. 74 41 85). Cheapest hotel in Brno. Singles around £8 ($12), doubles around £12 ($18). From the main train station take tram 4, 5 or 13 to Husova, then tram 10.

Europa, Jánská 1 (tel. 26611/26621). Singles £8.50 ($12.75), doubles around £15.50 ($23.25). Breakfast included. A short walk from the main train station. Head straight down Masarykova and the hotel is at the junction with Jánská, the fourth street on the right.

Astoria, Novabranska 3 (tel. 27526). Singles £12 ($18), doubles £16.50 ($24.75). Close to the Čedok office on Divadelní. A 10-minute walk from the main train station. Head straight down Masarykova from the station, turn right along Orli, then left after passing the Menin Gate. Tram 1, 2 or 18 from the station to Malinovskeho nám.

If the hotels above are full, the next three hotels as you move up the price scale are the U Jakuba at Jakubské náměstí 6 (tel. 22991), the Avion at Česká 20 (tel. 27606), and the Slovan at Lidická 23 (tel. 74 55 05); useful names to mention if Čedok are trying to be unreasonable.

PRIVATE ROOMS
Contact Čedok on Divadelní. Singles £6.50 ($9.75), doubles £11–13 ($16.50–19.50).

HI HOSTEL
Ubytovna Interservis, Lomená 38 (tel. 33 11 11). Bus 40 or 49, or tram 22.

INDEPENDENT HOSTEL
Ubytovna Komarov, Slatckeho ul 13 (tel. 33 93 41). Doubles from around £10 ($15). Tram 22 south to the last stop.

CAMPING
Both sites are about 16km out of town.

Bobrava, Modrice u Brna (tel. 32 01 10). Grade B site. Open 15 Apr.–15 Oct. Tram 2, 14 or 17 to the Modrice terminus, then a 10-minute walk, or a local train to Popovice, 500m from the site.
Obora, Brno-prehrada (tel. 79 11 05). Grade B site. Open 1 Apr.–31 Oct. More difficult to reach by public transport. A CSAD bus runs about every hour. In summer, you can reach the site by taking tram 3, 10, 14, 18, 20 or 21, followed by a trip on a boat or bus.

České Budějovice (tel. code 038)

TOURIST INFORMATION
Informační. In a red trailer on Švermovo náměstí. Open 9–11 a.m. and 2–6 p.m., weekends 9 a.m.–12 p.m. and 1–6 p.m. Good source of information on the city in English and German. From Žižkovo náměstí take 5 května and head straight on across the water and Na Sadech into Švermovo nám. From the bus and train stations head right, turn left up maršále Malinovského just past the train station, then left along Na sadech to Švermovo nám. A more permanent office may be found by 1994. If so the Srba International Travel Agency or CKM should be able to tell you the new location.

ACCOMMODATION AGENCIES

Srba International Travel Agency, 5 května 1 (tel. 25061). Open
Mon.–Fri. 2–8 p.m., weekends 9 a.m.–8 p.m. Map of the city
£0.35 ($0.50). 5 května runs out of Žižkovo náměstí.

CKM, Osvobození 14 (tel. 36138) Osvobození runs off Žižkovo
náměstí. Rents beds in student dorms in July and August.

Čedok, Žižkovo náměstí (tel. 38056). An office much criticized in
the past when they have changed money and booked hotels, but
made it quite plain they did not want to be bothered by other
enquiries. Also at N. Frýda 31.

BASIC DIRECTIONS

The bus and train stations are virtually side by side on Nádražní, a
ten-minute walk from the town centre. Just right of the train
station exit turn left on to maršále Malinovského. On the left-hand
side as you walk up this street is the PRIOR department store with
a supermarket. Continuing on down maršále Malinovského you
reach the junction with Na sadech, across which you can follow
Kanovnická into Žižkovo náměstí, the main square of the town.
Turning left along the side of the square brings you to the start of
Osvobození. If you continue straight on along the side of the square
from Kanovnická, you pass Čedok before arriving at the start of
5 Kvěětna.

FINDING ACCOMMODATION

Finding suitable accommodation is not the problem it was a couple
of years ago thanks to the increase in the number of rooms available
in private homes and small pensions. None the less, it can still
be tricky to find a cheap place to stay during July and August,
and especially so at weekends, as the town is highly popular
with Germans and Austrians taking weekend breaks, as well as
Czechs.

HOTELS

Enquiries about hotel accommodation should be made at the Čedok
office on Žižkovo náměstí.

Malše, Nádražní 31 (tel. 27631). Singles around £8.60 ($13),
doubles around £11 ($16.50). Across the street from the train
station.

Zvon, Žižkovo náměstí 28 (tel. 35361). Singles around £10.50
($15.75), doubles around £16.50 ($24.75). Payment in hard
currency only.

PENSIONS
In the past few years, the number of pensions has increased in and around the city. If you arrive by road you will see these advertised by the roadside as you enter town. Many of these 'pensions' are really just private rooms, advertised by enterprising owners. Your likeliest source of information on pensions is the Srba International Travel Agency (see above).

PRIVATE ROOMS
Book through the Srba International Travel Agency. Doubles range in price from £8–14 ($12–21). As well as booking rooms locally, the office books similarly priced rooms throughout south Bohemia, a particularly useful service if you are heading for some of the smaller towns in the region.

HI HOSTEL
Dům dětí a mládeže, U zimníhe stadionu 1 (tel. 38312). About 500m from the railway station.

CAMPING
There are two sites right beside each other on the fringes of the town, just off the road to Český Krumlov. Bus 6 from Na sadech stops close to the sites. Otherwise it is a 25-minute walk from the bus and train stations to the campsites. Head left along Nádražní from the train station on to Kasárenská. Turn right, then left along Dvořkova on to Mánesova. Turn right and follow Mánesova across the River Malše and towards the River Vltava. When the road forks near the Vltava head down to the left, and then along the main road. The campsites are signposted on the right.

Dlouhá Louka, Stromovka 8 (tel. 38308). Grade A site. Open May–Sept. Bungalows available.
Stromovka, Litvínovská (tel. 28807). Grade B site. Open Apr.–Oct. Bungalows available.

Karlovy Vary (tel. code 017)

ACCOMMODATION AGENCIES
Čedok operate at various locations in the town. Closest to the bus and train stations is the office at the junction of Dimitrova and Moskevská. In the town centre, there are offices at Karla IV 1

(tel. 26110), and in the Hotel Atlantic at Tržiště 23 (tel. 26705/24378).

'W', nám. Republiky (tel. 27768). Near the bus station (autobusová nádraží).

HOTELS
Turist, Dimitrovova 18 (tel. 26837). Doubles around £9 ($13.50). Near the bus station.

Nrodní dům, Masarykova 24 (tel. 23386). Singles £8.75 ($13), doubles £12.25 ($18.50). Close to the bus station.

Adria, Koněvova 1 (tel. 23765). Singles £10.50 ($15.75), doubles £15.50 ($23.25). Payment must be made in hard currency. Along the street from the bus station.

CKM Juniorhotel Alice, ul. Pětiletky 3 (tel. 24848). Singles around £10.50 ($15.75). Set in the woods about 5km out of town. A beautiful walk. From the Karlovy Vary horní nídraží train station take bus 11 to the market place, then bus 7. Take bus 7 direct from the bus station.

Jizena, Dimitrovova 7 (tel. 25020). £14.75 ($22) per person. Close to the bus station.

PRIVATE ROOMS
Čedok, Karla IV: doubles around £9 ($13.50). Office open mid-May–Sept. Mon.–Fri. 9 a.m.–5 p.m., Sat. 9 a.m.–12 p.m.; Oct.–mid-May 9 a.m.–4 p.m.

'W': £7–10.50 ($10.50–15.75) per person. Office open Mon.–Sat. 10 a.m.–6 p.m.

HOSTELS
Albion, Zamecky ur 43 (tel. 23473).
Hestia, Stará Kysebelská 43 (tel. 25985).

CAMPING
Březová, Slovenská č. 9 (tel. 25101). Grade A site. Open 1 May–30 Sept. Bungalows available. Close to CKM Juniorhotel Alice. See the entry in the **Hotels** section above for directions.

Olomouc (tel. code 068)

TOURIST OFFICES
Čedok, Horní nám 2 (tel. 28831) can book rooms, change money and sell a range of helpful brochures in English (10 kčs). Open

Mon.–Fri. 8 a.m.–12 noon and 1–5 p.m.; Sat. 9 a.m.–12 noon.
Olomouc Information Service, Horní nám 23 (tel. 26051) is situated inside the town hall arcade. Open Mon.–Fri. 9 a.m.–12 noon and 1–5 p.m.; Sat. 9 a.m.–12 noon.

ACCOMMODATION AGENCY
CKM, Denisova 4 (tel. 29009). German- and English-speaking staff.

HOTELS
Hotelový dům, Volgogradská (tel. 41 31 21). Cheapest hotel in the city, and consequently often full in the summer. Bus 16 runs along the street from its terminus on Kosmonautu near the train station.
Morava, Riegrova 16 (tel. 29671). Prices are a little higher than at the Hotelový dům. Excellent central location. The street runs off náměstí Míru.

PRIVATE ROOMS
Enquire at Čedok and CKM about the availability of private rooms.

HOSTELS
CKM control the letting of beds in student residences converted into temporary hostels in July and August.

CAMPING
Neither of the sites closest to Olomouc are easy to reach unless you have your own transport. Ask Čedok or CKM about precise directions by public transport before setting off to the sites. You can also try asking them about any *tábořiště* which may be more conveniently located.

Dolní Žleb, Šternberk (tel. 2300). Grade A site, open mid-June–mid-Sept. The site is located about 3km from the bus and train stations Šternberk, a small town about 16km to the north of Olomouc.
Přehrada, Mostkovice (tel. 0508–7279). Grade A site, open mid-May–mid-Sept. The town of Prostějov (19km from Olomouc) is on the main road and the railway line between Brno and Olomouc. Přehrada is a good campsite, with a pleasant lakeside setting, but it is 6km away from Prostějov.

Pilsen (Plzeň) (tel. code 019)

ACCOMMODATION AGENCIES

Čedok. On the corner of Sedláckova and Prešovská. The latter runs out of one corner of Nám Republiky, the centre of town. Opening hours: Mon.–Fri. 9 a.m.–12 p.m. and 1–6 p.m.; Sat. 9 a.m.–12 p.m.

CKM, Dominikanská. Just off Nám Republiky.

HOTELS

Enquire at the Čedok office above.

PRIVATE ROOMS

Enquire at Čedok about the availability of private rooms. Expect to pay 320Kčs per person.

HI HOSTEL

Hotel Armabeton Servis, Borská 53 (tel. 27 65 00). Bus 22 or tram 16.

HOSTELS

VŠ Kolej Lochotín, Bolevecká str. 30. Two to four-bed rooms available from 200–300Kčs per person. Student reductions available. Tram 1 or 4 from town centre (direction: Lochotín, first stop).

During July and August CKM let beds in converted student dormitories.

CAMPING

Bílá Hora (tel. 35611/62850). Grade A. Open 20 Apr.–15 Sept. Also lets bungalows. In the suburb of Bílá Hora. Bus 20 or 39.

Ostende (tel. 52 01 94). In Plzeň-Bolevec. Grade A, open 1 May–15 Sept. Bungalows available.

Prague (Praha) (tel. code 02)

TOURIST INFORMATION

Pražská Informačni služba (PIS), Na Příkopě 20 (tel. 54 44 44). Open Mon.–Fri. 9 a.m.–7 p.m., Sat. and Sun. 9 a.m.–6 p.m. The best source of general information on the city. No accommodation service. Metro: Náměstí Republiky. Na Přikopě runs out of nám. Republiky.

PIS, Staroměstré nám 22.

PIS, Hlavní nádraží.

ACCOMMODATION AGENCIES

Pragotur, U Obecního domu 2 (tel. 231 7200/231 7281/231 7234). Open Mon.–Fri. 8 a.m.–7 p.m., Sat. 9 a.m.–6 p.m., Sun. 9 a.m.–3 p.m. Metro: Náměstí Republiky. U Obecního domu runs off nám. Republiky. Pragotur can book rooms in hotels, pensions and hostels, as well as in private accommodation.

Čedok, Panská 5 (tel. 22 56 56/22 70 04). Open Mon.–Fri. 9 a.m.–10 p.m., weekends 8.30 a.m.–2 p.m. Metro: Náměstí Republiky. Follow Na Přikopě from nám. Republiky, then head left down Panská.

CKM, Žitná 12 (tel. 229 6526). Metro: I.P. Pavlova. Walk down Ječná.

Top Tour, Rybná 3 (tel. 229 6526/232 1077/232 0860). Open Mon.–Fri. 9 a.m.–8 p.m., weekends 10 a.m.–7 p.m. Metro: Nám. Republiky. From nám. Republiky walk a short distance down Celetná, turn right on to Královdorská, then left.

AVE Ltd, Wilsonova 80 (tel. 236 2560). AVE have two offices on the upper floor of Praha hlavní nádraží. They also operate an office at Ruzyne Airport (tel. 236 2541).

KONVEX, Kamziková 4 (tel. 236 6760). Open daily 10 a.m.–7 p.m. Metro: Staroměstská. The metro station is on Kaprova. Ask a local to point you in the direction of Staroměstské náměstí. Keep going more or less straight ahead until you reach the square. The KONVEX office is in a small street off Staroměstské nám., on the same side of the town hall as the astronomical clock.

Hello Ltd, nám. Gorkého-Senovážná 3 (tel. 22 42 83). Open daily 9 a.m.–10 p.m. Metro: Náměstí Republiky. From nám. Republiky walk down Hybernská, then turn right along Dlážděbá into the square.

Accommodation Service, Hastalske náměstí (tel. 231 0202). Double rooms in central and outlying Prague.

Contrans, Male náměstí 1 (tel. 262 313/236 6542). Rooms in private homes in the city centre.

Dispo-Travel, Washingtonova 23 (tel. 22 95 15). Close to the main railway station; offers double rooms only.

Euroagentur Zitna 13 (across from the CKM Juniorhotel). A new agency offering places in a hostel about 20 minutes from the centre.

Lisbona, Male náměstí 2 (tel. 26 55 15). Summer places in student dormitories, or more expensive private rooms.

Prague Suites, Melantrichova 8 (tel. 26 77 70/62 93 84). Specializes in long-term lets, but can arrange shorter stays in private homes.

Primo Agency, Zitna 17 (tel. 2491 0340). Places in a hostel about 10 minutes from the centre; also rather expensive central rooms and apartments.

Rekrea, Parizska 26 (tel. 231 2390). Good for cheap double rooms.

Universitas Tour, Opletalova 38 (tel. 22 35 43). Close to the main railway station. Offers reasonably priced pension rooms, as well as their own dormitory beds in the summer.

FINDING ACCOMMODATION

The growth in the number of private rooms and apartments available has gone some way to alleviating the terrible accommodation shortage in Prague. Nevertheless, there are still only around ten thousand beds in registered accommodation for ten million visitors, the vast majority of whom arrive between June and early September. If you are travelling at that time of year aim to get to Prague early in the morning and start looking for a bed right away. The accommodation situation worsens dramatically at weekends, as the city is exceptionally popular with Germans and Austrians taking a short break, so look to arrive between Monday and Thursday, if at all possible.

ARRIVING IN PRAGUE

Of the city's five main train stations your most likely point of arrival is Praha hlavní nádraží, a short walk from the Václavské náměstí, and within easy walking distance of the old town. Some international trains and overnight internal services drop you at Praha-Holešovice, in the northern suburb of Holešovice. Trains terminating at Praha-Smichov, Masarykovo nádraží (the old Praha-Stred), and Praha-Vysočany are usually local services, or slow trains from the provinces. Connections between Praha hlavní, Praha-Smichov and Praha-Holešovice are easy as all are served by the metro (line C: Hlavní nádraží; line B: Smichovské nádraží; line C: Nádraží Holešovice, respectively). The Masarykovo nádraží is a short walk along Wilsonova from Praha hlavní nádraží and, in the opposite direction, the Florenc metro station (lines B and C). From Praha-Vysočany tram 3 crosses Wilsonova a short distance from the Florenc metro stop. The main bus station, Praha-Florenc, is beside the Florenc metro station. The Masarykovo nádraží and Prah hlvaní nádraží are both within easy walking distance of Praha-Florenc, to the left along Wilsonova. Arriving at Ruzyně airport, your cheapest option is to take bus 119 (three an hour) from opposite the main exit to its terminus at the Dejvická metro station (line A). The CSA bus is dearer, but takes you direct to the CSA office on Revolučni, a short walk from náměstí Republiky.

HOTELS

Čedok deal in two-star hotels, but often claim not to in an attempt to persuade you to take a room in a more expensive hotel. Pragotur specialize in one-star hotels, and are unlikely to be dishonest about the availability of hotel rooms. Both agencies reallocate late cancellations and forfeited reservations from 5 p.m. onwards.

Hotel prices have fluctuated in the past few years. As a rough guide expect to pay from £11−16 ($16.50−24) for the cheapest doubles in a C/one-star hotel, and from £15−30 ($22.50−45) for their equivalent in a B/two-star hotel. Most hotel bills have to be settled in hard currency.

Two-star hotels

Adria, Václavské nám. 26 (tel. 235 2885). Metro: Museum or Můstek. A short walk left along Wilsonova from Praha hlavní nádraží.

Hvězda, Na Rovni 34 (tel. 36 80 37/36 89 65). Tram 18 from the Malostranská metro station to the Heyrovského náměstí terminus, or tram 1 or 18 from the Hradčanská metro station. From the tram terminus follow Polni until it crosses Na Rovni.

Hybernia, Hybernská 24 (tel. 22 04 31). Singles £13.50 ($20.25), doubles £19 ($28.50). Metro Náměstí Republiky. Walk down Hybernská from nám. Republiky.

Koruna, Opatovická 15 (tel. 293933). Metro: Národni tířda. From Spálená turn down Ostrovní (almost opposite Purkyňova), then head left at Opatovická.

Merkur, Těšnov 9 (tel. 231 6840). Metro: Florenc. Těšnov is a continuation of Na Florenci heading down towards the River Vltava, across Wilsonova from the bus station.

Meteor, Hybernská 6 (tel. 235 8517). See the Hybernia, above.

Moráň, Na Moráni 15 (tel. 29 42 51). Tram 9 from Hlavní nádraží runs along the street. A short walk from the Karlovo náměstí metro station.

Opera, Těšnov 13 (tel. 231 5609/231 5735). Singles £12 ($18), doubles £20 ($30). Price includes breakfast. See the Merkur above for directions.

Axa, Na poříčí 40 (tel. 232 7234). Metro: Náměstí Republiky. Na poříčí runs out of the square.

Botel Albatross, nábřeží L. Svobody (tel. 231 6996). A floating hotel moored on the Vltava by the Švermuv bridge. From the Náměstí Republiky metro station follow Revoluční down to the river.

Kriváň, Nám I.P. Pavlova 5 (tel. 29 33 41) Metro: I.P. Pavlova.

Praga, Plzeňská 29 (tel. 54 87 41). Tram 4 or 9 from Anděl metro station. A short walk from the Anděl metro station, left along Nádražní, then left up Plzeňská. Tram 9 runs from the stop to the right of Hlavní nádraží through Václavské náměstí and on up Plzeňská to the Motol terminus.

Savoy, Keplerova 6 (tel. 53 74 58/53 74 59). Singles £7.50 ($11.25), doubles £15 ($22.50). Undergoing renovation, so prices may rise sharply. From the Malostranská metro station take tram 22 heading uphill. The tram runs along Keplerova.

Solidarita, Soudružská 2081 (tel. 77 71 45). Metro: Strašnická. Walk along Volšinách about 300m, then turn left. If you see U Vesny on your left you are going the wrong way.

Transit, ul. 25 února 197 (tel. 36 71 08). On the outskirts of the city. From the Dejvická metro station take tram 20 or 26 to the terminus in Liboc, then change to bus 108.

U Blaženky, U Blaženky 1 (tel. 53 82 66). Tram 9 runs from the right of Hlavní nádraží through Václavské náměstí and up Plzeňská. Get off the tram at the junction of Plzeňská and Mozartova, walk down Mozartova and go right at U Blaženky.

Union, Jaromírova 1 (tel. 43 78 58/43 78 59). Metro: Vyšehrad. Follow the main road over the bridge. The hotel is on Jaromírova to the left of the bridge.

Modrá Hvězda, Jandova 3 (tel. 83 02 91). From the Florenc metro station walk right down Wilsonova towards the river. When you see the tram lines crossing Wilsonova follow them to the right and then take tram 3, 8 or 19 to nám. Lidových milicí and the start of Jandova.

One-star hotels

Stará Zbrojnice, Všehrdova 16 (tel. 53 28 15). Take tram 9 from the right of Hlavní Nádraží. Shortly after crossing the Vltava you will see Všehrdova on the right, off Vítězná.

Balkán, Svornosti 28 (tel. 54 07 77). From the Anděl metro station on Nádražní walk down either Na bělidle or Jindřicha Plachty on to Svornosti.

Liběň, Zenklova 2/37 (tel. 82 82 27). Tram 12 from the Malastranská metro station and tram 10 from Vltavská metro station both run along the street. After crossing the river the trams follow Liběňský most. At the point at which they turn left you are on Zenklova. The hotel is near the turn.

Moravan, U Uránie 22 (tel. 80 29 05). Metro: Nádraží Holešovice. From the station head left along Vrbenského which becomes U Uranie.

Národní dům, Bořivojova 53 (tel. 27 53 65). Doubles £11 ($16.50), triples £13.50 ($20.25), quads £18 ($27). Also dormitory accommodation, though this is frequently block-booked by visiting groups. From the right-hand side of Hlavní nádraží take tram 9, 10, 13 or 26 heading right towards Žižkov. Get off at Sladkovského nám., cross the square and follow one of the small streets on to Bořivojova. A 10-minute walk if you follow the tramlines.

Ostaš, Orebitská 8 (tel. 27 28 60). Within easy walking distance of Hlavní nádraží. Head right from the exit, then turn right and follow the tramlines. Take Rehořova (on the left after Přběnická) which leads into Orebitská.

Tichý, Seifertova 65 (tel. 27 30 79). A 10-minute walk from Hlavní nádraží, right from the main exit, right again and then follow the tramlines and the main road to the hotel, a few hundred metres past the stadium. Trams 9, 10, 13 and 26 pass the hotel.

PRIVATE ROOMS

With the removal of officially regulated prices, the cost of private rooms has soared so that they no longer offer the good value for money they once did. None the less, they are the most widely available accommodation possibility. Given the obvious potential in this market, new booking agencies are still emerging, so it is always worth asking around amongst other travellers and keeping your eyes open for adverts in the bus and train stations. Whichever office you deal with, try to get a room with a decent location. Ideally, you want a room in the centre, but these are scarce. Realistically, you should expect to be staying a few kilometres from the centre. Provided you can secure a room with an easy and frequent public transport service to the centre this is no problem, as public transport is cheap and reliable. When paying for a room you will probably be requested to do so in hard currency (Deutschmarks and US dollars are preferred).

HOSTELS

There are few year-round hostels in the city. By June, as the numbers of visitors begins to increase steadily, finding a hostel bed becomes extremely difficult. The conversion of vacant student dormitories into temporary hostels in July and August brings a welcome increase in the number of hostel beds available, but since these two months are the most popular time for visitors arriving in Prague you are still going to have to look early in the day if you want a hostel bed. It is possible to approach hostels in person, but it is better to head straight for CKM as they are well informed as to where beds are available, and will make reservations for you, as well as giving you directions to the hostel by public transport. As a rule, you can expect to pay from £2−4.50 ($3−6.75) for a hostel bed booked through CKM. Although at peak periods you should probably be glad to get any hostel bed at all, it can be worth asking CKM if they have beds in small rooms available, as dormitory beds at some hostels cost as much per person as singles and doubles at others. Top Tour also book beds in dormitory hostels, with prices ranging from £3.50−6.50 ($5.25−9.75) per person.

These hostels can be booked through CKM:

CKM Juniorhotel Žítna, Žítna 12 (tel. 29 29 84). HI hostel. Open year round. Only off-season are you likely to have any chance of getting a bed on arrival. Around £4.50 ($6.75) for HI members. See the CKM entry in the **Accommodation Agencies** section above for directions.

Admira, Ubytovna TJ, U školsé zahrady. HI hostel. Open year round. (Tel. 53 88 58). Trams 10 and 24 from the Vltavsk metro station run along Střelničá. Get off the tram when you reach the junction with Pakoměřická (left) and U měštanských škol (right). The latter crosses U školsé zahrady.

Hostel Braník, Vrbova 1233 (tel. 46 26 41). HI hostel a few kilometres from the centre. Around £6.50 ($10) per person in dorms. Metro: Smíchovské nádraží, then bus 196, 197 or 198.

Hotel Fasádostav, Jemnická 4 (tel. 43 12 44). HI hostel. Metro: Budějovická. From the station take bus 118 heading along Vyskočilova until the street is crossed by Michelská. Walking left up Michelská you will see Jemnická on your left. the hostel is a 10−15-minute walk from the metro stop.

TJ Čechie Karlin, Malého (tel. 22 20 09). Open all year. Around £2 ($3) per night, either in bunk beds or cots set up in the gym. If the hostel is full they may let you sleep on the floor. Close to the bus station. Metro: Florenc. From the station go right along Křižíkova. Turn right at the junction with Prvního pluku, followed by a short walk on to Malého.

TJ Huězda, zalány (tel. 316 5104). Metro to Dejvická, then tram 2, 20 or 26 to Homěřická, the fourth stop.

Akademie Výtanvych Umění (AVU), U Starého Vystaviště 188. £4.50 ($6.75) per person in doubles with a shower, £4.25 ($6.50) per person in ordinary doubles, £4 ($6) per person in dorms. Tram 12 from the Nádraží Holešovice metro station.

Domov Mládeže, Dykova 20. £3.50 ($5.25). Two-night maximum

stay. From the Náměstí Miru metro station take tram 16 to the second stop.

TJ Slavoj, V náklich (tel. 46 00 70). Four-bed rooms in a boathouse by the Vltava, close to the Braník terminus of trams 3 and 17. 150Kčs per person. From Hlavní nádraží head straight ahead across the gardens in front of the station and down Jeruzalémská on to Jindřišská. Head left along this street until you reach the stop for tram 3 (take the tram in the direction you were walking). Provides floor space even when full up.

TJ Dolní Měcholupy, Na paloučku 223 (tel. 70 57 48). Open year round. Singles £4 ($6). Eleven kilometres out in the eastern suburbs. From the Želivského metro station take bus 111, 228 or 229 to Dolnomécholupska.

ESTEC Students House, Kolej Strahov, Vaníckova 5, dríve Spartaki-ádní (5th building) (tel. 35 56 16). Open year round, but the full capacity of 400 beds is only available from July–mid-Sept. At other times only a few beds are available to visitors. Round-the-clock reception. £4.50 ($6.75) per person in doubles. From the Dejvická metro station take bus 217 to the sixth stop.

Koleje VŠCHT-VOLHA, Kosmonautu 950. £6.30 ($9.50) per person in doubles with showers. Bus 122, 145 or 154 from the Chodov metro station.

CAMPING

Pragotur distribute the brochure 'Praha Camping' listing all the sites. It is worth picking up a copy in case any of the telephone numbers have changed from those given below. Pragotur may simply say they have none left. If so, ask them to confirm the information given here. They may also tell you all the sites are full. Don't believe them. Call the sites yourself (all the better if you can speak German; if not, English should let you gather basic info).

All sites let bungalows except where indicated otherwise.

Expect to pay around £1.30 ($2.25) per tent and per person; £4.50 ($8) per person in a full bungalow

Sokol Trója, Trojská 171/82, (tel. 84 28 33). Grade A site, open 1 June–31 Aug. Bus 112 from the Nádraží Holešovice metro station passes the site. Take the bus to Na Kazance. If the site is full the house at Trojská 157 (a few minutes' walk away) has a small site to the rear of the house.

Caravancamp TJ Vysoké Školy, Plzeňská (tel. 52 47 14). Grade A, open 15 May–15 Sept. No bungalows. Trams 4, 7 and 9 run past the site. Walk right from the exit of Hlavní nádraží to catch tram

9 heading left along the street. From the Anděl metro station walk a short distance left onto Plzeňská to catch tram 4, 7 or 9.

Intercamp Kotva Braník, U ledáren 55 (tel. 46 17 12). Grade A, open 1 Apr.–30 Sept. Close to the Braník terminus of trams 3, 17 and 21. Shortly after passing the Zápotockého Bridge (the first after the islands), you can see the campsite down by the river. From Hlavní nádraží head across the gardens in front of the station and down Jeruzalémská onto Jindřišská. Head left along the street to the tram stop and take tram 3 in the direction you were walking.

Motol Sportcamp, Nad Hlinícken (tel. 52 18 02). Grade A, open 1 Apr.–31 Oct. Same directions as for the Caravancamp above. Take trams 4, 7 or 9 to their Motol terminus, from which the site is a 5-minute walk uphill, on the left.

Dolní Chabry, Ústeck. Public camping site. No bungalows.

Nad Iávkou 3 Džbán, Praha 6 (tel. 36 85 51). From Dejvická metro station take tram 20 or 26 heading along Benešova to last stop. From the terminus you follow the path around the left-hand side of the reservoir to reach the site (about 10 minutes' walk).

Autocamp Hájek, Trojská 337, Praha 7 (tel. 84 10 08). No bungalows.

Autocamp Sokol, Dolní Počernice, Nad rybníkem 290, Praha 9 (tel. 72 75 01).

Bušek, Březiněves, U Parku 6, Praha 8 (tel. 859 1852).

Eva, Zličín, Strojírenská 78, Praha 5 (tel. 301 9213). No bungalows.

Karavan Park, Císařská Iouka 599, Praha 5 (tel. 54 09 25). No bungalows.

Leinová, Trojská 157, Praha 7 (tel. 84 88 05).

Siesta, Pod Šancemi 51, Praha 9 (tel. 82 14 23). No bungalows.

Sky Club Brumlovka, Vyskočilova 2, Praha 4 (tel. 42 35 19). No bungalows.

Chalets only at the following sites:

Vlachovce, tř, Zenklova 217 (tel. 84 12 90). The bungalows are shaped like beer kegs. Follow the directions for the Hotel Liben (see **Hotels**, above), but do not get off the tram immediately after turning off Libeňský most. After the tram passes under the flyover look out for the site and the junction with Pod Vlachovkou on the left hand side of the street.

TJ Xaver Camp, Horní Měcholupy, Božanovská 2098, Praha 9 (tel. 685 5066).

Triocamp, Dolní Chabry, Obslužná, Praha 8 (tel. 84 28 39).

DENMARK (Danmark)

Few countries have responded as imaginatively and constructively to the growth in budget tourism as Denmark. Tourist Offices will take the time to explain the various cheap accommodation possibilities, in stark contrast to the way in which a leaflet is thrown at you in some other countries. Accommodation prices are noticeably lower than in the rest of Scandinavia, increasing the range of your options.

Hotels, however, are still likely to be outside your budget. The cheapest doubles in Copenhagen cost 400Dkr (£40; $60); elsewhere around 250–300Dkr (£25–30; $37.50–45). The concept of Bed and Breakfast is fast catching on in Denmark. A catalogue of those available is published by Dansk Bed and Breakfast and can be obtained by writing to them at Postbox 53, DK 2900, Hellerup. They are also available from any Danish tourist office both inside and outside Denmark and on ferries to and from Denmark. Rooms in **private homes** are more affordable, with singles costing around 130–180Dkr (£13–18; $19.50–27), doubles 200–290Dkr (£20–29; $30–43.50). The addition of an extra bed to a room generally costs around 50–100Dkr (£5–10; $7.50–15). Breakfast is optional: usually 25–35Dkr (£2.50–3.50; $3.75–5.25) for a hearty Danish breakfast. Private rooms are becoming more widely available each year, but they are still in short supply in some areas. For that reason, it is advisable to try and reserve rooms ahead. Where rooms are available Tourist Offices outside Copenhagen will accept requests for reservations made by letter or phone. A fee of around 12Dkr (£1.20; $1.80) is charged for making a reservation, the same fee paid by personal callers at the office.

Rooms do not have to be booked through the Tourist Office. If you see a house or farmhouse advertising rooms (rooms are invariably advertised in several languages) simply approach the owner. Another option, if there are a few of you, is to rent a **holiday home** for a week. In high season, a simple house sleeping four costs from 1,000–2,000Dkr (£100–200; $150–300) per week. If this appeals to you, it may be wise to contact the local Tourist Office for advice on booking ahead.

You will seldom be far from one of the hundred or so **HI hostels** spread throughout this small country. There is a hostel in all the main towns. In many hostels, you have the chance to stay in small rooms, as well as in dormitories. While you might baulk at the thought of paying £10–14 ($15–21) in some Norwegian hostels, prices here vary from 69–89Dkr (£6.90–8.90; $10.35–13.35) in four-bed rooms, with dormitory accommodation costing around

59Dkr (£5.90; $8.85). Prices are very reasonable considering the standard of Danish hostels. As a result of a drive by the hostel association to attract families, high standards of comfort exist. Outside the large towns and ports, hostels are rarely full but, as they may be a couple of kilometres out, phoning ahead is advisable in order to let you find out directions, as well as book a bed. Reservations are held until 5 p.m., unless you state that you will arrive later. Receptions close at 9 p.m. and, outside Copenhagen, an 11 p.m. curfew is normal. If advance warning is given, it is possible to arrive later than this but you may be charged 25Dkr (£2.50; $3.75) for this. Bring your own bed linen as it costs around 30Dkr (£3; $4.50) per night to hire. It is also advisable to have an HI card. Otherwise you will have to pay 25Dkr (£2.50; $3.75) for an overnight card, or 100Dkr (£10; $15) for a membership card.

In the main towns, there are often **independent hostels** and local authority run Sleep-Ins. The latter frequently operate only for a period of a few weeks in summer (usually early August), and may be as basic as a mattress on the floor to put your sleeping bag on. Sleep-Ins differ considerably in price, from the 80Dkr (£8; $12) for B&B in Copenhagen, to the free Sleep-In in Odense run by DSB, the state railway. In theory, age restrictions and one-night maximum stays exist, but they are seldom stringently enforced. Sleep-Ins apart, **Town Mission Hostels** can often provide the cheapest lodgings in town. Generally clean and well equipped, there is, however, a strict ban on alcohol. The local Tourist Office will inform you on whether a Sleep-In or Town Mission Hostel is in operation.

There is hardly a town of any size that does not have a **campsite**. Graded from one to three stars, the best are the three-star sites, at which one person will pay around 45Dkr (£4.50; $6.75) per night. All sites are open during the summer months; a fair number from April to September; and a few all year round. Unless you have an International Camping Carnet you will be obliged to buy either a Danish Camping Pass (valid all year, 28Dkr (£2.80; $4.20), or a one-night pass for 7Dkr (£0.70; $1). Many sites let cabins or caravans sleeping up to four people, which cost 1,200–3,000Dkr (£120–300; $180–450) per week.

Camping outside official sites is perfectly acceptable, provided you first obtain the permission of the landowner. Do not camp on the beaches as this is against the law and frequently results in an on-the-spot fine. It is also illegal to sleep rough, so it is asking for trouble to try sleeping in stations, parks, or on the streets.

Note: All Danish telephone numbers have eight digits. Dial eight digits at all times.

ADDRESSES

The Danish Tourist Board	55 Sloane Street, London SW1X 9SY (tel. 0171 259 5959)
Danish YHA	Landsforeningen Danmarks Vandrerhjem, Vesterbrogade 39, DK-1620 København V (tel. 3131 3612).
Camping	Camping Club Denmark, Horsens Turistforening, Søndergade 26, DK8700 Horsens (tel. 7562 3822). Official guide 'Camping Denmark' available from Tourist Offices, booksellers, campsites, and by post from Campinggrådet, Olaf Palmesgade 10, DK-2100 København (tel. 31423222). Not cheap. The National Tourist Office in London (or your capital city) has an abbreviated list, free on request.
Holiday homes	Feriehusudlejernes Brancheforening, Euro Tourist, Vesterbro 89, DK-9100 Aalborg. Sammenslutningen af Feriehususlejende Turistforeningen, Odsherreds Turistbureau, Algade 52, DK-5400 Nykøbing S.

Aalborg

TOURIST OFFICE

Turistbureauet, Østerå 8, DK-9000 Aalborg (tel. 9812 6022). Open 1 June–31 Aug., Mon.–Fri. 9 a.m.–5 p.m., Sat. 9 a.m.–4 p.m.; at other times, Mon.–Fri. 9 a.m.–4 p.m., Sat. 9 a.m.–noon.

HOTELS

Aalborg Sømandshjem, Østerbro 27 (tel. 9812 1900). B&B in doubles with a shower from 440Dkr (£44; $66).
Hotel Ansgar, Prinsensgade 14–16 (tel. 9813 3733). Doubles without shower around 550Dkr (£55; $82.50). Breakfast included.

PRIVATE ROOMS

Available from the Tourist Office.

HI HOSTEL
Fjordparken, Skydebanevej 50 (tel. 9811 6044). 60–84Dkr (£6–8.40; $9–12.60). Open 20 Jan.–5 Dec. By the marina, to the west of the town. Bus 8 from the town centre to the terminus. Chalets available, and camping from Apr.–Nov.

CAMPING
Strandparkens, Skydebanevej 20 (tel. 9812 7629). A few minutes' walk from the HI hostel. See above for directions. Open May–mid-Sept.

Lindholm, Lufthavnsvej 27, Nørresundby (tel. 9817 2683). Open mid-May–Sept. Near the airport, north of the Limfjord.

Århus

TOURIST OFFICE
Århus Turistbureauet, Radhuset, 8000 Århus (tel. 8612 1600). Open 14 June–20 June, Mon.–Sat. 9 a.m.–5 p.m.; 21 June–8 Aug., daily 9 a.m.–8 p.m.; 9 Aug.–12 Sept., daily 9 a.m.–7 p.m.; 13 Sept.–31 Dec., Mon.–Fri. 9.30 a.m.–4.30 p.m., Sat. 10 a.m.–1 p.m.; 1 Jan.–13 June, Mon.–Fri. 9 a.m.–4.30 p.m., Sat. 10 a.m.–1 p.m. A short walk from the train station. Head left from Banegard-spladsen then right along Park Alle.

HOTELS
Windsor, Skolebakken 17 (tel. 8612 2300). Doubles from 285Dkr (£28.50; $42.75) with breakfast.

Park, Sønder Allé 3 (tel. 8612 3231). Doubles from 340Dkr (£34; $51), without breakfast.

Eriksens, Banegårdsgade 6–8 (tel. 8613 6296). Doubles from 420Dkr (£42; $63). Breakfast included.

PRIVATE ROOMS
Available from the Tourist Office. Around 110Dkr (£11; $16.50) per person.

HI HOSTEL
Pavillonen, Marienlundsvej 10, Risskov (tel. 8616 7298). 70Dkr (£7; $10.50). Open 16 Jan.–15 Dec. 1.5km from the town centre, in the Risskov forest, about 500m from the beach. Bus 1 or 6. The hostel is signposted from the Marienlund terminus.

SLEEP-IN
Frederiksallé 20. Open 1 July–1 Sept. Check with the Tourist Office to see if this is in operation in 1995.

CAMPING
Blommehaven, Ørneredevej 35, Højbjerg (tel. 8627 0207). Open mid-Apr.–mid-Sept. In the Marselisborg forest, close to the Århus bay beach. In summer take bus 19 straight to the site, otherwise take bus 6 to Horhavevej. Chalets are also available.
Århus Nord, Randersvej 400, Lisbjerg (tel. 8623 1133). Open year round. Chalets available. Buses 117 and 118 run straight to the site.

Copenhagen (København)

TOURIST OFFICES
Danmarks Turistråd, Bernstorffsgade 1, DK-1577 København V (tel. 3311 1325). Open June–mid-Sept., daily 9 a.m.–8 p.m.; mid-Sept.–Apr., Mon.–Fri. 9 a.m.–5 p.m., Sat. 9 a.m.–2 p.m. May, open daily 9 a.m.–6 p.m. The office hands out a reasonable free map of the city and the informative *Copenhagen This Week*, as well as being an excellent source of information on the city and the country as a whole. On the first corner of the Tivoli amusement park from the main train station. Go left along the side of the park from the station.
USE-IT, Rådhusstræde 13 (tel. 3315 6528). Open 15 June–15 Sept., daily 9 a.m.–7 p.m.; at other times, Mon.–Fri. 10 a.m.–4 p.m. An office oriented towards the budget traveller. Free help with finding accommodation. Their free map is superior to that of the Tourist Office. The organization also publishes useful guides to seeing the city on foot, by bike, or by bus, as well as an entertainment guide.

FINDING ACCOMMODATION
During the summer, hostel beds can disappear at an alarming rate, so try to reserve ahead. If you arrive without reservations USE-IT (see **Tourist Offices**) are your best bet for finding a hostel bed. Otherwise, unless you have a tent, you will either have to sleep rough, or pay for a hotel room, neither of which is a good option.

HOTELS

Søfolkenes Mindehotel, Peder Skramsgade 19 (tel. 3313 4882). B&B in singles around 235Dkr (£23.50; $35.25), in doubles around 410Dkr (£41; $61.50). Bus 27 from Vesterbrogade or Rådhuspladsen passes the end of the street by the Inderhavnen.

Skt. Jørgen, Julius Thomsensgade 22 (tel. 3537 1511). B&B in doubles from 400Dkr (£40; $60).

Jørgensen, Rømersgade 11 (tel. 3313 8186). Doubles from around 440Dkr (£44; $66). See the entry in the **Hostels** section below for directions.

Amager, Amagerbrogade 29 (tel. 3154 4008/3154 5009). B&B in doubles starts around 500Dkr (£50; $75). Bus 30, 33 or 34 along Amager Boulevard to Amagerbrogade from Rådhuspladsen.

Cab Inn, Danasvej 3234 (tel. 3121 0400). Doubles with a shower around 550Dkr (£55; $82.50). With breakfast. Bus 29 from Vesterbrogade runs along the street. To walk follow Vester Farimagsgade away from Vesterbrogade by the train station. Turn left along Kampmannsgade and over the Skt Jøgens Sø into Dansavej.

Ibsens, Vendersgade 23 (tel. 3313 1913). Doubles around 600Dkr (£60; $90) per person with breakfast. S-tog to Nørreport, then walk down the street to the hotel.

Hotel Hebron, Helgolandsgade 4 (tel. 3131 6906). B&B in doubles around 500Dkr (£50; $75). From Banegardspladsen in front of Central Station turn left down Reventlowsgade then right along Istedgade into Helgolandsgade.

Turisthotellet, Reverdilsgade 5 (tel. 3122 9839). B&B in doubles from 500Dkr (£50; $75). From Banegardspladsen in front of Central Station turn left down Reventlowsgade then right at Reverdilsgade. A few minutes' walk.

Absalon, Helgolandsgade 15 (tel. 3124 2211). Doubles from 500Dkr (£50; $75), including breakfast.

Bertrams, Vesterbrogade 107 (tel. 3325 0405). Doubles from 575Dkr (£57.50; $86.25), including breakfast.

Boulevard, Sønder Boulevard 53 (tel. 3325 2519). Doubles from 460Dkr (£46; $69), including breakfast.

Carlton, Halmtorvet 14 (tel. 3121 2551). Doubles from 430Dkr (£43; $64.50), including breakfast.

Copenhagen Bed & Breakfast, Egilsgade 33 (tel. 3296 2727). Doubles from 457Dkr (£45.70; $68.55), including breakfast.

Metropol, Viktoriagade 2–4 (tel. 313 1839). Doubles from 500Dkr (£50; $75), including breakfast.

Missionshotellet Ansgar, Colbjørnsensgade 29 (tel. 3121 2196). Doubles from 500Dkr (£50; $75), including breakfast.

Saga, Colbjørnsensgade 18–20 (tel. 3124 4944). Doubles from 400Dkr (£40; $60), including breakfast.

Sct. Thomas, Frederiksberg Allé 7 (tel. 3121 6464). Doubles from 400Dkr (£40; $60), including breakfast.

West, Westend 11 (tel. 3124 2761). Doubles from 300Dkr (£30; $45).

PRIVATE ROOMS

Værelseanvisning, Bernstorffsgade 1 (tel. 3312 4045). Rooms found for a 13Dkr (£1.30; $2) commission. Prices start around 150Dkr (£15; $22.5). Personal callers only.

H.A.Y.4U, Kronprinsengade 10 (tel. 3333 0805). Prices start around 100Dkr (£10; $15) per person in private flats. Limited amount of accommodation available at these prices. From the Nørreport S-top station follow Frederiksborggade, cross Kultorvet, and then walk along Købmagergade until you see Kronprinsensgade on the left.

USE-IT (see **Tourist Offices**). No commission, and often capable of undercutting the prices of rooms from the two agencies above.

Skandinavisk Logi/Morgenmad (S.L.M.), St Kongensgade 94 (tel. 3391 9115).

Mihail Andonov, Kirkevænget 13 (tel. 3645 6540). Private rooms about 3km from the centre, bus 6 or metro: Valby. Singles 200Dkr (£20; $30), doubles 260Dkr (£26; $39).

HI HOSTELS

Bellahøj, Herbergvejen 8 (tel. 3128 9715). 55–60Dkr (£5.50–6; $8.25–9). Five kilometres from the town centre. From the station or from Rådhusplein take bus 2 or nightbus 902. Get off at Fuglsang Allé.

Amager, Vejlandsallé 200 (tel. 3252 2908). 60–70Dkr (£6–7; $9–10.50). Mon.–Fri. bus 46 from Central Station (9 a.m.–5 p.m.), or bus 37 from Holmens Bro. S-train B, C, H, or L to Valby station (S-trains free with railpasses) to join bus 37 saves a bit of time and money.

Lyngby Vandrerhjem, Rådvad 1 (tel. 4280 3074). 46–60Dkr (£4.60–6; $7–9). Far out, and not easy to get to. Fine if you are stuck for a first night. S-train A, B or L to Lyngby. From there, bus 182 or 183 to Lundtoftvej and Hjortekærsvej. The 3km walk to Rådvad is marked. Bus 187 provides a direct link between Central Station and the hostel, but only runs four times a day. The only HI hostel with a curfew, 11 p.m.

HOSTELS

City Public Hostel, Absalonsgade 8 (tel. 3131 2070). Open 5 May–31 Aug. No curfew and round-the-clock reception. More expensive than the HI hostels but central location. 90Dkr (£9; $13.50), or 105Dkr (£10.50; $15.75) if you want the breakfast, where you can eat as much as you like. In the Vesterbro Ungdomsgård. From the train station walk left along Vesterbro-gade to Vesterbros Torv. Absalonsgade is off Svendsgade on the left of the square.

KFUK (YWCA) Interpoint, Store Kannikestræde 19 (tel. 3111 3031). Open 1 July–22 Aug. Check in from 8 a.m.–12 p.m., or between 2.30 p.m. and the 12.20 a.m. curfew. 60Dkr (£6; $9). Excellent central location. The street runs from Frue Plads (site of Our Lady's Cathedral). From Rådhuspladsen walk away from the Town Hall down Vester Voldgade, right along Vester-gade, then left up Nørregade to Frue Plads. Walking down Nørregade from the Nørreport S-tog station is about half the distance.

KFUM/KFUK (YMCA/YWCA) Interpoint, Valdermarsgade 15 (tel. 3131 1574). Open 15 July–15 Aug. Same entry requirements as the KFUK hostel. Similar hours and prices. Outside the centre.

Hotel Jørgensen, Rømersgade 11 (tel. 3313 8186). From June–Aug. the hotel operates a mixed dorm in its basement. 70Dkr (£7; $10.50), 90Dkr (£9; $13.50) with breakfast. From the Nørre-port S-tog station Vendersgade and Frederiksborggade lead into Rømersgade.

SLEEP-IN

Per Henrik Lings Allé 6 (tel. 3126 5059). Open June–mid-Aug. Mixed dorms or mattresses on the floor. 80Dkr (£8; $12) with continental breakfast. Usually will find space for last-minute arrivals. Bus 1 from Rådhuspladsen or nightbus 953 to Per Henrik Allé. Alternatively bus 6 or 14 from Rådhuspladsen, or nightbus 914 to Vedidrætsparken.

CAMPING

There are a total of seven sites around Copenhagen. Expect to pay around 40Dkr (£4; $6) per person, tent included, at the following sites:

Strandmølle, Strandmølleveg 2 (tel. 4280 3883). Open mid-May–Sept. About 14.5km out, but only 20 minutes on S-train C dir. Klampenborg.

Absalon, Korsdalsvej 132 (tel. 3141 0600). Open year round. About 8km out of town. S-train B or L to Brøndbyøster, then a kilo-metre's walk. Ask locals for directions.

Bellahøj, Hvidkildevej (tel. 3110 1150). Open 1 June–31 Aug. Same buses as for the Bellahøj HI hostel, but get off at the stop after Hulgårdsvej.

Esbjerg

TOURIST OFFICE
Turistbureauet, Skolegade 33, DK-6700 Esbjerg (tel. 7512 5599). Open Mon.–Fri. 9 a.m.–5 p.m., Sat. 9 a.m.–12 p.m. (15 June–31 Aug., 9 a.m.–5 p.m.) The office is on the corner of the main square.

ARRIVING IN ESBJERG
Arriving by ferry from Harwich, Newcastle or Tórshavn, the town centre is a well-signposted 20-minute walk from the ferry terminal. Trains to Copenhagen depart from the train station by the ferry terminal. The main train station is located near the town centre, at the opposite end of Skolegade from the main square.

HOTELS
Tarp Kro, Tarpbyvej 50 (tel. 7516 7011). Doubles around 385Dkr (£38.50; $58), including breakfast.
Ølufvad Kro, Ølufvadhovedvej 85 (tel. 7516 9006). Doubles around 200Dkr (£20; $30).
Sømandshjemmet, Auktionsgade 3 (tel. 7512 0688). Doubles around 315Dkr (£31.50; $47.25). At the harbour.
St Darum Kro, Sviegade 2 (tel. 7517 9007). Doubles around 385Dkr (£38.50; $58), breakfast included.

PRIVATE ROOMS
Available from the Tourist Office.

HI HOSTEL
Gammel Vardevej 80 (tel. 7512 4258). 75Dkr (£7.50; $11.25). About 3km from the centre. Bus 1, 9, 11, 12 or 31 from Skolegade.

CAMPING
Strandskovens, Gl. Vardevej 76 (tel. 7512 5816). See the HI hostel above for directions.

Frederikshavn

TOURIST OFFICE
Brotorvet 1, DK-9900 Frederikshavn (tel. 9842 3266). Open 1 June–31 Aug., Mon.–Sat. 8.30 a.m.–8.30 p.m., Sun. 11 a.m.–8.30 p.m.; 1 Sept.–31 May, Mon.–Fri. 9 a.m.–4 p.m., Sat. 11 a.m.–2 p.m. By the Stena Line ferry terminal at the corner of Havnepladsen and Rådhus Allé, a 5-minute walk from the train and bus stations.

HOTEL
Discount Logi Teglgaarden, Teglgaardsvej 3 (tel. 9842 0444). Open all year. Singles from 170Dkr (£17; $25.50), doubles from 300Dkr (£30; $45).

HI HOSTEL
'Fladstrand', Buhlsvej 6 (tel. 9842 1475). 53–78Dkr (£5.30–7.80; $8–11.70).

CAMPING
Nordstrand, Apholmenvej 40 (tel. 9842 9350). Open Apr.–Sept.

Legoland

Situated in Billund, the mini-town made out of Lego is one of the main tourist attractions in Denmark. Legoland is open from May until mid-September, with a number of indoor exhibitions from Easter to mid-December. Hotels in Billund are expensive, so either camp at the local site, or visit Legoland on a daytrip from Vejle or Varde.

CAMPING
FDM-Camping Billund, Nordmarksvej 2 (tel. 7533 1521). Open 24 June–16 Sept. Very close to Legoland.

Vejle

Bus 912 to Billund. Most days an hourly service operates.

HOTEL
Grejsdalens Hotel and Kro, Grejsdalsvej 384 (tel. 7585 3004). Singles from 220Dkr (£22; $33), doubles from 360Dkr (£36; $54).

HI HOSTEL
Vejle Vandrerhjem, Gl. Landevej 80 (tel. 7582 5188). 75–84Dkr (£7.50–8.40; $11.25–12.60).

SLEEP-IN
In the Sports Hall, Vestre Engvej. Details from the Tourist Office (tel. 7582 1955).

CAMPING
Helligkilderej 5 (tel. 7582 3335).

Varde

HOTEL
Højskolehjemmet, Storegade 56 (tel. 7522 0140). Doubles around 350Dkr (£35; $52.50) including breakfast.

HI HOSTEL
Ungdomsgården, Pramstedvej 10 (tel. 7522 1091). 55–60Dkr (£5.50–6; $8.25–9). Open 15 May–1 Oct.

Odense

TOURIST OFFICE
Odense Tourist Information, Town Hall, DK-5000 Odense C (tel. 6612 7520). Open mid-June–Aug., Mon.–Sat. 9 a.m.–7 p.m., Sun. 11 a.m.–7 p.m.; Sept.–mid-June, Mon.–Fri. 9 a.m.–5 p.m., Sat. 10 a.m.–1 p.m. About 10 minutes' walk from the train station. Head right along Ostre Stationsvej then left at Jernbanegade, or walk through the park in front of the station on to Jernbanegade. At the end of Jernbanegade, turn left along Vestergade to the Town Hall. Booking fee for accommodation 25Dkr (£2.50; $3.75).

HOTELS
Doubles without breakfast around 330Dkr (£33; $49.50)

Ansgarhus Motel, Kirkegårds Alle 17—19 (tel. 6612 8800). Open Jan.—Sept.

B&B in doubles around 370—410Dkr (£37—41; $55.50—61.50)

Kahema, Dronningensgade 5 (tel. 6612 2821).
Ydes, Hans Tausensgade 11 (tel. 6612 1131).

B&B in doubles around 390Dkr (£39; $58.50)

Fangel Kro, Fangelvej 55 (tel. 6596 1011). Not central, but the bus stops about 100m from the hotel.

PRIVATE ROOMS
Available from the Tourist Office. Around 110Dkr (£11; $16.50) per person.

HI HOSTEL
Kragsbjerggården, Kragsbjergvej 121 (tel. 6613 0425). 64—72Dkr (£6.40—7.20; $9.60—10.80). Bus 62 or 63 from the train station. A 20-minute walk from the town centre.

HOSTEL
KFUM/KFUK (YMCA/YWCA) Interpoint, Rodegårdsvej 91 (tel. 6614 2314). Open 15 July—15 Aug. 60Dkr (£6; $9). Detailed map at station. Ring ahead to see if this hostel is open for 1995.

SLEEP-IN
Run by the State Railway DSB. Enquire by phone whether it is in operation either at the train station, or at the Tourist Office (tel. 6612 7520).

CAMPING
Odense, Odensevej 102 (tel. 6611 4702). Open Easter—mid-Oct. Around 35Dkr (£3.50; $5.25) per person, tent included. Bungalows available. Bus 13. The site is within easy walking distance of the Fruens Bøge train station on the line to Svendborg. Walk down Stationsvej, then right along Odensevej.
'Blommenslyst', Middelfartvej 494 (tel. 6596 7641). Open May—mid-Sept. Farther out than the site above, to the west of town.

FINLAND (Suomi)

In common with the other Scandinavian countries, simply feeding yourself in Finland costs a fair amount of money, making it all the more vital to keep the price of your accommodation down. Unless you are desperate you will want to avoid staying in **hotels**, as even the cheapest hotels charge around 140FIM (£18.20; $27.30) for singles, 200FIM (£26; $39) for doubles. In the main tourist destinations, you can expect to pay closer to 300FIM (£39; $58.50) for the cheapest doubles in town.

B&B accommodation is a cheaper option than hotels, with overnight prices generally in the 85–195FIM (£11.00–25.25; $16.50–38.00) range. A substantial breakfast and use of a sauna are usually included in the overnight price. Unfortunately B&B accommodation is nowhere near as widespread as hotel accommodation, and is available mainly in the north of the country, particularly on farms.

Hostelling is an excellent way to see Finland, especially if you are travelling outside the peak season of mid-July to mid-August. There are 165 **HI hostels** scattered around the country, with at least one operating in all the main tourist destinations during the summer. Finnish hostels are classified from one up to four stars. Prices in two-star hostels range from 35–55FIM (£4.50–7.00; $6.75–10.50), depending on whether you stay in a dorm or a small room. Most common in the larger towns are three-star hostels which charge 35–80FIM (£4.50–10.40; $6.76–15.60) per night in two- to eight-bed rooms. Prices in the four-star hostels (known as Finnhostels) start at 57FIM (£7.40; $11), rising to 160FIM (£21; $31.50). The largest rooms in four-star hostels are quads.

Only in the most expensive hostels are HI cards obligatory, but they do entitle you to a 15FIM (£2; $3) discount. Hiring sheets and towels will cost an extra 20–25FIM (£2.50–3.25; $4–5), so come well prepared and save your money. Only from June to August, and particularly from mid-July to mid-August, will you experience any difficulty in getting a hostel bed. At this time, hostels in the large cities and in areas popular with hikers are often full, making it imperative to reserve ahead, by letter or by telephone. Reservations are held until 6 p.m., unless you make it clear that you will be arriving later.

In contrast to other Scandinavian countries, Finland has seen little growth in the number of **independent hostels**. Converted student dorms, known as 'Summerhotels', are generally clean and modern. Accommodation is in singles or doubles: around 160FIM (£21;

$31.50) is the normal price for singles: 100—125FIM (£13.00—16.25;
$19.50—24.40) per person the usual price for doubles.

There are over 350 well-equipped official **campsites**, graded
from one to three stars, covering all the main tourist areas. Prices
vary from 25—80FIM (£3.25—10.40; $5—15.60) upwards, according
to the classification of the site. If you are not in possession of an
International Camping Carnet, you will have to buy a Finnish
camping pass at the first site you visit. Few sites remain open all
year round. Most open for the period May/June to August/Sep-
tember only. Many of the sites in and around the larger towns are
very big, with a tent capacity of 2,000. During July and August,
these sites become very busy at weekends. Some sites let cottages
(usually without bedding) for two to five people — well worth
enquiring about if there are several people prepared to share. Cottages are available for anything between 150—300FIM (£19.50—
39.00; $29.25—58.50) per day.

It is possible to **sleep rough** in Finland and stay within the law.
More advisably, you can take advantage of an old law which allows
you to camp anywhere as long as you have the landowner's permission. It is normal practice to camp out of sight of private homes.

ADDRESSES

Finnish Tourist Board   66—68 Haymarket, London SW1Y 4RF
                         (tel. 0171 839 4048). Lists of hotels,
                         hostels and campsites.
Finnish YHA   Suomen Retkeilymajajärjestö-SRM ry,
                         Yrjönkatu 38 B 15, 00100 Helsinki
                         (tel. 90 693 1347).

Helsinki (Helsingfors) (tel. code 90)

TOURIST OFFICES

Kaupungin Matkailutoimisto, Pohjoisesplanadi 19, 00100 Helsinki
(tel. 169 3757). Open mid-May—mid-Sept., Mon.—Fri.
8.30 a.m.—6 p.m., Sat. 8.30 a.m.—1 p.m.; otherwise, Mon.
8.30 a.m.—4.30 p.m., Tues.—Fri. 8.30 a.m.—4 p.m. A 10-minute
walk from the train station, left down Mannerheimintie, then
left again along Pohjoisesplanadi.

Hotellikeskus, train station (tel. 171133). Open in summer,
Mon.—Fri. 9 a.m.—9 p.m., Sat. 9 a.m.—7 p.m., Sun. 10 a.m.—6 p.m.;
at other times, Mon.—Fri. 9 a.m.—6 p.m. Dispenses city maps and

hotel/hostel lists but, first and foremost, the office is an accommodation service: 10FIM (£1.30; $2) commission for a hotel room, half that fee for a hostel bed. A few minutes' walk from the train station in the direction of the post office.

HOTELS
The least expensive hotels charge 200–300FIM (£26–39; $39.00–58.50) for their cheapest doubles.

Fenno, Franzeninkatu 26 (tel. 773 1661).
Kongressikoti, Snellmaninkatu 15 A (tel. 135 6839). Doubles from 200FIM (£26; $39).
Erottajanpuisto, Uudenmaankatu (tel. 642169).
Regina, Puistokatu 9 A 2 (tel. 656937).
Omapohja, Itäinen Teatterikuja 3 (tel. 666211). Near the train station.
Hotel Finn, Kalevankatu 3B (tel. 640904).

HI HOSTELS
Stadionin maja, Pohj Stadiontie 3 B (tel. 496071). Curfew 2 a.m. Three-star hostel. Prices for HI members start at 60FIM (£8; $12) in small dorms, rising to 80FIM (£10.40; $15.60) per person in doubles. Tram 3T or 7A to the Olympic Stadium, or a 25-minute walk.
Satakuntatalo, Lapinrinne 1A (tel. 695851). Student accommodation converted into a temporary four-star hostel. Open 1 June–31 Aug. 175FIM (£22.75; $34) for singles, 220FIM (£28.60; $43) for doubles, 60FIM (£8; $12) for dorms. Ask about student discounts (20–50%). A 10-minute walk from the train station. Tram 4 stops nearby.
Eurohostel, Linnankatu 9 (tel. 664452). Recently opened four-star hostel. Singles 145–160FIM (£19–21; $28.50–31.50), doubles 190–220FIM (£24.70–28.60; $37–43), 110FIM (£14.30; $21.50) for dorms. Close to the harbour, a 20-minute walk from the train station. Tram 4 stops nearby.
Finnhostel Academica, Hietaniemenkatu 14 (tel. 402 0206). Student accommodation converted into a temporary hostel. Open 1 June–1 Sept. Singles 245FIM (£32; $48), doubles 290FIM (£37.70; $56.60). Ask about student reductions. Bus 18 or tram 3T run to the hostel. A 10-minute walk from the train station.
Vantaan retkeilyhotelli, Valkoisenlähteentie 52, 01300 Vantaa (tel. 839 3310). Dorms for 45FIM (£6; $9), doubles for 120FIM (£15.60; $23.40). Four-star hostel. About 16km from the city centre; 1km from the Tikkurila train station.

HOSTELS

Kallion Retkeilymaja, Porthaninkatu 2 (tel. 7099 2590). Open June—Aug. 2 a.m. curfew. 50FIM (£6.50; $9.75). Only 30 beds. Run by the city's youth organization. Fifteen-minute walk from the train station along Unionkatu, or the metro to Hakaniemi.

YMCA Interpoint, Vuorikato 17 (tel. 173441). Open 12 July—20 Aug. Ring ahead to check that the hostel is open for 1995.

CAMPING

Rastila (tel. 316551). Open mid-May—mid-Sept. Prices at this municipal site start at 50FIM (£6.50; $9.75) p.p. (tent included). Also lets cabins. About 6.5km from the city centre. Metro to Itäkeskus, then bus 90, 90A or 96.

Rovaniemi (tel. code (9)60)

TOURIST OFFICE

Aallonkatu 1, 96200 Rovaniemi (tel. 346270). Open June—Aug., Mon.—Fri. 8 a.m.—7 p.m.; weekends, 9 a.m.—6 p.m.; rest of the year, Mon.—Fri. 8 a.m.—4 p.m. A short walk from the bus and train stations. Turn left from the bus station, right from the train station, on to Ratakatu, which leads into Hallituskatu. Turn left along Valtakatu, and continue until you see the Tourist Office.

HOTELS

Cheapest doubles 150FIM (£19.50; $29.25)

Matkakoti Matka-Kalle, Asemieskatu 1 (tel. 20130).
Outa, Ukkoherrantie 16 (tel. 312474).

Cheapest doubles 200FIM (£26; $39)

Aakenus, Koskikatu 47 (tel. 22051).

HI HOSTEL

Retkeilymaja Tervashonka, Hallituskatu 16 (tel. 344644). Dorms for 60FIM (£8; $12), doubles for 140FIM (£18.20; $27.30). Three-star hostel. For directions, see **Tourist Office**, above.

CAMPING

Ounaskoski (tel. 345304). Open 1 June—31 Aug. Just over the river from the centre of town.

Napapiirin Saari-Tuvat (tel. 60045). Open 24 May—30 Sept.

Savonlinna (tel. code (9)57)

TOURIST OFFICE
Savonlinna Tourist Service, Puistokatu 1, 57100 Savonlinna (tel. 273492). Open 28 June–1 Aug., daily 8 a.m.–10 p.m.; 31 May–27 June and 2–29 Aug., daily 8 a.m.–6 p.m.; at other times, Mon.–Fri. 9 a.m.–4 p.m. Accommodation-finding service available throughout the year (invaluable in July when the town is packed).

ARRIVING BY TRAIN
The most convenient stop for the town centre and the Tourist Office is Savonlinna-Kauppatori, one stop before the main station if you are arriving from Helsinki.

HOTEL
Hospits, Linnankatu 20 (tel. 515661). Cheapest doubles around 220FIM (£28.60; $43).

HI HOSTELS
Retkeilymaja Malakias, Pihlajavedenkuja 6 (tel. 23283). 240FIM (£31.20; $46.80) for doubles. Open 28 June–8 Aug. Just over 10 minutes' walk from the train station.
Retkeilymaja Vuorilinna, Kylpylaitoksentie (tel. 5750494). 240FIM (£31.25; $47) for doubles. Open 1 June–29 Aug.

CAMPING
Vuohimäki (tel. 537353). Open 4 June–22 Aug. About 6.5km from the centre. Bus 3 runs twice hourly.
Korkeamaen Majatalo, Ruokolahti, Kerimäki (tel. 312186 and, in summer, tel. 4827).

Turku (Turku/Åbo) (tel. code (9)21)

TOURIST OFFICES
The tourist office operates at two locations in the city:

The main office is at Käsityöläiskatu 3, 20100 Turku (tel. 233 6366), about 250m from the train station. Open June–Aug., Mon.–Fri. 8 a.m.–4 p.m.; at other times, Mon.–Fri. 8.30 a.m.–4 p.m.

Tourist Info, Aurakatu 4 (tel. 315262). Open 1 June–15 Sept., Mon.–Fri. 8.30 a.m.–7.30 p.m., Sat. and Sun. 10 a.m.–5 p.m.; 16 Sept.–31 May, Mon.–Fri. 8.30 a.m.–6 p.m., Sat. and Sun. 10 a.m.–5 p.m.

ARRIVING IN TURKU/ÅBO
If you arrive at the train station you are only a short walk from the centre of the town. The ferry terminal is about 3km from the city centre, but bus 1 runs frequently from the harbour to the Market Place in the town centre.

HOTELS
Cheapest doubles 250–300FIM (£32.50–39.00; $48.75–58.50)

Brahe, Humalistonkatu 13 (tel. 311973). The street leads away from the front of the train station.

Turisti-Aula, Käsityöläiskatu 11 (tel. 334484). The street leads away from the front of the train station.

St Birgittas Convent Guesthouse, Ursininkatu 15A (tel. 501910). Follow Käsityöläiskatu from the train station, right on Puutarhakatu, then left.

Ikituuri Summer Hotel, Pispalantie 7 (tel. 376111). Converted student accommodation. Open 1 June–31 Aug.

Asuntohotelli Astro, Humalistonkatu 18 (tel. 511107). See Brahe, above.

HI HOSTEL
Turku City Youth Hostel, Linnankatu 39 (tel. 316578). Dorms for 50FIM (£6.50; $9.75), doubles for 140FIM (£18.20; $27.30), singles for 110FIM (£14.30; $21.50). Three-star hostel. Bus 1 from the ferry terminal or a 20-minute walk along Linnankatu. A 15-minute walk from the train station.

CAMPING
Ruissalo (tel. 589249). Open 1 June–31 Aug. About 9.5km out of town. Bus 8 runs twice hourly from the Market Square.

FRANCE

As a rule, budget travellers should have little difficulty in finding a cheap place to stay in France. There is probably a wider range of good options here than anywhere else in Europe. Even in Paris there are plenty of cheap places to stay. For most of the year, you should be able to find a cheap bed on arrival anywhere outside the capital, unless there is a special event on in the town (such as the Festival d'Avignon). However, it is best to try and reserve hotels ahead in July and August when the French themselves are on holiday. In Paris, hotel reservations are a good idea at any time of year, but especially from Easter to late September when the city is buzzing with visitors. Youth hostels in Paris should be reserved in advance (around 3–4 months ahead if you are planning a visit in summer), while the two youth hostel associations advise advance reservations of hostels in popular tourist destinations between May and September.

Although the French have no national reservations centre on the Dutch model, they have made great strides in facilitating the easy booking of accommodation. While French hoteliers will invariably accept a request for a reservation over the phone you may be able to save yourself the trouble of phoning around to book in advance by using the 'Accueil de France' or 'Loisirs Accueil' services. Around fifty French cities' Tourist Offices are part of the 'Accueil de France' scheme, which allows you to book hotel accommodation in any other town which is also part of the system. (Details on whether a city included in this guide is a participant is given in the Tourist Office sections. As the number of cities taking part is increasing, this information may change, so it is always worth asking locally.) Reservations can be made for the same day or for up to eight days in advance; a small charge is made for this service to cover the cost of the phone call or telex. The 'Accueil de France' service is particularly useful if you are heading for Paris. Because looking for accommodation in Paris on your own can be frustrating, it makes sense to use one of the accommodation services in the capital to find you a bed, but it is even smarter to arrive with your accommodation already booked and bypass the very long queues which are common at these offices during the main tourist season. A variation on 'Accueil de France' are the 'Loisirs Accueil' services which have been established by many of the French départements (regional authorities). These offices reserve not just some hotels in the area but also campsites, more often than not free of charge. A list of such offices is available from the French

Government Tourist Office; simply send a stamped self-addressed envelope with your request.

The French Ministry of Tourism categories for **hotels** range from one star up to four stars, and then the deluxe 'four stars L', according to the facilities available and the level of comfort. The actual grading and inspection of hotels is carried out on a regular basis by the prefecture of the département (only a relatively small number of hotels remain unclassified). Standards of comfort and cleanliness in French hotels should give you little to worry about but, as is the case everywhere, there is always the occasional hotel which lets standards slip between inspections. Given that the authorities are committed to maintaining a consistently high standard of accommodation do not hesitate to contact them (c/o the local Tourist Office) if you have any grounds for complaint.

In contrast to other countries, two people can easily stay every night in a hotel without worrying unduly about their budgets as hotel prices are very low (Parisian hotels are ridiculously cheap when compared to their counterparts in London). French custom is to set a price for a room, which means that the charge is the same whether it is occupied by one or two people. In practice, some hoteliers will let rooms to solo travellers at a reduced rate (typically 70–75% of the cost of the room), but often only outside the peak season when trade is beginning to tail off. A third bed normally adds about 30% to the cost of a room.

One-star hotels will be of primary interest to budget travellers, though it is worth noting that many unclassified hotels, particularly in rural areas, offer perfectly adequate standards of accommodation. One-star hotels seldom offer more than the basic comforts, but they represent good value for what you pay. The cheaper two-star establishments are also within the range of the budget traveller. Despite the fact that these are described by the Ministry of Tourism as merely 'comfortable', you will probably find them a bit luxurious when compared to similarly priced accommodation in other west European countries. The cheapest one-star hotels charge around 100–110FF (£12.50–13.75; $18.75–20.50), except in Paris where you will do well to find a room for under 140FF (£17.50; $26.25). Prices for two-star hotels start at around 140–150FF (£17.50–18.75; $26.25–28.00) outside Paris, around 170–180FF (£21.25–22.50; $32.00–33.75) in the capital.

Although hotel rooms are cheap and good value for money, on the whole hotel breakfasts are not. You can expect to pay 15–25FF (£2–3; $3.00–4.50) for a basic continental breakfast; very poor value for money when you consider what that amount might buy at the supermarket or baker's, or even in a local café. Legally, hoteliers have no right to insist that you take breakfast (or any other meal), but in practice there are always a few who will try to force your hand in popular towns at the height of the season. While you have the right to refuse breakfast, they have the right to refuse your custom. Another cost over and above what you pay for a room may be a charge for taking a shower or a bath. You will normally be asked to pay from 10–25FF (£1.25–3; $2–4.50) to use the bath or shower when these are not included in the overnight price.

Throughout the provincial towns there are over 5,000 family-run hotels and inns belonging to an organization known as 'Logis de France', easily identifiable by their distinctive green-and-yellow emblem. These establishments have generally taken advantage of government grants and now provide guaranteed standards of service, mainly in one- or two-star accommodation, though a number of unclassified 'auberges' are also included in the association. A complete guide to these hotels and inns can be purchased from the Logis Department of the French Government Tourist Office. A considerably abridged list of these accommodations is available from 'Gîtes de France'.

Bed and Breakfast accommodation is found mainly in the countryside, though there are some B&B possibilities in a few of the larger cities. Rural chambres d'hôtes (B&B in private homes) are generally similar in price to cheap hotels, but probably offer even better value for money. Another alternative to hotel accommodation open to the budget traveller is to rent self-catering accommodation. Again, this is an option far more prevalent in rural France, most conspicuously in the form of 'Gîtes de France': self-catering accommodation let by an association of French families. Sleeping between four and six people, they can usually be rented for 900–1500FF (£112.50–187.50; $168.75–281.25) per week. The gîtes are normally located in and around small villages, and may be village houses, rural or farm cottages, or flats in private homes. Over 2,500 gîtes can be booked through the offices of 'Gîtes de France Ltd' in London. For an annual membership fee of £3 you receive an illustrated guide to all the properties, free use of the reservation service, and discounts on 21 ferry routes across the Channel if you are travelling by car or motorbike.

There are two **youth hostel** associations in France; the HI-affiliated Fédération Unie des Auberges de la Jeunesse (FUAJ), and the Ligue Française pour les Auberges de la Jeunesse (LFAJ). Relations between the two are strained, to say the least. The HI handbook lists the FUAJ hostels, but only a few of the LFAJ establishments. It is worthwhile finding out about the LFAJ hostels, as they fill in many of the gaps in the FUAJ network, so that there are not many places of major interest that lack a hostel (contact the associations' head offices for up-to-date hostel lists).

Most hostels stay open all year round, except perhaps for a few weeks in winter. Hostelling can certainly be a cheap way to see the country, at virtually any time of year, provided you take the trouble to reserve well ahead for hostels in the more popular tourist towns. The drawbacks are the poor quality of some of the hostels, and the curfews. Even the top-rated hostels vary enormously in quality. While some are well maintained and efficiently run, at the other extreme are those in dilapidated buildings, where the warden only appears at certain times and is not on the premises at night. In the very worst of this latter type, you may well have reason to worry about your personal safety. Curfews are normally 11 p.m. at the latest, except in a very small number of hostels.

Generally, hostel prices vary according to the grade of establishment. Prices can be as low as 30FF (£3.75; $5.60), but are normally around 40–50FF (£5.00–6.25; $7.50–9.40). However, in popular tourist destinations such as Paris, Strasbourg, Avignon and Bayeux even low-grade hostels may charge well above the normal hostel price. In these towns, expect to pay around 75–85FF (£9.40–10.60; $14–16) in the hostels of either association. The HI card permits entry to both FUAJ and LFAJ hostels. Technically, the HI card is obligatory at FUAJ hostels, but non-members are normally allowed to stay on the payment of a 10–20FF (£1.25–2.35; $1.75–3.55) supplement per night, or are restricted to a one-night stay.

In some of the larger towns, a further possibility available to HI members and students are the 'Foyers des Jeunes Travailleurs/ Travailleuses'. These are residential hostels, whose main function is to provide cheap living accommodation for young workers and students. As such, they tend to offer a higher standard of accommodation than hostels (mainly singles and doubles). Prices are usually on a par with local hostels, but you are getting better value for money. It is worth enquiring about 'foyers' at any time of year, but your chances of finding a place are obviously better during the student vacations.

Gîtes d'étapes (not to be confused with Gîtes de France) are widespread in rural areas, particularly those popular with hikers and cyclists. They provide basic, cheap accommodation; normally bunk-beds in dorms, and simple cooking and washing facilities. The LFAJ maintains 11 gîtes d'étapes in the Aveyron-Le Lot region, and another 27 in Corsica (details are included in the LFAJ hostel list). These are ideal for cycling or walking tours in two of the most beautiful areas of the country. Overnight fees range from about

25–45FF (£3.00–5.60; $4.50–8.40). If you are heading into the mountains, there is a plentiful supply of mountain huts, the majority of which are operated by the Club Alpin Français (CAF). Huts are open to non-members, but members of the CAF and its associated clubs receive a reduction on the usual overnight charge of 50FF (£6.25; $9.40).

Camping is very popular in France. Practically every town of any size has a campsite. There are over 7,000 in all, rated from one to four stars. The overnight fee varies from 5–20FF (£0.60–2.50; $0.90–4.00) per person, depending on the classification of the site. Usually, the cheapest you will find is a site run by the local authority (*camping municipal*). Charges are normally under 10FF (£1.25; $2) per night. Outside the main season there may not even be an attendant to collect the fees, so you can camp for free. At other times, these sites are clean and well maintained, and lack only the shopping and leisure facilities of higher-graded sites.

With a few exceptions, camping is a cheap, convenient and pleasant way to see France. There is no centrally located site in Lyon, so you will have to travel to one of the sites on the outskirts. The only site in Nice is pitifully small, and far from the centre. Along the Mediterranean, many sites become ridiculously overcrowded during the summer months; so much so that 11 regional information posts, 21 telephone information centres, and 59 local reception centres have been established to deal with the problem. The addresses and telephone numbers of these centres are listed in the brochure *Mémento du Campeur Averti*, available from Tourist Offices. Try to reserve coastal sites in advance.

In rural areas, many farms are part of a scheme which allows you to camp on the farm (*camping à la ferme*). These are listed in *Accueil à la Campagne*, a useful publication for anyone wanting to explore rural France. Facilities are very basic, yet prices are similar to those of other campsites. Many farmers will allow you to camp on their land free of charge, provided you ask their permission first. If you pitch your tent without their consent, expect a hostile confrontation.

Sleeping rough is legal, and the weather will seldom cause you any problems, except in the north outside the summer months. However, sleeping rough is not advisable, especially in the cities, or along the beaches of the Mediterranean. Petty criminals realized the easy pickings to be had from those sleeping in and around stations a long time ago (Paris and Marseilles are particularly unsafe). The beaches are 'worked' by French and North African gangs who steal for a living. If you are stuck for a place to stay, some stations have emergency lodgings. Ask for the 'Accueil en

Gare'. Failing this, you would be better to take an overnight train. If you are going to sleep rough, leave your pack at the station, and try to bed down beside other travellers. If you are attacked, hand over your money. Thieves have been known to become violent if their victims try to resist. If you have been sensible and taken out travel insurance you will incur only a small loss, which is preferable to risking serious injury.

Note: All French telephone numbers have eight digits and, with the exception of the capital, there are no dialling codes. Dial the eight digits for each number below at all times and when dialling Paris from outside the city, add 1 before the eight digits given.

ADDRESSES

French Government Tourist Office	178 Piccadilly, London W1V 0AL (tel. 0171 499 6911; 24-hours, recorded message). If purchasing any guides send cheques only, made payable to 'Maison de la France'.
Hotels	The Logis de France guide is available from the 'Logis Department' of the French Government Tourist Office from March onwards. The 1994 price was £6.50, plus £1 for postage and packing.
Gîtes de France	Gîtes de France Ltd, 178 Piccadilly, London W1V 9DB (tel. 0171 493 3480).
Youth hostels	Fédération Unie des Auberges de la Jeunesse, rue Pajol 27, 75018 Paris (tel. (1) 46 07 00 01). Ligue Français pour les Auberges de la Jeunesse, blvd Raspail 38, 75007 Paris (tel. (1) 45 48 69 84).
Camping	*The Camping Traveller to France 1995* is available from the French Government Tourist Office. £1, including postage and packing.
Rural Accommodation	The book *French Country Welcome*, available from bookshops, lists selections of chambres d'hôtes, gîtes, farms which are part of camping à la ferme, and mountain huts.

Aix-en-Provence

TOURIST OFFICE
Office du Tourisme, pl. du Général-de-Gaulle 2, 13100 Aix-en-Provence (tel. 42 26 02 93). 'Accueil de France' service unavailable. A few minutes' walk from the train station.

HOTELS
Cheapest doubles around 120FF (£15; $22.50)

Vendôme, cours des Minimes 10 (tel. 42 64 45 01).
Bellegarde, pl. Bellegarde 2 (tel. 42 23 43 37). From pl. Richelme head right along rue Paul Bert, left at the junction of rue Pierre et Marie Curie and rue Mathéron, then right along rue du Puits Neuf to pl. Bellegarde. Singles from 85FF (£10.60; $16).

Cheapest doubles around 140–160FF (£17.50–20.00; $26.25–30.00)

Paul, av. Pasteur 10 (tel. 42 23 23 89). From the foot of pl. Richelme near the Town Hall, rue Gaston de Saporta leads into av. Pasteur.
Vigouroux, rue Cardinale 27 (tel. 42 38 26 42). Right off av. Victor Hugo.

Cheapest doubles around 190–220FF (£23.75–27.50; $35.60–41.25)

Le Moulin, av. Robert Schumann 1 (tel. 42 59 41 68).
Des Arts (Sully), blvd Carnot 69 (tel. 42 38 11 77).
Le Concorde, blvd du Roi René 68 (tel. 42 26 03 95).
De France, rue Espariat 63 (tel. 42 27 90 15).
Du Globe, cours Sextius 74 (tel. 42 26 03 58).
Splendid, cours Mirabeau 69 (tel. 42 38 19 53).
Du Casino, rue Victor-Leydet 38 (tel. 42 26 06 88). The street runs between pl. des Augustins and pl. Niollon.

YOUTH HOSTEL
Av. Marcel Pagnol 3 (FUAJ), Quartier du Jas de Bouffan (tel. 42 20 15 99). HI cards obligatory. Sold at the hostel for 100FF (£12.50; $18.75). First night B&B 75FF (£9.40; $14), then 65FF (£8; $12) per night. 1.5km from the station. Bus 8 or 12 dir. Jas de Bouffan to the Etienne d'Orves Vasarely stop. Watch for the Vasarely building.

FOYERS
Club des Jeunes Travailleurs, Les Milles, av. Albert Einstein (Zone Industrielle) (tel. 42 24 41 38). 6.5km from the centre.
Foyer St Eloi, av. Jules Isaac 9 (tel. 42 23 44 99).
Foyer Hotel Sonacotra, av. du petit Barthélémy 16 (tel. 42 64 20 87). (Men only.)
Foyer La Provence, av. du Bon Pasteur 15 (tel. 42 23 33 98). Females only. At pl. Niollon go into the Old Town from the main roads. At the junction of rue Victor-Leydet and rue Lisse des Cordeliers follow the latter, on down rue de la Treille to the corner of rue des Bons Enfants.
Les Abeilles, av. Maréchal Leclerc (tel. 42 59 25 75). Men and women aged 16–25 only.

CAMPING
Airotel Chanteclere, Val St-André (tel. 42 26 12 98). Open all year.
Arc en Ciel, Pont des Trois Sautets (tel. 42 26 14 28). Off Route Nationale 7. Open mid-Mar.–Oct.

Avignon

TOURIST OFFICES
Office du Tourisme, cours Jean-Jaurès 41, 84000 Avignon (tel. 90 82 65 11). Head office. Open Mon.–Fri. 9 a.m.–6 p.m., Sat. 9 a.m.–12 p.m. and 2–6 p.m., except during the Festival when the office is open from 9 a.m.–7 p.m. daily. 'Accueil de France' service available.
Office du Tourisme, du Pont d'Avignon 'Le Châtelet'. Branch office. Open Apr.–Sept. daily 9 a.m.–6.30 p.m.; Oct.–Mar. open Tues.–Sun. 9 a.m.–1 p.m. and 2–5 p.m., closed Mondays.
Vaudure Tourisme Hébergements, B.P. 147, 84000 Avignon (tel. 90 82 05 81). Hotel reservations and 'Accueil de France' service. In the train station.

FINDING ACCOMMODATION
Accommodation in all price categories becomes difficult to find during the Festival d'Avignon (early July to late August) so reserve in advance if possible at this time.

HOTELS
Cheapest doubles 110–130FF (£13.75–16.25; $20.50–24.40)

Du Parc, rue Agricol-Perdiguier 18 (tel. 90 82 71 55). Right off cours Jean-Jaurès.
Hébergement Formule 1, Z.A.C. de Courtine 3 (tel. 90 86 48 55).
Innova, rue Joseph Vernet 100 (tel. 90 82 54 10).

Cheapest doubles 150–170FF (£18.75–21.25; $28–32)

Monclar, av. Monclar 13 (tel. 90 86 20 14). Head right on leaving the station. The street is on your right before you reach the Gare Routière.
Des Arts, rue de l'Aigarden 9 (tel. 90 86 63 87). Centrally located.
Le Splendid, rue Agricol-Perdiguier 17 (tel. 90 86 14 46). Right off cours Jean-Jaurès.
D'Angleterre, blvd. Raspail 29 (tel. 90 86 34 31). Left off cours Jean-Jaurès.

Cheapest doubles 180–200FF (£22.50–25.00; $33.75–37.50)

Medieval, rue Petite Saunerie 15 (tel. 90 86 11 06). Centrally located.
Mignon, rue Joseph Vernet 12 (tel. 90 82 17 30). Left off cours Jean-Jaurès.
Saint Roch, impasse Mérindol 9 (tel. 90 82 18 63). Close to the train station, just outside the city walls.
Saint George, route de Marseille 100/rue de l'Étoile 12 (tel. 90 88 54 34).
Les Balladins, av. du Grand Gigognan (tel. 90 86 88 92).
Le Relais d'Avignon, La Petite Castelette, R.N.7 (tel. 90 84 18 28).
De la Bourse, rue Portail Boquier 6 (tel. 90 82 34 43). Turn left off cours Jean-Jaurès immediately after passing the Chambre de Commerce to reach rue Portail Boquier.

Cheapest doubles 220–250FF (£27.50–31.25; $41.25–47.00)

Provençal, rue Joseph Vernet 13 (tel. 90 85 25 24). Left off 5 cours Jean-Jaurès.
Le Magnan, rue Portail Magnanen 63 (tel. 90 86 36 51). Head right from the train station and follow the city walls past the Port St-Michel to the Porte Magnanen, then turn left through the walls on to rue Portail Magnanen.
De Garlande, rue Galante 20 (tel. 90 85 08 85). Centrally located.

De Mons, rue de Mons 5 (tel. 90 82 57 16). Centrally located.
Regina, rue de la République 6 (tel. 90 86 49 45).

GUESTHOUSE
Ferme Etienne Jamet, Ile de la Barthelasse (tel. 90 86 16 74).

B&B
Mme Salaun, rue de la Masse 34 (tel. 90 86 19 05).
Les Logis St-Eloi, pl. de l'Oratoire 14 (tel. 90 25 40 36).

HOSTELS/FOYERS
The Squash Club, blvd Limbert 32 (tel. 90 85 27 78). Bed 50FF
(£6.25; $9.40).
Foyer Hameau de Champfleury, av. Eisenhower 33 (tel. 90 85 35
02). Open 15 June–15 Sept. B&B from 120–150FF (£15.00–
18.75; $22.50–28.00).
Residence Pierre Louis Loisil, av. Pierre Sémard (tel. 90 25 07 92).
Bed 57FF (£7; $10.50).
Foyer Bagatelle, Ile de la Barthelasse (tel. 90 86 30 39). Bed 52FF
(£6.50; $9.75).
Foyer International de Pont d'Avignon (YMCA), blvd de la Justice,
7 bis (tel. 90 25 46 20). B&B 85FF (£10.60; $16).
La Bastide de Bonpas, route de Cavaillon, Montfavet (tel. 90 23 04
57). Bed 77FF (£9.60; $14.40).

CAMPING
There are four sites grouped closely together on the Ile de la Barthelasse, just across the river. Within walking distance of the
station, or take the infrequent bus 10 from the Post Office (to the
left after passing through the Porte de la République).

Bagatelle (tel. 90 86 30 39). Open all year.
Camping Municipal Pont St-Benézet (tel. 90 82 63 50). Open 1
Mar.–31 Oct.
Camping Parc des Libertés (tel. 90 85 17 73). Open for a few weeks
around Easter, then from 15 June–15 Sept.
Les Deux Rhônes, Chemin de Bellegarde (tel. 90 85 49 70). Open
all year round.

Bordeaux

TOURIST OFFICES

Office du Tourisme Bordeaux Centre, cours du XXX Juillet 12,
33080 Bordeaux cedex (tel. 56 44 28 41). Open June–Sept.,
Mon.–Sat. 9 a.m.–9 p.m., Sun. 9 a.m.–7 p.m.; at other times,
Mon.–Sun. 9 a.m.–7 p.m. 'Accueil de France' service available.
Next to the Opera.
Office du Tourisme Bordeaux Gare St Jean (tel. 56 91 64 70).
Open June–Sept., daily 9 a.m.–7 p.m.; at other times, Mon.–Sat.
9 a.m.–7 p.m., Sun. 10 a.m.–7 p.m.
Office du Tourisme Bordeaux Aéroport (tel. 56 34 39 39). Open
Mon.–Sat. 8 a.m.–7 p.m., Sun. 9.30 a.m.–7 p.m.

BASIC DIRECTIONS

Bordeaux St-Jean is about 5km from the town centre. CGFTE buses
link the station to various points in the city centre. Maps of the
network are available from the Tourist Office. If you want to walk,
the simplest route (not the shortest, but the safest) is to follow
cours de la Marne from the station to pl. de la Victoire. Then you
can walk right along rue Sainte-Catherine into the heart of the
city, across cours Victor Hugo, cours d'Alsace et Lorraine and rue
de la Porte Dijeaux/rue St-Rémi, then on to the Opéra and
the beginning of cours du XXX Juillet. Going along cours du XXX
Juillet you reach the Girondins monument on Esplanade des
Quinconces.

HOTELS

*Centrally located hotels (one-star unless shown otherwise). Expect to pay
around 140–160FF (£17.50–20.00; $26.25–30.00)*

De la Boëtie, rue de la Boëtie 4 (tel. 56 91 76 68). Go left from the
Porte Dijeaux at the end of rue de la Porte Dijeaux.
D'Amboise, rue de la Vieille Tour 22 (tel. 56 81 62 67). Unclassified
hotel, slightly cheaper than the other hotels listed.
Abadie, rue Dubordieu 127 (tel. 56 91 60 85).
De Biarritz, rue de Loup 21 (tel. 56 44 38 51).
Le Blayais, rue Mautrec 17 (tel. 56 48 17 87). Near Notre-Dame.
From the Opéra, take Allées de Tourny, then left.
Le Bourgogne, cours Victor Hugo 16 (tel. 56 92 82 27). Near the
Porte des Salinières, down towards the River Garonne.
Dauphin, rue du Palais-Gallien 82 (tel. 56 52 24 62). From the

Opéra follow Allées de Tourny into pl. Tourny, then take rue Hugerie.

De Dax, rue Mautrec 7 (tel. 56 48 28 42). See the Le Blayais, above.

De Famille, cours Georges-Clemenceau 76 (tel. 56 52 11 28). From the Opéra follow Allées de Tourny, then go left from pl. Tourny.

Du Parc, rue de la Verrerie 10 (tel. 56 52 78 20). By the Jardin Public, on the fringe of the town centre. From the Girondins monument follow cours de Maréchal Foch, turn right at cours de Verdun, right again at cours Xavier Arnozan, then left.

Saint-François, rue de Mirail 22 (tel. 56 91 56 41). Rue du 5 Mirail faces the beautiful Grosse Cloche, on cours Victor Hugo heading down towards the river.

Saint-Rémi, rue Saint-Rémi 34 (tel. 56 48 55 48).

Lafaurie, rue Lafaurie-de-Monbadon 35 (tel. 56 48 16 33). The street crosses rue Hugerie (see the Dauphin, above).

Unotel, cours du Maréchal-Juin 37 (tel. 56 90 10 00). More expensive at 200FF (£25; $37.50), but the hotel has a very large capacity if you find you are having difficulty finding a room elsewhere. Follow cours d'Alsace et Lorraine away from the river past the Cathédrale St-André and along rue des F. Bonie.

One-star hotels near Gare St-Jean. Expect to pay around 140–160FF (£17.50–20.00; $26.25–30.00) for rooms without a shower/bath

Noël, rue St-Vincent-de-Paul 8 (tel. 56 91 62 48). The street runs diagonally right away from the station, between the arrival and departure halls.

San Michel, rue Charles-Domercq 32 (tel. 56 91 96 40). The street running along the front of the station.

Du Lion d'Or, pl. André-Meunier 38 (tel. 59 91 71 62). Follow rue St-Vincent-de-Paul (see the Noël, above) on to cours de la Marne, then head left until you see the square on your right.

Hôtel-Bar-Club Les Deux Mondes, rue St-Vincent-de-Paul 10 (tel. 56 91 63 03). See the Noël, above.

HOSTELS

Cours Barbey 22 (FUAJ) (tel. 56 91 59 51). Turn right on leaving the station, left up cours de la Marne, then fourth on the left. 11 p.m. curfew.

Maison des Etudiants, rue Ligier 50 (tel. 56 96 48 30). Open to women and men July–Sept., from Oct.–June women only. Bus 7 or 8 from the station to the Bourse du Travail stop on cours de la Libération.

CAMPING
No really convenient site. Two sites within reach of town are:

Les Gravières, Pont-de-la-Maye, Villeneuve d'Ornon, Courréjean (tel. 56 87 00 36). Open all year round. From the bus station on Quai Richelieu by the river take bus B to the end of the line (30-minute trip), then a couple of minutes' walk (800m).
Beausoleil, cours Général-de-Gaulle 371 (tel. 56 89 17 66). From the bus station on Quai Richelieu take bus G to the end of the line (45-minute trip).

Chamonix Mont-Blanc

TOURIST OFFICES
Office du Tourisme, pl. du Triangle de l'Amitié, 74400 Chamonix Mont-Blanc (tel. 50 53 00 24). Open daily July–Aug., 8.30 a.m.–7.30 p.m.; Sept.–June, 8.30 a.m.–12.30 p.m. and 2–7 p.m. Reserves rooms free of charge (tel. 50 53 23 33) or write in advance. 'Accueil de France' service not available. About 500m from the train station. Down av. Michel Croz, then round to the left of the Town Hall.

ACCOMMODATION IN CHAMONIX
As it can be very difficult to find accommodation on arrival, try to reserve ahead. If you have not done so you may have to stay outside Chamonix in one of the towns nearby. Those with a railpass will have no problem getting to accommodation outside Chamonix as most of the towns along the valley are served by SNCF (this includes all those mentioned below, unless stated otherwise).

HOTELS
Cheapest doubles 125–150FF (£15.60–18.75; $23.40–28.00)

Chaumière, route de Gaillands 322 (tel. 50 53 13 25).
Carrier, rue Charlet Straton 242 (tel. 50 54 02 16). In Argentière.
Chardonet, route du Plagnolet 39, Argentière (tel. 50 54 02 80).
Gorges de la Diosaz (tel. 50 47 20 97). In Servoz.
Valaisanne, av. Ravanel le Rouge 454 (tel. 50 53 17 98).
Dahu, rue Charlet Straton 325 (tel. 50 54 01 55). In Argentière.
Cimes Blanches (tel. 50 47 20 05). In Servoz.

Cheapest doubles 160–170FF (£20.00–21.25; $30–32)

Aiguille Verte, rue Joseph Vallot 683 (tel. 50 53 01 73).
Stade, rue Whymper 19 (tel. 50 53 05 44).
Les Grandes Charmoz, chemin de Cristalliers 468 (tel. 50 53 45 57).
Arve, impasse des Anémones 60 (tel. 50 53 02 31).
Boule de Neige, rue Joseph Vallot 362 (tel. 50 53 04 48).
Lion d'Or, rue du Docteur Paccard 255 (tel. 50 53 15 09).
Prairie, Chemin du Lavoussé (tel. 50 53 19 96). In Les Praz. No
    SNCF station in Les Praz, but the Les Bois station is a 10–
    15-minute walk away.

Cheapest doubles around 184FF (£23; $34.50)

Au Bon Coin, av. de l'Aiguille du Midi 80 (tel. 50 53 15 67).

YOUTH HOSTEL
Montée J. Balmat 103 (FUAJ), Les Pélerins (tel. 50 53 14 52). A
30-minute walk from Chamonix. Nearest train station Les Pélerins.
The hostel is about 1km uphill from the station. Alternatively, take
the bus dir. Les Houches from pl. de l'Eglise in Chamonix to the
school (école) in Les Pélerins.

DORMITORY ACCOMMODATION
Cheap accommodation is provided in several refuges, gîte d'étapes
and chalets in and around Chamonix:

Ski Station, route des Moussoux 6 (tel. 50 53 20 25). Bed only
    around 50FF (£6.25; $9.40). Up the hill from the Tourist Office.
Le Chamoniard Volant, route de la Frasse 45 (tel. 50 53 14 09). Beds
    around 50–60FF (£6.25–7.50; $9.40–11.25), breakfast around
    25FF (£3; $4.50), half-board starts around 133FF (£16.60; $25).
Le Belvédère, route du Plagnolet 501, Argentière (tel. 50 54 02 59).
    Beds around 50–58FF (£6.25–7.25; $9.40–11.00), breakfast
    around 20FF (£2.50; $3.75), half-board around 128–136FF
    (£16–17; $24.00–25.50).

CAMPING
Three sites are located about 10–15 minutes' walk from the centre
of town, just off the road to Les Pélerins (a full list of the 18 sites
in the area is available from the Tourist Office):

Les Arolles, Chemin du Cry-Chamonix 281 (tel. 50 53 14 30). Open
    25 June–30 Sept. 100 places.

L'Ile des Barrats (tel. 50 53 51 41). Open 1 June–30 Sept. 150 places.
Les Tissourds (tel. 50 55 94 97). Open 1 July–31 Aug. 20 places.
  Cold water only.
Les Moliasses (tel. 50 53 18 61). Open 1 June–15 Sept. A 15-minute
  walk from the town centre.

Dieppe

TOURIST OFFICE
Office du Tourisme-Syndicat d'Initiative de Dieppe, Pont Argo, B.P.
152, 76204 Dieppe cedex (tel. 35 84 11 77). 'Accueil de France'
service not available. To get there, see **Basic Directions** below.

BASIC DIRECTIONS
Trains from Paris connecting with ferry services run to Dieppe-
Maritime station, next to the ferry terminal. Other trains stop at
Dieppe station, about 10–15 minutes' walk from the ferry terminal.
From Dieppe station go straight ahead on to blvd G. Clemenceau.
On the right is the fishing port. Going along the side of the water
you pass blvd Général-de-Gaulle on the left, then rue d'Ecosse.
Continuing, you reach the Avant-Port and the ferry terminal.

HOTELS
Cheapest rooms 110–120FF (£13.75–15.00; $20.50–22.50)

La Pêcherie, rue Mortier-d'Or 3 (tel. 35 82 04 62). Near the fishing
  port. Take the second left off Quai Duquesne after rue d'Ecosse.
Du Havre, rue Thiers 13 (tel. 35 84 15 02). Left off blvd
  G.-Clemenceau.
Beauséjour, pl. Louis-Vitet 2 & 4 (tel. 35 84 13 90). Near the fishing
  harbour. Take the first right off Quai Duquesne after rue d'Ecosse.
De la Jetée, rue de l'Asile-Thomas 5 (tel. 35 84 89 98). In the area
  between the Quai Henri IV and Quai du Hable and the beach,
  around the Avant-Port from the ferry terminal.

Cheapest rooms around 150FF (£18.75; $28)

Au Grand Duquesne, pl. Saint-Jacques 15 (tel. 35 84 21 51). Great
  location near St James' Church in the heart of the Old Town.
  Take the third right off rue d'Ecosse.

L'Ancrage, arcades de la Poisonnerie 9 (tel. 35 84 21 45). Near the
ferry terminal.
Pontoise, rue Thiers 10 (tel. 35 84 14 57). Left off blvd
G.-Clemenceau.

Cheapest rooms around 170FF (£21.25; $32)

Tourist Hotel, rue de la Halle-au-Blé 16 (tel. 35 06 10 10). Straight
on from Quai Duquesne, then left after Grande Rue.
Les Arcades, av. de la Bourse 1 & 3 (tel. 35 84 14 12). Near the
ferry terminal.
Windsor, blvd de Verdun 18 (tel. 35 84 15 23). Cheapest of the
hotels on the seafront. A 15-minute walk from the station.
Straight on from Quai Duquesne, second left after Grande
Rue.

YOUTH HOSTEL
Rue Louis Fromager 48 (FUAJ), Quartier Janval, Chemin des
Vertus (tel. 35 84 85 73). Open from 15 June–15 Oct. Forty
minutes' walk from the station. Bus 2 dir. Val Druel to Château
Michel.

CAMPING
No really convenient site; the nearest are:

Camping du Pré St-Nicolas (tel. 35 84 11 39). Two-star site. Open all
year. Located near the golf course, just off the road to Pourville. A
25-minute walk from the station. Left along blvd G.-Clemenceau,
right at blvd Maréchal Joffre, left rue Cl. Groulard, left rue du
Faubourg de la Barre, then right at the fork in the road and
straight on.
Camping Vitamin, Dieppe-Les Vertus (tel. 35821111). Three-star
site. Open 1 Apr.–31 Oct.

Dijon

TOURIST OFFICE
Office du Tourisme-Syndicat d'Initiative de Dijon, Pavillon du Tourisme, pl. Darcy, 21022 Dijon (tel. 80 43 42 12). Open daily, June–
Aug. 9 a.m.–9 p.m.; mid-Apr.–1 June and 15 Sept.–mid-Nov.,
9 a.m.–8 p.m.; at other times of year, 9 a.m.–12 p.m. and 2–7 p.m.

Closed 1 Jan. and 25 Dec. If you arrive without reservations, the staff will find hotel rooms for you. 'Accueil de France' service available. When the office is closed an information board in front of the office gives round-the-clock information on the availability of hotel rooms in the city. A 5-minute walk from the train station.

HOTELS
Cheapest doubles 80–90FF (£10.00–11.25; $15–17)

Lamartine, rue Jules Mercier 12 (tel. 80 30 37 47). Right off rue de la Liberté near pl. de la Libération.
Diderot, rue du Lycée 7 (tel. 80 67 10 85).

Cheapest doubles 100–110FF (£12.50–13.75; $18.75–20.50)

Du Théâtre, rue des Bons Enfants 3 (tel. 80 67 15 41). The street is off pl. de la Libération.
KCNIL, av. Junot 11–13 (tel. 80 65 30 29). A 15–20-minute walk from the town centre.
De la Gare, rue Mariotte 16 (tel. 80 30 46 61). Left at the end of rue du Dr Rémy.
Du Lyée, rue du Lycée 28 (tel. 80 67 12 35).

Cheapest doubles 130–145FF (£16.25–18.00; $24.40–27.00)

Du Sauvage, rue Monge 64 (tel. 80 41 31 21). From the end of rue du Dr Rémy left on rue Mariotte and straight on to pl. St-Bénigne. Right into rue de la Prévote, left, then a quick right down rue Condorcet and first left into rue Monge.
Saint-Bernard, rue Courtépée 7 bis (tel. 80 30 74 67). From pl. St-Bernard go left down rue Bernard (virtually at a right angle to blvd des Brosses) into pl. Depuis, right along rue Devosge, then left at rue Courtépée.

Cheapest doubles 155–170FF (£19.40–21.25; $29–32)

Chateaubriand, 3 av. Maréchal Foch (tel. 80 41 42 18).
Thurot, Passage Thurot 4 & 6 (tel. 80 43 57 46). Rue Thurot is left off rue Guillaume Tell. Impasse Thurot is on the right-hand side.
Des Rosiers, rue de Montchapet 22 bis (tel. 80 55 33 11). A 15-minute walk from the train station.
Montchapet, rue Jacques Cellerier 26 (tel. 80 55 33 31). A

10-minute walk from the historic centre, slightly closer to the train station. See Hôtel des Rosiers, above.
De Paris, av. Maréchal Foch 9–11 (tel. 80 43 41 88/80 43 50 23).

Cheapest doubles 180–200FF (£22.50–25.00; $33.75–37.50)

Du Globe, rue Jeannin 67 (tel. 80 66 13 86). From pl. des Ducs go left up rue Verrerie, then a quick right.
Monge, rue Monge 20 (tel. 80 30 55 41). From the end of rue du Dr Rémy left on rue Mariotte and straight on to pl. St-Bénigne. Right into rue de la Prévote, left, then a quick right down rue Condorcet and first left into rue Monge.
Du Stade, blvd de Strasbourg 3 (tel. 80 65 35 32). See Hôtel KCNIL, above.
De la Poste, rue du Château 5 (tel. 80 30 51 64). Left off rue de la Liberté, a short distance from pl. Darcy.
La Résidence, rue Chancelier de l'Hôpital 17 bis (tel. 80 66 18 87). A 5-minute walk from pl. de la Libération. Straight on into pl. du Théâtre, then along rue Vaillant to pl. St-Michel. Right down rue Buffon, then left to the hotel.
Du Palais, rue du Palais 23 (tel. 80 67 16 26). Off pl. de la Libération.
Victor Hugo, rue des Fleurs 23 (tel. 80 43 63 45).
Le Chambellan, rue Vannerie 92 (tel. 80 67 12 67).
Republique, rue du Nord 3 (tel. 80 73 36 76).

HOSTEL
Blvd Champollion 1 (tel. 80 71 32 12). Take bus 5 from pl. Grangier to the last stop, Epirey; pl. Grangier is near pl. Darcy. From the latter, rue de la Poste runs into pl. Grangier. From rue de la Liberté take rue du Château. Bus 6 runs to pl. Grangier (blvd de Brosses stop) from the train station.

FOYER
Foyer International des Etudiants, av. Maréchal Leclerc 1 (tel. 80 71 51 01). Offers singles for about the same as you would pay for a dorm bed at the hostel, but is only open May–June. Bus 4 dir. Grésilles to Parc des Sports.

UNIVERSITY ACCOMMODATION
Singles in university dorms are let by CROUSS, rue Docteur Maret 3 (tel. 80 50 16 03). Again, prices are similar to those of dorm beds at the hostel. The office is open Mon.–Fri. 9–11.30 a.m. and 2–4.30 p.m. During the university vacation (July–Sept.) you can try the dormitories on your own if the CROUSS office is closed. The

Résidence Universitaire Mansard is on blvd Mansard (tel. 80 66 18 22), while the Résidence Universitaire Montmuzard is on blvd Gabriel (tel. 80 39 68 01). Bus 9 serves both dormitories.

CAMPING
Camping du Lac, blvd Kir 3 (tel. 80 43 54 72). Open 1 Apr.–15 Sept. 3FF (£0.40; $0.60) per tent, 6FF (£0.80; $1.20) per person. About 10 minutes' walk from the train station away from the town centre. At the end of rue du Dr Rémy turn right through the underpass, then follow av. Albert 1er to the right of the exit.

Lille

TOURIST OFFICE
Office du Tourisme de Lille, Palais Rihour, pl. Rihour, B.P. 205, 59002 Lille cedex (tel. 20 30 81 00). Open Mon. 2–6 p.m., Tues.–Sat. 10 a.m.–6 p.m. A well-stocked office with plenty of information on the city and the Pas de Calais. Rooms found in local hotels and bed and breakfast accommodation. 'Accueil de France' service available.

BASIC DIRECTIONS
The train station is about 10 minutes' walk from the Tourist Office in the heart of the old city. From pl. de la Gare follow rue Faidherbe towards pl. du Théâtre. At pl. du Théâtre, turn left down the side of the square and follow rue des Manneliers, then go straight ahead at the junction with pl. De Gaulle (right) and rue Neuve (left) into pl. Rihour.

HOTELS
Cheapest rooms 80–85FF (£10.00–10.60; $15–16)

Les Voyageurs, pl. de la Gare 10 (tel. 20 06 43 14).
Coq Hardi, pl. de la Gare 34 (tel. 20 06 05 89).

Cheapest rooms 100FF (£12.20; $19)

Floréal, rue Sainte-Anne 21 (tel. 20 06 36 21).
Faidherbe, pl. de la Gare 42 (tel. 20 06 27 93).
La Tradition, rue Masséna 73–75 (tel. 20 57 14 52). Rue Masséna crosses rue Nationale at pl. de Strasbourg.

Liberty, rue Baptiste-Monnoyer 16 (tel. 20 57 73 26). At the junction with blvd de la Liberté 169 .

Saint-Nicolas, rue Nicolas-Leblanc, 11 bis (tel. 20 57 73 26). The street runs off pl. de la République.

Cheapest rooms 110–120FF (£13.75–15.00; $20.50–22.50)

Central Hôtel, rue Boucher-de-Perthes 91 (tel. 20 54 64 63). The street crosses rue Nationale just beyond pl. de Strasbourg.

Du Globe, blvd Vauban 1 (tel. 20 57 29 58)

Du Moulin d'Or, rue du Molinel 15 (tel. 20 06 12 67).

De France, rue de Béthune 10 (tel. 20 57 14 78). From rue du Molinel turn right along rue des Tanneurs, then left at rue de Béthune. From pl. Rihour take rue de la Vieille Comédie, then turn right up rue de Béthune.

Cheapest rooms 140–150FF (£17.50–18.75; $26.25–28.00)

Saint Maurice, Parvis St-Maurice 8 (tel. 20 06 27 40). Between rue Sainte-Anne and rue de Paris.

Brueghel, Parvis St-Maurice 35 (tel. 20 06 06 69). Between rue Sainte-Anne and rue de Paris.

Cheapest rooms 165–170FF (£20.60–21.25; $31–32)

Minerva, rue Anatole-France 28 (tel. 20 55 25 11). From rue Faidherbe turn right down rue des Comines, left along rue Quenette, then left again on to rue Anatole-France.

Monte Carlo, place des Reigneaux 17 (tel. 20 06 06 93). Just off pl. de la Gare, to the right of rue Faidherbe.

HOSTEL

Av. Julien-Destrée 1 (FUAJ) (tel. 20 52 98 94). Around 45FF (£5.60; $8.40). Opposite the Foire Commercial (Métro station: Foire Commercial), a 10-minute walk from the train station. Follow rue de Tournai, head left on rue Javary, then right on to av. Julien-Destrée.

CAMPING

There are a number of campsites in the surrounding area. Information is available from the Tourist Office, or from the Camping Club de Lille, rue Baggio 13 (tel. 20 53 77 40).

If you are heading into Belgium there are two sites which may be of particular interest:

Sportstadion, Westerlaan 2, Waregem (tel. 056 606289). Around
65BF (£1.30; $2) per tent, 55BF (£1; $1.50) per person. Waregem is about 48km from Lille, on the Lille-Kortrijk-Gent-
Antwerpen railway line just beyond Kortrijk, and just off the
A14-E3.

Camping Communal de l'Orient, Vieux Chemin de Mons, Tournai
(tel. 069 222635). Open all year round. Around 70BF (£1.40;
$2.20) per tent, 60BF (£1.15; $1.75) per person. Tournai is about
32km from Lille, just over the Belgian border. There are good
road and rail links between Lille and Tournai, and onwards from
Tournai to Brussels or Mons.

Lyon

TOURIST OFFICES

Office du Tourisme/Bureau des Congrès de Lyon/Communauté, pl.
Bellecour, B.P. 2254, 69214 Lyon cedex 02 (tel. 78 42 25 75). The
Tourist Board operates several Tourist Information offices through-
out the city:

Pavillon du Tourisme, pl. Bellecour. Open mid-June—mid-Sept.,
Mon.–Fri. 9 a.m.–7 p.m., Sat. 9 a.m.–6 p.m., Sun. 10 a.m.–
6 p.m.; at other times of year, the office closes one hour earlier
each day. 'Accueil de France' service available. Métro: Bellecour,
or 10 minutes' walk along rue Victor Hugo from Lyon-Perrache
train station.

Bureau d'Information Perrache. In the Centre d'écharges de
Perrache, in front of Lyon-Perrache. Open Mon.–Fri. 9 a.m.–
12.30 p.m. and 2–6 p.m., Sat. 9 a.m.–5 p.m.

Fourvière. Open, in peak season, daily from 9 a.m.–12.30 p.m. and
2–6 p.m.

Agence de Villeurbane, av. Aristide Briand 3 (tel. 78 68 13 20)
Open Mon.–Fri. 9 a.m.–6 p.m., Sat. 9 a.m.–5 p.m.

FINDING ACCOMMODATION

Finding suitable accommodation in Lyon should be relatively easy.
Many of the cheapest hotels are in the area around Lyon-Perrache
train station. In contrast, the hotels around the Part-Dieu train
station are relatively expensive. If you arrive at Part-Dieu, there
are frequent connections to Lyon-Perrache by main line train,
while the two stations are also linked by the city's Métro. If for
any reason you cannot find a bed, head for the 'Accueil en Gare',

located in the covered walkway linking Lyon-Perrache train station to the Centre Perrache.

HOTELS
Cheapest rooms 110–120FF (£13.75–15.00; $20.50–22.50)

Vichy, rue de la Charité, 60 bis (tel. 78 37 42 58). Perrache district.
Vaubecour, rue Vaubecour 28 (tel. 78 37 44 91). Perrache.
Croix-Pâquet, pl. Croix-Pâquet 11 (tel. 78 28 51 49). Terreaux district.
Des Facultés, rue Sébastien-Gryphe 104 (tel. 78 72 22 65). Préfecture-Guillotière.
Hôtel de la Poste, rue Victor Fort 1 (tel. 78 28 62 67).

Cheapest rooms 140–150FF (£17.50–18.75; $26.25–28.00)

Simplon, rue Duhamel 11 (tel. 78 37 41 00). Perrache.
D'Ainay, rue des Remparts d'Ainay 14 (tel. 78 42 43 42). Perrache.
Alexandra, rue Victor-Hugo 49 (tel. 78 37 75 79). Perrache.
Du Tourisme, quai Jar, 44 bis (tel. 78 83 73 48). Vaise.
Victoria, rue Delandine 3 (tel. 78 37 57 61). Perrache.

Cheapest rooms 160–170FF (£20.00–21.25; $30–32)

Le Terme, rue Sainte-Cathérine 7 (tel. 78 28 30 45). Terreaux.
Valmy, rue des Tanneurs 15 (tel. 78 83 55 59). Vaie.
Celtic, pl. Saint-Paul 5 (tel. 78 28 01 12). Vieux Lyon.
La Loire, cours de Verdun 19 (tel. 78 37 44 29). Perrache. Closed 1–15 Aug.
Touring, cours de Verdun 37 (tel. 78 37 39 03). Perrache.
Morand, rue de Créqui 99 (tel. 78 52 29 96). Brotteaux.

Cheapest rooms 180–200FF (£22.50–25.00; $33.75–37.50)

Dauphiné, rue Duhamel 3 (tel. 78 37 24 19). Perrache.
Alias Hôtel, rue Pareille 9 (tel. 78 28 67 97).
La Marne, rue de la Charité 78 (tel. 78 37 07 46). Perrache. Closes for three weeks in August.
Normandie, rue de Bélier 3 (tel. 78 37 31 36). Perrache.
Le Boulevardier, rue de la Fromagerie 5 (tel. 78 28 48 22).

B & B
Association Bed & Breakfast, petite rue Tramassac 2. The office in Vieux-Lyon is open Mon.–Sat. 2–6 p.m. Singles from 90–200FF

(£11.25–25.00; $17.00–37.50), doubles from 75–130FF (£9.40–16.25; $14.00–24.40) per person.

HOSTELS
Lyon-Venissieux (FUAJ), rue Roger Salengro 51 (tel. 78 76 39 23). 50FF (£6.25; $9.40) for HI members, 20FF (£2.50; $3.75) supplement for non-members. About 4km from the centre. From Perrache, before 9 p.m., take the métro to Bellecour then bus 35 to av. Georges Levy. After 9 p.m., take bus 53 from Perrache to av. Viviani/blvd des Etats-Unis. From Part-Dieu, leave the station by the Vivier Merle exit and take bus 36 dir. Minguette to av. Viviani/blvd Joliot Curie.

Résidence Benjamin Delessert, 145 av. Jean Jaurès (tel. 78 61 41 41). Open July–Aug. Singles 80FF (£10; $15), doubles 125FF (£15.60; $23.40). Métro: Macé, then a 10-minute walk.

CISL, rue du Commandant Péqoud 46 (tel. 78 01 23 45). Near the FUAJ Hostel; doubles from 165FF (£20.50; $31).

CAMPING
All the sites are about 9.5km out of the city:

Dardilly, Camping International 'Porte de Lyon' (tel. 78 35 64 55). Four-star site. 50FF (£6.25; $9.40) per tent, 18FF (£2.25; $3.40) p.p. Open 1 Mar.–31 Oct. Bus 19 from the Town Hall (métro: Hôtel de Ville) dir. Ecully-Dardilly to the Parc d'Affaires stop.

'Les Barolles', Saint Denis Laval (tel. 78 56 05 56). One-star site to the south-west of the city. Open 1 Mar.–31 Dec.

There are another three sites at the Parc de Loisirs de Miribel Jonage, north-east of the city.

Marseilles (Marseille)

TOURIST OFFICES
Office Municipal de Tourisme de Marseille, La Canebière 4, 13001 Marseille (tel. 91 54 91 11). July–Sept., open daily 8.30 a.m.–8 p.m.; Oct.–June, 9 a.m.–7.15 p.m., Sun. 10 a.m.–5 p.m. Free accommodation service and a good range of information on the city. 'Accueil de France' service available. From Gare St-Charles (the main train station) go down the steps into blvd d'Athènes. Go straight ahead along blvd d'Athènes and then rue Dugommier into

La Canabière, then head left to the Tourist Office. Another branch operates in Marseille St Charles (tel. 91 50 59 18). Open, in summer, Mon.–Sat. 8.30 a.m.–8 p.m.; in winter, Mon.–Fri. 10 a.m.–6 p.m.

HOTELS

Cheapest doubles in the one-star hotels below cost 110–160FF (£13.75–20.00; $20.50–30.00). Most of the hotels are within easy walking distance of the train station.

Salvator, blvd Louis Salvator 6 (tel. 91 48 78 25). Métro: Estrangin or N.D. du Mont.

Gambetta, Allée Léon Gambetta 49 (tel. 91 62 07 88). Métro: Réformés or Noailles.

Provençal, rue Paradis 32 (tel. 91 33 11 15). Métro: Vieux-Port.

Sphinx, rue Sénac 16 (tel. 91 48 70 59). Métro: Réformés or Noailles.

Bearn, rue Sylvabelle 63 (tel. 91 37 75 83). Métro: Estrangin.

Manon, blvd Louis Salvator 36 (tel. 91 48 67 01). Métro: Estrangin or N.D. du Mont.

Montgrand, rue Montgrand 50 (tel. 91 33 33 81). Métro: Pierre Puget.

Guillemain, av. du Prado 357 (tel. 91 77 88 53). Métro: RD–PT du Prado.

Azur, cours Franklin Roosevelt 24 (tel. 91 42 74 38). Métro: Réformés.

Beaulieu Glaris, pl. Marseillaises 1 (tel. 91 90 70 59). By the main train station. Métro: St Charles.

De Bourgogne, allée Léon Gambetta 31 (tel. 91 62 19 49). Métro: Réformés or Noailles.

Little Palace, blvd d'Athènes 39 (tel. 91 90 12 93). Go down the steps from Gare St Charles. Métro: St Charles.

Sevigné, rue Bretueil 28 (tel. 91 81 29 20). Métro: Vieux-Port.

Monthyon, rue Montgrand 60 (tel. 91 33 85 55). Métro: Pierre Puget.

Fortia, rue Fortia 32 (tel. 91 33 33 75).

De Prado, av. Prado 80 (tel. 91 37 55 34).

Cheapest doubles at the two-star hotels below cost 150–200FF (£18.75–25.00; $28.00–37.50). Most are within easy walking distance of Marseille St Charles.

Estérel, rue Paradis 124 (tel. 91 37 13 90). Métro: Estrangin or Castellane.

La Préfecture, blvd Louis Salvator 9 (tel. 91 54 31 60). Métro:
  Estrangin or N.D. du Mont.
Du Velay, rue Berlioz 18 (tel. 91 48 31 37). Métro: Castellane.
Du Pharo, blvd Charles Livon 71 (tel. 91 31 08 71).
Peron, corniche Kennedy 119 (tel. 91 31 01 41).

YOUTH HOSTELS
Both the hostels are about 6.5km out from the city centre:

Marseille-Bois Luzy (FUAJ), av. de Bois Luzy 76 (tel. 91 49 06 18).
  The smaller of the two hostels, with 90 beds in summer. Also
  has space for tents. Bus 8 from Bourse, near La Canabière.
Marseille-Bonneveine (FUAJ), av. Joseph Vidal 47 (Impasse de
  Bonfils), Bonneveine (tel. 91 73 21 81). 185 beds. From
  St Charles train station take the métro to RDPT du Prado, then
  bus 44 dir. Roy d'Espagne to pl. Bonnefons.

Nice

TOURIST OFFICES
Nice Office du Tourisme, Acropolis, Esplanade Kennedy 1, B.P. 79,
06302 Nice cedex (tel. 93 92 82 82). Write to this office if you want
information on the city in advance. On arrival, head for one of the
information offices the Tourist Board operates in the city.

Bureau d'Accueil Gare SNCF, av. Thiers (tel. 93 87 07 07). Open
  July–Sept., Mon.–Sat. 8.45 a.m.–7 p.m., Sun. 8.45 a.m.–
  12.30 p.m. and 2–6 p.m.; Oct.–June, Mon.–Sat. 8.45 a.m.–
  12.30 p.m. and 2–6 p.m. Free plan of the city. Reserves local
  hotels for a 10FF (£1.25; $2) fee, but not before 10 a.m. 'Accueil
  de France' service available. The office is next to the train station.
Bureau d'Accueil, av. Gustave V 5 (tel. 93 87 60 60). This branch
  office near pl. Masséna is open July–Sept. Mon.–Sat. 8.45 a.m.–
  12.30 p.m. and 2–6 p.m.; Oct.–June open Mon.–Fri. only.
Bureau d'Accueil Nice-Ferber (tel. 93 83 32 64). Close to the airport. Open Mon.–Sat. 7.30 a.m.–6.30 p.m.

FINDING ACCOMMODATION
Beds are difficult to find in Nice at any time in summer, but especially so during the Jazz Parade in July. If you arrive early in the
morning at this time, try phoning a few hotels or searching for a

room in the area around the train station. If you are not having any success, try to get to the Tourist Office for about 9.30 a.m. and start queueing so you get the best rooms they have to offer.

HOTELS

All the hotels listed below are close to the station or the town centre. Some hotels offer reductions of up to 30% for single occupancy; others offer no reduction at all.
Cheapest doubles 100–110FF (£12.50–13.75; $18.75–22.50)

Le Commodore, rue Barbéris 10 (tel. 93 89 08 44).
Pastoral, rue Assalit 27 (tel. 93 85 17 22).
Chauvain, rue Chauvain 8 (tel. 93 85 34 01).
Interlaken, av. Durante 26 (tel. 93 88 30 15).
Les Mimosas, rue de la Buffa 26 (tel. 93 88 05 59).
Ostende, rue Alsace-Lorraine 3 (tel. 93 88 72 48).
Blue Sky, blvd A. Raynaud 3 (tel. 93 52 58 20).

Cheapest doubles 120–125FF (£15.00–15.60; $22.50–23.40)

De France, blvd Raimbaldi 24 (tel. 93 85 18 04/93 62 11 44).
Lyonnais, rue de Russie 20 (tel. 93 88 70 74).
Saint-François, rue Saint-François 3 (tel. 93 85 88 69/93 13 14 18)
La Belle Meunière, av. Durante 21 (tel. 93 88 66 15).
Lorrain, rue Gubernatis 6 (tel. 93 85 42 90).
Miron, rue Miron 4 (tel. 93 62 16 60).

Cheapest doubles 130–135FF (£16.25–16.85; $24.40–25.30)

Darcy, rue d'Angleterre 28 (tel. 93 88 67 06).
Idéal Bristol, rue Paganini 22 (tel. 93 88 60 72).
Rialto, rue de la Buffa 55 (tel. 93 88 15 04).

Cheapest doubles 140–150FF (£17.50–18.75; $26.25–28.00)

Astrid, rue Pertinax 26 (tel. 93 62 14 64).
Au Picardy, blvd Jean-Jaurès 10 (tel. 93 85 75 51).
Central, rue de Suisse 10 (tel. 93 88 85 08).
Novelty, rue d'Angleterre 26 (tel. 93 87 51 73).
Châteauneuf, rue Châteauneuf 3 (tel. 93 96 82 74).
Notre-Dame, rue de Russie 22 (tel. 93 88 70 44).
Mignon, rue de la Buffa 26 (tel. 93 88 07 43).
Wilson, rue Hôtel-des-Postes 39 (tel. 93 85 47 79).
D'Orsay, rue Alsace-Lorraine 1820 (tel. 93 88 45 02).

Cheapest doubles 160–170FF (£20.00–21.25; $30–32)

Carnot, blvd Carnot 8 (tel. 93 89 56 54).
Family, blvd Gambetta 34 (tel. 93 88 58 92).
Petit Louvre, rue Emma Tiranty 10 (tel. 93 80 15 54).
Les Orangers, av. Durante, 10 bis (tel. 93 87 51 41).
Du Centre, rue de Suisse 2 (tel. 93 88 83 85).
Carlone, blvd Francois Grosso 2 (tel. 93 44 71 61).
5 Les Cigales, rue Dalpozzo 16 (tel. 93 88 33 75).
Carlyna, rue Sacha-Guitry 8 (formerly rue St-Michel) (tel. 93 80
    77 21).

Cheapest doubles 180–210FF (£22.50–26.25; $33.75–39.50)

Crillon, rue Pastorelli 44 (tel. 93 85 43 59).
Imperial, blvd Carabacel 8 (tel. 93 62 21 40).
Le Congrès, rue du Congrès 11 (tel. 93 87 35 62).
Les Mouettes, rue du Congrès 11 (tel. 93 88 17 76).
Little Masséna, rue Masséna 22 (tel. 93 87 72 34).
Regency, rue Saint-Siagre 2 (tel. 93 62 17 44).
Soleda, av. St-Jean-Baptiste 16 (tel. 93 85 39 05).
Rex, rue Masséna 3 (tel. 93 87 87 38).
De Berne, av. Thiers 1 (tel. 93 88 25 08).
Camélias, rue Spitalieri 3 (tel. 93 62 15 54).
Paradis, rue Paradis 1 (tel. 93 87 71 23).
Canada, rue Halévy 8 (tel. 93 87 98 94).
Maru, rue Alexandre Mari 11 (tel. 93 80 06 83).
Des Flandres, rue de Belgique 6 (tel. 93 88 78 94).

UNIVERSITY ACCOMMODATION

Rooms in vacant student dormitories can often be let during the
summer. Details are available from CROUS, av. des Fleurs 18 (tel.
93 96 73 73). At any time of year, women can try calling Cité
Universitaire, Residence 'Les Collinettes', av. Robert Schumann 3
(tel. 93 97 06 64/93 89 23 64), where singles cost around 100FF
(£12.50; $18.75).

HOSTELS/FOYERS

Route Forestière du Mont Alban (FUAJ) (tel. 93 89 23 64). Mid-
    night curfew. B&B around 70FF (£8.75; $13). On top of a hill,
    about 5km from the train station. Bus 5 from the train station
    to pl. Masséna, then bus 14 to Alban Fort.
Let's Go Meublés, 3rd floor, rue Pertinax 22 (tel. 93 80 98 00).

Near the train station. No curfew. 51FF (£6.40; $9.60) including showers and blankets.

Espace Magnan, rue Louis de Coppet 31 (tel. 93 86 28 75). Open June–Sept. 55FF (£7; $10.50). Close to the beach and the Promenade des Anglais. From the train station, take bus 23.

Bale des Anges, Chemin de St-Antoine 55 (tel. 93 86 76 74).

Relais International de la Jeunesse 'Clairvallon', 26 av. Scudéri (tel. 93 81 27 63). Midnight curfew. B&B 70FF (£8.75; $13). Set in an old house in Cimiez, about 9.5km out of Nice. Easily reached by bus 15 from pl. Masséna.

Jean Médecin, Ancien Chemin de Lanterne 25 (tel. 93 83 34 61).

Forum Nice-Nord, blvd Comte de Falicon 10 (tel. 93 84 24 37).

Montebello, av. Valrose 96 (tel. 93 84 19 81).

Saint-Antoine, Chemin de St-Antoine 69 (tel. 93 86 37 19).

De la Plaine (tel. 93 29 90 04) and Des Bluets (tel. 93 29 90 05). Both at Route de Grenoble 273. Open to men aged 18 and over only.

'Les Sagnes', Route de Grenoble, 59 bis (tel. 93 83 76 28). Open to men aged 18 and over only.

Riquier, blvd du Mont-Boron 248 (tel. 93 55 44 28). Men aged 18 and over only.

CAMPING

No really convenient site in Nice. Camping Terry, Route de Grenoble St-Isidore 768 (tel. 93 08 11 58) has only 30 places. The site is 6.5km north of the airport, far from any bus route. There is a good choice of sites in Villeneuve-Loubet, only 8km along the coast on the railway line to Cannes. The Tourist Information Centre at Nice station can give you a map of these sites, some of which are listed below. Open all year unless otherwise stated.

L'Orée de Vaugrenier, blvd des Groules (tel. 93 33 57 30). Open 15 Mar.–31 Oct.

La Vieille Ferme, blvd des Groules (tel. 93 33 41 44). Two sites: four star and one star.

De l'Hippodrome, av. des Rives 2 (tel. 93 20 02 00).

L'Ensoleillado, av. de l'Eglise Christophe 49 (tel. 93 20 90 04). Open 15 Feb.–15 Oct.

Neptune, av. des Baumettes (tel. 93 73 93 81). Open 15 Mar.–15 Oct.

La Tour de la Madone, Route de Grasse (tel. 93 20 96 11). Open 15 Mar.–31 Oct.

Paris

Unless you have booked accommodation in advance the first thing you should do on arrival is head for a room-finding service. Making use of these room-finding services will probably save you time, frustration and money; except perhaps in winter, when the number of visitors has fallen off. The best rooms go early in the day, so the quicker you get there the better. If you arrive by train, there is at least one room-finding organization at all the stations, with the exception of St-Lazare (which is unfortunate if you are arriving on the boat-train from Dieppe, or from anywhere in Normandy).

ARRIVING BY BUS OR PLANE

The Gare Routière International at 8 pl. Stalingrad is the terminus for most international services arriving in Paris. Access to the city centre is easy from the Stalingrad métro station. Most international flights touch down at the Roissy—Charles de Gaulle airport. A free bus connects the airport to the Roissy train station, from which RER lines B and D run to Gare du Nord and Châtelet—Les Halles. Catch the bus from Aérogare 1 arrival gate 28, Aérogare 2A gate 5, Aérogare 2B gate 6 or Aérogare 2D gate 6. From Orly airport, a free bus service operates between Orly Sud gate H or Orly Ouest gate F and the Orly train station from which the RER runs into the city.

TROUBLE SPOTS

The areas around Pigalle and Montmartre (the Moulin Rouge and Sacré Coeur are the main attractions) are a favourite haunt of petty thieves and pickpockets during the day, so take care of your valuables. Some of the cheaper hotels in these districts (9ème and 18ème *arrondissements*) are used by prostitutes. In the evening, young women walking in these parts without a male companion are likely to be harassed, almost certain to be verbally abused. These areas can be dangerous for anyone after dark, but particularly if you are alone and noticeably foreign. Day and night you should avoid the Pigalle, Anvers and Barbes-Rocheouard métro stations.

TOURIST OFFICES

The Office du Tourisme et des Congrès de Paris operates seven offices in the city during the peak season. A fee of 15FF (£2; $3) per person is charged for finding a room in a one-star hotel (if this seems high to you, consider the fact that the same service in London costs over three times as much), while for beds in hostels/foyers the fee is 5FF (£0.60; $0.90) per person.

Bureau d'Accueil Central, av. des Champs-Élysées 127, 75008 Paris (tel. (1) 47 23 61 72). The head office. Open daily 9 a.m.–8 p.m. The 'Accueil de France' service is available at this office. Métro: Charles de Gaulle-Etoile.

Bureau Gare du Nord, rue de Dunkerque 18 (tel. (1) 45 26 94 82). Open, in peak season, Mon.–Sat. 8 a.m.–9 p.m., Sun. 1–8 p.m.; at other times, Mon.–Sat. 8 a.m.–8 p.m. Métro: Gare du Nord.

Bureau Gare de l'Est (tel. (1) 46 07 17 73). In the station arrivals hall. Open, in peak season, Mon.–Sat. 8 a.m.–9 p.m.; at other times, Mon.–Sat. 8 a.m.–8 p.m. Métro: Gare de l'Est.

Bureau Gare de Lyon (tel. (1) 43 43 33 24). By the exit from the main lines. Same hours as Gare de l'Est. Métro: Gare de Lyon.

Bureau Gare d'Austerlitz (tel. (1) 45 84 91 70). In the main line arrivals hall. Open, in peak season, Mon.–Sat. 8 a.m.–9 p.m.; at other times, Mon.–Sat. 8 a.m.–3 p.m. Métro: Gare d'Austerlitz.

Bureau Gare Montparnasse, blvd de Vaugirard 15 (tel. (1) 43 22 19 19). Same hours as Gare de l'Est. Métro: Montparnasse-Bienvenue.

Bureau Tour Eiffel, Champ de Mars (tel. (1) 45 51 22 15). Open May–Sept., daily 11 a.m.–6 p.m. Métro: Champ de Mars Tour Eiffel.

● **Accueil des Jeunes en France**

Accueil des Jeunes en France (AJF) is a tourist agency especially for young travellers. AJF is run on a non-profit-making basis, which helps keep charges low. The commission for finding a room in a hotel or hostel/foyer is 10FF (£1.25; $2) per person, except for beds in AJF hostels/foyers, which are located free of charge. Payment on booking with AJF is the norm. AJF operate four offices in the city, all of which will help with general tourist information as well as booking beds.

Beaubourg, rue Saint-Martin 119 (tel. (1) 42 77 87 80). The head office of AJF, opposite the Pompidou Centre. Open all year round, Mon.–Sat. 9.30 a.m.–7 p.m. The office also runs a poste restante service. Métro: Rambuteau or Les Halles; RER: Châtelet–Les Halles

Gare du Nord (tel. (1) 42 85 86 19). Inside the new suburban station. Open June–Oct., daily 8 a.m.–10 p.m. Métro: Gare du Nord.

Hôtel de Ville, rue du Pont Louis-Philippe 16 (tel. (1) 42 78 04 82).

Open all year round, Mon.–Fri. 9.30 a.m.–6.30 p.m. Métro: Hôtel de Ville or Pont Marie. From Hôtel de Ville, walk a short distance along the street and turn right. From Pont Marie, face the Seine and then follow the river along to your left.

Quartier Latin, blvd Saint-Michel 139 (tel. (1) 43 54 95 86). Open Mar.–Oct., Mon.–Fri. 9.30 a.m.–6.30 p.m. RER: Port Royal. Walk down blvd Saint-Michel from the RER station.

ACCOMMODATION AGENCY
La Centrale de Reservations (FUAJ-HI), blvd Jules Ferry 4, 4e (tel. 43 57 02 60), Métro: Republique. The best agency for hostels and all budget accommodation, can also book beds for the rest of France and even Europe. A 10FF (£1.25; $2) deposit is deducted from your bill. Open daily 8 a.m.–10 p.m.

HOTELS
The number after the street name (e.g. 7e) refers to the arrondisse-ment (district) of the city. Hotels in the 10e arrondissement are always within easy walking distance of Gare du Nord and Gare de l'Est (the two stations are virtually side by side).

Cheapest rooms around 120FF (£15; $22.50)

Cambrai, blvd de Magenta, 129 bis, 10e (tel. (1) 48 78 32 13). Métro: Gare de l'Est. From the station head right along rue de 8 mai 1945 on to blvd de Magenta. From Gare du Nord follow blvd de Denain away from the station, then head left down blvd de Magenta.

Cheapest rooms around 130FF (£16.25; $24.40)

De Lille, rue Montholon 2, 9e (tel. (1) 47 70 38 76). Off rue Lafay-ette between the Poissonière and Cadet métro stations.
De l'Industrie, rue Gustave Goublier 2, 10e (tel. (1) 42 08 51 79). Off blvd de Strasbourg between the Château d'Eau and Stras-bourg–St-Denis métro stations. You can walk straight down blvd de Strasbourg from Gare de l'Est.

Cheapest rooms around 150FF (£18.75; $28)

Pacific, rue du Château d'Eau 70, 10e (tel. (1) 47 70 07 91). Along rue du Château d'Eau from the Château d'Eau métro station. From the Jacques Bonsergent métro station, walk down rue de Lancry from blvd de Magenta on to rue du Château d'Eau. From the République métro station, walk up blvd de Magenta, then head left along rue du Château d'Eau.

Sthrau, rue Sthrau 1, 13e (tel. (1) 45 83 20 35). At the corner with rue Tolbiac 74. Walk along rue Tolbiac from the Tolbiac métro station.

Cheapest rooms around 160FF (£20; $30)

Sainte-Marie, rue de la Ville Neuve 6, 2e (tel. (1) 42 33 21 61). Off blvd de Bonne Nouvelle between the Bonne Nouvelle (closest) or Strasbourg—St-Denis métro stations.

Grand Hôtel d'Amiens, rue du Faubourg Poissonière 88, 10e (tel. (1) 48 78 71 18). The street runs between the Poissonière and Bonne Nouvelle métro stations.

Pierre-Dupont, rue Pierre-Dupont 1, 10e (tel. (1) 46 07 93 66). Off rue du Faubourg St-Martin between the Louis-Blanc and Château-Landon métro stations.

De l'Aveyron, rue d'Austerlitz 5, 12e (tel. (1) 43 07 86 86). Métro: Gare de Lyon (closest) or Bastille. Rue d'Austerlitz is off rue de Lyon, between the two métro stations.

De Bourgogne, rue Godefroy 15, 13e (tel. (1) 45 35 37 92). Métro: Place d'Italie. Rue Godefroy runs off the square.

Des Arts, rue Coypel 8, 13e (tel. (1) 47 07 76 32). Métro: Place d'Italie. The street runs between av. des Gobelins and blvd de l'Hôpital.

Arian-Hôtel, av. de Choisy 102, 13e (tel. (1) 45 70 76 00). Métro: Tolbiac or pl. d'Italie. Rue Tolbiac crosses av. de Choisy one block from the métro station. From pl. d'Italie, walk along av. de Choisy.

Cheapest rooms around 170FF (£21.25; $32)

Grand Hôtel des Arts-et-Métiers, rue Borda 4, 3e (tel. (1) 48 87 73 89). Off rue Turbigo at the junction with rue Volta, a short walk from the Arts-et-Métiers métro station.

Des Alliés, rue Berthollet 20, 5e (tel. (1) 43 31 47 52). Métro: Gobelins. From av. des Gobelins turn left along blvd du Port Royal, then right at rue Berthollet.

Brabant, rue des Petits Hôtels 18, 10e (tel. (1) 47 70 12 32). Métro: Poissonière. The street runs between rue Lafayette (at pl. Liszt) and blvd de Magenta.

De Chabrol, rue de Chabrol 46, 10e (tel. (1) 47 70 10 77). Métro: Poissonière or Gare de l'Est. From Gare de l'Est, head right along rue du 8 mai 1945.

Luna Park, rue Jacquard 1, 11e (tel. (1) 48 05 65 50). Left off rue Oberkampf, a short walk from the Parmentier métro station (follow descending street numbers along rue Oberkampf).

Des Beaux Arts, rue Toussaint-Féron 2, 13e (tel. (1) 44 24 22 60). Métro: Tolbiac. The street runs off av. d'Italie one block from the junction of rue Tolbiac and av. d'Italie.

Home Fleuri, rue Daguerre 75, 14e (tel. (1) 43 20 02 37). Métro: Denfert-Rochereau. From pl. Denfert-Rochereau follow av. du Général Leclerc until you see rue Daguerre on the right.

Atlas, rue de l'Atlas 12, 19e (tel. (1) 42 08 50 12). Métro: Belleville. The street runs right off blvd de la Villette.

Cheapest rooms around 180FF (£22.50; $33.75)

De Rouen, rue Croix-des-Petits-Champs 42, 1er (tel. (1) 42 61 38 21). Métro: Palais Royal Musée de Louvre. Turn left off rue St-Honoré.

Andrea, rue Saint-Bon 3, 4e (tel. (1) 42 78 43 93). Métro: Hôtel de Ville. Rue Saint-Bon is off rue de Rivoli as you head in the direction of blvd de Sebastopol and the Palais de Louvre.

Studia, blvd Saint-Germain 51, 5e (tel. (1) 43 26 81 00). Between the Odéon and Maubert-Mutualité métro stations.

Port-Royal, blvd du Port Royal 8, 5e (tel. (1) 43 31 70 06). Métro: Gobelins. Blvd du Port Royal runs from the end of av. des Gobelins.

Des Carmes, rue des Carmes 5, 5e (tel. (1) 43 29 78 40). Métro: Maubert-Mutualité. The street runs off pl. Maubert.

Blanche, rue Blanche 69, 9e (tel. (1) 48 74 16 94). Between the Blanche and Trinité métro stations.

Lux Hotel Picpus, blvd de Picpus 74, 12e (tel. (1) 43 43 08 46). Between the Picpus and Bel Air métro stations.

Wattignies, rue de Wattignies 6, 12e (tel. (1) 46 28 43 78). Métro: Dugommier. From blvd de Reuilly turn down rue de Charenton, then left at rue de Wattignies.

Royal, blvd Saint-Michel 65, 13e (1) 45 35 02 48). Between the Luxembourg and Port Royal RER stations.

Véronèse, rue Véronèse 5, 13e (tel. (1) 47 07 20 90). Off av. des Gobelins between the Place d'Italie and Gobelins métro stations.

Cheapest rooms around 190FF (£23.75; $35.60)

Sainte-Elisabeth, rue Sainte-Elisabeth 10, 3e (tel. (1) 42 72 03 95). Off rue de Turbigo between the Arts et Métiers and Temple métro stations.

De Chevreuse, rue de Chevreuse 3, 6e (tel. (1) 43 20 93 16). Off blvd du Montparnasse close to the Vavin métro station (follow ascending street numbers on blvd du Montparnasse).

D'Alsace, blvd de Strasbourg 85, 10e (tel. (1) 40 37 75 41). Between the Gare de l'Est and Château d'Eau métro stations.

Milan, rue de St-Quentin 17, 10e (tel. (1) 40 37 88 50). Métro: Gare du Nord. Off pl. de Roubaix, left of the train station exit.

Lafayette, rue Lafayette 198, 10e (tel. (1) 40 35 76 07). Métro: Gare du Nord or Louis-Blanc. From Gare du Nord, walk left along place Roubaix, then turn left up rue Lafayette. Louis-Blanc is on rue Lafayette.

Terminus et des Sports, cours de Vincennes 96, 12e (tel. (1) 43 43 97 93). Métro: Porte de Vincennes.

Floridor, pl. Denfert Rochereau 28, 14e (tel. (1) 43 21 35 53). Métro: Denfert Rochereau.

Du Mont Blanc, blvd Victor 11, 15e (tel. (1) 48 28 16 79). Métro: Porte de Versailles.

Paris Didot, rue Lédion 20, 14e (tel. (1) 45 42 33 29). Métro: Plaisance. Walk along rue d'Alésia, turn right at rue Didot, then left at rue Ledion.

Cheapest rooms around 200FF (£25; $37.50)

Gay-Lussac, rue Gay-Lussac 29, 5e (tel. (1) 43 54 23 96). The street runs off blvd St-Michel by the Luxembourg RER station.

Des Academies, rue de la Grande Chaumière 15, 6e (tel. (1) 43 26 66 44). Off blvd de Raspail by the Vavin métro station.

Delhy's, rue de l'Hirondelle 22, 6e (tel. (1) 43 26 58 25). Métro: St-Michel. The street runs off pl. St-Michel one block from the Seine.

Du Centre, rue Cler, 24 bis, 7e (tel. (1) 47 05 52 33). Métro: Ecole Militaire. Rue Cler is left off av. de la Motte Piquet, one block from the junction of the latter with av. Bosquet.

Grand Hôtel Léveque, rue Cler 29, 7e (tel. (1) 47 05 49 15). See Hôtel du Centre above for directions.

De Belgique, rue de Bruxelles 10, 9e (tel. (1) 49 74 93 12). Métro: Blanche or Place de Clichy. Rue de Bruxelles runs out of pl. Blanche, and off rue de Clichy, a short walk from pl. de Clichy.

De France, rue des Petites Ecuries 57, 10e (tel. (1) 47 70 15 83). Métro: Château D'Eau. The street runs off blvd de Strasbourg by the métro station.

Aviator, rue Louis Blanc 20, 10e (tel. (1) 46 07 79 24). Métro:

Louis-Blanc or Colonel-Fabien. The street runs out of place du Colonel-Fabien.

Grand Hôtel du Prince Eugene, rue du Château d'Eau 12, 10e (tel. (1) 42 39 89 13). See Hôtel Pacific. Jacques Bonsergent and République are closer than Château d'Eau.

Victoria, rue Bobillot 47, 13e (tel. (1) 45 80 59 88). Métro: Place d'Italie or Tolbiac. Walk down the street from pl. d'Italie. From Tolbiac follow the ascending street numbers on rue Tolbiac until it reaches rue Bobillot.

Celtic, rue d'Odessa 15, 14e (tel. (1) 43 20 93 53). Métro: Montparnasse-Bienvenue or Edgar-Quinet. Rue d'Odessa runs between blvd Edgar Quinet and rue du Départ in front of Gare Montparnasse.

De Blois, rue des Plantes 5, 14e (tel. (1) 45 40 99 48). Métro: Alésia. Walk up av. du Maine, then head left along rue de la Sablière into rue des Plantes.

Cheapest rooms around 210FF (£26.25; $39.40)

Printania, av. du Dr Arnold Netter 91, 12e (tel. (1) 43 07 65 13). Off cours de Vincennes between the Porte de Vincennes (closest) and Nation métro stations.

Novex, rue Caillaux 8, 13e (tel. (1) 44 24 22 00). Off av. d'Italie close to the Maison Blanche métro station.

Du Midi, av. René-Coty 4, 14e (tel. (1) 43 27 23 25). Métro: Denfert-Rochereau. The street runs out of pl. Denfert-Rochereau.

Le Royal, rue Raymond Losserand 49, 14e (tel. (1) 43 22 14 04). Métro: Pernety on rue Raymond Losserand.

Cheapest rooms around 220FF (£27.50; $41.25)

De la Vallée, rue Saint-Denis 84–86, 1er (tel. (1) 42 36 46 99). The street crosses rue Etienne Marcel close to the Etienne Marcel métro station.

Marignan, rue du Sommerard 13, 5e (tel. (1) 43 25 31 03). Métro: Maubert-Mutualité. At pl. Maubert turn off blvd St-Germain down rue des Carmes, then head right at rue du Sommerard.

Eiffel Rive Gauche, rue du Gros Caillou 6, 7e (tel. (1) 45 51 24 56). From the Ecole Militaire métro station head along av. Bosquet, turn left at rue de Grenelle, then left at rue du Gros Caillou.

Nievre, rue d'Austerlitz 18, 12e (tel. (1) 43 43 81 51). See Hôtel De l'Aveyron, above, for directions.

Lebrun, rue Lebrun 33, 13e (tel. (1) 47 07 97 02). Métro: Gobelins.

Rue Lebrun runs between av. des Gobelins and blvd St-Marcel.
De la Place des Alpes, pl. des Alpes 2, 13e (tel. (1) 45 35 14 14).
Place des Alpes is on blvd St-Vincent, between the pl. d'Italie
(closest) and Nationale métro stations.

Cheapest rooms around 230–240FF (£28.75–30.00; $43–45)

Palais Bourbon, rue de Bourgogne 49, 7e (tel. (1) 47 05 29 26).
Métro: Varenne. From blvd des Invalides both rue de Varenne
and rue de Grenelle lead into rue de Bourgogne.
Ribera, rue Lafontaine 66, 16e (tel. (1) 42 88 29 50). Métro: Jasmin.
From av. Mozart follow rue Ribera into rue Lafontaine.
Kuntz, rue des Deux Gares 2, 10e (tel. (1) 40 35 77 26). Métro:
Gare du Nord or Gare de l'Est.
Niel, rue Saussier-Leroy 11, 17e (tel. (1) 42 27 99 29). From the
Ternes métro station walk along av. des Ternes, turn right at rue
Poncelet, then left at rue Saussier-Leroy.
Tiquetonne, rue Tiquetonne 6, 2e (tel. (1) 42 36 94 58). Métro:
Etienne Marcel. From the métro station follow rue de Turbigo.
Rue Tiquetonne is one block away from rue de Turbigo down
both rue St-Denis and rue Française.
Du Midi, rue Traversière 31, 12e (tel. (1) 43 07 88 68). Métro:
Ledru-Rollin. The street runs left off av. Ledru-Rollin a short
distance from the métro station as you head in the direction of
av. Daumesnil.
Mistral, rue Chaligny 3, 12e (tel. (1) 46 28 10 20). Métro: Reuilly-
Diderot or Faidherbe Chaligny.

B&B
Pension les Marroniers, rue d'Assas 78, 6e (tel. (1) 43 26 37 71;
for reservations (1) 43 26 37 71). Bed, breakfast and evening
meal. Singles and doubles from around 160FF (£20; $30) per
person, slightly cheaper per person in triples. RER: Port Royal.
Bed & Breakfast 1, rue Campagne Premiere 7, 14e (tel. (1) 43
35 11 26). This organization has singles starting around 230FF
(£28.75; $43), doubles around 270FF (£33.75; $50.60). Métro:
Notre-Dame-des-Champs.

UNIVERSITY ACCOMMODATION
Cité Universitaire de Paris, blvd Jourdan 15, 14e (tel. (1) 45 89 35
79). In summer, there is a 7- to 10-night minimum stay. Singles
100–130FF (£12.50–16.25; $18.75–24.40), doubles around 95FF
(£12; $18) per person. Full payment in advance is usually required.
For further details and reservations contact: Général de Cité Univer-

sitaire de Paris, blvd Jourdan 19, 75690 Paris cedex 14. RER: Cité Universitaire. The closest métro stop is Porte d'Orléans Général-Leclerc, a 10-minute walk away along blvd Jourdan.

HOSTELS/FOYERS

AJF operate five Hôtels de Jeunes in the city, four of which are open all year round. Accommodation is usually in two- or four-bed rooms with B&B costing around 95FF (£12; $18). No reservations are accepted, so arrive early at an AJF office, or at one of the Foyers.

Le Fauconnier, rue de Fauconnier 11, 4e (tel. (1) 42 74 23 45). The largest of the five foyers. Métro: Pont Marie or St-Paul. From Pont Marie follow the Seine downstream about 100m, then turn left up rue de Fauconnier. From St-Paul turn left down rue Prévôt from rue Franois Miron, then left along rue Charlemagne until you see rue du Fauconnier on the right.

Le Fourcy, rue de Fourcy 6, 4e (tel. (1) 42 74 23 45). Off rue de Rivoli and rue Francois Miron, a short walk from the St-Paul métro station.

Maubisson, rue des Barres 12, 4e (tel. (1) 42 72 72 09). The smallest of the five foyers. Right off rue de l'Hôtel de Ville, a short walk from the Pont Marie métro station.

Résidence Bastille, av. Ledru-Rollin 151, 11e (tel. (1) 43 79 53 86). Some singles available. Between the Voltaire (closest) and Ledru-Rollin métro stations.

Residence Luxembourg, rue St-Jacques 270, 5e (tel. (1) 43 25 06 20). Open July–Sept. RER: Luxembourg. Rue St-Jacques runs parallel to blvd St-Michel, one block away. Follow Souflot from near the RER station.

Centre International de Paris (BVJ) run four foyers. Accommodation is mainly in multi-bedded rooms, though there are a few singles. B&B costs around 100FF (£12.50; $18.75). No reservations are accepted, so arrive early, preferably before 9 a.m. Three-night maximum stay.

Paris Quartier Latin, rue des Bernardins 44, 5e (tel. (1) 43 29 34 80). Métro: Maubert-Mutualité. Rue des Bernardins crosses blvd St-Germain about 150m from pl. Maubert.

Paris Louvre, rue Jean-Jacques Rousseau 20, 1er (tel. (1) 42 36 88 18). From the Louvre Rivoli métro station head up rue du Louvre from rue de Rivoli, turn left along rue St-Honoré, then right.

Paris Les Halles, rue du Pélican 5, 1er (tel. (1) 40 26 92 45). From the Louvre Rivoli métro station, follow the directions for the foyer above until you see rue du Pélican, going left off rue Jean-Jacques-Rousseau. From the Palais Royal/Musée du Louvre métro station, follow rue St-Honoré, turn left up rue Croix-des-Petits-Champs, then right.

Paris Opéra, rue Thérèse 11 (tel. (1) 42 60 77 23). Off av. de l'Opéra near the Pyramides métro station. An easy walk from the Opéra or Palais Royal/Musée de Louvre métro stations.

Centre International de Séjour de Paris (CISP) run two foyers. 140FF (£17.50; $26.25) for singles, 110FF (£13.75; $20.50) in two- to five-bedded rooms, 93FF (£11.60; $17.40) in 12-bedded dorms. Reception open 6.30 a.m.–1.30 a.m. The foyers are frequently full by 12 p.m.

CISP Ravel, av. Maurice Ravel 6, 12e (tel. (1) 43 43 19 01). Métro: Porte de Vincennes.

CISP Kellerman, blvd Kellerman 17, 13e (tel. (1) 45 80 70 76). Blvd Kellerman runs off av. d'Italie by the Porte d'Italie métro station.

Other independent hostels include:

Association des Etudiants Protestants de Paris (AEPP), rue de Vaugirard 46 (tel. (1) 46 33 23 30/43 54 31 49). Ages 18–25 only. Singles 92FF (£11.50; $16.80), doubles 83FF (£10.40; $15.60) per person, dorms 70FF (£8.75; $13). From pl. Edmond Rostand (by the Luxembourg RER station) follow rue des Médicis into rue de Vaugirard.

Jules Ferry (FUAJ), blvd Jules Ferry 8 (tel. (1) 43 57 55 60). Métro: République. 2 a.m. curfew. Reception open 8 a.m.–9 p.m. Fournight maximum stay. 95FF (£12; $18) for B&B in two- to six-bed rooms. The Jules Ferry hostel handles reservations for the temporary FUAJ hostel set up in the university during the summer vacation (July–mid-Sept.).

Le D'Artagnan (FUAJ), rue Vitruve 80 (tel. (1) 43 61 08 75). Métro: Porte de Bagnolet. No curfew. Round-the-clock reception. 103FF (£13; $19.50) for B&B in three- to eight-bed rooms. Will not accept reservations for individuals. Rue Vitruve is off blvd Davout between the Porte de Bagnolet (closest) and Porte de Montreuil métro stations.

Relais Européen de la Jeunesse (FUAJ), av. Robert Schumann 52, Athis Mons (tel. 64 84 81 39). No curfew. Round-the-clock reception. 95–105FF (£12–13; $18.00–19.50). About 500m from the RER station in Athis Mons (line C).

rue Marcel Duhamel 3 (FUAJ), Arpajon (tel. 64 90 28 55). Around
50FF (£6.25; $9.40). 400m from the RER station in Arpajon (line
C4 dir. Dourdan from Paris Austerlitz). Camping spaces available.

LFAJ hostels. The booking office for the six LFAJ hostels in the city
is opposite the Pompidou Centre at rue St-Martin 119 (tel. (1) 42
72 72 09). Métro: Rambuteau or Les Halles. RER: Châtelet-les-
Halles. LFAJ also let space in houseboats (peniches) along the Seine.

C.A.I. (LFAJ), rue de 8 mai 1945 25, Acheres (tel. 39 11 14 97).
Around 50FF (£6.25; $9.40). From Paris St-Lazare take the RER
dir. Cergy-St Christophe to Acheres. The hostel is about 700m
from the station.
Y&H Hostel, rue Mouffetard 80, 5e (tel. (1) 45 35 09 53). 1 a.m.
curfew. 87FF (£11; $16.50). Weekly rate 540FF (£67.50;
$101.25). Reserve in advance with the first night's payment, or
get to the hostel early. Métro: Place Monge. From pl. Monge
follow rue Ortocan until it is crossed by rue Mouffetard.
3 Ducks Hostel, pl. E. Pernet 6, 15e (tel. (1) 48 42 04 05). 1 a.m.
curfew. 83FF (£10.40; $15.60). Reservations accepted with one
night's payment. By the Jean Baptiste de Grenelle church. Métro:
Felix Fauré or Commerce. From Commerce, follow the ascending
street numbers on rue du Commerce.
Maison des Clubs UNESCO, rue de Glacière 43, 13e (tel. (1) 43 36
00 63). Three-night maximum stay. Singles 135−150FF
(£17.00−18.75; $25.50−28.00), two- to four-bed rooms 120FF
(£15; $22.50) per person. No reservations accepted for indi-
viduals. Rue de Glacière crosses blvd Auguste Blanqui by the
Glacière métro station.
Aloha Hostel, rue Borromée 42, 15e (tel (1) 42 73 03 03). Curfew
1 a.m. 83FF (£10.40; $15.60) per person in singles, doubles,
quads and six-bed rooms. Reservations accepted with the first
night's payment. Métro: Volontaires. Turn down rue Borromée
at rue Vaugirard 243.
Foyer Franco-Libannais, rue d'Ulm 15, 5e (tel. (1) 43 29 47 60).
No curfew. Singles 110FF (£13.75; $20.50), singles with shower
120FF (£15; $22.50), doubles 90FF (£11.25; $17), doubles with
shower 110FF (£13.75; $20.50) per person, triples with shower
90FF (£11.25; $17) per person.
Maison International des Jeunes, rue Titon 4, 11e (tel. (1) 43 71
99 21). Three-night maximum stay. Ages 18−30, but this rule is
not rigorously enforced. 100FF (£12.50; $18.75). Written
requests for reservations accepted. Métro: Faidherbe-Chaligny.
Foyer International des Etudiantes, blvd St-Michel 93, 6e (tel. (1)

43 54 49 63). July—Sept., open to both sexes; Oct.—June, women only. Singles 155FF (£19.40; $29), doubles 105FF (£13; $19.50) per person. Best reserved in writing two months in advance. A short walk along blvd St-Michel from the Luxembourg RER station.

CAMPING
Camping du Bois de Boulogne, allée du Bord de l'Eau (tel. (1) 45 24 30 00). Solo travellers pay around 60FF (£7.50; $11.25). Open all year. In summer, the site fills fast and becomes very crowded. Métro: Porte Maillot. Then bus 244, followed by a short walk.

There are several other campsites close to Paris:

Parc Etang (tel. 30 58 56 20). RER St Quentin-en-Yuelines. Open April—Sept.
Parc de la Colline (tel. 60 05 42 32). RER Torcy, then bus 421. Open all year.
Choisy-le-Roi (tel. 48 90 92 30). RER Choisy-le-Roi then bus 182. Open March—Nov.
Maisons Lafitte (tel. 39 12 21 91). Ten minutes from the RER station. Open all year.

Rheims (Reims)

TOURIST OFFICES
Office du Tourisme de Reims, Square du Trésor, rue Guillaume de Machault 2, B.P. 2533, 51071 Reims cedex (tel. 26 47 25 69). Open Easter—30 Sept., daily 9 a.m.—7.30 p.m., except Sun. and holidays 9.30 a.m.—6.30 p.m.; 1 Oct.—Easter, the office closes one hour earlier than the times above. 'Accueil de France' service available. By the cathedral, a 15-minute walk from the train station (see **Basic Directions**, below).

BASIC DIRECTIONS
On leaving the train station, blvd Joffre runs left to pl. de la République. Crossing the square in front of the station, blvd Foch heads left, parallel to blvd Joffre, to the Porte de Mars, while blvd Général Leclerc runs right to the canal. At the junction of these two boulevards, rue Noël leads off diagonally left. To the right of rue Noël, pl. Drouet d'Erlon heads towards St James's Church (St-Jacques),

beyond which is rue Vesle. Left of rue Noël, rue Thiers leads towards the Town Hall on pl. de l'Hôtel de Ville. Taking the third right off rue Thiers, you can follow cours J-B-Langlet to the Cathedral and the Tourist Office. From the station to the cathedral is about a 15-minute walk.

HOTELS
Cheapest doubles from 75FF (£9.40; $14)

Au Bon Accueil, rue de Thillois 31 (tel. 26 88 55 74). Right off pl. Drouet d'Erlon near St James's Church.

Linguet, rue Linguet 14 (tel. 26 47 31 89). Near the Town Hall and pl. de la République.

Cheapest doubles 85–95FF (£10.60–12.00; $16–18)

Thillois, rue de Thillois 17 (tel. 26 40 65 65). See Au Bon Accueil, above.

Le Parisien, rue Périn 3 (tel. 26 47 32 89). In the area immediately to the left of, and behind, the train station.

Saint-André, av. Jean Jaurès 46 (tel. 26 47 24 16). From the Town Hall follow rue Jean-Jacques Rousseau on to blvd Lundy, right to pl. Aristide Briand, then left, or go right round blvd Lundy from pl. de la République.

Cheapest doubles 100–120FF (£12.50–15.00; $18.75–22.50)

Central, rue Telliers 16 (tel. 26 47 30 08). Follow rue Noël into rue des Telliers.

Monopole, pl. Drouet d'Erlon 28 (tel. 26 47 10 33).

Jeanne d'Arc, rue Jeanne d'Arc 26 (tel. 26 40 29 62).

Alsace, rue du Général Sarrail 6 (tel. 26 47 44 08). The street runs between pl. de la République and pl. de Hôtel de Ville.

Porte-Paris, rue du Colonel Fabien 39 (tel. 26 08 73 50). Cross the canal by Pont de Vesle (left from the end of blvd du Général Leclerc) into rue du Colonel Fabien.

Saint-Maurice, rue Gambetta 90 (tel. 26 85 09 10). From cours J-B-Langlet, right on rue Carnot/rue de Vesle, then left along rue Chanzy which leads into rue Gambetta. About 20 minutes' walk from the station.

Ardenn'Hôtel, rue Caqué 6 (tel. 26 47 42 38). In the area bounded by blvd du Général Leclerc, rue Jeanne-d'Arc, the canal and rue de Vesle.

Cheapest doubles 140–160FF (£17.50–20.00; $26.25–30.00)

Alhambra, rue Emile Zola 38 (tel. 26 47 27 70).
Le Baron, rue de Vesle 85 (tel. 26 47 46 24).
Saint-Nicaise, pl. Saint-Nicaise 6 (tel. (26 85 01 26). Far from the
station, a 20–25-minute walk from the catheral. Head left at the
cathedral on rue R.-de Courcy, then right along cours A.-France.
Continuing straight on you reach pl. Saint-Nicaise.

Cheapest doubles 180–200FF (£22.50–25.00; $33.75–37.50)

Touring, blvd du Général Leclerc, 17 ter (tel. 26 47 38 15).
Le Madison, av. G. Clemenceau 70 (tel. 26 85 17 85).
Azur, rue des Ecrevées 9 (tel. 26 47 43 39). Near the Town Hall.
Crystal, pl. Drouet d'Erlon 86 (tel. 26 88 44 44).
Onestar, rue Louis Bréguet 7 (tel. 26 04 53 51).

Cheapest doubles from 220–245FF (£27.50–30.60; $41.25–46.00)

Gambetta, rue Gambetta 13 (tel. 26 47 41 64). About 15 minutes'
walk from the train station. See Hôtel Saint-Maurice, above.
Balladins, rue Maurice Hollande (tel. 26 82 72 10).
Resthotel Primevere, ZA du Mont St-Pierre (tel. 26 04 23 49). In
Tinqueux, west of the city centre.
Libergier, rue Libergier 20 (tel. 26 47 28 46).
Grand Hôtel de l'Univers, blvd Foch 41 (tel. 26 88 68 08).
Cottage Hôtel, rue Jacques Maritain, Val de Murigny (tel. 26 36 34
34).
Confortel, rue du Commerce 62 (tel. 26 82 01 02). In Cormontreuil,
south of the city centre.
Le Bon Moine, rue des Capucins 14 (tel. 26 47 33 64).
Au Tambour, rue de Magneux 60 (tel. 26 40 59 22).

UNIVERSITY ACCOMMODATION
Available July and August. Contact CROUS, 34 blvd Henri Vasnier
(tel. 26 85 50 16). Rooms are quite far from the centre.

HOSTELS
Centre International de Séjour et de Rencontres (FUAJ), Chaussée
Bocquaine 1 (tel. 26 40 52 60). A 15-minute walk from the
station. Cross the canal by Pont de Vesle (left from the end
of blvd du Général Leclerc), down rue du Colonel Fabien, then
left.
A.R.P.E.J., rue de Courcelles 66 (tel. 26 47 46 52). Open all year.

A 5—10-minute walk from the train station. Right from the exit along blvd Louis Röderer, then left on to rue de Courcelles.

Méridienne, rue de la Cerisaie 36 (tel. 26 85 65 17). Open all year except August. Around 100FF (£12.50; $18.75) per person in doubles.

CAMPING
Airotel de Champagne, av. Hoche (Route de Châlons) (tel. 26 85 41 22). Open 23 Mar.—30 Sept.

Rouen

TOURIST OFFICES
Office du Tourisme, 25 pl. de la Cathédrale, B.P. 666, 76008 Rouen cedex (tel. 35 71 41 77). Open May—Sept., Mon.—Sat. 9 a.m.—7 p.m., Sun. and holidays 9.30 a.m.—12.30 p.m. and 2.30—6 p.m.; at other times, Mon.—Sat. 9 a.m.—12.30 p.m. and 2—6.30 p.m. Finds rooms in local hotels for 15FF (£2; $3). 'Accueil de France' service available.

HOTELS
Cheapest rooms 65FF (£8; $12)

Normandy, rue du Renard 47 (tel. 35 71 13 69). From rue Jeanne-d'Arc go right down blvd de la Marne into pl. Cauchoise, then across the square into rue Renard.

Cheapest rooms 75—80FF (£9.40—10.00; $14—15)

Saint-Ouen, rue des Faulx 43 (tel. 35 71 46 44). From rue Thiers head to the right around the Church of St-Ouen into rue des Faulx.

De Lille, rue Lafayette 79 (tel. 35 72 89 91). From av. de Bretagne head left along rue A. Glatigny, across pl. des Emmurées and rue St-Sever to take rue de Lessard into rue Lafayette.

Cheapest rooms 85—90FF (£10.60—11.25; $16—17)

Du Square, rue du Moulinet 9 (tel. 35 71 56 07). Off rue Jeanne-d'Arc by rue Blanchard, a short distance after blvd de la Marne.

Napoléon, rue Beauvoisine 58 (tel. 35 71 43 59). Left from pl. Tissot along rue de la Rochefoucault, right down Champ des Oiseaux, over blvd de la Marne, and on down rue Bouvrreuil, then left along rue du Cordier which leads into Beauvoisine.

Du Sphynx, rue Beauvoisine 130 (tel. 35 71 35 86). See Napoléon, above.

Cheapest rooms 100–110FF (£12.50–13.75; $18.75–20.50)

Rochefoucauld, rue de la Rochefoucauld 1 (tel. 35 71 86 58). By the station, left off pl. Bernard-Tissot.

Du Palais, rue du Tambour 12 (tel. 35 71 41 40). Runs off pl. Maréchal Foch and rue aux Juifs to rue du Gros-Horloge.

Des Arcades, rue des Carmes 52 (tel. 35 70 10 30). Right off rue Thiers heading towards St. Ouen.

De la Gare, rue Maladrerie, 3 bis (tel. 35 71 57 90). To the right off pl. Tissot.

Beauséjour, rue Pouchet 9 (tel. 35 71 93 47). Rue Pouchet runs out of pl. Tissot to the right of rue Jeanne-d'Arc.

Du Chapeau Rouge, rue Lafayette 129 (tel. 35 72 23 72). See Hôtel de Lille, above.

Au Coin Fleuri, rue de Québec 8–10 (tel. 35 70 68 88).

Cheapest rooms 120–130FF (£15.00–16.25; $22.50–24.40)

Boieldieu, pl. du Gaillardbois 14 (tel. 35 70 50 75/35 88 73 96). From the cathedral, take rue Grand Pont towards the Seine, then left along rue de la Savonnerie into the square.

Regina, av. de Bretagne 2 (tel. 35 73 02 74).

De la Tour de Beurre, quai Pierre-Corneille 20 (tel. 35 71 95 17). Overlooking the Seine. From the foot of rue Jeanne-d'Arc go left.

De Nice, rue Lafayette 73 (tel. 35 72 21 72). See Hôtel de Lille, above.

Des Familles, rue Pouchet 4 (tel. 35 71 69 61/35 71 88 51). See Hôtel Beauséjour above.

Vieille-Tour, pl. de la Haute-Vieille-Tour 42 (tel. 35 70 03 27). To the left of pl. du Gaillardbois. See Hôtel Boieldieu, above.

Solferino, rue Thiers 51 (tel. 35 71 10 07). Right off rue Jeanne-d'Arc.

De l'Europe, rue aux Ours 87 (tel. 35 70 83 30). Crosses rue Jeanne-d'Arc one street on from rue du Gros-Horloge.

Cheapest rooms 140–160FF (£17.50–20.00; $26.25–30.00)

D'Albion, rue des Augustins 52 (tel. 35 70 05 15). From the St-Ouen church, rue de la République runs down to the Seine. Rue des Augustins is on the left near the river.

De Normandie, rue du Bec 19 (tel. 35 71 55 77). Near the Court. Left off Jeanne-d'Arc along rue aux Juifs at pl. Maréchal Foch, then right.

Celine, rue de Campulley 26 (tel. 35 71 95 23). From pl. Tissot head right on rue de la Maladrerie, then first left.

Du Gaillardbois, pl. du Gaillardbois 12 (tel. 35 70 34 28). See Hôtel Boieldieu, above.

Morand, rue Morand 1 (tel. 35 71 46 07). Left off rue Jeanne-d'Arc, about 250m from the station.

De Bordeaux, pl. de la République 9 (tel. 35 71 93 58). See Hôtel d'Albion, above. At the end of rue de la République by the Seine.

Cheapest rooms 170–180FF (£21.25–22.50; $32.00–33.75)

De Paris, rue la Champmeslé 12 (tel. 35 70 09 26). Right off rue du Gros-Horloge heading towards the cathedral.

Foch, rue Saint-Etienne-des-Tonneliers 6 (tel. 35 88 11 44). Right off rue Jeanne-d'Arc near the river along rue Général Leclerc, right down rue J-le-Lieur, then left.

De la Cathédrale, rue Saint-Romain 12 (tel. 35 71 57 95). The street runs along the left-hand side of the cathedral.

HI HOSTEL
Centre de Séjour, rue Diderot 17 (tel. 35 72 06 45). 57FF (£7; $10.50) in mixed dorms. Off av. de Bretagne. A 20-minute walk from the train station, or bus 12 to the end of rue Diderot.

UNIVERSITY ACCOMMODATION
CROUS, rue d'Herbouville 3 (tel. 35 71 46 15). This office lets singles to those with a student ID card for 50FF (£6.25; $9.40) from June–Sept. The university is in Mont-St-Aignan, far from the town centre but easily reached by bus 10.

CAMPING
Neither of the two sites are centrally located. Camping Municipal, rue Jules-Ferry (tel. 35 74 07 59) is in Déville-lès-Rouen, off the main road (Route National 27) to Dieppe. Camping 'L'Aubette', rue Vert-Buisson 23 (tel. 35 08 47 69) is in Saint-Leger-du-Bourg-Denis, in the direction of Beauvais.

St Malo

TOURIST OFFICES

Office du Tourisme, Port des Yachts, 35400 Saint-Malo (tel. 99 56 64 48). Open July–Aug., Mon.–Sat. 8.30 a.m.–8 p.m., Sun. 10 a.m.–6.30 p.m.; at other times, Mon.–Sat. 9 a.m.–12 p.m. and 2–6 p.m. 'Accueil de France' service not available.

HOTELS

Rooms can be very difficult to find in July and August, so reserve ahead if possible. If you want to stay in the Old Town, book as far in advance as you can.

Cheapest doubles 90–110FF (£11.25–13.75; $17.00–20.50)

Hôtel du Centre et du Canada, pl. du Canada 7 (tel. 99 56 96 16).
L'Arrivée, rue Ville Pépin 83 (tel. 99 81 99 57).
L'Europe, blvd de la République 44 (tel. 99 56 13 42).
Faisan Doré, rue de l'Orme 1 (tel. 99 40 91 70). In the Old Town, between the Halle-aux-Blés and the Marché-des-Légumes.
La Petite Vitesse, blvd de la République 42 (tel. 99 56 31 76). A short walk from the station.
L'Avenir, blvd de la Tour d'Auvergne 31 (tel. 99 56 13 33). Close to the train station. Right off blvd de la République.
Le Vauban, blvd de la République 7 (tel. 99 56 09 39). A few minutes' walk from the train station.
De la Vieille Ville, av. Aristide-Briand 40 (tel. 99 56 12 25). A 10–15-minute walk from the station. From blvd de la République, turn right on rue Jean-Jaurès, which leads into av. Aristide-Briand.
Les Chiens du Guet, pl. du Guet 4 (tel. 99 40 46 77). In the Old Town, beside the Porte St-Pierre.

Cheapest doubles 115–130FF (£14.40–16.25; $21.50–24.40)

Brasserie Armoricaine, rue du Boyer 6 (tel. 99 40 89 13). In the Old Town, near the post office (P.T.T.) between Place-aux-Herbes and the Porte des Bés.
Pomme d'Argent, blvd des Talards 24 (tel. 99 56 12 39). A short walk from the station.
Le Grand Jardin, rue Gustave Flaubert 40 (tel. 99 56 00 60).
Gambetta, blvd Gambetta 40 (tel. 99 56 54 70).

Les Charmettes, blvd Hébert 64 (tel. 99 56 07 31).
La Croix de l'Esperance, av. Aristide-Briand 111 (tel. 99 81 60 79).
Formule 1, rue de la Grassinais 28 (tel. 99 81 57 10).

Cheapest doubles 140–150FF (£17.50–18.75; $26.25–28.00)

Cap à l'Ouest, rue St-Benoît 2 (tel. 99 40 87 03). In the Old Town off rue Maclaw, near the Sous-Préfecture.
Le Tivoli, Chaussée du Sillon 61 (tel. 99 56 11 98). Near the main beach (Grande Plage). Follow blvd de la République to pl. Duguesclin, from which rue Roger Vercel heads down to the beach. A 10-minute walk from the station.
De la Mer, rue Dauphine 3 (tel. 99 81 61 05). In St-Servan, a 15–20-minute walk from the station. Head for the ferry terminal, then from the Quai de Trichet head left into rue Georges-Clemenceau, cross over and take one of the streets on the other side into rue Dauphine.
Armeric, blvd de la Tour d'Auvergne 5 (tel. 99 40 52 00). A 5-minute walk from the station, right off blvd de la République.
Antheus, pl. du Prieuré 2 (tel. 99 40 26 76).
La Gardelle, rue de la Gardelle 2 (tel. 99 56 00 69).

Cheapest doubles 160–180FF (£20.00–22.50; $30.00–33.75)

Hôtel des Voyageurs, blvd des Talards 2 (tel. 99 56 30 35). By the train station.
Paris, rue Alphonse Thébault 3 (tel. 99 56 31 44). Off pl. de l'Hermine, about 100m from the train station.
Victoria, rue des Orbettes 4 (tel. 99 56 34 01). In the Old Town. Follow the walls left from Porte St-Vincent, then right off rue Jacques-Cartier. The hotel offers a chance to play French billiards.
Auberge de l'Hermine, pl. de l'Hermine 4 (tel. 99 56 31 32). A few steps away from the train station.
Croiseur, pl. de la Poissonnerie 2 (tel. 99 40 80 40). Directions: see Bristol-Union, above.
Hostellerie la Grotte aux Fées, Chaussée du Sillon 36 (tel. 99 56 83 30).
Le Servannais, rue Amiral Magon 4 (tel. 99 81 45 50).
Le Bois Joli, av. de Marville 10 (tel. 99 40 74 00).

Cheapest doubles 185–205FF (£23.00–25.60; $34.50–38.40)

L'Arrivée, blvd de la République 52 (tel. 99 56 30 78). A 3-minute walk from the station.

Le Bristol-Union, pl. de la Poissonnerie 4 (tel. 99 40 83 36). In the
   Old Town. Diagonally left from Porte St-Vincent and down rue
   Ste-Marguerite.
Châteaubriand, blvd Hébert 8 (tel. 99 56 01 19). Directions: main
   FUAJ hostel below. To the left, off av. Louis-Pasteur.
Noquette, rue de la Fosse 9 (tel. 99 40 83 57).
La Poste, rue Godard 8 (tel. 99 81 60 55).
Saint-Hubert, blvd Chateaubriand 84 (tel. 99 56 07 65).
Le Saint-Maurice, av. du R.P. Umbricht 2 (tel. 99 56 07 66).

YOUTH HOSTELS
Av. du Révérend-Père-Umbricht 37 (FUAJ) (tel. 99 40 29 80). 65FF
   (£8; $12). Fills quickly in summer. Red bus 2 to rue Coutoisville,
   then a short walk along av. du R. P. Umbricht, or a 20-minute
   walk from the train station.
L'Hermitage (IFAJ), rue des Ecoles 13 (tel. 99 56 22 00). In Paramé,
   a 15-minute walk from the main FUAJ hostel. Singles and
   doubles for 44FF (£5.50; $8.25).

CAMPING
La Cité d'Aleth, Cité d'Aleth (tel. 99 81 60 91). The Cité d'Aleth
   adjoins the St-Servan district of town. This municipal site overlooks the Old Town and, less enchantingly, the ferry terminal.
Les Nielles, av. John Kennedy (tel. 99 40 26 35). This municipal
   site is located near one of the beaches (Plage du Minihic), beyond
   the Paramé district. Open mid-June to mid-Sept.
Du Nicet, av. de la Varde (tel. 99 40 26 32). This municipal site is
   far from the centre in the Rotheneuf district, near the coast at
   the Pointe du Nicet. Open Easter to Sept.
Les Ilôts, av. de la Guimorais (tel. 99 56 98 72). Also in Rotheneuf,
   this municipal site is well inland from the coast, but close to the
   coastal route to Mont-St-Michel. Open July to mid-Sept.
De la Fontaine, rue de la Fontaine-aux-Pélerins (tel. 99 81 62 62).
   Open mid-April to mid-Oct. Well out from the centre, on the
   main route to Mont-St-Michel.

Strasbourg

TOURIST OFFICES
Office du Tourisme de Strasbourg et de sa Région, pl. de la Cathédrale 17, 67000 Strasbourg cedex. Head office of the Tourist Board.

Contact this office if you want information in advance. Open 1
June–30 Sept., 8 a.m.–7 p.m.; Easter–31 May and 1–31 Oct.,
9 a.m.–6 p.m.; 1 Nov.–Easter, Mon.–Sat. 9 a.m.–6 p.m., Sun.
9.30 a.m.–12.30 p.m. and 2–5 p.m.
Accueil Gare, pl. de la Gare (tel. 88 32 51 49). In front of the train
station. Open June–Sept., 8 a.m.–7 p.m. daily; Easter–May and
Oct., daily 9 a.m.–12.30 p.m. and 1.45–6 p.m.; 1 Nov.–Easter,
Mon.–Fri. 9 a.m.–12.30 p.m. and 1.45–6 p.m.
Accueil Pont de l'Europe (tel. 88 61 39 23). Same hours as Accueil
Gare.

BASIC DIRECTIONS
From pl. de la Gare in front of the train station, blvd de Metz runs
right into pl. Ste-Aurélie and blvd de Nancy, which leads in turn
into pl. de la Porte Blanche and blvd de Lyon. Diagonally left across
pl. de la Gare from the station is rue Kuhn, to the right of which
(almost opposite the station exit) is rue du Maire Kuss. Following
this street and then crossing the Pont du Maire Kuss you arrive at
the church near the intersection of rue du Vieux-Marché-aux-Vins
(to the left) and Grand' Rue (right of the church). Grand' Rue leads
into rue Gutenberg, which ends at pl. Gutenberg with the statue
of the famous printer facing the cathedral. From the train station
to pl. Gutenberg is about 15 minutes' walk. Going right from pl.
Gutenberg, you can follow rue du Vieux-Marché-aux-Poissons
down to the river Ill, across which is pl. du Corbeau.

HOTELS
Cheapest doubles around 115FF (£14.40; $21.60)

Michelet, rue du Vieux-Marché-aux-Poissons 48 (tel. 88 32 47 38).
One-star hotel.
La Cruche d'Or, rue des Tonneliers 6 (tel. 88 32 11 23). One-star
hotel. Closed 1–15 Aug. In the area between Grand' Rue and
the Ill.
Henriette, rue Leclerc 69 (tel. 88 78 03 84) One-star hotel in the
suburb of Wolfisheim.

Cheapest doubles around 125FF (£15.60; $23.40)

Astoria, rue de Rosheim 7a (tel. 88 32 17 22). Two-star hotel. Left
off blvd de Nancy near pl. Ste-Aurélie.
Grillon, rue Thiergarten 2 (tel. 88 32 36 47). No star. Opposite the
train station and left at the crossroads.

Au Cygne, rue de la 1ère Division Blindée 38 (tel. 88 64 04 79). One-star hotel in the suburb of Eschau.

Weber, blvd de Nancy 22 (tel. 88 32 36 47). One-star hotel.

Patricia, rue des Puits 1a (tel. 88 32 14 60). One-star hotel. In the area between Grand' Rue and the Ill.

Cheapest doubles around 170FF (£21.25; $32)

Gutenberg, rue des Serruriers 31 (tel. 88 32 17 15). Two-star hotel. From Grand' Rue turn right down rue des Cordonniers then left at rue des Serruriers.

De l'Ill, rue des Bateliers 8 (tel. 88 36 20 01). Two-star hotel. From pl. du Corbeau head left along quai des Bateliers, then right at rue des Bateliers. A 5–10-minute walk from the town centre.

Du Rhin, pl. de la Gare 7–8 (tel. 88 32 35 00). Two-star hotel.

De Bruxelles, rue Kuhn 13 (tel. 88 32 36 47). Two-star hotel.

Schutzenbock, av. Jean Jaurès 81 (tel. 88 34 04 19). One-star hotel. Closed 1–25 Aug. A 20-minute walk from the centre. Off pl. l'Etoile near the city council offices.

Auberge du Grand Duc, route de l'Hôpital 33 (tel. 88 34 31 76). One-star hotel. About 20 minutes' walk from the city centre, near the city council offices.

Cheapest doubles 190–220FF (£23.75–27.50; $35.50–41.25)

Du Couvent du Franciscain, rue Faubourg de Pierre 18 (tel. 88 32 93 93). Two-star hotel. From the train station walk left along blvd du Président Wilson, then right along blvd du Président Poincaré to pl. du Faubourg de Pierre and the start of rue du Faubourg de Pierre.

Eden, rue d'Obernai 16 (tel. 88 32 41 99). Two-star hotel. Left off blvd de Lyon.

Pax, rue du Faubourg National 24/26 (tel. 88 32 14 54). Two-star hotel. Petite rue de la Course (diagonally right across pl. de la Gare from the train station exit) leads into rue du Faubourg National. Alternatively you can walk right from the station along blvd de Metz and then turn left.

YOUTH HOSTELS

'René Cassin' (FUAJ), rue de l'Auberge de Jeunesse 9 (tel. 88 30 26 46). 1 a.m. curfew. 65FF (£8; $12) for B&B. Also has space for 60 tents. Bus 3, 13, or 23 from Marché Ste-Marguérite (follow Petite rue de la Course and then rue St-Michel from pl. de la Gare), or a 20-minute walk from the train station.

Centre International de Rencontres du Parc du Rhin (FUAJ), rue
des Cavaliers (tel. 88 60 10 20). Bus 1, 11 or 21 from Strasbourg
train station to Pont-du-Rhin. The nearest train station is Kehl/
Rhein, 1km away in Germany.
Amitel Galaxie (LFAJ), rue de Soleure 8 (tel. 88 25 58 91). About
2.5km from the train station. Ten minutes' walk from the town
centre.
CIARUS, rue Finkmatt 7 (tel. 88 32 12 12). 75FF (£9.40; $14). A
10–15-minute walk from the train station.
Altrheinweg 11, Kehl/Rhein (tel. 19 49 78 51/19 49 23 30). DM17
(£7.25; $11). Although the pleasant town of Kehl/Rhein is in
Germany it is virtually a suburb of Strasbourg. Trains run more
or less hourly from Strasbourg and there is a frequent bus service.

FOYERS
Du Jeune Travailleur, rue du Macon (tel. 88 39 69 01).
Du Jeune Ouvrier Chrétien, rue de Bitche 6 (tel. 88 35 12 75).
De l'Ingenieur, blvd d'Anvers 54 (tel. 88 61 59 89).
De l'Etudiant Catholique, pl. St-Etienne 17 (tel. 88 35 36 20).
De la Jeune Fille, rue de Soleure 8 (tel. 88 36 15 28). Women only.

CAMPING
Rue l'Auberge de Jeunesse 7 (tel. 88 30 26 46). Next to the 'René
Cassin' hostel. For directions see above. Camping is also available
at the hostel itself.

Toulouse (Tolosa)

TOURIST OFFICES
Office du Tourisme Syndicat d'Initiative de Toulouse, Donjon du
Capitole, place du Capitole, 31000 Toulouse (tel. 61 23 32 00).
Open daily May–Sept., 9 a.m.–7 p.m.; Oct.–Apr., Mon.–Sat.
9 a.m.–6 p.m. A branch office operates in the train station.

BASIC DIRECTIONS
Trains arrive at Toulouse Matabiau, about 1.5km from the city
centre. Almost directly across the canal from the station is rue de
Bayard, which leads down to blvd de Strasbourg. Slightly to the
right across blvd de Strasbourg is rue de Remusat, which takes you
right into pl. du Capitole, site of the Tourist Office.

HOTELS
Cheapest doubles around 80FF (£10; $15)

Beauséjour, rue Caffarelli 4 (tel. 61 62 77 59). Right off Allée Jean-Jaurès.

Cheapest doubles around 100FF (£12.50; $18.75)

Antoine, rue Arnaud Vidal 21 (tel. 61 62 70 27). Left off Allée Jean-Jaurès.

Des Arts, rue Cantegril, 1 bis (tel. 61 23 36 21). Off rue des Arts. From pl. Wilson follow rue St-Antoine-du-T. into pl. St-Georges, across which is rue des Arts.

Astrid, rue Denfert Rochereau 12 (tel. 61 23 36 21). Between rue de Bayard and Allée Jean-Jaurès, rue Bertrand-de-Born runs parallel to these two streets into pl. du Belfort, across which is rue Denfert Rochereau.

Splendid, rue Caffarelli 13 (tel. 61 62 43 02). See Beauséjour, above.

Donjon, rue du Poids de l'Huile 12 (tel. 61 21 86 44). The street runs between pl. du Capitole and rue d'Alsace-Lorraine. Head left from rue Lafayette as you walk from pl. Wilson.

Excelsior, rue Riquet 82 (tel. 61 62 71 25). Left off Allée Jean-Jaurès, close to the canal.

Cheapest doubles around 110FF (£13.75; $20.50)

Anatole France, pl. Anatole France 46 (tel. 61 23 19 96).

Héliot, rue Héliot 3 (tel. 61 62 47 66). From rue de Bayard turn left down rue Maynard into pl. de Belfort. Rue Héliot is directly across the square.

Le Lutetia, rue Maynard 33 (tel. 61 62 51 57). Left off rue de Bayard.

Bourse, rue Clémence Isaure 11 (tel. 61 21 55 86). Follow rue Gambetta from pl. du Capitole, turn left along rue Ste-Ursule. Rue Clémence Isaure is off to the right near the junction with rue de Cujas.

Nouvel Hôtel, rue du Taur 13 (tel. 61 21 13 93). The street runs from pl. du Capitole.

Cheapest doubles around 120FF (£15; $22.50)

Olivier, av. Honoré-Serres 75 (tel. 61 21 39 94). From rue de Bayard head right along blvd de Strasbourg on to blvd d'Arcole, then right down av. Honoré-Serres.

Palais, Allée Paul Feuga 4 (tel. 61 52 96 23). Between the Palais de Justice and the Point St-Michel. From pl. Wilson walk down rue Lapeyrousse on to rue d'Alsace-Lorraine, turn left, and go straight ahead until you eventually reach Grande rue de Nazareth. Turn right, then left at the end of the street to reach Allée Paul Feuga.

Brasserie Pierre, rue de Périole 48 (tel. 61 48 58 75). In the area to the rear of Gare Matabiau. Head left from the station along the canal, turn left down the main road, and watch for rue Périole on the left-hand side, off Allée Georges-Pompidou.

Unic, Allée Jean-Jaurès 26 (tel. 61 62 38 19).

Au Père Leon, pl. Esquirol 2 (tel. 61 21 70 39). From pl. Wilson walk down rue Lapeyrousse on to rue d'Alsace-Lorraine. Turn left, and then right down rue de Metz to reach pl. Esquirol.

Francois 1er, rue d'Austerlitz 4 (tel. 61 21 54 52). Off pl. 5 Wilson.

Grand Balcon, rue Romiguières 8 (tel. 61 21 48 08). Off pl. du Capitole.

Cheapest doubles 130–160FF (£16.25–20.00; $24.40–30.00)

Real, Allée Jean-Jaurès 30 (tel. 61 62 94 34).
Le Toulouse, rue de Bayard 63 (tel. 61 62 41 03).
Chaumond, rue Lafayette 19 (tel. 61 21 86 42).
Croix Baragnon, rue Croix Baragnon 17 (tel. 61 52 60 10). From pl. Wilson follow rue St-Antoine-de-T. into pl. St-Georges, then take rue des Arts, which is crossed by rue Croix Baragnon.
Guillaume Tell, blvd Lazare-Carnot 42 (tel. 61 62 44 02).
Riquet, rue Riquet 92 (tel. 61 62 55 96). See Hôtel des Arts, above.
Saint-Severin, rue de Bayard 69 (tel. 61 62 71 39).

Cheapest doubles 170–200FF (£21.25–25.00; $32.00–37.50)

Jacobins, rue Pargaminières 52 (tel. 61 21 86 42). From pl. du Capitole follow rue Romiguières into rue Pargaminières.
Grand Hôtel d'Orléans, rue Bayard 72 (tel. 61 62 98 47).
Trianon, rue Lafaille 7 (tel. 61 62 74 74).
Cosmos, rue Caffarelli 20 (tel. 61 62 57 21). See Hôtel Beauséjour.
Junior, rue du Taur 62 (tel. 61 21 69 67).
Le Bristol, rue de Bayard 75 (tel. 61 62 90 76).
Clocher de Rodez, pl. Jeanne d'Arc 14–15 (tel. 61 62 42 92). From rue de Bayard turn right along rue des Moutons into the square.
Lafayette, rue Caffarelli 5 (tel. 61 62 75 73). See Hôtel Beauséjour.
Metropole, rue d'Austerlitz 18 (tel. 61 21 68 51). See Hôtel François.

L'Ours Blanc, rue Victor Hugo 2 (tel. 61 21 62 40). Off blvd de Strasbourg, left from the end of rue de Bayard.

HOSTELS

Villa des Rosiers, av. Jean-Rieux 125 (FUAJ) (Tel. 61 80 49 93). Curfew 11 p.m. Around 45FF (£5.60; $8.40). Bus 14 from the train station, then bus 22 to the hostel, or a 25-minute walk. Head left from the train station along the canal, then head left up av. Jean-Rieux at the fifth roadbridge.

UCJG (YMCA) San Francisco, 92 Route d'Espagne (tel. 61 40 29 28). Around 56FF (£7; $10.50). Bus 12 to Barrier de Muret.

CAMPING

Camping Municipal du Pont de Rupé, av. des Etats-Unis, Chemin du Pont de Rupé (tel. 61 70 07 35). On the northern fringe of the city. Take bus P from the train station.

GERMANY (Deutschland)

The money already ploughed into tourism in the east of the country has, even at this early stage, ensured that the old DDR has a tourist infrastructure much more akin to the western European norm than any of the other former Eastern bloc countries. There is no discernible difference in the amount or quality of tourist information on offer between the east and the west of the country. However, there are great differences in the standard of accommodation: Germany will still be two separate countries for several years to come, though the difference is only really apparent if you are looking for a room of your own. In that case your most likely options are cheap hotels, Pensionen, Gästhause and private rooms. It is the relative abundance of these different forms of accommodation that is as good a guide as any to whether you are in the east or west of the country.

Cheap hotels, **Pensionen** and **Gästhause** are widely available in the west. Prices in the main tourist destinations generally start around DM32,50–35 (£14–15; $21.00–22.50) per person in singles and doubles, elsewhere around DM27,50 (£11.75; $17.50). The west also boasts a good supply of **farmhouse accommodation** (available mainly in summer) and **private rooms** (found mainly in the smaller towns). Prices for farmhouse accommodation and private rooms start around DM25–30 (£10.75–13.00; $16.25–19.50) per person. The standards of comfort and cleanliness in all the forms of accommodation mentioned above are invariably high, so you are virtually assured excellent value for money, particularly if you make comparisons with similarly priced accommodation in Italy or the UK. In the east of the country, cheap hotels, Pensionen and Gästhause are few and far between when compared to the west. Here it is **private rooms** which are the mainstay of the accommodation scene. They are by far the most widely available cheap accommodation possibility, no matter where you travel in the east. The increase in the number of private rooms available to let since the practice was legalized in the DDR in 1990 has averted a potentially serious accommodation shortage in the east. Now there is an ample supply of rooms, even in particularly popular destinations such as Dresden, Weimar, Potsdam and Eisenach. On average, prices are in the DM20–30 (£8.50–13.00; $12.75–19.50) per person range, in singles or doubles. While the standards of comfort in private rooms in the east may not yet match their western counterparts, rooms are normally scrupulously clean so that, on the whole, reasonable value for money is guaranteed. Tourist Office accommodation services throughout Germany are usually more than willing to help you find a room in any of the types of accommodation listed above. In smaller towns, it is feasible to look for rooms on your own. Simply make enquiries at hotels, or wherever you see a '*Gasthof*' or '*Zimmer frei*' sign. With the possible exception of staunchly Roman Catholic rural Bavaria, unmarried couples are unlikely to face any difficulties when requesting to share a room.

At a first glance, the impressive network of nearly 700 **HI hostels** created in 1991 by the fusion of West Germany's Deutsches Jugendherbergswerk (DJH) and the Jugendherbergsverband der DDR would suggest that the budget traveller need look no further for a cheap bed. It is certainly possible to see the country cheaply if you hostel, as there is one in almost every town you are likely to visit, even during a four-month trip. As in other countries, hostelling is a good way to meet other travellers. One thing that should not deter you from hostelling in Germany is the image of German hostels as highly institutional and impersonal establishments, run by dour and officious staff. This is no more true than in most countries. Generally, the staff are approachable and happy to provide you with any information to help you enjoy your stay in town. However, there are some real drawbacks to hostelling as a means of visiting Germany. German hostels are open to HI members only. In Bavaria, there is a maximum age restriction of 26; elsewhere hostels are open to people of all ages. Curfews, which are rigorously enforced, are normally 10 p.m., except in the larger cities where hostels may stay open until midnight or 1 a.m. Whether you are in a small town or a large city, the curfew coincides with the time that the local nightlife starts to get going.

The Association recommends that hostels should be reserved in advance at all times, but particularly between 15 June and 15 September (good advice, but not always possible to adhere to). Unless your reservation is for a longer period, you will be limited to a three-night stay, except where there is plenty of space at a hostel. If you have a reservation be sure to arrive before 6 p.m. unless you have notified the hostel that you will arrive later, otherwise your reservation will not be held, and your bed may be given to someone else. If you turn up without a reservation, priority is given to visitors aged up to 27 until 6 p.m. where beds are available. In theory, this means anyone older is not assigned a bed until after 6 p.m. in case younger guests arrive. In practice, this rule is often ignored. The association handbook states that no beds are let after 10 p.m., even in the city hostels which are open late. Again this is a rule that many wardens choose to ignore, so if you are stuck there is nothing to be lost by approaching city hostels after 10 p.m.

There are six types of hostel and prices vary according to the standard of comfort, facilities available, location, and the time of the curfew. Prices at the different types of hostel also vary according to the age of the user, with those aged 25 and over paying a surcharge of around DM5 (£2.15; $3.25) at all hostels. The main price divide amongst the various grades of hostel is between **Jugendherbergen** (youth hostels) and **Jugendgästhause** (youth guest houses). Juniors (age 24 and under) pay between DM12,50–20 (£5.35–8.50; $8.00–12.75) for B&B in dormitories at a Jugendherberge. Unless you have your own sheet sleeping bag, you will also have to pay for sheet hire: the charge varies between the 15 regional associations, but you can expect to pay at least DM5 (£2.15; $3.25) for the duration of your stay. In a Jugendgästhaus, prices for juniors range from DM21–37 (£9–16; $13.50–24.00), with DM26–32 (£11.00–13.75; $16.50–20.50) being normal. Accommodation is mainly in two- or four-bed rooms, with breakfast and the hire of bed-linen included in the overnight price.

Jugendgästhause are more expensive partly because they have been modernized in an effort to attract groups. This means that individual travellers are obliged to pay extra for leisure and recreation facilities that will rarely be available for their use. Groups can be a great source of annoyance to individual travellers. Hostels are frequently full of school and youth groups. This is especially true of hostels in the cities, along the Rhine and in the Black Forest, and in the more picturesque small towns; in short, all the places you are most likely to visit. The worst times are weekdays during the summer months, and weekends throughout the rest of the year. Space for individual travellers in hostels is often at a premium, and even by 9.30 a.m. you may be turned away. Even if you do squeeze into a hostel packed with groups it may not be too pleasant. As groups bring in a lot of money, wardens tend to turn a blind eye to poorly controlled or noisy groups, no matter what the rules say. While the various problems discussed above are by no means peculiar to Germany (English hostels can be just as bad), the sheer number of groups you encounter here causes greater irritation than in most other countries. Possibly the best advice is neither to avoid the hostels, nor to try and stay in them all of the time.

As well as the HI hostels, the western part of Germany has a network of hostels run by the 'Naturfreundehaus' organization (Friends of Nature Hostels). Most are located in the countryside just outside the towns. Accommodation is in singles, doubles, or small dorms, and prices are on a par with those of Jugendgästhause. Again, you may have problems finding a bed because of groups:

not of schoolchildren this time, but of middle-aged guests, with whom the hostels are very popular.

Camping is an excellent way to see Germany cheaply, and without worrying about the likelihood of finding a cheap bed. The chances of you being turned away from a site because it is full are virtually nil (Munich's campsites manage to cope with the huge influx at the time of the Oktoberfest). At present, the sites in the east of the country are very quiet, since the numbers of campers coming from the west has failed to compensate for the loss of East European holidaymakers (primarily from the DDR and Czechoslovakia). In the west of Germany there are over 2,000 sites, covering all the main places of interest, and most towns and villages with even a minimal tourist trade. The two main operators are local authorities and the Deutscher Camping Club (DCC). Municipal sites are usually cheaper than those run by the DCC, but the standards of amenities and cleanliness are normally very high, irrespective of who operates the site. Some DCC sites are quite exceptional. Charges are around DM3–6 (£1.25–2.50; $2.00–3.75) for a tent, DM4,50–7 (£2–3; $3.00–4.50) per person, which, considering the standards of the sites, represents excellent value for money. Sites in the east tend to be similarly priced to those in the west, or slightly cheaper. While levels of cleanliness are now on a par with sites in the west, the standards of facilities are generally lower. The one drawback to camping in the east is that you may still have to make a short journey of about 8km from one of the main towns to a smaller town nearby to find the closest campsite. This is rarely the case in the west, with sites usually being within the limits of the main towns (Heidelberg is one notable exception). In any large city where there is a choice of sites with similar prices, railpass holders may save on transportation costs if there is a site located near a local train station or an S-Bahn stop (railpasses are often valid on city S-Bahn systems). Even if they are not primarily interested in camping, anyone travelling extensively in Germany would be well advised to take a tent, as this will stand you in good stead if you happen to arrive in town during one of the many trade fairs or local festivals that take place in German cities throughout the year. At these times all the cheaper beds fill rapidly, so unless you can camp you will most likely have to either pay for an expensive hotel room, sleep rough, or leave town.

In an effort to safeguard the environment **camping outside official sites** has been made illegal, but it is still possible to sleep rough, providing you obtain the permission of the landowner and/ or the police. There is little point trying to sleep out in parks or town centres. Apart from this being dangerous in some cities, the police will send you on your way if they find you. Police attitudes to **sleeping in stations** vary from place to place. In some of the smaller towns and cities they will wake you to check if you have a valid rail ticket, and if you have they will then let you lie until around 6 a.m., but when they come back at that time be prepared to move sharpish. If you do not have a ticket you will be ejected from the station, and arrested if you return later. In Munich, tolerance is shown (especially during the Oktoberfest) but do not expect a peaceful night before you are asked to move on in the morning. The stations of the northern ports and the central cities around Frankfurt are rough, and potentially dangerous at night. It is also unwise to try sleeping in the stations of the large towns in the east of the country. Although the media tends to overstate the level of neo-fascist activity in the former DDR, it is not unusual to see small groups of young neo-fascists in and around train stations late at night.

Railpass holders can always take a **night train** if they are stuck for somewhere to sleep. Trains leave the main stations for a multitude of destinations, internal and international. In the central area around Mainz-Heidelberg-Mannheim-Würzburg-Nuremberg there are trains leaving at all hours through the night. Alternatively, there is the 'Bahnhofsmission', a church-run organization which operates in the stations of all reasonably sized towns in the west of the country (shelters will no doubt be opened in the east as well). They are meant for travellers who have no place to stay, or who are leaving early in the morning. If you approach the Bahnhofsmission during the day it is likely that you will be told to return before 8 p.m. This highly restrictive curfew helps prevent abuses of the system by those who are simply looking to fix themselves up with a cheap bed. You cannot stay more than one night in the shelter. B&B and use of the showers usually costs DM10–15 (£4.25–6.50; $6.50–9.50).

Note: There is no unified telephone system in Germany, so codes quoted for eastern cities may be useless if phoning from the west of the country (and vice versa). As the telephone system in the east is overhauled codes quoted may also become obsolete, even for phone calls within the east of the country. Check which code you should be using when you telephone across the old border. Most telephone boxes have a panel showing main city codes; if not, enquire at a post office or contact directory enquiries.

ADDRESSES

German National Tourist Office	Nightingale House, 65 Curzon Street, London W1 7PE (tel. 0171 495 3990).
German YHA	Deutsches Jugendherbergswerk (DJH), Hauptverband, Bismarckstraße 8, Postfach 1455, D-4930 Detmold (tel. 0523 174010).
Friends of Nature Hostels	NaturfreundeJugend, Großglockner Straße 28, D-7000 Stuttgart 60 (tel. 0711 481076).
Camping	Deutscher Camping-Club (DCC), Mandlestraße 28, D-8000 Munchen 23 (tel. 0893 34021).
	The DCC sell the official, comprehensive guide to Germany's campsites. Expect to pay around DM25 (£10.75; $16.25) for the guide.
	A considerably abridged list is available from the German National Tourist Office.

Berlin (tel. code 030)

TOURIST OFFICES

Berlin-Tourist-Information, Europa Center, Budapesterstraße 45 (tel. 262 6031) (Charlottenburg). Open Mon.–Sat. 8 a.m.–10.30 p.m., Sun. 9 a.m.–9 p.m. Basic plan of the city. Rooms found in local hotels for a fee of DM5 (£2.15; $3.25). From the Zoologischer Garten train station (main line, S-Bahn and U-Bahn) head along Budapester Straße past the ruins of the Kaiser-Wilhelm-Gedächtniskirche. The Europa Center is on the right after about 500m. There are branch offices at the Zoologischer Garten station (tel. 313 9063/313 9064; closed Sun.) and at Tegel Airport (tel. 4101 3145), both open 8 a.m.–11 p.m.

Informationszentrum am Fernsehturm, Panoramastraße 1 (tel. 242 4675/242 4512) (Mitte). Open daily 8 a.m.–8 p.m. This office should provide the same services as the other offices, but (on past performance) do not head here first. At the foot of the radio tower on Alexanderplatz (S-Bahn and U-Bahn: Alexanderplatz).

HOTELS, PENSIONS & GUESTHOUSES
Cheapest doubles DM50–55 (£21.50–23.50; $32.25–35.25)

Berlin City-Apartments Mahlsdorf, Waldowstraße 47 (tel. 527 7497) (Hellersdorf). Singles DM30 (£13; $19.50). Breakfast not included.

Pension Monika, Schräger Weg 26 (tel. 949 4502) (Weißensee). Without breakfast.

Pension Haus Schliebner, Dannenwalder Weg 95 (tel. 416 7997) (Reinickendorf). Without breakfast.

Cheapest doubles DM60 (£25.50; $38.25)

Pension 22, Schambachweg 22 (tel. 365 5230) (Spandau). Breakfast not included.

Hotel-Pension Elton, Pariser Straße 9 (tel. 883 6155/883 6156) (Wilmersdorf).

Berlin City-Apartments, Rhinstraße 159 (tel. 975 3122) (Lichtenberg). Apartments available.

Cheapest doubles around DM70 (£30; $45)

Hotel-Pension Trautenau, Trautenaustraße 14 (tel. 861 3514) (Wilmersdorf).

Pension Zum Alten Fischerdorf, Dorfstraße 14 (tel. 648 9320) (Köpenick).

Privatzimmer Wolfram, Steinkirchener Straße 8 (tel. 415 1362) (Reinickendorf). Without breakfast.

Hotel Hamburger Hof, Kinkelstraße 6 (tel. 333 4602) (Spandau).

Hotel-Pension Wien, Brandenburgische Straße 37 (tel. 891 8486) (Wilmersdorf).

Berlin City-Apartments Wilhelmsberg, Landsberger Allee 203 (tel. 49774–0) (Hohenschönhausen). Without breakfast.

Berlin City-Apartments Prenzlauer Berg, Storkower Straße 114 (tel. 429 4103) (Prenzlauer Berg). Without breakfast.

Pension Steinert-Rosteck, Machnower Straße 13 (tel. 815 6097) (Zehlendorf). Without breakfast.

Cheapest doubles DM75–78 (£32.00–33.50; $48.00–50.25)

Hotel-Pension München, Güntzelstraße 62 (tel. 854 2226) (Wilmersdorf).

Wirtshaus zum Finkenhanel, Steinkirchener Straße 17 (tel. 415 4953) (Reinickendorf).

Hotel-Pension Bialas, Carmerstraße 16 (tel. 312 5025) (Charlottenburg).

Pension Kreuzberg, Großbeerenstraße 64 (tel. 251 1362) (Kreuzberg). Three- to four-bed rooms for DM30 (£13; $19.50) per person. Breakfast DM5 (£2.15; $3.25).

Cheapest doubles DM80 (£34.50; $51.75)

Hotel Zur Reichspost, Urbanstraße 84 (tel. 691 1035) (Kreuzberg).

Hotel An der Gropinsstadt, Neuköllner Straße 284 (tel. 661 3031) (Neukölln).

Cheapest doubles DM85 (£36.50; $54.75)

Motel Grünau, Libboldallee 17 (tel. 681 4198) (Köpenick).

Hotel Pension Majesty, Mommsenstraße 55 (tel. 323 2061) (Charlottenburg).

Hotel Charlottenburger Hof, Stuttgarter Platz 14 (tel. 324 4819) (Charlottenburg). Without breakfast.

Hotel-Pension Pariser Eck, Pariser Straße 19 (tel. 881 2145) (Wilmersdorf). Breakfast not included.

Cheapest doubles DM90 (£38.50; $57.75)

Pension Helga, Formerweg 19 (tel. 662 1010) (Neukölln). Breakfast not included.

Gästehaus Ingeborg, Ruthnerweg 15 (tel. 817 7632) (Steglitz).

Pension Am Elsterplatz, Plöner Straße 25 (tel. 826 2880) (Wilmersdorf). Without breakfast.

Haus Tannenhöhe, Ulricistraße 31 (tel. 805 1531) (Zehlendorf).

Pension 'Dorf-Aue', Alt-Lichtenrade 128 (tel. 744 4581) (Tempelhof).

Hotelpension Cortina, Kantstraße 140 (tel. 313 9059) (Charlottenburg).

Hotel Crystal, Kantstraße 144 (tel. 312 9047/312 9048/312 9049) (Charlottenburg).

Pension Silvia, Knesebeckstraße 29 (tel. 881 2129) (Charlottenburg). Breakfast not included.

Pension Cäcilie, Motzstraße 52 (tel. 211 6514) (Schöneberg). Breakfast not included.

Haus zur Linde am See, Alt-Gatow 1–3 (tel. 362 6094) (Spandau). Without breakfast.

Pension Dalg, Woltmannweg 46 and Ritterstraße 6B (tel. 773 4908) (Steglitz). Without breakfast.

Hotel-Pension Insel Rügen, Pariser Straße 39/40 (tel. 881 8204) (Wilmersdorf).

Hotel-Pension Nürnberger Eck, Nürnberger Straße 24a (tel. 218 5371) (Charlottenburg). Without breakfast.

Pension Blumenbach, Blumenbachweg 40 (tel. 545 5377) (Marzahn).

Pension Boche, Harbertssteg 19 (tel. 545 5220) (Marzahn).

Hotel-Pension Conti, Potsdamer Straße 67 (tel. 261 2999) (Tiergarten). Without breakfast.

Pension Maas, Rublanderstraße 3 (tel. 459 4735) (Weißensee).

Cheapest doubles DM95—98 (£40.75—42.00; $61—63)

Pension Finck, Güntzelstraße 54 (tel. 861 2940/861 8158) (Wilmersdorf).

City-Pension Alexandra, Wielandstraße 32 (tel. 881 2107) (Charlottenburg).

Hotel Transit, Hagelberger Straße 53—54 (tel. 785 5051) (Kreuzberg).

Pension Schultze, Friedrichrodaer Straße 13 (tel. 779 9070) (Steglitz). Breakfast not included.

Hotel-Pension Charlottenburg, Grolmanstraße 32/33 (tel. 881 5254) (Charlottenburg).

Hotel-Pension Leibniz, Leibnizstraße 59 (tel. 323 8495) (Charlottenburg).

Hotel-Pension Haus Konstanz, Konstanzer Straße 30 (tel. 860268) (Wilmersdorf).

Hotel Bogota, Schlüterstraße 45 (tel. 881 5001) (Charlottenburg).

Hotel-Pension Modena, Wielandstraße 26 (tel. 885 7010/883 5404) (Charlottenburg).

Pension Kramer, Eitelsdorfer Straße 35 (tel. 657 5656) (Köpenick).

Pension Ilse Altermann, Battenheimer Weg 10 (tel. 742 6977) (Neukölln).

Hotel Süden, Neuköllner Straße 217 (tel. 661 6093) (Neukölln).

Hotel-Pension Sickinger Hof, Beusselstraße 44 (tel. 345 3787) (Tiergarten).

Hotel-Pension Becker, Tranteraustraße 19 (tel. 861 8078/861 8079) (Wilmersdorf).

Hotel-Pension 'Paris 9', Ludwigkirchstraße 9 (tel. 881 8462/881 3080) (Wilmersdorf).

Cheapest doubles DM100—105 (£42.50—45.00; $65.00—67.50)

Hotelpension 'a b c', Grolmanstraße 32/33 (tel. 881 1496) (Charlottenburg).

Hotel Am Park-Pension, Sophie-Charlotten-Straße 57/58 (tel. 321 3485) (Charlottenburg).

Hotel-Pension Curtis, Pariser Straße 39/40 (tel. 883 4931) (Wilmersdorf).

Hotel Pichlers Viktoriagarten, Leonorenstraße 18–22 (tel. 771 6088) (Steglitz).

Pension Arkade, Kantstraße 34 (tel. 310824) (Charlottenburg).

Hotel 'Eremitage' Berlin, Schlüterstraße 54 (tel. 882 7151) (Charlottenburg).

Hotel-Pension Funk, Fasanenstraße 69 (tel. 882 7193) (Charlottenburg).

Pension Galerie 48, Leibnizstraße 48 (tel. 324 2658) (Charlottenburg).

Hotel-Pension 'Messe', Neue Kantstraße 5 (tel. 321 6446) (Charlottenburg).

Hotel-Pension Alster, Eisenacher Straße 10 (tel. 218 6952/214 1524) (Schöneberg).

Hotel Hospiz Friedenau, Fregestraße 68 (tel. 851 9017/851 9018) (Schöneberg).

Hotel Siemensstadt, Jugendweg 4 (tel. 382 8128) (Spandau).

Pension Werth, Kettinger Straße 56 (tel. 742 6439) (Tempelhof).

Hotel-Pension Margrit, Brandenburgische Straße 24 (tel. 883 7717) (Wilmersdorf).

Hotel-Pension Postillion, Gasteiner Straße 8 (tel. 875232) (Wilmersdorf).

Pension am Rüdesheimer Platz, Rüdesheimer Platz 7 (tel. 827917–0) (Wilmersdorf).

PRIVATE ROOMS & APARTMENTS

Berlin-Tourist-Information, Europa Center, Budapester Straße 45 (tel. 262 6031) (Charlottenburg). Around DM35 (£15; $22.50) per person, with breakfast for private rooms. Two-night minimum stay. For opening hours and directions, see the **Tourist Office** section above.

Europäisches Reisebüro, Alexanderplatz 5 (tel. 245 4415) (Mitte). Rooms DM18–30 (£7.75–13.00; $11.50–19.50) per person. Office open Mon.–Fri. 10 a.m.–6 p.m., Sat. 10 a.m.–5 p.m. S-Bahn and U-Bahn: Alexanderplatz.

Zeitraum, Horstweg 7 (tel. 325 6181) (Charlottenburg). From DM30 (£13; $19.50) per person in rooms and apartments. Office open Mon.–Fri. 9 a.m.–1 p.m. and 3–8 p.m., Sat. 10 a.m.–3 p.m. and 4–7 p.m.

Mitwohnzentrale, Kurfürstendamm 227/228, 2nd floor (tel. 883051) (Charlottenburg). Prices for apartments start around

DM35 (£15; $22.50) per person for one night, falling with the length of your stay. Open Mon.–Fri. 10 a.m.–6 p.m., Sat. 11 a.m.–3 p.m.

Mitwohn-Börse, Katzlerstraße 15 (tel. 217 0040/217 0041) (Schöneberg). U-Bahn: Yorckstraße.

Freiraum, Marienburger Straße 47 (tel. 426 5447) (Prenzlauer Berg). Also at Wiener Straße 14 (tel. 618 2008) (Kreuzberg), U-Bahn: Görlitzer Bahnhof, or bus 129.

Wohnagentur 'Last Minute', Yorckstraße 72 (tel. 786 5284/786 4836) (Schöneberg). U-Bahn: Yorckstraße, or bus 119.

Agentur 'Wohnwitz', Holsteinische Straße 55 (tel. 861 8222) (Wilmersdorf). Open Mon.–Fri. 10 a.m.–7 p.m., Sat. 11 a.m.–2 p.m. U-Bahn: Blissestraße.

HI HOSTELS

Advance reservation is advisable, particularly if you are travelling in summer, or will be arriving in Berlin at the weekend. Requests for reservations should be sent to the head office of the regional hostel association in Tempelhof: DJH Landesverband Berlin-Brandenburg, Tempelhofer Ufer 32, D-1000 Berlin 61 (tel. 262 3024). The hostels are open to HI members only. Cards can be purchased from the regional head office for around DM36 (£15.40; $23). Office open 10 a.m.–3 p.m. Mon., Wed. and Fri., and from 2–5.30 p.m. Tues. and Thurs.

'Ernst Reuter', Hermsdorfer Damm 48–50 (tel. 404 1610) (Hermsdorf). Midnight curfew. Juniors DM22 (£9.40; $14) for B&B. U-Bahn: Tegel (line 6), then bus 125 dir. Frohnau to the fourth stop.

Jugendgästehaus Berlin, Kluckstraße 3 (tel. 261 1097) (Tiergarten). Midnight curfew. Juniors DM27 (£11.50; $17.25) for B&B. Bus 129 from Kurfurstendamm towards Oranienplatz or Hermannplatz.

Jugendgästehaus Wannsee, Badeweg 1 (tel. 803 2034) (Wannsee). Midnight curfew. Juniors DM27 (£11.50; $17.25) for B&B. S-Bahn: Nikolassee (line 3) then a 10-minute walk towards the beach. The hostel is at the junction of Badeweg and Kronprinzessinnenweg.

HOSTELS/DORMITORY ACCOMMODATION

Jugendgästehaus Am Zoo, Hardenbergstraße 9a (tel. 312 9410) (Charlottenburg). Singles DM47 (£20; $30); doubles DM85 (£36.50; $54.75). DM35 (£15; $22.50) per person in quads. Without breakfast. U-Bahn: Ernst-Reuter-Platz.

Studentenhotel, Meininger Straße 10 (tel. 784 6720) (Schöneberg). B&B in doubles DM37 (£16; $24) per person, in quads DM33 (£14; $21) per person. U-Bahn: Rathaus Schoneberg, or bus 146 from Zoologischer Garten train station to the same stop.

Studentenwohnheim Hubertusallee, Hubertusallee 61, at the junction with Delbrückstraße (tel. 891 9718) (Wilmersdorf). Open Feb.–Oct. Students with ID pay DM40 (£17; $25.50) for singles, DM60 (£25.50; $38.25) for doubles, and DM70 (£30; $45) for triples. The prices for non-students are DM75 (£32; $48) for singles, DM90 (£38.50; $57.75) for doubles, and DM100 (£42.50; $65) for triples. Breakfast included. Bus 110 or 129.

Jugendgästehaus Central, Nikolsburger Straße 2–4 (tel. 870188) (Wilmersdorf). 1 a.m. curfew. Two- to six-bed rooms. DM31 (£13.25; $20) for B&B. Bed-linen DM7 (£3; $4.50). U-Bahn: Güntzelstraße.

Jugendgästehaus Feurigstraße, Feurigstraße 63 (tel. 781 5211/781 5212) (Schöneberg). DM32 (£13.75; $20.50) for B&B. Bed-linen DM3,50 (£1.50; $2.25). U-Bahn: Kleistpark.

Gästehaus Luftbrücke, Kolonnenstraße 10 (tel. 784 1037) (Schöneberg). Singles, doubles, triples and quads for DM40 (£17; $25.50) per person. Breakfast included. U-Bahn: Kleistpark.

Haus Sonnenland, Gartenfelder Straße 1 (tel. 334 4492) (Gartenfeld). DM28 (£12; $18) per person, including breakfast and evening meal. U-Bahn: Paulsternstraße.

Jugendgästehaus Deutsche Schreberjugend, Franz-Künstler-Straße 4–10 (tel. 615 1007) (Kreuzberg). DM31 (£13.25; $20) per person in doubles and triples. Breakfast DM1,50 (£0.60; $0.90). Bed-linen DM6 (£2.50; $3.75). U-Bahn: Hallesches Tor.

Jugendgästehaus Koloniestraße, Koloniestraße 23–24 (tel. 493 5075/493 5076) (Wedding). Dorms DM32 (£13.75; $20.50). Breakfast and evening meal DM3 (£1.25; $2). Bed-linen DM3,50 (£1.50; $2.25). U-Bahn: Osloer Straße.

Jugendgästehaus Nordnfer, Nordnfer 28 (tel. 451 7030) (Wedding). DM35 (£15; $22.50), including breakfast and bed-linen. U-Bahn: Westhafen. Buses: 105, 126.

Jugendgästehaus Tegel, Ziekowstraße 161 (tel. 433 3046) (Tegel). Quads DM35 (£15; $22.50) per person. Breakfast, evening meal and bed-linen included. U-Bahn: Tegel. Bus: 222.

Jugendhotel Berlin, Kaiserdamm 3 (tel. 322 1011) (Charlottenburg). Triples DM42 (£18; $27) per person for juniors (under 27 years). Breakfast included. Bed-linen DM7 (£3; $4.50). U-Bahn: Sophie-Charlotte-Platz.

Karl-Renner-Haus, Ringstraße 76 (tel. 833 5029/833 5030) (Lichterfelde). Two- to six-bed rooms for DM28 (£12; $18) per person.

Breakfast included. Bed-linen DM5 (£2.15; $3.25). S-Bahn: Lichterfelde West. Bus: 283.

Gästehaus 'Haus Wichern', Waldenser Straße 31 (tel. 395 4072) (Tiergarten). DM35−47 (£15−20; $22.50−30.00), including breakfast.

Touristenhaus Grünan, Dahmestraße 6 (tel. 676 4422) (Grünau). Quads DM35 (£15; $22.50) per person, including breakfast. Open all day. S-Bahn: Grünau (then take tram 86, direction Köpenick, to the second stop).

CVJM-Haus, Einemstraße 10 (tel. 264 9100) (Schöneberg). Singles and doubles DM40 (£17; $25.50) per person, including breakfast.

Jugend- and Sporthotel Gensler Straße, Gensler Straße 18 (tel. 976 5801) (Hohenschönhausen). Triples DM40 (£17; $25.50) per person, including breakfast.

INTERNATIONAL YOUTH CAMP

Internationales Jugendcamp, Ziekowstraße 161 (tel. 433 8640) (Reinickendorf-Hermsdorf). A similar idea to 'The Tent' in Munich; a large covered area, with mattresses and sheets provided. Open 21 June−31 Aug. Age limit 27. DM9 (£4; $6) per night. Bus 222 from the Tegel U-Bahn station.

CAMPING

The campsites below are open all year round. DM8 (£3.50; $5.25) per person is the standard charge at all four sites. Advance reservations can be made by contacting the Deutscher Camping Club e.V. at Geisbergstraße 11, D-1000 Berlin 30 (tel. 246071) (Schöneberg).

Kladow, Krampnitzerweg 111/117 (tel. 365 2797) (Spandau). From the Rathaus Spandau U-Bahn station take bus 135 to its terminus, then continue along Krampnitzerweg about 500m.

Haselhorst, Pulvermühlenweg (tel. 334 5955). From the Haselhorst U-Bahn station follow Daumster into Pulvermühlenweg.

Dreilinden, Kremnitz Ufer (Albrechts-Teerofen) (tel. 805 1201) (Wannsee). Bus 118 from the Oskar-Helene Heim U-Bahn station, then a 20-minute walk along Kremnitz Ufer to Albrechts-Teerofen.

International Campsite Krossinsee, Wernsdorfer Straße (tel. 685 8687) (Schmöckwitz). A 2.5km walk from the terminus of tram 86, across the bridge, then down the third turning on the right.

SLEEPING ROUGH

The Grunewald is the most obvious, but there are lots of places at the end of the S-Bahn lines, or along the shores of the Krossinsee.

If you are stuck for a bed, but do not want to sleep out, go to the Bahnhofsmission in Zoologischer Garten station, where you will be given a bed for DM15 (£6.50; $9.50). One night only.

Bremen (tel. code 0421)

TOURIST OFFICES

Verkehrsverein der Freien Hansestadt Bremen, Hillmannplatz 6, D-2800 Bremen 1 (tel. 30800–0). Open Mon.Thurs. 9 a.m.– 4 p.m., Fri. 9 a.m.–1.30 p.m. Contact this office only for information on hotels and for reservations.

Tourist-Information am Hauptbahnhof. Open Mon.–Wed., Fri. 9.30 a.m.–6.30 p.m., Thurs. 9.30 a.m.–8.30 p.m., Sat. 9.30 a.m.– 2 p.m., Sun. 9.30 a.m.–3.30 p.m. Information on the city and on accommodation. Outside the main train station (Bremen Hbf).

Tourist-Information Bremen-Nord, Alte Hafenstraße 30 (tel. 663031). Open Mon. 2–6 p.m., Tues.–Fri. 10 a.m.–6 p.m., Sat. 10 a.m.–2 p.m. Information on the city and on accommodation.

HOTELS, PENSIONS & GUESTHOUSES

Few of the city's cheaper hotels are located close to the centre, or to the train station.

Cheapest doubles DM70–75 (£30–32; $45–48)

Grollander Krug, Oldenburger Straße 11 (tel. 510755).

Gästehaus Walter, Buntentorsteinweg 86–88 (tel. 558027) Off Friedrich-Ebert-Straße, across the Kleine Weser.

Haus Neustadt, Graudenzer Straße 33 (tel. 551749). In the Süder-vorstadt district.

Enzensperger, Brautstraße 9 (tel. 503224). Reasonable location. Just across the Weser, between the Bürgermeister-Smidt-Brücke and the Wilhelm-Kaiser-Brücke.

Pension Kosch, Celler Straße 4 (tel. 447101). Close to the Weserstadion (home of Werder Bremen).

Hotel Falk, Osterholzer Heerstraße 154 (tel. 405600).

Cheapest doubles DM80 (£34.50; $51.75)

Pension Galerie, Thedinghauser Straße 46 (tel. 530753). In the area off Friedrich-Ebert-Straße.

Lutkemeyer, Rockwinkeler Landstraße 83 (tel. 259461).

Regenbogen Aopartements, Hastedter Osterdeich 206 (tel. 442769).

Hotel-Pension Weidmann, Am Schwarzen Meer 35 (tel. 494055). In the area close to the Weserstadion.

Cheapest doubles DM85 (£36.50; $54.75)

Krone, Hastedter Osterdeich 209b (tel. 443151).

Cheapest doubles DM90–95 (£38.50–40.75; $57.75–61.00)

Weltevreden, Am Dobben 62 (78015). Reasonable location, just outside the historic centre.

Pension Haus Bremen, Verdener Straße 47 (tel. 498 7777/498 7778). In the area close to the Weserstadion.

Heinisch, Wachmannstraße 26 (tel. 342925). By the Burgerpark, a 10-minute walk from Bremen Hbf. From the train station, head left and then turn left under the lines. At the fork in the road, head right along Hermann-Böse-Straße. Wachmannstraße is directly across the junction with Hollerallee when you reach the park.

Pension Atlantik, Hastedter Osterdeich 205 (tel. 444593/494225).

Haus Wiegmann, Kattenturmer Heerstraße 75 (tel. 874643).

Gasthof Zur Börse, Arster Heerstraße 35–37 (tel. 822658).

HI HOSTELS

Jugendgästehaus Bremen, Kalkstraße 6 (tel. 171369). 1 a.m. curfew. DM24–30 (£10.25–13; $15.50–19.50). Fine location by the Weser, a short walk from the city centre. From the train station walk down Bahnhofstraße, cross the water, and turn right along Am Wall past the windmill. Turn left off Am Wall down Bürgermeister-Smidt-Straße, then go right when you reach the river.

Jugendherberge Blumenthal, Bürgermeister-Dehnkamp-Straße 22 (tel. 601005). DM17,50–21,50 (£7.50–9.25; $11.25–14.00). Far from the centre.

HOSTELS

Seemannsheim Bremen, Jippen 1 (tel. 18361). Singles DM20–31 (£8.50–13.25; $12.75–20.00), doubles DM31–51 (£13.25–22.00; $20–33). In the same part of town as the DJH Jugendgästhaus, only slightly further out from the centre.

HI HOSTELS NEARBY

Jugendherberge Worpswede, Hammeweg 2, Worpswede (tel. 04792 1360). DM18,50−22,50 (£8−9.50; $12−14). Worpswede is about 16km from Bremen. No train service, but regular buses.

CAMPING

Campingplatz Freie Hansestadt Bremen, Am Stadtwaldsee 1 (tel. 212002). Close to the university. Bus 28 passes close to the site.

Cologne (Köln) (tel. code 0221)

TOURIST OFFICE

Verkehrsamt der Stadt Köln, Unter Fettenhennen 19, D-5000 Köln 1 (tel. 221 3345). May−Oct. open daily from 8 a.m.−10.30 p.m. (except Sun. and public holidays 9 a.m.−10.30 p.m.); Nov.−Apr. open daily from 8 a.m.−9 p.m. (except Sun. and public holidays 9.30 a.m.−7 p.m.). The office accepts requests to book hotel accommodation in advance by letter, but not by telephone. Room-finding service for those who arrive without prior reservation. DM5 (£2.15; $3.25) commission.

BASIC DIRECTIONS

Leaving Köln Hbf by the main exit on to Bahnhofvorplatz the vast bulk of the cathedral is to your left. Going right along the front of the train station as far as you can, and then following the street which runs away to your left, you arrive at the junction with Marzellanstraße. Across Bahnhofvorplatz from the train station, almost opposite the main entrance to the cathedral is the Tourist Office on Unter Fettenhennen. Running away from the cathedral near the Tourist Office is Hohe Straße. To the left of Hohe Straße is the old market (Alter Markt) and the Town Hall, beyond which is the Rhine. The Hohenzollern-brücke crosses the Rhine by the cathedral. The next bridge downstream is the Deutzer Brücke. Along the Rhine between the two are the Frankenwerft and the Rheingarten. Buses 32 and 33 from Köln Hbf wind their way through the area around the Town Hall before running the whole length of Severinstraße and on beyond the Severinstor.

HOTELS, PENSIONS & GUESTHOUSES
Cheapest doubles around DM60–65 (£25.50–28.00; $38.25–42.00)

Pension Kirchner, Richard-Wagner-Straße 18 (tel. 252977). A 20-minute walk from Köln Hbf. From the Neumarkt, follow Hahnenstraße, then go left at Pilgrimstraße, which leads into Richard-Wagner-Straße.

Hubertushof, Mühlenbach 30 (tel. 217386). A 10-minute walk from Köln Hbf, left off Hohe Pforte.

Schützenhof, Mengenicher Straße 12 (tel. 590 2739). Far from the centre in the suburb of Pesch. Take a train to Köln Westbahnhof then take tram 3 to the terminus on Venloerstraße. Continue on down Venloerstraße then go right at the fork in the road along Grevenbroicherstraße and Nüssenbergerstraße.

An der Oper, Auf der Ruhr 3 (tel. 245065). Just over 5 minutes' walk from Köln Hbf. Turn right off Hohe Straße along Minoritenstraße and continue straight on until Auf der Ruhr crosses Breite Straße.

Rossner, Jakordenstraße 19 (tel. 122703).

Cheapest doubles around DM70 (£30; $45)

Thielen Tourist, Brandenburger Straße 1–7 (tel. 123333).

Am Rathaus, Bürgerstraße 6 (tel. 216293). By the Town Hall, about 8 minutes' walk from Köln Hbf. Turn left off Hohe Straße at Große Budengasse, go straight on, then right at Bürgerstraße.

Flintsch, Moselstraße 16–20 (tel. 232142/237011). Take a local train to Köln Südbahnhof. Moselstraße is the street running along the front of the station.

Ziegenhagen, Plankgasse 62 (tel. 136461).

Cheapest doubles around DM75 (£32; $48)

Dom-Pension, Domstraße 28 (tel. 123742).

Friedrich, Domstraße 23 (tel. 123303).

Im Fuchsbau, Tempelstraße 26 (tel. 814602).

Cheapest doubles around DM80 (£34.50; $51.75)

Brandenburger Hof, Brandenburger Straße 2–4 (tel. 122889).

Pension Jansen, Richard-Wagner-Straße 18 (tel. 251875). See Pension Kirchner above for directions.

City-Hotel, Ursulagartenstraße 26 (tel. 133646). In a quiet street by St Ursula's Church, just under 10 minutes' walk from Köln Hbf. Follow Marzellanstraße to its end and turn left into Ursulaplatz from which Ursulagartenstraße is off to the right.

Heinzelmännchen, Hohe Pforte 5–7 (tel. 211217).

Haus Trost, Thebäerstraße 17 (tel. 516647). Take a local train to Köln Ehrenfeld then follow Stammstraße from the station and turn right along Simrockstraße into Thebäerstraße. A 5–10-minute walk from Köln Ehrenfeld.

Lindenhof, Lintgasse 7 (tel. 231242). From Hohe Straße turn left down Große Budengasse and continue on along Kleine Budengasse and Mühlengasse. Turn right down Unter Käster and then right again. Buses 132 and 133 from Köln Hbf pass the end of the street, but it takes just over 5 minutes to walk.

Graf Adolph, Adolphstraße 12 (tel. 816611). From Ottoplatz by the Köln Deutz train station, take Neuhöfferstraße and continue straight ahead until you reach Adolphstraße.

Weisser Schwan, Thieboldsgasse 133/135 (tel. 217697). The street runs off the Neumarkt. A 15–20-minute walk from Köln Hbf, but an easy walk from the U-Bahn station on the Neumarkt.

Zum Boor, Bonner Straße 217 (tel. 383998). Bus 32 from Köln Hbf runs along Bonner Straße.

Cristall, Ursulaplatz 9–11 (tel. 16300).

Berg, Brandenburger Straße 6 (tel. 121124).

Autohof SVG, Kreuznacher Straße 1 (tel. 380535/380536). Well out from the centre in the suburb of Raderberg. From Köln Hbf, take bus 133 to the junction of the Brühlerstraße with Raderthaler Gürtel and Raderberger Gürtel. Walk up Raderbergerstraße and take the first left.

Cheapest doubles around DM85 (£36.50; $54.75)

Rhein-Hotel St Martin, Frankenwerft 31–33 (tel. 234031/234032/234033).

Im Kupferkessel, Probsteigasse 6 (tel. 135338). From Bahnhofvorplatz, head away from the station down Ketzerstraße and then An den Dominikan. Keep on going straight ahead until you see Probsteigasse on the right off Christophstraße.

Haus Schallenberg, Bergisch-Gladbacher Straße 616 (tel. 633091/633092). Far from the centre but easy to reach. From Evertplatz take tram 16 to the junction of Isenburgstraße with Maria-Himmelfahrt, then walk up the latter on to Bergisch-Gladbacherstraße. The hotel is nearby.

Einig, Johannisstraße 71 (tel. 122128/137158)

Tagungs- und Gästehaus St Georg, Rolandstraße 61 (tel. 937 0200). Bus 32 or 33 from Köln Hbf or a 25-minute walk. Rolandstraße is to the right off Bonnerstraße just beyond the Severinstor.

Cheapest doubles around DM90 (£38.50; $57.75)

Alter Römer, Am Bollwerk 23 (tel. 212385/216290). One street back from the Frankenwerft, between Bischofsgartenstraße and Große Neugasse.
Weber, Jahnstraße 22 (tel. 233282). A 15—20-minute walk from the Köln Hbf. From the Neumarkt take Hahnenstraße, turn left down Mauritiussteinweg and go around the church to the start of Jahnstraße. You can take the U-Bahn to the Neumarkt from Köln Hbf. From Ottoplatz in front of the Köln Deutz train station, trams 1 and 2 run along Jahnstraße.
Breslauer Hof, Johannisstraße 56 (tel. 123009).
Em Blomekörvge, Josephstraße 15 (tel. 323660).

HI HOSTELS
Deutz, Siegestraße 5a (tel. 814711). Curfew 12.30 a.m. DM22 (£9.50; $14.25). Fills quickly. Reception opens 12.30 p.m. 150m from Köln-Deutz station. Well signposted.
Jugendgästehaus Köln-Riehl, An der Schanze 14 (tel. 767081). Reception opens at 11 a.m. DM29 (£12.50; $18.75). About 3km from the main train station. From Breslauer Platz, walk right down to the river, turn left, on under the Zoobrücke, along Niederlander Ufer into An der Schanze. From Köln Hbf take U-Bahn lines 5, 16 or 18 to Boltensternstraße.

HI HOSTELS NEARBY
'Jugendhof', Macherscheiderstraße 113, Neuss-Uedesheim (tel. 02101 39273). There are frequent connections between Cologne and Neuss by train and S-Bahn.

CAMPING
All the sites are quite a distance from the centre. If you take tram 16 to Marienburg there are two sites on the opposite side of the Rhine, about 15 minutes' walk over the Rodenkirchener Brücke in Köln-Poll.

Campingplatz der Stadt Köln, Weidenweg (tel. 831966). Open 1 May—10 Oct. Intended mainly for families, but you will not be turned away.
Alfred-Schutte-Allee (tel. 835989). Open 1 July—15 Sept. Site for young people.
Campingplatz Berger, Uferstraße 53a is in Köln-Rodenkirchen (tel. 392421). Open all year round.
Campingplatz Waldbad, Peter-Baum-Weg is in Köln-Dünnwald (tel. 603315). Open all year round.

Dresden (tel. code 0351/30603)

TOURIST OFFICES

Dresden-Werbung und Tourismus GmbH, Goetheallee 18, D-8053 Dresden (tel. 35621). Contact this office in advance for information on the city and help in planning your visit. On arrival in Dresden, you can obtain information and book accommodation at either of the two offices the Dresden Tourist Board operate in the city.

Tourist-Information, Prager Straße 10, D-8010 Dresden (tel. 495 5025). Open Apr.–Sept., Mon.–Sat. 9 a.m.–8 p.m., Sun. 9 a.m.–1 p.m.; Oct.–Mar., Mon.–Fri. 9 a.m.–8 p.m., Sat. 9 a.m.–2 p.m., Sun. 9 a.m.–1 p.m. A 5-minute walk from Dresden Hbf. You cannot miss the tall Hotel Newa on Pragerstraße on leaving the Dresden Hbf.

Tourist-Information (Branch Office), Neustädter Markt (tel. 53539). Open Mon.–Fri. 9 a.m.–6 p.m., weekends 9 a.m.–4 p.m. A 5–10-minute walk from Bahnhof Dresden-Neustadt. From the square in front of the statin, head left along Antonstraße into Platz der Einheit from which Straße der Befreiung runs to the Neustadter Markt with the famous Goldener Reiter statue. The Tourist Office is in the underpass leading to the Augustusbrücke.

ARRIVING BY TRAIN

Trains not terminating in Dresden frequently stop at Bahnhof Dresden-Neustadt only. However, there are regular connnecting trains between the two stations. It is unlikely that you will have to wait more than 15 minutes for a connection. Dresden Hbf and Dresden Neustadt are also linked by a frequent tram service (lines 3 and 11).

PUBLIC TRANSPORT

The Dresdner Verkehrsbetriebe AG operate an integrated transport system consisting mainly of the suburban railway (SV-Bahn), trams and buses. Their head office is near the Dresden-Neustadt station at Antonstraße 2a (tel. 52001). There is an information booth in front of Dresden Hbf. Dresden Transport sell a particularly cheap day-ticket for visitors at DM2 (£0.80; $1.25) in 1994). As well as the trams, buses and SV-Bahn, the ticket covers the Elbe ferry (on the route to the Pillnitz Palace) and the funicular railway.

TROUBLE SPOTS

Unlike in most German cities, the 1FC Dynamo Dresden football stadium is close to the main train station, so opposition fans walk to the ground, inevitably accompanied by groups of local fans taunting their rivals, and the police, complete with dogs, and riot police waiting in the wings. While the police in eastern Germany have learned from their western counterparts how to deal with the novel and hence very dangerous problem of football hooliganism which emerged in the wake of reunification, the spectacle can be unnerving for anyone unaccustomed to such a scene. There is virtually no chance of you being set upon, but, as with all such situations, there is no knowing what damage the throwing of even one missile can do. The best advice is to avoid the area between Dresden Hbf and the Altmarkt and Pirnaischer Platz before and after matches (usually Saturday afternoons, occasionally Wednesday evenings; match posters are displayed by Dresden Information).

FINDING ACCOMMODATION

Dresden is highly popular, so accommodation is best reserved in advance. The cheapest hotels and pensions are all located outside central Dresden, as are the majority of the private rooms on offer, which means you are going to have to use the public transport system to get to them. Several of the accommodation options listed below are in Radebeul which is, effectively, a suburb of Dresden. Those with a railpass can travel free to Radebeul by taking one of the frequent local trains.

HOTELS, PENSIONS & GUESTHOUSES

All hotel and pension prices include breakfast, except where indicated.

Doubles from DM55 (£23.50; $35.25)

Pension Schuster, Weinbergstraße 5, Boxdorf (tel. 460 9003).

Cheapest doubles DM60–65 (£25.50–28.00; $38.25–42.00)

Gästehaus Strehlen, August-Bebel-Straße 46 (tel. 471 9495).
Pension Omsewitz, Gompitzer Straße 24 (tel. 434650).
Pension Lorenz, Lindenplatz 1 (tel. 432 1014).
Pension Ullrich, Kauschaer Straße 37 (tel. 493 6146).

Cheapest doubles DM70–76 (£30.00–31.50; $45.00–48.75)

Pension Lößnitzer Hof, Meißner Straße 202, Radebeul (tel. 75353).
Pension Magvas, Gondelweg 3 (tel. 223 6084).

Pension Megiér, Lessingstraße 3 (tel. 575305).
Pension Steiner, Plattleite 49 (tel. 37376).
Touristenhotel Haus der Kultur und Bildung, Maternistraße 17 (tel. 484 5204).

Cheapest doubles DM80–85 (£34.50–36.50; $51.75–54.75)

Pension Im Grünen an der Elbe, Pillnitzer Landstraße 174 (tel. 376517). From Dresden Hbf take tram 10 to Altenbergerplatz, then change to bus 85, which runs along Pillnitzer Landstraße.
Pension Haus Höhenblick, Wachwitzer Höhenweg 28, Pappritz (tel. 36363). All rooms have shower and WC. Breakfast not included.
Pension Renate Deckwer, Rädestraße 26 (tel. 432 7192). All rooms have a shower and WC.
Pension Reiche, Meißner Landstraße 77 (tel. 434404).
Pension Augenwide, Wachwitzer Bergstraße 30 (tel. 376181).
Pension Edith, Prießnitzstraße 63 (tel. 579058).
Pension Trauschke, Eduard-Bilz-Straße 18, Radebeul (tel. 762757).

Cheapest doubles DM90–95 (£38.50–40.75; $57.75–61.00)

Fremdenheim Bellmann, Kretschmerstraße 16 (tel. 38150).
Pension Elchlepp, Dr-Rudolph-Friedrichs-Straße 15, Radebeul (tel. 728742). All rooms have shower and WC.
Hotel Stadt Rendsburg, Kamenzer Straße 1 (tel. 51551).
Pension Jarosch, Wilh.-Müller-Straße 3 (tel. 432 6790).
Gasthof Wilschdorf, Warnemünder Straße 1 (tel. 728127).

PRIVATE ROOMS
Available from the Tourist Office. Singles DM20–30 (£8.50—13.00; $12.75–19.50), doubles and larger rooms DM30–80 (£13.00–34.50; $19.50–51.75). 5DM (£2.15; $3.25) booking fee.

HI HOSTELS
Hübnerstraße 11 (tel. 471 0667). DM13,50 (£6; $9) for juniors, DM17,50 (£7.50; $11.25) for seniors. Tram 3 from Dresden Hbf to the Südvorstadt terminus, or a 10-minute walk from the station. Out of the exit to the right of the main exit, head right along Juri-Gagarin-Straße, then right again at Reichenbach, then straight on, along Altenzellerstraße to Hübnerstraße.
Oberloschwitz, Sierksstraße 33 (tel. 36672). DM12,50 (£5.35; $8) for juniors, DM16 (£7; $10.50) for seniors. Tram 5 to Nürnburger

Platz, then bus 61 or 93 to the second stop over the River Elbe, followed by a short walk.

Weintraubenstraße 12, Radebeul (tel. 74786) DM12,50 (£5.35; $8) for juniors; DM16 (£7; $10.50) for seniors. On the edge of the city. Short train trip to Radebeul, then a 10-minute walk to the hostel.

HI HOSTELS NEARBY

Pirna-Copitz, Birkwitzer Straße 51, Pirna (tel. 04 2388). Juniors DM12,50 (£5.35; $8), seniors DM17 (£7; $10.50). About 15 minutes' walk from the train station, bus L dir. Sportplatz. Pirna is about 16km from Dresden.

CAMPING

Mockritz, Boderitzer Straße 30 (tel. 471 8226/471 5250). Open all year. Bungalows for hire, sleeping up to four people. DM15−20 (£6.50−8.50; $9.50−12.75) p.p.

Wostra, Trieskestraße 100 (tel. 223 1903). Open Apr.−Oct. Tents for hire.

Caravan Camping, Werner Schmidt, Elsterweg 13 (tel. 460 9263). Open all year. Caravans for hire.

Bad Sonnenland, Dresdner Straße 115, Reichenberg (tel. 472 7788). Open Apr.−Oct. Four-bed bungalows available for DM50 (£21.50; $32.25) per night.

Mittelteich Moritzburg, Kalkreuther Straße, Moritzberg (tel. Moritzburg 423). Open Apr.−Oct. About 16km north-west of Dresden. The site offers a view over the lake to Moritzburg, the magnificent baroque hunting lodge of the Electors of Saxony. Take the Moritzburg bus from the bus station (100m to the right of the main exit of Dresden Hbf).

Eisenach (tel. code 0623)

TOURIST OFFICE

Fremdenverkehrsamt Eisenach-Information, Bahnhofstraße 3−5, D-5900 Eisenach (tel. 76162/2284 for general information; tel. 4895 for enquiries regarding accommodation). Open Mon. 10 a.m.−6 p.m., Tues.−Fri. 9 a.m.−6 p.m., Sat. 9 a.m.−3 p.m. After the office closes, the accommodation line is open for several hours. The accommodation service covers hotels, private rooms and apartments.

FINDING ACCOMMODATION

Just outside Eisenach is the Wartburg, the most visited tourist attraction in the former DDR. Although large numbers of coach tourists come to Eisenach, most stay somewhere else, which means that at most times of year finding a bed is easier than you might imagine. Nevertheless, finding a room can be difficult if you arrive at the weekend during the summer, as the town is very popular with people taking weekend breaks.

HOTEL

Burghof, Karlsplatz 24/26 (tel. 3387). The cheapest hotel in the town. B&B starts around DM38 (£16.25; $24.40) per person. From the Tourist Office continue along Bahnhofstraße through the old town gate into Karlsplatz.

PENSIONS

Anita Meister, Querstraße 11a. No telephone. B&B DM28 (£12; $18) per person. From Bahnhofstraße go through the old town gate into Karlsplatz. Both Alexanderstraße and Karlstraße on the opposite side of the square across Querstraße.

Palmental Haus II (tel. 72045). Bed only from DM28 (£12; $18) per person.

Haus Schönblick, Fritz-Koch-Straße 12 (tel. 2722). B&B from DM32,50 (£14; $21) per person.

PRIVATE ROOMS

Book through the Tourist Office. B&B from DM25 (£10.75; $16.25) per person.

APARTMENTS

Available from the Tourist Office. Well worth enquiring about if there are three or four of you. Stays of one night are possible, though your chances of finding a vacant apartment for a short stay are much slimmer if you are travelling in summer.

HI HOSTELS

Mariental 24 (tel. 3613). DM13,50 (£6; $9) for those aged under 27, DM16,50 (£7; $10.50) otherwise. About 25 minutes' walk from the bus and train stations. From Bahnhofstraße, turn left along Wartburg-Allee. Shortly after passing the Automobil-Pavilon, the street bends right to the junction of Marienstraße (right) and Mariental (left).

Bornstraße 7 (tel. 2012) Similar in price to the hostel on Mariental. A 15–20-minute walk from the bus and train stations. From

Bahnhofstraße head left along Wartburg-Allee, then turn left down Johann-Sebastian-Bach-Straße. At the fork in the road go left, then right down Bornstraße.

Frankfurt-am-Main (tel. code 069)

TOURIST OFFICES
In addition to two branch offices at the airport, there are two main offices in the city:

Tourist Information Hauptbahnhof (tel. 2123 8849/8851). At the main train station. Information and room-finding service (DM3 (£1.25; $2) commission). Open Mon.–Sat. 8 a.m.–9 p.m., Sun. 9.30 a.m.–8 p.m.
Tourist Information Römer, Römerberg 27 (tel. 2123 8708/8809). In the heart of the old town, a short walk from U-Bahn Römer. Open Mon.–Fri. 9 a.m.–6 p.m., Sat. & Sun. 9.30 a.m.–6 p.m.

TROUBLE SPOTS
Kaiserstraße (see **Basic Directions** below) is the main thorough-fare leading from Frankfurt Hbf to the city centre. The Red Light district is in the area to the left of Kaiserstraße. Kaiserstraße itself is safe, as is the Red Light district until the small hours of the morning. Even then it is not really violent, but it is the place you are most likely to find trouble in the city centre. The crowds drawn to the famous flea market (Flohmarkt), over the River Main from the Flosserbrücke, create opportunities for pickpockets. Use some common sense and you will have no problems.

BASIC DIRECTIONS
In front of Frankfurt Hbf is the busy Am Hauptbahnhof. To the right, this street runs into Baselerstraße, to the left, into Düsseldor-ferstraße which takes you to Platz der Republik. Of the streets opposite the station Kaiserstraße (take the underpass from Frank-furt Hbf) offers the simplest route if you are walking to the town centre. Follow Kaiserstraße into the Rossmarkt and on to the Hauptwache. The main shopping street Zeil begins at Hauptwache. From Zeil, you can reach the Römerberg, the heart of the beautiful Old Town, by turning right down Liebfrauenstraße, past the church and on down Neue Krame into the Römerberg. The walk from

Frankfurt Hbf to the Hauptwache takes about 15 minutes, another few minutes takes you to the Römerberg.

HOTELS, PENSIONS & GUESTHOUSES
Cheapest doubles around DM65 (£28; $42)

Goldener Stern, Karlsruherstraße 8 (tel. 233309). A 5-minute walk from the Hbf. Mannheimerstraße runs along the side of the station, right from the main exit. Karlsruherstraße is off Mannheimerstraße

Am Schloß, Bolongarostraße 168 (tel. 301849). Well out from the centre in the area between the Nied and Höchst S-Bahn stations.

Cheapest doubles around DM75 (£32; $48)

Atlas, Zimmerweg 1 (tel. 723946). Just over 5 minutes' walk from Frankfurt Hbf. From Platz der Republik head right along Mainzer Landstraße, then left at Zimmerweg. The S-Bahn station Taunus-anlage (all lines) is closer. Walk a short distance along Mainzer Landstraße, then right.

Bruns, Mendelssohnstraße 42 (tel. 748896). A 15-minute walk from Frankfurt Hbf. From Platz der Republik follow Friedrich-Ebert-Anlage, then go right along Wilhelm-Hauff-Straße, which leads into Mendelssohnstraße. Tram 19 heading left from Frankfurt Hbf passes the hotel. From U6: Westend, the hotel is only a short walk, left off Bockenheimer Landstraße.

Cheapest doubles around DM85 (£36.50; $54.75)

Backer, Mendelssohnstraße 92 (tel. 747992). Just over 15 minutes' walk from the Hbf. Easily accessible by tram or U-Bahn. See Hotel Bruns, above.

HI HOSTEL
'Haus der Jugend', Deutscherrnufer 12 (tel. 619058). Midnight curfew. DM20 (£8.50; $12.75). During the morning and evening rush hours, take bus 46 from Frankfurt Hbf to the Frankensteinerplatz stop, only 50m from the hostel. After 7.30 p.m., take tram 16 to Textorstraße, again leaving you a short walk. The closest S-Bahn station is about 8 minutes' walk away.

HI HOSTELS NEARBY
Beckerstraße 47, Aschaffenburg (tel. 06021 92763). Trains hourly (at least), 45-minute journey.

Schützengraben 5, Gelnhausen (tel. 06051 4424). Hourly trains, 40-minute trip.

Blücherstraße 66, Wiesbaden (tel. 0611 48657/449081). Forty-five minutes by S–14 or regular train, every 20–30 minutes.

CAMPING

Heddernheim, An der Sandelmühle 35 (tel. 570332). U2: Sandel-mühle is a short walk from the site by the River Nidda. S6: Escherheim is about 5 minutes' walk away.

Niederrad, Niederräder Ufer 2 (tel. 673846). Tram 15 runs past the Hbf to the site by the River Main. A 15–20-minute walk from the Hbf. Follow Baselerstraße into Baseler Platz, then cross the Main by the Friedensbrücke. Then turn right and walk along the side of the Main to the site, just beyond the next bridge (Main-Neckar-Brücke).

Freiburg-im-Breisgau (tel. code 0761)

TOURIST OFFICE

Freiburg-Information, Rotteckring 14, Postfach 1549, D-7800 Frei-burg-im-Breisgau (tel. 36890–90). Two blocks down Eisenbahn-straße from the train station. Open May–Oct., Mon.–Wed. and Sat. 9 a.m.–6 p.m., Thurs.–Fri. 9 a.m.–9 p.m., Sun. and public holidays 10 a.m.–12 p.m.; Nov.–Apr., Mon.–Fri. 9 a.m.–6 p.m., Sat. 9 a.m.–3 p.m. If you have not reserved accommodation in advance the staff will find hotel rooms and private rooms (*Privat-zimmer*) for a DM3 (£1.25; $2) commission. Private rooms are nor-mally only available for stays of three days and longer.

HOTELS, PENSIONS & GUESTHOUSES
Cheapest doubles around DM60 (£25.50; $38.25)

Gasthaus Zur Sonne, Hochdorferstraße 1 (tel. 07665–1288). In Hochdorf, 9.5km from the town centre.

Waldheim, Schauinslandstraße 20 (tel. 290494).

Cheapest doubles DM64–68 (£27.50–29.00; $41.25–43.50) B&B

Dionysos, Hirschstraße 2 (tel. 29353). A 20-minute walk from the centre, in the Guntersal area of town, 3km from the main train station. Nearest train station is Freiburg-Wiehre, a 15-minute walk away.

Gasthaus Löwen, Dürleberg 9 (tel. 07664 1260). In Opfingen, 9.5km from the centre.

Gasthaus Schauinsland, Grostalstraße 133 (tel. 69483). Rooms with showers. About 9.5km from Freiburg Hbf in Kappel.

Gasthaus Zur Tanne, Altgasse 2 (tel. 07664 1810). In Opfingen, about 9.5km from the centre.

Cheapest doubles around DM70 (£30; $45) B&B

Adler, Im Schulerdobel 3 (tel. 65413). In Kappel, 8km from the train station.

Zum Löwen, Breisgauer Straße 62 (tel. 84661). Three kilometres from the station in the opposite direction from the centre.

Cheapest doubles DM75 (£32; $48) with breakfast (unless otherwise indicated)

Schemmer, Eschholzstraße 63 (tel. 272424). Only 400m from Freiburg Hbf. From Bismarckallee, follow Wannerstraße past the bus station and the church into Eschholzstraße, then left.

Stadt Wien, Habsburgerstraße 48 (tel. 36560/39898). A 10–15-minute walk from the train station. Down Friedrichstraße and Friedrichring, then left. A 5–10-minute walk from the town centre.

Cheapest doubles around DM80 (£34.50; $51.75) B&B

Gasthaus Goldener Sternen, Emmendinger Straße 1 (tel. 278373). A 10-minute walk from Freiburg Hbf. Go left, then left off Stefan-Meier-Straße at Lortzingstraße. A 15-minute walk from the town centre.

Sonne, Basler Straße 58 (tel. 403048). About 15 minutes' walk from the stations, and from the centre. Cross the River Dreisam, down Heinrich-von-Stephan-Straße, then left.

Gasthaus St Ottilien, Kartauserstraße 135 (tel. 83470). On the Schloßberg, 6.5km from the station, 3km from the centre, uphill from the HI hostel.

PRIVATE ROOMS

Private rooms are best reserved in advance. However, although private rooms arranged through the Tourist Office are normally only available to those staying at least three days, if you are stuck for a bed it is doubtful if any owner with a room available will quibble about letting you stay one night if you ring up in the evening.

All of the following are only available to non-smokers, unless otherwise stated.

Cheapest rooms around DM19 (£8; $12) per person

Sumser, Neuhäuserstraße 2 (tel. 63623). No singles available. About 6.5km from the stations.

Burger, Waldallee 14 (tel. 84357). Singles and doubles. About 3km from the stations, in the opposite direction from the town centre.

Cheapest rooms around DM20–23 (£8.50–10.00; $12.75–15.00) p.p.

Faubert, Häherweg 25 (tel. 131651). Singles and doubles, with shower and WC. About 3km from the stations, in the opposite direction from the town centre.

Höll, Haierweg 30 (tel. 445343). Singles not available. About 1.5km from the stations, slightly further from the centre.

Brodmann, Langackern 21 (tel. 29397). Singles about 20% more expensive. About 15–20 minutes' walk from the centre. About 3km from Freiburg Hbf. Closest train station is Freiburg-Wiehre.

Heise, Kleintalstraße 58 (tel. 62927). No singles. About 6.5km from the stations.

Kern, Im Bohrer 46 (tel. 29474). Doubles only. About 15–20 minutes' walk from the centre. About 3km from Freiburg Hbf. Closest train station is Freiburg-Wiehre.

Beneke, Darriwald 1 (tel. 07665 40893). On the north-west outskirts of the city.

Brüstle, Kleintalstraße 62 (tel. 63021/63308). Smokers welcome.

Schuler, Großtalstraße 18 (tel. 67193).

Wehrle, Kleintalstraße 36 (tel. 65474). Smokers welcome.

Cheapest rooms around DM24–25 (£10.25–10.75; $15.40–16.25) p.p.

Tritschler, Ziegelhofstraße 40 (tel. 86077). Singles only. About 3km from the stations in the opposite direction from the centre of town. Smokers welcome.

Busse, Waldseestraße 77 (tel. 72938). Singles and doubles. Singles are slightly more expensive. Near the Mösle-Park campsite. Tram 1 dir: Litterweiler from Freiburg Hbf to Stadthalle or the terminus.

Ihde, Marchstraße 5 (tel. 273421). No singles. A 10-minute walk from the stations.

Hug, Kleintalstraße 40 (tel. 67714). Rooms on a farm in Kappel, south-east of the city centre. Smokers welcome.

Cheapest rooms around DM26,50 (£11.40; $17) p.p.

Schuler, Eulenweg 6 (tel. 131230). Smokers welcome.

Cheapest rooms around DM30 (£13; $19.50) p.p.

Ehret, Mozartstraße 48 (tel. 33387). Two singles only. A 15–20-minute walk from the stations. Follow the ring road from Friedrichstraße, then go left after Stadtstraße, along the side of the park where Leopoldring joins Schloßbergring. A 10-minute walk from the centre.

HI HOSTEL
Kartäuserstraße 151 (tel. 67656). Curfew 11.30 p.m. DM19 (£8; $12). Far from the centre. Tram 1 dir. Littenweiler from the station to Römerhof. Along Fritz-Geiges-Straße, over the water, then right.

UNIVERSITY ACCOMMODATION
Enquiries about the availability of rooms during the university vacation to 'Studentenhaus Alte Universität', Wohnraumabteilung, Bertoldstraße 12, D-7800 Freiburg (tel. 210 1272).

CAMPING
Hirzberg, Kartäuserstraße 99 (tel. 35054). Open 1 Apr.–15 Oct. DM3 (£1.25; $2) per tent, DM6 (£2.50; $3.75) per person. Tram 1 dir. Littenweiler to Messeplatz from Freiburg Hbf. A 20-minute walk from the nearest train station, Freiburg-Wiehre on the Höllentalbahn. Go right from the station along Turkenlouisstraße, left up Hildastraße, then right along Kartäuserstraße. A 10–15-minute walk from the town centre. Go right from the Schwabentor, then left along Kartäuserstraße.

Mösle-Park (tel. 72938). Open 20 Mar.–31 Oct. DM3–5 (£1.25–2.15; $2.00–3.25) per tent, DM7,50 (£3.25; $4.75) per person. Near the FFC stadium. Tram 1 dir. Littenweiler from Freiburg Hbf to the Stadthalle. A 15–20-minute walk from the nearest train station, Freiburg-Wiehre. Right from the station to the end of Turkenlouisstraße, left up Dreikönigstraße, right along Talstraße, then right down Schützenallee, from which you can see the stadium complex. A 20-minute walk from the town centre.

St Georg, Basler Landstraße 62 (tel. 43183). Open all year. DM4–
5 (£1.75–2.15; $2.75–3.25) per tent, DM6,50 (£2.75; $4.25) per
person. A 25-minute walk from the centre, and from Freiburg
Hbf. Cross the Dreisam, on down Heinrich-von-Stephan-Straße,
then right. Closest station is Freiburg St Georgen, about 5–10
minutes' walk from the site.

There are another two sites in Freiburg-Hochdorf, about 6.5km out
from the centre, but these sites cater more for those with caravans/
caravanettes. Although prices per person are similar to those at the
sites above, prices for tents are much higher at around DM7,50–
8,50 (£3.25–3.75; $5.00–5.50).

Tunisee (tel. 07665 2249/1249). Open 1 Apr.–31 Oct. The cheaper
of the two sites.
Breisgau (tel. 07665 2346). Open all year.

HI HOSTEL NEARBY
Rheinuferstraße 12, Breisach-am-Rhein (tel. 07667 7665). DM16
(£7; $10.50). Breisach is a beautiful small town about 19km from
Freiburg. Trains and/or German railway buses hourly. (German
railpasses are valid on these DB buses.)

Hamburg (tel. code 040)

TOURIST OFFICES
Tourist Information im Hauptbahnhof (tel. 30051 230). By the
main exit on to Kirchenallee. Open daily 7 a.m.–11 p.m.
Tourist Information am Hafen, St Pauli Landungsbrücken (tel.
30051 200). Between landing stages 4 and 5 of the port. Open
daily Mar.–Oct., 9 a.m.–6 p.m., at other times, 10 a.m.–5 p.m.
Tourist Information im Flughafen (tel. 30051 240). In the airport
at Terminal 3 (Arrivals). Open daily 8 a.m.–11 p.m.
Tourismus-Zentrale Hamburg GmbH, Postfach 10 22 49, D-2000
Hamburg (tel. 30051 0). Contact this office to reserve hotel
accommodation in advance.

BASIC DIRECTIONS
The area around Hamburg Hbf contains some of the city's least
expensive hotels. Leaving the train station by the main exit on to
Kirchenallee and heading left you arrive at Hachmannplatz. At this

point, Kirchenallee runs into St Georg-Straße, while Lange Reihe runs away to your right. Turning around so that Lange Reihe is on your left, then walking along Kirchenallee, you come to Ellmenreichstraße on the left. This street leads into Hansaplatz, as does the next street on the left, Bremer Reihe. Continuing along Kirchenallee, you reach Steintorplatz, from which three streets run off to the left: sharp left is Steintorweg, leading into Bremer Reihe, then Steindamm, then, almost at a right angle to Kirchenallee is Adenauerallee. While there are relatively inexpensive hotels in all of these streets, Bremer Reihe and Steindamm offer the most possibilities. Unfortunately, the cheapest hotels in these streets are often used by prostitutes, which, even though the hotels are invariably safe for you and your belongings, hardly makes for a peaceful night.

HOTELS
Cheapest doubles around DM70 (£30; $45)

Inter-Rast, Reeperbahn 154166 (tel. 311591). S-Bahn: Reeperbahn. In the Red Light district. Street noise is a problem, unless you are a sound sleeper.

Cheapest doubles around DM75 (£32; $48)

Kochler, Bremer Reihe (tel. 249511). S-Bahn/U-Bahn: Hauptbahnhof.
Schanzenstern, Bartelsstraße 13 (tel. 439 8441). S-Bahn: Sternschanze. Bartelsstraße runs between Schanzenstraße and Susannenstraße.

Cheapest doubles around DM80 (£34.50; $51.75)

Auto-Hotel 'Am Hafen', Spielbudenplatz 11 (tel. 316631). S-Bahn: Reeperbahn. Walk up the Reeperbahn, right at Davidstraße, then left.
Benecke, Lange Reihe 54–56 (tel. 245860). S-Bahn/U-Bahn: Hauptbahnhof.
Wernecke, Hartungstraße 7a (tel. 455357). U-Bahn: Hallerstraße, then a few minutes' walk down Rothenbaumchaussee, passing Hermann-Behn-Weg to Hartungstraße on the right. A 10-minute walk from mainline S-Bahn station Dammtor. Follow Rothenbaumchaussee from Theodor-Heuss-Platz to Hartungstraße on the left.

Cheapest doubles around DM85 (£36.50; $54.75) S-Bahn/U-Bahn stop Hauptbahnhof, unless otherwise indicated

Village, Steindamm 4 (tel. 246137).
Polo, Adenauerallee 7 (tel. 280 3556).
Sarah Petersen, Lange Reihe 50 (tel. 249826).
Hager, Hansaplatz 7 (tel. 243404).
Kieler Hof, Bremer Reihe 15 (tel. 243024).
Remstal, Steintorweg 2 (tel. 244560).
Pfeifer, Hallerstraße 2 (tel. 447830). U-Bahn: Hallerstraße.
Ingeborg, Hartungstraße 7a (tel. 455357). See Hotel Wernecke above.
Garni Schaub, Martinistraße 12 (tel. 460 3430). U-Bahn: Eppen-
    dorfer Baum. Follow Eppendorfer Baum across Hegestraße into
    Curschmannstraße, which is crossed by Martinistraße.

HI HOSTELS
'Auf dem Stintfang', Alfred-Wegener-Weg 5 (tel. 313488). Curfew
    1 a.m. DM15–17,50 (£6.50–7.50; $9.50–11.25) From the
    Hauptbahnhof, take S1, S2, S3 (S-Bahn free with railpasses) or
    the U3 to Landungsbrücke. The hostel is on top of the hill.
Jugendgästehaus 'Horner-Rennbahn', Rennbahnstraße 100 (tel.
    651 1671). Open Mar.–Dec. DM15–17,50 (£6.50–7.50; $9.50–
    11.25) Curfew 1 a.m. Quite far out. U3 to Horner-Rennbahn,
    then a 10-minute walk. Alternatively take the Wandsbek bus
    from the centre.

HOSTELS
Zeltdorf Hamburg, Sylvesterallee 3 (tel. 831 9939). DM17,50 (£7.50;
    $11.25). Open May–Sept. S21, S3 to Stellingen, and bus 180.
Kolpinghaus St Georg, Schmilinskystraße 78 (tel. 246609). Recep-
    tion open round the clock. Singles DM41 (£17.50; $26.25),
    doubles DM65–80 (£28.00–34.50; $42.00–51.75), triples
    DM100 (£42.50; $65). A 10-minute walk from Hamburg Hbf.
Jugendhotel MUI, Budapester Straße 45 (tel. 431169). Singles
    around DM48 (£20.50; $30.75), doubles from DM65 (£28; $42),
    larger rooms around DM28 (£12; $18). U-Bahn: St Pauli, then
    walk along Budapesterstraße.
Sternschanze, Schanzenstraße 101 (tel. 433389). S-Bahn: Stern-
    schanze. Singles DM45 (£19.25; $29), doubles DM75 (£32; $48).

HI HOSTELS NEARBY
Soltauerstraße 133, Luneberg (tel. 04131 41864). The beautiful
    town of Luneberg is about 48km from Hamburg. Frequent trains.
    About 45 minutes from Hamburg Hbf.

Konrad-Adenauer-Ring 2, Bad Oldesloe (tel. 04531 504294). Trains at least twice hourly, 25–45 minute trip depending on classification of train.

CAMPING

Buchholz, Kielerstraße 374 (tel. 540 4532). Near the Hamburger SV football stadium. S3 dir. Pinneberg, or S21 dir. Elbgaustraße to the Stellingren (Volksparkstadion) stop.

Ramcke, Kielerstraße 620 (tel. 570 5121).

Anders, Kielerstraße 650 (tel. 570 4498).

City Camping Park, Kronsaalweg, 86/Kielerstraße (tel. 540 4994).

Hannover (tel. code 0511)

TOURIST OFFICES

Hannover Information, Ernst-August-Platz 2 (tel. 301422). Near Hannover Hbf. Open Mon.–Fri. 8.30 a.m.–6 p.m., Sat. 8.30 a.m.–2 p.m.

Amt für Fremdenverkehrs und Kongreßwesen, Friedrichswall 5, Postfach 404, D-3000 Hannover. Write to this office at least three weeks before your arrival if you want to reserve accommodation (including private rooms).

TRADE FAIRS

Unlike in most other German cities, there are no hotel rooms available in the DM30–40 (£13.00–17.00; $19.50–25.50) per person range, as accommodation prices are inflated by the large number of trade fairs the city plays host to. If possible, try not to arrive during a fair, as finding a bed of any sort becomes very difficult. Dates of the fairs are available from Tour Consult in the UK, Nyumbani, Lynwick Street, Rudgwick, Sussex RH12 3DJ (tel. 040382 2837), from the German National Tourist Office in London, from the Hannover Trade Fair Organization in Croydon (tel. 081 688 9541), or from Tourist Offices in Germany.

HOTELS
Cheapest doubles around DM80 (£34.50; $51.75)

Heise, Fritz-Erler-Straße 1 (tel. 401335). About 10km west of Hannover Hbf, in Seelze.

Flora, Heinrichstraße 36 (tel. 342334). Triples are available at around the same price p.p. as doubles. Only 800m from Hannover Hbf. From the rear exit walk right until you see Volgersweg heading left off Augustenstraße. Heinrichstraße runs parallel to the right of Volgersweg on the other side of Berliner Allee.

Cheapest doubles around DM90 (£38.50; $57.75)

Hotel Haus Tanneneck, Brehmstraße 80 (tel. 818650). About 3km from the train station. Bus 39 from Hannover Hbf runs along Brehmstraße. Closest train station is Hannover-Bismarckstraße.
Hospiz am Bahnhof, Joachimstraße 2 (tel. 324297). A few minutes' walk from the train station, to the left of Ernst-August-Platz.
Hotel Eilenriede, Guerickestraße 32 (tel. 547 6652). About 5km from Hannover Hbf. Follow Klingerstraße from Klingerstraße U-Bahn stop. Guerickstraße is to the left.
Hotel Eden, Waldhausenstraße 30 (tel. 830430). A short walk from U-Bahn Döhrener Turm.

PRIVATE ROOMS
Bed and breakfast accommodation is available with local families during the Hannover Fair. Singles cost around DM60 (£25.50; $38.25), doubles around DM100 (£42.50; $65). Book in advance (see above), or make enquiries on arrival at the Tourist Office, or at the airport (Arrival Level A, Gates 1–6).

HI HOSTELS
Ferdinand-Wilhelm-Fricke-Weg 1 (tel. 131 7674). DM16 (£6.70; $10). A more expensive Jugendgästehaus operates at the same location. Five minutes away from the football stadium (Niedersachsen-Stadion, home of Hannover 96).
Naturfreundhaus in der Eilenriede, Hermann-Bahlsen-Allee 8 (tel. 691493). Stadtbahn U3 dir. Lahe or U7 dir. Fasanenkrug to Spannhagengarten, or a 30-minute walk from the station.

HI HOSTELS NEARBY
If the hostels in Hannover are full and you cannot afford a hotel or private room, there are HI hostels in three towns near Hannover, all of which are well worth visiting in their own right.

Weghausstraße 2, Celle (tel. 05141 53208). At least two trains each hour, 20 minutes by express train, 30–45 minutes by local train.
Fischbeckerstraße 33, Hameln (of Pied Piper fame) (tel. 05151 3425). Hourly trains, 45-minute trip.
Schirrmannweg 4, Hildesheim (tel. 05121 42717). Trains at least once an hour, 25-minute trip by local train.

CAMPING
Birkensee, Hannover-Laatzen (tel. 529962). Laatzen is a 10-minute journey from Hannover Hbf. Frequent local trains.

Heidelberg (tel. code 06221)

TOURIST OFFICES
Verkehrsverein Heidelberg, Postfach 10 58 60, D-6900 Heidelberg 1 (tel. 10821). Room reservations and information in advance.

Tourist-Information am Hauptbahnhof (tel. 21341). On the square outside the main train station. General information and a room-finding service. DM4 (£1.75; $2.50) commission. Open Mar.–Oct., Mon.–Sat. 10 a.m.–6 p.m., Sun. 10 a.m.–3 p.m.; at other times, Mon.–Sat. 9 a.m.–7 p.m.; Sun. 10 a.m.–3 p.m. When closed, details of hotels with rooms available at closing time are posted outside.

Tourist-Information am Schloß, Neue Schloßtraße 54. Open 10 a.m.–5 p.m. At the top of the Bergbahn funicular railway, a short walk from the castle.

Tourist-Information Neckarmünzplatz. Open 9 a.m.–6.30 p.m. (closed in winter). Follow the River Neckar upstream from the Karl-Theodor-Brücke (Alter Brücke) along Am Hackteufel to the coach park.

BASIC DIRECTIONS
The main train station (Heidelberg Hbf) is about 20 minutes' walk from the town centre. Buses 10 and 11 link Heidelberg Hbf with Universitätsplatz. Bus 33 runs from the station to the Kornmarkt, just beyond Marktplatz, while bus 11 continues from Universitats-platz to the Bergbahn stop, close to the Kornmarkt at the foot of the funicular railway leading up to the castle and the Königsstühl. Railpass holders can save money by taking a train from Heidelberg Hbf to Heidelberg-Karlstor, about 8 minutes' walk from the Marktplatz.

FINDING ACCOMMODATION
Finding suitable accommodation can be difficult in Heidelberg because the city is popular with older, more affluent tourists, guaranteeing the hotels a steady trade and pushing hotel prices above the norm for Germany. As the city also receives large numbers of young visitors, you cannot always count on getting a

bed in the HI hostel, even with its large capacity (451 beds). Even camping is not without its problems: the two sites are about 8km out of town, and although there is a train station nearby, the service is so infrequent that you will almost certainly have to travel by bus, adding to the cost of an overnight stay at either of the sites.

HOTELS
Cheapest doubles around DM45 (£19.25; $29)

Jeske, Mittelbadgasse 2 (tel. 23733). Two- to five-bed rooms. All the same price p.p. Right in the centre of the Old Town. Understandably popular, so try to reserve ahead. Mittelbadgasse runs off the Marktplatz. Also has dorm beds from DM22,50 (£9.75; $14.50).

Cheapest doubles around DM55 (£23.50; $35.25)

Waldhorn, Peter-Wenzel-Weg 11 (tel. 800294). Beautifully located, high in the hills above the suburb of Ziegelhausen. Fine if you have your own transport.

Cheapest doubles DM70–80 (£30.00–34.50; $45.00–51.75)

Alter Kohlhof, Kohlhof 5 (tel. 21915). Near the Königsstuhl, in the hills above the castle.
Goldenes Lamm, Pfarrgasse 3 (tel. 480834).
Elite, Bunsenstraße 15 (tel. 25734). Turn right off Bahnhofstraße down Landhausstraße, then left along Bunsenstraße.
Endrich, Friedhofweg 28 (tel. 801086). In the suburb of Ziegelhausen.
Haus Sedlmayer, Gerhart-Hauptmann-Straße 5 (tel. 412872/402372). In Neuenheim. A 15-minute walk from Heidelberg Hbf. Cross the Neckar by the Ernst-Walz-Brücke, go straight ahead on Berlinerstraße, then right at Gerhart-Hauptmann-Straße.

Cheapest doubles DM85–90 (£36.50–38.50; $54.75–57.75)

Auerstein, Dossenheimer Landstraße 82 (tel. 480798).
Goldene Rose Kirchheim, Hegenichstraße 10 (tel. 782058).
Kohler, Goethestraße 2 (tel. 24360/166088). Right off Bahnhofstraße shortly after Landhausstraße.
Burgfreiheit, Am Schloßeingang (tel. 22768). By the entrance to the castle.

Zum Pfalzgrafen, Kettengasse 21 (tel. 20489). Centrally located. Kettengasse runs off the Marktplatz.

PRIVATE ROOMS
The staff in the second-hand clothes shop **Flic-Flac** at Untere Straße 12 can help young travellers find lodgings with local people. Untere Straße runs between the Heumarkt and the Fischmarkt.

HI HOSTEL
Tiergartenstraße 5 (tel. 412066). DM18 (£7.75; $11.50). About 4km from Heidelberg Hbf. Bus 33 from the station, or Bismarckplatz. After 8 p.m., tram 1 to Chirurgische Klinik, then bus 330 to the first stop after the zoo.

HI HOSTELS NEARBY
'Lindenhof', Rheinpromenade 21, Mannheim (tel. 0621 822718). DM15 (£6.50; $9.50). In many ways the best hostel option for anyone with a railpass. Set on the banks of the Rhine, the Mannheim hostel is both cheaper and more pleasant to stay in than the Heidelberg hostel. Midnight curfew. 10—15 minutes' walk from Mannheim Hbf (main station). Train journey from Heidelberg around 12—20 minutes.

As well as the hostel in Mannheim, railpass holders stuck for a bed have the option of staying in the HI hostels in Worms or Speyer, two towns well worth a visit in their own right. There are frequent trains between Mannheim and Worms. Local trains take about 20 minutes. Journey time from Heidelberg to Speyer is about 1 hour. You may have to change at Mannheim or Ludwigshafen. Deutsche Bundesbahn bus 7007 provides a direct connection between the two towns (1 hour trip, railpasses valid). The bus leaves from Stance 2 at Heidelberg Hbf.

Dechaneigasse 1, Worms (tel. 06241 27580). The hostel is about 15 minutes' walk from Worms Hbf, looking out on to the cathedral (Dom). Walk right from the cathedral along Bahnhofstraße, left up Kriemhildenstraße and then right along Lutherring to the cathedral.
Geibstraße 5, Speyer (tel. 06232 75380). About 3km from Speyer Hbf. Bus 2 (phone the hostel or the Tourist Office in Speyer tel. 06232 14395, to check this).

CAMPING
Haide (tel. 06223 2111). Located between Ziegelhausen and Kleingemünd. Bus 35 to the Orthopedic Clinic in Schlierbach-

Ziegelhausen, about 8km out of town. The site is across the Neckar. Popular with groups on camping holidays.

Neckartal (tel. 06221 802506). Same bus as above, but get off at the Im Grund stop. The site is near the clinic. More basic than the site across the river, but perfectly adequate. Tends to be free of groups. Passports held at reception, which means you cannot leave before the office opens at 8 a.m.

CAMPING NEARBY
'Strandbad', Karin Ebner, Mannheim-Neckarau (tel. 0621 856240). Probably the best site if you have a railpass. The site is close to Mannheim-Neckarau station. Frequent trains from Mannheim Hbf. Last train around 11.45 p.m. except Sat. and Sun. night. Also local buses. About 3km from Mannheim Hbf, so you will pay less travelling by bus to this site than those above. If you stay late in Heidelberg there are trains to Mannheim Hbf at 11.49 p.m., 1.20 a.m. and various trains between 2–3 a.m. (check times locally).

Kiel (tel. code 0431)

TOURIST OFFICE
Tourist Information Kiel e.V., Sophienblatt 30, D-2300 Kiel 1 (tel. 67910–18). A few minutes' walk from the train station.

HOTELS, PENSIONS & GUESTHOUSES
Cheapest doubles around DM40 (£17; $25.50)

Pension Schnoor, Hof Wulfsdorf 5 (tel. 04348 1479/8266). About 9.5km out of town in Probsteierhagen.

Cheapest doubles around DM50 (£21.50; $32.25)

Hotel Neu-Schonberg, Strandstraße 207 (tel. 04344 8083). In Schonberg, 14.5km from the centre.

Cheapest doubles DM55–66 (£23.50–28.25; $35.25–42.50)

Pension-Gasthof Margarethenhöh, Kirschberg 17 (tel. 202725). In Kiel-Dietrichsdorf, 6km from the centre.

Gasthaus Landwehr, Am Plotzenbrook 3 (tel. 04346 289). Singles are similarly priced. In Landwehr, 6km from the town centre.

Gasthaus Meyer, Rosenkranzer Weg 15 (tel. 04346 6596). In Schinkel, 6km from centre.

Gaststätte-Pension Villa Fernsicht, Fernsichtweg (tel. 04307 222). In Raisdorf, 6.5km from the centre.

Pension Waldeck, Tröndelweg 11 (tel. 722311, 727605). In Kiel-Ellerbek, 5km from the centre.

Hotel Dietrichsdorfer Hof, Heikendorfer Weg 54 (tel. 26108). In Kiel-Dietrichsdorf. 5km from the centre. Some basic doubles for DM66 (£28.25; $42.50).

Cheapest doubles around DM70–75 (£30–32; $45–48)

Pension Acht, Julienstraße 11 (tel. 721113/729080). In Kiel-Ellerbek.

Privat Pension Karin Krauthammer, Grabastraße 73 (tel. 722810). In Kiel-Ellerbek, 3km from the centre.

Hotel Zur Kreuzung, An der B4 (tel. 04322–4586). In Bordesholm, about 19km from the centre.

Hotel Runge, Elisabethstraße. 16 (tel. 731992). In Kiel-Gaarden, 2.5km from the centre.

Cheapest doubles around DM78–85 (£33.50–36.50; $50.25–54.75)

Reimers Gaststatte, Dorfstraße 2 (tel. 783108). In Kiel-Elmschenhagen, 5km from the centre.

Pension Petra, Gravensteiner Straße 4 (tel. 362100/362021). In Kiel-Holtenau, 6km from the centre.

Hotel Zum Fritz Reuter, Langer Segen 5a (tel. 561016).

Hotel Rendsburger Hof, Rendsburger Landstraße 363 (tel. 690131).

Hotel-Pension Altenholz, Kronsberg 18 (tel. 321073). In Kiel-Altenholz.

Pension Haus Lucija, Schusterkrug 11 (tel. 391366). In Kiel-Holtenau.

HI HOSTEL
Johannesstraße 1 (tel. 731488). In Kiel-Gaarden, about 1.5km from the centre. Bus 4, 24, 34 or 64 to Karlstal, then walk up Schulstraße into Johannesstraße and go left.

HI HOSTEL NEARBY
'Haus der Jugend', Franz-Rohwer-Straße 10, Neumünster (tel. 04321 403416). Hourly trains, 20-minute journey.

CAMPING
Campingplatz Falckenstein, Palisadenweg 171 (tel. 392078). DM5 (£2.15; $3.25) for a small tent; same fee per person. In Kiel-Friedrichsort, 12km from the town centre.

Leipzig (tel. code 0341)

TOURIST OFFICES
Rat der Stadt Leipzig, Fremdenverkehrsamt und Kongreßamt, Hainstraße 16–18, D-7010 Leipzig. The office offers a full information and accommodation service if you contact them in advance. The Tourist Board operate several offices in the city and at the airport:

Tourist-Information/Zimmervermittlung Sachsenplatz 1 (tel. 79590). General information and a room-finding service for those arriving without prior reservations. Tourist Information open Mon.–Fri. 9 a.m.–7 p.m., Sat. 9 a.m.–2 p.m. Accommodation Service open Mon.–Fri. 9 a.m.–8 p.m., Sat. and Sun. 9.30 a.m.–2 p.m. A five-minute walk from Leipzig Hbf. Head straight on from the station across Platz der Republik and Richard-Wagner-Straße until you reach Bruhl. Head right, then left at Katharinenstraße to Sachsenplatz.
Leipzig-Information, Hauptbahnhof (tel. 275318). Open Mon.–Fri. 9 a.m.–6 p.m., Sat. 9 a.m.–12 p.m. In the Westhalle of Leipzig Hbf.
Flughafen Leipzig-Halle. Open Mon.–Fri. 7 a.m.–9 p.m., Sat. and Sun. 9 a.m.–6 p.m.

HOTELS
All of the following include breakfast, except where indicated.

Cheapest doubles DM60–70 (£25.50–30.00; $38.25–45.00)

Grünau, Gäartnerstraße 177 (tel. 412 6156).
Pension Hillerman, Rosa-Luxemburg-Straße 2 (tel. 282482). Breakfast not included.

Cheapest doubles DM80–85 (£34.50–36.50; $51.75–54.75)

Am Park, Grünauer Allee 37 (tel. 412 6156).
Schönan, Garskestraße 5 (tel. 411 5013).

Pension Am Zoo, Pfaffendorfer Straße 23 (tel. 291838).
Pension Prima, Dresdner Straße 82 (tel. 63481). Doubles DM85
(£36.50; $54.75), breakfast DM5 (£2.15; $3.25) extra.

Cheapest doubles DM90–95 (£38.50–40.75; $57.75–61.00)

Am Lisztplatz, Rosa-Luxemburg-Straße 36 (tel. 60592).
Hans Ingeborg, Nordstraße 58 (tel. 294816).

Cheapest doubles around DM100 (£42.50; $65)

Hotel Am Auewald, Paul-Michael-Straße 12–14 (tel. 451 1003/
451 1025).
Zur Parthe, Löhrstraße 15 (tel. 299490).

PRIVATE ROOMS
Available from Tourist-Information on Sachsenplatz. Single rooms
for DM40–60 (£17.00–25.50; $25.50–38.25), double rooms for
DM60–80 (£25.50–34.50; $38.25–51.75). DM10 (£4.25; $6.50)
surcharge if you stay for only one night.

HI HOSTELS
Käthe-Kollwitz-Straße 6266 (tel. 475888/470530). DM17 (£7.25;
$11). Tram 2 from the front of Leipzig Hbf, or tram 1 from the
stop to the far right of the main exit, or a 10–15-minute walk.
Am Auensee, Gustav-Esche-Straße 4 (tel. 57189). DM15,50 (£6.75;
$10). About 8km from the town centre, but easily reached by
tram 11 or 28 from Leipzig Hbf. The hostel is about 10 minutes'
walk from the Wahren station, down Linkelstraße into Straße
der Jungen Pioniere.
Hauptstraße 23, Großdeuben (tel. 034299 651). DM17 (£7.25;
$11). S-Bahn to Gaschwitz, then a 10–15-minute walk towards
Großdeuben. Bus 1 dir: Zwenkau to the first stop in Großdeuben
leaves you with an 8-minute walk.

HI HOSTEL NEARBY
'Halle', August-Bebel-Straße 48a, Halle (tel. 0345 24716). DM17
(£7.25; $11). Halle is a historically interesting city about 35km from
Leipzig. The two cities are linked by frequent express trains.

CAMPING
Am Auensee, Gustav-Esche-Straße 5 (tel. 52648). Same directions
as the HI hostel of the same name. Pleasant site near the lake. DM4
(£1.75; $2.50) per person, DM3 (£1.25; $2) per tent. Also lets bunga-

lows and *Finnhütten*. Twin-bedded bungalows DM30 (£13.00; $19.50) per night, triple-bedded bungalows DM45 (£19.25; $29) per night, four-bed bungalows DM40 (£17; $25.50) per night. A twin-bedded *Finnhütte* costs DM20 (£8.50; $12.75) per night.

Lübeck (tel. code 0451)

TOURIST OFFICES
Amt für Lübeck-Werbung und Tourismus, Postfach 2132, D-2400 Lübeck 1. Contact this office if you want information on the city in advance. The organization operates two information points in the city: Touristbüro am Markt (tel. 122 8106), open Mon.–Fri. 9.30 a.m.–6 p.m., weekends 10 a.m.–2 p.m.; Touristbüro Beckergrube, Beckergrube 95 (tel. 122 8109). Open Mon.–Fri. 8 a.m.–4 p.m. Beckergrube runs between An der Untertrave and Breite Straße.

Lübecker Verkehrsverein e.V., Postfach 1205, Breite Straße 75 (tel. 72339/72300). Write to this office to reserve accommodation in advance. On arrival you can use their accommodation service. DM5 (£2.15; $3.25) commission. Breite Straße runs from the Markt.

Informationsschalter im Hauptbahnhof (tel. 72300). Operated by the Lübecker Verkehrsverein. Same commission for finding accommodation. Relatively poor information service.

BASIC DIRECTIONS
From the train station you can follow Beim Retteich or Konrad-Adenauer-Straße down to the Puppenbrücke. After crossing the bridge the road forks, but either way will take you to the Holstentor, the old gate which is the symbol of the city. Crossing the Holstenbrücke, you arrive at the start of Holstenstraße. Going up Holstenstraße, you arrive at the Kohlmarkt, from which you can turn left into the Markt. From Lübeck Hbf to the Markt is about 12 minutes' walk.

HOTELS, PENSIONS & GUESTHOUSES
Cheapest doubles around DM75 (£32; $48) B&B

Pension am Park, Hüxtertorallee 57 (tel. 797598). Just outside the Old Town. From Wahmstraße follow Kranenstraße into Hüxtertorallee, then go right.

Hotel Stadtpark, Roeckstraße 9 (tel. 34555). B&B.
Pension Köglin, Kottwitzstraße 39 (tel. 622432/623733).

Cheapest doubles around DM80 (£34.50; $51.75)

Hotel Marienburg, Katharinenstraße 41 (tel. 42512). B&B. Left
  from the station, left at Fackenburger Allee across the railway
  line, first right, then first right again, then left along Katharinenstraße.
Hotel Weißer Hirsch, Krempelsdorfer Allee 27 (tel. 493342).

Cheapest doubles around DM90 (£38.50; $57.75) B&B

Hotel Hanseatic, Hansestraße 19 (tel. 83328). Buffet breakfast. The
  street runs off Beim Retteich.
Hotel Petersen, Hansestraße 11a (tel. 84519). The street runs off
  Beim Retteich.
Hanse-Hotel Schwarzbunte, Bei der Lohmühle 11a (tel. 44777–8).
Hotel Zur Waage, Schwartauer Allee 84 (tel. 46039).

Cheapest doubles around DM100 (£42.50; $65) B&B

Hotel Stadt Lübeck, Am Bahnhof 21 (tel. 83883/864194). Buffet
  breakfast. By Lübeck Hbf.
Hotel Victoria, Am Bahnhof 17/19 (tel. 81144/81145/81146).
Hotel Herrenhof, Herrendamm 8 (tel. 46027).
Hotel Astoria, Fackenburger Allee 68 (tel. 46763).
Altstadt-Hotel, Fischergrube 52 (tel. 72083).
Hotel Priebe, Hansestraße 11 (tel. 81271).
Hotel Zum Scheibenstand, Fackenburger Allee 76 (tel. 473382).
HOTELchen, Schönböckenerstraße 64 (tel. 41013).

PRIVATE ROOMS

Famile Schräger, Ginsterweg 5 (tel. 891407). B&B in singles and
  doubles DM35 (£15; $22.50) per person.
Frau Reimer, Vermehrenring 11e (tel. 65596). B&B DM35 (£15;
  $22.50) per person.
Frau Zingel, Vermehrenring 119 (tel. 625029. Room for up to three
  persons. B&B DM35 (£15; $22.50) per person.

APARTMENTS

Herr Nickel, Engelsgrube 61 (tel. 593139/705120). DM40 (£17;
  $25.50) per person per day for two sharing. DM35 (£15; $22.50)
  per person per day for three sharing.

Familie Nickel, Kahlorststraße 1a (tel. 593139). Sleeps 2–4. DM80 (£34.50; $51.75) per day.

Ferienwohnung Kottwitzstraße 42 (tel. 64289) DM90–100 (£38.50–42.50; $57.75–65.00) per day. Sleeps up to three persons.

Pension 'Santa Monika', Monika Schlei, Kronsdorfer Allee 101a (tel. 581328). DM40 (£17; $25.50) p.p. per day for two sharing.

Historisches Altstadt-Ferienhaus, Hartengrube 44 (Heynathsgang). DM50 (£21.50; $32.25) p.p. per day for two sharing: DM45 (£19.25; $29) p.p. per day for three sharing: DM35 (£15; $22.50) p.p. per day for four sharing. In the Old Town. Contact Engelsgrube 85 (tel. 74629/3909181).

E. Lorenz, Steinstraße 2 (tel. 791708). In the Old Town. Similar prices to the Historisches Altstadt-Ferienhaus, above.

HI HOSTELS
Folke-Bernadotte-Heim, Am Gertrudenkirchhof 4 (tel. 33433). Curfew 11.30 p.m. DM17,50 (£7.50; $11.25). Outside the historic centre, about 5 minutes' walk from the Bürgtor. A 25–30 minute walk from Lübeck Hbf. From the station take bus 1 or 3 to Am Burgfeld.

Lübeck Jugendgästehaus, Mengstraße 33 (tel. 70399). DM26,50 (£11.50; $17). In the Old Town. Turn right off An der Untertrave.

HOSTELS
Sleep-In (YMCA), Groß Petersgrube 11 (tel. 78982). Open to men and women. Midnight curfew. DM15 (£6.50; $9.50). Turn left off An der Obertrave.

Rucksackhotel, Kanalstraße 70 (tel. 706892). DM75 (£32; $48) for doubles, DM100 (£42.50; $65) for triples, DM19–24 (£8–10.25; $12–15.50) per person in larger rooms. About 20 minutes' walk from Lübeck Hbf.

CAMPING
Steinrader Damm 12, Lübeck-Schönböcken (tel. 893090/892287). DM10 (£4.25; $6.50) per tent, DM8 (£3.50; $5.25) p.p. Open 1 Apr.–31 Oct. From the centre of town only a 10-minute trip on bus 7 or 8 dir. Dornbreite. Both stop near the entrance to the site.

Meissen (tel. code 03521)

TOURIST OFFICE

Kultur- un Tourismusamt der Stadt Meissen, Meissen-Information, An der Frauenkirche 3, D-8250 Meissen (tel. 454470). Open Mon.–Fri. 10 a.m.–6 p.m. and, during the main tourist season, Sat. 11 a.m.–3 p.m. From the Meissen Hbf, head left until you reach the Elbe. Cross the bridge and go straight ahead, or down Elbstraße until you reach the Marktplatz. The Frauenkirche and the Tourist Office are on the left of the Marktplatz.

HOTELS AND PENSIONS

Pension Am Berkaer Bahnhof, Peter-Cornelius-Straße 7 (tel. 2010). Doubles DM82 (£35; $52.50).

Pension Dorotheenhof, Dorotheenhof 1, 0–5301 Weimar-Schöndorf (tel. 420068). Doubles DM99 (£42; $64.50).

Pension Flurblick, Am Sportplatz 15 (tel. 59738). Doubles DM90 (£38.50; $57.75).

Pension Sarina, Nembrandtweg 13. Doubles DM90 (£38.50; $57.75).

Hotel-Pension Schöndorf Waldstadt, Ernst-Busse-Straße 4 (tel. 420011). Doubles from DM100 (£42.50; $65).

PRIVATE ROOMS

Rooms must be booked through the Kultur- un Tourismusamt Meissen-Information. Prices for B&B are normally in the range DM25–55 (£10.75–23.50; $16.25–35.25) per person.

Cheapest price around DM17,50 (£7.50; $11.25) p.p.

Ilse Stelzner, Weinberggasse 8b. Doubles/triples only. Price does not include breakfast.

Cheapest price DM20–23 (£8.50–10.00; $12.75–15) p.p.

Herbert Börsdorf, Dresdnerstraße 101 (tel. 734158). Double/triple only.

Edelgard Bursche, Trinitaskirchweg 20 (tel. 732945). Singles only.

Ingrid Kanis, Am Hohen Gericht 12 (tel. 733777). No singles or doubles. Larger rooms only.

Pia Hampf, Tonberg 10. Doubles only.

Helmut Queisser, Oberspaarerstraße 55. Doubles only.

Frank Lützner, Niederspaarerstraße 17. Doubles only.
Jutta Weder, Stadtparkhohe 11d (tel. 454006). Single and doubles. The single room is DM29 (£12.25; $19).

Cheapest price around DM25 (£10.75; $16.25) p.p.

Sabine Göckert, Bohnitzscherstraße 12. Doubles/triples.
Elisabeth Kursawe, Großenhainerstraße 136. Doubles only.
Ingeborg Müller, Gelegegasse 9b. Doubles only.
Ingeborg Münch, Grüner Weg 8. Doubles/triples.
Claus Reichenbach, Rauhentalstraße 67. No singles. Doubles and larger rooms. Price does not include breakfast.

Cheapest price DM28−30 (£12−13; $18.00−19.50) p.p.

Steffen Zimmermann, Stadtblick 27 (tel. 453641). Doubles only.
Werner Bartscht, Gelegegasse 6b (tel. 737519). Doubles/triples.
Hans Fölck, Heinrich-Heine-Straße 54. Doubles/triples.
Helga Nickel, Großenhainerstraße 95 (tel. 733365). Doubles only.
Helmut Porsche, Korbitzerstraße 18b. No singles. Doubles and larger rooms.

APARTMENTS
Also available through the Kultur- un Tourismusamt Meissen-Information. DM40−55 (£17.00−23.50; $25.50−35.25) per person, including breakfast.

HI HOSTEL
Wilsdruffer Straße 58 (tel. 453065). DM12,50 (£5.35; $8). No lock-out or curfew, but tends to be booked solid.

CAMPING
Campingplatz Scharfenberg (tel. 452680). By the River Elbe, in the direction of Dresden. For further information contact Dietmar Sieber, Siebeneichen 6b, D-8250 Meissen.

Munich (München) (tel. code 089)

TOURIST OFFICES
Fremdenverkehrsamt der Landeshauptstadt München, Postfach, D-80313 München 1 (tel. 233 0300/fax 233 0233). Hotels can

be reserved in advance by writing to this office. The Fremdenverkehrsamt operate three branches in the city which will book
rooms for you on arrival. A fee of DM5 (£2.15; $3.25) is payable
for this service.

München Hauptbahnhof (tel. 239 1256/239 1257). Open
Mon.–Sat. 8 a.m.–10 p.m., Sun. 11 a.m.–7 p.m. Opposite track
11 in the main train station, by the Bayerstraße exit. Queues can
be lengthy in summer, expect to wait 15–30 minutes. If all you
want is a simple city map with the main tourist attractions, these
are normally available from the self-service brochure stand.

Flughafen München 'Franz Josef Strauss' (tel. 9759 2815). In the
central building of the airport. Open daily 8.30 a.m.–10 p.m.,
except Sun. and public holidays: 1–9 p.m.

FINDING ACCOMMODATION

Munich is one of the most popular destinations in Europe, so
advance reservation of accommodation is advisable at any time of
year, as far in advance as possible. To reserve hotel accommodation
write directly to the hotel, or to the Tourist Office (you can give
the names of a few hotels in order of preference). The city is exceptionally busy between June and August, then, in September, just
when it is becoming easier to find accommodation elsewhere,
Munich receives a huge influx of visitors for the start of the
Oktoberfest. If you are arriving without reservations at this time
it is highly unlikely you will find a hostel bed, or even a room in
one of the cheaper hotels listed below. Railpass holders totally stuck
for a bed should refer to the Sleeping Rough section below for
details of a useful train service.

HOTELS, PENSIONS & GUESTHOUSES

Note: Roman numerals in an address refer to the floor of the
building.
*Singles around DM35 (£15; $22.50) doubles around DM50 (£21.50;
$32.25)*

Maisinger, Pippinger Straße 105 (tel. 811 2920). S2: Obermenzing,
then bus 75 along Verdistraße and into Pippingerstraße, or a
10-minute walk along the same route.

Cheapest doubles around DM65 (£28; $42)

Eberl, Josef-Frankl-Straße 56 (tel. 313 2638).

Cheapest doubles around DM80 (£34.50; $51.75)

Schiller, Schillerstraße 11 (tel. 592435). About 300m from Munich Hbf. Leaving the station by the main exit, Schillerstraße begins almost opposite the right hand end of Bahnhofplatz, across Bayerstraße.

Cheapest doubles DM80–90 (£34.50–38.50; $51.75–57.75)

Am Kaiserplatz, Kaiserplatz 12 (tel. 349190). U3, U6: Münchener Freiheit, then a few minutes' walk along Herzogstraße, first left, then right along Kaiserstraße.

Fleischmann, Bischof-Adalbert-Straße 10 (tel. 359 5379/350 8126). U2, U3: Petuelring. From Petuelring, a short walk down Riesenfeldstraße, right after Keferloherstraße, then left.

Theresia, Luisenstraße 51 (tel. 523 1250/523 3081/523 3082). U2: Theresienstraße. Follow Theresienstraße two blocks in the direction of the Alte Pinakothek, then right on Luisenstraße (about 300m in all).

Würmtalhof, Eversbuschstraße 91 (tel. 812 2185). S2: Allach, then a 250m walk along Versaliusstraße into Eversbuschstraße. The hotel is near the junction.

Augsburg, Schillerstraße 18 (tel. 597673). See Hotel Schiller, above. About 300m from Munich Hbf.

Härtl, Verdistraße 135 (tel. 811 1632). S2: Obermenzing, then a 5-minute walk along Verdistraße or bus 73 or 75.

Isabella, Isabellastraße 35 (tel. 271 3503). U2: Hohenzollernplatz, a 400m walk along Kurfürstenstraße, then right down Isabellastraße.

Zöllner, Sonnenstraße 10/IV and V (tel. 554035). A 5–10 minute walk from Munich Hbf, left along Bayerstraße from Bahnhofplatz, then right down Sonnenstraße, or take tram 20, 25 or 27 heading right from Bahnhofplatz.

Sollner Hof, Herterichstraße 63–65 (tel. 792090/794045).

Strigl, Elisabethstraße 11/II (tel. 271 3444/271 6250). U2: Hohenzollernplatz, then a few minutes' walk down Tengstraße and left along Elisabethstraße.

Beck, Thierschstraße 36 (tel. 225768). Tram 20 heading right from the front of the Munich Hbf runs along the street. S1–S7: Isartor, then a 5-minute walk along Thierschstraße from Isartorplatz.

Diana, Altheimer Eck 15/3 (tel. 260 3107). Excellent central location, 5–10 minutes' walk from Munich Hbf. Through the underground shopping centre to Karlsplatz (S1–S7/U4, U5: Karlsplatz/

Stachus is the nearest stop to the hotel), along Neuhauserstraße, right at Eisenmannstraße, then left along Altheimer Eck.

Josefine, Nordendstraße 13 (tel. 271 0043). U2, U3: Scheidplatz, then tram 13 to Nordendstraße, or U3, U6: Giselastraße, then a 500m walk along Leopoldstraße in the direction of the university (Universität) right along Georgenstraße, left at Nordendstraße.

Am Knie, Strindbergstraße 33 (tel. 886450). Tram 19 from Munich Hbf heading towards Pasinger Marienplatz. Get off by the junction of Landsbergerstraße and G.-Habel-Straße. Walk down the latter, then left.

Doria, Hohenstaufenstraße 12/IV (tel. 333872). U3, U6: Giselastraße, then a 5-minute walk. Down Leopoldstraße toward the university (Universität), right along Georgenstraße, right again at Friedrichstraße, then left.

Frankfurter Ring, Riesenfeldstraße 79a (tel. 351 1309). Good value, as rooms have a shower/bath. U3, U6: Münchener Freiheit, then bus 43 or 143 to the junction of Frankfurter Ring and Riesenfeldstraße (the hotel is near the junction), or U2, U3: Petuelring, then a 600m walk along Riesenfeldstraße from Petuelring.

Herzog Heinrich, Herzog-Heinrich-Straße 3 (tel. 532575/538 0750). A 10-minute walk from Munich Hbf. Exit on to Bayerstraße, right, left down Paul-Heyse-Straße and across Georg-Hirth-Platz into Herzog-Heinrich-Straße. Exit left from the station on to Arnulfstraße and you can take bus 58 to Georg-Hirth-Platz.

Hungaria, Brienner Straße 42/II (tel. 521558). A 10-minute walk from Munich Hbf. Exit left on to Arnulfstraße, cross over and take Dachauer Straße, second right, across Karlstraße, on down Augustenstraße into Brienner Straße. The hotel is located roughly 250m from both. U1: Stiglmaierplatz and U2: Königsplatz.

Lutz, Hofenfelsstraße 57 (tel. 152970).

Marie-Luise, Landwehrstraße 37/IV (tel. 554230). A 5-minute walk from Munich Hbf, right when Landwehrstraße crosses Schillerstraße (see Hotel Schiller above).

Olympia, Maxhofstraße 23 (tel. 754063/754064).

Clara, Wilhelmstraße 25 (tel. 348374). U3, U6: Münchener Freiheit, then a few minutes' walk along Herzogstraße from Leopoldstraße, then left at Wilhelmstraße.

Frank, Schellingstraße 24 (tel. 281451). Schellingstraße runs off of Ludwigstraße. A 5-minute walk from the U-Bahn station.

Haydn, Haydnstraße 9 (tel. 531119). A 10–15-minute walk from Munich Hbf, left off Herzog-Heinrich-Straße at Kaiser-Ludwig-Platz (see Hotel Herzog-Heinrich, above). U3, U6: Goetheplatz, then a few minutes' walk along Mozartstraße, then right.

Lugano, Schillerstraße 32 (tel. 591005). A 5-minute walk from Munich Hbf, see Hotel Schiller, above.

Cheapest doubles around DM85 (£36.50; $54.75)

Erika, Landwehrstraße 8 (tel. 554327). A 5-minute walk from Munich Hbf, left where Landwehrstraße crosses Schillerstraße (see Schiller, above).

Fraunhofer, Fraunhoferstraße 10 (tel. 260 7238). U1, U2: Fraunhofer, then a 150m walk. Tram 25 or 27 heading right from Munich Hbf to Müllerstraße also leaves 150m walk down Fraunhoferstraße.

Alba, Mühlbaurstraße 2 (tel. 472458). U4: Prinzregentenplatz. The hotel is right at the start of Muhlbaurstraße as it leaves Prinzregentenplatz.

Am Nordbad, Schleißheimer Straße 91 (tel. 180857). U2: Hohenzollernplatz, then a short walk along Hohenzollernstraße, then left on Schleißheimer Straße.

Armin, Augustenstraße 5 (tel. 593197). About 800m from Munich Hbf (see Hotel Hungaria, above). U1: Stiglmaierplatz, then a few minutes' walk down Dachauerstraße, left at Karlstraße, then left again.

Beim Haus der Kunst, Bruderstraße 4/I (tel. 222127). Tram 20 heading right from Munich Hbf to the junction of Wagmüllerstraße and Prinzregentenstraße. Go left along the latter, then left at Bruderstraße.

Gebhardt, Goethestraße 38 (tel. 539446).

Peter im Park, Neufeldstraße 20 (tel. 881356). S4: Westkreuz.

Schillerhof, Schillerstraße 21 (tel. 594270).

Cheapest doubles around DM90 (£38.50; $57.75)

Brunner, Untere Mühlstraße 13 (tel. 813 1528). Rooms have shower/bath. S2: Allach, then a few minutes' walk along Vesaliusstraße, then left.

Flora, Karlstraße 49 (tel. 597067). Just over 5 minutes' walk from Munich Hbf, left off Dachauerstraße (see Hotel Hungaria, above).

Lex, Brienner Straße 48 (tel. 522091). See Hotel Hungaria, above, then left off Augustenstraße.

Lucia, Linprunstraße 12 (tel. 523 4016). A 15-minute walk from Munich Hbf. Right along Dachauerstraße into Stiglmaierplatz, (U1: Stiglmaierplatz) left along Brienner Straße, right Sandstraße, then left.

Mariandl, Goethestraße 51 (tel. 534108). U3, U6: Goetheplatz.

München, Valpichlerstraße 49 (tel. 564045). U4, U5: Laimer Platz is about 200m away. Follow Fürstenriederstraße from the station, then left.

Erbprinz, Sonnenstraße 2 (tel. 594521/594522) A 5–10-minute walk from Munich Hbf (see Hotel Zöllner, above).

Köberl, Bodenseestraße 222 (tel. 876339). West of the city centre. S5: Neuaubing.

Verdi, Verdistraße 123 (tel. 811 1484). S2: Obermenzing.

Westend, Landsberger Straße 20 (tel. 504004).

Winhart, Balanstraße 238 (tel. 683117/682226). South of the city centre.

Atlanta, Sendlinger Straße 50 (tel. 263605).

Lipp, Herzogstraße 11 (tel. 332951). U3, U6: Münchener Freiheit.

Luna, Landwehrstraße 5 (tel. 597833).

St Augustinus, St-Augustinus-Straße 6 (tel. 425191/429321). South-east of the city centre.

Agnes, Agnes Straße 58 (tel. 129 3061). U2: Josephsplatz.

Post-Sport-Park, Franz-Mader-Straße 11 (tel. 149 1055).

Wachau, Heiglhofstraße 13 (tel. 714 1854). U-Bahn: Großhadern.

HI HOSTELS

The HI hostels in Munich are part of the Bavarian section of the Deutsches Jugendherbergswerk, which admits only those aged 27 or under to hostels under its control. Because of the popularity of the hostels in Munich there is virtually no chance of this rule being ignored, as can be the case in some cities in the region.

DJH Jugendgästehaus München, Miesingstraße 4 (tel. 723 6550/ 723 6560). 1 a.m. curfew. Singles DM33 (£14; $21), doubles DM29 (£11.50; $17.25) per person, larger rooms DM27 (£11.50; $17.50) p.p. Prices include breakfast. Take the underground (U-Bahn 3) directly from Marienplatz (direction 'Fürstenried-West' to Thalkirchen, the 200 stop. 15-minute ride. Hostel is then signposted from station (5-minute walk).

DJH München, Wendl-Dietrich-Straße 20 (tel. 131156). 1 a.m. curfew. B&B in dorms around DM22,50 (£9.50; $14.50) p.p. U1: Rotkreuzplatz, then a short walk along Wendl-Dietrich-Straße. The entrance is on Winthirplatz, second on the right.

DJH Burg Schwaneck, Burgweg 4–6, Pullach (tel. 793 0644). 1 a.m. curfew. B&B in dorms DM15,50–17,50 (£7.00–7.50; $10.50–11.25) p.p. About 11km from the city centre, but the trip on the S7 to Pullach from the main train station or city centre only takes about 25 minutes. From the S-Bahn station the hostel is a well signposted 10-minute walk.

HOSTELS

CVJM-Jugendgästehaus, Landwehrstraße 13 (tel. 552141–0). YMCA hostel, but open to girls as well. 12.30 a.m. curfew. Singles DM41–56,35 (£17.50–24.00; $26.25–36.00), doubles DM35–44,85 (£15.00–19.25; $22.50–29.00), per person, larger rooms DM32–41,40 (£13.75–17.25; $20.50–26.50) p.p. Overnight price includes breakfast. Prices fall after two nights. A 5–10-minute walk from Munich Hbf.

Haus International, Jugendhotel, Elisabethstraße 87 (tel. 12006–0). All rooms have showers and WC. Singles DM51–79 (£22–34; $33–51), doubles DM48–66 (£20.50–28.50; $30.75–42.75) p.p., larger rooms DM38–43 (£16.50–18.50; $24.75–27.50) p.p. U2: Hohenzollernplatz, then a 5-minute walk along Hohenzollernplatz and left down Schleißheimer Straße into Elisabethstraße

Jugendhotel Marienherberge, Goethestraße 9 (tel. 555891). Women only. Age limit 25. Midnight curfew. Singles DM35 (£15; $22.50), doubles and larger rooms DM30 (£12.75; $19.50) p.p. Overnight price includes breakfast. A 5-minute walk from Munich Hbf.

Kolpinghaus St Theresia, Hanebergstraße 8 (tel. 126050). Singles DM45 (£19.25; $29), doubles DM39 (£16.75; $25) p.p., larger rooms DM29 (£12.25; $18.50) p.p. From Munich Hbf, take tram 20, 25 or 27 heading left from the station to the stop after Dachauerstraße crosses Landshuter Allee. Walk back, then right down Landshuter Allee, then right again at Hanebergstraße (a 5-minute walk).

HI HOSTEL NEARBY

Beim Pfaffenkeller 3, Augsburg (tel. 0821 33909). DM18 (£7.75; $11.50) for B&B in dorms. Trains run to Augsburg every 20–30 minutes from Munich, a 30–40-minute trip. To get to the hostel from Augsburg Hbf, take tram 2 to Stadtwerke. As Augsburg is a popular destination itself (and rightly so), the hostel is often full in summer so phone before making the trip out to Augsburg.

THE TENT

Jugendlage Kapuzinerhölzl, Franz-Schrank-Straße 8 (tel. 141 4300). Actually two circus tents, with mattresses and blankets provided. Open 5 p.m.–9 a.m., late June–early September. DM7 (£3; $4.50). Three-night maximum stay. Maximum age 24, not rigorously enforced. Leave your pack at the station. U1 to Rotkreuzplatz, then tram 12 dir. Amalienburgstraße to the Botanischer Garten stop on Miesingerstraße. Along Franz-Schrank-Straße and left at the top on to In den Kirschen. 'The Tent' is on the right.

CAMPING
Munich-Thalkirchen, Zentralländstraße 49 (tel. 723 1707). Cheap, municipal site. Open 15 Mar.−31 Oct. Crowded, especially during the Oktoberfest. From the train station, S1−S7 to Marienplatz, then U3 dir. Forstenrieder Allee to Thalkirchen (Tierplatz), followed by bus 57 to Thalkirchen (last stop).
Munich-Obermenzing, Lochhausener Straße 59 (tel. 811 2235). S2: Obermenzing, then bus 75 to the junction of Pippingerstraße and Lochhausenerstraße, followed by a 5-minute walk along the latter. Open 15 Mar.−31 Oct.

SLEEPING ROUGH
The police tolerate people sleeping in the main train station during the Oktoberfest, though make sure you move quickly when they wake you in the morning (usually around 6 a.m.). For obvious reasons, you cannot expect a peaceful night's sleep. A useful train for railpass holders stuck for a bed is the D14164, which leaves Munich Hbf at 1.23 a.m. and runs as a local service to Stuttgart, arriving at 5.12 a.m. At 5.38 a.m., the D2111 Norddeich-Munich train arrives in Stuttgart, departing at 5.53 a.m. and arriving in Munich at 8.45 a.m. Leave your pack at Munich Hbf.

Nuremberg (Nürnberg) (tel. code 0911)

TOURIST OFFICES
Nuremburg's Tourist Information (tel. 23360) has two branches: one in Nürnberg Hbf, open Mon.−Sat. 9 a.m.−7 p.m., the other in the Rathaus (Town Hall) off Hauptmarkt, open Mon.−Sat. 9 a.m.−1 p.m. and 2−6 p.m. To reserve hotels in advance, write to: Congress- und Tourismus-Zentrale Nürnberg, Frauentorgraben 3, D-8500 Nürnberg 70.

BASIC DIRECTIONS
The historic core of Nuremberg is quite small, so in 20 minutes you can walk from the train station to the castle on the opposite side of the Old Town. From the station, take the underpass to Königstor, then walk down Königstraße to reach St Lawrence's Church on Lorenzplatz. Go downhill over the River Pegnitz by the Museum-

sbrücke and into Hauptmarkt. Head diagonally left across the square, turn right into Rathausplatz, from which Burgstraße leads uphill to the castle. Near the Church of St Lawrence (just over one third of the way) is the Lorenzkirche U-Bahn stop, linked to Nürnberg Hbf by U-Bahn lines 1 and 2.

HOTELS, PENSIONS & GUESTHOUSES
Cheapest doubles around DM60–65 (£25.50–28.00; $38.25–42.00)

Zum Schwänlein, Hintere Sterngasse 11 (tel. 225162). First left off Königstraße from the Königstor.

Cramer-Klett, Pillenreuther Straße 162 (tel. 449291). Singles DM30 (£13; $19.50). U-Bahn lines 1 and 11 to Frankenstraße take you virtually to the door.

Süd, Ingolstädter Straße 51 (tel. 445139). U-Bahn line 1 or 11 to Frankenstraße. Head right from the junction with Pillenreutherstraße, then right again a few blocks on.

Cheapest doubles around DM70 (£30; $45)

Melanchthon, Melanchthonplatz 1 (tel. 412626/66). A 20-minute walk from Nürnberg Hbf. Left from the exit, left through the Celtis underpass, across Celtisplatz and down Pillenreutherstraße, then right along Breitscheidstraße and Wiesenstraße. U-Bahn line 1 or 11 to Aufsessplatz will save you half the walk.

Vater Jahn, Jahnstraße 13 (tel. 444507). A 15-minute walk from Nürnberg Hbf. From Celtisplatz (see Melanchthon above) go right along Celtisstraße and Tunnelstraße, then left.

Fischer, Brunnengasse 11 (tel. 226189). Left off Königstraße, just before the Lorenzkirche.

Humboldtklause, Humboldtstraße 41 (tel. 413801/413841).

Weinländer, Rothenburger Straße 482 (tel. 612761).

Cheapest doubles around DM75–80 (£32.00–34.50; $48.00–51.75)

Brendel, Blumenstraße 1 (tel. 225618). Follow Königstor-Marientorgraben from the Königstor, then right.

Keim, Peuntgasse 10 (tel. 225940). A short walk down Königstraße from the Königstor, then right.

Christl, Laufamholzstraße 216c (tel. 501249). Well out from the centre, but a 10–15-minute walk from the Nürnberg-Laufamholz S-Bahn stop.

Keiml, Luitpoldstraße 7 (tel. 226240). To the left off Königstraße, a short walk from the Königstor.

Altstadt, Hintere Ledergasse 4 (tel. 226102). Walking from Lorenzplatz towards the River Pegnitz, go left on Kaiserstraße which leads into Hintere Ledergasse.

Peter Henlein, Peter-Henlein-Straße 15 (tel. 412912). Over the street from the Hannweber (directions above).

Royal, Theodorstraße 9 (tel. 533209). A 15-minute walk from the Nürnberg Hbf. Follow Gleissbühlstraße into Laufertorgraben, right at Kesslerstraße, then sharp right.

Blaue Traube, Johannesgasse 22 (tel. 221666). A short walk from the Königstor, right on Theatergasse, then right.

Pfälzer Hof, Am Gräslein 10 (tel. 221411). A short walk from the Königstor along Königstraße, left at Hallplatz across the Kornmarkt, then left after Kartäusergasse.

Goldener Adler, Hallplatz 21 (tel. 208500/221360). The entrance is on Klaragasse, left off Königstraße a short distance from the Königstor.

Spitzweg, Valznerweiherstraße 110 (tel. 407206).

Birkenwald-Keller, Herriedener Straße 38 (tel. 682855/687068).

Übelacker, Mathildenstraße 13 (tel. 553158).

Großmarkt, Leyher Straße 101 (tel. 313321).

Kronfleischküche, Kaiserstraße 22 (tel. 227845/224932).

Kreuzeck, Schnepfenreuther Weg 1 (tel. 34961/34962/341474).

Probst, Luitpoldstraße 9 (tel. 203433/222227)

Cheapest doubles around DM85 (£36.50; $54.75)

Sonne, Königstraße 45 (tel. 227166). A short walk from the Königstor. The entrance is on Theatergasse.

Noris, Prinzregentenufer 3 (tel. 552818).

More double rooms in the DM55–75 (£23.50–32.00; $35.25–48.00) range are available in nearby Fürth and Erlangen, both about 15–30 minutes' journey by frequent local trains. In both Fürth and Erlangen there is a branch of the Tourist Office near the train station (tel. 74912–0 for the office in Fürth; tel. 09131 25074 for the office in Erlangen).

HI HOSTEL

Jugendgästehaus 'Kaiserstallung', Bürg 2 (tel. 221024). DM25 (£10.75; $16.25). Age limit 27. 1 a.m. curfew. Formerly the castle stables. A 20-minute walk from Nürnberg Hbf (see **Basic Directions**), or take tram 9 dir. Thon to Krelingstraße. The castle is on the left. Walk through the grounds to the hostel.

HOSTELS

Jugend-Hotel Nürnberg, Buchenbuhl, Rathsbergstraße 300 (tel. 521 6092). Small dorms cost DM21–26 (£9–11; $13.50–16.50) depending on whether the dorm has its own shower and toilet. Breakfast included. Thirty minutes' walk from the centre. Tram 3 to the terminus, then bus 41 to Felsenkeller.

Jugend- und Economy-Hotel, Gostenhofer Hauptstraße 47–49 (tel. 92620). Doubles start around DM70 (£30; $45).

HI HOSTEL NEARBY

'Frankenhof', Südlicher Stadtmauerstraße 35, Amt für Freizeit, Erlangen (tel. 09131 862555/862274). DM16 (£7; $10.50). Frequent local trains make the 30-minute trip to Erlangen. From the station go straight ahead on to Hauptstraße, turn right, then left along Friedrichstraße. The hostel is in the sport and leisure area to the right of Friedrichstraße.

CAMPING

Campingplatz im Volkspark Dutzendteich, Hans-Kalb-Straße 56 (tel. 811122). Open May–Sept. Those with a railpass can take a train to Nürnberg-Dutzendteich. The site is behind the football stadium. The U-Bahn stop Messenzentrum is slightly closer.

Naturfreunde Erlangen, Wohrmuhle 6, Erlangen (tel. 09131 28499). Year round site. Near the station in Erlangen, a 30-minute trip by frequent local trains from Nürnberg. From the rear of the station, go right until you see the road heading left under the A73 road.

Potsdam (tel. code 0331)

TOURIST OFFICE

Potsdam-Information, Touristenzentrale am Alten Markt, Friedrich-Ebert-Straße 5, D-1561 Potsdam (tel. 23385). Open Apr.–Oct. Mon.–Fri. 9 a.m.–8 p.m., Sat. and Sun. 9 a.m.–6 p.m.; Nov.–Mar. Mon.–Fri. 10 a.m.–6 p.m., Sat. and Sun. 11 a.m.–3 p.m. From Potsdam Stadtbahnhof, cross the Havel by the Lange Brücke and go right at the fork in the end of the road, down Friedrich-Ebert-Straße to the Tourist Office.

ARRIVING BY TRAIN

In contrast to most German cities, do not get off at the Hauptbahnhof as it is far from the centre. Potsdam-Stadt is closest to the

Tourist Office and the town centre. Potsdam Charlottenhof (also known as Potsdam West) is the closest station to the Sanssouci Palace and the New Palace.

HOTELS, PENSIONS & GUESTHOUSES

There is a shortage of hotels offering doubles in the DM60–80 (£25.50–34.50; $38.25–51.75) range in Potsdam, though there are rooms available around these prices in neighbouring towns.

B&B in doubles around DM60 (£25.50; $38.25)

Haus Havelblick, Dorfstraße 17, Töplitz (tel. 033202 214). Singles from DM30 (£13; $19.50).

B&B in doubles DM70–75 (£30–32; $45–48)

Haus Glindowsee, Puschkinstraße 21, Werder (tel. 03327 2342).
DEFA Gästehaus, Stahnsdorfer Straße 81 (tel. 965 3188). Breakfast not included.
Hotel Schloß Petzow, Zelterstraße 5, Werder (tel. 03327 3153/ 2678).

B&B in doubles DM80–90 (£34.50–38.50; $51.75–57.75)

Hotel Am Schwielowsee, Am Schwielowsee 100, Werder (tel. 03327 2850).
Pension Haus Frühling, Berliner Straße 109, Werder (tel. 03327 2953).
Babelsberg, Stahnsdorfer Straße 68 (tel. 78889). The closest train station is S-Bahn: Griebnitzsee, about 750m away. Walk from the station to Stahnsdorferstraße, then go right along the street.

PRIVATE ROOMS AND APARTMENTS

The Tourist Office book rooms and apartments in Potsdam and within a 19km radius of the town. If no rooms are available in town, railpass holders should ask for a room in a town on the railway. Prices range from DM15–50 (£6.50–21.50; $9.50–32.25) per person per night, depending on the quality of the accommodation. Bookings can be made at any time the Tourist Office is open.

CAMPING

Potsdam-Stadt, Potsdam-Gaisberg, Geltow (tel. 03327 55680). Open 1 Apr.–15 Oct. DM5 (£2.15; $3.25) per person, DM6 (£2.50; $3.75) per tent. By the Templiner See.

Werder-Riegelspitze, Werder (tel. 03327 2397/2331). Open 15
Apr.–15 Oct. Beside the Glindower See. Bus D-631 runs to the
site from Potsdam Hbf.
Caputh-Himmelreich, Caputh (tel. 03327 475). Open May–Oct.
Caputher Flottstelle, Caputh (tel. 033209 497).

Stuttgart (tel. code 0711)

TOURIST OFFICES
'I-Punkt', Königstraße 1a. Open May–Oct. Mon.–Sat. 8.30 a.m.–
10 p.m., Sun. 11 a.m.–6 p.m.; Nov.–Apr. Mon.–Sat. 8.30 a.m.–
9 p.m., Sun. 1–6 p.m. Opposite the main train station.
Stuttgart Marketing GmbH, Lautenschlagerstraße 3, Postfach 10 01
55, D-7000 Stuttgart 10 (tel. 2228–0). Advance reservation of
hotel rooms can be made free of charge through this office.

HOTEL, PENSIONS & GUESTHOUSES
Cheapest doubles around DM75–80 (£32.00–34.50; $48.00–51.75)

Solitude, Hohewartstraße 10 (tel. 854919). In the Feuerbach district. U-Bahn line 6 to Feuerbach Krankenhaus. With the hospital
on your right, follow Stuttgarter Straße until you see Hohewartstraße on your right.
Eckel, Vorsteigstraße 10 (tel. 290995). About 20 minutes' walk
from the centre, further from Stuttgart Hbf. Bus 40 (heading
right from in front of the train station) to Hölderlinplatz.
Schwarzwaldheim, Fritz-Elsas-Straße 20 (tel. 296988). Central
location. S-Bahn lines 1–6 to Stadtmitte. The street runs off
Rotebuhlplatz. A 10-minute walk from the train station down
Lautenschlägerstraße and Theodor-Heuss-Straße to Rotebühl-
platz.
Adler, Filderbahnstraße 25 (tel. 711304). In Möhringen. U-Bahn
lines 5 and 6 to Möhringen Bahnhof. From Filderbahnplatz, a
short walk down Filderbahnstraße.
Traube, Kornwestheimerstraße 11 (tel. 802696). In Stammheim.
U-Bahn line 15 to Korntalerstraße.
Bronni, Stierlenstraße 2 (tel. 335266). In the Untertürkheim dis-
trict. S-Bahn 1 to Untertürkheim, and bus 60 to Im Hag.
Pflugfelder, Ostendstraße 20 (tel. 262 2730). U-Bahn 9 to Berg-
friedhof.
Lamm, Karl-Schurz-Straße 7 (tel. 267328). U-Bahn line 14 to Min-
eralbäder. Karl-Schurz-Straße runs out of Am Schwanenplatz.

Cheapest doubles around DM85 (£36.50; $54.75)

Silberwald, Kirchheimerstraße 58–60 (tel. 474503). In Sillenbuch.
  U-Bahn lines 15 and 16 to Eduard-Steinle-Straße. At the end of
  Eduard-Steinle-Straße, on the main road passing through Sil-
  lenbuch.
Museum-Stube, Hospitalstraße 9 (tel. 296810). Central location.
  S-Bahn lines 16 to Stadtmitte. From Theodor-Heuss-Straße, take
  Langestraße one block into Hospitalstraße. Just over 5 minutes'
  walk from Stuttgart Hbf, along Lautenschlägerstraße, then right
  on Willi-Bleicher-Straße into Hospitalstraße.

Cheapest doubles around DM90 (£38.50; $57.75)

Haus Berg, Karl-Schurz-Straße 16 (tel. 261875). See Lamm, above.
Krämer's Bürgerstuben, Gablenberger Hauptstraße 4 (tel. 465481).
  In Gablenberg. Bus 40 or 42 (heading left from the front of
  Stuttgart Hbf) to Wagenburg/Ostendstraße.
Schnaich, Paulinenstraße 16 (tel. 602679). Just outside the centre.
  U-Bahn line 14 to Österreichischer Platz, then a short walk along
  Paulinenstraße.
Stoll, Brunnenstraße 27 (tel. 562331). In Bad Cannstatt. S-Bahn
  lines 1–3 to Bad Cannstatt. A 5–10-minute walk from the
  station. Left along Bahnhofstraße, across Wilhelmsplatz and
  down Wilhelmstraße into Brunnenstraße.

HI HOSTEL
Haußmannstraße 27 (tel. 241583) DM18 (£7.75; $11.50). The
entrance is on the corner of Werastraße and Kernerstraße. U-Bahn
lines 15 and 16 to Eugensplatz then a short walk along Kernerstraße, or a 10-minute walk from Stuttgart Hbf. Leave the station
by the ZOB exit (right, facing the tracks), under the tunnel then
right. At the monument, go into Schillerstraße, across Neckarstraße
at the crossing, up the path to the right of the police station, past
the school, then up the steps to the corner of Werastraße and
Kernerstraße.

HI HOSTELS NEARBY
There are hostels in two towns nearby which are well worth a visit.
Esslingen-am-Neckar has retained much of its historic core, while
Ludwigsburg has a superb palace. Esslingen is easily reached by
frequent local trains, or by S-Bahn line 1 dir. Plochingen (15–30
minute journey). There are regular local trains to Ludwigsburg
(10–15 minute journey). Unfortunately, both hostels are located

far from the respective stations. For details on which buses to take contact the hostels or the local Tourist Information Offices: for Ludwigsburg (tel. 07141 910252); in Esslingen the office is a 10-minute walk from the train station on the Marktplatz (along Bahnhofstraße, over the Neckar and straight on).

Neuffenstraße 65, Esslingen (tel. 0711 351 2441/351 2645).
Gemsenbergstraße 31, Ludwigsburg (tel. 07141 51564).

CAMPING
By the Neckar on the Cannstätter Wasen (tel. 556696/561503). Not central, but easily reached from the centre or the train station. The site is only a few minutes' walk from U-Bahn stop Hedelfingen (lines 9 and 13). S-Bahn station Bad Cannstatt (lines 1–3) is a 10-minute walk away. Head right from the station, then right down Daimlerstraße to the Cannstätter Wasen. The site is within walking distance of the fabulous Daimler-Benz Museum and off the football stadium (Neckarstadion, home of VfB and Stuttgarter Kickers).

Trier (tel. code 0651)

TOURIST OFFICE
Verkehrsamt der Stadt Trier, Simeonstift an der Porta Nigra, Postfach 3830, D-5500 Trier (tel. 978080). Open Apr.–mid-Nov., Mon.–Sat. 9 a.m.–6.30 p.m., Sun. 9 a.m.–3.30 p.m.; mid-Nov.–Dec., Mon.–Fri. 9 a.m.–6 p.m., weekends, 9 a.m.–1 p.m.; Jan.–Feb., Mon.–Fri. 9 a.m.–5 p.m., Sat. 9 a.m.–1 p.m.; Mar., Mon.–Fri. 9 a.m.–6 p.m., Sat. 9 a.m.–1 p.m. Contact the office in writing to reserve hotels in advance.

HOTELS, PENSIONS & GUESTHOUSES
All the hotels and pensions listed at DM60 or less are out in the suburbs of the city.

Cheapest doubles around DM45 (£19.25; $29)

Weinhaus E. Thiel, Ruwererstraße 10 (tel. 52233).
Pension Anna Rudolf, Peter-Klöckner-Straße 28 (tel. 69449). In Trier-Quint.

Cheapest doubles around DM50 (£21.50; $32.25)

Maximin, Ruwererstraße 12 (tel. 52577).
Haus Magda, Biewererstraße 203 (tel. 66372).

Cheapest doubles around DM60 (£25.50; $38.25)

Gasthaus Filscher Häuschen, Filscher Häuschen 1 (tel. 10600).
Pension Ursula Monzel, Fröbelstraße 9 (tel. 86376).
Pension Fritz Metzen, Wolkerstraße 2 (tel. 37575).
Pension Waltraud Heinz, Marianholzstraße 26 (tel. 57231). In Trier-Ruwer.

Cheapest doubles around DM65–70 (£28–30; $42–45)

Saarbrücker Hof, Saarstraße 45 (tel. 75161). An easy walk from Trier Süd.
Zur Glocke, Glockenstraße 12 (tel. 73109). Great location. Off Simeonstraße.

Cheapest doubles around DM75 (£32; $48)

Klosterklause, Balthasar-Neumann-Strasse 1 (tel. 25613). From Theodor-Heuss-Allee, turn right down Göbenstraße, then right again at Thebäerstraße. Follow the street towards the St Paulin church until you see Balthasar-Neumann-Strasse on the left.
In der Olk, In der Olk 33 (tel. 41227). Near the junction of the Hauptmarkt and Fleischstraße, turn down Dietrichstraße, head left along Zuckerbergstraße (opposite Walramsneustraße), right at Salvianstraße, then left at In der Olk.
Haus Marianne, Eurenerstraße 190a (tel. 800103). All rooms have bath/shower and WC. On the other side of the Mosel from the centre, close to the Konrad-Adenauer-Brücke. The closest train station is Trier West.

Cheapest doubles around DM80 (£34.50; $51.75)

Grund, Paulinstraße 7 (tel. 25939). Right off Theodor-Heuss-Allee at the Porta Nigra.
Kurfürst Balduin, Theodor-Heuss-Allee 22 (tel. 25610).
Neutor, Neusstraße 50 (tel. 48626). Trier Süd is the closest train station.
Weinhaus Haag, Stockplatz 1 (tel. 72366). Well located. From

Simeonstraße a short walk down Stockstraße takes you into Stockplatz.

HI HOSTEL
Jugendherberge Trier, Am Moselufer 4 (tel. 29292). Midnight curfew. DM24 (£10.25; $15.50). Pleasant setting by the Mosel, within easy walking distance of the centre. About 20 minutes' walk from Trier Hbf. Follow Theodor-Heuss-Allee to the Porta Nigra, turn right up Paulinstraße, then left down Maarstraße. Bus 2 dir: Trierweilerweg, or bus 8 dir: Pfalzel/Ehrang/Quint stop at Georg-Schmidt-Platz, about 500m from the hostel. Take the footpath and follow the river downstream.

HOSTEL
Jugendgästehaus Kolpinghaus, Dietrichstraße 42 (tel. 75131). DM22 (£9.50; $14.25). Well located. Near the junction of the Hauptmarkt and Fleischstraße head along Dietrichstraße.

CAMPING
Campingpark Trier-City, Luxemburger Straße 81 (tel. 86921). Cheap private site. Across the Mosel from the city centre, close to the Konrad-Adenauer-Brücke. Trier West is the closest train station.

Weimar (tel. code 03643)

TOURIST OFFICE
Weimar-Information, Marktstraße 4, D-05300 Weimar (tel. 2173). From the train station head downhill on Carl-August-Allee, straight on until you reach Goetheplatz (a 15-minute walk), or take bus 1. From the far end of Goetheplatz, head left along Geleitstraße, turn right at Windischenstraße, then left.

HOTELS, PENSIONS & GUESTHOUSES
Cheapest doubles around DM80 (£34.50; $51.75)

Hotel Kaiserin Augusta, Carl-August-Allee 17 (tel. 2162). Singles start at DM45 (£19.25; $29). Just over 100m downhill from the train station.
Guest House of the Hotel Belvedere, Ernst-Busse-Strasse 9 (tel. 61566).

Cheapest doubles around DM90 (£38.50; $57.75)

Hotel Thüringen, Brennerstraße 2 (tel. 3675). Brennerstraße runs downhill from the left-hand side of the square in front of the train station.

Hotel-Pension Liszt, Lisztstraße 3 (tel. 61911). Close to the centre. From Goetheplatz (see **Tourist Office** above), take Heinrich-Heine-Strasse at the bottom right of the square, left on Sophienstiftsplatz, right on Philipp-Müller-Strasse, right again into Steubenstraße, then left.

PRIVATE ROOMS
From the Tourist Office. Mar.–Oct., Mon.–Fri. 9 a.m.–7 p.m., Sat. 9 a.m.–4 p.m.; Nov.–Feb., 9 a.m.–1 p.m. only. Prices range from DM20–30 (£8.50–13.00; $12.75–19.50) per person without breakfast.

HI HOSTELS
'Germania', Carl-August-Allee 13 (tel. 2076). B&B DM19,50 (£8.50; $12.75). A 100m walk downhill from the train station.

'Am Poseckschen Garten', Humboldtstraße 17 (tel. 64021). B&B DM18 (£7.75; $11.50). Just outside the centre. From Goetheplatz (see **Tourist Office** above), take Wielandstraße at the bottom left of the square, straight on through Theaterplatz, right along Schützengasse, left at Steubenstraße, then a quick right into Humboldtstraße.

'Maxim Gorki', Zum Wilden Graben 12 (tel. 3471). B&B, DM22,50 (£9.50; $14.50). A 15-minute walk from the town centre. From Schützengasse (see the hostel above), head left into Wielandplatz, right down Amalienstraße, then along the sides of the cemeteries until you see Zum Wilden Graben on the right.

CAMPING
Although there are no campsites in Weimar itself, it is easy to get to sites in the vicinity by public transport. The closest site is in Öttern, 9.5km from Weimar and accessible by bus. 24km out of town is the site at Lake Hohenfelden, which can be reached by bus or local trains (a 40-minute trip).

Würzburg (tel. code 0931)

TOURIST OFFICES
Fremdenverkehrsamt Würzburg, Am Congress Centrum, D-97070 Würzburg (tel. 37371/37436). Handles the advance reservation of rooms (written enquiries preferred).

Tourist Information, Pavillon am Hauptbahnhof (tel. 37436). Open Mon.–Sat. 8 a.m.–8 p.m. Room reservation on arrival. DM3 (£1.25; $2) commission. By the train and bus stations.

Tourist Information, Haus zum Falken am Markt (tel. 37398). Open Mon.–Fri. 9 a.m.–6 p.m., Sat. 9 a.m.–2 p.m. Room reservation on arrival. DM3 (£1.25; $2) commission.

HOTELS, PENSIONS & GUESTHOUSES
Cheapest doubles around DM60 (£25.50; $38.25)

Gasthof Schlier (tel. 09367 501) and Pension Schlier (tel. 09367 448) are both in Bergtheim, about 16km out of Würzburg. Local trains to Schweinfurt stop in the town. There are trains every 90 minutes through the day. The last train leaves just before 9 p.m. and does not run on Saturdays, but there are later buses.

Hotel Groene, Scheffelstraße 2 (tel. 74449). About 2km from the town centre.

Cheapest doubles around DM65 (£28; $42)

Hotel Fischzucht, Julius-Echter-Strasse 15 (tel. 64095). About 4km from the centre.

Cheapest doubles around DM80 (£34.50; $51.75)

Pension Spehnkuch, Röntgenring 7 (tel. 54752).

Gasthof Jägerruh, Grombühlstraße 55 (tel. 281412/21892). Three kilometres from the centre.

Gasthof Zur Klinge, Rathausplatz (tel. 62122). About 4km from the town centre in the suburb of Heidingsfeld. Tram 3 from Würzburg Hbf.

Pension Siegel, Reisgrubengasse 7 (tel. 52941/52964). Excellent central location.

Cheapest doubles around DM90 (£38.50; $57.75)

Hotel Zum Winzermännle, Domstraße 32 (tel. 54156/17456).
   Excellent central location.

Gasthof Hemmerlein, Balthasar-Neumann-Promenade 5 (tel.
   51300). Good location on the street running past the Residenz
   (Palace of the Prince-Bishops). Follow Theaterstraße to its end,
   then go left.

Hotel Dortmunder Hof, Innerer Graben 22 (tel. 56163). Central
   location. First right off Schönbornstraße.

HI HOSTEL

DJH-Jugendgästehaus, Burkarder Straße 44 (tel. 42590). B&B
DM24 (£10.25; $15.50). A 20–25-minute walk from Würzburg Hbf
(left after crossing the Alte Mainbrücke, then straight on), or tram
3 dir: Heidingsfeld from the station.

CAMPING

Kanu-Club, Mergentheimerstraße 13b (tel. 72536). Tram 3 dir:
   Heidingsfeld from Würzburg Hbf to Judenbühlweg, then a short
   walk following the signs for the canoe club. Check in at the
   restaurant.

Kalte Quelle, Winterhäuserstraße 160 (tel. 65598).

GREECE (Hellas)

Although accommodation prices have risen relatively sharply over the past few years, by European standards accommodation in Greece is still a bargain. At most times of the year, there is an ample supply of cheap beds and, except in the peak months of July and August, you are unlikely to encounter any trouble in finding a place to stay, even if you arrive late in the day. However, finding a cheap bed in Athens during the peak season becomes a bit of a problem (especially if you start looking after midday), while the supply of reasonably priced accommodation on most of the islands fails miserably to satisfy the huge demand.

Hotels are graded into six categories; deluxe, and then downwards from A to E. D-and E-class hotels are well within the range of the budget traveller, with singles in the 1500–3300dr (£4.25–9.50; $6.50–14.25) range, and doubles from 1700–4000dr (£4.75–11.00; $7.00–16.50) (prices are for rooms without a shower/bath). Prices in C-class hotels generally start around 3250dr (£9.50; $14.25) for singles and 5400dr (£15; $22.50) for doubles, though some C-class hotels offer much cheaper rooms. Beds in triples or quads invariably work out much cheaper per person than those in singles or doubles. During the peak season, hotels may levy a 10% surcharge if you stay for less than three nights. Off-season, hotels cut their rates by up to 40%. At this time of year, hoteliers are often prepared to negotiate about room prices, as they know you can easily take your custom elsewhere.

Pensions are cheaper than hotels. Though you may not notice much of a difference between the prices of pensions and those of cheap hotels in Athens, the difference is readily apparent elsewhere: even in such popular destinations as Rhodes where pensions are often cheaper than private rooms, but especially so in rural areas, where prices can be as low as 600dr (£1.75; $2.50) per person.

Private rooms (*dhomatia*) are normally a fair amount cheaper than hotels. These are also officially classified, from A down to C. C-class rooms start around 1300dr (£3.75; $5.50) for singles, 1900dr (£5.25; $8) for doubles and 2500dr (£7; $10.50) for triples. Comparable A-class rooms start around 2000dr (£5.50; $8.50), 2300dr (£6.50; $9.50) and 3200dr (£9; $13.50) respectively. Private rooms are most common on the islands and in the coastal resorts. In most towns with a considerable supply of rooms, they can be booked through the local Tourist Office or Tourist Police. In some places, these offices operate an annoying policy of only booking rooms when the local hotels are filled to capacity. It is possible to look for rooms on your own: they are frequently advertised in several languages in an effort to attract tourists' attention (typically Greek, German, English, French and Italian). At the height of the tourist season, travellers arriving by bus or ferry in popular destinations are almost certain to encounter locals touting rooms in their homes at train and bus stations, or ferry terminals. Given the severe accommodation shortage on most of the islands, it makes sense to accept any offer where the price and the location are reasonable. Few private rooms remain open during the period from November to April. For any small group looking to stay put for a week or so, renting a house or a flat can be an excellent option, particularly on the islands. Unfortunately, you will have to make enquiries locally on arrival to see what possibilities exist.

The **youth hostel** network is not extensive, numbering around 30 hostels in total. Generally, they are a bit ramshackle, but the atmosphere is usually quite relaxed. Only rarely are HI membership cards asked for. Even then you can buy a card at the hostel, or will be allowed to stay on the payment of a small surcharge. The overnight fee ranges from 1400–2500dr (£4–7; $6.00–10.50). Between June and September, curfews are usually 1 a.m.; at other times of the year, midnight. However, there are some hostels which close as early as 10 p.m. With the warden's agreement, you can stay longer than the normal three-day maximum. In Athens, there are a number of **student houses**. These are non-official hostels which offer cheap dormitory accommodation. As international trains approach Athens, young people from various student houses often board the train to hand out leaflets advertising their establishment. The leaflets are always flattering, of course, but some of these places are fine. Others, however, are of very poor quality. By and large, the cheapest of these hostels are also the least secure for your belongings. The average price for dorms is 1300dr (£3.75; $5.50).

Student houses frequently offer sleeping accommodation on their roof, as do some hotels and HI hostels. In the countryside, and on the islands, the best bet for renting **roof space** are the local 'tavernas'. To find out about availability you will have to ask in person, question the hostel touts, or rely on word of mouth. The Tourist Office are unlikely to be very expansive regarding the availability of roof space, as the practice was made illegal in 1987, ostensibly because the government was concerned about hoteliers overcharging. At present, the law is flouted on a wide scale, and renting a spot on a roof to throw down a mat and a sleeping bag remains a cheap and pleasant way to spend the summer nights. In Athens, you can expect to pay about 750dr (£2; $3), but elsewhere you will rarely pay as much as this – around 600dr (£1.75; $2.50) being more normal.

There are around 90 official **campsites**, of which 13 are run by the Greek National Tourist Organization (EOT); the rest are privately operated. The EOT sites are usually large, regimented establishments. The standard of the private sites varies widely. While some are very pleasant, others, especially those on the islands, are often little more than fenced off patches of land (or sand). Typical prices are around 450dr (£1.25; $1.75) for a small tent, 650dr (£1.80; $2.75) per occupant. While private sites may be prepared to drop their prices a little, there is no chance of this at state-run sites. If you are travelling between late June and early September, it is advisable to pack a tent as it guarantees you a cheap night's sleep. Travelling without a tent in the peak season, you are going to have to be incredibly fortunate to find a cheap bed every night of your trip.

Freelance camping and **sleeping rough** were made illegal as long ago as 1977, although many travellers are completely unaware of this. In part this is because many people still camp and sleep rough without encountering any difficulties with the authorities. Certainly, the law is not always stringently enforced. In the rural parts of the mainland there is virtually no chance of you having any problems, provided you ask permission before you pitch a tent, and do not litter the area. Even on the islands, the police are tolerant of transgressions of the law, within certain limits. You will usually be all right if you show some discretion in your choice of site. This is important because in July and August your chances of finding a room or hostel bed are slim, so at some point you are likely to have to camp or sleep rough. *Avoid the main tourist beaches as the local police patrol them regularly.* Raids are also likely if the police hear that large numbers are beginning to congregate in one spot. The police are increasingly prone to using force to clear people away.

In most of the mountainous regions of the country the Hellenic Alpine Club (HAC) maintains **refuge huts** for the use of climbers and hikers. Some of these are unmanned, so you have to visit the local HAC office in advance to pick up a set of keys. Unless you are a member of the HAC, or one of its foreign associates, you will have to pay a surcharge on the normal overnight fee.

ADDRESSES

EOT	National Tourist Organization of Greece, 4 Conduit Street, London W1R 0DJ (tel. 0171 734 5997).

Hotels	Advance reservations. Greek Chamber of Hotels, Stadiou Street 24, Athens 105–64 (tel. 01 323 6962).
Greek YHA	Greek Youth Hostel Association, Dragatsaniou Street 4, Athens 105–59 (tel. 01 323 4107/323 7590).
Camping	Greek Camping Association, Solanos Street 76, Athens 106–80 (tel. 01 362 1560).
Mountain Refuges	Hellenic Alpine Club (HAC), Karageorgi Street 7, Athens (tel. 01 323 4555).

Athens (Athina) (tel. code 01)

TOURIST OFFICES

Greek National Tourist Organization (EOT), Amerikis 2, Athens 10564 (tel. 3223111). EOT head office. Contact this office for information on the city or the country before you set off on holiday. On arrival, you can obtain information at any of the information counters they operate in the city, but most will not give help with finding accommodation.

Karageorgi Servias 2 (tel. 322 2545). The office is located in the National Bank on Syntagma Square. Open Mon.–Fri. 8 a.m.–6.30 p.m., Sat. 9 a.m.–2 p.m., Sun. 9 a.m.–1 p.m.

Ermou 1 (tel. 323 4130). In the General Bank of Greece on Syntagma Square. Open Mon.–Fri. 8 a.m.–8.30 p.m., Sat. 8 a.m.–2 p.m.

Airport (tel. 961 2722). Round-the-clock service in the East Air Terminal.

Pireaus, Zea Marina (tel. 4135716). Information and help with accommodation is available.

Hellenic Chamber of Hotels. Room-finding service. A–C-class hotels only. In the National Bank on Syntagma Square. Open Mon.–Fri. 8 a.m.–2 p.m., Sat. 9 a.m.–2 p.m.

FINDING ACCOMMODATION

Unless you arrive late in the day during July or August you should find a reasonably cheap place to stay quite easily. Expect to pay from 2500dr (£7; $10.50) for a single, upwards of 3500dr (£9.75; $14.50) for a double, around 1500dr (£4.25; $6.50) for a dormitory bed, and 600–1000dr (£1.70–2.75; $2.50–4.25) for a mattress on a hostel roof.

PENSIONS/STUDENT HOSTELS

There's plenty of cheap accommodation close to the railway station and around Omonia Square, which is handy if you're passing through Athens but rather inconvenient for the main sights and night life. For Omonia Square, turn right outside the station along Theodorou Diligiani to Karaiskaki Square, then turn left along Agiou Konstandinou.

Olympos (tel. 522 3433). Right opposite the train station.

Diethnes, Peoniou 52 (tel. 883 6855). Walk left from the station, then turn right on to Peoniou.

Aphrodite, Einavdou 12 (tel. 881 0589). Walk left from the station, past the end of Peonious, then turn right up Karditsas on to Liossion. Cross the street, head left, and then almost immediately right at Einavdou.

Athens Connection, Ioulianou 20 (tel. 821 3940). Free baggage storage. Beds go swiftly.

San Remo, Nissirou 8 (tel. 522 2404). Left off Theodorou Diligiani, just before Mezonos.

Santa Mavra, Mezonos 74 (tel. 522 3138/522 5149).

Athens Inn, Viktoros Ougo 13 (tel. 524 6906). Singles 2400dr (£6.75; $10), doubles 3400dr (£9.50; $14.25). Dorms 1300–1700dr (£3.75–4.75; $5.50–7.25). Free baggage storage. Viktoros Ougo crosses Theodorou Diligiani a short distance from Karaisaki Square.

Argo, Viktoros Ougo 25 (tel. 522 5939). Singles 1800dr (£5; 7.50), doubles 3400dr (£9.50; $14.25), triples 3600dr (£10; $15), quads 4800dr (£13.50; $20). Free luggage storage.

Rio, Odisseos 13 (tel. 522 7075). Singles 3000dr (£8.50; $12.75), doubles 3600dr (£10; $15), triples 4800dr (£13.50; $20), quads 5800dr (£16.20; $24.25). Free baggage storage. Right off Theodorou Diligiani, virtually at Karaiskaki Square.

Annabel, Koumoundourou 28 (tel. 524 5834). Dorms 1500dr (£4.25; $6.50), roof 600dr (£1.70; $2.50). Free baggage storage. From Theodorou Diligiani go left along Viktoros Ougo after crossing Marni.

Appia, Menandrou 21 (tel. 524 5155/4561). Singles 2500dr (£7; $10.50), doubles 4000dr (£11; $16.50). Cafeteria and 24-hour. Free luggage storage. Left off Agiou Konstandinou.

Lydia, Liossion 121 (tel. 821 9980).

Joy's, Feron 38 (tel. 823 1012). A few blocks beyond Liossion turn

left off Ioulianou up Mihail Voda, then turn right along Feron.
The pension is at the junction with Aharnon.

Feron, Feron 43 (tel. 823 2083). See Joy's, above.

Pergamos, Aharnon 104 (tel. 523 1991).

Elli, Heiden 29 (tel. 881 5876). Left up Aharnon, then right.

Angela, Stournara 38 (tel. 523 3262/3263/4263). Off Aharnon and
Marni, one block from Anexartissias Square.

Sun Light, Filis 68 (tel. 881 1956). Filis crosses Ioulianou one block
after Aharnon.

Athens House, Aristotelous 4 (tel. 524 0539). Single 2400dr (£6.75;
$10), doubles 3600dr (£10; $15), triples 4800dr (£13.50; $20),
quad 6000dr (£17; $25.50). Aristotelous crosses Ioulianou a
couple of blocks after Aharnon.

Iokastis' House, Aristotelous 65 (tel. 822 6647). At the junction
with Ioulianou.

Hellas, Tritis Septemvriou 5 (tel. 522 4540/8544). Singles 1900dr
(£5.25; $8), doubles 3100dr (£8.75; $13), triples 3300dr (£9.25;
$14). Free luggage storage.

Zorba's, Gilfordou 10 (tel. 823 2543). Turn left up Tritis Septemvriou from Ioulianou, then head right.

Patissia, Patission 221 (tel. 862 7511/865 7512).

Athens City, Patission 232 (tel. 862 9115/9116).

Diana, Patission 70 (tel. 822 3179).

Milton, Kotsika 4 (tel. 821 6806). From Ioulianou turn left up
Patission, then right along Kotsika.

Accommodation around Syntagma Square is slightly more expensive than on average, but is conveniently located near the centre
and the places of interest. As you look across Syntagma with the
Parliament to your rear, Ermou is the road leading out of the centre
of the square. Kar. Servias (which becomes Perikleous) runs from
the far right-hand corner, Mitropoleos from the far left. Filelinon
runs from the left-hand side of the square.

Festos, Filelinon 18 (tel. 323 2455). 2 a.m. curfew. Doubles 4400dr
(£12.25; $18.50), dorm 1600dr (£4.50; $7), roof 1000dr (£2.75;
$4.25). Baggage storage 100dr (£0.30: $0.45) per day.

George's, Nikis 46 (tel. 322 6474). Doubles 3500dr (£9.75; $14.50),
dorms 1500dr (£4.25; $6.50). Nikis crosses Ermou and Mitropo-
leos one block from Syntagma.

Peter's, Nikis 32 (tel. 322 2697). See George's, above.

Myrto, Nikis 40 (tel. 322 7237/323 4560). See George's, above.

Christ, Apolonos 11 (tel. 322 0177/323 4581). From Mitropoleos
turn left down Nikis, then turn right along Apolonos.

Aphrodite, Apolonos 21 (tel. 323 4357/322 6047). See Christ, above.

Amazon, Pentelis 7 & Mitropoleos (tel. 323 4002/4004). Pentelis is off Mitropoleos, three blocks from Syntagma.

John's Place, Patroou 5 (tel. 322 9719). Off Mitropoleos, four blocks from Syntagma.

Theseus, Thissios 10 (tel. 324 5960). Curfew 1 a.m. Doubles 3500dr (£9.75; $14.50), small dorms 1500dr (£4.25; $6.50). Right off Perikleous.

Hermion, Ermou 66c (tel. 321 2753). Singles 3500dr (£9.75; $14.50), doubles 5500dr (£15.50; $23.25). In an alleyway off Ermou.

Ideal, Eolou 39 (tel. 321 3195/322 0542). Eolou crosses Ermou about 1km from Syntagma, beyond the Kapnikarea church.

Pella Inn, Ermou 104 (tel. 325 0598). Singles 6000dr (£17; $25.50), doubles 7000dr (£20; $30). Free baggage storage. The entrance is on Karaisaki. A 10-minute walk from Syntagma, close to the Monastariki underground station.

Athenian Inn, Haritos 22 (tel. 723097/7239552). From Syntagma walk past the left-hand side of the parliament. At the Benaki Museum turn left away from the National Garden up Koumbari into Filikis Eterias Square. Cross the square and head right along Patriarhi Iokm, turn left up Irodotou, then right into Haritos.

The Plaka, beneath the Acropolis, is both centrally located, and a cheap area to stay in.

Dioscouri, Pitakou 6 (tel. 324 8165).

Student Inn, Kidathineon 16 (tel. 324 4808). 1.30 a.m. curfew. Small dorms 1200dr (£3.50; $5). Luggage storage. Turn right off Filelinon as you walk from Syntagma Square (see below).

Kouros, Kodrou 11 (tel. 322 7431). Walking from Syntagma Square along Mitropoleos (see below), turn left down Voulis and continue straight on across Nikodimou into Kodrou.

Acropolis House, Kodrou 6–8 (tel. 322 2344/6241). Singles 5100dr (£14.25; $21.50) for one night, 7200dr (£20; $30) for two nights. Doubles 6650dr (£18.50; $28). Adding an extra bed to a room increases the original price by 20%. Luggage storage. See Kouros, above.

Adonis, Kodrou 3 & Voulis (tel. 3249737/3249741). Cheapest doubles 8000dr (£22; $33). See Kouros.

Veikou, Koukaki, Arditos and Pangrati districts: on the other side of the Acropolis from the Plaka, these are quieter residential areas.

Art Gallery, Erehthiou 5 (tel. 923 8376/1933). Singles from 5900dr
(£16.50; $24.75), doubles from 7100dr (£19.75; $29.75). Luggage storage.
Greca, Singrou 48 (tel. 921 5262). Singles 3100dr (£8.75; $13).
Marble House, An. Zini 35 (tel. 923 4058). Singles 3500dr (£9.75;
$14.50), doubles 6000dr (£17; $25.50). Free luggage storage.
Take trolleybus 1 or 5 to the Zini stop.
Joseph House, Markou Moussouro 13 (tel. 923 1204). Singles from
2750dr (£7.50; $11.25), roof 1000dr (£2.75; $4.25).
Youth Hostel No. 5, Damareos 75 (tel. 751 9530). Dorms 1500dr
(£4.25; $6.50), roof from 1000dr (£2.75; $4.25). Take trolleybus
2, 11 or 12 to Pangratiou Square, then walk down Frinis until
it is crossed by Damareos.

HI HOSTEL
Kypselis 57 (tel. 822 5860). Kipseli district. Trolleybus 2, 4 or 9
from Syntagma to Zakinthou.

YMCA HOSTEL
XAN, Omirou 28 (tel. 362 4291). From Syntagma Square (standing
with your back to the parliament), take Stadiou, the main road
heading right. Walk past the junction with Amerikis and the GNTO
head office, then take the next right.

YWCA HOSTEL
XEN, Amerikis 11 (tel. 362 4291). Cheapest doubles 4000dr (£11;
$16.50). For directions, see the YMCA hostel above.

CAMPING
Athens Camping, Leoforos Athinon 198, Peresteri (tel. 581 4114).
Bus 822 or 823 from Eleftherias Square (Underground: Thission).
Open all year, 7km from the centre.
Dionissioti Camping (tel. 807 1494). 18km north of the city on the
national road at Nea Kifissia.
Acropolis Camping (tel. 807 5253). 16km north at the Athens–
Lania crossing on the national road at Nea Kiffissia. 430dr
(£1.25; $2) per person.
Voula, 2 Alkyonidon (tel. 895 2712). Bus 118, 122 or 153 from
Vass. Olgas Avenue.
Dafni Camping. About 13km out in Dafni (tel. 581 1562/1563).
Bus 853 or 870.

SLEEPING ROUGH
Definitely not to be advised. It is illegal and the police make regular
checks on the city's parks, especially those located close to the train

station. The police, however, are likely to be the least of your worries given the considerable numbers of travellers who are robbed or assaulted while sleeping rough.

Corfu Town (Kerkira) (tel. code 0661)

TOURIST OFFICES
EOT and the local Tourist Police both have offices in the palace (tel. 37520/37638). Follow the street along the waterfront from the new port. The EOT office distributes a list of local hotels and has information on the availability of private rooms. Another office operates in the Governor's House between Dessila and Mantzarou. For information, tel. 30298/30360.

FINDING ACCOMMODATION
At most times of year you should find yourself an E-class hotel without too much trouble, either from the list given out by the EOT office or simply by looking round on your own (the streets between the Igoumentsa Dock and N. Theotki are your best bet, especially if it is singles you are after). In summer, you are more likely to have to ask the Tourist Office about a private room, but it is worth noting that many of the tourist agencies lining Arseniou (between the Old Port and the Old Fortress) and Stratigou (beside the New Port) book rooms in pensions, frequently without commission.

HOTELS
Europa (tel. 39304). Not far from the new port ferry terminal.
Cyprus, Agion Pateron 13 (tel. 40675). Close to the National Bank on Voulgareos. Doubles 5000dr (£14; $21), triples 6000dr (£17; $25.50).
Elpis, Parados N. Theotki 4,5H (tel. 30289). In an alley across from 128 N. Theotki, near the Old Port.
Konstantinoupoli, Zavitsanou 11 (tel. 31595). At the end of N. Theotki. Doubles from around 5000dr (£14; $21).
Crete, N. Theotki 43 (tel. 38691). Doubles 4000dr (£11; $16.50).
Spilia, Solomou 2 (tel. 25648). Close to the KTEL bus station.

HI HOSTEL
Kontokali Beach (tel. 91202). About 5km north of town, a 20-minute trip on bus 7 from Platia San Rocco, every 30 minutes.

Cheapest accommodation in Corfu: 1000dr (£2.75; $4.25) per person. No curfew, and handy for the beach.

CAMPING
Kontokali Beach International (tel. 91170). Same bus as the hostel. 600dr (£1.70; $2.50) per person, plus 600dr per tent.

Camping Dionysus, Dafnilas Bay, P.O.Box 185 (tel. 91417). About 9km north of the town, connected by a morning bus service.

Crete (Kriti) – Agios Nikolaos
(tel. code 0841)

TOURIST OFFICE
Akti I. Koundourou 20 (tel. 22357/24165). By the bridge near the port. Room-finding service.

FINDING ACCOMMODATION
The best places to look for rooms are the streets up the hill from the HI hostel, or the side streets leading off the roads heading out of town. However, in summer when it is exceptionally difficult to find rooms, you will probably save yourself a lot of effort by heading straight to the Tourist Office.

HOTELS
Pension Katerina, Koraka Street 33 (tel. 22766). Six blocks from the HI hostel.

Christodoulakis Pension, Stratigou Koraka Street 7 (tel. 22525). Doubles around 5000dr (£14; $21). Kitchen facilities available. Next to the HI hostel.

Argiro Pension, Solonos Street 1 (tel. 28707). Doubles from 3500dr (£9.75; $14.50). From the Tourist Office head up 25th Martirou, turn left along Manousogianaki, then right at Solonos.

The Green House, Modatsou Street 15 (tel. 22025). Doubles 3500dr (£9.75; $14.50). From the Tourist Office follow Koudourou to the left, go left again at Iroon Polytechniou, then right at Modatsou.

Pension Perla, Salaminos 4 (tel. 23379). Doubles 5700dr (£16; $24).

HI HOSTEL
Odos Stratigou Koraka 3 (tel. 22823). Walk up the concrete steps from the bridge at the harbour.

CAMPING

Although some people camp on the beach in front of the bus station, this is not to be recommended. It is better to head out of town to some of the beaches along the coast. The cove at Kalo Horio, about 13km out, is one of the best places to pitch a tent.

Crete (Kriti) – Hania (Xania)
(tel. code 0821)

TOURIST OFFICE

EOT, 'Pantheon' building (4th floor), 40 Kriari (tel. 26426). Head office. Well organized, and extremely helpful. A branch office operates in the old mosque at the east end of the harbour (tel. 43300). Open Mon.–Sat. 8.30 a.m.–2 p.m. and 3–8 p.m., Sun. 9 a.m.–3 p.m.

FINDING ACCOMMODATION

Finding a reasonably priced room is considerably easier in Hania than in the other main towns on the island. Even in high season, you should not have to contemplate staying in one of the local C-class hotels. There are concentrations of cheap pensions around the harbour, and slightly further afield, around the cathedral, and in the slightly dilapidated Spiantza district. Outside the peak season, you will rarely have to stray far from the harbour to find suitable accommodation.

HOTELS

Hotel Piraeus, Zambeliou 10 (tel. 54154). Singles 2500dr (£7; $10.50), doubles 3800dr (£10.50; $15.75). At the junction of Halidon and Zambeliou.

Meltemi Pension, Angelou Street 2 (tel. 40192). Singles 4000dr (£11; $16.50). By the Naval Museum, at the western end of the harbour.

Pension Teris, Zambeliou 47 (tel. 53120). Singles 3500dr (£9.75; $14.50), doubles 4000dr (£11; $16.50).

Hotel Viennos, Skalidi Street 27 (tel. 22470). Singles 1200dr (£3.50; $5), doubles 1900dr (£5.25; $8). Dormitory 700dr (£2; $3). Beyond 1866 Platia as you walk from the harbour.

Hotel Fidias, Sarpaki Street 6 (tel. 52494). Doubles 3500dr (£9.75; $14.50), dorms from 1250dr (£3.50; $5.25). Turn right off

Halidon at the cathedral, along Athinagora which subsequently becomes Sarpaki.

Pension Kasteli, Kanevaro Street 39 (tel. 57057). Singles 3000dr (£8.50; $12.75), doubles 4000dr (£11; $16.50). The owner also lets apartments with kitchen facilities in a house nearby. Kanevaro runs from the eastern end of the harbour.

Pension Efi, Sorvolou Street 15 (tel. 23986). Signposted from the market.

Hotel Manos, Zambeliou 17 (tel. 52152). Although the entrance is on Zambeliou, the hotel overlooks the shore from above the Dionisos Taverna.

Rooms for Rent No.47, Kandanolou 47 (tel. 53243). Doubles around 3500dr (£9.75; $14.50). On Kastelli Hill. Follow Kanevaro from the eastern end of the harbour, then turn off to the left.

Antonis Rooms, Kountoriotou Street 8 (tel. 20019). Doubles 1700dr (£4.75; $7.25), triples 2200dr (£6.20; $9.25). Overlooking the western end of the harbour.

HI HOSTEL

Drakonianou Street 33 (tel. 53565). Open Mar.–Nov. No curfew. Well out from the centre on the outskirts of Hania. Bus 4, 11, 12 or 13 from the junction of Apokoronou and Yianari.

CAMPING

Hania (tel. 31490). 450dr (£1.25; $2) for a small tent, 600dr (£1.75; $2.50) per person. Close to the beach. About 2km west of Hania, reached by taking the Kalamaki bus from 1866 Platia.

Agia Marina (tel. 68555/68556/68596). In the village of Agia Marina, 9.5km west of Hania. Close to the beach. The Kastelli bus serves Agia Marina.

Crete (Kriti) – Heraklion (Iraklion)
(tel. code 081)

TOURIST OFFICES

EOT, Xanthoudidou Street 1 (tel. 228203/228225). Open Mon.–Fri. 8 a.m.–2.30 p.m. Plans of the town, lists of local hotels. Just off Platia Eleftherias, across from the Archaeological Museum. A branch office operates at the airport (tel. 225636), open 9 a.m.–9 p.m. daily. The Tourist Police office is at Dhikeosinis Street 10 (tel. 283190), on the way from Platia Eleftherias to the market.

FINDING ACCOMMODATION

Rooms become very difficult to find in the peak season. The majority of the cheaper rooms are located in the area between Platia Venizelou and the shore, especially Handakos Street and the streets on either side. On leaving the port head right, then go right again when you reach the town walls and follow the water for about 1km, until you see Handakos on the left after the Xenia Hotel.

HOTELS

Hotel Rea, Kalimeraki Street 1 (tel. 223638). Doubles 4000dr (£11; $16.50). Off Handakos, close to the Historical Museum, a couple of blocks from the shore.

Rent-a-Room Vergina, Hortatson 32 (tel. 242739). Doubles 4000dr (£11; $16.50). Between the OTE office (telephone company) and the Morosini Fountain.

Kretan Sun, 1866 Street 10 (tel. 243794). Singles 4000dr (£11; $16.50), doubles 5300dr (£14.75; $22). Above the market.

Hotel Ideon Andron, Perdikari Street 1 (tel. 283624). Singles 1650dr (£4.50; $7), doubles 2200dr (£6.25; $9.25), triples 2750dr (£7.60; $11.60). From Platia Venizelou walk along Dedalou Street, then turn left and follow Perdikari to its end.

Rent Rooms Mary, Handakos 67 (tel. 281135).

HI HOSTEL

Vironos Street 5 (tel. 286281). Open year all round. 11.30 p.m. curfew. 700dr (£2; $3) per person. Luggage storage. Bar serves beer 350dr (£1; $1.50) and breakfast 350dr (£1; $1.50). Vironos is off 25th Augustou.

HOSTEL

Yours Hostel, Handakos 24 (tel. 280858). Rooms from 800dr (£2.25; $3.50). Very central. Rooftop bar; breakfast 450–600dr (£1.25–1.75; $2.00–2.50).

Crete (Kriti) – Rethimno (tel. code 0831)

TOURIST OFFICE

E. Venizelos Ave. (tel. 29148/24143). Open Mon.–Fri. 9 a.m.–3.30 p.m. Local maps and bus and ferry schedules. Contact this office for details of private rooms for rent. By the waterfront.

FINDING ACCOMMODATION

Rooms in the cheaper D- and E-class hotels become very hard to find during the summer season, so start looking for a room as early as possible. The majority of the cheaper rooms are located in the streets to your left as you make your way down from the bus station to the shore.

HOTELS

Vrisinas, Hereti Street 10 (tel. 26092). Doubles 2300dr (£6.50; $9.50). Off Arkadiou Street, a short walk from the bus station.

Olga's Pension, Souliou 57 (tel. 29851). Singles 3500dr (£9.75; $14.50), doubles 4000dr (£11; $16.50), roof space 600dr (£1.75; $2.50). Souliou is off Ethnikis Antistaseos.

Hotel Paradisos, Igoum Gavril Street 35 (tel. 22419). Singles 2700dr (£7.50; $11.50), doubles 3600dr (£10; $15). From the bus station head for the Venizelou monument, then go left along Kountou-roitou, which runs into Igoum Gavril.

Hotel Zania, Pavlou Vlastou Street 3 (tel. 28169). Doubles 5000dr (£14; $21). Off Arkadiou.

Hotel Achillo, Arkadiou 151 (tel. 22581). Singles 3000dr (£8.50; $12.75), doubles 4000dr (£11; $16.50).

Hotel Acropol, Makariou Street 2 (tel. 21305). Off Iroon Square, close to the shore.

Rent Rooms. To the rear of the Taverna Helona, at the junction of Eleftheriou Venizelou and Petichaki. Doubles 2700dr (£7.50; $11.50).

Barbara Dokimaki, Plastira Street 14 (tel. 22319). Doubles 4000dr (£11; $16.50). All rooms have a private bath. Roof space 1500dr (£4.25; $6.50).

Pension Anna, Katehaki (tel. 25586). Close to the fortress.

HI HOSTEL

Topazi Street 45 (tel. 22848). No curfew. 900dr (£2.50; $4) per person.

CAMPING

Camping Elizabeth (tel. 28694). 1200dr (£3.50; $5) per person, 600dr (£1.75; $2.50) per tent. On the beach at Myssiria Rethimno, 3km from town at the start of the old Iraklion road (buses from Iraklion pass the site). Buses run frequently from Rethimno bus station to the site. Grassed areas for pitching tents.

Ios – Ios Town (Hora) (tel. code 0286)

TOURIST OFFICE
The Tourist Office (tel. 91028) is by the bus stop in Ios Town. Open daily 9 a.m.–3 p.m. and 4.30–10.30 p.m. Local information and ferry schedules. Ios Town is easily reached from the ferry port in Yialos by bus, or by a 20-minute walk up the hill.

FINDING ACCOMMODATION
Accommodation on Ios is noticeably cheaper than on most of the Cyclades, with the exception of the ferry port of Yialos. That said, singles are in short supply at any time of year, while rooms of any type become difficult to find during the peak season of July and August.

HOTELS
Draco Pension. Immediately to the right of the bus stop.
Francesco's (tel. 91223). Up the hill from the bank.
The Wind (tel. 91139). Doubles 5000dr (£14; $21). Below the George Irene Hotel.
Marko's Pension (tel. 91060). Doubles 6000dr (£17; $25.50). Just to the left of The Wind.
Petradi's (tel. 91510). Doubles 4000dr (£11; $16.50). On the main road between the beach and the Old Town.

CAMPING
Camping Ios (tel. 91329). About 1000dr (£2.75; $4.25) per person. In Yialos, close to the ferry terminal.

There are two sites in Milopotamos, about 2km away. Both charge much the same price as Camping Ios, but are much more pleasant:

Stars (tel. 91302, or 01 4821083) (Athens number of the company who run the site).
Souli (tel. 91554, or 01 8940657).

SLEEPING ROUGH
Sleeping on the beach is no longer to be recommended, despite its past popularity. Not only is there a considerable risk of theft but police patrols are becoming increasingly regular, as is their readiness to clear the beach forcibly. Although it is still illegal, you should

have little trouble with the authorities if you stick to quieter beaches such as Koumbara or Manganari.

Kos – Kos Town (tel. code 0242)

TOURIST OFFICE
Municipal Tourist Information, Akti Kountouritou 7 (tel. 28724/24460). Open daily 7.30 a.m.–9.30 p.m. from 15 Apr.–31 Oct; Mon.–Fri. 7.30 a.m.–3 p.m. at other times. Information on accommodation, local maps and transport schedules. On the shore, at the junction of Akti Kountouritou with Vas. Pavlou.
   Tourist Police (tel. 28227). Next door to the Tourist Office.

FINDING ACCOMMODATION
Looking towards town from the harbour, the majority of the cheaper establishments are located over to your right. In July and August, you will struggle to find a bed in a pension or private room if you look on your own, unless you begin your search early in the day. At this time of year, it is better to accept any reasonable offer you receive from locals touting at the ferry port.

HOTELS & PENSIONS
Pension Alexis, Irodotou 9 (tel. 28798). Doubles from 4000dr (£11; $16.50). The owners will often accommodate those stuck for a room in beds on the patio for 1000dr (£2.75; $4.25). Off Megalos Alexandrou Street.
Xenon Australia, Averof 39 (tel. 23650). In summer, reservations four weeks in advance are virtually essential. Close to the town's northern beach.
Pension Popi, Averof 37 (tel. 23475). Doubles 5000dr (£14; $21). Next door to the Xenon Australia.
Hotel Dodecanissos, Alex. Ipsilantou 2 (tel. 28460/22860). Singles 4000dr (£11; $16.50), doubles 6000dr (£17; $25.50). From the Tourist Office head away from the shore, then take the first right.
Hotel Hara, Halkonos (tel. 22500). Doubles 6500dr (£18; $27). Close to Arseniou Street, one street back from the town's eastern shore.

CAMPING
Kos Camping (tel. 23910/23275). Open Apr.–Oct. 1000dr (£2.75; $4.25) per person, 600dr (£1.75; $2.50) per tent, but cheaper off-season. In the village of Psaldi, 2.5km from Kos.

Mykonos – Mykonos Town (Hora)
(tel. code 0289)

TOURIST OFFICE
Tourist Information (tel. 23990) is beside the Town Hall, at the other end of the waterfront from the ferry port and the Olympic Airways office. Open daily 9 a.m.–9 p.m. Free local accommodation service and information on ferry schedules. The Tourist Police office (tel. 22716/22482) (open round the clock) can also help with accommodation. Follow the signs marked 'Bus to Plati Yialos' as far as Platia Dim. Koutsi, at which point you turn left.

FINDING ACCOMMODATION
In the high season (May–Oct.) cheap rooms can be almost impossible to find, especially if you do not start looking until after midday. At this time of year, unless you are prepared to camp, or to sleep rough, it makes sense to accept any offer from the touts at the port that seems reasonable, bearing in mind the inflated price of accommodation on the island. In peak season, doubles in local pensions are rarely available for under 7000dr (£19.50; $29.50).

HOTELS
Hotel Phillipi, Kalogera Street 32 (tel. 22294). Open 1 Apr.–30 Oct. only. Singles 5700dr (£16; $24), doubles 10,300dr (£28.75; $43).
Hotel Maria, Kalogera Street 18 (tel. 24213). Doubles with bath 12,500dr (£35; $52.50).
Rooms Chez Maria, Kalogera Street 30 (tel. 22480). Open Apr.–Oct. Doubles 4400dr (£12.25; $18.50), doubles with baths 8000dr (£22; $33).
Apollon Hotel, Mavroyenous (tel. 23271/22223). Open Apr.–Oct. Singles from 7000dr (£19.50; $29.50). By the harbour.
Mina Hotel (tel. 23024). Doubles with bath 7000dr (£19.50; $29.50). Breakfast included. By the beach.
Panorama Hotel (tel. 22337). Singles 3300dr (£9.25; $14), doubles 6000dr (£17; $25.50). By the beach.
Angela's Rooms, Taxi Square (tel. 22967).
Delfines, Mavroyenous (tel. 22292).
Karbonaki, 21 Panahrandou (tel. 23127).
Karbonis, Andronikou Matoyianni (tel. 22475).

CAMPING
Paradise Beach (tel. 22129/22852/22937). A van meets all incoming ferries, offering free transport to the site.

FREELANCE CAMPING AND SLEEPING ROUGH
Despite being illegal both are widely practised on the Paradise, Super Paradise and Elia beaches. All three beaches are periodically cleared by the police.

Naxos – Naxos Town (Hora)
(tel. code 0285)

TOURIST OFFICE
The Tourist Office (tel. 24525/24358) is on the waterfront. Open daily 8 a.m.–12.30 a.m. from 15 Mar.–31 Oct; at other times, open daily 8 a.m.–9.30 p.m. Free local accommodation service and bus/ferry timetables. Luggage storage 150dr (£0.45; $0.65).

FINDING ACCOMMODATION
Unless you arrive during July or August, you should be able to find a double for 2000–3000dr (£5.50–8.50; $8.50–12.75), even less if you are travelling in the winter, when rates can be cut by anything up to 50%. The best area to search for accommodation is up the hill from the OTE office (the telephone company) where there is a substantial concentration of pensions and cheap hotels. In summer, incoming ferries are met by locals touting rooms: typical prices are 2000dr (£5.50; $8.50), for singles, 3100dr (£8.75; $13) for doubles, and 3500dr (£9.75; $14.50) for triples. As a rule, rooms offered at the port are more expensive than many of the rooms on offer in the town, but it can save you a lot of effort and frustration to fix up a room at the port.

HOTELS
Hotel Okeanis (tel. 22436). Directly opposite the docks.

Hotel Pantheon, Old Market Street (tel. 22379).

Hotel Dionyssos, Amfitritis (tel. 22331). Doubles 2500dr (£17; $10.50); roof/dorms 1000dr (£2.75; $4.25). Close to the Venetian Kastro in the Old Market quarter, straight up the hill from the docks. Painted red hands mark the way to the pension, while arrows point the way to the Annixis next door.

Eleni (tel. 24042). Doubles 3500dr (£9.75; $14.50). Turn left before the post office, and then watch for the white house with the brown balcony on your left.

Anna Legaki's (tel. 22837). Singles 3000dr (£8.50; $12.75). Over the road from the Eleni, above.

Hotel Annixis, Amfitritis 330 (tel. 22112). Next to the Dionyssos.
  See above for directions.
Hotel Proto, Protopapaki 13 (tel. 22394)

CAMPING
Naxos (tel. 41291/23500). 250dr (£0.75; $1.15) per tent, 750dr
(£2.10; $3.25) per person. Located by the Agios Giorgios beach.

Paros – Parikia (tel. code 0284)

TOURIST OFFICE
In the old windmill by the port (tel. 22079). Open 8 a.m.–10 p.m.
daily. Local maps and transport schedules, but no accommodation
service.

FINDING ACCOMMODATION
Paros is not only one of the most popular of the Cyclades in its
own right, but it is also an island many people pass through due
to its importance as a ferry hub. Consequently, finding hotels in
the peak season can be a frustrating experience (many are block-
booked by tour operators). At this time of year, locals touting private rooms await the arrival of every ferry. Provided the price is
not extravagant you should take the first offer you receive. Outside
the peak season you should have no trouble finding a double for
around 5000dr (£14; $21) in a local pension.

HOTELS
Hotel Dina (tel. 21325). Open May–Oct. Doubles 7000dr (£19.50;
  $29.25). Advanced reservation advised, preferably in writing.
  Just off the main street, at the foot of Market Square, past the
  National Bank.
Rooms Mimikos (tel. 21437). Doubles 6000dr (£17; $25). Close to
  the National Bank, just off Agorakitau (signposted).
Hotel Kontes (tel. 21246). All rooms have private baths. Behind
  the Tourist Office.
Hotel Kypreou (tel. 21383/22448). Not far from the Tourist Office,
  by the Olympic Airways office.
Hotel Parko (tel. 22213). Doubles 3900dr (£10.75; $16); doubles
  with bath 6000dr (£17; $25.50). Along the street from the
  Olympic Airways office.

CAMPING

Koula (tel. 22081/22082/84400). 250dr (£0.75; $1.15) per tent, 800dr (£2.25; $3.50) per person. At the northern end of the town's beach, only 400 metres from the centre.

Parasporas (tel. 21394/21944). About 2km out of town, but less crowded than the site above. Buses run from the port.

Krios (tel. 21705). On Krios Beach across the harbour. A small boat makes the trip to Krios Beach from the port.

Rhodes (Rodos) – Rhodes Town

(tel. code 0241)

TOURIST OFFICES

EOT, Archbishop Makariou/Papagou Street 5 (tel. 23255/23655). Open Mon.–Fri. 7.30 a.m.–3 p.m. Open all year.

City of Rhodes Tourist Office, Rimini Square (tel. 35945). Open Mon.–Sat. 8 a.m.–8 p.m., Sun. 9 a.m.–12 p.m. Closed during the winter. Accommodation service. Free town plan and bus and ferry information.

FINDING ACCOMMODATION

You should not have much trouble finding suitably priced accommodation in Rhodes Town. There are plenty of cheap pensions, virtually all of which are conveniently situated within the Old Town, in the area roughly bounded by Sokratous on the north, Perikléos on the east, Omirou on the south, and Ippodhamou on the west. In the winter, many pension owners close their doors; those that remain open will often drop their rates if you haggle.

HOTELS

Steve Kefalas's Pension, Omirou Street 60 (tel. 24357). Above a lively folk theatre. From the beginning of Sokratous go left on to Ag. Fanourious, then turn right into Omirou.

Billy's Pension, Perikléos Street 32 (tel. 35691). Doubles around 4000dr (£11; $16.50).

Dionisos Pension, Platonos Street 75 (tel. 22035). Down the alley between 73 and 75 Sokratous Street.

Pension Massari, Irodotou Street 42 (tel. 22469). All rooms with private baths. The pension is signposted on Omirou.

Minos Pension, Omirou 5 (tel. 31813). Doubles around 6000dr (£17; $25.50).

Artemis Pissa, Dimosthenes Street 12 (tel. 34235). 700dr (£2; $3) per person in beds in small rooms, in the hallway or in the garden.

Hotel Faliron, Faliriki (tel. 85483).

Kastellorizios Filippos, Aristofanous L27 (tel. 36181).

Christoforou Michael, Sofokleous 39 (tel. 25115).

Hazivasiliou Maria, Athenasiou Piakou 28 (tel. 29552).

Santorini (Thira) – Fira (tel. code 0286)

TOURIST OFFICE
The Tourist Police office (tel. 22649) is close to the main square on 25th Martiou, the road leading to Oia.

FINDING ACCOMMODATION
Fira has a large number of pensions and cheap hotels, but in summer these are frequently full by midday. You might be well advised to take up the first reasonable offer you receive from the locals with rooms to let, who are on hand every time a boat docks in the harbour. If you are having no luck finding a room in Fira, there are good supplies of pensions and private rooms in many of the small towns nearby, such as Karteradhos (only 20 minutes' walk away), Messaria, Pirgos and Emborio.

HOTELS/PENSIONS
Villa Litsa, 25th Martiou (tel. 22267) Doubles 8000dr (£22; $33).

Delfini (tel. 71272). Near the HI hostel.

Hotel Tataki (tel. 22389).

Villa Maria (tel. 22168). Next door to the Kamares Hostel (see below). Doubles 5000dr (£14; $21).

HI HOSTELS
Kontohori Youth Hostel, Agios Eleftherios (tel. 22722/22577). Dorm beds 900dr (£2.50; $3.75), roof space 650dr (£1.75; $2.50). About 400m north of the town, uphill from 25th Martiou (signposted).

Kamares Hostel (tel. 23142). Dorm beds and roof space at the same prices as the Kontohori hostel. Also uphill from 25th Martiou (follow the yellow signs).

CAMPING
Perissa (tel. 81343). On the beach.
Camping Santorini (tel. 22944). 500dr (£1.40; $2) per tent, 800dr
  (£2.25; $3.50) per person. 400m east of Plateia Theotocopoulou.

Thessalonika (Thessaloniki) (tel. code 031)

TOURIST OFFICE
EOT, Aristotelous Square 8 (tel. 222935/271888). Hotel lists, town
plans and transport schedules. Very helpful office. Bus 3 from the
train station.
  Tourist Police, Egnatia 10 (tel. 251316).

FINDING ACCOMMODATION
With the exception of the festival season (Sept.–Oct.) finding a bed
in an E- or D-class hotel, or in one of the city's hostels should be
relatively simple.

HOTELS
Iliasa, Egnatia 24 (tel. 528492). Singles 4000dr (£11; $16.50).
Tourist, Mitropleos 21 (tel. 276335). Very central, one block away
  from Aristotelous Square. Doubles around 6600dr (£18; $27).
Kastoria, (tel. 536280). At the junction of Egnatia and Leontos
  Sofou. Doubles 4000dr (£11; $16.50).

HI HOSTEL
Alex, Svolou 44 (tel. 225946). 11 p.m. curfew. Tram 8, 10, 11 or
31 from Egnatia to the Arch of Galerius. Walk towards the water
for a few blocks, then turn left along Alex. Svolou (also known as
Pringipos Nikolaou). 1500dr (£4.25; $6.50) per person.

YWCA HOSTEL
XEN, Agias Sofia 11 (tel. 276144). Women only. Dormitory accommodation similar in price to the HI hostel.

CAMPING
There are no really convenient sites. There is a site on the beach
Agia Trias, but it is about 21km away. Around 1000dr (£2.75;
$4.25) per tent, 800dr (£2.25; $3.50) per person. Bus 69 from Platia
Dicastirion, or bus 72.

HUNGARY

You should have few problems finding accommodation in Hungary, except during the peak season in Budapest and Lake Balaton. The excellent hotel guide from the Tourist Board includes cheap pension-type hotels as well as youth hostels, and together with the camping guide this should keep you up to date with any changes for 1995. Outside the capital, you are more or less assured a cheap bed if you arrive when the accommodation agencies are open. Even in Budapest, you will get a bed, though you may have to pay £12–15 ($18–22.50) if you want a room to yourself. Inflation is currently running at around 20% in Hungary, so all prices are quoted in hard currency. Although prices in forints (Ft) will increase, the real cost should remain approximately the same from the Western tourist's point of view.

Neither the local offices of the national tourist agency IBUSZ, nor the regional or local tourist agencies, will attempt to pressure you into staying in expensive hotels (uniquely for the Soviet Bloc, this was the case even before 1989). On the contrary, they will generally do their best to arrange the type of accommodation you want, or at the very least direct you to organizations who will help you out. IBUSZ can be an expecially useful organization for travellers as their nationwide presence allows them to operate an advance reservation system so that you can book hotels or private rooms ahead for a fee of around £1.50 ($2.25). This service is well worth using if you are heading for Budapest in peak season, when queues at accommodation agencies can be horrendous, or if you know you will arrive at a future destination in late evening or on a Saturday afternoon or a Sunday (many accommodation agencies outside Budapest are closed at these times).

Hotels (*szálló* or *szálloda*) are rated from one up to five stars. There is a shortage of singles throughout the country in all the various grades of hotels. Unless you are looking for a private bathroom, rooms in one-star hotels are normally perfectly acceptable, assuming you can find them: in recent years the number of one-and two-star hotels has dwindled considerably. Outside of Budapest and the Lake Balaton area, where prices are normally about 30% higher, the remaining one-star hotels charge on average around £12–15 ($18–22.50) for doubles. Three-star hotels are much more common, but with prices for doubles with a shower starting at around £53 ($79.50), these are unlikely to be of interest to budget travellers, unless you are travelling in the winter months when rates can be cut to around £25 ($37.50) for doubles with showers.

The Hungarian National Tourist Office or local offices will provide details on any three-star hotels offering substantially reduced rates. Beware: the 10% tax on hotel bills which was introduced in 1993 should be included in the quoted price, not added on afterwards.

Rooms in a **pension** (*penzio* or *panzio*) or **inn** (*fogado*) are normally slightly cheaper than at a one-star hotel, with singles (more widely available than in hotels) costing around £7–10 ($10.50–15), doubles £10–13 ($15–19.50). Breakfast is included in the overnight price at all hotels, pensions and inns. This may be only an uninspiring continental breakfast, but on other occasions you may be treated to a substantial buffet of cold meats. In the countryside it is possible to stay in **farm cottages** and **B&Bs**. Details of these establishments are contained in the brochure 'Holidays in the Countryside' available from IBUSZ, although in the vast majority of cases it is the regional tourist agencies rather than IBUSZ with whom you must make reservations.

Probably the best accommodation bargains in Hungary are **private rooms** (*fizetovendégszolgáat* or *Fiz* for short). Although there's a general shortage of singles, the low prices mean even doubles are usually within reach for the solo traveller. The vast majority of private rooms are controlled by the old state tourist organizations IBUSZ or EXPRESS (the student travel organization), or by more specialized local agencies such as Szegedtourist or Egertourist (in the towns of those names), or Balatontourist (around Lake Balaton). Some new agencies have been established, and, with such a potentially lucrative market to be tapped, further growth cannot be ruled out. However, in the more popular towns, long queues can act as a deterrent to finding out what various agencies are charging. As a rough guide, IBUSZ offers the best service in Budapest as they control the major share of the market and have a good supply of very cheap rooms. If you arrive in Budapest from another Hungarian town, it is well worth getting the local IBUSZ to reserve one of the cheaper rooms for you. Outside the capital, IBUSZ generally cannot compete with more local agencies in terms of price, or the numbers of rooms they control. However, if you are arriving late at your next destination it is probably worth paying a little extra to reserve a room through IBUSZ.

You should have little cause for complaint about the standard of rooms booked through an agency, but try to make sure the location is acceptable. It might be hoping for a bit much to get a centrally located room in one of the cities, but make a point of asking for one that is well served by public transport. There is a shortage of singles (especially in Budapest), so solo travellers might want to find someone to share with. If you do not want to share, the option of taking a cheap or moderately priced double for yourself is usually available until reasonably late in the day. Only in Budapest are you likely to have to pay out for one of the more expensive doubles, as these tend to be the only rooms remaining after 5 p.m. in peak season. Expect to pay around £4 ($6) for doubles outside the capital and from £7 ($10.50) in Budapest. A surcharge may be added to the price of the room if you stay less than four days (common in Budapest); for example, another 30% for one-night stays. It is standard practice to pay the agency rather than the householder.

In peak season, it is still quite common to be approached by locals offering rooms; most likely in and around the train stations and outside IBUSZ offices. Outside Budapest these rooms are likely to be fine, but you should be wary of offers made in Budapest. The rooms on offer in the capital are generally of an inferior standard to rooms booked through an agency and are likely to be poorly located as well, although the asking price will be similar. However, solo travellers arriving late in the afternoon might want to consider such offers for the first night. If you do accept a private offer, keep an eye on your valuables or, better still, leave them at the station. In the smaller towns, it is feasible to look for rooms on your own. Watch out for houses displaying a 'szobe kiado' or 'Zimmer frei' sign, then simply approach the owner to view the rooms on offer.

EXPRESS operates a chain of 30 **youth hostels** and **youth hotels**, a number of which are listed in the HI handbook. They also control the letting of some of the non-EXPRESS hostels listed in the HI handbook, and many of the temporary hostels set up in college dormitories during the summer vacation (late June to the end of August). You can expect to pay around £2–3 ($3.00–4.50) per person in a dormitory (except in Budapest, where it costs twice as much). Couples wishing to share a double will encounter no difficulties. There are no curfews in EXPRESS accommodation, but you are expected to remain quiet after midnight.

It is advisable to try and reserve hostels in advance, as it is not unusual for EXPRESS accommodation to be filled to capacity by school groups and youth organizations. The HI handbook advises the use of Advance Booking Vouchers which should effect a reservation, and to put a deposit against it. Unfortunately, this is not certain to succeed, as EXPRESS make a habit of sending vouchers back and explaining that their value was less than that of the accommodation requested, so you may have no choice but to try and book at an EXPRESS office on arrival in Hungary. Dealing with the companies who have recently begun to operate hostels in the capital is a more straightforward proposition, as they say they will accept requests for reservations made in writing.

As well as youth hostels, there are also a number of local hostels, which are known by different names according to their location. In provincial towns, enquiries should be made regarding the availability of beds in *turistaszalló* but, in highland areas, they are referred to as *turistahaz*. Local and regional accommodation agencies are generally the best source of information on these hostels. Standards vary much more than the simple A or B grading implies. While some are spartan, others can be very comfortable. As a rule, however, the overnight price of £3–13 ($4.50–19.50) tends to match the level of comfort provided.

Camping is highly popular with Hungarians, and the Magyar Camping and Caravanning Club (MCCC) is very active. Both the MCCC and an organization called Tourinform produce excellent, easy-to-follow lists of the sites, complete with opening times, facilities available, and a map showing their locations. The recently revised, comprehensive guide *Camping Hungary* is generally available from IBUSZ, or from local tourist agencies. There are about 140 sites in total, the heaviest concentration of which are along the shores of Lake Balaton, though there are sites in all the places you are likely to visit. The season runs from May to October inclusive, but many sites only open for the peak months of July and August. Outside July and August, there is usually no need to make reservations, or to check about the availability of space before heading out to the site, and even at peak times this should only be necessary in Budapest and the Lake Balaton area. Sites are graded from one up to three stars. The three-star sites usually have a supermarket and leisure facilities, whereas the one-star sites seldom offer more than the basic necessities. A solo traveller can expect to pay £6–9 ($9–13.50) for an overnight stay at a two- or three-star site, though discounts are available to members of the International Camping and Caravanning Club (FICC). Prices in a one-star site can be as little as £1.50 ($2.25) per tent, plus a similar charge per person. Either side of the high season, most sites reduce their prices by 25–30%. At the larger sites it is possible to rent bungalows (*faház*). To hire a typical bungalow sleeping two generally costs around £15 ($22.50), four-person bungalows around £16 ($24). You pay for the bungalow, so there is no discount for unoccupied bed space. Details of sites letting bungalows are contained in the various camping lists mentioned above. Freelance camping is illegal but is practised by many young people (Hungarians especially); most likely because offenders are rarely heavily punished. Favourite locations are the forests of the Danube Bend, and the highland regions of the country where rain shelters (*esöház*) are common.

ADDRESSES

Danube Travel Agency	6 Conduit Street, London W1R 9TG (tel. 0171 493 0263).
Youth hostels and youth hotels	Magyar Ifjusági Házak-EXPRESS, Szabadsg tér 16, 1395 Budapest V (tel. 112 9887/153 0660).
Camping	Magyar Camping & Caravanning Club (MCCC), Üllői útja 6, 1085 Budapest (tel. 336536).
	Tourinform, Süto u.2, 1052 Budapest (tel. 117 9800)

Lists of sites are available from the Hungarian National Tourist Office.

Budapest (tel. code 01)

TOURIST OFFICE

Tourinform, Suto u.2 (tel. 1179800). Open daily 8 a.m.–8 p.m. Not only a good source of general information on the city, but the multilingual staff do their best to answer more unusual enquiries. The staff can advise you on accommodation possibilities, but the office does not make bookings. About 50m from the Károly körút exit of the Deák tér metro station.

ACCOMMODATION AGENCIES

IBUSZ has the best supply of private rooms. The head office is at Károly körút 3c (tel. 142 3140), a short walk from the Károly körút exit of the Deák tér metro station. Open Mon.–Fri. 8.30 a.m.–5 p.m., Sat. 8 a.m.–1 p.m. There are branch offices in the three main train stations, open daily 8 a.m.–8 p.m.; at Ferenciek tere 10 (tel. 118 6866), open Mon.–Fri. 8 a.m.–7 p.m.; and at Petőfi tér 3 (tel. 118 5707) open round the clock. The latter two offices are best approached from the Ferenciek tere metro station. From the station, walk down Kossuth Lajos u. to Ferenciek tere. Continuing on you reach the Elisabeth Bridge. Petőfi tér is to the right along the riverside.

Budapest Tourist book private rooms, and two- and four-bed bungalows at the city's campsites. Roosevelt tér 5–6 (tel. 118 6600). Open Mon.–Sat. 8 a.m.–8 p.m., Sun. 9 a.m.–3 p.m. About ten minutes' walk from the Deák tér metro station. From the

Károly körút exit, head left along Bajcsy-Zsilinszky út, then left down József Attila u. into Roosevelt tér.

EXPRESS book beds in hostels and converted student dorms. The EXPRESS head office is at Semmelweis utca 4 (tel. 1117860). From the Deák tér metro station, exit on to Károly körút, walk along the street then turn right down Gerlóczy u., and then first left. An EXPRESS branch office operates at the Keleti train station (tel. 114 2772). Open daily 8 a.m.–9 p.m. As well as hostel beds, this office books private rooms.

Coopturist books private rooms. Their office is at Bajcsy-Zsilinszky út 17 (tel. 131 0992). From the Deák tér metro station, exit on to Károly körút, and then head left along Bajcsy-Zsilinszky út.

HungarHotels at Petőfi utca 16 (tel. 118 3393), Pannonia Service at Kigyó utca 4/6 (tel. 118 3910), and Danubius Travel at Martinelli tér 8 (tel. 117 3652) all make hotel bookings.

HOTELS

The prices of hotels and pensions have risen sharply over the last few years, with the result that few remain within the budget category. The exception is if you are travelling in winter when hotels often drop their rates substantially. Enquire about current prices at IBUSZ on Petőfi tér or at HungarHotels, Pannonia Service or Danubius Travel.

Cheapest doubles generally around £10–15 ($15–22.50)

Citadella, Gellérthegy (tel. 166 5794). Doubles £11 ($16.50), quads £15 ($22.50). Recommended. Advance reservation advised. From the Deák tér or Kalvin tér metro stations take tram 49 to Móricz Zsigmond körtér, then change to bus 27 which runs up to the Citadel. Also dorm rooms – see under **Hostels**.

Haladás Motel, Udülő sor 7 102 (tel. 189 1114). Doubles £7 ($10.50). By the Danube, across from Szentendre Island. From the Ujpest-Városkapu metro station take bus 104 or 104A along Váci út. Rev u. runs right off Váci út down to Udülő sor.

Hotel Kandó, Bécsi út 104–108 (tel. 168 2032). Doubles £9 ($13.50), triples £11 ($16.50), quads £12.50 ($18.75). Bus 60 from the Batthyány tér metro station runs along the street.

Strand penzió, Pusztakúti út 3 (tel. 167 1999). Doubles £10 ($15). Next to the Arpád baths. A short walk from the Csillaghegy HÉV. Catch the HÉV at the Batthyány tér metro station.

Trio penzió, Ördögorom u. 10 (tel. 865742). Open 15 May–15 Oct. No singles. From Marcius 15 tér near the Ferenciek tere metro station take bus 8 to its terminus in the Buda hills. The pension is a 10-minute walk from the bus stop.

Saturnus, Pillangó u. 10 (tel. 421789). Reasonably located in the east of Pest, a short walk from the Pillangó u. metro station.

Ifjúság, Zivatar u. 1–3 (tel. 353331/154260). Well located. From Moszkva tér metro station bus 84 runs along Rómer Flóris u., passing the end of Zivatar u. Bus 191 from the Nyugati train station runs down Margit u. before turning into Apostol u., Zivatar u. is a short walk from the junction of these two streets.

EBEN, Nagy Lajos Király útja 15–17 (tel. 1840677). From the Örs vezér tér metro station, bus 32 and tram 62 run along Nagy Lajos Király útja.

PRIVATE ROOMS

IBUSZ have the best supply of rooms, and the largest stock of well-located rooms. Prices start around £5 ($7.50), for singles, £8 ($12) for doubles. During the summer, you will have to get to one of their offices early to be sure of getting one of the cheaper rooms. Otherwise you may find that only the more expensive doubles are left – around £12 ($18). If the offices at the train stations have allocated their whole stock, or if you arrive before they open, or after closing time, head for the IBUSZ office on Petőfi tér. On the whole, the rooms on offer at Coopturist, Budapest Tourist, and the EXPRESS office at the Keleti train station are slightly more expensive than those controlled by IBUSZ. The touting of rooms in the train stations (particularly outside the IBUSZ offices) is still common in summer. As a rule, these will be of lower quality than the rooms you can book through an agency, and possibly poorly located as well. If you can agree on a suitable price the main thing to find out is how easy it is to get to the room.

HOSTELS

Visitors are spoilt for choice for hostel accommodation in Budapest, especially in summer. Besides the 21 hostels currently listed in the HI handbook, there are more independent hostels springing up every year. In summer many of the city's college and university dorms become temporary hostels. Only a few of the HI hostels require a membership card, and these can be bought for around £2 ($3) at any EXPRESS office.

It's often easier to make bookings through a hostel's group headquarters:

EXPRESS is the largest chain, with offices at Semmelweis utca 4 (tel. 117 8600), Szabadság tér 16 (tel. 131 7777), and Andrassy ut 55 (tel. 142 5341).

Universum, Pusztaszeri út 24/B, 1025 Budapest II (tel. 156 8726).
More than Ways, Dozsa Gy ut 152 (tel. 129 8644/266 6107).
Panda, Bajcsy-Zsilinszky út 17, Budapest IV.
City Centre Hostels, Irinyi Jozsef u 42, 1117 Budapest XI.
Strawberry Youth Hostels (tel. 111 1780). Summer accommodation
only.

*Dormitory beds from around £4 ($6); single rooms no more than £7
($10.50)*

The Citadella Hostel (tel. 166 5794). See **Hotels** above for direc-
tions. Dramatic setting, with dorm beds at around £3 ($4.50).
Schonhertz, XI Irinyi Jozsef utca 42 (tel. 166 5422). This 22-storey
summertime hostel boasts a sauna and disco. Hundreds of beds
at £4 ($6). Tram 4 or 6 from Pest, or bus 86 from Buda.
Backpack Guesthouse, XI Takacs Menyhert u 33 (tel. 185 5089).
Information, bike rental, no curfew. Beds from £3 ($4.50). Bus
1, 7 or 7A from the city centre, alight at Tetenyi út.
Hostel Diàksportszálló, Dózsa György út 152 (tel. 140 8585). Agent:
More Than Ways. Open all year round. Singles £3 ($4.50),
doubles £4 ($6). From the Dózsa György út metro station, walk
one block down Dózsa György út. The hotel entrance is on
Angyyalföldi út, left off Dózsa György út.
Csillebérci Gyermek-és Ifjusági Kozpont, Konkoly Thege Miklós u.
21 (tel. 156 5772). Agent: EXPRESS. Open all year round. High
in the Buda hills. Dificult to reach by public transport.
Asmara Youth Hostel, Bajcsy-Zsilininszky út 51 (tel. 131 7777).
Agent: EXPRESS. Open all year. Far from the centre, near the
airport, but easy to reach. From the Határ út metro station bus
50 runs along Üllői út, passing Bajcsy-Zsilinszky út on the left.
Hotel Lidó, Nánási út. 67 (tel. 1886865/805576). Agent: EXPRESS.
Open all year round. A 10-minute walk from the Római-Fürdo
HÉV stop (take the HÉV from Batthyány tér metro station). Cross
the main road and continue in the direction the train was going.
Turn right down Emőd út, which leads into Nánási út.
Landler, Bartók Béla út 17 (tel. 185 1444). Agent: Universum.
Open 1 July–1 Sept. Two-, three-, and four-bed rooms. £3.50
($5.25). Free luggage storage. Well located. Tram 49 from the
Deák tér or Kalvin tér metro stations runs along the street.
Vásárhelyi, Kruspér u. 2–4 (tel. 185 3794). Agent: Universum.
Open 1 July–1 Sept. Two- and four-bed rooms. £4.25 ($6.50)
per person. Free luggage storage. Good location, close to the
Landler hostel. Taking the same tram, walk down Bertalan Lajos
u. from Bartók Béla út, turn right along Budafoki út, then take

the first left. From the Batthyány tér metro station bus 86 runs along Budafoki út passing the end of Kruspér u.

Rózsa, Bercsényi u. 28–30 (tel. 166 6677). Agent: Universum. Open 1 July–1 Sept. Two- and three-bed rooms. £4 ($6) per person. Free luggage store. Also close to the Landler hostel. Take tram 49, get off at Móricz Zsigmond körtér and walk down Karinthy Frigyes út, which is crossed by Bercsényi u.

Hostel Donáti, Donáti u. 46 (tel. 169 0788). Agent: EXPRESS. Open 22 June–24 Aug. Dorms £3.50 ($5.25). Free baggage storage. Great location. From the Batthyány tér metro station follow Batthyány u. until you see Donáti u. on your left. Keep your eyes open for the painted footprints showing the way to the hostel.

Hostel Felvinci, Felvinci u. 8 (tel. 116 8932). Agent: EXPRESS. Open 16 June–22 Aug. Dorms £3.50 ($5.25). Free baggage storage. Good location. From the Moskva tér metro station, walk uphill a little then turn right down Ezredes u. to cross Fillér u. and Alvinci út. Take the first street on the left after passing Marczibányi tér.

Sote Balassa Kollégium, Tömö u 39/43 (tel. 133 0135). Agent: More Than Ways. Open 5 July–23 Aug. From the Kliniták metro station on Üllöi út Szigony u. runs across Tömö u.

Hostel Schönherz, Irinyi József u. 42 (tel. 166 5021). City Centre Agency. Open 1 July–31 Aug. Tram 6 from the Nyugati train station or from the Blaha Lujza tér or Ferenc körút metro station runs along the street. From the Ferenc körút station it is an easy walk down the street of that name, over the Danube by the Petöfi bridge, and straight on to the hostel.

Hostel Bárczy, Damjanich u. 41–43 (tel. 213526). City Centre Agency. Open 1 July–25 Aug. Within easy walking distance of the Keleti station (mainline trains and metro). The main street leading away from Keleti is Rákóczi út. Take Rottenbiller út to the right of Rákóczi út and keep going until you see Damjanich u. on the right.

Student Hostel 'KEK', Szüret u. 218 (tel. 185 2369). Agent: More Than Ways. Open 1 July–25 Aug. From the Deák tér or Kalvin tér metro stations take tram 49 to Móricz Zsigmond körtér. Here you can change to bus 27 which runs along Szüret u. but it is an easy walk down Villányi út until you see Szüret u. on the right.

CAMPING

Budapest Tourist book two- and four-bed bungalows at the city's campsites. A two-bed bungalow costs around £10 ($15), a four-bed bungalow around £14 ($21). Budapest Tourist is the best organization to approach with any enquiries regarding camping. Solo travellers can now expect to pay £2–3.50 ($3–5.25) to camp. By the time you add on the cost of leaving your pack at the station, camping becomes a poor option in comparison to a hostel bed.

Hárs-hegyi, Hárshegyi út 57 (tel. 115 1482/176 1921). Open mid-May–mid-Oct. Bungalows available. Bus 22 from the Moszkva tér metro station stops about 100m from the site.

Római, Szentendrei út 189 (tel. 168 6260). Open all year round. Bungalows available. From Batthyány tér take the HÉV to Római-fürdo. The site is just over the road from the HÉV station.

Zugligeti 'NICHE', Zugligeti út 101. Open mid-Mar.–mid-Oct. Bungalows available. From the Moszkva tér metro station take bus 158.

Tündérhegyi 'Feeberg', Szilassy út 8. Open year round. Bungalows available. Close to the Istenhegy stop on the cog railway. To reach the foot of the cog railway, walk uphill from the Moszkva tér metro station.

Rosengarten, Pilisi út 7. Open mid-June–mid-Sept. Bungalows available. From the Örs vezér tere metro station take bus 45 along Kerepesi ut. Pilisi út is right off Kerepesi út.

FREE CAMPSITE
In the Budapest X district, close to the Jászberényi út bridge. From the Örs vezér tere metro station, take bus 61 to the Jászberényi út bridge. Do not leave anything at the site during the day. Before making your way out, check with Tourinform or Budapest Tourist as to whether the site is operating in 1995.

Eger (tel. code 36)

TOURIST INFORMATION
Tourinform-Eger, Dobó tér 2 (tel. 321807).

The accommodation agencies below hand out a small photo-copied map of the town which will be quite sufficient if you have a good guide book to help you locate the sights. If you want a more detailed plan there is one with a street index which costs around £0.20 ($0.30).

ACCOMMODATION AGENCIES
Egertourist, Bajcsy-Zsilinszky utca 9 (tel. 311724). Open Mon.–Sat. 8 a.m.–6 p.m. Well-informed staff speaking excellent English and German. Singles from £4 ($6), doubles from £8 ($12).

IBUSZ, Bajcsy-Zs. tombbelső (tel. 312652). Located in a passage behind the Egertourist office. Open Mon.–Fri. 8 a.m.–12 p.m. Doubles from £8 ($12).

EXPRESS, Széchenyi István u. 28 (tel. 310757/311865). Open Mon.–Fri. 8 a.m.–4 p.m. Hostel beds, as well as student dorm accommodation in summer from £3 ($4.50).

Cooptourist, Dobó tér 3 (tel. 311998). Open Mon.–Fri. 9 a.m.–4.30 p.m., Sat. 9 a.m.–12 p.m. Doubles from £6 ($9).

Erlau Reisen, Szálloda u. 4–6 (tel. 413091).

HOTELS
The Tourist at Mekcsey utca 2 (tel. 310014) is good value with doubles around £7 ($10.50). The hotel is just along from the castle. There are cheap pensions at Kapasi u. 35a and at Deák Ferenc utca 11. Enquire at Egertourist about rooms in these. More expensive is the Hotel Minaret, Harangönto utca 5 (tel. 362020), across the street from the minaret. Doubles around £21 ($31.50).

HOSTELS
Dobó tér 6. Open all year round. £2 ($3) for a bed. Enquire about the availability of beds in this hostel at Egertourist or EXPRESS.

Középiskolai Kollégium, Dobó tér 25. Excellent central location. Summer only.

Berzeviczy Gizella Kollégium, Leányka u. 2 (tel. 312399). Summer only.

Kun Béla Kollégium, Leányka u. 6 (tel. 312399). Summer only.

Mezögazdasági Kollégium, Mátyás Király u. 132–134. Summer only.

Mátyás Hotel, Mátyás Király u. 140.

Sas Hotel, Sas u. 92. Four-bedded rooms £7 ($10.50) per person.

Unicornis Hotel, Dr Hibay Károly utca 2 (tel. 312886). Dorm beds £2 ($3), including breakfast.

CAMPING
Egercamping, Rákóczi út 79 (tel. 10558). Open mid-May–mid-Oct. Bungalows available. Book in advance at Egertourist, or at the site. A 10-minute walk from the town centre. Bus 5, 10, 11 or 12.

Esztergom (tel. code 27)

ACCOMMODATION AGENCIES
The following agencies all arrange private rooms and hotel accommodation. Private doubles start at around £12 ($18).

IBUSZ, Lörinc u. 1 (formerly Martirok u.) (tel. 12552). Open Mon.–Fri. 8 a.m.–11.50 a.m. and 12.30–4 p.m., Sat. 8–11 a.m. IBUSZ book hotels and private rooms.
Komtourist, Lörinc u. 6 (tel. 12082). Open Mon.–Fri. 9 a.m.–5 p.m., Sat. 9 a.m.–12 p.m.
EXPRESS, Szechenyi tér 7 (tel. 13133/13712).

HOTELS
Fürdo, Bajcsy-Zsilinszky utca 14 (tel. 11688). Doubles from £10 ($15).
Volán, József Attila tér 2 (tel. 11257/12714). Doubles from £14 ($21).

HOSTELS
The Tourist Hostel at Dobó u. 8 (near Béke tér) (tel. 12714) is very cheap, as is the turistaszallo at Dobozi Mihály út 8 (close to the cathedral). You can enquire about beds in these hostels or in other turistaszalle at Komtourist. For information on temporary summer hostels, contact Komtourist or EXPRESS.

CAMPING
Vadvirág, Bánomi-dűlő (tel. 12234). Open 15 Apr.–15 Oct. Bungalows available. About 3km from the train station.
Gran Tours, és üdültőlep, Primás-sziget, Nagyduna-sétány. Open 1 May–30 Sept. Bungalows available. About 2km from the train station. Ten minutes' walk from the nearest bus stop.

Pécs (tel. code 72)

ACCOMMODATION AGENCIES
All the following agencies offer hotel and hostel rooms as well as private accommodation where singles cost from £6 ($9), doubles from £8 ($12):

IBUSZ, Széchenyi tér 8 (tel. 312176). Open Mon.–Thurs. 8 a.m.–
5 p.m., Fri. 8 a.m.–2 p.m., Sat. 8 a.m.–12 p.m.
Mecsek Tourist, Széchenyi tér 9 (tel. 313300).
EXPRESS, Bajcsy-Zsilinszky u. 6. Close to the bus station. Open
Mon.–Thurs. 8 a.m.–4 p.m., Fri. 8.15 a.m.–2 p.m.
MAV Travel Agency. In the train station (tel. 324523).

HOTELS
Rooms in hotels and pensions from around £8 ($12) can be booked
through Mecsek Tourist (see above).

Mini Motel, Kóczián Sandor ut 2 (tel. 321399).
Fonix Hotel, Hunyadi ut. 2 (tel. 311680).
Toboz Panzio, Fenyues sor 5 (tel. 325232).

HOSTELS
Hotel Laterum, Hajnóczy u. 37–39 (tel. 315829). HI hostel. Bus
20, 21, or 27 from the centre.
Szent Mór Kollégium, .48-es tér 4 (tel. 311199). A beautiful old
building. Doubles from £5 ($7.50).

CAMPING
Mandulás, Ángyán J.3 (tel. 15981). Open mid-Apr.–mid-Oct.
Around £4–5 ($6–7.50) for two persons. Bungalows are available
for £8.50 ($12.75) for two persons. To reserve on the day call the
campsite, to book ahead contact Mecsek Tourist. Located close to
the zoo, in the woods under the television tower. Bus 34 runs
infrequently to the site. Bus 35 stops at the zoo, five minutes' walk
away. Bus 44 runs past the site. Get off the bus at Demokrácia út.

Siófok (tel. code 84)

TOURIST OFFICES
Siótour, Szabadság tér 6 (tel. 10800). Off Fo utca. Open Mon.–Sat.
8 a.m.–8 p.m., Sun. 9 a.m.–1 p.m. and 2–6 p.m.
IBUSZ, Fő utca 174 (tel. 11066). Head left from the bus or train
station to reach Fö utca.

HOTELS
Not a good idea for the budget traveller, especially in summer when
doubles (starting at around £16 ($24) are usually booked solid.

Radio Inn, Beszédes Jósef Sétány 77 (tel. 311634).
Panorama, Beszédes Jósef Sétány 77 (tel. 311637).

PRIVATE ROOMS
Some rooms can be a considerable distance from the beach. Try to coax the agencies into giving you a room near the lake.

Siótour: doubles from £8 ($12).
IBUSZ: doubles from £9 ($13.50).

Doubles at around £10 ($15) are available in a number of the elegant houses which line Batthyány Lajos u. Excellent value, and close to the beach. Look for the 'Zimmer frei' or 'szoba kiado' signs and then approach the owner to book a room.

HOSTELS
Altálános School, Fő tér. Open 1 July–20 Aug.
Trade School Holiday Home, Erhel Ferenc utca 46 (tel. 310131).
 Dorm rooms June–Sept.

CAMPING
Kék Balaton (tel. 10851). Open 15 June–31 Aug. One of several sites near Aranypart (the so-called 'Golden Beach'). Close to Siófok, but sandwiched between the train lines and the road.
Aranypart Nyaralótelep (tel. 11801). Open 1 May–30 Sept. Bungalows available.
Ifjúság, Pusztatorony tér (tel. 11471). Open 15 May–25 Sept. With bungalows. Close to the lakeside, as is Gamasza campsite, open July and Aug.
Főfza, Szőlő-hegy, Fő u. 7/a. Open July and Aug. Bungalows available.
Strand, Szent László u. 183, Fürdőtelep (tel. 11804). Open 15 May–15 Sept. By the lake. Bus 2 runs from Siófok train station 4km away. Nearest train station is 100m from the site.
Mini Camping, Szent László út 74. Open 1 May–15 Sept.
TOT, Viola u. 19–21, Fürdőtelep. Open 1 June–31 Aug. 500m from the nearest train station.

Sopron (tel. code 99)

ACCOMMODATION AGENCIES
IBUSZ, Várkerület 41 (tel. 12455). Open Mon.–Fri. 8 a.m.–4 p.m.,
Sat. 8 a.m.–12 p.m.
Ciklámen Tourist, Ogabona tér 8 (tel. 12040). In summer, open
Mon.–Fri. 7.30 a.m.–4 p.m., Sat. 7.30 a.m.–8 p.m., Sun. 8 a.m.–
12 p.m.; in winter, Mon.–Fri. 7.30 a.m.–4 p.m., Sat. 7.30 a.m.–
1 p.m., closed on Sundays.

HOTELS
Lövér, Várisi út (tel. 11061).
Sopron, Fövényverem u. 7 (tel. 14254).
Palatinus, Uj u. 23 (tel. 11395).

PENSIONS
Bástya, Patak u. 40 (tel. 34061). Book through Ciklámen Tourist.
Bianco, Arahy J. u. 17 (tel. 19227).
Diana, Lövér körút 64 (tel. 29013).

PRIVATE ROOMS
IBUSZ: singles and doubles are both around £6 ($9).
Ciklámen Tourist: Singles around £4 ($6), doubles around £7
($10.50).

CAMPING
Lövér, Kőszegi út (tel. 11715). Around £3.50 ($5.25) for a solo
traveller. Two- and four-bed bungalows available: £6.50 ($9.75)
and £9 ($13.50) respectively. Bus 12 runs hourly from Várkerület
until 9.50 p.m. The site is about 25 minutes' walk from the train
station.

Szentendre (tel. code 26)

ACCOMMODATION AGENCIES
IBUSZ, Bogdányi u. 11 (tel. 10333). Open Mon.–Fri. 10 a.m.–4 p.m.
Private doubles from around £9 ($13.50).
Dunatour, Bogdányi u. 1 (tel. 11311). Open June–Aug., Mon.–Fri.
8 a.m.–4 p.m., Sat. 7 a.m.–7 p.m., Sun. 10 a.m.–4 p.m.

HOTELS
Expect to pay £7 ($10.50) for singles, and £10 ($15) for doubles

Party, Ady utca (tel. 12491).
Danubius, Ady utca (tel. 12511).

PENSIONS
Doubles are around £8–9 ($12.00–13.50); similar in price to a private room

Coca Cola, Dunakanyar körút 50 (tel. 10410).
Hubertus, Tyukosdulo 10 (tel. 10616).

HOSTELS
ET Hostel 'Duna-Parti Diakhotel', Szentendre Somogyi Bacso Part 12. Open mid-July to mid-Aug. About £1.50 ($2.25). Ask Duna-tours about the availability of space at this hostel (or at any others).

CAMPING
Pap-sziget (tel. 10697). On Pap Island. Open 1 May–30 Sept. Bungalows available. About 1km from the town centre.

There is also a smaller site on Szentendrei Island. This site lacks many of the facilities of the three-star Papsziget campground, but is much less crowded. Take the ferry from the northern landing stage.

REPUBLIC OF IRELAND

Budget travellers should have few problems finding reasonably priced accommodation in the Irish Republic. **Bed & Breakfast** accommodation is the most widely available option throughout the country as hotels are expensive. Prices for B&B start around IR£12 (£12; $18) per person in doubles, but in the most popular tourist towns you can expect to pay IR£13 (£13; $19.50) per person. A supplement is charged for the single occupancy of a double room; usually around IR£3 (£3; $4.50), but occasionally as high as IR£8 (£8; $12). In the countryside, B&B is often available at farmhouses. Again, prices start around IR£12 (£12; $18). Many farmhouses offering B&B are members of the Irish Farm Holidays Association.

Hostelling is probably the best way to see the Irish Republic. There are around 50 **HI hostels** throughout the country, operated by the Irish YHA, An Óige. Many of these are set out in the country, ideally spaced for a day's walking or cycling, and most (but not all) of the main towns have a hostel. Impeccable levels of cleanliness are virtually guaranteed at An Óige hostels. Prices are normally IR£4−5 (£4−5; $6.00−7.50) for dormitory accommodation between October and May, rising to IR£5−6.50 (£5−6.50; $7.50−9.75) in the peak season of June to September. A few hostels are more expensive. Peak season prices for the hostels in Dublin and Galway are around IR£10 (£10; $15), with the price of the main Dublin hostel falling to IR£7.70 (£7.70; $11) off season (the Galway hostel and the other Dublin hostels operate in summer only). There are no daytime lockouts, and the midnight curfew at all hostels is late by HI standards. Booking other hostels ahead is easy as wardens will do this for you free of charge. Although you are expected to do any domestic duties required by the warden, An Óige hostels are more friendly and easygoing than is the norm. Indeed, the high esteem in which An Óige hostels are held by hostellers is reflected by their consistently high rating in surveys of European HI members.

Few countries have seen such a growth in **independent hostels** as the Irish Republic. Around 50 of these hostels have joined together to form the Independent Hostel Owners (IHO) association, while another 21 are united under the name Irish Budget Hostels (marketed as Irish Approved Independent Hostels). Both organizations issue lists of their establishments. Like the An Óige hostels, a number of these independent hostels (currently around 60, but likely to increase) have been officially approved by the Irish Tourist Board. Such hostels are referred to as 'holiday hostels' (all the

Irish Budget Hostels are officially approved). Independent hostels frequently fill in the gaps in the An Óige network, as well as offering an alternative to An Óige hostels in some towns. Unlike An Óige hostels where HI membership is obligatory, these hostels have no such requirements, and they are almost always free of curfews. Most independent hostels cost around IR£5.00–7.50 (£5.00–7.50; $7.50–11.25) for dormitory accommodation, although several in Dublin charge IR£8–10 (£8–10; $12–15). A feature of some independent hostels is the availability of more expensive singles and doubles, as well as dormitory accommodation.

Unless you are planning on getting right out into the countryside, carrying a tent may not be particularly worthwhile, other than as insurance in case you cannot find suitably priced accommodation. Some of the official **campsites** serving the main towns are located well outside town. With prices generally in the range of IR£2–5 (£2–5; $3.00–4.50), a solo traveller can spend almost as much as the cost of a hostel bed once the cost of getting to the site is taken into account. Where there is no convenient site, one possibility can be camping in the grounds of an independent hostel. For around IR£2.50 (£2.50; $3.75) you can camp outside some of the independent hostels, and make use of their facilities. In rural areas, farmers seldom object to you pitching a tent on their land if you ask their permission. It is also quite legal to **sleep rough**, though this leaves you open to a soaking at any time of year.

ADDRESSES

Irish Tourist Board	150–51 New Bond Street, London W1Y 0AQ (tel. 0171 493 3201). The office sells a guide to all the registered B&Bs, officially approved hostels and official campsites.
B&B	Town and Country Homes Association, Donegal Road, Ballyshannon, Co. Donegal (tel. 072 51377).
	The Secretary, Irish Farm Holidays Association, Glynch House, Newbliss Co. Monaghan (tel. 047 54045).
Youth Hostels	An Óige, 61 Mountjoy Street, Dublin 7 (tel. 01 304555).
	Paddy and Josephine Moloney, Irish Budget Hostels, Doolin Village, Co. Clare (tel. 065 74006).
	Independent Hostel Owners (IHO), Dooey Hostel, Glencolumcille, Co.

Donegal (tel. 073 30130).Co. Donegal
(tel. 073 30130).

Camping   Irish Caravan Council, 20 Park View,
Northbrook Avenue, Ranelagh,
Dublin 6.

Cork (Corcaigh) (tel. code 021)

TOURIST OFFICE
Tourist House, Grand Parade (tel. 273251). Open July—Aug.,
Mon.–Sat. 9 a.m.–7 p.m.; June, closes at 6 p.m.; Sept.–May,
Mon.–Fri. 9.15 a.m.–5.30 p.m. (closes for lunch), Sat. 9.15 a.m.–
5.30 p.m. Just over 10 minutes' walk from the train station. Walk
left along Lower Glanmire Road, turn left at the end of the street
and cross the River Lee, walk right along the riverside then left at
the next bridge down St Patrick's Street into Grand Parade.

B&Bs
*Expect to pay around IR£13 (£13; $19.50) p.p. in doubles, and around
IR£15 (£15; $22.50) for a single*

Mrs Lelia Holmes, Olivet, Bishopstown Road, Bishopstown (tel.
543105). City centre 1.5km away. Bus 8.
Mrs Kay O'Donavan, 38 Westgate Road, Dunderg, Bishopstown
(tel. 543078). City centre 1.5km away. Bus 5 or 8.
Mrs Mary O'Leary, Belrose, 50 Maryville, Ballintemple, Blackrock
(tel. 292219). City centre 1.5km away. Bus 2.
Mrs Rita O'Herlihy, 55 Wilton Gardens, Wilton/University (tel.
541705). 1.5km from the centre. Bus 5 or 8.
Mrs Catherine Whelan, Rose Villa, 1 Dons Court, Bishopstown
Road, Wilton/University (tel. 545731). City centre 1.5km away.
Bus 8.
Mrs M. Flynn, Kent House, 47 Lower Glanmire Road (tel. 504260).
A 10-minute walk from the centre. Close to the train station.
Mrs B. Higgins, 7 Ferncliff Villas, Bellevue Park, St Lukes (tel.
508963). A 10-minute walk from the centre. Rooms are cheaper
than on average.
Mrs E. Murray, Oakland, 51 Lower Glanmire Road (tel. 500578).
A 10-minute walk from the centre of Cork. Close to the train
station.

Mrs Nuala Kennedy, San Antone, 10 Park View, Victoria Road (tel. 963513). Less than 400m from the centre.

HI HOSTEL
1–2 Redclyffe, Western Road (tel. 543289). Curfew 11.55 p.m. June–Sept., IR£5.90 (£5.90; $9); Oct.–May, IR£4.50 (£4.50; $6.75). Prices fall slightly for the rest of the year. Bus 5 or 8.

HOLIDAY HOSTELS
Kinlay House, Bob & Joan Walk, Shandon (tel. 508966). Irish Budget Hostel. No curfew. Round-the-clock reception. B&B around IR£7 (£7; $10.50). In an alley beside St Anne's Church in Shandon.

ISAACS, 48 MacCurtin Street (tel. 500011). Irish Budget Hostel. Twenty-four hour reception. Six-bed rooms around IR£5.50 (£5.50; $8.25). A few more expensive small rooms are available. Near the bus and train stations. From the train station head left along Lower Glanmire Road to the junction with MacCurtin Street. From the bus station cross the River Lee and head straight on to the same junction.

Sheila's Hostel, Belgrove Place, Wellington Road (tel. 505562). No curfew. Reception open 8 a.m.–10 p.m. Around IR£5.50 (£5.50; $8.25). Near the bus and train stations.

Campus House, 3 Woodland View (tel. 343531). Around IR£5.50 (£5.50; $8.25) in dorms; singles IR£10 (£10; $15). Close to the HI hostel, 1.5km from the centre on Western Road. Bus 5 and 8.

HOSTELS
Cork City Hostel, 100 Lower Glanmire Road (tel. 509089). No curfew. Around IR£6 (£6; $9). Along the road from the train station. From the bus station cross the River Lee and go straight ahead, then right along Lower Glanmire Road.

CAMPING
Cork City Caravan and Camping Park (tel. 961866). Three-star site. Open Easter–30 Sept., and during the Jazz Festival. Bus 14 stops at the gate. Small tent IR£3.50 (£3.50; $5), large tent IR£4.50 (£4.50; $6.75), IR£1 (£1; $1.50) per adult.

Bienvenue Caravan and Camping Site (tel. 312171). One-star site. Open Easter–31 Oct. On the main road to Kinsale (R600). Free pick-up from the bus station or the Tourist Office. IR£4 (£3.80; $5.70) for all tents, IR£0.75 (£0.70; $1.70) per adult.

Dublin (Baile Átha Cliath) (tel. code 01)

TOURIST OFFICES

Tourist Information, 14 Upper O'Connell Street (tel. 284 1765).
Open July—Aug., Mon.—Sat. 8.30 a.m.—8 p.m., Sun. 10.30 a.m.—
3 p.m.; June, Mon.—Sat. 8.30 a.m.—6 p.m.; otherwise, Mon.—Fri.
9 a.m.—5 p.m. Books rooms locally for IR£1 (£1; $1.50).
Tourist Information, Dublin Airport (tel. 376387). Open June—
Sept. 8 a.m.—10.30 p.m.; May 8 a.m.—8 p.m.; Sept.—Dec. 8 a.m.—
6.30 p.m.; Jan.—Apr. 8 a.m.—6 p.m.
Tourist Information, North Wall Ferryport (B&I Terminal), Alexander Road. Open only from late June until early Sept.

FINDING ACCOMMODATION

On the whole, you should have little trouble finding a bed in a
hostel or in one of the cheaper B&Bs. The one time of year when
it can become tricky to find cheap accommodation are the days
leading up to and after one of Ireland's home games in the Five
Nations rugby championship, when hordes of visiting rugby fans
descend on the city. However, it is doubtful if you will be in Dublin
at that time as the games are played in the winter months.

PUBLIC TRANSPORT

Although most of the cheaper B&Bs are outside the city centre,
you will have no trouble getting to them as the city has an efficient
bus service while the DART commuter train can be useful,
depending on where you are staying (same price as buses to similar
destinations). Information on the city's bus network is available
from the office at 59 Upper O'Connell Street (tel. 836 6111 during
office hours, tel. 873 4222 thereafter). Most city buses depart from
the streets off Upper O'Connell Street (see **Tourist Office** for directions), especially the Eden Quay, Abbey Street and Talbot Street.
B&B proprietors will invariably be able to tell you which bus to get
to their establishment, where to catch the bus and where to get
off.

TROUBLE SPOTS

The area around the Connolly train station is one of the more
depressed parts of the city. Most of the hostels are in this part of
town. Although the district is in no way dangerous it is advisable
not to leave rucksacks and valuables lying in the hostels. Either

make use of hostel storage facilities (where available) or leave your pack at the station.

B&Bs

All prices quoted below are per person and based on two people sharing a room without a bath/shower. A supplement is added for single occupancy, usually around IR£4–5 (£4–5; $6–7.50). During public holidays and special events some owners increase their prices, usually by IR£1.50–2.50 (£1.50–2.50; $2.25–3.75) per person.

Around IR£11 (£11; £16.50)

Mrs E. Trehy, 110 Ringsend Park, Sandymount (tel. 668 9447). Single supplement IR£2.50 (£2.50; $3.75).

Around IR£12 (£12; $18)

Mrs M. Birmingham, 8 Dromard Terrace, Sandymount (tel. 668 3861). Single supplement IR£1.50 (£1.50; $2.25).
Mrs R. Casey, Villa Jude, 2 Church Avenue, Sandymount (tel. 668 4982). Single supplement IR£2 (£2; $3).
Mrs Ryan, 10 Distillery Road, Clontarf (tel. 837 4147).

Around IR£14 (£14; $21)

Mrs D. Abbot-Murphy, 14 Sandymount Castle Park, Sandymount (tel. 269 8413). Off the Guildford Road.
Mrs E. Byrne-Poole, Sea-Front, 278 Clontarf Road, Clontarf (tel. 833 6118). Bus 30.
Mrs C. Canavan, 81 Kincora Road, Clontarf (tel. 833 1007). Bus 30.
Mrs B. Creagh, St Aidan's, 150 Clonliffe Road, Clontarf (tel. 837 6750).
Mrs Margo Harahan, Jaymara, 67 Hampton Court/Vernon Avenue, Clontarf (tel. 833 6992).
Mrs Mary Hosford, 1 Park View, Kincroa Court, Clontarf (tel. 833 0694).
Mrs Moira Kavanagh, Springvale, 69 Kincora Drive, Clontarf (tel. 833 3413). Off Kincora Grove. Bus 28, 29A, 31, 32 or 44A.
Mrs C. Drain, Bayview, 265 Clontarf Road, Clontarf (tel. 833 9870). Bus 30.
Mrs Oonagh Egan, Currow, 144 Kincora Road, Clontarf (tel. 833 9990). Bus 30.

Mrs Erna Doherty, 16 Beechlawn Avenue, Woodville Estate, Art-
ane (tel. 847 4361). Bus 27A or 27B.

Mrs Rita Kenny, Seaview, 166 Bettyglen, Raheny (tel. 831 5335).
Bus 31, 31A, 32, 32B or the DART.

Mrs Mai Bird, St Dunstans, 25A Oakley Road, Ranelagh (tel. 497
2286). Just under 1.5km from the centre. Bus 11, 11A, 11B or
13.

Mrs A. Boyle, St Judes, 6 Fortfield Terrace, Upper Rathmines (tel.
497 2517).

Mrs M. MacMahon, 64 Sandford Road, Ranelagh (tel. 497 0654).

Mrs E. O'Brien, 24 Ormond Road, Rathmines (tel. 497 7801).

Mrs Roma Gibbons, Joyville, 24 St Alphonsus Road, Drumcondra
(tel. 8303221). Bus 3, 11, 11A, 16, 16A, or 41A.

Mrs M. Smyth, 21 Sandymount Road, Sandymount (tel. 668 3602).

HI HOSTELS

Dublin International Youth Hostel, 61 Mountjoy Street (tel.
301776/301396). Relatively flexible midnight curfew. B&B
June–Sept. IR£9 (£9; $13.50); Oct.–May IR£7 (£7; $10.50).
Best reserved in advance during July and Aug. Free luggage
lockers. Near the city centre. From the airport take bus 41A to
Dorset Street. A free bus meets incoming ferries.

Scoil Lorcáin, Monkstown (tel. 284 4255). Open July–Aug.,
IR£5.90 (£5.90; $9). About 9km from the centre.

69/70 Harcourt Street (tel. 750430). Open 24 June–31 Aug., IR£9
(£9; $13.50). Breakfast included. Just off St Stephen's Green, a
15-minute walk from the Connolly Station across the Liffey.
Buses 11, 13 and 46A run to St Stephen's Green.

OTHER HOSTELS

Old School House, Eblana Avenue, Dun Laoghaire (tel. 280 8777).
20 minutes from the city centre by DART train. Beds from IR£8
(£8; $12) with breakfast from IR£1.25 (£1.25; $2) and dinner
from IR£4.25 (£4.25; $7).

The Dublin Tourist Hostel (ISAACS), 2–5 Frenchman's Lane (tel.
363877/749321). Irish Budget Hostel. No curfew. 24-hour reception. Basic dorms IR£5.50 (£5.50; $8.25), 6- and 8-bed dorms
IR£6 (£6; $9), singles IR£13 (£13; $19.50), doubles IR£17 (£17;
$25.50). Free baggage storage, lockers available. Close to the
Connolly Station, off Lower Gardiner Street.

Kinlay House, 2–12 Lord Edward Street (tel. 679 6644). Irish
Budget Hostel. Dorms from IR£7.50 (£7.50; $11.25), doubles
from IR£11.50 (£11.50; $17.25) per person. Prices increase by
IR£0.50–1.00 (£0.50–1.00; $0.75–1.50) July–Sept. Breakfast

included. Lockers available. Centrally located near Christ Church Cathedral.

Avalon House, 55 Aungier Street (tel. 475 0001). No curfew. Dorms IR£7–10 (£7–10; $10.50–15.00), quads IR£11 (£11; $16.50) per person, doubles IR£12.50 (£12.50; $19.25) per person, singles IR£17.50 (£17.50; $26.25). IR£0.50 (£0.50; $0.75) supplement in high season. 250m from St Stephen's Green, a 15-minute walk from the Connolly Station across the Liffey.

YWCA, Radcliffe Hall, St John's Road, Sandymount (tel. 269 4521). Open June–Sept. 11 p.m. curfew. IR£9 (£9; $13.50) for dorms, IR£13–14 (£13–14; $19.50–21.00) per person in small rooms. 700m from the Sydney Parade DART station. On the number 3 bus route.

Marlborough Hostel, 81–82 Marlborough Street (tel. 747629). Dorms IR£7.50 (£7.50; $11.25), doubles IR£11 (£11; $16.50) per person. Beside St Mary's Pro-Cathedral.

M.E.C., 43 North Great George Street (tel. 726301). Round the clock reception. Dorms IR£7.50 (£7.50; $11.25), doubles IR£10 (£10; $15) per person, singles IR£14 (£14; $21) with breakfast. Reduced weekly rates available. Off Parnell Street. Follow O'Connell Street away from the quayside into Parnell Street.

Young Traveller, St Mary's Place (tel. 305000). 24-hour reception. B&B IR£9.50 (£9.50; $14.25). Close to the Connolly Station, off Talbot Street.

Goin' My Way/Cardijn House, 15 Talbot Street (tel. 788484/741720). Midnight curfew. B&B IR£6 (£6; $9). Baggage room with a safe. No lockers. Over Tiffany's shoe shop, close to the Connolly train station.

CAMPING

Shankhill Caravan & Camping Park (tel. 282 0011). Open all year round. IR£5 (£5; $7.50) per tent, IR£0.50 (£0.50; $0.75) per person in peak season (27 June to 28 Aug.). The price for tents falls slightly at other times of the year. The closest site to Dublin, 16km south of the city on the N11 to Wexford. Bus 45, 45A, 84, or the DART to Shankill.

North Beach Caravan and Camping Park, Rush (tel. 843 7131/7602). Open all year round. IR£3 (£3; $4.50) per person, tent included. About 27km north of the city.

Galway City (Gaillimh) (tel. code 091)

TOURIST OFFICE
Tourist Information, Victoria Place, off Eyre Square (tel. 63081).
July–Aug. open daily 9 a.m.–6.45 p.m.; Sept.–June Mon.–Fri.
9 a.m.–5.45 p.m., Sat. 9 a.m.–12.45 p.m. Accommodation service.
IR£1 (£1; $1.50) commission. One block from the bus and train
stations.

FINDING ACCOMMODATION
Throughout most of the year finding suitable accommodation in
Galway is straightforward, but this is not the case in late July and
August. The International Busking Festival on the last weekend in
July draws many visitors to the city, as does the Westend Traditional Festival on the last weekend in August. Sandwiched
between these two events are the Galway Races (last week in July)
and the Galway Arts Festival (mid to late July), which attract even
more visitors. Unless you have a tent, reservations are essential if
you are arriving during this period.

B&Bs
All prices quoted below are per person based on two people sharing
a room without a bath/shower. A supplement is added for single
occupancy, usually around IR£2–3 (£2–3; $3.00–4.50). During
public holidays and special events some owners increase their
prices, usually by IR£2–3 (£2–3; $3.00–4.50) per person. All the
B&Bs listed below are within the central area of the city or within
10–15 minutes' walking distance. There are plenty of similarly
priced B&Bs further out.

Around IR£12 (£12; $18)

Mrs T. Collins, 31 Grattan Court, Lower Salthill (tel. 63667).
Mrs D. Glynn, Montmartre, 41 Whitestrand Park (tel. 64927).
Mrs P. Heffernan, Merrion House, 28 Lower Salthill (tel. 25964).
Mrs B. Lyons, Mount Perpetua, 28 Whitestrand Park, Lower Salthill
(tel. 65563).
Mrs C. Ruane, 25 Grattan Court, Fr. Griffin Road (tel. 66513).

Around IR£13 (£13; $19.50)

Mrs Mary Corless, 22 Newcastle Road (tel. 22415).

Mrs K. Stephens, Inishmore House, 109 Fr. Griffin Road, Lower Salthill (tel. 62639).
Mrs Eileen Storan, Dunree, 57 Lower Salthill (tel. 23196).
Mrs C. Carey, The Greenways, 9 Glenard Crescent (tel. 22308).
Mrs S. Comer, Towerhill, 33 Glenard Crescent (tel. 22150).
Mrs M. O'Gorman, Setanta, 2 D'Alton Place (tel. 23538). Off Dr Mannix Road.
Johnny & Helen Geraghty, Cill Dara, 23 Rockhill Avenue (tel. 22401). Off Dalysfort Road.

Around IR£14 (£14; $21)

Avalon, 11 College Road. 200m from the city centre.
Mrs S. Davy, Ross House, 14 Whitestrand Avenue (tel. 67431).
Mrs M. Tarpey, The Dormers, Whitestrand Road, Lower Salthill (tel. 65034).

HI HOSTEL
St Mary's College, St Mary's Road (tel. 27411). Open 26 June–28 Aug. B&B IR£8 (£8; $12). In the Salthill area of the city, 1.5km from the train station.

OTHER HOSTELS
Great Western House, Frenchville Lane, Eyre Square (tel. 61139). A brand new budget accommodation complex, close to the train and bus stations in the city centre. Dorms from IR£7 (£7; $10.50) and doubles from IR£12 (£12; $18) including breakfast.
Arch View Hostel, 11 Upper Dominick Street (tel. 66661). Irish Budget Hostel. IR£6.00–7.50 (£6.00–7.50; $9.00–11.25). Prices fall slightly Oct.–May. Right in the centre of town.
The Stella Maris Holiday Hostel, 151 Upper Salthill (tel. 21950/ 26974). No curfew. IR£7–8 (£7–8; $10.50–12.00). Price falls slightly Oct.–June.
Grand Holiday Hostel, 244 Upper Salthill (tel. 21150). No curfew. IR£6–7 (£6–7; $9.00–10.50). Bus 1.
Woodquay Hostel, 23–24 Woodquay (tel. 62618). IR£7–8 (£7–8; $10.50–12.00).
Galway City Hostel, 25–27 Dominick Street (tel. 66367). IR£5.00–6.50 (£5.00–6.50; $7.50–9.75).
Corrib Villa, 4 Waterside (tel. 62892). No curfew. IR£5.50 (£5.50; $8.25). Centrally located. Follow Eglinton Street past the court to Waterside.
Owens, Upper Dominick Street (tel. 66211). No phone reservations,

but phoning ahead will let you know if there is space. No curfew. IR£6 (£6; $9). In the centre of town.

Eyre Hostel, 35 Eyre Street. No telephone. Central location.

Galway Tourist Hostel, Gentian Hill, Knocknacarra, Salthill (tel. 25176).

CAMPING

The Ballyloughane Caravan Park on the Dublin Road has space for tents. Open Apr.–Sept. Hunter's Silver Strand, 6.5km west of the city along the coast is the best of a number of sites in Salthill.

No one will object to you pitching a tent on the grassy area by the Spanish Arch, although this is actually illegal.

There are two sites on the coast west of Galway at Barna:

Hunter's Silver Strand Caravan & Camping Park (tel. 92452/ 92040).

Barna House Caravan & Camping Park (tel. 92469).

Limerick City (Luimneach)

(tel. code 061)

TOURIST OFFICE

Tourist Information, Arthur's Quay (tel. 317522). Open June–Aug., Mon.–Fri. 9 a.m.–6.30 p.m., Sat. and Sun. 9.30 a.m.–5.30 p.m.; Sept. and May, Mon.–Fri. 9.30 a.m.–6 p.m.; Sat. 9.30 a.m.–5.30 p.m.; Oct.–Apr., Mon.–Fri. 9.30 a.m.–5.30 p.m., Sat. 9.30 a.m.–1 p.m.

B&Bs

The Ennis Road, running from the River Shannon in the direction of the airport, and the streets leading off it, are the best places to look for Bed & Breakfast accommodation in Limerick. Buses 2, 3, 10 and 59 all run along parts of the Ennis Road.

Expect to pay around IR£13 (£13; $19.50) p.p. in doubles, IR£15 (£15; $22.50) if you want a single

Mrs Noreen Marsh, Shannon Grove House, Athlunkard, Killaloe Road (tel. 345756/343838). Only slightly more expensive than the prices quoted above. All rooms have private shower/bath and toilet. About 1km from the city centre.

Mrs B. Feeney, Dellastrada House, 136 Upper Mayorstone Park (off the Ennis Road) (tel. 452300). Cheap rooms. Singles cost less than usual price for doubles. A 10-minute walk from the town centre.

Mrs S. Roche, St Martin's, 4 Clanmorris Gardens (off the Ennis Road) (tel. 455013). Cheap rooms. Singles less than usual price for doubles.

Mrs M. Volke, Coolgreen, Ennis Road (tel. 454375). A 15-minute walk from the town centre.

Mrs Mary Power, Curraghgower House, Ennis Road (tel. 454716). Singles are more expensive than average. About 1km from the city centre. Buses 2, 3, 59 and 10 stop 100m away.

Mrs Carole O'Toole, Gleneagles, 12 Vereker Gardens, Ennis Road (tel. 455521). Singles are more expensive than normal. Within easy walking distance of the town centre.

Mrs C. Beresford, Annesville (Bogside House), Ennis Road (tel. 452703). Doubles only. 2km from the centre.

Mrs F. Houn'gan, 6 Elm Drive, Caherdevin Lawn, Ennis Road (tel. 451756). 2km from the centre. Open May to September.

Mrs M. Collins, St Anthony's, 8 Coolraine Terrace, Ennis Road (tel. 452607). Doubles only.

Mrs C. Gavin, Shannonville, Ennis Road (next to the Limerick Ryan Hotel) (tel. 453690). Doubles only. Open May to September.

Mrs J. McSweeney, Trebor, Ennis Road (tel. 454632). Singles £18.

Mr Dermot Walsh, Santa Cruz, 10 Coolraine Terrace, Ennis Road (tel. 454500).

Mrs S. Lowney, Garnish, 15 Merval Drive, Clareview (tel. 453465). 1km from the centre.

Mrs Mary Frost Walsh, Casa Marie, 16 Westfield Park, North Circular Road (tel. 453865).

Mrs N. Coyne, Mount Gerard, O'Connell Avenue (tel. 314981/411886). Singles £17. 500m from the centre.

HI HOSTEL
1 Pery Square (tel. 312107). June–Sept. IR£5.90 (£5.90; $9); Oct.–May IR£4.50 (£4.50; $6.75). Midnight curfew. Close to the bus and train stations.

ITALY (Italia)

Anyone who thinks of Italy as a place where accommodation prices are low is likely to be disappointed. Compared to Greece, Portugal and Spain, accommodation is no bargain and, in some ways, this is also true when comparisons are made with northern Europe. In the major Italian cities, hostels are around the same price as those in the Netherlands and Denmark, but rarely approach the standard of hostels in those countries. Similarly, cheap Italian hotels cost roughly the same as their German counterparts, but the latter offer much higher standards of comfort and cleanliness.

In the main places of interest, accommodation options for solo travellers can be restricted to hostelling or camping, unless they can find someone to share a room with, or can afford to pay upwards of 20,000–30,000L (£8.30–12.50; $12.50–18.75) for one of the limited supply of singles. For two or more people travelling together, hostelling or staying in cheap hotels are the best, easily available options. Rooms in private homes (*camere libere*) can be much cheaper than hotels, but are not easy to find. Ask the Tourist Office for details of their availability.

Hotels are rated from one up to five stars. Charges, which are fixed by the Provincial Tourist Board, should be clearly displayed in the room. It should also be stated whether overnight price is inclusive of breakfast, showers and IVA (VAT), as these are often charged separately. If there is no notice in the room, ask the management for written confirmation of the relevant details. At the lower end of the hotel market IVA is charged at 10%. Showers normally cost 1,500–3,000L (£0.60–1.25; $1–2). Breakfast can add anything from 3,000–10,000L (£1.25–4.00; $2–6) to the overnight price per person, but, legally, breakfast is optional for those staying only a few days. Hoteliers can insist, however, that you take half-board if you stay for a lengthy period.

In most of the main towns you should consider yourself fortunate if you find a double in the region of 35,000L (£14.50; $21.75). It is more likely that you will have to pay around 45,000–50,000L (£18.75–21.00; $28.00–31.50). For triples, you will rarely pay more than another third on top of the price of doubles. Florence, Milan, Bologna and Venice are the places most likely to cause you problems in your search for one of the cheaper rooms, due to a combination of higher than average prices and demand exceeding supply. If you are beginning to despair in Venice, consider staying in nearby Mestre, or Padua (regular trains leave right up to midnight; 10 and 30 minute trips respectively). In the off-season, hotels often reduce their prices. If they have not already done so, you can expect some success if you try to bargain them down.

The **Italian YHA** operates about 50 hostels, split into three grades. Even the top-rated hostels can vary dramatically in quality. Prices start at around 12,000L (£5; $7.50), but normally you will pay around 14,000–16,000L (£6.00–6.70; $9–10). In some of the main cities, such as Rome, Venice, Florence, Milan and Naples, prices range from 18,000–20,000L (£7.50–8.30; $11.25–12.50). At hostels charging 15,000L (£6.25; $9.50) and over, breakfast is included in the price. Non-members are usually admitted on the payment of a small surcharge of 2,000L (£0.85; $1.25) per night. In Venice, non-members are only admitted if they buy a membership card, costing 15,000L (£6.25; $9.50). In summer, hostel curfews are normally 11.30 p.m. Hostels are seldom conveniently located in the centre of town and many of the smaller towns of particular interest have no hostel.

In the cities, there are also a number of **independent hostels** and some run by local authorities. Prices and curfews are similar to those of HI hostels. In most of the larger cities, women have the option of staying in one of the dormitories run by the various religious orders. These establishments, known as 'Protezione della Giovane', offer high standards of accommodation and security to female travellers. Prices are normally around 18,000L (£7.50; $11.25) in singles, 12,500L (£5.25; $8) per person in doubles, but can reach 28,000L (£11.75; $17.50) per person in some institutions in Venice. Curfews are usually between 10 and 11.30 p.m. During university vacations, it is possible to stay in vacant **student residences**. The *Guide for Foreign Students*, available from the Ministry of Education, Viale Trastavese, Roma, is a useful source of information. Applications should be made to the local 'Casa dello Studente'. Ask the local Tourist Office for the location and the telephone number.

There are over 2000 registered **campsites**. Strictly speaking, you are not supposed to camp outside these sites, but the authorities are unlikely to trouble you if you are camping on privately owned land with the permission of the owner. Unless you are planning to do a considerable amount of touring outside the main cities there is not much to commend taking a tent, other than as an insurance should all else fail. Sites serving the cities are usually large, crowded, noisy and located far from the centre; by and large, they are more suited to those travelling by car than those relying on public transport. Camping is also quite expensive. Normally, charges are around 3,500L (£1.50; $2.25) per tent, and 5,500L (£2.30; $3.50) per occupant, but can rise well above this at city sites. It is not unusual to be charged 6,500L (£2.70; $4) per tent and per person. Some of the sites near Venice charge a ridiculous 15,000L (£6.25; $9.50) per tent, 6,000L (£2.50; $3.75) per person, and above, in peak season. Security is also a problem, so you can add the cost of storing your pack at the station (1,500L (£0.60; $0.90) per day, or each time you want access to it within that period, to the cost of camping and of public transport.

Sleeping in train stations has recently been made illegal, and the police are not too well disposed to those sleeping rough elsewhere. If you are **sleeping rough**, however, the police are likely to be the least of your problems. Places which seem well suited to sleeping out also tend to be the places where naïve and foolish travellers are stripped of their cash and belongings (and, where the thieves have a sense of humour, their clothes too). The Borghese Gardens in Rome is one prime example. Naples is especially dangerous, but you should avoid sleeping rough in Italy as a whole.

Anyone who would like to spend some time in the countryside might consider **renting a cottage** or a farmhouse. These can be rented for as little as 4,000–10,000L (£1.70–4.00; $2.50–6.00) per person per night, which represents excellent value for money. Hikers and climbers should contact the Italian Alpine Club for details of the 465 refuge huts in the Italian Alps. The overnight fee is normally around 7,000L (£3; $4.50), but this rises by 20% in winter.

ADDRESSES

Italian State Tourist Office	1 Princes Street, London W1R 8AY (tel. 0171 408 1254).
Italian YHA	Associazione Italiana Alberghi per la Gioventù, Via Cavour 44 (terzo piano), I-00184 Roma (tel. 06 474 6755/487 1152).
Student accommodation	Relazioni Universitari, Associazione Italiana per il Turismo e gli Scambi Universitari, Via Palestro 11, 00185 Roma (tel. 06 475 5265).
Camping	Federcampeggio, Casella Postale 23, I-50041 Calenzalo (Firenze) supplies lists and maps, as does the Italian State Tourist Office.If you want to buy a guide while in Italy, the *Euro Camping* guide is easy to pick up and one of the best available, for around 10,000L (£4; $6).

Farmhouses and cottages	Agriturist, Corso V Emanuele 101, Roma (tel. 06 651 2342).
Mountain Refuges	Club Alpino Italiano (Rifugi Alpini), Via Ugo Foscolo 3, Milano (tel. 02 720 22555).

Assisi (tel. code 075)

TOURIST OFFICE
Azienda di Promozione Turistica, Piazza del Comune 12 (tel. 812534). Opposite the Roman Temple of Minerva. Open 9 a.m.– 1 p.m. and 3.30–6.30 p.m.

ARRIVING BY TRAIN
Trains stop in Assisi-Santa Maria degli Angeli, 5km from the Old Town. A regular bus service operates between the station and the Old Town.

FINDING ACCOMMODATION
Despite the fact that relatively few of those who visit Assisi actually stay there (most pass through on coach trips) it can be difficult to find a cheap place to stay the night. The Tourist Office will book hotel rooms for you, either in the Old Town or in Assisi-Santa Maria degli Angeli. Unfortunately, hotel prices have been rising sharply over the past few years with the result that there are now relatively few hotels in the budget category. If you want to stay in the Old Town but cannot afford a hotel room, the Tourist Office has lists of local families and religious institutions which accept paying guests.

HOTELS
Cheapest doubles around 30,000–40,000L (£12.50–16.75; $18.75–25.00)

Dal Moro, Via G. Becchetti 12, Santa Maria degli Angeli (tel. 804 1666). One-star hotel.
Porziuncola, Piazza Garibaldi 10, Santa Maria degli Angeli (tel. 804 1020). Two-star hotel. The hotel has the best location possible in Santa Maria degli Angeli, on the square facing the Basilica of St Mary amongst the Angels.
Anfiteatro Romano, Via Anfiteatro (tel. 813025). One-star hotel.
Italia, Vicolo della Fortezza (tel. 812625). One-star hotel.

Marconi, Piazza Dante Alighieri 3 (tel. 804 0277). One-star hotel.

Donnini, Via Los Angeles 47, Santa Maria degli Angeli (tel. 804 0260). One-star hotel. Singles start around 25,000L (£10.50; $15.75), singles with bath/shower around 30,000L (£12.50; $18.75), doubles with bath/shower around 45,000L (£18.75; $28).

La Rocca, Via Porta Perlici 27 (tel. 816467). One-star hotel. Follow signs for the Duomo.

Cheapest doubles around 45,000L (£18.75; $28)

Belvedere, Via Borgo Aretino 13 (tel. 812460). Two-star hotel.

Porziuncola, Via Micarelli, Santa Maria degli Angeli (tel. 804 1020). One-star hotel. An annex of the two-star hotel listed above. The price here is for doubles with a bath/shower, which is a good deal lower than at the two-star hotel. The annex has no basic doubles.

Patrono d'Italia, Via Patrono d'Italia 48, Santa Maria degli Angeli (tel. 804 0221). One-star hotel.

Montecavallo, Viale Patrono d'Italia 46 (tel. 804 0867). One-star hotel

Il Duomo, Vicolo S. Lorenzo (tel. 812742). One-star hotel.

Da Angelo, Via S. Rufino Campagna 35/c, S. Potente (tel. 812821). Two-star hotel.

Cheapest doubles around 50,000–55,000L (£21–23; $31.50–34.50)

Villa Cherubino, Via Patrono d'Italia 39, Santa Maria degli Angeli (tel. 804 0226). One-star hotel. Doubles with shower/bath only.

Europa, Via Metastasio 2 (tel. 812412). Two-star hotel.

Los Angeles, Via Los Angeles, Santa Maria degli Angeli (tel. 804 1339). One-star hotel. An annex of the two-star hotel of that name. Price quoted is for doubles in the annex with shower/bath.

Rina, Piaggia S. Pietro 20 (tel. 812817). Two-star hotel.

Victor, Via S. Maria della Spira, Rivotorto (tel. 806 5562). One-star hotel.

Fontanella, Via S. Maria della Spira, Rivotorto (tel. 806 4400). One-star hotel.

Da Giovanna, Via A. Diaz, Santa Maria degli Angeli (tel. 804 0607). One-star hotel.

Cavallucci, Via S. Pietro Campagna 4 (tel. 813279). One-star hotel.

Bellavista, Via S. Pietro Campagna 140 (tel. 804 1636). One-star hotel.

Sole, Corso Mazzini 20 (tel. 812922). Two-star hotel. An annex of the hotel of the same name listed below.

HI HOSTEL
Della Pace, Via Valecchi (tel. 816767). 16,000L (£6.75; $10). Open all year. Closed from 9 a.m.–5 p.m. daily. 11 p.m. curfew.

HOSTEL
In the small village of Fontemaggio, 1.75km outside the old town, at Strada Eremo delle Carceri 8 (tel. 813636). Around 15,000L (£6.25; $9.50), including breakfast.

CAMPING
Strada Eremo delle Carceri 8, Fontemaggio. Same telephone number as the hostel. 4,500L (£2; $3) per tent, 6,000L (£2.50; $3.75) per person.
Internazionale Assisi, Via S. Giovanni Campiglione 110 (tel. 813710). Open Mar.–Oct. 6,000L (£2.50; $3.75) per tent, 7,000L (£3; $4.50) per person.

Bari (tel. code 080)

TOURIST OFFICE
Piazza Aldo Moro. Beside the train station. Open Mon.–Fri. 8.30 a.m.–1 p.m., Sat. 8.30–11 a.m.
• **Stop-over in Bari**
Between mid-June and mid-Sept, the Stop-over in Bari organization operate a site where travellers under 30 can **camp** or **sleep out** for free for one night at Pineta San Francesco (tel. 441186, 24 hours). The site is on the fringe of the city, but is easily reached by bus 5 from the train station, or by bus 1 from Corso Cavour. Toilet and washing facilities are available on site, as is free luggage storage. Stop-over in Bari also offer two-night stays in **private flats** for 30,000L (£12.50; $18.75), great value if you want to spend a couple of days looking around Bari. Any of the four Stop-over offices will give you details of the other offers open to under-30s for one day, such as free bus travel, free bike hire. Stop-over offices:

OTE, Via Dante 111 (tel. 521 4538).
Piazza Aldo Moro. By the main train station.

Maritime Station, c/o the Adriatica Office.
Registration desk at Pineta San Francesco.

HOTELS
Doubles around 40,000L (£16.75; $25)

Smeralda, Via Capruzzi 234 (tel. 64400). No singles.

Cheapest doubles around 60,000L (£25; $37.50)

Residenza Universitaria, Via de Rossi 23 (tel. 235226). Singles
around 35,000L (£14.50; $21.75).
Pensione Giulia, Via Crisanzio 12 (tel. 523 5030). Close to the
station. Singles from 45,000L (£19; $28.50).

Cheapest doubles around 65,000L (£27; $40.50)

Maria, Via Crisanzio 26 (tel. 232592). Singles around 40,000L
(£16.75; $25).
Loizzo, Via Crisanzio 46 (tel. 521 1284). Singles around 35,000L
(£14.50; $21.75).
Pensione Romeo, Via Crisanzio 12 (tel. 521 6380).

Cheapest doubles around 70,000L (£29.25; $44)

Fiorini, Via Imbriani 69 (tel. 540185). Singles around 40,000L
(£16.75; $25).
Modernissimo, Corso Vittorio Emanuele 30 (tel. 210203). Singles
around 40,000L (£16.75; $25).
Casa della Studentessa, Via Carruba 58 (tel. 512415). Two-star.
Open to women only. Singles around 40,000L (£16.75; $25),
with bath/shower 45,000L (£18.75; $28).
Patricia, Via Fiume 5 (tel. 235702). Singles around 40,000L
(£16.75; $25).
Serena, Via Imbriani 69 (tel. 540283). Singles around 35,000L
(£14.50; $21.75).

PRIVATE ROOMS
The Tourist Office has a list of private rooms available in the city.

HI HOSTEL
'Del Levante', Via Nicola Massaro 33 (tel. 520282). In Bari-Palese,
about 6.5km from the town centre. Take bus 1 from Corso Cavour.

CAMPING

San Giorgio (tel. 491175). Open all year round. By the SS16, about 6.5km south of the centre. From the Teatro Petruzzeli take bus 12.

Bologna (tel. code 051)

TOURIST OFFICES

Azienda di Promozione Turistica (APT), Via Marconi 45 (tel. 237413). Open 8 a.m.–2 p.m. The administrative office. Contact for information in advance.

IAT, Piazza della Medaglia d'Oro (tel. 246541). Outside the train station. Open Mon.–Sat. 9 a.m.–12.30 p.m. and 2.30–6.30 p.m. The staff will find you a room or phone any suggestions you have. After closing time a list of hotels with vacancies is displayed.

IAT, Piazza Maggiore 6 (tel. 239660). Open Mon.–Sat. 9 a.m.– 7 p.m., Sun. 9 a.m.–1 p.m. The main information office, located in the Palazzo Communale. Same hours and services as the office at the train station, but this office has a greater range of information.

BASIC DIRECTIONS

After leaving the train station, cross Piazza della Medaglia d'Oro and go left along the busy Viale Pietro Pietramellara until you see the square on the right-hand side with the Porta Galliera. Via Galliera and Via dell'Indipendenza run from this square. After about 300m both streets meet Via dei Mille. Going right along Via dei Mille, and then turning left at Via Montebello, you arrive at the start of Via del Porto. Continuing straight on down Via dell'Indipendenza you reach the end of the street opposite Piazza del Nettuno. At this point, Via Ugo Bassi heads right. Going to the left you can join Via Rizzoli, which leads to the two towers ('Due Torri') on Piazza di Porta Ravegna which are the symbol of the city. Crossing the street from the end of Via dell'Indipendenza you can walk through Piazza del Nettuno into the larger Piazza Maggiore, the main square in the city.

HOTELS

Hotel prices in Bologna are comparatively high due to the large number of students and business travellers. Expect to pay around 40,000L (£16.75; $25) for a single and 60,000L (£25; $37.50) for a double in a one star hotel.

Cheapest doubles from 40,000–47,000L (£16.75–19.60; $25.00–29.40)

Touring, Via Mattuiani 1/2 (tel. 584305). This two-star hotel offers some cheap rooms of all types. Singles from 30,000L (£12.50; $18.75), singles with bath/shower from 48,000L (£20; $30), doubles from 47,000L (£19.60; $29.40), and doubles with bath/shower from 70,000L (£29.25; $44).

Rossini, Via Bibbiena 11 (tel. 237716). Singles from 30,000L (£12.50; $18.75).

Accademia, Via Belle Arti 6 (tel. 232318). This two-star hotel offers a few cheap rooms of all types. Singles from 30,000L (£12.50; $18.75), singles with bath/shower from 40,000L (£16.75; $25), doubles from 40,000L (£16.75; $25), doubles with bath/shower from 50,000L (£21; $31.50). From Via dell'Indipendenza go left along Via A. Righi, then straight on down Via delle Moline into Via Belle Arti.

Atlantic, Via Galliera 46 (tel. 248488). A few cheap rooms of all types in this two-star hotel. Singles from 25,000L (£10.50; $15.75), singles with bath/shower from 40,000L (£16.75; $25), doubles 40,000L (£16.75; $25), doubles with bath/shower from 50,000L (£21; $31.50).

Due Torri, Via degli Usberti 4 (tel. 269826). Three-star hotel with some singles at 30,000L (£12.50; $18.75). Go right at the end of Via Galliera along Via Parigi and watch out for Via degli Usberti on the left.

Cheapest doubles around 50,000–56,000L (£21.00–23.50; $31.50–35.25)

Saragozza, Via Senzanome 10 (tel. 330258). Three-star hotel. Some singles from 30,000L (£12.50; $18.75), some doubles from 50,000L (£21; $31.50). About 10 minutes' walk from the centre, 20 minutes' walk from the train station. Walking from the station, turn right off Via Galliera at Via Riva de Reno, left at Via N. Sauro, across Via Ugo Bassi and on down Via Cesare Battisti, left at Via Barberia, right at Via del Riccio, first right along Via Lo Stradellaccio, right at Via del Fossato, left at Vicolo della Neve, then left.

Tuscolano, Via Tuscolano 29 (tel. 324024). Two-star hotel. Only a few rooms at this price. Singles 35,000L (£14.50; $21.75).

Apollo, Via Drapperie 5 (tel. 223955). Some singles at 30,000L (£12.50; $18.75) and some doubles at the prices quoted above. Otherwise rooms at this one-star hotel are the standard price.

Right off Via Rizzoli at Via Calzolerie, and straight on into Via Drapperie.

Nuovo, Via del Porto 6 (tel. 247926). This three-star hotel also has singles available from 28,000L (£11.70; $17.50). Most are twice that price.

Cheapest doubles around 60,000L (£25; $37.50)

S. Orsola, Via Palonieri 25 (tel. 302997).

Centrale, Via della Zecca 2 (tel. 225114).

Berlino, Via S. Mamolo 143 (tel. 581104).

Cristallo, Via San Giuseppe 5 (tel. 248574).

Panorama, Via Livraghi 1 (tel. 221802). Right at Via Ugo Bassi, then left after Via della Zecca. Singles 35,000L (£14.50; $21.75).

Garisenda, Galleria del Leone 1 (tel. 224369). Singles 38,000L (£16; $24).

Villa Azzurra, Via Felsina 49 (tel. 535460). One-star hotel. Singles 35,000L (£14.50; $21.75).

Pensione Marconi, Via Marconi 2 (tel. 262832). Singles 38,000L (£16; $24).

Doubles 65,000L (£27; $40.50)

Perla, Via San Vitale 77/2 (tel. 224579). A few singles at this one-star hotel cost about 38,000L (£16; 24). Otherwise singles and doubles are the same price as at most one-star hotels. Via S. Vitale begins at the 'Due Torri'.

Minerva, Via De Monari 3 (tel. 239652). Doubles without bath/shower only at this one-star hotel. Most rooms are priced at the standard rate. Left off Via Galliera after Via Volturno. Singles 45,000L (£19; $28.50).

Ideale, Via Sirani 5 (tel. 358270). One-star hotel. Standard price for most doubles. Singles from 35,000 (£14.50; $21.75).

HI HOSTEL

San Sisto I, Via Viadagola 14 (tel. 519202). Open all year. About 6.5km from the main train station. From Via Irnerio (near the main station, off Via dell'Indipendenza) take bus 93 (Mon.–Sat., last bus 8.15 p.m.) heading east. Sundays and from 1–24 August take bus 301.

San Sisto II, Via Viadagola 5 (tel. 501810). 16,000L (£6.70; $10). See San Sisto I for directions.

WOMEN'S HOSTEL
Protezione della Giovane, Via Santo Stefano 45 (tel. 225573). Clean
but tends to be packed with students. 15,000L (£6.25; $9.50) per
person, breakfast and shower included. 10.30 p.m. curfew.

CAMPING
No convenient site. Piccolo Paradiso is in Marzabotto, 17km away
(tel. 842680). 13,700L (£5.70; $8.50), plus 5,500–7,900L (£2.30–
3.30; $3.50–5.00) per person (cheaper off-season). Open
Mar.–Dec. Ask the Tourist Office how to get to the site, and for
details of the new campsites in Bologna that will be open for 1995.

Brindisi (tel. code 0831)

TOURIST OFFICE
Ente Provincial per il Turismo (EPT), Viale Regina Margherita 5 (tel.
21944). Open Mon.–Sat. 8.30 a.m.–12.30 p.m. and 4.30–7.30 p.m.
Very helpful office.

ARRIVING IN BRINDISI
The train station is on Piazza Crispi, about 20 minutes' walk from
the ferry terminal at the Stazione Marittima down Corso Garibaldi
to its end, then along Via del Mare. There are plenty of buses which
make the journey along the length of Corso Garibaldi (around 800L
(£0.35; $0.50) for the trip).

FINDING ACCOMMODATION
Finding a place to stay in Brindisi is seldom a problem as most of
the people who arrive in town depart on one of the overnight
ferries.

HOTELS
*Cheapest singles around 12,000L (£5; $7.50), doubles around 14,000L
(£6; $9)*

Doria, Via Fulvia 38 (tel. 26453). The cheapest in town, but best
  avoided by women travelling alone. Well out from the centre.
  Follow Via Appia into Via Arione, from which Via Fulvia is the
  second street on the right.

Cheapest doubles around 36,000–38,000L (£15–16; $22.50–24.00)

Villá Blanca, Via Armengol 23 (tel. 25438). Singles around 25,000L
(£10.50; $15.75). Doubles with a shower/bath are only slightly
more expensive than basic doubles.
Venezia, Via Pisanelli 6 (tel. 25411). Singles around 25,000L
(£10.50; $15.75).

Cheapest doubles around 40,000L (£16.75; $25)

Europa, Piazza Cairoli 5 (tel. 528546/528547). Singles around
30,000L (£12.50; $18.75).
Altair, Via Tunisi 2 (tel. 524911). Singles around 25,000L (£10.50;
$15.75).

HOSTEL
Via Brandi 2 (tel. 413123). About 1.5km from the centre, but easily
reached by bus 3, 4 or 5 from the train station. Call ahead to make
sure that the hostel is open before making the trip. 11,000L (£4.85;
$7.25) per person.

Florence (Firenze) (tel. code 055)

TOURIST OFFICES
Azienda di Promozione Turistica (APT), Via Manzoni 16 (tel.
23320). Open Mon.–Sat. Contact this office if you want information in advance. Not open to the public.
Informazione Turistiche. In a booth outside Firenze Santa Maria
Novella train station (take the exit by track 16). Open daily
8 a.m.–9 p.m. Free map of the city.
Informazione Turistiche Alberghiere. Beside track 16 in the train
station. Open daily, mid-Apr.–mid-Nov., 8 a.m.–8.30 p.m.; at
other times, 9 a.m.–8.30 p.m. Room-finding service. Commission
around 2,000L (£0.85; $1.25) per person. State clearly the price
range you are interested in, as otherwise they will offer you
expensive rooms.

BASIC DIRECTIONS
The vast majority of the accommodation suggestions below are
within reasonable walking distance of the Santa Maria Novella train
station. The cathedral is 10–15 minutes' walk away from the

station. Piazza della Stazione is the square in front of the train station. Via Nazionale leads out of the left-hand side of the square. Within a short distance, Via Nazionale passes one end of Via Fiume and crosses Via Faenza, two streets with a good supply of relatively inexpensive hotels. A few blocks further on Via Faenza crosses Via Guelfa. There are also a number of cheap hotels in the streets running off Via Guelfa, parallel to the right of Via Nazionale. At the bottom left of Piazza della Stazione is Piazza della Unità Italiana, from which Via de' Panzani runs to Via de' Cerretani, crossing Via del Giglio on the way. Going along Via de' Cerretani you arrive at Piazza S. Giovanni with the baptistry, beyond which is the cathedral. If from Piazza della Unità Italiana you head round the Santa Maria Novella church you arrive at Piazza Santa Maria Novella.

● **Street numbers**
The city's streets are not numbered in the conventional manner. Instead, there are two sets of numbers: red indicating business premises and blue or black denoting residential properties. Most hotels have blue or black numbers. In local publications, an *r* is added to the street number of commercial buildings.

HOTELS
Room prices in Florence's one-star hotels are more or less standard. With a few exceptions, you can expect to pay around 29,500L (£12.30; $18.50) for a single; 37,500L (£15.75; $23.50) for a single with bath/shower; 43,000L (£18; $27) for a double; and 54,000L (£22.50; $33.75) for a double with bath/shower. Hotels 1–8 in the list below offer slightly cheaper rooms, generally around 26,000L (£11; $16.50) for a single; 33,000L (£13.75; $20.50) for a single with bath/shower; 39,000L (£16.25; $24.40) for a double; and 48,000–51,000L (£20.00–21.25; $30–32) for a double with shower/bath. All other hotels charge the standard rate.

1. Rina, Via Dante Alighieri 12 (tel. 213209). A few really cheap rooms. Single around 13,500L (£5.65; $8.50), double around 26,000L (£11; $16.50). Others as described above. No rooms with shower/bath. Near the Badia. Follow Via della Studio from the cathedral and go straight on into Via Dante Alighieri.
2. Ausonia e Rimini, Via Nazionale 24 (tel. 496547).
3. Colorado, Via Cavour 66 (tel. 217310).
4. La Mia Casa, Piazza Santa Maria Novella 23 (tel. 213061). No singles with bath/shower.
5. Montreal, Via della Scala 43 (tel. 262331).
6. Marilena Tourist House, Via Fiume 20 (tel. 261705). No doubles with bath/shower.

7. Sampaoli, Via San Gallo 14 (tel. 284834). The street runs off Via Guelfa, three blocks to the right of Via Nazionale.
8. San Marco, Via Cavour 50 (tel. 284235).
9. ABC, Borgo Ognissanti 67 (tel. 218882).
10. Accademia, Via Faenza 7 (tel. 293451).
11. Adria, Via Montebello 49 (tel. 212029).
12. Aline, Via XXVII Aprile 14 (tel. 483256).
13. Antica, Via Pandoltini 27 (tel. 239 6644).
14. Asso, Via Lamarmota 27 (tel. 576729).
15. Azzi, Via Faenza 56 (tel. 213806).
16. Bavaria, Borgo degli Albizi 26 (tel. 234 0313). From the cathedral, head down Via del Proconsolo, then left.
17. Bellavista, Largo Alinari 15 (tel. 284528).
18. Brunori, Via del Proconsolo 5 (tel. 263648).
19. Burchianti, Via del Giglio 6 (tel. 212796).
20. Canada, Borgo San Lorenzo 14 (tel. 210074). Left from the end of Via de' Cerretani, by the baptistry.
21. Casci, Via Cavour 13 (tel. 211686). Via Cavour crosses Via Guelfa, four blocks to the right of Via Nazionale.
22. Cely, Piazza Santa Maria Novella 24 (tel. 218755).
23. Cestelli, Borgo SS Apostoli 25 (tel. 214213). From the Piazza Santa Maria Novella, take Via delle Belledonne (just to the right of Via de' Banchi). At the end of the street head left until you reach Via de'Tornabuoni. Turn right down this street and continue on, passing Via Porta Rossa on the left as you enter Piazza S. Trinità. Borgo SS Apostoli is then the second street on the left. Walking from the train station to Piazza S. Trinità takes just over 15 minutes.
24. Colomba, Via Cavour 21 (tel. 263139). See 21.
25. Concordia, Via dell'Amorino 14 (tel. 213233).
26. D'Errico, Via Faenza 69 (tel. 214059).
27. Delle Rose, Via Cantodei Nelli 2 (tel. 239 6372).
28. Duilio, Corso Italia 13 (tel. 287331).
29. Elite, Via della Scala 12 (215395). Cheapest doubles 60,000L (£25; $37.50).
30. Enza, Via S. Zanobi 45 (tel. 490990). The street runs off Via Guelfa, one block to the right of Via Nazionale.
31. Erina, Via Fiume 17 (tel. 284343). No singles
32. Esplanade, Via Tornabuoni 13 (tel. 287078).
33. Etrusca, Via Nazionale 35 (tel. 213100).
34. Fani, Via Guelfa 28 (tel. 283731).
35. Ferdy, Via S. Gallo 39 (tel. 475302). Cheapest doubles 40,000L (£16.75; $25). See 7.

36. Fiorentina, Via dei Fossi 12 (tel. 219530). No singles. The street runs from the far end of Piazza Santa Maria Novella.
37. Fiorita, Via Fiume 20 (tel. 283693). Cheapest singles 30,000L (£12.50; $18.75).
38. Genzianella, Via Cavour 112 (tel. 573909). See 21.
39. Giacobazzi, Piazza Santa Maria Novella 24 (tel. 294679).
40. Giappone, Via dei Banchi 1 (tel. 210090).
41. Gigliola, Via della Scala 40 (tel. 287981).
42. Giovanna, Via Faenza 69 (tel. 238 1353).
43. Graziella, Via Pier Capponi 89 (tel. 592807).
44. Guelfa, Via Guelfa 28 (tel. 215882).
45. Il Bargellino, Via Guelfa 87 (tel. 238 2658).
46. Iris, Piazza Santa Maria Novella 22 (tel. 296735).
47. Joli, Via Fiume 8 (tel. 292079). No singles. Cheapest doubles 60,000L (£25; $37.50).
48. Kursaal, Via Nazionale 24 (tel. 496324).
49. La Romagnola, Via della Scala 40 (tel. 211597).
50. La Scala, Via della Scala 21 (tel. 212629).
51. Le Vigne, Piazza Santa Maria Novella 24 (tel. 294449).
52. Orologio, Via dell Oriuolo 17 (tel. 234 0706).
53. Losanna, Via v. Alfieri 9 (tel. 245840).
54. Magliani, Via Santa Reperata 1 (tel. 287378). The street runs off Via Guelfa two blocks to the right of Via Nazionale.
55. Marcella, Via Faenza 58 (tel. 213232).
56. Margaret, Via della Scala 25 (tel. 210138). Cheapest doubles 55,000L £23; $34.50).
57. Mariella, Via Fiume 11 (tel. 212302).
58. Marini, Via Faenza 56 (tel. 284824).
59. Merlini, Via Faenza 56 (212848).
60. Mia Cara, Via Faenza 58 (tel. 216053).
61. Monica, Via Faenza 66 (tel. 283804).
62. Mirella, Via degli Alfari 36 (tel. 247 8170).
63. Nella, Via Faenza 69 (tel. 284256).
64. Palazzuolo, Via Palazzuolo 71 (tel. 214611).
65. Pina, Via Faenza 69 (tel. 212231).
66. Orchidea, Borgo degli Albizi 11 (tel. 248 0346). See 16.
67. Polo Nord, Via Panzani 7 (tel. 287952).
68. Residenza Universitaria, Viale Don Manzoni 25 (tel. 576552).
69. Rudy, Via S. Gallo 51 (tel. 475519). See 7.
70. San Giovanni, Via Cerretani 2 (tel. 213580).
71. Scoti, Via Tornabuoni 7 (tel. 292128). See 23.
72. Serena Tourist House, Via Fiume 20 (tel. 213643). No singles.
73. Sofia, Via Cavour 21 (tel. 283930).

74. Sole, Via del Sole 8 (tel. 239 6094). The street runs left from the far end of Piazza Santa Maria Novella.
75. Tamerici, Via Fiume 5 (tel. 214156).
76. Tirreno, Via Bonifacio Lupi 21 (tel. 490695).
77. Tony's Inn, Via Faenza 77 (tel. 217975).
78. Toscana, Via del Sole 8 (tel. 213156). See 74.
79. Universo, Piazza Santa Maria Novella 20 (tel. 211484).
80. Varsavia, Via Panzani 5 (tel. 215615).

HI HOSTEL
Viale Augusto Righi 2–4 (tel. 601451). Members only. Reservations by letter only. 18,000L (£7.50; $11.25) per night. About 5.5km from the town centre. Bus 17B from the station.

HOSTELS
Ostello Santa Monaca, Via Santa Monaca 6 (tel. 268338). Midnight curfew. Around 17,000L (£7; $10.50), sheets 3,000L (£1.25; $2). No reservations, so arrive anytime after 9.30 a.m. to sign the list and put some form of ID in the box. Go back to check in between 4–4.30 p.m. No toilet facilities for female guests. Bus 36 or 37 from Piazza Santa Maria Novella to the first stop over the river, or 20 minutes on foot. Via Santa Monaca is right off Via dei Serragli, opposite Via S. Agostino.

Pensionato Pio X, Via de' Serragli 106 (tel. 225044). Midnight curfew. Two-day minimum stay. No reservations accepted, so get there early. Bus 36 or 37 from Piazza Santa Maria Novella to the second stop after crossing the Arno, or just over 20 minutes' walk. See 81 for directions.

Istituto Gould, Via de' Serragli 49 (tel. 212576). No curfew. No arrivals or departures on Sundays. Bus 36 or 37 from Piazza Santa Maria Novella to the first stop after crossing the river, or a 20-minute walk.

Suore Oblate dell'Assunzione, Via Borgo Pinti 15 (tel. 248 0582). Open mid-June–July and Sept. Midnight curfew. Singles and doubles around 25,000L (£10.50; $15.75) per person. From the Duomo, follow Via dell'Oriuolo to the start of Via Borgo Pinti.

Suore Oblate dello Spirito Santo, Via Nazionale 8 (tel. 239 8202). Open mid-June–Oct. Midnight curfew. Singles, doubles and triples from around 25,000L (£10.50; $15.75) per person with breakfast.

CAMPING
Parco Communale. Viale Michelangelo 80 (tel. 681 1977). Open Apr.–Oct. 6,500L (£2.70; $4) per tent, 6,000L (£2.50; $3.75) per

person. Frequently crowded. Tend to say they are full if you phone during the peak season, but usually find space if you turn up. Bus 13 from the station.

Villa di Camerata, Viale Augusto Righi 2–4 (next to the youth hostel) (tel. 610300). Open Apr.–Oct. 6,000L (£2.50; $3.75) per tent, 5,000L (£2; $3) per person. Bus 17b from the station.

'AREA DE SOSTA'
A covered area where you can put down a mat and a sleeping bag. Run by the city authorities at Via Rocca Tedalda in Villa Favard, about 6.5km from the town centre. Washing and toilet facilities are available at the site. No charge. Maximum stay one week. Open from 7 p.m.–10 a.m. (tel. 690022). Bus 14a, 14b or 14c from the station. Leave your pack at the station.

Genoa (Genova) (tel. code 010)

TOURIST OFFICES
The head office is at Via Roma 11 (tel. 581407/541541). Open Mon.–Fri. 8 a.m.–1.30 p.m. and 2–5 p.m., Sat. 8 a.m.–1 p.m. There are branch offices at the two main train stations, both open daily 8 a.m.–8 p.m.; Porta Principe (tel. 262633) and Brignole (tel. 562056/583398). Other branch offices operate at the airport (tel. 241 5247) and at Piazza Pittaluga 4r (tel. 321504/326283) in the Nervi district.

BASIC DIRECTIONS
● **Around the Porta Principe Station**
Genova Porta Principe occupies one side of Piazza Acquaverde. At the right-hand end of the square, Via Andrea Doria runs back along the side of the train station. From the far right-hand end of Piazza Acquaverde, Salita S. Giovanni leads out of the square into Via Pre'. On the opposite side of the square from the station, past the Columbus monument, is Via Balbi. Taking this street and continuing more or less straight ahead through Piazza dell'Annunziata and along Via Bensa, Largo Zecca and Galleria G. Garibaldi you arrive at Piazza Portello, from which Galleria N. Bixio leads past Piazzale Mazzini into Piazza Corvetto. Via Roma runs from Piazza Corvetto down towards Piazza de Ferrari.
● **Around the Brignole Station**
In front of Genova Brignole is Piazza Verdi. Going right from the station exit brings you to Via de Amicis. From the end of this street,

Via Serra runs into Piazza Corvetto. Also on the right of Piazza
Verdi, Via Fiume runs away from the station to Via Cadorna, across
which is the large Piazza della Victoria. Going right at this point,
Via Cadorna leads into Via XX Settembre which ends at Piazza de
Ferrari. Via S. Vicenzo runs between Via Fiume and Via XX Settembre. Heading left from Piazza Verdi along Via Tolemaide you pass
the end of Corso Torino on the right.

TROUBLE SPOTS
Genoa's Old Town is dangerous at night (roughly the area bounded
by the waterfront, Piazza Carignano, Piazza Dante, Piazza de Ferrari
and Piazza Caricamento). For the most part, it is safe during the
day, though you may not want to venture into the labyrinthine
area between Piazza Cavour and the Porta Siberia o del Molo.

HOTELS
Cheapest doubles around 25,000L (£10; $15)

Bona, Via Assarotti 36/5 (te . 870124).
Gina, Via Goito 20 (tel. 839 1512).
Federale, Salita San Siro 2 (tel. 201729).

Cheapest doubles 35,000L (£14.50; $21.75)

Balbi, Via Balbi 21/3 (tel. 280912).
Major, Vico Spada 4 (tel. 293449).
Parigi, Via Pré 72/1 (tel. 252172).
Rinascente, Via Pré 59 (tel. 261113).
Riviera Ligure, Vico Colalanza 2 (tel. 201996).
Switzerland, Piazza Santa Brigida 16 (tel. 256776).
Valle, Via Groppalo 4/11 (tel. 882257).

Cheapest doubles around 40,000L (£16.75; $25)

Colombo, Via Porta Soprana 27 (tel. 206843).
Cristallo, Vico San Pancrazio 9 (tel. 294639).
Da Gioia, Piazza Colombo 4/11 (tel. 580145).
Diana, Salita San Siro 1 (tel. 298531).
Mini Hotel, Via Lomellini 6 (tel. 280589).
Romano, Via A. Doria 4/4 (tel. 261070).

Cheapest doubles around 45,000L (£18.75; $28)

Acquaverde, Via Balbi 29/8 (tel. 265427).
Alicia, Via Balbi 15/5 (tel. 280166).

Arcobaleno, Corso Torino 17/7 (tel. 570 5477).
Bologna, Piazza Sup. del Roso 3 (tel. 208879).
Carola, Via Gropallo 4/12 (tel. 839 1340).
Delfino, Via Pré 29 (tel. 200673).
Doria, Vico dei Garibaldi 3 (tel. 200645).
Genziana, Vico Mele 7 (tel. 398052).
La Capannina Dipendenza, Via T. Speri 5/3 (tel. 362 2692).
Nettuno Lido, Via Mercantini 16 (tel. 362 8106).
Panson, Salita Pollaiuoli 13/3 (tel. 203919).
Piemontese, Via A. Doria 6 (tel. 261812).
Ricci, Piazza Colombo 4/8 (tel. 592746).
Stella, Via Fassolo 1/1 (tel. 265991).

Cheapest doubles around 50,000L (£21; $31.50)

Bruxelles Margherita, Via XX Settembre 19/7 (tel. 589191).
Fieramare, Corso Torino 17/5 (tel. 540450).
Nuovo Nord, Via Balbi 155R (tel. 257363).
Rita, Via Gropollo 8C (tel. 870207).
Virginia, Vico Primo dello Scalo 1 (tel. 265820).

HI HOSTEL
Genova, Via Costanzi 120 (tel. 242 2457). 18,000L (£7.50; $11.25), including breakfast. Bus 40 from Stazione Brignole, 35/40 from Stazione Porta Principe. Opens for check-in at 3 p.m.

WOMEN'S HOSTEL
Casa della Giovane, Piazza Santa Sabina 4 (tel. 206632). Women only. B&B 13,000–20,000L (£5.45–8.30; $8.15–12.50).

CAMPING
Villa Doria, Via Vespucci (tel. 680613). Open year round. Far from the centre in the Genova-Pegli district. Train or bus 1, 2 or 3 to Pegli. 5,000L (£2; $3) per person, 12,000L (£5; $7.50) per tent.

Milan (Milano) (tel. code 02)

TOURIST OFFICES
Azienda di Promozione Turistica (APT), Via Marconi 1, 20123 Milano. Contact this office if you want information in advance. A

Tourist Information office operates at the same address (tel. 809662). Open Mon.–Fri. 9.45 a.m.–12.30 p.m. and 1.30–5 p.m., Sat. 9 a.m.–12.30 p.m. and 1.30–5 p.m. The office is near the cathedral (metro: Duomo). This office has a more efficient and wide-ranging room-finding service than the other office, located in Milano Centrale train station (tel. 669 0532/0432). Open 9 a.m.– 12.30 p.m. and 2.15–6 p.m. Hotel Reservation Milano is at Via Palestro 24, 20121 Milano (tel. 7600 6095).

BASIC DIRECTIONS

In front of the Milano Centrale station is Piazza Duca d'Aosta, to the right running alongside of the station is Piazza IV Novembre, to the left also running alongside the station is Piazza L. di Savoia. Along the side of the station, Via Tonale leads out off Piazza IV Novembre. Diagonally right from the main exit of Milano Centrale is the start of Via Galvani. Via Copernico runs right off Via Galvani after one block. The main road leading away from Piazza Duca d'Aosta in the direction of the city centre is Via Pisani. At the start of Via Pisani, Via Vitruvio runs left out of Piazza Duca d'Aosta to Corso Buenos Aires at Piazza Lima (metro MM1: Lima), across which is Via Plinio. Walking down Via Pisani, you pass the ends of Via S. Gregorio and then Viale Tunisia on the left-hand side. The next street on the left after Viale Tunisia leads into Via Castaldi. Continuing on to the end of Via Pisani you arrive in Piazza Repubblica. Heading left at this point brings you into Via V. Veneto, which ends at the Porta Venezia (metro MM1: Porta Venezia). Via Lazzaretto runs parallel to the left of Via Piani between Via Vitruvio and Piazza Repubblica.

HOTELS
Doubles around 30,000L (£12.50; $19)

Firenze Mare, Via Porpora 143 (tel. 284 6223).
Vitruvio, Via B. Marcello 65 (tel. 271 1807).
Ballarin, Via Soncino 3 (tel. 800822). Within easy walking distance of Piazza del Duomo (metro MM1: Duomo). Follow Via Torino into Largo Carrobbio then left).
Cecconi, Via Settembrini 54 (tel. 224514).

Doubles around 35,000L (£14.50; $22)

Comercio, Via Mercato 1 (tel. 804 8003). Price quoted is for doubles with bath/shower. Singles with bath/shower 21,000L (£9.75;

$13). Close to the city centre. Metro M2: Lanza is a few minutes' walk from the hotel.

Andrea Doria, Via Andrea Doria 16 (tel. 669 2372). Singles 17,000L (£7; $10.50).

Mongelli, Via Iulli 20 (tel. 236 1265).

Doubles around 40,000L (£16.75; $25)

Isolabella, Viale Montegrappa 6a (tel. 659 9865). From Stazione Porta Garibaldi (train station and metro M2), a short walk down Corso del Como towards the Porta Garibaldi and then left near the gate. From metro M2: Moscova walk towards the gate.

ABC, Via Molino delle Armi 12 (tel. 867501). Near the San Lorenzo Maggiore church, off Corso Italia.

Doubles around 45,000L (£19; 28.50)

Arlecchino, Via Paganini 7 (tel. 278174). Singles 26,000L (£11; $16.50).

Golden Gate, Corso di Porta Vittoria 58 (tel. 545 8096). Singles 25,000L (£10.50; $15.75). Metro M1: Palestro. From Piazza S. Babila follow Via Durini into Via Verziere, go left and cross the road into Corso di Porta Vittoria.

Helen, Via Paganini 8 (tel. 204 2001). Singles 27,000L (£11.25; $17).

Internazionale, Via Dante 15 (tel. 873697). Singles 26,000L (£11; $16.50). Excellent location, a few minutes' walk from Piazza del Duomo. Metro MM1: Cairoli. The street runs out of Piazza Cairoli.

Ischia, Via F. Lippi 43 (tel. 266 6235). Singles 22,000L (£9.50; $14).

Mercurio, Via Ascanio Sforza 73 (tel. 846 6774). Singles 24,500L (£10.25; $15.50). From Porta Genova (mainline and metro M2 station) walk to the harbour (*Darsena*), right along the waterfront into Piazza XXIV Maggio, then right down Via Ascanio Sforza.

Paganini, Via Paganini 6 (tel. 278443). No singles.

Rovello, Via Rovello 18a (tel. 873956). Singles 25,500L (£10.50; $16). Excellent location, a few minutes' walk from Piazza del Duomo. Metro M1: Cordusio. The street runs out of Piazza Cordusio.

Argentario, Corso di Porta Vittoria 58 (tel. 545 8172). Singles 27,000L (£11.25; $17). See Hotel Golden Gate for directions.

Doubles around 50,000L (£21; $31.50)

Bussentina, Via Settala 3 (tel. 288517). Singles 27,000L (£11.25; $17).

Canna, Viale Tunisia 6 (tel. 224133). Singles 26,000L (£11; $16.50).

Dante, Via Dante 14 (tel. 866471). Singles 27,000L (£11.25; $17). Well located, a short walk from Piazza del Duomo. See Hotel Internazionale for directions.

Nicosia, Corso Vercelli 1 (tel. 481 4411). Singles 27,000L (£11.25; $17).

Trentina, Via F. Lippi 50 (tel. 236 1208). No singles.

Ullrich, Corso Italia 6 (tel. 873177). About 8 minutes' walk from Piazza del Duomo.

Eva, Via Lazzaretto 17 (tel. 659 2898).

Iride, Via Porpora 170 (tel. 266 6695).

Sorriso, Corso di Porta Vittoria 51 (tel. 5519 2226). See Hotel Golden Gate for directions.

Doubles around 60,000L (£25; $37.50)

Adri, Via Iulli 18 (tel. 235692).

Arthur, Via Lazzaretto 14 (tel. 204 6294).

Brera, Via Pontaccio 9 (tel. 873509). Close to the city centre. Metro M2: Lanza is a very short walk from the hotel.

Charly, Via Settala 78 (tel. 278190).

Cremona, Via Porpora 168 (tel. 235312).

Giglio, Via P. Castaldi 26 (tel. 2940 6995).

Italia, Via Vitruvio 44 (tel. 669 3826).

Kennedy, Viale Tunisia 6 (tel. 2940 0934).

Marte, Via Ascanio Sforza 81 (tel. 843 3136). See Hotel Mercurio for directions.

Doubles around 70,000L (£29.25; $44)

Aurora, Corso Buenos Aires 18 (tel. 278960).

Ca'Grande, Via Porpora 87 (tel. 285 0295).

Casa Mia, Via Vittorio Veneto 30 (tel. 657 5249). An easy walk from Stazione Centrale. Closest metro is M1: Porta Venezia.

Eden, Via Tonale 2 (tel. 6698 0609).

Jolanda, Corso Magenta 78 (tel. 463317). From metro M1 M2: Cadorna, follow Via Carducci out of Piazza Cadorna then right at Corso Magenta.

Manzoni, Via Senato 45 (tel. 791002). Good location off Piazza Cavour, within easy walking distance of Piazza del Duomo.

HI HOSTEL
Ostello Piero Rotta, Via Martino Bassi 2/Viale Salmoiraghi 2 (tel.
3926 7095). Curfew 11.30 p.m. 20,000L (£8.50; $12.75). Members
only, but HI cards are sold at the hostel. 16,000L (£6.75; $10).
From Central Station metro line 2 to Cadorna, then line 1 heading
for S. Leonardo to QT8/San Siro. Line 1 splits, so make sure you
don't get on a train to Inganni.

WOMEN'S HOSTEL
Casa Famiglia ACISJF, Corso Garibaldi 121a–123 (tel. 659 5206).
Women under 30 only. Around 23,000L (£9.60; $14.40) per night.
Very safe, but a 10.30 p.m. curfew. A 5–10-minute walk from
Milano Porta Garibaldi train station. Take a train from Milano Cen-
trale, walk down Corso Como which leads into Corso Garibaldi.
Metro MM2: Moscova is much closer.

CAMPING
The three closest sites are all a considerable distance away:

Il Barregino, Via Corbettina, Bareggio (tel. 901 4417). Open all
year.
Autodromo, Parco di Monza, Monza (tel. 387771). Open Apr.–Sept.
Close to the famous Formula One circuit. Accessible by bus from
Milano Centrale train station.
Agip Metanopoli, Via Emilia, San Donato Milanese (tel. 527 2159).
Open all year.

Naples (Napoli) (tel. code 081)

TOURIST OFFICES
Ente Provinciale per il Turismo (EPT), Piazza dei Martiri 58 (tel.
405311). The main EPT office on the bay near Villa Communale.
Open Mon.–Fri. 8.30 a.m.–2 p.m. Free city maps and information
on accommodation possibilities.
EPT, Stazione Napoli Centrale (tel. 268779). Open Mon.–Sat.
8.30 a.m.–8 p.m., Sun. 8.30 a.m.–2 p.m. The office will phone
hotels to see if they have vacancies. Free city map.
EPT, Piazza Gesù Nuovo (tel. 552 3328). Open Mon.–Sat. 9 a.m.–
7 p.m., Sun. 9 a.m.–2 p.m. The best of the EPT offices for information on the city and surrounding area.
Azienda di Turismo, Piazza Reale (tel. 418744). Open Mon.–Sat.

8.30 a.m.–2.30 p.m. The best of all the offices for information on the city.

There are two other information offices which open on an irregular basis, one in the Napoli Mergellina train station and the other at the Capodochino Airport.

BASIC DIRECTIONS

In front of the Napoli Centrale train station is Piazza Garibaldi. Immediately to the right of the station Corso Novara runs off the square. Parallel to Corso Novara, one street back from Piazza Garibaldi, Via Aquila runs away from the side of Stazione Napoli Centrale. Continuing along the right-hand side of Piazza Garibaldi from Corso Novara, you pass the ends of Via Bologna, Via Torino and Via Milano before arriving at Corso Giuseppe Garibaldi, which runs across the far end of Piazza Garibaldi. Turning right up Corso Garibaldi, you arrive at Piazza Principe Umberto. The small Vico Ferrovia runs between Via Milano and Piazza Principe Umberto. Walking along Corso Novara from Piazza Garibaldi after one block you arrive at the junction with Via Firenze (heading left to Piazza Principe Umberto) and Corso Meridionale (going right). One block further on down Corso Novara, Via Palermo leads off to the left, ending at Via Milano, while Via Genova goes off to the right. After another block Via Venezia runs left from Corso Novara, running parallel to Via Firenze and Via Palermo, and crossing Via Bologna, Via Torino and Via Milano. Via Giuseppe Pica runs parallel to the left-hand side of Piazza Garibaldi, one block back from the square. Corso Umberto I runs from the far left-hand corner of Piazza Garibaldi as you look out from Napoli Centrale station.

FINDING ACCOMMODATION

Hotel prices in Naples are lower than in the other major cities, and you should seldom struggle to get a room in a cheap one-star hotel. Unfortunately, on the whole, the standard of accommodation in Neapolitan one-star hotels does not compare favourably with their more northern counterparts, especially as regards cleanliness and security for your belongings. You might want to leave your pack at the station. There are a few two-star hotels which are reasonably cheap, and which are safer for your belongings. Do not allow hotel owners to cheat you (reputedly, this is second nature to many of them). The price for rooms must be clearly displayed on the door of the room.

Finding a hotel with a decent location can be difficult. Many of the hotels listed below are in the area around the Napoli Centrale train station. Although this part of town is hardly choice, it is intimidating rather than dangerous (unless you are stupid enough to wander through it with your pack at night). The area around the Mergellina train and metro station is one of the best, but unfortunately hotel options here are limited. The HI hostel is in this part of town. Even those who are usually none too keen on hostels might want to consider staying here. The hostel is one of the best in Italy, and you will have no problems with personal security (although you are probably still best to leave your pack at the train station).

TROUBLE SPOTS

As is the case with many cities, Naples suffers from a reputation gained in the past. Many travellers bypass the city or visit it with trepidation, yet walk around more dangerous places with no qualms at all. That is not to say that Naples is safe to wander about in, but it has long surrendered its title as the mugging capital of Europe. Two areas which are dangerous at night are the university quarter (around Via Roma and Piazza Dante) and the Santa Lucia district (down towards the bay). Sadly some of the best hotels in the city are in those areas.

HOTELS
Cheapest doubles around 30,000L (£12.50; $19)

Tirreno, Via Giuseppe Pica 20 (tel. 281750). No singles.
Annadea, Via Milano 77 (tel. 554 3311).
Fiore, Via Milano 109 (tel. 553 8798). No singles.
Manzoni, Vico Ferrovia 6 (tel. 554 2960).
Sorrento, Via Milano 77 (tel. 282948).
Vittorio Veneto, Via Milano 96 (tel. 201539).

Cheapest doubles around 40,000L (£16.75; $25)

Bella Napoli, Via Carraciolo 10 (tel. 680234). Two-star hotel. Singles start around 14,250L (£6; $9). Via Carraciolo lines the waterfront near the Mergellina train station, so just walk down to the sea from the station. Temporarily closed during 1994; ring ahead to check that it is open for 1995.
Potenza, P. Garbaldi 120 (tel. 286330).
Teresita, Via Santa Lucia 90 (tel. 764 0105). A very safe and pleasant hotel, but in unsafe surroundings at night.
Zara, Via Firenze 81 (tel. 287125).
Aurora, Piazza Garibaldi 60 (tel. 201920).

Crispi, Via Francesco Giordani 2 (tel. 668048). From the Mergellina train station, walk away from the sea, turn right along Via A. d'Isernia, then left on to Via Giordani. From Piazza Garibaldi you can take bus 4 to Via M. Schipa which is crossed by Via Giordani.

Cheapest doubles around 45,000L (£19; $28.50)

Casanova, Via Venezia 2 (tel. 268287).
Ginevra, Via Genova 116 (tel. 283210).
Imperia, Piazza Miraglia 386 (tel. 459347). Singles around 21,000L (£9; $13.50). Another very good hotel, but the area is unsafe at night. Take bus 185, CD or CS from Piazza Garibaldi to Piazza Dante in the heart of the university quarter.
Muller, Piazza Mergellina 7 (tel. 669056). A good two-star hotel near the Mergellina train station.
Giglio, Via Firenze 16 (tel. 287500).
Sayonara, Piazza Garibaldi 59 (tel. 554 0313).

Cheapest doubles around 50,000L (£21; $31.50)

Ausonia, Via Carraciolo 11 (tel. 682278). Two-star hotel on the waterfront near the Mergellina train station. Walk down to the sea from the station.
Speranza, Via Palermo 31 (tel. 269286) Two-star hotel.
Primus, Via Torino 26 (tel. 554 7354).
Viola, Via Palermo 23 (tel. 269368).
Garden, Corso Garibaldi 92 (tel. 533 6069).

HI HOSTEL
'Mergellina', Salita della Grotta a Piedigrotta 23 (tel. 761 2346). A fine hostel in a good location. 11.30 p.m. curfew. Three-day maximum stay in July and August. 18,000L (£7.50; $11.25). Only 300m from the Mergellina train station. Turn right, then right again from the station. From Napoli Centrale take a local train or the metro to Mergellina, or bus 152 from Piazza Garibaldi.

CAMPING
Camping Vulcano Solfatara, Via Solfatara 161, Pozzuoli (tel. 526 7413). On the edge of a volcano crater. Open Apr.–Oct. Bus 152 from Piazza Garibaldi runs right to the site. Alternatively, you can take the metro or a local train (free with railpasses) to Pozzuoli. The site is an 800m walk from the station in Pozzuoli, mostly uphill. When this site is closed ask the Tourist Office for details of the sites in Pompeii or Sorrento.

Padua (Padova) (tel. code 049)

TOURIST OFFICE
Azienda di Promozione Turismo di Padova, Riviera dei Mugnai 8, I-35100 Padova. Write to this office if you want information on the city in advance. On arrival, head for one of the three APT information offices in the city:

Train station (tel. 875 2077). Open Mon.–Sat. 8 a.m.–6 p.m., Sun. 8 a.m.–12 p.m.
Museo Civico Eremitani, Piazza Eremitani (tel. 875 1153). Open daily 9 a.m.–6 p.m.
Basilica S. Antonio, Prato della Valle (tel. 875 3087). Open Mon.–Sat. 9.30 a.m.–4.30 p.m. from Mar.–Oct.

FINDING ACCOMMODATION
Except in the period June to early September, when many tourists unable to find suitable accommodation in Venice make their way to Padua (shamefully many never even bother to visit the wonderful attractions of Padua itself), you should have little trouble finding a reasonably priced bed in the city.

HOTELS
Prices for rooms without showers are more or less standard in the city's one- and two-star hotels. In one-star hotels you can expect to pay around 30,000L (£12.50; $18.75) for a single, 40,000L (£16.75; $25) for a double. Rates in a two-star hotel are around 35,000–50,000L (£14.50–21.00; $21.75–31.50) and 70,000L (£29.25; $44) respectively. At the few one-star hotels offering singles with showers, prices range from 40,000–45,000L (£16.75–19.00; $25.00–28.50). Doubles with showers are more common, and usually cost in the region of 60,000L (£25; $37.50).

One-star hotels. Normal price for doubles; singles slightly cheaper at around 23,500L (£10; $15)

Piccola Vienna, Via Beato Pellegrino 133 (tel. 871 6331/872 0020). From P. Stazione take Viale Codalunga and head straight on until you see Via Beato Pellegrino on your right.
Junior, Via L. Faggin 2 (tel. 611756). In the area between Via T. Aspetti and Via A. Da Bassano. The former runs out of P. Sta-

zione, heading into the part of town to the rear of the train station.

One-star hotels. Normal prices for singles and doubles

Al Camin, Via Felice Cavallotti 44 (tel. 687835). At the opposite end of the old town from the train station. From Prato delle Valle head down Corso Vittorio Emanuele. Go straight ahead across Piazzale S. Croce into Via Felice Cavallotti.

Al Santo, Via del Santo 147 (tel. 875 2131). Singles with showers are relatively cheap. Normal price for doubles with showers. Central location. From Piazza Eremitani follow Via degli Zabarelli into Via del Santo.

Bellevue, Via Luca Belludi (tel. 875 5547). No basic doubles. Doubles with showers at the normal price. Singles with showers are available at the top of the price range quoted above. The street runs between Prato delle Valle and Piazza del Santo.

Da Marco, Via Sorio 73 (tel. 871 7296). Doubles with showers at the usual prices. Outside the city walls on the way to the airport.

Dante, Via San Polo 5 (tel. 876 0408). From Piazza Garibaldi follow Via S. Fermo into Via S. Pietro, then turn left.

Eden, Via Cesare Battisti 255 (tel. 650484). Doubles with showers available at the usual price. From Piazza Eremitani follow Via degli Zabarella, then turn left.

Giotto, Via Catania 1 (tel. 871 1003). Outside the old town.

La Perla, Via Cesarotti 67 (tel. 875 8939). From Piazza degli Eremitani follow Via degli Zabarella and then Via del Santo into Piazza del Santo, from which Via Cesarotti runs off to the left.

Pace, Via Papafava 3 (tel. 875 1566). From Via Roma take the right turning after Solferino and look for Via Papafava running left off Via Marsala.

Pavia, Via Papafava 11 (tel. 661558). See the Pace above.

Riviera, Via Rodena 12 (tel. 665413). Doubles with showers available at the usual price. From Piazza Eremitani follow Via degli Zabarella and then Via del Santo. Via Rudena runs left off Via del Santo.

Venezia, Via Venezia 30 (tel. 807 0499). Doubles with showers at the normal price. Head left from the station exit on to Via Nicol Tommasseo, which leads into Via Venezia.

Verdi, Via Dondi dell'Orologio 7 (tel. 875 5744). Good location, close to Piazza del Signori.

Two-star hotel. Singles around 40,000L (£16.75; $25), doubles around 55,000L (£23; $34.50)

Casa del Pellegrino, Via Cesarotti 21 (tel. 875 2100). See the La Perla, above.

Two-star hotels. Singles around 36,000L (£15; $22.50), doubles around 58,000L (£24.25; $36.50)

Vienna, Via Beato Pellegrino 106 (tel. 872 0020). See the Piccola Vienna above.
Alla Fiera, Via Ugo Bassi 20 (tel. 875 5094). From the train station head left on to Via Nicoló Tommaseo. Continue straight ahead until you see Via Ugo Bassi on the right.
Buenos Aires, Via Luca Belludi 37 (tel. 651844). See the Bellevue, above.

HOSTEL
Centro Ospitalità Città di Padova, Via A. Aleardi 30 (tel. 875 2219). Curfew 11 p.m. B&B around 16,000L (£6.75; $10). Bus 3, 8 or 18 from the train station.

WOMEN'S HOSTEL
Casa della Famiglia, Via Nino Bixio 4 (tel. 875 1554). Christian hostel. Women under 29 only. Open July–Aug. Beds from around 20,000L (£8; $12).

HI HOSTEL NEARBY
'Rocca degli Alberi', Castello degli Alberi (Porta Legnago), Montagnana (tel. 429 81076/81320). Open Apr.–mid-Oct. B&B around 13,500L (£5.75; $8.50). Montagnana is about 40km from Padua, accessible by local train and bus. The hostel is 500m from the train station.

CAMPING
Strada Romana Aponense 104, Montegrotto Terme (tel. 793400). Open Mar.–Dec. The closest site to Padua. Bus M runs to Montegrotto Terme, just over 16km away.

Pisa (tel. code 050)

TOURIST OFFICES

Azienda di Promozione Turistica (APT), Lungarno Mediceo 42, I-56100 Pisa (tel. 541800/542344). The administrative office of APT in Pisa. Contact this office if you require information in advance.

APT branch office, Piazza del Duomo (tel. 560464). Open all year, Mon.–Sat. 8 a.m.–8 p.m.; at other times, 8.30 a.m.–12.30 p.m. and 2.30–6.30 p.m. The staff will help you find accommodation. Bus 1 from the station, or a 15–20-minute walk. Near the Leaning Tower.

HOTELS

In any of Pisa's one-star hotels you can expect to pay around 35,000–40,000L (£14.50–16.75; $21.75–25.00) for a single, 40,000L (£16.75; $25) for a double, though some hotels do have a limited number of rooms available at lower prices. Normal prices in two-star hotels are 34,000L (£14.20; $21.30) for singles, 45,000–50,000L (£18.75–21.00; $28.00–31.50) for singles with bath/shower, 53,000L (£22; $33) for doubles, and 65,000–70,000L (£27.00–29.25; $40.50–44.00) for doubles with bath/shower.

Clio, Via San Lorenzo 3 (tel. 28446). One-star hotel. Cheapest doubles 44,000L (£18.40; $27.55).

Di Stefano, Via Sant'Apollonia 35 (tel. 553559). One-star hotel.

Galileo, Via Santa Maria 12 (tel. 40621). A few singles slightly cheaper than the norm for one-star hotels.

Giardino, Via C. Cammeo (tel. 562101). One-star hotel. Some doubles for 40,000L (£16.75; $25). Cheapest doubles with bath/shower 50,000L (£21; $31.50).

Gronchi, Piazza Arcivescovado 1 (tel. 561823). One-star hotel with a few singles slightly cheaper than normal and some doubles around 36,000L (£15; $22.50). A short walk from Piazza del Duomo.

Helvetia, Via Don G. Boschi 31 (tel. 553084). One-star hotel with some singles available for around 20,000L (£8.30; $12.50) and some doubles at around 30,000L (£12.50; $18.75). Also has doubles with shower/bath for 40,000–55,000L (£16.75–23.00; $25.00–34.50). A short walk from Piazza del Duomo.

Milano, Via Mascagni 14 (tel. 23162). One-star hotel.

Rinascente, Via del Castelletto 28 (tel. 580460). Some doubles as cheap as 20,000L (£8.30; $12.50).

San Rocco, Via Contessa Matilde 110 (tel. 553248). One-star hotel with some singles and doubles slightly cheaper than average. Via Contessa Matilde is the street at the back of the wall behind the Cathedral and the Leaning Tower. Go through the wall near the Leaning Tower.

Serena, Via D. Cavalca 45 (tel. 580809). Singles start around 18,000L (£7.50; $11.25), doubles around 25,500L (£10.65; $16) in this one-star hotel.

Cecile, Via Roma 54 (tel. 29328). Prices in this two-star hotel start around 20,000L (£8.30; $12.50) for singles, 30,000L (£12.50; $18.75) for singles with bath/shower, 35,000L (£14.50; $21.75) for doubles and 45,000L (£18.75; $28) for doubles with bath/shower.

Roseta, Via P. Mascagni 24 (tel. 42596). Two-star hotel. Cheapest doubles 35,000L (£14.50; $21.75).

Villino Aurora, Via Pietro da Pisa 4 (tel. 25201). One-star hotel. Singles from 18,000L (£7.50; $11.25), doubles from 23,000L (£9.60; $14.40).

Moderno, Via Corridoni 103 (tel. 25021). Two-star hotel. Cheapest doubles 45,000L (£18.75; $28).

Terminus e Plaza, Via Colombo 45 (tel. 500303). Three-star hotel. Some singles from 23,000L (£9.60; $14.40), some doubles from 33,000L (£13.75; $20.50).

Royal-Victoria, Lungarno Pacinotti 12 (tel. 940111). Three-star hotel. Some singles from 28,000L (£11.70; $17.50), some doubles from 35,000L (£14.50; $21.75).

La Pace, Via Gramsci, Galleria B (tel. 48863). Three-star hotel. Some singles from 25,000L (£10.50; $15.75), some doubles from 35,000L (£14.50; $21.75).

HOSTEL

Centro Turistico Madonna dell'Acqua, Via Pietrasantina 15 (tel. 890622). Bus 3. Single rooms 15,000–20,000L (£6.25–8.30; $9.50–12.50).

WOMEN'S HOSTEL

Casa della Giovane, Via Corridoni 31 (tel. 22732). Women only. Around 18,000L (£7.50; $11.25) per night, including breakfast. Reception open until midnight. A short distance from the station. Turn right on leaving the station.

CAMPING

Torre Pendente, Viale delle Cascine 86 (tel. 560665). Open mid-Mar.–Sept. About 5 minutes' walk from the Leaning Tower, past the cathedral and baptistry, out through the old walls, turn right, then left.

Rome (Roma) (tel. code 06)

TOURIST OFFICES

Ente Provinciale per il Turismo (EPT), Via Parigi 5 (tel. 488 3748). EPT Head Office, open Mon.–Sat. 8.15 a.m.–7 p.m. Much shorter queues than at the EPT branch office in the Roma Termini train station. Only 500m from Termini. On leaving the station, head for the far left-hand corner of the square in front of you (Piazza dei Cinquecento), go up Viale L. Einaudi, around Piazza della Repubblica to the right, then along Via G. Romita to the start of Via Parigi on the right.

EPT, Stazione Termini (tel. 487 1270/482 4078). Platform 3. Open daily 9 a.m.–1 p.m. and 3–8 p.m. Very long queues are the norm in summer. The office claims to have no information on campsites.

EPT, Aeroporto Intercontinentale 'Leonardo da Vinci' (tel. 600 0255). In the arrivals hall of the airport.

EPT, Autostrada del Sole A1 (Salaria services).

EPT, Autostrada del Sole A2 (Frascati services).

Ente Nazionale per il Turismo (ENIT), Via Marghera 2/6 (tel. 497 1282). Open Mon.–Tues. and Thurs.–Fri. 9 a.m.–1 p.m., Wed. 4–5 p.m. Information on the rest of the country only.

CTS (Student Travel Centre), Via Nazionale 66 (tel. 479931). Open Mon.–Fri. 9 a.m.–1 p.m. and 4–7 p.m., Sat. 9 a.m.–1 p.m. As well as the usual travel services the office will help find you accommodation.

Enjoy Rome Information Centre, Via Varese 39 (tel. 445 1843). Open Mon.–Fri. 8.30 a.m.–1 p.m. and 3.30–6 p.m, Sat. 8.30 a.m.–1 p.m. This office books accommodation in hostels, hotels and private rooms, gives out free maps and offers free luggage storage. Near to Termini Station.

FINDING ACCOMMODATION

Rome has a vast stock of hotel rooms, so even in July and August when hordes of visitors flock into the city, there are still enough beds to go round. Nevertheless, finding one can still be frustrating. The area around the Termini station has the largest concentration of rooms and is the cheapest area of the city to stay in. Understandably, this is the area most popular with budget travellers. The sheer number of rooms in the area means you can make personal enquiries at a lot of hotels without having to walk very far, but consider leaving your pack at the station as many establishments are on the upper floors. Prices are generally higher in the city centre, and over the River Tiber around the Vatican City. Few owners will show you their cheapest rooms if they have others available. Cheaper rooms are usually only offered if you are on the point of leaving. The price set by the Tourist Authority for a room should be displayed in the room. Make sure what you are being asked to pay tallies with the price shown. It is not really wise to try and haggle an owner down from the official price in summer, as they can send you packing, safe in the knowledge that someone else will be along shortly. Although both the EPT offices in the city centre find rooms, they are not interested in finding rooms at the prices you will want to pay. Usually, however, they can be persuaded to phone any suggestions you give them, but do not expect them to consider such requests during July and August. At these times, the Student Travel Office (CTS) is likely to be more help. Railpass holders stuck for a bed should refer to the **Sleeping Rough** section below.

TROUBLE SPOTS
There is no area of the city you are likely to visit that is really violent, although the area around Termini station can get rough late at night. Unless you are stupid enough to sleep rough, there is little chance of you being robbed at knifepoint, but there is a high incidence of non-violent petty theft, particularly amongst crowds where wallets can be taken or rucksacks cut open. Obviously, the metro and buses offer a perfect setting for the sneak thief, so pay particular attention to your belongings as you travel about (keep your rucksack in front of you; hold small daysacks to your chest).

BASIC DIRECTIONS
The *Centro Storico* (historical centre) of Rome lies on the east bank of a bend of the River Tiber, which runs north to south through the city. The main railway station, Termini, is to the east of the centre, while Vatican City lies over the river to the west. The familiar landmarks of the Colosseum and the Roman Forum are located just to the south of the centre, while to the north are the plush, expensive suburbs which surround the Spanish Steps.

   Emerging from Termini Station you face Piazza dei Cinquecento. To the left Via Cavour leads off towards the Forum and Colosseum, a walk of around 12 minutes. From the top left corner of Piazza dei Cinquecento, Viale L. Einaudi leads into Piazza della Repubblica. From here, Via Nationale runs off to the left. An 8 minute walk brings you to Piazza Venezia and the Vittorio Emanuele II monument on the eastern edge of the Centro Storico. Key locations are the Piazza Navona, to the north of Corso Vittorio Emanuele II, and Campo dei Fiori to the south — both can also be reached on bus 64 (night bus 70) from Termini Station.

To the right of Piazza dei Cinquecento, Via Solferino leads into Piazza Indipendenza, from which Via San Martino della Battaglia, Via Magenta, Via dei Mille, Via Varese and Via Castelfidardo all run, scattered with some of the cheapest accommodation in Rome.

Down to the right of Termini Station runs Via Marsala, which connects with Via Marghera, Via Milazzo and Via Vicenza. In the opposite direction, up the right-hand side of Piazza dei Cinquecento, Via Marsala becomes Largo Montemartini and then Via Volturno.

HOTELS
Cheapest doubles from 20,000L (£8.30; $12.50)

Allo Statuto, Via dello Statuto 32 (tel. 487 2721).
Cambridge, Via Calabria 32 (tel. 484930).
Margherina, Via Marghera 13 (tel. 491625).
Malta, Via Rattazzi 64 (tel. 446 6395).
Moscatello, Via Principe Amedo 51 (tel. 733675).
Paolo, Via Cairoli 88 (tle. 474 5380).
Sibilla, Via Marghera 29 (tel. 495 2336).

Cheapest doubles from 30,000L (£12.50; $19)

Andreina, Via G. Amendola 77 (tel. 481 8657).
Aquila, Via Milazzo 8 (tel. 491837).
Brugnetti, Via Merulana 43 (tel. 734134).
Cressy, Via Voturno 27 (tel. 484917).
Di Rienzio, Via Principe Amedeo 79/a (tel. 446 7131).
Ghenciu, Via Collina 48 (tel. 474 3266).
Irpinia, Via Principe Amedeo 76 (tel. 481 8016).
Montestella, Via Palestro 88 (tel. 491269).
Ortensia, Via Magenta 53 (tel. 446 3206).
Pax Romana, Via Villafranca 10 (tel. 445 1365).
Rita, Via Volturno 42 (tel. 444 0639).
Sud America, Via Cavour 116 (tel. 474 5521).
Valparaiso, Viale G. Cesare 47 (tel. 321 3184). Near the Vatican

City. Metro stations Lepanto and Ottaviano are on the Viale
Giulio Cesare.

Cheapest doubles from 40,000L (£16.75; $25)

Antigua, Via Salandra 1 (tel. 486788).
Beatrice, Via dei Serpenti 137 (tel. 482 4007).
Blanda, Via Castelfidardo 31 (tel. 494 1378).
Camilla, Via Carlo Alberto 13 (tel. 730784).
Danubio, Via Palestro 34 (tel. 404 1305).
Katty, Via Palestro 35 (tel. 444 1216).
La Fontanella, Via Palestro 87 (tel. 445 5770).
Mena, Via Marsala 64 (tel. 445 0164).
Ottaviano, Via Ottaviano 6 (tel. 383956). A short walk from
   St Peter's Square. Metro: Ottaviano. 20,000L (£8.30; $12.50) per
   person in dorm bunkbeds.
Perugia, Via del Colosseo 7 (tel. 679 7200). Near the Colosseum,
   off Via Cavour. Metro: Colosseo or Cavour.
Rubino, Via Milazzo 3 (tel. 445 2323). Immaculately clean. A
   second hotel, Pensione Alvisini, is at the same address.
Sandy, Via Cavour 136 (tel. 483121). On the 4th floor next door
   to Hotel Valle. Hostel-style beds for 20,000L (£8.30; $12.50) per
   person; 15,000L (£6.25; $9.50) in winter.
Tokyo, Via Marsala 64 (tel. 445 0365).

Cheapest doubles from 50,000L (£21; $31.50)

Belfiore, Via Giovanni Giolitti 453 (tel. 7030 0032).
California, Via Principe Amadeo 47 (tel. 482 2002).
Castelfidardo, Via Castelfidardo 31 (tel. 474 2894). Recently reno-
   vated. Accepts credit cards.
Catherine, Via Volturno 27 (tel. 483634). Very close to Termini
   Station.
Cervia, Via Palestro 55 (tel. 491056). A large hostel with helpful
   management.
Delfina, Via Principe Amedeo 82 (tel. 466 5416).
Ercoli, Via Collina 48 (tel. 474 5454). Above Pensione Tizi on the
   3rd floor.
Eureka, Piazza della Repubblica 47 (tel. 482 5806). Off the far left
   corner of P. dei Cinquecento as you leave Termini Station.
Ferraro, Via Cavour 266 (tel. 474 3755). Very comfortable, a stone's
   throw from the Colosseum.
Galli, Via Milazzo 20 (tel. 445 6859). Close to Termini Station, off
   Via Marsala.

Gexim, Via Palestro 34 (tel. 444 1311).
Giulia, Via Calatafimi 19 (tel. 481 7582).
Lazzari, Via Castelfidardo 31 (tel. 494 1378).
Magic, Via Milazzo 20 (tel. 495 9880).
Oriente, Via della Statuto 56 (tel. 487 3119).
Orlanda, Via Principe Amedeo 76 (tel. 488 0637). Midnight curfew.
Resi, Via G. Amendola 77 (tel. 481 4302).
Sandra, Via Villafranca 10 (tel. 445 2612).
Selene, Via del Viminale 8 (tel. 474 4781).
Tizi, Via Collina 48 (tel. 474 3226). A 15 minute walk from Termini
  Station.

Cheapest doubles from 60,000L (£25; $37.50)

Azzurra, Via del Boccaccio 25 (tel. 474 6531).
Boccaccio, Via del Boccaccio 25 (tel. 488 5962). Off Via del Tritone.
Carmel, Via Goffredo Mameli 11 (tel. 580 9921).
Dei Mille, Via dei Mille 7/b (tel. 491313)
Esedra, Piazza della Repubblica 47 (tel. 482 5806).
La Rosa, Via Carlo Alberto (tel. 445 5770).
Liz, Via Marsala 98 (tel. 401413).
Pisa, Via Pietro Micca 10 (tel. 7045 1514).
Restivo, Via Palestro 55 (tel. 446 2172). Large clean rooms. Credit
  cards accepted.
Rossi, Via Rattazzi 65 (tel. 446 6415).
Sileo, Via Magenta 39 (tel. 445 0246).
Tony, Via Principe Amedeo 79/d (tel. 446 6887). 10% discount
  Nov.–Mar.

Cheapest doubles from 70,000L (£29.25; $44)

Amalia, Via Germanico 66 (tel. 316407). On the east side of the
  river.
Argentina, Via Cavour 47 (tel. 488 3263).
Bell Oriente, Via Domenichio 7 (tel. 487 3275).
Bianca, Via Volturno 48 (tel. 444 0680).
Everest, Via Cavour 47 (tel. 488 1629).
Fiorella, Via del Babuino 196 (tel. 361 0597). Near the Spanish
  Steps. Metro: Spagna or Flaminio. 1 a.m. curfew.
Giolitti, Via Giolitti 441 (tel. 7030 0058).
Ida, Via Germanico 198 (tel. 324 2164). First-floor hostel near the
  Vatican City. Metro: Ottaviano. Several other hostels are located
  in the same building and next door.
Il Castello, Via Vittorio Amedeo II 9 (tel. 757 7784).

Jonella, Via della Croce 41 (tel. 679 7966). Near the Spanish Steps.
Via della Croce runs off Piazza di Spagna. Metro: Spagna.
Mari, Via Palestro 55 (tel. 446 2137).
Navona, Via dei Sediari 8 (tel. 686 4203). Right in the centre of
the city. Via dei Sediari runs out of Piazza Navona.
Onella, Via Principe Amedeo 47 (tel. 488 5257).
Primavera, Piazza San Pantaleo 3 (tel. 654 3109). Piazza San Panta-
leo is on Corso Vittorio Emanuele II, near Piazza Navona in the
heart of the city.

HI HOSTELS
'Foro Italico-A.F. Pessina', Viale delle Olimpiadi 61 (tel. 396 4709).
11 p.m. curfew. About 20,000L (£8.30; $12.50) for B&B. Well
out from the centre, by the Olympic stadium. Metro A to Ottaviano, then bus 32.

The Italian YHA also let rooms in three university halls from about
20 July to 20 Sept. The price for B&B at these three residences is
similar to that of the HI hostel. Enquiries for all three residences
tel. 324 2571 or 324 2573, or ask at EPT. Advance reservation:
AIG, Via Carlo Poma 2, 00195 Roma.

Via Cesare de Lollis 20. About 1.5km from Roma Termini. Bus 492
from the station.
Viale del Ministerio degli Affari Esteri 6. Near the HI hostel. The
hostel is the check-in point for this residence.
Via Domenico de Dominicis 13. Just over 3km from Roma Termini.
Metro A to Colli Albani, then bus 409.

HOSTELS
YWCA, Via Cesare Balbo 4 (tel. 460460). Midnight curfew. Women
only. Safe, if not cheap. Singles around 40,000L (£16.75; $25),
doubles around 62,000L (£25.85; $38.80). Near Roma Termini.
Follow Via D'Azeglio from Piazza d. Cinquecento, go right at Via
Torino, then left along Via Cesare Balbo. No single men admitted.
Locando del Conservatorio, Via del Conservatorio 62 (tel. 659612).
Singles around the price you will pay for dorms at the HI hostel,
doubles slightly cheaper. Central location. Understandably popular, so write in advance.
Centro dei Giovani, Via degli Apuli 40 (tel. 495 3151). Near the
station. Fills fast.

CAMPING

No central site, but the following are within reach:

Flaminio, Via Flaminia Nuova (tel. 333 2604). Open Mar.–Oct. Quite expensive. One of the closest to the centre (8km out). Metro A to Flaminio, then bus 202, 203, 204 or 205.

Roma, Via Aurelia 831 (tel. 662 3018). Open all year. Bus 38 from Termini station to Piazza Fiume, then bus 490 to the last stop. Change to bus 246.

Nomentano, Via Nomentana (corner of Via della Cesarina) (tel. 610 0296). Open Mar.–Oct. Bus 36 from Termini to Piazza Sempione, then bus 336 to Via Nomentana.

Salaria, Via Salaria 2141 (tel. 888 7642). Open June to Oct. About 16km from the centre.

Capitol, Via Castelfusano 195, Ostia Antica (tel. 566 2720). Open all year. About 3km from the ruins. Metro to Piramide, train to Lido Centro then bus 5 to the campsite. The train from Piramide to Ostia Antica leaves you a 3km walk to the site.

SLEEPING ROUGH

Lunacy. Even putting all your valuables in the left luggage and sleeping in the station is not advisable. Far better to sleep out at one of the campsites after leaving your pack and valuables at the station (Nomentano and Flaminio are the closest). Railpass holders can check in their luggage and valuables and then take the 1.10 a.m. from Roma Termini to Ancona. The train arrives in Ancona at 4.35 a.m. Ten minutes later you can catch a train back to Rome (arrives 8.45 a.m.). If you want to be absolutely sure of catching the return train get off in Falconara, the station before Ancona (arrives 4.27 a.m., departs 4.54 a.m.).

Siena (tel. code 0577)

TOURIST OFFICE

The city Tourist Office is located on the main square at Piazza del Campo 56 (tel. 280551). Open summer Mon.–Sat. 8.30 a.m.–7.30 p.m.; winter Mon.–Fri. 9 a.m.–12.30 p.m. and 3.30–7 p.m., Sat. 9 a.m.–12.30 p.m. Hotel accommodation can be booked at the Cooperative booth near the church of San Domenico on Viale Curtatone (tel. 288084). Open summer Mon.–Sat. 9 a.m.–8 p.m.; winter Mon.–Sat. 9 a.m.–7 p.m.

FINDING ACCOMMODATION

With the exception of the days around the Palio (2 July and 16 August), finding suitable accommodation has been relatively straightforward in the past. Although the city has few one-star hotels, private rooms are available and the city has one of the best HI hostels in Italy, with a capacity of 110 beds.

BASIC DIRECTIONS

The train station is about 2.5km from the city centre. Incoming trains are met by a bus which drops passengers at Piazza Matteotti, a short walk from Piazza del Campo. From the square, head down Via dei Termini and turn left down any of the small streets on to Banchi di Sopra. Turn right and follow Banchi di Sopra to Piazza del Campo (head right from the end of the street to reach Via di Città). Intercity buses stop on Viale Curtatone, close to the church of San Domenico; again a short walk from Piazza del Campo. From the church, follow Via d. Paradiso, head right along Via della Sapienza, then right again at Costa S. Antonio. Going straight ahead, Via d. Galluzza and then Via d. Beccheria bring you on to Via di Citta, just off Piazza del Campo.

HOTELS

Doubles from 40,000L (£16.75; $25)

Bernini, Via della Sapienza 15 (tel. 289047).
Cannon d'Oro, Via Montanini 28 (tel. 443211). Two-star hotel. No basic singles. Only a few doubles at the price quoted above. Others are much more expensive.

Doubles from 50,000L (£21; $31.50)

Tre Donzelle, Via delle Donzelle 5 (tel. 280358). Just off Piazza del Campo.
Garibaldi, Via G. Duprè 18 (tel. 284204). Off Piazza del Campo to the right of the Palazzo Pubblico.
Moderno, Via Peruzzi 19 (tel. 288453). Just outside the old city walls. From Piazza del Campo, take Banchi di Sopra and head straight on, turn right along Via di Vallerozzi, then right after passing through the town gate. Three-star hotel. Only some rooms at these prices.

Doubles from 60,000L (£25; $37.50)

Lea, Viale XXIV Maggio 10 (tel. 283207). Two-star hotel. Only a few rooms at these prices.

Piccolo Hotel Etruria, Via delle Donzelle 1/3 (tel. 288088). Just off Piazza del Campo.

La Toscana, Via C. Angiolieri 12 (tel. 46097). Three-star hotel. Singles from 38,000L (£16; $24).

Santa Caterina, Via E. S. Piccolomini 7 (tel. 221105). Three-star hotel. Some doubles from 50,000L (£21; $31.50).

Piccolo Hotel Il Palio, Piazza del Sale 19 (tel. 281131). Some doubles with shower from 53,000L (£22; $33).

La Perla, Via delle Terme 25 (tel. 47144). Singles with shower from 34,000L (£14.20; $21.30), doubles with shower from 53,000L (£22; $33).

PRIVATE ROOMS

The Tourist Office has a list of rooms that is updated daily, but they do not book accommodation. Around 43,000L (£18; $27) for a double.

HI HOSTEL

'Guidoriccio', Via Fiorentina (loc. Stellino) (tel. 52212). A 20-minute walk from the city centre. Bus 10 or 15 from Piazza Gramsci. Arriving by bus from Florence you can ask the driver to let you off at Lo Stellino. 18,000L (£7.50; $11.25).

CAMPING

Campeggio Siena Colleverde, Strada di Scacciapensieri 47 (tel. 280044). Open 21 Mar.–10 Nov. About 1.5km from the city centre. Until 10 p.m. you can take either bus 8 or 10 from Piazza Gramsci to the site.

Turin (Torino) (tel. code 011)

TOURIST OFFICES

Azienda di Promozione Turistica (APT), Via Roma 226 (tel. 535181/535901). The main APT office. Open Mon.–Fri. 9 a.m.–5 p.m., Sat. 9 a.m.–12 p.m. An APT branch office (tel. 531327) operates in the main hall of the Porta Nuova train station, open Mon.–Sat. 9 a.m.–7 p.m.

BASIC DIRECTIONS

Torino Porta Nuova (the main train station) is located on the Corso Emanuele II. Just under 15 minutes' walk away is Corso Regina

Margherita. The remarkably compact historic centre of Turin is located between these two main thoroughfares. Across Corso Vittorio Emanuele II from Porta Nuova is Piazza Carlo Felice, from which Via Roma runs into the impressive Piazza San Carlo. Crossing the square, Via Roma leads into a second important square: Piazza Castello with the Palazzo Madama. Via Garibaldi leads out of the left-hand side of Piazza Castello in the direction of Piazza d. Statuto by the Porta Susa train station. From the right-hand side of the Piazza Castello, Via Giuseppe Verdi runs into Corso San Maurizio, close to the River Po, while Via Po leads into Piazza Vittorio Veneto, across which is the Ponte Vittorio Emanuele I.

TROUBLE SPOTS
To the right of the main exit of Torino Porta Nuova Via Nizza runs off Corso Vittorio Emanuele II down the side of the train station. The area bounded by Via Nizza, Corso Vittorio Emanuele II and the Parco Valentino contains many of the cheapest hotels in the city. Women travelling without a male companion, and certainly those travelling alone, would be better to look for accommodation elsewhere in the city. Although the area is not dangerous to walk about in, it is slightly run down and on the sleazy side, and unaccompanied women are likely to face harassment. The area on the opposite side of Corso Vittorio Emanuele is fine, with hotels convenient to both the train station and the city centre.

HOTELS
Cheapest doubles 30,000L (£12.50; $19)

Casa Placidia, Via Medici 54 (tel. 744949).
Nelly, Via Palmieri 23 (tel. 480279). A 15-minute walk from Porta
    Nuova. Head left until you see the street heading right off Corso
    Vittorio Emanuele II.
Nettuno, Via Po 4 (tel. 839 7291).
Pine, Via Rismondo 10 (tel. 606 8350).

Cheapest doubles from 35,000L (£14.50; $21.75)

Canelli, Via San Dalmazzo 7 (tel. 546078).
Casa Impiegate e Studentesse, Via Nizza 25 (tel. 657857).

Cheapest doubles from 40,000–45,000L (£16.75–18.75; $25–28)

Serenella, Via Tarino 4 (tel. 837031). By the River Po, well out
    from the centre.

Passatempo, Corso Francia 318 (tel. 779 3330). Out from the city centre. Corso Francia runs out of Piazza d. Statuto.

Doria, Via Accademia Albertina 42 (tel. 839 7328).

La Consolata, Via Nizza 21 (tel. 669 8979). Go right from the exit of Porta Nuova, then right down the side of the station.

Lux, Via B. Galliari 9 (tel. 657257). Head right from the exit of Porta Nuova, turn right down the side of the station along Via Nizza then left at Via B. Galliari.

Alfieri, Via G. Pomba 7 (tel. 839 5911).

Casa ex Allieri Salesiani, Via Revello 27 (tel. 447 0122).

Centrale, Via Mazzini 13 (tel. 812 4182).

Maggi, Via San Secondo 31 (tel. 502593).

Michelangelo, Via M. Buonarroti 11 (tel. 687033).

Porta Susa, Corso San Martino 4 (tel. 542375).

Cheapest doubles from 48,000–49,000L (£20.00–20.50; $30.00–30.75)

Centauro, Via Camerana 8 (tel. 534973).

Ferrucci, Via San Paolo 2 (tel. 385 9765).

Vinzaglio, Corso Vinzaglio 12 (tel. 561 3793).

Cheapest doubles 50,000–55,000L (£21–23; $31.50–34.50)

Kariba, Via San Francesco d'Assisi 4 (tel. 534856). Head left from the exit of Porta Nuova until you see the street running right off Corso Vittorio Emanuele II.

San Maurizio, Corso San Maurizio 31 (tel. 882434). The street runs between the Po and Corso Regina Margherita.

Edelweis, Via Madama Cristina 34 (tel. 650 7208). Head right from the exit of Porta Nuova until you see the street running right off Corso Vittorio Emanuele II.

Palmieri, Via Palmieri 23 (tel. 482226). See Hotel Nelly.

Domus, Via Giulia di Barolo 5 (tel. 830229). The street runs out of Piazza Vittorio Veneto.

Soggiorno Flora, Via Nizza 3 (tel. 669 8691). Right from the exit of Porta Nuova, then right again down the side of the station.

Aurora, Via Carlo Alberto 47 (tel. 839 7011). Head right from the exit of Porta Nuova until you see the street running left off Corso Vittorio Emanuele II.

Graziella, Via Mazzini 22 (tel. 877810). From Corso Vittorio Emanuele II take Via Lagrange, the street parallel to the right of Piazza Carlo Felice. Via Mazzini is on the right as you walk down Via Lagrange.

HI HOSTEL
'Torino', Via Alby 1 (tel. 660 2939). Around 17,500L (£7.30; $11). Bus 52 from Corso Vittorio Emanuele II, or a 20-minute walk from Porta Nuova. Head right from the station, cross the Po by Ponte Umberto I, and head straight on. At the fork in the road, go right on to Corso Giovanni Lanza. Cross the road and follow Viale Enrico Thovez, from which the hostel is off to the right.

CAMPING
Campeggio Villa Rey, St Sup. Val S. Martino 27 (tel. 819 0117). Buses 61 and 56 from Corso Vittorio Emanuele II. 4,000L (£1.75; $2.50) per person, 3,500L (£1.50; $2.25) per tent.

Venice (Venezia) (tel. code 041)

TOURIST OFFICES
The APT Head Office at Ascensione 71f near Piazza San Marco (tel. 522 6365) does not find rooms, which means anyone wanting information only should go to this office to avoid the queues at other APT offices. Open Mon.–Sat. 8.30 a.m.–7 p.m. The APT office in Venezia Santa Lucia train station (tel. 715016) finds rooms and gives out information. Open 8 a.m.–8 p.m. daily. Exceptionally long queues in summer. From May–Sept., the AVA Hotel Information at the bus station on Piazzale Roma offers advice on accommodation and books hotel rooms (tel. 522 7402). Open Mon.–Sat. 9.30 a.m.–7.30 p.m., Sun. 1.30–5 p.m. The Centro Turistico Studentesco (CTS) at Dorsoduro 3252 on the Fondamenta Tagliapietra will help find rooms (tel. 705660). Open Mon.–Fri. 7 a.m.–12.30 p.m. and 3.30–6.30 p.m., Sat. 9 a.m.–12.30 p.m. Queues are shorter than at the train station.

● **Addresses**
Streets and buildings in Venice are not numbered in the normal manner. Instead, districts are numbered at once, so that the number a house bears is its district number rather than a street number. There are six districts in the city: Cannaregio, San Polo, Santa Croce, Dorsoduro, San Marco and Castello.

FINDING ACCOMMODATION
If you arrive in Venice during the summer it is safe to say you will never have seen a city so packed with tourists. Ideally, you should reserve hotels in writing well in advance (Italian or English) stating

clearly the type of room you want. Inform the hotelier at what time you expect to arrive, but if you get to Venice early go to the hotel as soon as you arrive just to make sure the room has been held. You can try phoning ahead, but even if you can communicate with an owner, they are generally loath to reserve one of their cheaper rooms. If you arrive in Venice early in the morning, start queueing at one of the offices before opening time, as it could make the difference between getting one of the cheaper rooms or not. As reasonably inexpensive singles are few and far between, solo travellers might also find someone in the queue to team up with and get a double.

The Tourist Office hands out *Dormire Giovane*, a publication listing all the youth accommodations and their respective prices. If you want to stay in the HI hostel, reservations are recommended at all times. In the summer, you have to spend about three hours in a queue to have a hope of getting in without a reservation. Reservations for the city-run hostels are best made in writing one month in advance.

If you are having trouble finding suitably priced accommodation, consider staying in nearby Venezia-Mestre, where hotel prices are slightly lower, or in Padua. Both are linked to Venice by frequent trains, right up to midnight (Mestre is a 10-minute trip, Padua is only 30 minutes away).

HOTELS
Most of the city's one-star hotels charge around 60,000L (£25; $37.50) in doubles, though some do have a number of rooms which are cheaper than this.

Cheapest doubles around 40,000L (£16.75; $25)

Alle Guglie, Rio Terra San Leonardo, Cannaregio 1523 (tel. 717351). Head left from the station along Lista da Spagna, cross the Ponte d. Guglie. The hotel is not far from the bridge on Rio Terra San Leonardo.
Caneva, Ramo della Favia, Castello 5515/5518 (tel. 522 8118).
San Salvador, Calle Galiazza, San Marco 5264 (tel. 528 9147).
Alla Fava, Campo della Fava, Castello 5525 (tel. 522 9224).
Atlantico, Castello 4416 (tel. 709244).
Diana, Calle Specchieri, San Marco 449 (tel. 520 6911). A short walk from St Mark's Square. Calle Specchieri runs from S. Zulian towards San Marco.
Serenissima, Calle Goldoni, San Marco 4486 (tel. 700011).

Tivoli, Dorsoduro 3838 (tel. 523 7752). In the off-season prices are reduced by 20%.

Trovatore, Calle delle Rasse, Castello 4534 (tel. 522 4611). Excellent location, a few minutes' walk from St Mark's Square. Left from the waterfront at the second street after passing the Bridge of Sighs ('Ponte dei Sospiri').

Firenze, San Marco 1490 (tel. 522 2858).

Walter, Fondamenta Tolentini, Santa Croce 240 (tel. 528 6204).

Canal, Santa Croce 553 (tel. 523 5480).

Alla Torre, Via Calle del Sale 52/54, Mestre (tel. 984646). Doubles only.

Col di Lana, Via Fagarese 19, Mestre (tel. 926879).

Primavera, Via Orlanda 5 (tel. 531 0550).

Doubles around 45,000L (£18.75; $28)

Casa Linger, Castello 3451 (tel. 528 5920).

Cavallino, Via S. Dona 39, Mestre (tel. 611191). Doubles only.

Trento, Via Fagare 2, Mestre (tel. 926090).

Bernardi Semenzato, SS Apostoli, Cannaregio 4363/4366 (tel. 522 7257). English-speaking owner. Just off Strada Nuova, near the Church of the Holy Apostles. Walk left from the station along Lista de Spagna and keep going straight on until you reach Strada Nuova, or take a boat to the stop by the Ca d'Oro.

Da Bepi, Fondamenta Minotto, Santa Croce 160 (tel. 522 6735). Cross the bridge near the station, turn left and follow the Grand Canal to the Rio dei Tolentini. Do not cross the water, but turn left and keep going, past the S. Nicola da Tolentino church, then left onto Fondamenta Minotto.

Eden, Cannaregio 2357 (tel. 720228).

Cheapest doubles around 50,000L (£21; $31.50)

Antiche Figure, S. Simeon Piccolo, Santa Croce 686a (tel. 718290). The hotel is near S. Simeon Piccolo, the church directly across the Grand Canal from the train station.

Basilea (dipendenza), Rio Marin, Santa Croce 804 (tel. 718667). Close to the station. Cross the Grand Canal and head up Calle Lunga, left across the Rio Marin, then right along Fondamenta Rio Marin.

Da Pino, Crossera S. Pantalon, Dorsoduro 3941 (tel. 522 3646). Near the S. Pantaleone Church, a short walk from Campo S. Rocco across the Rio della Frescada.

Dalla Mora, Salizzada San Pantalon, Santa Croce 42a (tel. 523 5703). In the off-season prices are reduced by 20%.

Fiorita, Campiello Nuovo, San Marco 3457a (tel. 523 4754).

Marin, Ramo del Traghetto, Santa Croce 670b (tel. 718022).

Toscana-Tofanelli, Via Garibaldi, Castello 1650–1653 (tel. 523 5722). Near the Arsenal in Castello. From Pier 18 on the Piazzale Roma-Lido service cross the Rio di S. Giuseppe and walk down Viale Garibaldi into Via Garibaldi.

Villa Rosa, Calle della Misericordia, Cannaregio 388 (tel. 716569).

San Gallo, San Marco 1093a (tel. 522 7311). Two-star hotel.

Stella Alpina-Edelweiss, Calle Priuli, Cannaregio 99d (tel. 715179). Two-star hotel. Head left from the train station past the Church of the Barefooted and then left at Calle Priuli.

Al Veronese, Via Cappuccina 94a (tel. 926275). From Venezia-Mestre station, head right along the Via Della Giustizia, then take the left turn after Via Dante.

Montiron, Via Triestina 246, Mestre (tel. 541 5068).

Roberta, Via Sernaglia 21, Mestre (tel. 929355).

Trieste, Piazzale Stazione 2, Mestre (tel. 921244). By the station.

Vidale, Via G. Parini 2, Mestre (tel. 931968).

Cheapest doubles around 55,000L (£23; $34.50)

Adua, Lista da Spagna, Cannaregio 233a (tel. 716184). Close to the train station. Head left into Lista da Spagna.

Rossi, Calle del Procurate, Cannaregio 262 (tel. 715164).

Florida, Cannaregio 106 (tel. 715251). Two-star hotel.

Gorizia a La Valigia, Calle dei Fabbri, San Marco 4696a (tel. 522 3737). Two-star hotel. Near St Mark's Square. From the Rialto Bridge head right along the Grand Canal (past Pier 7 of the *vaporino* service) and take the first left after crossing the Rio di S. Salvador.

Da Giacomo, Via Altinia 49, Mestre (tel. 610536).

Dina, Via G. Parini 2/4, Mestre (tel. 531 4673).

Doubles around 60,000L (£25; $37.50)

Ai do Mori, Calle Larga San Marco, San Marco 658 (tel. 520 4817). Excellent location, a few minute's walk from St Mark's Square. Right off Mercerie, just behind the Clock Tower.

Casa Carrettoni, Lista da Spagna, Cannaregio 130 (tel. 716231). A short walk from the train station. Head left on to Lista da Spagna.

Corona, Calle Corona 4464 (tel. 522 9174).

Piccolo Fenice, San Marco 3614 (tel. 520 4909).

Stefania, Fondamenta Tolentino, Santa Croce 181a (tel. 520 3757). In the off-season prices are reduced by 20%. A 5-minute walk from the train station. Over the bridge, right along the Grand Canal then left before the bridge over the Rio de Tolentini. Watch out for the small lantern which marks the entry to the hotel.

Tiepolo, SS. Filippo e Giacomo, Castello 4510 (tel. 523 1315). Excellent location, a short walk from St Mark's Square. Calle d. Albanesi, just past the Bridge of Sighs, leads into Campo SS. Filippo e Giacomo.

Adria, Via Cappuccina 34, Mestre (tel. 989755). See Al Veronese for directions.

Cortina, Via Piave 153, Mestre (tel. 929206). The main road heading away from Venezia-Mestre station off Via della Giustizia.

Giovanni, Via Dante 113, Mestre (tel. 926396). See Al Veronese for directions.

Johnny, Via Orlanda 223, Mestre (tel. 541 5093).

La Triestina, Via Orlanda 62, Mestre (tel. 900168).

Le Perroquet, Via Orlanda 256a, Mestre (tel. 541 5170).

Montepiana, Via Monte S. Michele, Mestre (tel. 926242).

Riva, Via Pescheria Vecchia 24b, Mestre (tel. 972566).

Doubles around 65,000L (£27; $40.50)

Al Gazzetino, Calle delle Acque, San Marco 4971 (tel. 528 6523).

Al Piave-Da Mario, Ruga Giuffa, Castello 4840 (tel. 528 5174). Good location. A 5-minute walk from St Mark's Square and the Rialto Bridge. From Piazza San Marco follow Mercerie to S. Zulian. From the church, head right along Calle d. Guerra and go on down Calle d. Bande to the S. Maria Formosa church. Go round the right-hand side of the church to the start of Ruga Giuffa. From the Rialto Bridge take Salizzada S. Lio to Calle d. Bande, then turn left.

Canal, Fondamenta Remedio, Castello 4422c (tel. 522 8118).

Minerva e Nettuno, Lista da Spagna, Cannaregio 230 (tel. 715968). A short walk from the train station. Head left into Lista da Spagna.

Montin, Fondamenta di Borgo, Dorsoduro 1147 (tel. 522 7151). From Pier 11 of the Piazzale Roma-Lido *vaporino* service, walk down past the S. Barnaba Church, then go left over Rio Malpaga after passing through the square.

Tintoretto, San Fosca, Cannaregio 2316–2317 (tel. 721522). Head left from the station on to Lista da Spagna and continue straight on until you reach S. Fosca church on Rio Terra d. Maddalena. The hotel is nearby.

Doubles 70,000L (£29.25; $44)

Atlantide, Cannaregio 375a (tel. 716901).

Bartolomeo, Calle dell'Orso, San Marco 5494 (tel. 523 5387).

Canada, San Lio, Castello 5659 (tel. 523 5852). Near Campo S. Bartolomeo at the foot of the Rialto Bridge.

Caprera, Lista da Spagna, Cannaregio 219 (tel. 715271). Head left from the train station on to Lista da Spagna.

Centauro, Campo Manin, San Marco 4297a (tel. 522 5832). From the Rialto Bridge, head left along the Grand Canal (past Pier 7 of the *vaporino* service) then turn left near the end of Riva d. Carbon down Calle Cavalli into Campo Manin.

Città di Milano, San Marco (tel. 522 7002).

Da Bruno, San Lio, Castello 5726a (tel. 523 0452). Near Campo S. Bartolomeo at the foot of the Rialto Bridge.

Hesperia, Cannaregio 459 (tel. 715251).

Lux, Castello 4541−4542 (tel. 523 5767).

Madonna dell'Orto, Cannaregio 3499 (tel. 719955).

Al Gambero, Calle del Fabbri, San Marco 4687−4689 (tel. 522 4384). See Hotel Gorizia a La Valigia for directions.

Al Gobbo, Campo S. Geremia, Cannaregio 312 (tel. 715001). In the off season prices fall by 20%. A short walk from the train station at the end of Lista da Spagna. Head left from the exit.

Alex, Rio Terrà Frari, San Polo 2606 (tel. 523 1341). Pleasant location near St Roch's (Chiesa di S Rocco). Prices are reduced by 20% in the off season.

Antico Capon, Campo S. Margherita, Dorsoduro 3004/3008 (tel. 528 5292). Just off the Rio di Ca' Foscari. Vaporino service to Pier 11 by the Ca' Foscari. Walk down to the S. Barnaba Church, diagonally across the square then left, right over the Rio S. Barnaba and straight on to the end of R.T. Canal then left.

Belvedere, Via Garibaldi, Castello 1636 (tel. 528 5148). For directions, see Hotel Toscana-Tofanelli.

Bridge, SS Filippo e Giacomo, Castello 4498 (tel. 520 5287). Excellent location, close to St Mark's Square. See Hotel Tiepolo for directions.

Budapest, Corte Barozzi, San Marco 2143 (tel. 522 0514).

Ca'Foscari, Calle della Frescada, Dorsuduro 3888 (tel. 522 5817).

Casa Boccassini, Calle del Fumo, Cannaregio 5295 (tel. 522 9892).

Casa de Stefani, Calle Traghetto S. Barnaba, Dorsuduro 2786 (tel. 522 3337). Near the S. Barnaba church and the Ca' Foscari. The street running from Pier 11 of the *vaporino* service.

Casa Petrarca, Calle delle Colonne, San Marco 4386 (tel. 520 0430). English speaking owner. From Riva d. Carbon, turn left up Calle

d. Carbon into Campo S. Luca. Take Calle dei Fuseri on the other side of the square, second left, then first right.

Doni, S. Zaccaria, Castello 4656 (tel. 522 4267). Not far from St Mark's Square. From the square go past the Bridge of Sighs (Ponte dei Sospiri) and Pier 16 of the *vaporino* service, over the Rio del Vin, then first left to S. Zaccaria.

Galleria, Accademia, Dorsoduro 878a (tel. 520 4172). Near the Accademia. Pier 12 of the *vaporino* service.

Guerrato, Calle Dietro la Scimmia, San Polo 240a (tel. 522 7131).

Marte, Ponte della Guglie, Cannaregio 338 (tel. 716351). A short walk from the train station. Head left along Lista da Spagna to the Guglie bridge.

Messner, Salute, Dorsoduro 236 (tel. 522743). Near the Basilica della Salute. Pier 14 of the *vaporino* service.

Moderno, Lista da Spagna, Cannaregio 154b (tel. 716679).

Raspo de Ua, Piazza Galuppi 560 (tel. 730095).

Rio, SS Filippo e Giacomo, Castello 4356 (tel. 523 4810). Good location, close to St Mark's Square. See Hotel Tiepolo for directions.

Riva, Ponte dell'Anzolo, Castello 5310 (tel. 522 7034).

San Geremia, Campo San Geremia, Cannaregio 290a (tel. 716245). Near the train station. See Hotel Al Gobbo for directions.

San Samuele, Piscina S. Samuele, San Marco 3358 (tel. 522 8045).

Sant'Anna, Sant'Anna, Castello 269 (tel. 528 6466). Near the Arsenal. See Hotel Marin above for directions. Turn right on Via Garibaldi and follow the street into Sant'Anna.

Santa Lucia, Calle Misericordia, Cannaregio 358 (tel. 715180). Head left from the train station into Lista da Spagna, then go left.

Silva, Fondamenta Remedio, Castello 4423 (tel. 522 7643).

HI HOSTEL
'Venezia', Fondamenta di Zitelle 86, Isola della Giudecca (tel. 523 8211 Fax 041 523 5689). On Giudecca island. 11 p.m. curfew. 20,000L (£8.30; $12.50). Members only, but membership cards are sold at the hostel: 15,000L (£6.25; $9.50). Waterbus 5 from the train station, or 8 from S. Zaccaria (left along the canal as you leave St Mark's Square) to Zitelle, then walk right. Hostel opens 6 p.m. Queue from 3 p.m. if you have not reserved in advance.

CITY HOSTELS
In the past, the city authorities have operated hostels during the summer (mid-July to mid-Sept.). Prices and curfews similar to those of the HI hostel, but the city hostels are more conveniently located. Reservations for the city hostels are handled by the HI

hostel (address above). It is always advisable to write at least one month before your date of arrival.

S. Caboto, Cannaregio 1105f (tel. 716629). By the Canale di Cannaregio, 10 minutes from the station. Head left along Lista da Spagna to the Guglie Bridge and the Canale di Cannaregio. The hostel is signposted from the bridge. Various accommodation options. Cheapest of all is throwing down a mat and a sleeping bag in the grounds; then camping in your tent in the grounds; followed by a night in the tents they hire out; and, lastly, dorm beds.

R. Michiel, Dorsoduro 1184 (tel. 522 7227). Close to the Accademia (waterbus 1, 2 or 34).

S. Fosca, Cannaregio 2372 (tel. 715775). A short walk from Campo S. Fosca. Dorm beds 18,000L (£7.50; $11).

HOSTELS/DORMITORIES

Istituto Canossiane, Fondamento del Ponte Piccolo 428, Isola della Giudecca (tel. 522 2157). Curfew 10.30 p.m. Dorms. Women only. Run by nuns. 14,500L (£6; $9). Same waterbuses as the HI hostel above, but get off at the Sant'Eufemia stop. Short walk to your left.

Foresteria Valdese, Castello 5170 (tel. 528 6897). No curfew. B&B from 21,000L (£9; $13.50). *Vaporetto* stop: S. Zaccaria. Walk away from the water to the S. Zaccaria church then head left. Go right along S. Provolo, then left over the Rio dell'Osmarin and down Ruga Giuffa into Campo S. Maria Formosa. From the right-hand side of the square follow Calle Lunga to its end. The hostel is by the bridge.

Domus Civica, Calle Chiovere & Calle Campazzo, San Polo 3082. Near the Frari church (tel. 522 7139). Open June–July and Sept–mid-Oct. Curfew 11.30 p.m. Singles around 27,000L (£11.25; $16.85); doubles around 50,000L (£21; $31.50) per person.

Domus Covanis, Rio Terra Foscarini, Dorsoduro 912 (tel. 528 7374). Open June–Sept. 11.30 p.m. curfew. Doubles 49,000L (£20.45; $30.65). Separate rooms for men and women in this church-run hostel.

Archie's House, Rio Terra San Leonardo, Cannaregio 1814b (tel. 720884). Open to those aged 21 and over only. 14,500–18,500L (£6.00–7.70; $9.00–11.60). Head left from the train station along Lista da Spagna, over the Guglie Bridge and into Rio Terra San Leonardo.

CAMPING

Waterbus 15 will take you to the Littorale del Cavallino, a peninsula with a string of campsites along its beach. Some charge ridiculously high prices.

Marina da Venezia, Via Hermada (tel. 966146). Open all year. 10,000–20,000L (£4.00–8.30; $6.00–12.50) per tent; 3,500–7,000L (£1.50–3.00; $2.25–4.50) p.p. depending on the time of year.

Ca' Pasqualli, Via Fausta (tel. 966110). Only slightly cheaper than the site above.

Camping Fusina, Via Moranzani, Fusina (tel. 547 0055). 25,000L (£10.50; $15.75) per tent, 5,000L (£2; $3) per person. From Mestre, bus 13 from opposite the Pam supermarket to the last stop. Last bus at 10 p.m., a one-hour trip. In summer, *vaporetto* 5 to Zattere, then 16 to Fusina takes about 30 minutes. Mosquito repellent is essential.

San Nicolo, on the island of Lido (tel. 767415). Ferry to Lido, then bus A.

See also the **City Hostels** section above.

SLEEPING ROUGH

Thieves patrol the beaches of the Lido island looking for easy targets. If you choose to sleep here, bed down beside other travellers. Even then ants and mosquitoes can make for an unpleasant night. Sleeping on the train station forecourt is illegal, and the police occasionally use water hoses to clear people away.

Verona (tel. code 045)

TOURIST OFFICES

Azienda di Promozione Turistica (APT), Piazza delle Erbe 42 (tel. 803 0086). Contact this office if you want information before setting off on holiday. On arrival, head for the office at Via Leoncino 61, lato Palazzo Barbieri, behind the Roman Arena (tel. 592828). Open Mon.–Sat. 8 a.m.–8 p.m., Sun. (July and August only) 9 a.m.–1.30 p.m. If you are arriving by car or motorbike from Milan or Venice, there is a city information office at the turn-off from the motorway (Viale del Lavoro 7).

BASIC DIRECTIONS

The Verona Porta Nuova train station is about 20 minutes' walk from the Piazza delle Erbe in the centre of the Old Town. Going right from the station, you arrive at the Porta Nuova, the old city gate from which the station takes its name. Turning right at this point, you can follow the road under the railway lines and down Viale Piave and Viale delle Lavoro to the Milan—Venice highway. Turning left at the Porta Nuova, you can follow Corso Porta Nuova towards the town centre. Passing through the old city walls, you arrive at Piazza Bra' with the famous Roman Arena. To the left as you enter the square, Via Roma leads off in the direction of the Castelvecchio by the River Adige. Going around the Arena, you can take Via Giuseppe Mazzini from the opposite side of Piazza Bra' into the Piazza delle Erbe. Buses 1, 2 and 8 run from Verona Porta Nuova to the Piazza Bra', if you want to save yourself about two thirds of the walk.

HOTELS
Doubles from 30,000L (£12.50; $18.75)

Alla Cancellata, Via Col. Fincato 4/6 (tel. 532820). Normal rate for singles.
Ciopeta, Vic. Teatro Filarmonico 2 (tel. 800 6843).

Doubles around 40,000L (£16.75; $25)

Catullo, Via V. Catullo 1 (tel. 800 2786). Singles 24,000—32,000L (£10.00—13.35; $15—20). Left off Via Mazzini between the Piazza Bra' and the Piazza Erbe.
Volto Cittadella, Via Volto Citadella 8 (tel. 800 0077).

Doubles around 50,000L (£21; 31.50)

Da Romano, Via Tombetta 39 (tel. 505228). In the area behind Porta Nuova station, left off Viale Piave. A 5—10-minute walk from the station.
Alla Grotta, Via Bresciana 16 (tel. 890 3865).
Selene, Via Bresciana 81 (tel. 851 0318). Other rooms of these types in this two-star hotel are 50% dearer. No rooms without bath/shower.

Two-star hotels with some doubles available from around 60,000L (£25; $37.50)

Scalzi, Via Scalzi 5 (tel. 590422). Singles from 30,000L (£12.50; $18.75), doubles from 40,000L (£16.75; $25).
Trento, Corso Porto Nuova 36 (tel. 596037).
Valverde, Via Valverde 91 (tel. 803 3611). A 10-minute walk from Porta Nuova. Straight on from the station, across the gardens to the canal. Over the canal and then virtually straight on down Via Città di Nimes into Piazza Simone, then take Via Giberti on the right hand side of the square into Via Valverde.
Garda, Via Gardesane 35 (tel. 890 3877).
Sanmicheli, Via Valverde 2 (tel. 800 3749).
Elena, Via Mastino della Scala 9 (tel. 500911).

HI HOSTEL
Salita Fontana del Ferro 15 (tel. 590360). Curfew 11 p.m., extended for opera goers. 14,000L (£6; $9). Camping permitted 8,000L (£3.35; $5). Behind the Teatro Romano, 3km from the station, but only 10 minutes' walk from the town centre. Bus 2 or minibus 32 from Verona Porta Nuova.

WOMEN'S HOSTELS
Normal curfews are extended if you are going to the opera.

Casa della Giovane, Via Pigna 7 (tel. 596880). Curfew 10.30 p.m. Beds from 15,000L (£6.25; $9.50).
Casa della Studentessa, Via G. Trezza 16 (tel. 800 5278).
Pensionato Ns. Sig. di Lourdes, Via Nicola Mazza 49 (tel. 594068).

CAMPING
Giulietta e Romeo, Via Bresciana 54 (tel. 851 0243). Open all year. About 3km from the centre on the road to Brescia.
Castel San Pietro, Via Castel San Pietro (tel. 592037). Near the HI hostel, a 10-minute walk from the centre.
Salita Fontana del Ferro 15 (tel. 590360). In the grounds of the HI hostel. 8,000L (£3.35; $5) for a solo traveller.

LUXEMBOURG (Lëtzebuerg)

If you arrive in Luxembourg having previously visited Belgium, you will notice a similarity both in the types of accommodation on offer, and in the prices of different accommodation options. On the whole, with the exception of HI hostels, standards in the various types of accommodation are also on a par with those in Belgium. Prices in **hotels** and **pensions** start around 800LF (£14.50; $21.50) in singles, 1,300LF (£23.50; $35.25) in doubles. A less expensive option in the more popular tourist towns such as Echternach, Vianden, Clervaux and Wiltz is the availability of rooms in private homes. Prices for **private rooms** range from 500–1000LF (£9–18; $13.50–24.00). These tend to fill quickly, so it is best to make enquiries as early in the day as possible. You can either ask about their availability at the local Tourist Office (i.e. not the National Tourist Office in the city), or approach the owner of any house advertising rooms to let (signs are usually printed in French, German, Dutch and English).

Considering their price, the facilities on offer, and the high standards of comfort and cleanliness, the Grand-Duchy's small network of **HI hostels** must rank among the best in Europe. All the hostels are open from mid-April to September but, at other times, different hostels are closed for anything between two days to six weeks. Curfews are normally 11 p.m. (midnight in Luxembourg). To stay at one of the hostels, a valid membership card is essential. The cost of B&B varies between 300–350LF (£5.50–6.50; $8.00–9.75), except in Luxembourg where prices range from 350–420LF (£6.50–7.50; $9.75–11.25). Duvets (rather than the usual blanket) are supplied, but you must have a linen sheet sleeping bag – either your own, or one hired from the hostel at a cost of 100LF (£2; $3). The maximum stay at any hostel is limited to three days, and only one day at peak periods (July and August). These rules are only enforced when the hostel is full, but it is as well to be aware of them.

Most of the main places of interest have a hostel. One notable exception is Clervaux, but here there is the choice of two of the small network of **gîtes d'étapes**. Most are open all year and prices range from 80–120LF (£1.50–2.25; $2.25–3.50).

Of the 120 or so **campsites**, only around 30 are open for the whole year. However, the vast majority are open March/April to September. The pamphlet 'Camping Grand-Duché de Luxembourg' clearly lists both opening periods and amenities. Two people can expect to pay roughly 325LF (£6; $9) per night. The 'Camping Guidage' service of the National Tourist Office will give advice on sites with vacancies (tel. 481199 from 11 a.m.–7.30 p.m.).

ADDRESSES

Luxembourg National Tourist Office	36/37 Piccadilly, London W1V 9PA (tel. 0171 434 2800).
Luxembourgeois YHA	Centrale des Auberges de Jeunesse Luxembourgeoises, 18 Place d'Armes, BP 374, L-2013 Luxembourg (tel. 22 55 88).
Camping	List available from the Luxembourg National Tourist Office in London or your capital city.
Gîtes d'Étapes	Gîtes d'Étapes de Grand-Duché de Luxembourg, blvd Prince Henri 23, L-1724 Luxembourg (tel. 23698/ 472172).

Luxembourg (Lëtzebuerg)

TOURIST OFFICES

Office National du Tourisme, Place de la Gare, Luxembourg (tel. 48 11 99). Open daily, from July–mid-Sept., 9 a.m.–7.30 p.m.; at other times, daily from 9 a.m.–12 p.m. and 2–6.30 p.m. except mid-Nov.–mid-March when the office is closed Sundays. By the Luxair terminal to the right of the train station. There is another branch at Luxembourg-Findel airport. Both offices provide information and services covering the whole country.

Syndicat d'Initiative et de Tourisme de la Ville de Luxembourg, Place d'Armes, B.P. 181, Luxembourg (tel. 22 28 09). Open July–mid-Sept., Mon.–Fri. 9 a.m.–1 p.m. and 2–8 p.m., Sat. closes at 7 p.m., Sun. 10 a.m.–12 p.m. and 2–6 p.m.; at other times, open Mon.–Sat. 9 a.m.–1 p.m. and 2–6 p.m. Information and services for the city only. Place d'Armes is right in the heart of the city.

HOTELS

All the hotels listed are about a 5–10-minute walk from Place de la Gare in front of the train station, unless otherwise stated.

Cheapest doubles around 1250LF (£22.50; $33.75). Singles as shown

Carlton, 9 rue de Strasbourg (tel. 48 48 02/48 17 45). Singles from 600LF (£11; $16.50). Head right past the Luxair terminal. Rue de Strasbourg is across the road on the left.

Bristol, 11 rue de Strasbourg (tel. 48 58 29/48 58 30). Singles from 800LF (£14.50; $21.75). Directions Hotel Carlton above.

Cheapest doubles around 1400LF (£25.25; $38). Singles as shown

Axe, 33–34 rue Joseph Junck (tel. 49 09 53). Singles from 900LF (£16.25; $24.50). The street is at the right end of Place de la Gare.

Family, 38 av. du X Septembre (tel. 45 26 69). Singles start around 1000LF (£18; $24). Not central.

Cheapest doubles around 1500LF (£27; $40.50). Singles as shown

Le Parisien, 46 rue Ste-Zithe (tel. 49 23 97). Singles start around 950LF (£17; $25.50). Right from pl. de la Gare. At the fork left down Av. de la Liberté. Rue Ste-Zithe is left off pl. de Paris.

Papillon, 9 rue Origer (tel. 49 44 90). Singles from 1000LF (£18; $24). Right from pl. de la Gare. At the fork right down Av. de la Gare, then left.

Paradiso, 23 rue de Strasbourg (tel. 48 48 01/40 36 91). Singles start around 950LF (£17; $25.50). Directions see Hotel Carlton, above.

Cheapest doubles around 1700LF (£30.50; $45.75). All rooms have baths/ showers. Similar rooms are available for about the same amount at all the hotels above with the exception of Hotels Axe and Bristol

Mertens, 16 rue de Hollerich (tel. 48 26 38). Off to the right at the left-hand end of Place de la Gare.

New Chemin de Fer, 4 rue Joseph Junck (tel. 49 35 28). Directions Hotel Axe above.

HI HOSTEL
2 rue de Fort Olisy (tel. 22 68 89). 1 a.m. curfew, reasonably flexible. About 2.5km from the station. Bus 9 from the station (or the airport) to the Vallée d'Alzette.

CAMPING
Luxembourg-Kockelscheur (tel. 47 18 15). Open Easter/mid-Apr. to Oct. About 4km from the train station. Bus 2 from the station. 90LF (£1.60; $2.40) per person.

MOROCCO (Maroc)

The price of accommodation in Morocco is so low that a decent hotel room should be well within your budget. **Hotels** are divided into two main categories, classé and non-classé. The former are regulated by the National Tourist Authority, which both grades them on a scale rising from one star to five-star luxury, and fixes their prices. The one- to four-star grades are further subdivided A and B. The classé hotels are listed in a free hotel guide which you can get from any tourist office. At the lower end of the scale there is only a small variation in prices, and in the facilities offered. Even the one-star establishments offer a level of comfort and cleanliness you are unlikely to find in a non-classé hotel. As a rule, classé hotels are situated in the ville nouvelle – the new town or administrative quarters built during the French colonial period. All classé hotels are listed in the publication *Royaume de Maroc Guide des Hôtels*.

Non-classé hotels enjoy two advantages over classé hotels: location, and, outside peak periods, price. In peak season (August, Christmas and Easter) it is not uncommon for non-classé hotels to raise their prices sharply, so that they actually exceed the price of one-star B and one-star A establishments. Non-classé hotels, which are neither listed nor regulated by the National Tourist Authority, are generally located in the medina, the old, Arab-built part of the town. Staying here, you will be close to the markets, historic buildings and the bewildering array of street performers. However, the medina, with its twisting, narrow streets, can be an intimidating place. The quality of hotels varies greatly: while some offer spotless, whitewashed rooms looking out on to a central patio, there are also a considerable number that are filthy and flea ridden. You are also far more likely to encounter problems with a poor water supply and primitive toilet facilities in the medina.

A room in the medina should cost in the region of 30–40dh (£2–3; $3.00–4.50). A spacious, more comfortable room in a classé hotel in the ville nouvelle might cost about 60–80dh (£4–6; $6–9), possibly with a small extra charge for showers. At this lower end of the price scale, hot water may only be available at certain times of the day. Only during the peak season are you likely to have any problem finding a room, although any difficulties will probably be restricted to Tangier, Fez, Agadir, Rabat (in July) and, occasionally, Tetouan.

For those reaching the end of their funds, even cheaper possibilities exist. Prices at Morocco's 46 **campsites** are extremely cheap, at around 7dh (£0.50; $0.75) per tent, and 10dh (£0.70; $1) per person. On no account should you leave any valuables unattended. All the major towns have a campsite, and most also have an **HI hostel**. The 11 hostels differ tremendously in quality. Prices range from 10–30dh (£0.70–2.00; $1–3). Anyone without a membership card is usually permitted to stay on the payment of a small supplement, and some hostels sell cards on the spot for 75dh (£5.50; $8.25). All but one of the hostels are situated in the larger towns. The other, at Asni, is well worth considering as a base by those interested in hiking in the Atlas Mountains. The French Alpine Club (CAF) have a network of **refuge huts** for the use of those hiking in the Atlas.

ADDRESSES

Moroccan National Tourist Office	205 Regent Street, London W1R 7DE (tel. 0171 437 0073).
Moroccan YHA	Fédération Royale Marocaine des Auberges de Jeunes, blvd Okba Ben Nafii, Meknès (tel. 05 52 46 98).
Refuge huts	Club Alpin Français, rue de la Boëtie, F-75008 Paris (tel. 01 47 42 38 46).

Fez (Fès) (tel. code 05)

TOURIST OFFICES

Office National Marocaine du Tourisme (ONMT), pl. de la Résistance (tel. 62 34 60/62 62 97). Open Mon.–Fri. 8 a.m.–12 p.m. and 2–6 p.m., Sat. 8 a.m.–12 p.m. At the end of av. Hassan II, in the Immeuble Bennani. From the train, follow rue Chenguit, go left at pl. Kennedy, then turn left on to av. Hassan II. From the CTM bus station, follow blvd Mohammed V, then go right at av. Hassan II. There are Syndicats d'Initiative on pl. Mohammed V (tel. 62 47 64) by Bab Boujeloud, the main entrance to the medina, and outside the more expensive hotels (generally open Mon.–Sat. 8 a.m.–7 p.m.).

FINDING ACCOMMODATION

Fez lacks sufficient hotel accommodation of all types, which means that prices are higher than elsewhere in the country. It is best to phone ahead and try to get a reservation. The best of the cheap rooms in the new town are located just to the west of blvd Mohammed V, between av. Hassan II (near the Post Office) and av. Mohammed es Slaoui (near the CTM bus terminal). Rooms in the medina are concentrated around Bab Boujeloud.

UNCLASSIFIED HOTELS
Du Commerce, pl. des Alouites, Fes el-Jdid. Across from the royal palace. The cleanest and best hotel in the medina. Singles 35dh (£2.50; $3.75), doubles 70dh (£5; $7.50).
Renaissance, rue Abdekrim el-Khattabi (tel. 62 21 93). Singles 40dh (£3; $4.50); doubles 70dh (£5; $7.50). Near pl. Mohammed V.
Du Jardin Public, Kasbah Boujeloud 153 (tel. 63 30 86). Singles 40dh (£3; $4.50); doubles 66dh (£4.75; $7). Considerably cleaner than other hotels in the area. Close to Bab Boujeloud down an alleyway by the Boujeloud mosque.
Regina, av. Mailay Slimone 25. Fine rooms. Prices are raised considerably during the summer.
Maghrib, av. Mohammed es Slaoui 25. Another hotel offering good rooms, again at considerably inflated prices during the summer months.
Rex, pl. de l'Atlas. No frills, but cheap and very clean.
Du Parc, Grand rue de Fés el-Jdid.

CLASSIFIED HOTELS
Two-star A:

Olympic, blvd Mohammed V (tel. 62 45 29/62 24 03). Singles with shower 116dh (£8.25; $12.50), doubles 135dh (£9.50; $14.25).

Two-star B:

Amor, rue du Pakistan 31 (tel. 62 33 04/62 27 24).
Royal, rue d'Espagne 36 (tel. 62 46 56).
Lamdaghri, Kabbour El Mangad 10 (tel. 62 03 10). Doubles from 84dh (£6; $9).

One-star A:

Kairouan, rue du Soudan 84 (tel. 62 35 90). Singles from 60dh (£4; $6), doubles from 75dh (£5.50; $8.25).

One-star B:

Central, rue du Nador 50 (tel. 62 23 33). Singles 55dh (£4; $6), singles with showers 76dh (£5.50; $8), singles with baths 100dh (£7; $10.50); doubles with showers 84dh (£6; $9), doubles with baths 100dh (£7; $10.50). Very popular, so get there early. Off blvd Mohammed V.

CTM, blvd Mohammed V (tel. 62 28 11). Singles from 50dh (£3.50; $5.50), doubles from 70dh (£5; $7.50). Near the bus station.

Excelsior, rue Larbi el-Kaghat (tel. 62 56 02). Singles with shower 72dh (£5; $7.50), doubles with shower 84dh (£6; $9), double with bath 100dh (£7; $10). Right off blvd Mohammed V, three blocks up from the main Post Office.

HI HOSTEL
Rue Abdesslam Serghini 18 (tel. 62 40 85). 10 p.m. curfew. 15dh (£1; $1.50) for HI members, 17,50dh (£1.25; $2) for non-members. Roof space available when the dormitories are filled. A clean hostel with friendly staff.

CAMPING
Camping Moulay Slimane, rue Moulay Slimane (tel. 62 24 38). Camping Diament Vert, off the Ilfrane road, 6km away. 25dh (£1.75; $2.50) per person. Bus 218.

Marrakech (tel. code 04)

TOURIST OFFICES
Office National Marocaine du Tourisme (ONMT), av Mohammed V (tel. 43 02 58/43 10 88/43 88 89). At pl. Abd el Moumen Benall. Open Mon.–Fri. 8.30 a.m.–12 p.m. and 2.30–6.30 p.m., Sat. 8.30 a.m.–12.30 p.m.; during Ramadan, 9 a.m.–3 p.m. only. Further down the street in the direction of the medina is the Syndicat d'Initiative at av. Mohammed V 170 (tel. 43 30 97). Open July–mid-Sept., Mon.–Fri. 9 a.m.–1.30 p.m. and 4–7 p.m., Sat. 9 a.m.–1.30 p.m.; at other times, Mon.–Fri. 8 a.m.–12 p.m. and 3–6 p.m., Sat. 8 a.m.–12 p.m. Bus 1 runs along av. Mohammed V from the Koutoubia Minaret near the Djemaâ El Fna.

UNCLASSIFIED HOTELS
Café de France, Djemaâ El Fna (tel. 43901). The centre of the medina. Relatively expensive, but the best of the unclassified hotels around the square. Double room for 90dh (£6.50; $9.75).

De la Jeunesse, Derb Sidi Bouloukate 56 (rue de la Recette) (tel. 44 36 31). Singles 40dh (£3; $4.50), doubles 50dh (£3.50; $5.50), triples 62dh (£4.50; $6.75). Facing Hotel CTM on the Djemaâ El

Fna go through the first arch to your right, then down the little street.

Hotels Afriquia, Nouzah and Eddakia are in the same street as the Hôtel de la Jeunesse above. These four establishments are the pick of the many hotels along Derb Sidi Bouloukate.

De France, Riad Zitoune el-Kedim 197 (tel. 44 30 67). Singles 35dh (£2.50; $3.75), doubles 50dh (£3.50; $5.50). Recently renovated.
Chellah (tel. 44 19 77). The Chellah is in an alley left off Zitoune el-Kedim about 50m down the street from the Hôtel de France above. Watch out for the sign pointing to the hotel. Singles around 40dh (£3; $4.50).
Medina. A particularly good unclassified hotel, in an alley to the right off Zitoune el-Kedim.
Oukaimedon, Djemaâ El Fna. One of the best unclassified hotels around the square.

Near Djemaâ El Fna, Hôtel des Amis and Hôtel Cecil charge around 50dh (£3.50; $5.50) in doubles.

CLASSIFIED HOTELS
Two-star A:

Koutoubia, blvd Mansour 51 Eddahbi (tel. 43 09 21).
Les Ambassadeurs, av. Mohammed V 2 (tel. 44 71 59).
Ali, rue Moulay Ismail 10 (rue du Dispensaire/pl. de Foucauld) (tel. 44 49 79). Singles with shower 85dh (£6; $9); doubles with shower 120dh (£8.50; $13) with good breakfast. Extremely popular. Near Djemaâ El Fna, behind the post office.

Two-star B:

De Foucauld, av El Mouahidine (tel. 44 54 99). A fine hotel, but particularly good value if three or four people share one of the larger rooms. Rooftop terrace.
Gallia, rue de la Recette 90 (tel. 44 59 13). Singles 68–103dh (£5–£7.50; $7.50–11.00), doubles 84–125dh (£6–£9; $9.00–$13.50).
Grand Hôtel Tazi (tel. 44 21 52/44 27 87). In the medina at the corner of av. El Mouahidine & Bab Agnaou. Singles around 115dh (£8.25; $12.50), doubles around 140dh (£10; $15).
La Palmeraie, rue Souraya (tel. 43 10 07). In the New Town.

One-star A:

CTM, Djemaâ El Fna (tel. 44 23 25). Over the old bus station. Singles 50dh (£3.50; $5.50); with shower 75dh (£5.50; $8.25), doubles 64dh (£4.50; $6.75), with shower 100dh (£7; $10.50).
La Mouatamid, av. Mohammed V 94 (tel. 44 88 54/44 88 55). Doubles from 125dh (£9; $13.50).
Oasis, av. Mohammed V 50 (tel. 44 71 79).

One-star B:

Des Voyageurs, av. Zerktouni 40 (tel. 44 72 18). 100m from the ONMT office. Singles from 50dh (£3.50; $5.50), doubles 68dh (£5; $7.50).

HI HOSTEL
Rue El Jahid, Quartier Industriel (tel. 43 28 31/44 47 13). Technically an HI card is obligatory, but non-members are usually admitted outside the peak season. 20dh (£1.50; $2.25). Very clean. Lockout between 9 a.m.–12 p.m. and from 2–6 p.m. About 700m from the train station. Turn right after crossing av. Hassan II, then take the first left and keep on going until you see the hostel on the right.

CAMPING
Camping Municipal, rue El Jahid (tel. 43 17 07/44 60 85). 10dh (£0.70; $1) per person, 11dh (£0.80; $1.25) per tent. About 10 minutes' walk from the train station, on down the road from the HI hostel (see above for directions).

Rabat (tel. code 07)

TOURIST OFFICES
Office National Marocaine du Tourisme (ONMT), rue el-Jazair (tel. 72 12 52/73 05 62). Open July–mid-Sept, Mon.–Fri. 8 a.m.–2.30 p.m.; at other times, Mon.–Fri. 8.30 a.m.–12 p.m. and 2.30–6.30 p.m., except Ramadan, Mon.–Fri. 9 a.m.–3 p.m. A very helpful office but, unfortunately, not well located. Follow av. Mohammed V from the train station to the Grande Essouna Mosque then go left down av. Moulay Hassan until you see rue el-Jazair (formerly rue d'Alger) on the right. The Syndicat d'Initiative on rue Patrice

Lumumba (tel. 72 32 72) is more conveniently located. Across from the post office on av. Mohammed V go right along rue el-Kahira for a few block. Open Mon.–Fri. 8 a.m.–7 p.m., Sat. 8 a.m.–12 p.m.

UNCLASSIFIED HOTELS
Marrakesh, rue Sebbahi 10 (tel. 72 77 03). Singles 40dh (£3; $4.50); doubles 70dh (£5; $7.50). Turn right three blocks after entering the medina from av. Mohammed V.
Dohrmi, av. Mohammed V 313 (tel. 72 38 98). Doubles 100dh (£7; $10.50).

Also in the medina: Hôtel el Alam and Hôtel Regina. Both in rue Gebbali.

CLASSIFIED HOTELS
Two-star A:

Royal, rue Amman 1 (tel. 72 11 71/72 11 72).
Splendid, rue de Ghazzah 24 (tel. 72 32 83). Singles from 77dh (£5.50; $8.25), doubles from 102dh (£7.25; $11). Off av. Mohammed V. See also the Hôtel de la Paix close by.
Des Oudaïs, blvd el Alou 132 (tel. 73 23 71). In the medina, over from the kasbah area. Considerably better than the other hotels in the medina.

One-star A:

Capitol, av. Allal Ben Abdellah 34 (tel. 73 12 36). Singles 60dh (£4; $6); with shower 80dh (£6; $9); doubles 80dh (£6; $9); with shower 100dh (£7; $10.50).
Central, rue el-Basra 2 (tel. 72 21 31/76 73 56). Singles 58dh (£4; $6), singles with showers 68dh (£4.75; $7), doubles 80dh (£6; $9), doubles with showers 90dh (£6.50; $9.75). To the right off av. Mohammed V, a couple of blocks from the train station in the direction of the medina.
Gauloise, Zankat Hims 1 (tel. 72 30 22/73 05 73).
Majestic, av. Hassan II 121 (tel. 72 29 97). Singles from 58dh (£4; $6), doubles from 70dh (£5; $7.50). The hotel fills quickly, so try to get there before 12 p.m. at least.
Dahir, av. Hassan II 429 (tel. 73 30 26/72 20 96).
Dakar, rue Dakar (tel. 72 16 71).

HI HOSTEL
Rue Marassa, Bab El Had (blvd Misr) (tel. 72 57 69). Just outside the medina. Members only. 25dh (£1.75; $2.50) per person.

CAMPING

Camping de la Plage (tel. 78 23 68). 5dh (£0.35; $0.50) per tent, 10dh (£0.70; $1) per person. In Salé, across the River Bou Regreg. Bus 6 leaves av. Hassan II for Salé. Also bus 24. Get off at Bab Bou Haja, then follow the signs to the site on the beach.

Tangier (Tanger) (tel. code 09)

TOURIST OFFICES

Office National Marocaine du Tourisme (ONMT), blvd Pasteur 29 (tel. 93 29 96). Open Mon.–Sat. 8 a.m.–2 p.m. Within walking distance of the port, but it is more advisable to take a petit taxi from the port to the office — only 4dh (£0.30; $0.60) or so.

TROUBLE SPOTS

If you venture into the medina or the kasbah at night keep your wits about you at all times, especially if you are on your own, and stick to the main streets. Tourists are pestered in Tangier to a degree unparalleled in the rest of the country. Although this can become annoying do not adopt an aggressive manner in trying to rid yourself of unwanted attention or you could find yourself in serious trouble. If a dangerous situation does develop (for whatever reason) it is up to you to extricate yourself, as there is little chance of anyone else intervening.

FINDING ACCOMMODATION

Tangier has a large number of hotels and pensions, so even in July and August when the city becomes very busy you should find a room without too much trouble, though you may pay over the odds at this time of year (unclassified hotels often up their prices in July and August, by up to 100%). If you are looking for accommodation near the port or the main train station (Gare de Ville) Zankat Salah Eddine el-Ayoubi (previously rue de la Plage) is well supplied with reasonably priced hotels. Walk left along Avenue d'Espagne from the Gare de Ville, then take the first right. If you would prefer to stay in the medina, one of the best places to look for a room is rue Mokhtar Ahardan (formerly rue de la Poste), just off the Petit Socco. Turn right on leaving the port and enter the medina at rue de Cadiz. Head along the street towards the lower gateway to the kasbah. Just before the gate turn left off rue de Cadiz and follow the steps into rue Mokhtar Ahardan.

If your pension has no showers, there's a hamman at rue des Cheretiéns 80, off the Petit Socco. Showers are 6dh (£0.40; $0.60).

PENSIONS/UNCLASSIFIED HOTELS
In the medina:

Pension Palace, rue Mokhtar Ahardan 2 (tel. 93 61 28). Around 50dh (£3.50; $5.50) p.p. Large and spotless rooms.
Hôtel Grand Socco (tel. 93 31 26). On Grand Socco.
Hôtel Fuentes, Petit Socco (tel. 93 46 69).
Hôtel Mauretania, Petit Socco (tel. 93 46 77).
Pension Becerra, Petit Socco (tel. 93 23 69).

Also located on Petit Socco are Pension Amal, Pension Fes, Pension Karlton and Pension Tan-Tan.

In the new town:

Pension Miami, rue Salah Eddine el-Ayoubi 126 (tel. 93 29 00). Singles 35dh (£2.50; $3.75); doubles 56dh (£4; $6), triples 90dh (£6.50; $9.75).

CLASSIFIED HOTELS
Two-star A:

Marco Polo, av. d'Espagne (tel. 93 82 13/93 60 87).

Two-star B:

Anjou, rue Ibn El Banna 3 (tel. 93 43 44/93 42 44).
Djenina, rue Grotins 8 (tel. 93 47 59/93 60 75).
Lutetia, av. My Abdellah 3 (tel. 93 18 66). Doubles 70–125dh (£5–9; $7.50–13.50).
Valencia, av. d'Espagne 72 (tel. 93 17 14).

One-star A:

Andalucia, rue Vermeer 14 (tel. 94 13 34).
Astoria, rue Ahmed Chaouki 10 (tel. 93 72 02). 180dh (£13; $19.50) for a double.
Biaritz, av. des F.A.R. 102 (tel. 93 24 73).
Continental, rue Dar el Baroud (tel. 93 10 24/93 11 43).
De Paris, blvd Pasteur 42 (tel. 03 81 26/93 18 77). Singles 50dh

(£3.50; $5.50); with shower 72dh (£5.15; $7.70); doubles 66dh (£4.75; $7), with shower 90dh (£6.50; $9.75).

Mamora, rue Mokhtar Ahardan 19 (tel. 93 41 05). Singles 125dh (£9; $13.50); doubles with shower 120dh (£8.50; $13), doubles with bath 165dh (£11.75; $17.50). The best hotel in the medina.

Hotel Residence Ritz, rue Soraya 1 (tel. 93 80 74/93 80 75).

One-star B:

Al Farabi, Zankat Essadia 10 (tel. 93 45 66).

Miramar, av. des F.A.R. (tel. 93 89 48). The best of the reasonably priced hotels along the beach.

Hotel Magellan, rue Magellan (tel. 93 87 26). Doubles 80dh (£6; $9).

Hotel El Munina. William Burroughs wrote *The Naked Lunch* here. Singles 100dh (£7; $10.50), doubles 120dh (£8.50; $12.75), showers included.

HI HOSTEL
Tanger Youth Hostel, rue El Antaki 8, av. d'Espagne (tel. 946127). 20dh (£1.50; $2.25) per night.

CAMPING
Miramonte (tel. 937138). Just under 3km west of the kasbah. Bus 1, 2 or 21 from Grand Socco. 6dh (£0.45; $0.70) per tent, 10dh (£0.70; $1) p.p.

Tingis (tel. 940191). Bus 15 from Grand Socco. 10dh (£0.70; $1) per person, 6dh (£0.45; $0.70) per tent. Facilities include tennis court and swimming pool.

Camping Sahara. About 1.5km north of train station, on the beach.

THE NETHERLANDS (Nederland)

It is a pleasure to travel in The Netherlands, not least because the Dutch are responding particularly well to the growth in independent, budget tourism. Reserving accommodation before you set off on holiday is easy. Local Tourist Offices (VVV) will book hotel rooms and B&Bs accommodation if you write to them in advance, though if you plan to travel around a fair bit you can save yourself the trouble of writing to individual offices by using the services of the wonderful Netherlands Reservations Centre in Leidschendam. They will book hotels, B&Bs, and even campsites all over the country for you. Campsites are reserved free of charge, though a deposit of 25% may be requested for other types of accommodation, which you forfeit if you make a late cancellation. There is now a Netherlands Reservations Centre in the UK (tel. 0171 931 0801), but they do charge a fee of £7 ($10.50) per reservation. If you want to reserve a bed in an HI hostel all you need do is write to the hostel in Dutch, English or German, enclosing an International Reply Coupon. Try to reserve as early as possible if you want to stay in either of the HI hostels in Amsterdam. You can also book rooms on arrival through local Tourist Offices. Staff are generally very helpful, and fully appreciate what you mean when you say you want cheap accommodation. You need have no worries that they are trying to offer you expensive rooms when there are cheap rooms available. For a small fee, any VVV will reserve ahead for you. This is a service you might wish to use if you know you will be arriving late at your next destination, or if you are heading for Amsterdam in summer, as queues at the VVV Amsterdam Tourist Office can be horrendous at any time of day, with the cheapest rooms disappearing fast.

If you are very fortunate you may find a **hotel** or **pension** in one of the main towns with singles and doubles available for around 30Dfl (£11.25; $17) per person, but these are few and far between. More likely you will pay 40Dfl (£15; $22.50) per person and upwards for singles and doubles. The local VVV can advise you on the availability of **B&B** in private homes, which is a cheaper option than pensions or hotels. Prices range from 23–50Dfl (£8.50–18.75; $12.75–28.00) per person, with around 30Dfl (£11.25; $17) being the norm. B&B accommodation offers good value for money, as rigorous standards of cleanliness and comfort are enforced, while a traditional Dutch breakfast is a rare treat compared to the meagre offerings you get in most countries.

A similar hearty breakfast is also available at some of the country's 40–45 **HI hostels**. Depending on the location and the time of year B&B will cost you 20–28Dfl (£7.50–10.50; $11.25–15.75). Full board is available at reasonable prices with meals that are good value for money. Basically, the HI hostels are good value all round; usually spotlessly clean, comfortable, equipped with a bar and games room, and staying open later than is usual for official hostels. Unfortunately, not all the main places of interest have an HI hostel in town, but those with a railpass will invariably find one in a town nearby. Hostels in the major towns are open all year. Most of the others are open from Easter to late September, but a few are open for the summer only. If you stay in an HI hostel a valid membership card will usually bring a discount.

As well as the HI hostels you may have the option of staying in **privately run hostels** or **youth hotels**. Both the prices and standards of these can vary dramatically. Prices can be as low as 15Dfl (£5.50; $8.50), but on the other hand they may be as high as 40Dfl (£15; $22.50). In most cases, when you pay 40Dfl this gets you a single or a double, but there are some hostels which charge this price for larger rooms, representing very poor value compared to a cheap hotel. The local VVV will inform you of the whereabouts of any private hostels operating in town. It is also worth asking whether there is a local **Sleep-In**, as several towns have followed the example set by Amsterdam and established dorm hostels (sometimes open in summer only) which charge around 17–25Dfl (£6.50–9.50; $9.75–14.25) for B&B.

No matter where you choose to visit you will never be far from one of the Netherlands' 2000 **campsites**. Sites are generally clean, well maintained and equipped with all the essentials. Prices for a solo traveller will normally be around 6–12Dfl (£2.25–4.50; $3.50–6.75), but there are a few sites – primarily aimed at caravans – whose prices will bring a tear to the eye of those with a small tent. In such sites, you pay for a little hedged enclosure, designed to accommodate a caravan, plus a fee per person. For a solo traveller this is likely to amount to at least 17,50Dfl (£6.50; $9.75).

Camping outside official sites is illegal, as is sleeping in cars, or **sleeping rough** in any public place. If you are sleeping in any public place the police are likely to wake you up and, most likely move you on, though they may press vagrancy charges if you have no money on you, so, ironically, to avoid being charged with vagrancy you have to make yourself an attractive target for muggers. Just as the police are well aware of the spots in which travellers are most likely to try to bed down, so are the would-be thieves. If you try to sleep in the main train stations in Rotterdam or, especially, Amsterdam, it is likely to be touch and go whether the police get to you before the thieves do. Even worse, there is a fair chance you will be assaulted in Amsterdam Central if you are lying sleeping.

ADDRESSES

Netherlands Board of Tourism	PO Box 523, London SW1E 6NT (tel. 01891 200 277 – premium rate)
Dutch YHA	Stichting Nederlandse Jeugdherberg Centrale NJHC, Prof Tulplein 4, ND-1018 GX Amsterdam (tel. 020 551 3155).
Sleep-Ins	MAIC, Hartenstraat 16–18, Amsterdam (tel. 020 240977).
Netherlands Reservation Centre	P O Box 404, ND-2260 AK Leidschendam (tel. 070 317 5454).
Bed & Breakfast Holland	Warmondstraat 1291e, ND-1058 KV Amsterdam (tel. 020 615 7527).
Camping	Stichting Vriije Recreatre, Broekseweg 75–77, ND-4231 VD Meerkerk (tel. 018 372741).

Amsterdam (tel. code 020)

TOURIST OFFICES

VVV Amsterdam Tourist Office, P O Box 3901, 1001 AS Amsterdam (tel. 06 3403 4066). Contact this office if you want information in advance.

VVV Amsterdam Tourist Office, Stationsplein 10 (tel. 626 6444). Open Easter–Sept. daily 9 a.m.–11 p.m.; Oct.–Easter open daily 9 a.m.–6 p.m.

VVV Amsterdam Tourist Office, Leidsestraat 106. Open Easter–Sept., daily 9 a.m.–11 p.m.; Oct.–Easter, Mon.–Sat. 9 a.m.–5 p.m. Tram 1, 2 or 5 from Amsterdam Centraal.

TROUBLE SPOTS

There are a few wild stories about drug-crazed gangs roaming around the city mugging tourists. Wild stories are all they are! Because of the number of tourists visiting it, the Red Light area is particularly safe, at least until the early hours of the morning although, as in the most crowded areas of all cities, pickpockets are to be found plying their trade amongst the hustle and bustle. Although you are more likely to be offered drugs in Amsterdam than in almost any other city, pushers are rarely aggressive. Amsterdam drug culture has become so integrated that the pushers almost see themselves as a public service! One place you might want to avoid after dark is the Nieuwemarkt (location of the Waag), only a short walk from Oudezijds Achterburgwal in the Red Light district down Bloedstraat or Barndesteeg. Many of the casualties of the hard drug scene congregate around the square, as do those who supply them.

BASIC DIRECTIONS
From Stationsplein in front of Amsterdam Centraal, head across the bridge (avoiding the trams) before crossing Prins Hendrikkade to the start of Damrak. Walking up Damrak, turning left at the end of the water takes you to Oude Brug Steeg, across Warmoesstraat and down Lange Niezel into the Red Light district. Continuing up Damrak you arrive at Dam, the large square containing the Royal Palace and the National Monument. To the right, behind the palace, Raadhuisstraat leads off across the ring of canals which encircle the town centre. Directly across Dam from Damrak is Rokin, which leads to Muntplein. The walk from Amsterdam Centraal to Dam takes about 10 minutes, that from Dam to Muntplein slightly less. Trams 4, 5, 9, 16, 24 and 25 run from the station to Muntplein.

FINDING ACCOMMODATION
Of all the cities in Europe, only Rome, Paris and London receive more visitors than Amsterdam, so if you want to be sure of reasonably cheap accommodation you should reserve as far in advance as possible, particularly in summer. If you have not reserved ahead but are stopping in another Dutch town before visiting Amsterdam you can ask the local VVV to reserve ahead for you. Otherwise, try to arrive in Amsterdam as early as possible because, for obvious reasons, the cheapest accommodation goes quickly. In the sections below, directions are given for most accommodation options, often from a reference point in the **Basic Directions** section above. All hotels listed below have the full approval of the VVV Amsterdam Tourist Office, but do not hesitate to contact them in the unlikely event that you should have any cause for complaint.

HOTELS
Cheapest doubles around 65Dfl (£24.50; $36.75)

Schröder, Haarlemerdijk 48b (tel. 626 6272). Without breakfast. Two-night minimum stay in peak season. Right along Prins Hendrikkade, left at Singel, then right along Haarlemerstraat into Haarlemerdijk. A 5—10-minute walk from Amsterdam Centraal.

Pax, Raadhuisstraat 37 (tel. 624 9735). Without breakfast. A 10—15-minute walk from Amsterdam Centraal or take tram 13 or 17 along the street from the station.

Amstel Boat Hotel (Botel Cruises Amstel), Osterdok 2—4 (tel. 626 4247). B&B. This two-star hotel is moored a short walk from the front exit of Amsterdam Centraal.

De Bloeiende Ramenas, Haarlemerdijk 61 (tel. 624 6030). Turn right from the station.

Cheapest doubles around 70Dfl (£26.25; $39.50)

Westertoren, Raadhuisstraat 35b (tel. 624 4639). B&B. See Hotel Pax.

Oosterpark, Oosterpark 72 (tel. 693 0049). B&B. Metro: Weesperplein, then change to tram 6 which runs along Oosterpark. A 5—10-minute walk from Amsterdam-Muiderpoort train station. Follow Wijtenbachstraat into Oosterpark.

Old Nickel, Nieuwe Brugsteeg 11 (tel. 624 1912). B&B. Left along the waterside at the start of Damrak into Nieuwe Brugsteeg. A few minutes' walk from Amsterdam Centraal.

Cheapest doubles around 75Dfl (£28; $42)

Weber, Marnixstraat 397 (tel. 627 0574). Without breakfast. Tram 1 or 2 from Amsterdam Centraal to Leidse Plein, then a few minutes' walk along Marnixstraat.

Casa Cara, Emmastraat 24 (tel. 662 3135). B&B. Good value, a two-star hotel. Out by the Vondelpark. Trams 2 and 16 from Amsterdam Centraal cross the Emmastraat.

Bema, Concertgebouwplein 19b (tel. 679 1396). B&B. Tram 16 from Amsterdam Centraal.

Rokin, Rokin 73 (tel. 626 7456). B&B. Two-star hotel in excellent location.

Apple Inn, Koninginneweg 93 (tel. 662 7894). B&B. Two-star hotel near the Vondelpark. Tram 2 from Amsterdam Centraal runs along the street.

Aspen, Raadhuisstraat 31 (tel. 626 6714). Without breakfast. See Hotel Pax.

Cheapest doubles around 80Dfl (£30; $45)

La Bohème, Marnixstraat 415 (tel. 624 2828). Without breakfast. See Hotel Weber.

Sphinx, Weteringschans 82 (tel. 627 3680). B&B. From Amsterdam Centraal tram 4 to Frederiksplein, or tram 16, 24 or 25 to Weteringplein.

Galerij, Raadhuisstraat 43 (tel. 624 8851). Without breakfast. See Hotel Pax.

Van Rooyen, Tweede Helmersstraat 6 (tel. 618 4577). B&B. Tram 1, 2 or 5 to Leidse Plein from Amsterdam Centraal. Walk right along Nassaukade, past the end of 1e Helmerstraat then left on 2e Helmerstraat.

Clemens, Raadhuisstraat 39 (tel. 624 6089). B&B. See Hotel Pax.

Brian, Singel 69 (tel. 624 4661). B&B. A 5–10-minute walk from Amsterdam Centraal. Right along Prins Hendrikkade, then left.

Impala, Leidsekade 77 (tel. 623 4706). From Amsterdam Centraal take tram 1, 2 or 5 to Leidse Plein.

Kitty, Plantage Middenlaan 40 (tel. 622 6819). B&B. Tram 9 from Amsterdam Centraal runs along the street.

Ronnie, Raadhuisstraat 41 (tel. 624 2821). See Hotel Pax.

Liberty, Singel 5 (tel. 620 7307). Right and then left from station.

Cheapest doubles around 90Dfl (£33.75; $50.50)

Arena Budget Hotel, 's-Gravesandestraat 51 (tel. 6947 444). Tram 9, Metro 'Weesperplein', Bus 22. Nightbus 77. Cheaper dormitories also available. Also cultural centre and café-restaurant.

Kap, Den Texstraat 5b (tel. 624 5908). B&B. Tram 16, 24 or 25 to Weteringplein from Amsterdam Centraal. Facing the canal, head right on Weteringschans, right at Weteringplantsoen, then left.

Internationaal, Warmoesstraat 1–3 (tel. 624 5520). Without breakfast. Right off Oude Brug Steeg. On the fringe of the Red Light district.

Amstelzicht, Amstel 104 (tel. 623 6693). Two-star hotel in a good location between Muntplein and the Blauwe Brug (Blue Bridge). B&B. Tram 4 from Amsterdam Centraal runs down part of Amstel before turning off into Rembrandtsplein. From the metro stop on Waterlooplein you can take tram 9 the whole length of Amstel.

Verdi, Wanningstraat 9 (tel. 676 0073). B&B. From Amsterdam Centraal take tram 2 to the first stop after it turns off Van Baerle Straat onto Willems Parkweg. Go left down Jacob Obrecht Straat, left again at Van Bree Straat, then right.

Peters, Nicolaas Maesstraat 72 (tel. 673 3454). B&B. The street crosses Van Baerle Straat shortly after tram 5 from Amsterdam Centraal passes the National Museum on Museumplein.

HI HOSTELS
'Vondelpark', Zandpad 5 (tel. 683 1744). Open all year. Curfew 2 a.m. Written reservations only. Arrive early if you have not reserved. B&B 23,50Dfl (£8.75; $13) p.p. in doubles; 22,50Dfl (£8.50; $12.75) in dorms. From Amsterdam Centraal take tram 1, 2 or 5 to Leidseplein. Zandpad is off Stadhouderskade at the left-hand end of Leidseplein.

'Stadsdoelen', Kloveniersburgwal 97 (tel. 624 6832). Open 1 Mar.–1 Nov. and 27 Dec.–2 Jan. Curfew 1.30 a.m. B&B 20,50Dfl (£7.75; $11.50) in dorms. Between Muntplein and the Nieuwmarkt. From Muntplein follow Nieuwe Doelen Straat into Klovenierburgwal. A 15 minute walk from Amsterdam Centraal, through the Red Light district. From Lange Niezel follow Korte Niezel, then go right at Oudezijds Achterburgwal then left at Oude Hoogstraat into Kloveniersburgwal.

CHRISTIAN HOSTELS
Both are safe, cheap, and not as rule-bound as you might imagine. 1 a.m. curfew Fri. and Sat., midnight the rest of the week. Both 15Dfl (£5.50; $8.50) for B&B.

Eben Haëzer, Bloemstraat 179 (tel. 624 4717). Tram 13 or 17 from Amsterdam Centraal to the Marnixstraat stop. Walk back to Rozengracht, and Bloemstraat is parallel to the left.

The Shelter, Barndesteeg 21–25 (tel. 625 3230). A 10-minute walk from Amsterdam Centraal to the hostel in the Red Light district. From Lange Niezel follow Korte Niezel, go right on Oudezijds Achterburgwal, then left at Barndesteeg.

HOSTELS
Adam & Eva, Sarphatistraat 105 (tel. 624 6206). Dorms 23Dfl (£8.50; $12.75). Metro: Weesperplein, then a few minutes'walk along Sarphatistraat.

Bob's Youth Hostel, Nieuwezijds Voorburgwal 92 (tel. 623 0063). B&B in dorms works out cheaper if you have a mattress on the floor. Good location, close to Dam, about 8 minutes' walk from Amsterdam Centraal. Trams 1, 2 and 5 run along the street from Amsterdam Centraal.

Keizersgracht, Keizersgracht 15 (tel. 625 1364). Dorms 24Dfl (£9; $13.50), doubles about 90Dfl (£33.75; $50.50), without breakfast. A pleasant location, about 8 minutes' walk from Amsterdam Centraal.

Kabul, Warmoesstraat 38–42 (tel. 623 7158). No curfew. Dorms 23Dfl (£8.50; $12.75), doubles from 70–90Dfl (£26.25–33.75; $39.50–

50.50). Without breakfast. In the Red Light district, 5 minutes' walk from Amsterdam Centraal. Right off Oude Brug Steeg.

Jeugdhotel Meeting Point, Warmoesstraat 14 (tel. 627 7499) Dorms 25Dfl (£9.50; $14.25). Without breakfast. See Kabul.

Hans Brinker, Kerkstraat 136 (tel. 622 0687). B&B in dorms 38,50Dfl (£14.50; $21.75). Doubles are more expensive than in the hotels listed above. Tram 16 from Amsterdam Centraal crosses Kerkstraat on its way down Vijzelstraat.

Zeezicht, Piet Heinkade 15 (tel. 617 8706). B&B in dorms 30Dfl (£11.25; $17). A 10 minute walk from the rear exit of Amsterdam Centraal, right along De Ruijter Kade which leads into Piet Hein Kade.

Frisco Inn, Beursstraat 5 (tel. 620 1610). No curfew. Dorms start at around 25Dfl (£9.50; $14.25), more expensive doubles and triples are available. Just over 5 minutes' walk from Amsterdam Centraal.

Bill's 'Happy Hours' Youth Hostel, Binnen Wieringerstraat 8 (tel. 625 5259). B&B in dorms 20Dfl (£7.50; $11.25). Off Haarlemerstraat near the end of Herengracht.

Euphemia Budget Hotel, Fokke Simonszstraat 1–9 (tel. 622 9045). Dorms 30Dfl (£11.25; $17), doubles 85Dfl (£32; $48), triples 115Dfl (£43; $64.50). With breakfast. Tram 16, 24 or 25 from Amsterdam Centraal to Weteringschans. Go back over the canal (Lijnbaansgracht), then turn right.

't Ancker, De Ruijterkade 100 (tel. 622 9560). Dorms 27.50–35Dfl (£10.50–13.00; $15.75–19.50). Includes a buffet breakfast where you can eat as much as you like. More expensive doubles available. About 100m to the right from the rear exit from Amsterdam Centraal.

Arena, s'-Gravesandestraat 51 (tel. 694 7444). The original Sleep-In has reopened as the largest budget hostel in Amsterdam, with more than 600 beds. Cheapest dorm beds 17,50Dfl (£6.75; $10). Sheet hire 5Dfl (£2; $3) with 20Dfl (£7.50; $11.25) deposit. Beside the Oosterpark, 15 minutes from the city centre.

CAMPING

Zeeburg, Zuider-Ijdijk 44 (tel. 694 4430). Open mid-Apr.–Oct. 6Dfl (£2.25; $3.50) per person plus 2,50Dfl (£1; $1.50) per tent. Aimed at young travellers. Live music regularly. Direct ferry from Central Station, or take bus 22 or 37. Night bus 71 or 76.

Gaasper, Loosdrechtdreef 7 (tel. 696 7326). 4,75Dfl (£1.75; $2.50) p.p. with tent. Metro to Gaasperplas or night bus 75. Approx. 20-minute trip from Central Station.

Vliegenbos, Meeuwenlaan 138 (tel. 636 8855). 5,50Dfl (£2; $3)

p.p. with tent. Also travellers' huts at 46Dfl (£17.25; $26). From
Central Station tram 1, 2 or 5 to Leidseplein, then bus 172.
De Badhoeve, Uitdammerdijk 10 (tel. 490 4294). 4Dfl (£1.50;
$2.25) per person, 6Dfl (£2.25; $3.50) per tent.
Het Amsterdamse Bos, Kleine Noorddijk 1 (tel. 641 6868). 7,60Dfl
(£2.75; $4.25) per person, 2,60Dfl (£1; $1.50) per tent.

SLEEPING ROUGH
Sleeping rough is not to be recommended in Amsterdam as a whole,
and certainly not in Amsterdam Centraal train station. Even if you
are not physically attacked, it is almost guaranteed someone will
try to rob you as you sleep. If you do decide to sleep rough, at
least try to gain some extra security by bedding down beside other
travellers, rather than in some quiet spot on your own. The most
popular spots for sleeping out are the Vondelpark, the Julianapark
and the Beatrixpark. Those with a railpass who are totally stuck
but do not want to sleep rough should put their luggage and all
but a little of their money into the left luggage office (or the lockers)
and then ride the trains, which keep up a virtually constant service
between Amsterdam and Rotterdam through the night. You will
not get a lot of sleep, but it is much safer than trying to sleep in
Amsterdam Centraal.

Delft (tel. code 015)

TOURIST OFFICES
VVV Delft, Markt 85, 2611 GS Delft (tel. 126100). Write in advance
for information or free hotel reservations. Open Apr.–Sept.,
Mon.–Fri. 9 a.m.–6 p.m., Sat. 9 a.m.–5 p.m., Sun. 11 a.m.–3 p.m.;
Oct.–Mar. closed Sun. The office is about 10 minutes' walk from
the train station. Leaving the station, head left along the main road,
turn right up Binnenwatersloot with its tree-lined canal, across
Oude Delft and straight on at the top of Binnenwatersloot, left
along the canal at the Wijnhaven, then right over the first bridge
and straight on into the Markt. The office is at the top right-hand
end of the square near the Nieuwe Kerk.

HOTELS
Cheapest doubles around 65Dfl (£24.50; $36.75)

Den Dulk, Markt 61/65 (tel. 158255). Prime location.
Van Domburg, Voldersgracht 24 (tel. 123029). Also excellently

located on a canal just off the Markt. Continue along the Wijnhaven (see **Tourist Office** above) until you see Voldersgracht on the right.

De Vos, Breerstraat 5a (tel. 123258).

Rust, Oranje Plantage 38 (tel. 126874). Singles the same price as doubles. About 10 minutes' walk from the centre, 15 minutes' walk from the station. Oranje Plantage runs between the Oostpoort and the end of Nieuwe Langendijk, the street leading out of the Markt beside the Nieuwe Kerk.

Cheapest doubles around 70Dfl (£26.25; $39.50)

Parallel, Parallelweg 5–6 (tel. 126046). On the street immediately behind the train station. Head right from the station, right under the underpass and you arrive at the end of Parallelweg.

Van Leeuwen, Achterom 143 (tel. 123716). Singles the same price as doubles. About 5 minutes' walk from the centre and the train station. Take the small street opposite the station into Oude Delft then continue more or less straight on across the canals into Achterom.

PRIVATE ROOMS
Available from the Tourist Office. Doubles around 60Dfl (£22.50; $33.75).

HOSTELS
There are no hostels in Delft. The nearest hostels (both HI and privately run) are in Rotterdam and the Hague, both a short rail trip from Delft.

STUDENT FLATS
Krakeelhof, Jacoba Van Beierlaan 9 (tel. 135953/146235). Open June–Aug. Singles 20Dfl (£7.50; $11.25); doubles 36Dfl (£13.50; $19.75). Prices fall by about 25% if you stay more than seven days. As you leave the station turn right along Van Leeuwenhoeksingel, right at the end of the road, through the underpass, right at the first set of traffic lights, left on to Van Beierlaan, and left again over the bridge.

CAMPING
Delftse Hout (tel. 570515/130040/602323). Expensive. About 12Dfl (£4.50; $7) to pitch a tent, 6Dfl (£2.25; $3.50) p.p. In a wood about 20 minutes' walk from the town centre. From the train

station, bus 60 runs every 20 minutes to the Delftse Hout entrance on Korftlaan.

The Hague (Den Haag) (tel. code 070)

TOURIST OFFICES
The Hague Visitors & Convention Bureau, Postbus 85456, 2508 CD Den Haag (tel. 364 8286). Hotels can be booked in advance through this office, either by letter or by telephone (Mon.–Fri. 8.30 a.m.–5 p.m., Sat. 9 a.m.–1 p.m.).

VVV-i, The Hague Information Office, Koningin Julianaplein 30, ND-2595 Den Haag AA (tel. 354 6200). Open mid-Apr.–mid-Sept., Mon.–Sat. 9 a.m.–9 p.m., Sun. 10 a.m.–5 p.m.; at other times, Mon.–Sat. 9 a.m.–6 p.m., Sun. 10 a.m.–5 p.m. In the Babylon shopping centre, to the right of Den Haag Centraal train station.

VVV-i, Scheveningen Information Office, Gevers Deynootweg 1134–1136. Same hours as the VVV-i above. In the Palace Promenade shopping centre.

ARRIVING BY TRAIN
There are two main stations in The Hague, Den Haag Centraal and Den Haag Hollandse Spoor (usually abbreviated to Den Haag CS and Den Haag HS). Den Haag Central is the most convenient for the Tourist Office and for the tourist attractions. Paris/Brussels-Amsterdam trains stop at Hollandse Spoor only, but there are frequent connecting trains between the two stations.

FINDING ACCOMMODATION
Cheap accommodation in the centre of the city is in limited supply. Most of the cheaper hotels are in Scheveningen, on the coast to the north-west of the city and the various hostels are also outside the central area. Trams link Scheveningen to The Hague.

HOTELS
Cheapest doubles around 60Dfl (£22.50; $33.75)

Hotel Pension Scheveningen, Gevers Deynootweg 2 (tel. 354 7003). Enak, Keizerstraat 53, Scheveningen (tel. 355 6169).

Cheapest doubles around 70Dfl (£26.25; $39.50)

Duinroos, Alkmaarsestraat 27, Scheveningen (tel. 354 6079).
Meijer, Stevinstraat 34, Scheveningen (tel. 355 8138).
Huize Rosa, Badhuisweg 41, Scheveningen (tel. 355 7796).
Neuf, Rijswijkseweg 119 (tel. 399 2600). Just under 10 minutes' walk from the Hollandse Spoor train station (Den Haag HS). Through the underpass to the right of the main exit, then down Rijswijksweg to the hotel.
De Minstreel, Badhuiskade 4–5, Scheveningen (tel. 352 0024).
Schuur, Badhuiskade 2 (tel. 355 6583).

Cheapest doubles around 80Dfl (£30; $45)

Aristo, Stationsweg 164–166 (tel. 389 0847). A 5-minute walk down the street in front of Hollandse Spoor train station.
Clavan, Badhuiskade 8, Scheveningen (tel. 355 2844).
Jodi, Van Aerssenstraat 194–196 (tel. 355 9208). Technically not in Scheveningen, but far closer to Scheveningen than the centre of The Hague.
Astoria, Stationsweg 139 (tel. 384 0401). A 5-minute walk down the street in front of Hollandse Spoor station.
Empire, Keizerstraat 27a–29, Scheveningen (tel. 350 5752).
Lunamare, Badhuisweg 9 (tel. 354 6075).
Mont Blanc, Stevinstraat 66, Scheveningen (tel. 355 9785).
De Zonnehoek, Groningestraat 19, (tel. 354 1879).
El Cid, Badhuisweg 51 Scheveningen (tel. 354 6667).

PRIVATE ROOMS
These are arranged through VVV; occasionally they will not let private rooms until the hotels are full. Expect to pay around 35Dfl (£13; $19.50).

HI HOSTEL
Ockenburgh, Monsterseweg 4 (tel. 397 0011). About 8km from the city centre in Kijkduin. Bus 122, 123 or 124 from Central Station. Ask the driver for the nearest stop. A 10-minute walk, follow the signs. Midnight curfew. B&B in dorms 23–28Dfl (£8.50–10.50; $12.75–15.75).

HOSTELS
Marion, Havenkade 3/3a, Scheveningen (tel. 354 3501). Singles around 30Dfl (£11.25; $17) with breakfast, doubles 50–60Dfl (£18.75–22.50; $28.00–33.75).

Duinrell Duinhostel, Duinrell 1, Wassenaar (tel. 01751 19314). By the camping site. Around 23Dfl (£8.50; $12.75).

Scheveningen, Gevers Deynootweg 2, Scheveningen (tel. 354 7003). Singles around 40Dfl (£15; $22.50), doubles around 30Dfl (£11.25; $17) per person.

CAMPING

Duinhorst, Buurtweg 135, Wassenaar (tel. 324 2270). Open 1 Apr.–1 Oct. 6Dfl (£2.25; $3.50) p.p., 8,75Dfl (£3.25; $5) per site.

Duinrell, Duinrell 5, Wassenaar (tel. 01751 12339/19314). Open year round. 15Dfl (£5.50; $8.50) per camping site, 2,50Dfl (£1; $1.50) p.p.

Ockenburgh, Wijndaelerweg 25 (tel. 325 2364). Open 3 Apr.–20 Oct. 11Dfl (£4; $6) per camping site; 6Dfl (£2.25; $3.50) p.p. Tram 3 from Den Haag Centraal.

Vlietland, Oostvlietweg 60, Leidschendam (tel. 071 612200). Open 11 Apr.–1 Oct. 17,50Dfl (£7; $10.50) per camping site, 5Dfl (£2; $3) p.p.

Rotterdam (tel. code 010)

TOURIST OFFICES

Rotterdam VVV Tourist Information, Coolsingel 67, ND-3012 AC Rotterdam (tel. 06 3403 4065). Open Apr.–Sept., Mon.–Thurs. 9 a.m.–5.30 p.m., Fri. 9 a.m.–9 p.m., Sat. 9 a.m.–5 p.m., Sun. 10 a.m.–4 p.m.; Oct.–Mar. same hours except Sundays, when the office is closed. The head office of Rotterdam VVV Tourist Information. Information on the city and the country as a whole. Contact this office if you want to reserve hotel rooms in advance. Located near the Town Hall, a 10-minute walk from Rotterdam Centraal, left along Weena after crossing Stationsplein, then right down Coolsingel from Hofplein, or take tram 1 or the metro to Stadhuis.

Rotterdam VVV Tourist Information, Rotterdam Centraal. Branch office in the hall of the main train station. Open Mon.–Sat. 9 a.m.–10 p.m., Sun. 10 a.m.–10 p.m.

HOTELS

Doubles 47Dfl (£17.50; $26.50), doubles with bath/shower 70Dfl (£26.25; $39.50) for B&B

Keeldar, Virulyplein 10 (tel. 477 7400). Bus 38 or 45.

Cheapest doubles around 65Dfl (£24.50; $36.75) without breakfast

Bagatelle, Provenierssingel 26 (tel. 467 6348). A few minutes' walk from the main train station. Leave Rotterdam Centraal by the rear exit on to Proveniersplein. Provenierssingel runs out the right hand side of the square.

Heemraad, Heemraadssingel 90 (tel. 477 5461). Tram 1, 7 or 9, or a 10–15 minute walk from Rotterdam Centraal. From Stationsplein head right along Weena and Beukelsdijk, then left at Heemradssingel.

Bharat/Mathenesser, Mathenesserlaan 399 (tel. 477 6921). Tram 1, 4 or 7.

Cheapest doubles around 70Dfl (£26.25; $39.50)

Metropole, Nieuwe Binnenweg 13a (tel. 436 0319). Overnight price includes breakfast. A 15-minute walk from Rotterdam Centraal. Head directly across Stationsplein and keep going until you see Nieuwe Binnenweg on the right at the end of Westersingel. Metro: Eendrachtsplein leaves a short walk along Nieuwe Binnenweg from the square, or you can take tram 5 or 6.

Rox-Inn, s'-Gravendijkwal 14 (tel. 436 6109). Without breakfast. Tram 1, 7 or 9, or a 15-minute walk from Rotterdam Centraal. Head straight from the exit across Stationsplein and down Kruisplein. Turn right at West-Kruiskade, and keep on going until you see s'-Gravendijkwal on the left.

De Gunst, Brielselaan 190–192 (tel. 485 0940). Metro: Maashaven, then tram 2.

Cheapest doubles around 75Dfl (£28; $42)

Traverse, s'-Gravendijkwal 70–72 (tel. 436 4040). B&B. Tram 6 or 9, or bus 32, or a 20-minute walk from Rotterdam Centraal. Follow the directions for the Rox-Inn, above.

Bienvenue, Spoorsingel 24 (tel. 466 9394). Overnight price includes breakfast. A few minutes' walk from Rotterdam Centraal. Go out the rear exit and across Provenisplein into Spoorsingel.

HI HOSTEL

Rochussenstraat 107–109 (tel. 436 5763). Curfew 2 a.m. B&B 23Dfl (£8.50; $12.75), 28Dfl (£10.50; $15.75) for non members. Metro or tram 4 to Dijkzigt on Rochussenstraat, or a 20-minute walk from Rotterdam Centraal. Across Stationsplein and straight on to Eendrachtsplein from which Rochussenstraat runs off to the right.

SLEEP-IN
Sleep-in Rotterdam, Mauritsweg 29b (tel. 414 3256/412 1420). Open July–Aug. 112,50Dfl (£42; $63) including breakfast.

CAMPING
Kanaalweg 84 (tel. 415 9772). Bus 33. 7Dfl (£2.50; $3.75) p.p., plus 5Dfl (£2; $3) per pitch.

Utrecht (tel. code 030)

TOURIST OFFICE
VVV Utrecht, Vredenburg 90, ND-3511 Utrecht BD (tel. 06 3403 4085). Open Mon.–Fri. 9 a.m.–6 p.m., Sat. 9 a.m.–4 p.m. Accommodation service, town plans and leaflets with suggested walking tours. When closed, information and accommodation listings are available from the vending machine outside the office. To reach the office in the Muziekcenter from Utrecht Centraal Station you have to negotiate your way through the Hoog Catherine shopping complex (watch out for signs pointing to the VVV).

HOTELS
There is a dire shortage of cheap hotels in the city.

Pension Van Ooyen, Dantelaan 117 (tel. 938190). Doubles from 75Dfl (£28; $42). From Utrecht Centraal Station take bus 8 dir. Oog in Al to Everard Meijsterlaan.

Hotel Ouwi, F.C. Donderstraat 12 (tel. 716303). From Utrecht Centraal take bus 4 dir. Wilhelminapark, or bus 11 dir. Uithof to F.C. Donderstraat.

Parkhotel, Tolsteegsingel 34 (tel. 516712). Doubles from 85Dfl (£32; $48). From Utrecht Centraal take bus 2 dir. Kanaleiland to Ledig Erf.

B&Bs
Local Bed & Breakfast accommodation can be booked through the VVV Utrecht. Prices start around 35Dfl (£13; $19.50) per person.

HI HOSTEL

'Ridderhofstad Rhijnauwen', Rhijnauwenslaan 14, Bunnik (tel. 03405 61277). 12.30 a.m. curfew. 23Dfl (£8.50; $12.75). Bus 40 from Utrecht Centraal stops about 5 minutes' walk away from this excellent hostel set in the countryside outside Utrecht (ask the driver for the Jeugdherberg).

CAMPING

De Berekuil, Ariënslaan 5 (tel. 713870). Open Apr.–Oct. 5Dfl (£2; $3) per tent and per person. Within walking distance of the town centre. Bus 57 from Utrecht Centraal Station to Biltse Rading.

NORWAY (Norge)

Not surprisingly, cheap accommodation options are severely limited in Norway, reputedly the most expensive country in mainland Europe. Even if the prices below seem affordable to you, remember that you are also going to spend a considerable amount of money simply feeding yourself. Even in summer when **hotels** reduce their prices, it is rare to find prices lower than 250kr (£24; $36) for singles, 400kr (£38.50; $57.75) for doubles. The only consolations are the excellent standards, and the chance of gorging yourself on the buffet breakfast. A room in a small **boarding house**, known as a *pensjonat* or *hospit* is cheaper, but you can still expect to pay at least 170kr (£16.50; $24.75) for a single, 300kr (£29; $43.50) for a double, without breakfast. These are usually available in the more popular tourist towns.

More affordable is a **room in a private home**, at 100–160kr (£9.50–15.50; $14.25–23.25) for singles and 180–220kr (£17.50–21.25; $26.25–32.00) for doubles, without breakfast. These have to be booked through the local Tourist Office, which charges a fee of 15kr (£1.50; $2.25). Unfortunately, private rooms may be difficult to find outside the larger towns, and may also have a specified minimum stay.

There are around 90 **HI hostels** around the country, with convenient clusters in the western fjords, the popular hiking areas of the centre, and in the vicinity of Oslo. Standards are unquestionably excellent, but prices are high. Overnight fees start at around 60kr (£5.75; $8.50), but are normally around 90–120kr (£8.50–11.50; $12.75–17.25). However, prices can be as high as 140–160kr (£13.50–15.50; $20.25–23.25) in some hostels. One slight consolation is that a substantial buffet breakfast is included in the overnight price at most hostels charging over 130kr (£12.50; $18.75); otherwise most serve breakfast for 40–50kr (£4–5; $6.00–7.50) or evening meals for 70–80kr (£6.50–7.50; $9.75–11.25). It is advisable to have an HI card, otherwise you will have to pay an extra 25kr (£2.50; $3.75), assuming you are admitted to the hostel. Only a few hostels operate throughout the year. Most open from June to September only; some for even shorter periods.

Groups of three to seven travellers planning to stay in the same area for a while might consider hiring a chalet. **Chalets** (*hytte*) are let by the week only and prices vary from 60–150kr (£5.75–14.50; $8.50–21.75) per person per night. In the peak period of late June to mid-August expect to pay about 90–110kr (£8.50–10.50; $12.75–15.75) p.p. per night. At other times prices fall, so that in

May, or September to December, chalets are let out for perhaps two thirds of the peak-season price. Most chalets are located in rural areas, ideal for hiking and fishing. Just occasionally, a chalet can be found in the suburbs of the main towns.

There are some 1300 **campsites**, rated with from one to three stars according to the facilities available. There are no fixed prices, so charges can vary considerably. Most cost 50–60kr (£5.00–5.75; $7.50–8.50) for a tent, with a fee of 5–10kr (£0.50–1.00; $0.75–1.50) per occupant. Sites do not accept reservations, but these are not necessary in any case, and while the FICC camping carnet is valid, it is not essential. An increasing number of sites offer self-catering chalets for rent, with one-night stays possible. Sleeping between four and six people, these chalets have fully equipped kitchens and prices range from 250–350kr (£24.00–33.75; $36.00–50.50) per night. All the sites, complete with addresses, telephone numbers, facilities and opening times are listed in the brochure 'Camping in Norway', published annually by the Norwegian Tourist Board.

As in neighbouring Sweden and Finland, the right to **sleep rough** is written into the law, with certain restrictions. You are allowed to camp for two days on any uncultivated land or open area without asking permission, provided you pitch your tent at least 150 metres away from the nearest habitations. Between 15 April and 15 September, avoid setting fires in open fields or woodland areas. Wherever you may be camping or sleeping rough, it is likely to get very cold at night, even during the summer, so a good sleeping bag and tent with a flysheet is recommended. Nor is there any time of the year that is particularly free of rain (Bergen especially is renowned for its wet weather). It is also advisable to have a good mosquito repellent.

Anyone heading out into the countryside who would prefer a roof over their head should contact the Norwegian Mountain Touring Association for a list of the simple **mountain huts** they operate throughout the country. Open at Easter, and from late June to early September, these huts cost 50–150kr (£5.00–14.50; $7.50–21.75) per night. Non-members pay an additional 50kr (£5; $7.50) surcharge. Mountain huts can provide an alternative to hostelling, or act as a supplement in areas where there are no hostels. In the Lofoten Islands, it is possible to rent old **fishermen's cabins** (*rorbuer*), although advance booking is essential.

Note: There are no longer any telephone area codes as such in Norway. A full 8-digit number which includes the area code is now dialled.

ADDRESSES

Norwegian Tourist Board	Charles House, 5–11 Lower Regent Street, London SW1Y 4LR (tel. 0171 839 6255).
Norwegian YHA	Norske Vandrerhjem, Dronningensgate 26, N-0154 Oslo 1 (tel. 0242 1410).
'Hytte' (Chalets)	Den Norske Hytteformidling, Kierschowsgate 7, Boks 3207 Sagene, N-0405 Oslo 4 (tel. 0235 6710). Fjordhytter, Jan Smrgsgate 11, N-5011 Bergen (tel. 0523 2080).
'Rorbuer'	Lofoten Reiselivslag, Boks 210, N-8301 Svolvaer (tel. 0887 1053).
Mountain huts	Den Norske Turistforening, Stortinsgate 28, Oslo 1.
Camping	Norges Campingplassforbund, Dronningensgate 10–12, N-0152 Oslo 1 (tel. 0242 1203).

Bergen

TOURIST OFFICES

Bergen Reiselivslag, Slottsgt. 1, N-5003 Bergen (tel. 5531 3860). Contact the Bergen Tourist Board if you want information on the city in advance.

Turistinformasjon (tel. 5532 1480). From the train and bus stations on Strømgaten, walk left and right respectively before turning down Kaigaten and then along Starvhusgaten to the pavilion on Torgalmenning (a 10-minute walk). Open May–Sept., Mon.–Sat. 8.30 a.m.–9 p.m., Sun. 10 a.m.–7 p.m.; Oct.–Apr., Mon.–Fri. 10 a.m.–3 p.m.

HOTELS

Kalmar Inn, Jon Smørsgate 11 (tel. 5523 1860). Doubles from 500kr (£48; $72).

Steens Frokosthotel, Parkveien 22 (tel. 5532 6993). Expect to pay around 590kr (£56.75; $85.25) in doubles.

Håkon, Håkonsgaten 27 (tel. 5523 2028). Doubles from 435kr (£42; $63).

PENSIONS/GUESTHOUSES

Fagerheim Pensjonat, Kalvedalsveien 49A (tel. 5531 0172). Singles around 170kr (£16.50; $24.75); doubles around 300kr (£29; $43.50).

Mrs Bernstens, Klosteret 16 (tel. 5523 3502). Doubles around 320kr (£31; $46.50).

Kloster Pension, Klosteret 12 (tel. 5590 2158).

Myklebust Pensjonat, Rosenbergsgt. 19 (tel. 5531 1328). Doubles 380–400kr (£36.50–38.50; $54.75–57.75).

Olsnes Guesthouse, Skirebakken 24 (tel. 5531 2044). Singles around 135kr (£13; $19.50), doubles around 245kr (£23.50; $35.25). From railway station turn uphill towards the Leprosy Museum.

PRIVATE ROOMS
Available at the Tourist Office. Singles 160–190kr (£15.50–18.25; $23.25–27.50); doubles 260–320kr (£25–31; $37.50–46.50). Commission of 15kr (£1.50; $2.25) for one person, 20kr (£2; $3) for two people.

HI HOSTEL
Montana, Johan Blyttsveien 20 (tel. 5529 2900). Open 15 Feb.–15 Nov. 141kr (£13.60; $20.50) for HI members. Best reserved ahead. The HI Information Office at Strandgaten 4 (tel. 5532 6880) will inform you whether there are beds available. Strandgaten runs off Torgalmenning. The hostel is 4km from the town centre, roughly halfway up Mt Ulriken. Take bus 4 from the head post office (right off Kaigaten/Starvhusgaten) to Lægdene.

HOSTELS
Intermission, Kalfarveien 8 (tel. 5531 3275). Open mid-June–mid-Aug. from 5 p.m. Mixed dorm 90kr (£8.50; $12.75). See the hostel immediately above for directions.

Vågenes, J. L. Mowinckelsvej (tel. 5516 1101) 110kr (£10.50; $15.75) p.p. for doubles with kitchen facilities, mattresses on the floor, 85kr (£8; $12). Call ahead. A 10-minute trip on bus 19.

Bergen Interpoint, Kalfarveien 77 (tel. 5531 8125). Open 1 July–mid-Aug. 90kr (£8.50; $12.75). Turn right out of the station and walk along Kalfarveien for 10 minutes.

CAMPING
Bergenshallen, Vilhelm Bjerknesveien 24 (tel. 5527 0180). Open 24 July–10 Aug. 50kr (£5; $7.50) per tent and all occupants. A 10-minute trip on bus 3 from Strandgaten (see **Tourist Offices** above).

Lone (tel. 5524 0820). Not cheap. Far from the centre.

FREELANCE CAMPING
Provided you follow the normal rules you can pick your spot. Camping on top of Mt Fløyen is popular. To reach the top it is an hour's walk by a well-maintained path, or a funicular ride costing 26kr (£2.50; $3.25) (half price for students).

Oslo

TOURIST OFFICES
Oslo Tourist Board, Rådhuset, N-0037 Oslo 1 (tel. 2233 4386). Contact this office to reserve hotels, pensions or guesthouses in advance.
Turistinformasjon Rådhusplassen (tel. 2283 0050). Open May–Sept. Mon.–Fri. 9 a.m.–6 p.m., Sat. 9 a.m.–4 p.m.; the rest of the year open Mon.–Fri. 9 a.m.–5 p.m.
Turistinformasjon Centralstasjon. Open daily 8 a.m.–11 p.m.
USE IT, Trafikanten (tel. 2217 2728). Open mid-June until late Aug., Mon.–Fri. 7 a.m.–5 p.m., Sat. 9 a.m.–2 p.m. Lists of the cheapest accommodation possibilities in the city. In front of Oslo Sentral.

HOTELS
Expect to pay around 500kr (£48; $72) for doubles, with breakfast included

Astoria, Dronningers Gate 21 (tel. 2242 0010). Price valid mid-June–mid-Aug. and at weekends.
Gyldenløve, Bogstadveien 20 (tel. 2260 1090). Price valid mid-June–mid-Aug. only. Tram 1 from the National Theatre.
Majorstuen, Bogstadveien 64 (tel. 2269 3495). Price applies late June–early Aug. only, at other times cheapest doubles start at 550kr (£53; $79.50). Metro to Majorstuen, or tram 1, 2 or 11 from the National Theatre.
Munch, Munchsgatan 5 (tel. 2242 4275). Centrally located.
Smestad, Sørkedalsvn 93 (tel. 2214 6490). Price valid June–Aug.

PENSIONS/GUESTHOUSES
Bella Vista, Årrundveien 11b (tel. 2265 4588). Singles around 200kr (£19.25; $29), doubles around 350kr (£33.75; $50.50).
Cochs Pensjonat, Parkveien 25 (tel 2260 4836). Doubles start around 490kr (£47; $70.50). Beside the royal park, at the corner of Hegdehaugsveien. The entrance is on Hegdehaugsveien.

Ellingsens Pensjonat, Holtegte 25 (tel. 2260 0359). Singles around 190kr (£18.25; $27.50); doubles around 300kr (£29; $43.50). Tram 1 to the Uranienborg Church (Uranienborgveien) from the National Theatre.

Oslo Sjømannshjemmet, Fred Olsen Gate 2/Tollbugata (tel. 2241 2005). Singles around 260kr (£25; $37.50); doubles around 310kr (£30; $45) p.p. Central location, near the harbour.

St Katarinahjemmet, Majorstuveien 21b (tel. 2260 1370). Open mid-June—mid-Aug. Run by nuns. Doubles around 320kr (£31; $46.50) p.p. Tram 1 from the National Theatre to Valkyrie Plass.

Holtekilen Sommerhotell, Micheletsveien 55 (tel. 2253 3853). Open 1 June—20 Aug. Singles around 245kr (£23.50; $35.25), doubles 390kr (£37.50; $56.25).

Hotell-Pension Hall, Fritznorgst. 21 (tel. 2244 3233). Open all year. Singles from 250kr (£24; $36), doubles from 500kr (£48; $72).

PRIVATE ROOMS

Innkvartering in the Central Station book rooms with a two-day minimum stay. Singles are in short supply at 160kr (£15.50; $23.25); doubles 270kr (£26; $39). Commission 20kr (£2; $3).

HI HOSTELS

Haraldsheim, Haraldsheimveien 4 (tel. 2222 2965). No curfew. B&B 145kr (£13.50; $20) for HI members, 170kr (£16.50; $24.75) for non-members from May—Sept. At other times, these prices are increased slightly. Tram 1 or 7 from Storgata to the Sinsen terminus, or a local train to Grefsen.

Holtekilen Sommerhotell, Micheletsveien 55 (tel. 2253 3853). Open 1 June—20 Aug. Dorms 140kr (£13.50; $20.25).

HOSTEL

KFUM (YMCA), Møllergata (tel. 2242 1066). Open July—Aug. Midnight curfew. 75kr (£7; $10.50) for a mattress on the floor. About 500m from Oslo Sentral, just past the cathedral (hostel entrance on Grubbegata).

CAMPING

Bogstad, Ankerveien 117 (tel. 2250 7680). Open year round. 70kr (£6.50; $9.75) to pitch a tent. Chalets for rent at around 400kr (£38.50; $57.75) per night. Bus 41 from the National Theatre to Bogstad.

Ekeberg, Ekebergveien 65 (tel. 2219 8568). Open June—Aug. 70kr (£6.50; $9.75) to pitch a tent. No charge per person. About 3km from the centre. Bus 24 or 72 from Oslo Sentral, or bus 72 from the National Theatre.

FREELANCE CAMPING
You can pitch a tent in the woods to the north of Oslo, provided you stay clear of public areas. Take the metro to Sognsvann. Free camping is also allowed on the Oslofjord island of Langøyene.

Stavanger

TOURIST OFFICE
Turistinformasjon, Jernbaneveien 3, P.O. Box 11, N-4001 Stavanger (tel. 5153 5100). Turn left down Jernbaneveien from the train and bus stations. Open June–Aug. 8.30 a.m.–4 p.m.; Sept.–May. Mon.–Fri. 8.30 a.m.–4 p.m.; Sat. 9 a.m.–1 p.m.

HOTELS
Commandør, Valberggt. 9 (tel. 5189 5300). Doubles from 495kr (£47.50; $71.25) from June–Aug. In the centre of the old town.
Havly Hotel, Valbergyt 1 (tel. 5189 6700). Doubles 490kr (£47; $70.50). From 29 June–15 Aug. Close to the harbour. You need a Fjord Pass – 50kr (£5; $7.50) – to qualify for the summer rates.

PENSIONS/GUESTHOUSES
Gjestehuset Phønix, Lagårdsveien 47 (tel. 5152 0437). Doubles around 360kr (£34.75; $51) from mid-June until mid-Aug. Right at the opposite end of Jernbaneveien from the Tourist Office.
Bergeland Gjestgiveri, Vujedaksgata 1a (tel. 5153 4110). B&B around 220kr (£21.25; $32) per person.
Melands Gjestgiveri, Nedre Holmeg. 2 (tel. 5189 5585). Around 450kr (£43.25; $65) for doubles from mid-June until August. In the centre of the old town.
Paradis Hospits, Lyder Sagensgt. 26 (tel. 5152 9655).
Rogalandsheimen, Muségata 18 (tel. 5152 0188). 290kr (£28; $42) for singles, 390kr (£37.50; $56.25) for doubles; groups of three or four pay 150kr (£14.50; $21.75) per bed. Ten minutes' walk south of the railway station.
Skogstuen Hospits, Stasjonsveien 26 (tel. 5158 5117).
Øglaend Hospits, Jens Zetlitzgt. 25 (tel. 5152 0832). The street begins near the Tourist Office.

HI HOSTEL

Mosvangen YH, Henrik Ibsensgate 21 (tel. 5187 0977). Open June–Aug. 120kr (£11.50; $17.25) for HI members, 150kr (£14.50; $21.75) for non-members, without breakfast. Double rooms are available from 280kr (£27; $40.50). Bus 78 from the train station, or a half hour walk. Kannikgata (near the station) leads into Madlaveien. Left off Madlaveien along the E18, then follow the cycle path round.

CAMPING

Mosvangen, Henrik Ibsensgate 21 (tel. 5187 0977). Open 29 May–1 Sept. 60kr (£5.75; $8.50) per tent and all its occupants. Cabins available. Located by Lake Mosvatn, beside the HI hostel (see above for directions).

Trondheim

TOURIST OFFICE

Trondheim Reiselivslag, P.O. Box 2102, N-7001 Trondheim. Contact the Tourist Board at this address if you want information on the city in advance. On arrival go to their Turistinformasjon on the Market Square (Torvet) (tel. 7352 7201). Open June–mid-Aug., Mon.–Fri. 8.30 a.m.–8 p.m., Sat. 8.30 a.m.–6 p.m., Sun. 10 a.m.–6 p.m.; rest of the year, Mon.–Fri. 9 a.m.–4 p.m., Sat. 9 a.m.–1 p.m. The main bus station is close to Torvet. From the train station head straight ahead from the exit, then turn right at the end of Søndregate.

HOTELS

Trondheim, Kongensgt. 15 (tel. 7352 7030). Doubles around 595kr (£57.25; $86) from late June until early August. Kongensgt. runs out of Torvet.

Singsaker Sommerhotell, Rogertsgate 1 (tel. 7352 0092). Open mid-June–mid-Aug. Singles around 250kr (£24; $36), doubles around 400kr (£38.50; $57.75), with breakfast. About 15 minutes' walk from the train station. Head straight down Søndregate, left at the end of the street, then right along Kjøpmannsgt, over the Nidelva by the Old Town Bridge (Bybrua) and straight on.

Trondheim Leilighesthotell, Gardemoenst. 1A (tel. 7352 3969). Open all year. Singles from 300kr (£29; $43.50), doubles 400–

600kr (£38.50−57.75; $57.75−86.50) with breakfast. About 3km north-east of the city centre.

Gildevangen Hotell, Søndre Gate 22 (tel. 7352 8340). Doubles around 450kr (£43.25; $65) in summer.

PRIVATE ROOMS

Available from the Tourist Office. Singles around 165kr (£16; $24) doubles around 280kr (£27; $40.50), plus a 20kr (£2; $3) commission.

HI HOSTELS

Rosenborg, Weidemannsv. 41 (tel. 7353 0490). B&B 150kr (£14.50; $21.75) for HI members, 180kr (£17.50; $26.25) for non-members. Bus 63 or a 20-minute walk from the train station. Head straight on from the exit down Søndregate, left at the junction with Olav Tryggvasonsgt, and over the Nidelva by the Bakke bru, left along Innherredsveien past the Bakke kirke, right at Nonnegt. then left along Weidemannsv.

Jarlen, Kongensgt. 40 (tel. 7351 3218). 150kr (£14.50; $21.75) for members, 180kr (£17.50; $26.25) for non-members. Doubles available at 400kr (£38.50; $57.75). The street runs out of Torvet.

HOSTELS

Singsaker Sommerhotell, Rogertsgate 1 (tel. 7352 0092). Mattresses on the floor 110kr (£10.50; $15.75). See the entry in **Hotels** section above for directions.

Studentersamfundet (tel. 7389 9538). Five minutes south of the cathedral. Open mid-July−Aug. Mattress 60kr (£5.75; $8.50). Operated by university students.

CAMPING

Sandmoen (tel. 3388 6135) 20kr (£2; $3) per person, 20kr (£2; $3) per tent. About 8km out of Trondheim. Bus 44 or 45 to Sandbakken.

FREELANCE CAMPING

Not permitted in the area around Trondheim.

POLAND (Polska)

While Poland has recently been receiving unprecedented numbers of visitors, good quality tourist information is available in most of the main towns and finding reasonably priced accommodation is relatively straightforward. This said, if you arrive late in a popular town like Cracow or Warsaw you are no longer guaranteed a cheap bed. Prices are also increasing steadily, but remain cheap by Western standards.

Although in Warsaw you will struggle to find doubles in **hotels** for under £20 ($30), elsewhere there are some excellent hotels offering doubles for as little as £10–13 ($15–19.50). Even in Cracow there are several hotels offering singles for £7–9 ($10.50–13.50). These days it is advisable to try and reserve ahead, preferably in writing (use German if you can) a month or so in advance.

PTTK, the Polish Tourist Association, runs a network of cheap hotels known as *Dom Turysty* and *Dom Wycieczkowy*, offering accommodation in singles, doubles, triples, quads and eight-bed dormitories. The local PTTK or Tourist Office will inform you of the whereabouts of any such hotels operating in the locality. The prices of PTTK hotels vary substantially across the country: whereas in Lublin you can get a single for around £4 ($6), the same amount will only get you a bed in a four- or eight-bed room in Warsaw.

It is the widespread availability of **private rooms** that has helped Poland avoid a dire accommodation shortage. In most well-visited towns, private rooms can be arranged through the Biuro Zakwaterowania (and occasionally by other organizations). Prices are generally very low, with singles available for £4 ($6) in destinations as popular as Danzig and Poznan. Even in Warsaw you can find singles for around £6 ($9), with rooms in Cracow being the most expensive, from £7.75 ($11.50) for singles, £11 ($16.50) for doubles. Payment is to the booking agency rather than to your host. It is not uncommon to be approached by locals offering rooms, particularly in the vicinity of the train stations and Tourist Offices. These rooms are normally clean, and safe for you and your belongings. As a rule, prices are a bit lower than rooms fixed up through the local Biuro. The one problem you might have with such offers is the location of the rooms. Try to find out if they are centrally located, or, at the very least, well served by public transport. If you are not specifically asked to pay in hard currency you can often obtain a reduction on the asking price by offering to do so (Deutschmarks and US dollars are especially welcome).

During the university/college summer holidays (July to Aug./

mid-Sept.) the student travel organization ALMATUR runs 'International Student Hostels' in vacant **student residences**. Accommodation is usually in two-or four-bed rooms. While rooms are supposedly only available to holders of the ISIC/IUS card who are aged under 35, this rule is rarely enforced if there is space. There is very little chance of simply turning up and finding a bed in the hostels in Cracow, Danzig or Warsaw, and this is likely to become the case in other cities as well. Possibly your only chance of getting a bed on arrival is to head for the local ALMATUR office early in the morning and enquire if there are any beds available (the office is invariably much easier to reach than the hostel as the latter tends to be situated out from the centre). **International Student Hostels** can be reserved in advance using ALMATUR vouchers, and with these reservations you can reserve a bed until 2 p.m., but thereafter reservations are invalid. It is probably worth making the effort to reserve International Student Hostels in this manner, at least in the main cities, because although initially you pay a bit more this way, you are still getting reasonable value for money as the hostels are by and large very comfortable, and a good place to meet other travellers. Moreover, you will save yourself time looking for accommodation on arrival, and perhaps save yourself money as well.

The Polish affiliate of the HI, the Polish Federation of **Youth Hostels** (PTSM), runs a network of 1,500 hostels known as *Schroniske Mlodziezowe*. A comprehensive list of Polish hostels is available from PTSM, but the abbreviated list in the HI handbook covers the towns that you are most likely to visit. Again, hostels in the main towns should be reserved in advance, preferably by means of a reservation card. At all hostels priority is given to schoolchildren and students, but there is no maximum age limit. All hostels have a 10 p.m. curfew, but you must arrive before 9 p.m. Prices are low (but increasing all the time), with dormitory accommodation ranging in price from £3–5 ($4.50–7.50). Unfortunately, standards are also low, hostels tend to be very crowded, and facilities are rudimentary, while standards of cleanliness at many hostels leave a lot to be desired.

The camping season runs from April/May to September/October. There are **campsites** in all the places you are likely to visit. Polish campsites are certainly cheap, with prices for an overnight stay rarely rising above £3 ($4.50) for a solo traveller. Although facilities at some sites can be very basic, prices are generally set accordingly, so you seldom have cause to grumble about lack of value for money. At many sites it is possible to hire bungalows sleeping two to four people. Average prices work out at around £4 ($6), assuming all the beds are taken. The first-class publication *Polskie Campingi* lists details of all the sites, and shows their locations on a map. Copies are available from main bookstores, or from PZMot (the National Automobile Club). ALMATUR also operates a chain of sites in summer. Any of their local offices will supply you with a list. A few of the HI hostels also allow camping in their grounds, but this is not usually permitted.

ADDRESSES

Polish National Tourist Office	82 Mortimer Street, London W1N 7DE (tel. 0171 636 2217/637 4971)
Hostels	ALMATUR, ul Ordynacka 9, 00364 Warszawa (tel. 262356). Polskie Towarzystwo Schronisk Mlodziezowych, ul Chocimska 28, 00791 Warszawa (tel. 498354/ 498128).
Camping	Polska Federacja Campingu i Caravaningu, ul Króléwska 27a, Warszawa. PZMot, ul. Krucza 6/14, Warszawa (tel. 290467/293541).

Cracow (Kraków) (tel. code 012)

TOURIST OFFICE
Centralny Ośrodek Informacji Turystycznej, ul. Pawia 8, 31–016 Kraków (tel. 220471/226091). Open Mon.–Fri. 8 a.m.–4 p.m., Sat. 8 a.m.–12 p.m. A good source of books, maps and general information on the city and its surroundings. *A Tourist Map of Cracow* is a good basic guide to the city.
ORBIS are at Rynok 41 (tel. 224035) and at the Hotel Cracovia (ul. F. Focha 1, tel. 224632).

BASIC DIRECTIONS
The main bus station is beside the main train station, Kraków Głowny. When you finally make your way through the market stalls in front of the stations, you arrive on ul. Pawia. Crossing the street and heading left, you pass the Tourist Office and the Hotel Warszawski before arriving at the junction of ul. Pawia with ul. Basztowa (right), ul. Westerplatte (more or less straight ahead)

and ul. Lubicz (left). Turning right on ul. Basztowa you pass the information booth for the tram network on the left, and then, again on the left, the end of ul. Szpitalna. Next on the left is the Barbican (Barbakan). Turning left through the Barbican and going straight ahead you can follow Floriańska into Rynek Głowny, the market square at the heart of the city. The walk from the train station to Rynek Głowny takes around 10 minutes.

FINDING ACCOMMODATION

Over the past few years, Cracow has (understandably) become exceptionally popular, especially during the period mid-June to August. If you are travelling at this time it makes sense to try and reserve accommodation as far in advance as possible. Wawel Tourist, ul. Pawia 6 (inside the Hotel Warszawski) books hotels in advance, or on arrival. Write to the office or telephone 221509 to reserve in advance (tel. 229370 or call in person for same-day bookings). Even in peak season, you will probably be able to get a private room if you arrive while the Biuro Zakwaterowania is open, though the later in the day you arrive the less likely you are to get a reasonably located room, or one of the cheaper rooms.

HOTELS

Singles around £5.50 ($8.25), doubles around £7 ($10.50), triples around £8.75 ($13)

Holiday Hotel Mercury al. 29, Listopada 48a (tel. 118826). Operated by the students of the Kraków Academy of Economics. Bus 105 or 129 from Krakw Głowny.

Singles around £7 ($10.50), doubles around £10 ($15), triples around £11 ($16.50) if available

Student Hotel Zaczek, ul. Karasia (tel 335477). One to six beds per room. Open summer only. Near the Biblioteka Jagiellońska on al. Zygmunta Krasińskiego. Tram 15 crosses this street before heading along al. 3 Maja. Either walk right along ul. Krasińskiego then left or walk right along ul. Oleandry from al. 3 Maja into ul. Karasia.

Wisła, ul. Reymonta 22 (tel. 334922). Near the Wisła Kraków football stadium (one of Poland's best teams over the years). Bus 144 stops nearby. Alternatively, you can take tram 15 along al. 3 Maja to the Cichy Kacik terminus, followed by a short walk along ul. D. Chodowieckiego into wł. Reymonta.

Korona, ul. Pstrowskiego 9/15 (tel. 666511). On the fringe of the wartime Jewish ghetto.

Singles around £10 ($15), singles with baths/showers around £12.75 ($19), doubles around £13.35 ($20), doubles with baths/showers around £18.75 ($28)

Warszawski, ul. Pawia 6 (tel. 220622).
Europeijski, ul. Lubicz 5 (tel. 220911).
Saski, ul. Sławkowska 3 (tel. 214222).
Polonia, ul. Basztowa 25 (tel. 221661). Triples around £14.25 ($21.50), triples with bath/shower £17 ($25.50), quads £17.50 ($26.25). Prices may rise following recent renovations.
Pollera, ul. Szpitalna 30 (tel. 221044). Fine location, a 5-minute walk from both Kraków Głowny and the Rynek Głowny.

PRIVATE ROOMS
Biuro Zakwaterowania, ul. Pawia 8 (tel. 221921). Open Mon.–Fri. 7 a.m.–9 p.m.; Sat. 1–6 p.m. Singles from £7.75 ($11.50), singles with bath £9.50 ($14.25), doubles £11 ($16.50), doubles with bath £14 ($21).

PTTK DOM TURYSTY
Westerplatte 15–16 (tel. 229566) Eight-bed dorms £5 ($7.50) per person, singles around £10 ($15), doubles £15–18 ($22.50–27), doubles with bath £20 ($30). Good location, near the main Post Office, within easy walking distance of the town centre and the bus and train stations. Friendly, English-speaking staff.

HI HOSTELS
Ul. Oleandry 4 (tel. 338822). Open all year. Doubles £6 ($9) per person, three-to five-bed rooms £4 ($6), sixteen-bed dorms £3 ($4.50). Tram 15 along al. 3 Maja, until you see ul. Oleandry, the first street on the right. The hostel is a 10–15-minute walk from the centre.
Ul Kościuszki 88 (tel. 221951). Open all year. Tram 1, 2 or 6. Above an Augustine convent. £3 ($4.50) per person.

INTERNATIONAL STUDENT HOSTEL
ALMATUR, Rynek Głowny 7–8 (tel. 215130/226352). ALMATUR will inform you of the current location, as it changes almost annually. Open July–mid-Sept.

CAMPING
Krak, ul. Radzikowskiego 99 (tel. 372122). Category I site. Open

May—Sept. £3 ($4.50) p.p., tent included. Far from town centre.
Tram 8 or 12 to Fizyków, or bus 208.
Krakowania, ul. Zywiecka Boczna (tel. 664191). A good category
II site, cheaper and quieter than Krak. £2 ($3) p.p., tent included.
Bungalows from £8 ($12). Take tram 19 to the Borek Fałecki
terminus along Zakopiańska from ul. Basztowa (or any tram to
Łagiewniki, then change to tram 19). From the terminus, head
in the direction of the housing estate to the right, then take the
path which leads away to the right.

Częstochowa (tel. code 034)

TOURIST OFFICE
Informacji Turystycznej, al. Najświetszej Marii Panny 65, 42—200
Częstochowa (tel. 41360). Open Mon.—Fri. 9 a.m.—6 p.m., week-
ends 10 a.m.—4 p.m. In the underpass at the junction of al.
Najświetszej with ul. Pułaskiego, near Jasna Góra.

FINDING ACCOMMODATION
The constant influx of pilgrims to Częstochowa means that accommodation can be difficult to find on arrival at any time, with the
task becoming virtually impossible at the time of major pilgrimages
and religious festivals. It is advisable to make finding a bed your
first priority on arrival so that if there is nothing suitable available
you can check times for moving on to another town (Cracow is 2—
3 hours away by train, Opole about the same). Those with a railpass
can always take a night train out of Częstochowa if they cannot
find a place to stay (trains leave for a variety of destinations). If
you want to reserve a couchette or sleeper you will find ORBIS at
al. Najświetszej Marii Panny 40/42 (tel. 47987/41769).

HOTELS
Two hotels near the train station are relatively cheap. The better
and cheaper — doubles £10 ($15) — of the two is the Mały, ul.
Katedralna 18 (tel. 43391); the other is the Centralny, ul. Piłsudski-
ego 9 (tel. 44076). Doubles there cost £16.75 ($25).

PRIVATE ROOMS
Enquire at LOGOS, ul. Najświetszej Marii Panny 56 (tel. 42925).
Around £3 ($4.50) per person.

HI HOSTEL
Ul Jasnogórska (tel. 24321). Open June–Aug. only.

INTERNATIONAL STUDENT HOSTELS
Details of any such hostels operating in the city in 1995 will be available from ALMATUR, ul. Armii Krakowej 29 (tel. 54106/44368).

PILGRIM HOSTELS
Dom Pielgrzyma, ul. Wyszynskiego 1–31 (tel. 43302). The hostel is by the car park, directly behind Jasna Góra as you approach the monastery from al. Najświetszej Marii Panny. Quads for £3.35 ($5). Strict 10 p.m. curfew.
Dom Rekolekcyjny, ul. Sw. Barbary 43 (tel. 41177). Near St Barbara's Church. From the end of al. Najświetszej Marii Panny head left along ul. Pułaskiego, turn right down ul. Sw. Kazimierza, then left at ul. Sw. Barbary.

CAMPING
Ul. Olénki 6 (tel. 47495). Category I site.
Ul. Mukusyńskiego 57 (tel. 46755). Category II site.

Gdańsk (tel. code 058)

TOURIST OFFICES
Gdański Ośrodek Informacji Turystycznej, ul. Heweliusza 27, 80–890 Gdańsk (tel. 316637/314355). The head office of the Tourist Board and the main Informacji Turystycznej (IT) point. Open Mon.–Sat. 8 a.m.–4 p.m. Good range of maps and guides and a knowledgeable staff who do their best to answer any enquiries. A short walk from the main train station.
ALMATUR, Długi Targ 11/13 (3rd floor, to the rear) (tel. 317801/317818). Open Mon.–Fri. 9 a.m.–3 p.m. Limited range of publications, but again the staff are very helpful if you have any questions. Near the Town Hall.
ORBIS, ul. Heweliusza 22 (tel. 314944), opposite the 'it' office.

BASIC DIRECTIONS
Gdańsk Dworzec Głowny, the main train station, and the main bus station behind it, are both within 10–15 minutes' walk of Długi Targ, the centre of Gdańsk's Old Town. From the train station take

the underpass to the other side of Podwale Grodzkie. Two streets run off Podwale Grodzkie opposite Gdańsk Dworzec Głowny: ul. Heweliusza and ul. Elzbietańska. Turning right along Podwale Grodzkie then left .along ul. Wały Jagiellonskie and straight on, you arrive at the old Upland Gate (Brama Złota) into Ulica Kługa, which opens out into Długi Targ by the imposing Town Hall.

THE TRI-CITY
Gdańsk, Sopot and Gdynia combine to make up a conurbation often referred to as the Tri-City (population around 1 million). Travelling around the conurbation is relatively easy. Trams run within but do not cross the boundaries of the three constituent parts of the Tri-City. Buses do run between the different parts, as do frequent local trains. The journey time from Gdańsk Dworzec Głowny to Gdynia Dworzec Głowny by local train is around 25–30 minutes, but there are frequent express trains which make the trip in about half that time.

FINDING ACCOMMODATION
Hotels and hostel accommodation are best reserved in advance if you are arriving in Gdańsk during the summer, especially in July and August. Not only are increasing numbers of visitors coming to see the historic Old Town but the beaches of Gdańsk and Sopot are the most popular in Poland, which ensures that hotels and hostels in the Tri-City are frequently filled to capacity during the summer.

HOTELS
Expect to pay around £9.50–11.50 ($14–17) for singles, £13.50–16.50 ($20–25) for doubles, and £16.00–22.50 ($24–34) for doubles with a shower bath

Jantar, Długi Targ 19 (tel. 312716). Also triples with showers around £18 ($27).
Piast, ul. Piastowska 199/201 (tel. 530928).
Żabianka, ul. Dickmana 15 (tel. 522772).
Dom Harcerza, ul. Zam Urami 2/10 (tel. 313621).
Mesa, ul. Waly Jagelliońskie 36 (tel. 318052). Recommended.
OPO, ul. Wiejska 1 (tel. 524636).
Students' Home, ul. Polanki 65 (tel. 524212).
Pensjonat Irena, ul. Chopina 36 (tel. 512074). In Sopot.
Pensjonat Maryla, ul. Sepia 22 (tel. 510034). In Sopot.
Antracyt, ul. Korzeniowskiego 19d (tel. 206811). In Gdynia.
Miastral, ul. Ejsmonda 2 (tel. 221542). In Gdynia.

PRIVATE ROOMS

Singles in the Tri-City cost around £4 ($6), doubles around £6 ($9). The relevant agencies are located as follows: in Gdańsk at ul. Elżbietańska 10–11 (tel. 319444/338840), in Sopot at ul. Dworcowa 4 (tel. 512617), and in Gdynia at ul. Dworcowa 7 (tel. 218265). The offices in Sopot and Gdynia are down the street from the train stations. In summer, there are usually locals offering rooms outside the office in Gdańsk.

DOM TURYSTY

In Sopot/Sopot Kamienny Potok at ul. Zamkowa Góra 25 (tel. 518011).

HI HOSTELS

Ul. Smoluchowskiego 11 (tel. 323820). £4 ($6) for dorms. In Gdańsk-Wrzeszcz, about 1.5km from Gdańsk Dworzec Główny. From the train station, take tram 2, 8, 12, 13 or 14 as far as ul. Zwyciestwa, from which the hostel is only a short walk.

Ul. Wałowa 21 (tel. 312313). 10 p.m. curfew. £4 ($6) for dorms. Smaller rooms are available. A 10-minute walk from Gdańsk Dworzec Główny station. Turn left off Heweliusza along Rajska, and then right at Wałowa.

Grunwaldzka 238/240 (tel. 411660). £4 ($6) for dorms. In a sports centre in Gdańsk-Wrzeszcz, near the boundary with the suburb of Oliwa. Tram 2, 4, 7, 8 or 14. The closest train station to the hostel is Gdańsk-Zaspa.

Ul. Morska 108c (tel. 270005). In Gdynia, close to the Gdynia-Grabowek train station. Tram 22, 25, 26 or 30, or bus 109, 125 or 141.

Ul. Kartuska 245b (tel. 324187).

INTERNATIONAL STUDENT HOSTELS

Dom Studencki nr. 3, ul. Polanki 65, Oliwa (tel. 524212). Tram 6 or 12.

Hotel Studencki nr. 7, ul. Hibernia 32, Gdansk-Wrzeszcz.

HOSTEL

YMCA, ul. Zeromskiego 26, Gdynia (tel. 203115). Open 15 June–31 Aug. £5 ($7.50). In the town centre, about 10 minutes' walk from Gdynia Dworzec Głowny.

CAMPING

Gdańsk-Jelitkowo, ul. Jelitkowska 32 (tel. 532731). Open June–mid-Sept. £2.50 ($3.75) p.p. tent included. Bungalows around

£10.50 ($15.75) per night. Clean, well-maintained site. Tram 6 from Gdańsk Dworzec Główny to the Jelitkowo terminus, past the pond and out on to the main road, then left along to the site entrance.

Gdańsk-Brzeźno, ul. Gen. Hallera 234 (tel. 566531/435531). Open mid-May—Oct. Tram 7, 13 or 15, or bus 124 or 148 all stop reasonably close to the site.

Gdańsk-Sobieszewo-Orle, ul. Lazurowa 5 (tel. 380739). Well out to the east of the centre. Bus 112 runs by the site.

Lublin (tel. code 081)

TOURIST OFFICE

Informacji Turystycznej, ul. Krakowskie Przedmieście 78, 20–101 Lublin (tel. 24412). Open Mon.–Fri. 9 a.m.–5 p.m., Sat. 10 a.m.–2 p.m. Well supplied with maps and other information. Exceptionally helpful staff. Bus/trolleybus 50 and 150 from the train station. From the bus station walk right along the main road (al. Tysiaclecia, left up ul. Lubartowska into pl. Łokietka, then right along ul. Krakowskie Przedmieście.

ALMATUR, ul. Langiewicza 10 (tel. 33238). Open Mon.–Fri. 9 a.m.–4.30 p.m.

ORBIS, ul. Narotowicza 31–33 (tel. 22256/22259).

HOTELS

Lublinianka, ul. Krakowskie Przedmieście 56 (tel. 24261). Singles around £6 ($9), doubles around £11 ($16.50). Good central location, between pl. Łokietka and the Tourist Office.

Motel PZM, ul. B. Prusa 8 (tel. 34232). Singles £9–12 ($13.50–18.00), doubles with bath £18 ($27). From the bus station go right along the main road (al. Tysiaclecia), then right at ul. B. Prusa. From pl. Łokietka go down ul. Lubartowska, left along al. Tysiaclecia, then right.

ZNP Dom Noclegowy, ul. Akademicka 4 (tel. 38285). Singles £4 ($6), doubles with bath £7 ($10.50). By the Marie Skłodowskiej-Curie university. From the train station take trolleybus 150 along ul. Krakowskie Przedmieście into al. Racławickie to the junction with ul. Łopacińskiego. Walk down the latter, go left at the end of the street, then almost immediately right down ul. Akademicka.

PTTK DOM WYCIECZKOWY

Ul. Krakowskie Przedmieście 29 (tel. 22102). Singles £4—6 ($6—9), doubles £5.00—7.50 ($7.50—11.25), triples £7.25—9.00 ($11.00—13.50). Prices per person are very low in the four-bed dormitories. Excellent location, a short distance along ul. Krakowskie Przedmieście from pl. Łokietka.

HI HOSTEL

Ul. Długosza 6a (tel. 30628). Seniors pay around £3 ($4.50), juniors slightly less. Usually you can camp in the hostel garden. Trolleybus 160 from the train station or ul. Krakowskie Przedmieście. Just after ul. Krakowskie Przedmieście runs into al. Racławickie you will see a large park (Ogrd Saski) on the right. al. Długosa is off al. Racławickie to the right at the end of the park.

CAMPING

There are several sites in Lublin, details of which are available from the Tourist Office, as well as the directions how to get to the sites.

Ul. Stawinkowska 46 (tel. 32231). Bungalows available. From ul. Krakowskie Przedmieście take bus 18 or 32 (ask the Tourist Office for exact directions if you can).

Ul. Nad Zalawem 12 (tel. 40831). Take bus 49.

Poznań (tel. code 061)

TOURIST OFFICE

Informacji Turystycznej, Stary Rynek 77, 61—772 Poznań (tel. 526156). Open Mon.—Fri. 9 a.m.—5 p.m., Sat. 10 a.m.—2 p.m. *A Tourist Guide to Poznań* contains a good street map of the central area.

ALMATUR, ul. Fredy 7 (tel. 523645).

ORBIS (tel. 330281) are in the Orbis-Poznań Hotel at pl. Dąbrowskiego 1.

BASIC DIRECTIONS

The main train station (Poznań Głowny) is about 15—20 minutes' walk from the Stary Rynek at the heart of the old town. The main bus station is about 500m from Poznań Głowny, to the right along ul. Towarowa. Trams 5 and 21 run from the main exit of the train station (between platforms 1 and 4) and the city centre.

HOTELS
Because of the Poznań Trade Fair, hotel prices in Poznań are relatively high by Polish standards. The cheapest hotels are all out from the centre.

Olimpia, ul. Warmińska 1 (tel. 45821/415025). Tram 9 or 11.
Naramowice, ul. Naramowicka 150 (tel. 2006612). In the suburb of Naramowice. Bus 67 or 105.
POSiR, ul. Marcina Chwiałkowskiego 34 (tel. 330511). A sports hotel located just outside the city centre.
Miejskiego, ul. Chwiałkowskiego 34 (tel. 332444).

Near the centre of the old town are three three-star hotels at which you can expect to pay around £11.50 ($17.25) for singles and £12.75 ($19) for doubles.

Poznański, al. Karola Marcinkowskiego 22 (tel. 528121).
Wielkopolska, ul. Sw. Wojciech 67 (tel. 527631).
Lech, ul. Sw. Wojciech 74 (tel. 530151). Take tram 5.

PRIVATE ROOMS
There is a Biuro Zakwaterowania at ul. Głogowska 16 (tel. 60313), across the road from the side entrance to Poznań Głowny. Open Mon.–Fri. 9 a.m.–7 p.m., Sat. 9 a.m.–3 p.m. Around £4 ($6) per person. The ORBIS office is in the Hotel Poznań at pl. Henryka Dabrowskiego 1 (tel. 331811). Singles around £5.75 ($8.50) doubles around £7.00–8.50 ($10.50–13.00). The hotel overlooks the Henryka Dabrowskiego park, not far from the bus station, about 10 minutes' walk from Poznań Głowny. A short distance from the main exit, head right along ul. Towarowa. Go left at the first main junction, then turn right immediately after passing ul. Kosciuszki on the left.

PTTK DOM TURYSTY
Stary Rynek 91 (tel. 528893). Singles around £10 ($15), doubles around £16 ($24). Prices per person in the eight-bed dorms are very low if you are lucky enough to get a bed. Excellent location.

HI HOSTELS
Ul. Berwińiskiego 2/3 (tel. 663680). A 5–10 minute walk from Poznań Głowny. Leave the station by the side exit on to ul. Głogowska, go left and then keep on going until you see ul. Berwińskiego on the right.

Ul. Biskupinska 27 (tel. 221063). Price includes breakfast. Bus 60 or 95.

Ul. Głuszyna 127. This hostel has the largest capacity of the five, but rather frustratingly is both inconveniently located and lacking a telephone. To get there, take a local train to Starołeka, then bus 58 from the station.

INTERNATIONAL STUDENT HOSTELS
The ALMATUR office at ul. Aleksandra Fredry 7 (tel. 523645/520344) will have details of where any hostels may be operating in 1995, as the locations vary from year to year.

CAMPING
The two campsites are about 9km from the city centre. Bungalows are available at both sites.

Strzeszynek, ul. Koszalińska 15 (tel. 417224). Open May–Sept. Pleasantly located by a lake in the north-west of Poznań. Bus 95.

Ławica, ul. Wichrowa 100 (tel. 43225). On the western fringe of the city. Bus 122 takes a long route to the site.

Stettin (Szczecin) (tel. code 091)

TOURIST OFFICES
A Tourist Map of Szczecin provides a good basic guide to the city. For further information or help in finding accommodation, contact:

Informacji Turystycznej, ul. Wyszynskiego 26 (tel. 337918).
ORBIS, pl. Zwyciestwa 1 (tel. 45154/43106).
Pomerania, pl. Brama Portowa 4 (tel. 47208). Can book private accommodation.

HOTELS
The two cheapest hotels are both sports hotels located out from the city centre. The most conveniently sited is the Pogon, ul. Twardowskiego 12 (tel. 72878), near the Pogon Szczecin football stadium, a 5-minute walk from Szczecin-Turzyn train station. The Wojewdzki Dom Sportu, ul. Unisławy 29 (tel. 222856) is far from the centre.

Reasonably priced rooms are available at three hotels in the

central area. Cheapest of these is the Pomorski, by the Harbour
Gate at Brama Portowa 4 (tel. 36051). The Piast, pl. Zwyciestwa 3
(tel. 3071) is slightly more expensive than the Brama Portowa. The
Gryf, al. Wojska Polskiego 49 (tel. 34035) is a little bit dearer than
the Piast but is definitely the choice hotel amongst the three centrally located hotels listed here. Doubles cost around £14.50 ($22).
Al. Wojske Polskiego runs off pl. Zywciestwa.

PRIVATE ROOMS
Enquire at ORBIS on pl. Zywciestwa or Pomerania at pl. Brama
Portowa for private rooms.

PTTK DOM TURYSTY
Pl. Batorego 2 (tel. 45833). Near the main bus and train stations,
off ul. Korzeniowskie which runs parallel to ks. Swietopetka. Quads
around £5 ($7.50).

HI HOSTELS
Ul. Monte Cassino 19a (tel. 224761). Open all year. 100 beds.
Ul. Grodzka 22 (tel. 332924). Open July–Aug. Central location:
walk north along Odra and turn west at Stary Rynek.

INTERNATIONAL STUDENT HOSTELS
Locations of the hostels change each year. ALMATUR, ul.
Wawrzyniaka 7 (tel. 233678) will inform you of the latest details.

CAMPING
Expect to pay around £2 ($3) per person

PTTK Camping, ul. Przestrzenna 24, Szczecin-Dabie (tel. 613264).
Open May–Sept. Bungalows available. About 3km from the city
centre. Easily reached from the Szczecin-Dabie train station.
Ul. Szosa Stargardzka 45 (tel. 621288).

Toruń (tel. code 056)

TOURIST OFFICE
PTTK, pl. Rapackiego 2 (tel. 24926). Open Mon.–Fri. 8 a.m.–
4.30 p.m., weekends 10 a.m.–1 p.m.
ORBIS, ul. Żeglarska 31 (just off Rynek Staromiejskie) (tel. 22553/
24346). Can provide brochures on the town. Open Mon.–Fri.

9 a.m.–5 p.m., Sat. 9 a.m.–2 p.m. Tyrusta, at ul. Kopernika 42 (tel. 21523) can provide travel information.

BASIC DIRECTIONS
Most trains stop at the main station (Toruń Głowny), about 3km from the centre, across the River Vistula (Wisła). Buses 12 and 22 maintain a frequent service between the bus terminal near the station and the city centre. The PTTK office is close to the old city gate. The main bus station on ul. Dabrowskiego is within easy walking distance of the old town (Stare Miasto).

HOTELS
Trzy Korony, ul. Stary Rynek 21 (tel. 26031). Singles around £7 ($10.50), doubles around £10 ($15). Communal bathrooms. On the fringe of Rynek Staromiejskie, looking out on to the Town Hall.

Wileński, ul. Mostowa 15 (tel. 25024). Singles around £6.50 ($9.75), doubles around £10 ($15). A considerable step up in quality from the Trzy Korony. Best reserved ahead. Follow ul. Szeroka from Rynek Staromiejskie, then turn right down ul. Mostowa.

Polonia, ul. Szosa Chełmińska (near pl. Teatrainy) (tel. 23028). Singles around £8 ($12), doubles around £14 ($21). A short walk along ul. Chełmińska from Rynek Staromiejskie.

Wodnik, Bulwar Filadelfijski. Singles around £7.50 ($11.25), doubles around £13.50 ($20.25).

Zajazd Starapolski, ul. Żeglarska 10/14 (tel. 26061/26063). Singles around £16.75 ($25), doubles around £23.40 ($35). The street runs out of Rynek Staromiejskie down to the Vistula.

Kosmos, ul. Ks. J. Popiełuszki 2 (tel. 28900). Singles around £13 ($19.50), doubles around £19.50 ($29.25).

PRIVATE ROOMS
Book through the office at Rynek Staromiejskie 20.

PTTK DOM WYCIECZKOWY
Ul. Legionów 24 (tel. 23855). Singles around £4.75 ($7), doubles around £8.50 ($12.75), triples around £11 ($16.50), quads around £14 ($21). A fair distance north of the city centre. From pl. Rapackiego take bus 10 to the third stop to reach the hostel. Before making the trip enquire whether space is available at the PTTK office on pl. Rapackiego (tel. 24926).

HI HOSTEL
Ul. Rudacka 15 (tel. 27242). Around £2.25 ($3.50) per night. Take bus 13 from the centre; the hostel is one stop beyond the main train station.

INTERNATIONAL STUDENT HOSTELS
During the summer, university accommodation is converted into temporary hostels. The ALMATUR office (tel. 20470) located near the university at ul. Gargarina 21 will provide details.

CAMPING
Tramp, ul. Kujawska 14 (tel. 24187). Open May–Sept. Bungalows available. The site is 600m from the main train station.

Warsaw (Warszawa) (tel. code 02 or 022)

TOURIST OFFICES
Centrum Informacji Turystycznej, pl. Zamkowy 1–13 (tel. 6351881). Open daily 10 a.m.–6 p.m. Although the 'IT' office does not book accommodation, it does sell a very useful guide listing all the hotels and accommodation offices. Around £1.75 ($2.75). Take bus 128 from al. Jerozolimskie or bus 150 from ul. Świetokrzyska (see **Basic Directions** below). Both stop near the castle at the foot of the Ślasko-Dabrowski bridge. Buy tickets at a *Ruch* kiosk and cancel both ends on the bus.

ORBIS (tel. 273673/2660271), at the junction of Marzałkowska and Krlewska. Queues at this office are frequently very long. Information is also available at the 'it' points in ORBIS hotels.

'IT', Okecie airport and Warszawa Centralna train station. Long queues are the norm at these two very basic information points.

PTTK, ul. Świętokrysta 36 (tel. 203201). Good for students.

BASIC DIRECTIONS
The main road running past Warszawa Centralna Station is al. Jerozolimskie. Opposite the station are the IOT terminal and the multi-storey Hotel Marriott. Facing these buildings al. Jerozolimskie runs right towards pl. Artura Zawiszy, and then on to the Zachodnia train station and the main bus station. Going left, the street crosses Emilii Plater and Marszałkowska before continuing straight on Most

Ks. Józefa Poniatowskiego which crosses the river Wisła. Going left up Emilii Plater from al. Jerozolimskie takes you round the back of the Palac Kultury and onto ul. Świetokrzyska.

HOTELS

Expect to pay around £8–12 ($12–18) for singles, £10–14 ($15–21) for singles with bath/shower, from £11 ($16.50) for doubles, and around £18–24 ($27–36) for doubles with bath/shower

ZNP (Teachers' Hotel), Wybrzeźe Kościuszki 33 (tel. 279211/6250571). Admits non-teachers when space permits. Prices are at the lower end of the scales quoted above. The hotel is down by the River Wisła.

Pensjonat Stegny, ul. Idzikowskiego 4 (tel. 422768). Far out, on the road to Wilanow Palace.

Skra, ul. Wawelska 5 (tel. 225100). In the Ochota suburb beside the Skra stadium. See Camping Gromada for buses and directions to the stadium.

Orzel, ul. Podskarbińska 11/15 (tel. 105060). In the Praga suburb. Bus 102 or 115.

Druh, ul. Niemcewicza 17 (tel. 6590011). West of the train station. Take tram 7, 8, 9 or 25. Popular with students.

Sokrates, ul. Smyczkowa 9 (tel. 133889/439551) Around the top of the price range quoted above. Overnight price includes breakfast. Tram 4, 19, or 33.

Federacja Mełalowcy, ul. Długa 29 (tel. 314021). From pl. Zamkowy, take ul. Gen. Swierczewskiego west to ul. Długa.

Domu Literatury, Krakowskie Przedmiescie 87–89 (tel. 6850404). Slightly more expensive than the hotels above.

Harctur, ul. Niemcewicza 17 (tel. 6590011). Triples £17 ($25.50), quads £17.50–21.00 ($26.25–31.50). Doubles with bath/shower are at the bottom of the price range quoted above. No doubles, and no singles of any kind. The street is off ul. Raszyńska. Within walking distance of Warszawa Centralna. Take bus 136, 175 or 512, or tram 7, 9 or 25.

Dom Chłopa, pl. Postańców (tel. 279251). No doubles without a bath. Prices at the top of the range quoted above. Located between Nowy Świat and the Palc Kultury.

PRIVATE ROOMS

Syrena, ul. Krucza 17 (tel. 628 7540). Open 8 a.m.–8 p.m. Singles around £6 ($9), doubles around £8.50 ($12.75). Right off al. Jerozolimskie after Marsałkowska.

Romeo and Juliet, Emilii Plater 30 (third floor) (tel. 292993).

Doubles around £22 ($33). Centrally located rooms (opposite the station).

Polonaise, ul. Swietojerska 4/10 (tel. 635 0765). Doubles around £6.75—10.00 ($10—15) per person.

PTTK DOM TURYSTY
Krakowskie Przedmieście 4/6 (tel. 263011/262625). Singles £10 ($15), doubles £8.75 ($13) per person. Well located, near the university. Within walking distance of Warszawa Centralna and the Old Town. From Centralna, head right along Świetokrzyska to the start of Krakowskie Przedmieście. Otherwise take bus 175 heading along al. Jerozolimskie towards the river to the Uniwersytet stop.

HI HOSTELS
Ul. Karolkowa 53a (tel. 328829). 11 p.m. curfew. £5 ($7.50) per person in quads, £4.50 ($6.75) in dorms. Clean, but not central. Out in the Wola suburb. From al. Jerozolimskie take tram 22 or 24 to al. Świerczewskiego, close to the Wola shopping centre.

Ul. Smolna 30 (tel. 278952). 10 p.m. curfew. £4 ($6) for dorms. Well located, off Nowy Świat, opposite the National Museum on al. Jerozolimskie. Within walking distance of Warszawa Centralna.

There are three further HI hostels, all some distance from the city centre:

Ul. Lokalna 51 (tel. 129521).
Ul. Klapotowskiego (tel. 185317).
Ul. Solidarnosci 61 (tel. 184989).

INTERNATIONAL STUDENT HOSTELS
Dziekanka, Krakowskie Przedmiescie 58—60 (tel. 264012). £3 ($4.50) per night.

Wackacyjny, ul. Kickiego 12 (tel. 100985/100981) £6 ($9).

ALMATUR, ul. Kopernika 23 (tel. 263512). ALMATUR office open Mon.—Fri. 8.30 a.m.—8 p.m., Sat. 10 a.m.—6 p.m., Sun. 10 a.m.—3 p.m. Restricted hours Sept.—June, Mon.—Fri. 9 a.m.—3 p.m. Even when the student hostels are not open ALMATUR may help students to find reasonably priced accommodation.

Hotel Studenski, ul. Smyczkowa 5—7 (tel. 438621). £4 ($6) per person. Tram 4, 19 or 33.

CAMPING
Expect to pay around £2.25 ($3.50) p.p. including tent

Gromada, ul. Żwirki i Wigury 32 (tel. 254391). Twin-bedded bungalows £6 ($9) per night. Bus 136, 175, 188 or 512 heading along al. Jerozolimskie towards pl. Artura Zawiszy.

PTTK Camping, ul. Połczyńska 6a (tel. 366716). In the suburb of Wola. Bus 105.

Wisła, u. Bitwy Warszawskiej 1920 (tel. 233748). A short distance south of the bus station and Warszawa Zachodnia train station. Bus 154, 167, 173 or 191.

Wrocław (Breslau) (tel. code 071)

TOURIST OFFICES
ORBIS, Rynek 45 (tel. 447946/447679/444109) is the best office for general tourist information. Open Apr.–Sept., Mon.–Sat. 8 a.m.–5 p.m.; Oct.–Mar., same hours but closed on Sat. A second ORBIS office is located at ul. Gen. Karola Swierczewskiego 62 (tel. 444714), useful for travel information and tickets.

A small Tourist Information operates at Rynek 38 (tel. 443111), open Mon.–Sat. 10 a.m.–4 p.m.

Biuro Usług Turystycznych, ul. Gen. Karola Swierczewskiego 98 (tel. 444101), opposite the station. Open Mon.–Fri. 9 a.m.–5 p.m. and the first Sat. each month 9 a.m.–2 p.m.

ALMATUR, ul. Tadeusza Kościuszki 34 (tel. 443003), open Mon.–Fri. 10 a.m.–4 p.m. offers assistance to students.

If you can get a copy, the publication *A Tourist Map of Wroclaw* is indexed and has basic background information on the main places of historical interest, which are marked on the plan.

BASIC DIRECTIONS
Arriving in Wrocław by train, your most likely point of arrival is Wrocław Głowny, which is about 1.5km to the south of the Rynek. The two bus terminals are both by Wrocław Głowny; one is situated behind it on ul. Sucho, the other diagonally across the square from it on pl. Konstytucji 3 Maja. Most trains from Jelenia Góra, and some from Legnica and Głogów arrive at Wrocław Świebodzki, to the left of the junction of ul. Gen. Karola Swierczewskiego and Podwale, from which Wrocław Głowny is easily reached on foot

by following the inner ring road round to the right from Swie-
bodzki. Trains from Łodź, Trzebnica and Oleśnica arrive at Wrocław
Nadodrze on pl. Staszica, about 2km north of the centre.

HOTELS
The cheapest hotels in Wrocław are all situated well out from the
centre, but there are a number of hotels in and around the centre
which fall within the budget category.

Cheapest hotels

Zeglarz, ul. Władysława Reymonta 4 (tel. 212996). Near the Wro-
    cław Nadodrze train station (the street runs off pl. Staszica on
    tram route 14.
Oficerski, ul. Adama Prchnika 130 (tel. 603303). Far out in the
    south-west of the city. Trams 13, 14 and 20 pass close by the
    hotel.
Ślask (tel. 611611). Far out to the west of the city, located in a
    park close to ul. Oporowska. Trams 1, 4, 5, 13, 16, 18 or 20.
DOSiR, ul. Wejherowska 2 (tel. 550198). Sports hotel, out to the
    west, near the terminus of bus 127.
Nauczycielski, ul. Nauczycielska 2 (tel. 229268). About 20–25
    minutes' walk from the centre off Marii Skłodowskiej-Curie
    beyond the Most Grunwaldzki. Trams 0, 1, 2, 10 or 12.

*Singles around £8.50 ($12.75), singles with baths around £10 ($15),
doubles around £15 ($22.50), doubles with baths around £9 ($13.50).
By Wrocław Głowny unless otherwise stated*

Odra ('Piast II'), ul. Stawowa 13 (tel. 37560/45447).
Piast I, ul. Gen. Karola Swierczewskiego 98 (tel. 30033).
Polonia, ul. Gen. Karola Swierczewskiego 66 (tel. 31021).
Europejski, ul. Gen. Karola Swierczewskiego 88 (tel. 31071).
Grand, ul. Gen. Karola Swierczewskiego 100 (tel. 36071).
Dom Kultury, ul. Kazimierza Wielkiego 45 (tel. 442866). A short
    walk from the Rynek. Rooms at this hotel are a bit cheaper than
    the prices quoted above.

PRIVATE ROOMS
Available from the Biuro Ustug Turystycznych (ODRA-tourist), ul
Gen. Karola Swierczewskiego 98 (tel. 444101). See **Tourist Offices**
for opening hours. Across the street from Wrocław Głowny. Singles
£7.30 ($11), doubles £12 ($18).

PTTK DOM TURYSTY

Ul. Karola Szajnochy 11 (tel. 443073). Close to the Rynek. Walking from Wrocław Głowny turn left along ul. Kazimierza Wielkiego from Świdnicka, right at ul. Gepperta, then left into ul. Karoly Szajnochy. Ul Gepperta continues into pl. Solny, which adjoins the Rynek.

HI HOSTELS

Ul. Kołłataja 20 (tel. 38856). £5 ($7.50). Near Wrocław Głowny.
Ul. Kiekzowska 43 (tel. 253076). Large family hostel. Take bus N from the centre.

INTERNATIONAL STUDENT HOSTELS

ALMATUR (see Tourist Offices) will inform you of any hostels operating in the city in 1995.

CAMPING

Camping Stadion Olimpijski, ul. Paderewskiego 35 (tel. 484651). Chalets available. The better of the two sites. Further out, but easier to reach. The site is close to the Olympic Stadium, left off ul. Adama Mickiewicza. Trams 16 and 17 pass close by.

Camping Skaza, ul. Na Grobli (tel. 34442). Chalets available. Near the HI hostel in ul. Na Grobli, by the Oder. About 3km from Wrocław Głowny and the city centre. Difficult to reach by public transport; trams 3, 4 and 5 take you closest, but it's a 20-minute walk from the nearest stop.

Zakopane (tel. code 0165)

TOURIST OFFICES

Tatry, ul. Kościuszki 7. The main information office for Zakopane and its surroundings.

PTTK, ul. Krupówki 37. A good selection of maps and guidebooks, plus information on the mountain refuges operated by PTTK in the area (the vast majority of local refuges are run either by PTTK or ALMATUR).

Biuro Obsługi Ruchu Turystycznego, ul. Krupówki 12 (tel. 2429). Information on refuges.

ORBIS, ul. Krupówki 22 (tel. 4609). Books trains, buses and local excursions, and hotels and private rooms.

HOTELS

Słoneczny, ul. Słoneczny 2a (tel. 666026/66253). A student hotel run by Juventur. Singles £6 ($9), singles with a bath £10 ($15), doubles £11 ($16.50). doubles with a bath £16.50 ($24.75). Prices include breakfast. The hotel is between the train station and the centre of town.

Gazda, ul. Zaruskiego 2 (tel. 5011). Singles £7–10 ($10.50–15.00), singles with a bath £12.00–13.50 ($18.00–20.25), doubles with a bath £18 ($27). Without breakfast.

Tatry Centre, ul Kosciuszki 7 (tel. 4000). £4 ($6) per person in quads.

Rooms at the Morskie Oko, Krupówki 30 (tel 5076), the Imperial, ul. Balzera 1 (tel. 4021), and the Warszawianka, Jagiellońska 7 (tel. 3261) are similar in price to those of the Gazda. Expect to pay around £14.75–17.50 ($22–26) for doubles.

PRIVATE ROOMS

Biuro Zakwaterowania, ul. Kościuszki 7 (tel. 4000). Singles £2.50–3.50 ($3.75–5.25), doubles £4–5 ($6.00–7.50).

ORBIS, ul. Krupówki 37 (tel. 4609) £3.25 ($5) per person.

PTTK DOM WYCIECZKOWY

Ul. Zaruskiego 5 (tel. 3281/3282). Singles with a bath £6 ($9), doubles with a bath £6.25 ($9.50) per person, larger rooms £3 ($4.50) p.p. Near the Post Office.

HI HOSTEL

Ul. Nowotarska 45 (tel. 66203). £3–5 ($4.50–7.50). From the train and bus stations, head towards the centre, go right along ul. Sienkiewiza, then straight across.

CAMPING

Pod Krokiwa, ul. Żeromskiego (tel. 2256). Open May–Aug. Opposite the foot of the ski jump. Tent space £1 ($1.50), plus £1.50 ($2.25) per person.

PORTUGAL

By northern European standards accommodation is cheap here, and there are plenty of possibilities open to budget travellers. In most places it should be quite easy to find somewhere cheap to stay, but it can be difficult on the Algarve in peak season, where it is advisable to write or telephone ahead as early as possible.

Pensions and cheap hotels are inexpensive and convenient options. They are graded and priced by the municipal authority, albeit in a manner which at times seems quite arbitrary. Location does not affect the price, so you have the bonus of being able to stay in the town centre, or near the train station, without having to pay extra for the privilege. **Hotels** are rated from one star up to five stars, with the less expensive *pensoes* and *residencias* graded from one up to three stars. In general, three-star pensions and one-star hotels are roughly similar in price. However, it is quite possible to pay more for a very poor one-star hotel than for a comfortable three-star pension, and vice versa. Prices in one-star hotels/three-star pensions range from 2400–7000$ (£10–29; $15.00–43.75) for singles, 4000–8500$ (£16.75–35.50; $25.00–53.25) per person for doubles. In the lower-rated pensions, singles cost around 1700–2500$ (£7.00–10.50; $10.50–15.75), doubles around 2800–3200$ (£11.75–13.50; $17.50–20.25).

In the smaller towns, seaside resorts, and areas particularly popular with tourists, **rooms in private homes** (*quartos* or *dormidas*) can be both less expensive and more comfortable than pensions. Private rooms are sometimes offered to travellers at bus and train stations. Such offers may be worth considering as private rooms are generally more difficult to find than pensions. Local Tourist Offices have lists of private rooms available in the locality. Alternatively, simply enquire at any house with a sign in the window advertising private rooms (signs are frequently written in several languages).

Hostelling can be a cheap way to see much of the country, but, especially during the peak periods, you may not feel it is worth the added effort, considering the restrictions hostelling imposes. However, hostelling can be a more attractive option in the off-season, as the hostels offer an excellent opportunity to meet other travellers, especially outside Lisbon and Oporto. There are 19 HI hostels and most of the main places of interest have a hostel of some sort, or can be reached on a day-trip from the nearest hostel. Depending on the standard of the hostel, the age of the user and the time of year, the overnight charge for B&B and sheets varies from 900–1500$ (£3.75–6.25; $5.50–9.50). Hostels are open to HI members only, but it is possible to buy a membership card at the hostels, though the 2400$ (£10; $15) fee is roughly twice what under-25s pay to join one of the British associations in advance. Unless the warden agrees to you staying longer, you are limited to three consecutive nights in any hostel. Curfews (midnight 1 May–30 Sept.; 11.30 p.m. at other times) can be a real nuisance, since bars and clubs stay open late, many football matches kick off at 9 p.m., and cinemas often show late films in English. The peak periods for the hostels are June to September, around Christmas, and Holy Week. At these times, it is advisable to write or phone ahead to reserve a bed. As the hostel in Oporto is pitifully small considering the numbers who visit the town, to have a chance of getting a bed at any time of year you will either have to write in advance, or arrive at the hostel or phone ahead between 9–10.30 a.m.

In contrast to Mediterranean countries, **camping** is well worth considering in Portugal. Sites tend to be more conveniently located in and around the main towns than in Greece, Italy or neighbouring Spain. Portuguese sites are seldom more than 5km out from the town centre, and usually have a direct bus link. Nor will you have problems carrying around your tent as left luggage stores are available at all train stations. Camping is a great way to meet the locals as the Portuguese themselves are enthusiastic campers. The relative unpopularity of camping with budget travellers is due to the widespread availability of other cheap accommodation, and nothing to do with the standard of the campsites, which is actually quite high. There are 97 official sites, graded from one star up to four stars, many of which require a Camping Carnet. All the sites have the basic, essential facilities – most even have a café and a supermarket – so bearing in mind the facilities available, prices are very reasonable. Even at some of the more expensive sites around Lisbon and on the Algarve charges are unlikely to exceed 500$ (£2; $3), with around 400$ (£1.50; $2.25) per tent and per person being the norm elsewhere. **Camping outside official sites** is permitted with the consent of the landowner, but is not allowed in towns, at any spot less than one kilometre from a beach, or from an official site, or in the vicinity of a reservoir.

ADDRESSES

Portuguese National Tourist Office	22–25a Sackville Street, London W1X IDE (tel. 0171 494 1441).
Portuguese YHA	Assoçiaão de Utentes das Pousadas de Juventude, Rua Andrade Corvo No. 46,

	1000 Lisboa (tel. 3511 571054).
Camping	Federaçao Portuguesa de Campismo, 5 Rua Voz de Operario, Lisboa (tel. 01 862350).
	Orbitur, Av. Almirante Gago Coutinho 25d, Lisboa. Orbitur operates 15 sites which are amongst the best managed, but also the most expensive, in Portugal.
	A free list of the 97 official sites, 'Portugal Camping', is available from the Portuguese National Tourist Office, and from local Tourist Offices.

Coimbra (tel. code 039)

TOURIST OFFICE
Posto de Turismo, Largo da Portagem (tel. 23886/33019/33028). Open Apr.–Sept., Mon.–Fri. 9 a.m.–7 p.m., weekends 9 a.m.– 12.20 p.m. and 2–5.30 p.m.; Oct.–Mar., Mon.–Fri. 9 a.m.–6 p.m., Sat. 10 a.m.–1 p.m. A short walk from Coimbra A train station. Follow the main road (Avenida Emidio Navarro) with the Mondego river on your right until you see the office.

ARRIVING BY TRAIN
Most long-distance trains stop at the Coimbra B station on the outskirts of the town, about 3km from the centre. From Coimbra B, there are frequent connecting trains to the centrally situated Coimbra A.

FINDING ACCOMMODATION
The area around Coimbra A has the least expensive accommodation in town, particularly Rua da Sota and the streets running off it. While this is not the most attractive of areas, the pensions are generally perfectly acceptable and safe.

HOTELS
Expect to pay around 2800–4300$ (£11.75–18.00; $17.50–27.00) for doubles

Flor de Coimbra, Rua da Poo 8. Good inexpensive meals available to residents. Singles around 1700$ (£7; $10.50).

Residencia Luis Atenas, Avda Fernão de Magalhães 68 (tel. 26412/29357). Singles around 2750$ (£11.50; $17.25), doubles around 3850$ (£16; $24), triples around 5500$ (£23; $34.50) with breakfast. The avenue running away to the left from the station.

Residencial Internacional de Coimbra, Avda Fernão de Magalhães (opposite the train station) (tel. 25503). Doubles around 2600$ (£11; $16.50). Prices per person are lower in triples and quads.

Aviz, Avda Fernão de Magalhães 64 (tel. 23718).

Rivoli, Praça do Comercio 27 (tel. 25550). Two-star pension. Doubles around 3800$ (£16; $24).

Madeira, Fernão de Magalhães 26 (tel. 20569).

Atlântico, R. Sargenta Mor 42 (tel. 26496).

Casa Branca, R. Elisio de Moura (tel. 723019/96).

Gouveia, Rua João de Rouão 21 (tel. 29793). Not central, but close to the station.

Jardim, Avda Emidio Navarro 65 (tel. 25204). Two-star pension. The street runs alongside the river.

Parque, Avda Emidio Navarro 42 (tel. 29202). Two-star pension. Doubles around 3200$ (£13.50; $20.25), doubles with bath around 3800$ (£16; $24).

Diogo, Praça da República 18–2. In the university area.

Antunes, Rua Castro Matoso 8 (tel. 23048). University quarter, beneath the aqueduct. Advance reservation advised.

HI HOSTEL
Rua Henriques Seco 14 (tel. 22955). Excellent hostel. B&B 1400$ (£6; $9), doubles available at 3500$ (£14.50; $21.75). Close to the Parque de Santa Cruz. From Coimbra A take bus 7, 8, 29 or 46 to Praça República. From the square, walk up Rua Lourenco de Almeida Azevdo along the side of the park until you see Rua Henriques Seco.

CAMPING
Parque de Campismo Municipal de Coimbra, Praça 25 de Abril (tel. 712997). 500$ (£2; $3) per tent, including person.

Évora (tel. code 066)

TOURIST OFFICE
Turismo, Praça do Giraldo 73 (tel. 22671). Open June–Sept., Mon.–Fri. 9 a.m.–7 p.m., weekends 9 a.m.–12.30 p.m. and 2–5.30 p.m.; Oct.–May., Mon.–Fri. 9 a.m.–6 p.m., weekends 9 a.m.–12.30 p.m. and 2–5.30 p.m. Turismo will help you find private rooms. The office is on the town's main square, about 15 minutes' walk from the train station (no buses). Follow Rua de Baronha from the train station, then straight on when the street runs into Rua da República. Also Av. de S. Sebastião (tel. 31296).

HOTELS
Évora is a particularly popular destination, with the result that hotel prices in peak season are higher than usual (prices fall by 10–20% in the off-season). The vast majority of the cheaper hotels are located within a radius of about 1km from Praça do Giraldo.

Os Manuéis, Rua do Raimundo 35a 1st floor (tel. 22861). Singles 2200$ (£9; $13.50), doubles from 3500$ (£14.50; £21.75). The street runs off Praça do Giraldo.

Casa Portalegre, Travessa do Barão 18 (tel. 22326). Another (relatively) cheap establishment close to Praça do Giraldo, in a street off Rua do Raimundo.

O Eborense, Larga da Misericórdia 1 (tel. 22031). B&B in doubles from 9000$ (£37.50; $56.25). Off Rua da República, close to Praça do Giraldo.

Giraldo, Rua Meroadores 15 (tel. 25833). Singles from 2850$ (£11.80; $17.75), doubles from 4200$ (£17.50; $26.25). Prices per room fall by around 1000$ (£4; $6) in winter. Two blocks from Praça do Giraldo.

Policarpo, Rua da Freira de Baixo 16 (tel. 22424). B&B in doubles from 4000$ (£16.75; $25). Near the cathedral.

CAMPING
Parque de Campismo Évora (tel. 25190) Orbitur site. 350$ (£1.45; $2.20) per tent, 400$ (£1.50; $2.25) p.p. The site is off Estrada das Alcácovas, about 4km from the centre, served by just one bus each day. From Praça do Giraldo walk down Rua Raimundo then turn along Estrada das Alcáçovas at the end of the street.

Faro (tel. 089)

Many telephone numbers in Faro have recently been changed as part of the national system. If you have difficulty getting through, check the number with the tourist office.

TOURIST OFFICE
Turismo, Rua da Misericordia 8 (tel. 803604). By the harbour. Open daily 9 a.m.–7 or 8 p.m.

FINDING ACCOMMODATION
During the summer, cheap accommodation can be difficult to find in Faro unless you look early in the day. Many people only stay one night in Faro (before flying out or after flying in) so if you can start your search early you have a fair chance of benefiting from this turnover of visitors. The Tourist Office will supply you with a list of pensions, but leave it up to you to phone around or call in person. The best streets in which to look for pensions are Filipe Alistão, Alportel, Conselheiro Bivar, Infante Dom Henrique and Vasco da Gama. Not only are beds difficult to find in July and August, but, in response to the high level of demand, hoteliers often increase their prices. At the very height of the season, private rooms may be your best option.

HOTELS
Expect to pay from 2000–2700$ (£8.50–11.25; $12.75–17.00) for singles, 2700–3400$ (£11.25–14.00; $17–21) for doubles

One-star:

Mirense, Rua Capitão Mor 5(tel. 22687).
Nunes, Rua Horta Machado 28 (tel. 27876).

Two-star:

Dandy, Rua Filipe Alistão 62 (tel. 824791). Recommended.
Delfim, Rua da Alportel 121–1 (tel. 22578).
Carminho, Rua da Alportel 169a (tel. 23709).
Dina, Rua Teofilo Braga 43 (tel. 23897).
Avenida, Av. da Republica (tel. 23347).
Madalena, Rua Conselheiro Bivar 109 (tel. 805806). One of the best.

Novo Lar, Rua Infante Dom Henrique 85 (tel. 24389).
Tivoli, Praça Alexandre Herculano 6–1 (tel. 82854).
Tinita, Rua do Alportel 58 (tel. 25040).

Three-star:

Rest. O Faraó, Largo da Madalena 4 (tel. 823356).
Marim, Rua Gonçalo Barreto 1 (tel. 24063).
Oceano, Travessa Ivens 2–1 (tel. 823349). Doubles around 5000$
  (£21; $31.50).
Afonso III, Rua Gomes Freire (tel. 27042/27054).
Solar do Alto, Rua de Berlim 53 (tel. 22091).
Samé, Rua do Bocage 66 (tel. 24375/23370).
Residencial Galo, Rua Filipe Alistão 41 (tel. 26435). Doubles around
  3200$ (£13.50; $20.25).

PRIVATE ROOMS
The Tourist Office have a good supply of rooms, some well located,
others less so. In peak season, take what you get. As is the case
throughout the Algarve during the summer, touts frequently offer
rooms at the bus and train stations. Expect to pay 2000–3000$
(£8.50–12.50; $12.75–18.75) for doubles.

CAMPING
Parque de Campismo Municipal da Ilha de Faro, Ilha de Faro (tel.
817876). Year-round site. Often full. Very crowded in summer.
Camping Carnet required. Bus 16 from the airport or town centre
to Praia de Faro. May–Sept. bus runs twice hourly from 7.30 a.m.–
8 p.m., hourly the rest of the year. Infrequent service at weekends.

Lisbon (Lisboa) (tel. code 01)

TOURIST OFFICES
Turismo, Palácio da Foz, Praça dos Restauradores (tel. 346 3314/
346 3643). Open Mon.–Sat. 9 a.m.–8 p.m., Sun. 10 a.m.–6 p.m.
The office distributes a simple plan of the city and lists of accommodation. Branch offices operate at the Santa Apolónia station, open
Mon.–Sat. 9 a.m.–7 p.m., and at the airport, open daily round-the-
clock. Both the branch offices can be very busy so you might prefer
to just head to the main office.

ARRIVING AND BASIC DIRECTIONS

Most long-distance trains arrive at the Lisboa Santa Apolónia station, by the River Tajus (Rio Tejo), just over 15 minutes' walk from the Tourist Office. Bus 9 or 9A from the side of the station by the Tajus will take you to Praça dos Restauradores. To walk, simply keep the river on your left and go straight on until you see the broad expanse of Praça do Comércio with the statue of Dom José I on your right, off Terreiro do Paco. Diagonally right across this square is the start of Rua do Ouro, which you can follow into Praça Dom Pedro IV, commonly known as Rossio (the streets to the right of Rua do Ouro are laid out on a grid pattern, an area known as the Baixa). Turning left from the National Theatre brings you to the Rossio train station (services to Queluz and Sintra) at the foot of Praça dos Restauradores. On the left as you walk up Praça dos Restauradores is the Elevador da Gloria which provides an easy means of reaching the Bairro Alto.

Arriving by train the other two railway stations are within easy reach of the centre. Trains from the Algarve and the south terminate at the Barreiro train station across the Tajus, from which there are frequent services to the terminal on Terreiro do Paco, a short walk from Praça do Comércio. The Cais do Sodré station by the Tajus on Praça Duque da Terceira handles traffic from Cascais, Estoril and Oeiras. Walking away from Cais do Sodre with the river on your right you reach Praça do Commércio after about 5 minutes' walk.

The terminal for buses of the state-run Rodoviária Nacional is on Avenida Casal Ribiero, close to Praça Saldanha, and lined to Praça dos Restauradores by buses 1, 21, 32 and 36. Arriving at the airport, you can take bus 44 or 45 to Avenida da Liberdade, or the quicker *linha verde* (green line express). At around 300$ (£1.25; $2) the trip on the *linha verde* costs roughly twice that of the normal service buses.

TROUBLE SPOTS

Although prostitutes use some of the cheapest hotels around the Rossio station, this area is not really the red light district of the city. The crowds of people in this part of town mean it is quite safe for women to walk around in until the early hours of the morning. More dangerous (for women especially) are the Bairro Alto (which contains the red light district) and Mouraria (around the castle); quarters which many travellers head for to try and escape the noise and bustle of Rossio. Women are advised not to walk alone in these parts of town after dusk.

FINDING ACCOMMODATION

At most times of the year finding a cheap room near Rossio should be quite easy: singles 2000–2500$ (£8.50–10.50; $12.75–15.75); doubles 3400–4000$ (£14.00–16.75; $21–25). Because of their location, pensions on Avenida da Liberdade fill quickly; those in the streets off the avenue are more likely to have space. In the summer months, however, you may have difficulty finding accommodation at the prices quoted above as the amount of rooms available just manages to satisfy demand. If you arrive in the afternoon be prepared to take something slightly more expensive, and then look around early next morning. If you are willing to pay 5000–6000$ (£21–25; $31.50–37.50) for a double the main tourist office will find rooms in this price range free of charge.

HOTELS

Rossio area:

Ibérica, Praça da Figueira 10–2 (tel. 886 7026). Doubles around 3300$ (£13.75; $20.50) with breakfast.

Londres, Praça Dom Pedro IV 53–1 (tel. 346 2203). Doubles around 3800$ (£16; $24).

Coimbra e Madrid, Praça de Figueira 3–3&4 (tel. 342 1760). Doubles around 4800$ (£20; $30).

Evora, Rossio/Praça Dom Pedro IV 59–2 (tel. 346 7666). Doubles around 3000$ (£12.50; $18.75).

Do Sul, Rossio/Praça Dom Pedro IV 59–2 (tel. 342 2511).

Beira-Minho, Praça de Figueira 6–2 (tel. 346 1846). B&B. All rooms have baths. Singles around 3800$ (£16; $24), doubles around 4800$ (£20; $30).

Baixa – the lower town; a roughly rectangular area stretching from Praça Dom Pedro IV & Praça de Figueira down to Praça do Comercio:

Arco Bandeira, Rua Arco Bandeira 226–4 (tel. 342 3478). Around 5400$ (£22.50; $33.75) for doubles. Not cheap, but a very comfortable pension. Just off Rossio.

Moderna, Rua dos Correiros 205–4 (tel. 346 0818). Doubles around 4400$ (£18.50; $27.75). Clean rooms.

Angoche, Rua dos Douradores 121–4 (tel. 870711). Doubles around 3600$ (£15; $22.50). Very clean.

Bom Conforto, Rua dos Douradores 83–3 (tel. 878 328). Doubles around 3500$ (£14.50; $21.75).

Norte, Rua dos Douradores 159–1&2 (tel. 878941). Doubles around 4000$ (£16.75; $25).

Santiago, Rua dos Douradores 222–3 (tel. 874353).
Prata, Rua da Prata 71–3 (tel. 346 8908). Reasonably priced and very good. Singles from around 2750$ (£11.50; $17.25), doubles from 3100$ (£13; $19.50).
Galiza, Rua do Crucifixio 50–5 (tel. 328430).
Estrela de Serra, Rua dos Fanqueiros 122–4 (tel. 874251). Doubles around 4500$ (£18.75; $28).

Around São Jorge castle and close to the Alfama:

São João da Praça, Rua São João da Praça 97 (tel. 862591). Cheap and high quality.
Ninho das Aguias, Rua Costa do Castelo 74 (tel. 867008). Slightly more expensive than the prices quoted above, but an excellent pension set in a garden. Doubles start around 4500$ (£18.75; $28). Highly recommended.

To the west of the Baixa, around San Roque and the Rossio railway station:

Estacio Central, Calçada do Carmo 17–2 (tel. 346 4947). Behind the train station. Doubles around 4000$ (£16.75; $25).
Henriques, Calçada do Carmo 37–11 (tel. 326886).
Do Duque, Calçada do Duque 53 (tel. 346 3444). Inexpensive and very clean.

Avenida da Liberdade area:

D. Maria II, Rua Portas de Santo Antao 9–3 (tel. 371128). Large, well-kept rooms. Doubles around 3300$ (£13.75; $20.50).
Iris, Rua da Gloria 2a–1 (tel. 323157). Doubles around 3600$ (£15; $22.50). A simple pension, but highly recommended for women travelling on their own.
Pembo, Avda da Liberdade 11–3 (tel. 325010). Singles 1750–2250$ (£7.25–9.50; $11.00–14.25), doubles with bath 2750–3300$ (£11.50–13.75; $17.25–20.50).
Mucaba, Avda da Liberdade 53–2 (tel. 346 5647).
Lis, Avda da Liberdade 180 (tel. 521084).
Dom Sancho I, Avda da Liberdade 202–3&5 (tel. 548648).
Ritz, Avda da Liberdade 240–4 (tel. 521084).
Mansarde, Avda da Liberdade 141–5 (tel. 372963).
Do Sul, Avda da Liberdade 53 (tel. 346 5647).
Modelo, Rua das Portas de Santo Antão 12 (tel. 327041).

Flor de Baixa, Rua das Portas de Santo Antão 81–2 (tel. 323153). Doubles around 5000$ (£21; $31.50).

Floroscente, Rua das Portas de Santo Antão 99 (tel. 342 6609). Large capacity with some very cheap rooms. Singles and doubles start around 2250$ (£9.25; $14).

Monumental, Rua da Gloria 21 (tel. 346 9807). Doubles around 5500$ (£23; $34.50).

Virginia, Rua da Gloria 72–2 (tel. 347 5498). Doubles around 2500$ (£10.50; $15.75).

'13 da Sorte', Rua do Salitre 13–2 (tel. 531851). Doubles around 2500$ (£10.50; $15.75).

Madeirense, Rua da Gloria 22–1 (tel. 396 1992). Doubles around 3000$ (£12.50; $18.75).

Milanesa, Rua da Alegria 25–2 (tel. 346 6456).

Sevilha, Praça da Alegria 11–2&3 (tel. 346 9579).

Alegria, Praça da Alegria 12–1 (tel. 347 5522). Doubles around 4900$ (£20.50; $30.75).

Solar, Praça da Alegria 12–2 (tel. 346 5964). Doubles around 4000$ (£16.75; $25).

Dos Restauradores, Praça dos Restauradores 13–4.

Imperial, Praça dos Restauradores 78 (tel. 342 0166).

Luso, Praça de Algeria 12–2 (tel. 328740).

Avenida Almirante Reis. A main thoroughfare beginning at Lg. Martin Moniz, close to Praa de Figueira:

Almirante Reis, Avda Almirante Reis 98–2 (tel. 823773). Doubles around 5000$ (£21; $31.50).

Portugalia, Avda Almirante Reis 112–1 (tel. 823653). Doubles around 2500$ (£10.50; $15.75).

HI HOSTELS

Rua Andrade Corvo 46 (tel. 353 2696). Metro: Picoas. Bus 1 or 45 from Rossio or Cais do Sodré. Twenty-minute walk from the centre, off Avda Fontes Pereira de Melo, in the area beyond the Pombal statue.

Lisboa-Catalazete, Estrada da Marginal, Oeiras (tel. 443 0638). 11.30 p.m. curfew. 1000–1250$ (£4.00–5.25; $6–8). A good hostel, but with a relatively small capacity, so phone ahead to check on the availability of beds. Frequent trains from Cais do Sodré; a 20-minute trip. On leaving the station, go through the underpass, to the right beneath the Praia sign. Look for the sign pointing out the way to the hostels. It's about 1km and well signposted.

CAMPING
Parque de Campismo Municipal de Lisboa Monsanto (tel. 704413/
708384). Open all year round. Four-star campsite. 150$ (£0.50;
$0.75) per tent, 550$ (£2.25; $3.50) per person. Bus 14 runs
from Praça de Figueira.
Parque de Campismo Municipal de Oeiras, Rua de S. Pedro do
Areeiro (tel. 243 0330). Train from Cais do Sodré to Oeiras. Open
May–Oct.

There are six sites on the Costa da Caparica. Ask the tourist office
which metro and/or bus you should take for the different sites.
Open all year round unless indicated:

Costa da Caparica, Estrada da Trafaria (tel. 290 0661). Orbitur site.
Bungalows available. From Praça de Espanha a bus 5 runs right
to the site, or take the metro to Palhava.
Um Lugar ao Sol, Estrada da Trafaria (tel. 290 1592).
Costa Velha, Estrada da Trafaria (tel. 290 0100/0374).
C. do Concelho de Almada, Praia da Saúde (tel. 290 1862).
Costa Nova, Estrada da Costa Nova (tel. 290 3078). Closed Jan.
Piedense, Praia da Mata (tel. 290 2004).

Oporto (Porto) (tel. code 02)

TOURIST OFFICE
Turismo, Rua Clube Fenianos 25 (tel. 312740). Open June–Sept.,
Mon.–Fri. 9 a.m.–7 p.m., Sat. 9 a.m.–2 p.m., Sun. 10 a.m.–2 p.m.;
Oct.–May., Mon.–Fri. 9 a.m.–12.30 p.m. and 2–5.30 p.m., Sat.
9 a.m.–4 p.m. From São Bento train station follow Avenida dos
Aliados to the Town Hall, from which the Tourist Office is over to
the left.

ARRIVING BY TRAIN
Your most likely point of arrival is Porto Campanha, which is quite
a distance from the city centre. Rather than start walking you
should wait for a connection to the São Bento station in the heart
of the city (you will rarely have to wait over 20 minutes, the trip
takes 5 minutes). A few trains arrive at the Trinidad station by the
Trinidad Church, just to the rear of the Town Hall.

FINDING ACCOMMODATION

Most of the city's pensions are on and around Avenida dos Aliados, particularly on the western side of Aliados (on the left as you walk up the street towards the Town Hall). You should be able to find a single for around 2300–3000$ (£9.50–12.50; $14.25–18.75) or a double for around 3800–4800$ (£16–20; $24–30) without too much difficulty, though in July and August prices may rise a little. The cheapest rooms in the city are to be found along Rua do Loureiro, close to São Bento train station, but this is the red-light area of Oporto.

PENSIONS

Estoril, Rua de Cedofeita 193 (tel. 200 2751). Doubles around 4000$ (£16.75; $25). Very smart rooms. From the western side of Aliados, near the Tourist Office, follow Rua Fabrica into Praça Carlos Alberto. Rua do Cedofeita runs from the right hand end of this square.

São Marino, Praça Carlos Alberto 59 (tel. 325499). Doubles with breakfast around 4000$ (£16.75; $25). See the Estoril, above, for directions.

Astoria, Rua Arnaldo Gama 56 (tel. 200 8175). In a quiet area of town to the rear of the city wall. Very popular, so reserve ahead.

Monumental, Avda dos Aliados 151–4 (tel. 23964). Large rooms, good value. Next door to Monumental and above the Bel Arte there is another good pension. Unfortunately, this pension is nameless.

Norte, Rua Fernandes Tomás 579 (tel. 314482). East off Aliados from the Trinidad church. The pension is at the junction with Rua Santa Catarina.

Vera Cruz, Rua da Ramalho Ortigão 14–4 (tel. 323396). B&B. Doubles 6500$ (£27; $40.50). The street off Aliados before the tourist office.

Dos Aliados, Rua Elisio de Melo 27–2 (tel. 200 4853). B&B. Doubles 6500$ (£27; $40.50). Off Aliados.

Novo Mundo, Rua Conde de Vizela 92 (tel. 25403). West of Aliados. Off Rua Clerigos, the street going up the hill to the Clerigos Tower from São Bento station.

União, Rua Conde Vizela 62 (tel. 200 3078).

Duas Nações, Praça Guilherme Gomes Fernandes 59 (tel. 26807). Along Rua Carmelitas from the Clerigos Tower. See the Novo Mundo, above.

Grand Oceano, Rua da Fabrica 45 (tel. 382447). Joins Aliados on the west side near the Tourist Office. Doubles start at 2200$ (£9; $13.50).

Franco, Praça Parada de Leitão 41 (tel. 381201). To the west of Aliados.

D'Ouro, Praça Parada de Leitão 41 (tel. 381201).

Nobreza, Rua do Breyner 6 (tel. 312409). Rundown and not the cleanest of places. Rua do Breyner is on the left as you walk up Cedofeita from Praça Carlos Alberto. See the Estoril, above.

Porto Rico, Rua do Almada 237 (tel. 318785). Doubles from 4000$ (£16.75; $25).

Europa, Rua do Almada 398 (tel. 200 6971). Two-star pension.

Moderna, Rua de Estacão 74 (tel. 571280). A short walk from Porto Campanha train station.

Continental, Rua Mousinho da Silveira 14 (tel. 320355). West of Aliados, close to the São Bento station.

Madariz, Rua Cimo da Vila. Very cheap pension, close to the São Bento station.

Visconde, Rua Visconde de Setúbal 79 (tel. 484798). Cheap pension off Rua do Constituição, north of the city centre.

Portuguesa, Traversa Coronel Pachero 11 (tel. 200 4174).

HI HOSTEL
Rua Rodrigues Lobo 98 (tel. 606 5535). Very small and usually full by midday. Curfew midnight. 950–1200$ (£3.85–5.00; $5.75–7.50). Twenty-minute walk from the town centre. Bus 3, 19, 20 or 52 from Praça da Liberdade (at the foot of Avda dos Aliados) runs to nearby Rua Júlio Dinis.

STUDENT ACCOMMODATION
Colegio de Gaia, Rua Padua Correia 166, Vila Nova de Gaia (tel. 304007). On the other side of the River Douro from Porto. Frequent train connections, as well as local buses.

CAMPING
Parque de Campismo da Prelada, Rua Monte dos Burgos (tel. 812616). Open all year. Around 300$ (£1.25; $2) per tent, 375$ (£1.55; $2.35) per person. Bus 6 from Praça da Liberdade; bus 9 from Bolhao (last bus 9 p.m.); bus 50 from Cordoaria. Closest site to the town centre, but 5km from the beach.

There are three sites in Vila Nova da Guia, closer to the beaches than Prelada:

Salguieros-Canidelo (tel. 781 0500). Open May–Sept.

Madalena, Lugar da Marinha (tel. 714162). Open June–Sept. Bus 50 from Rua Mouz, near Porto Sao Bento train station.

Marisol, Rua Alto das Chaquedas 82, Canidelo (tel. 715942).

Sintra (tel. code 01)

TOURIST OFFICE
Turismo, Praça República 19 (tel. 923 1157/923 3919).

FINDING ACCOMMODATION
Finding a bed in a pension can be a problem during the summer
unless you arrive early in the day, so a private room is probably
your best option if you want to stay in Sintra. Trains from Lisbon's
Rossio station take only 50 minutes to reach Sintra, so you might
want to consider visiting the town on a day-trip from the capital
to save yourself the trouble of finding a room.

PENSIONS
Cyntia Café. From the station, head away from the town centre
along Avda Dr. Miguel Bombarda until you see the pension.
Nova Sintra, Largo Alfonso de Albuquerque 25 (tel. 923 0220).
Further along from the Cyntia Café through Largo D. Manuel I.
Doubles around 5000$ (£21; $31.50).
Familiar. Past the Nova Sintra. About 10 minutes' walk from the
station.
Casa Adelaide, Avda Guilherme Gomes Fernandes 11−1 (tel. 923
0873). Near the Town Hall, roughly halfway between the train
station and the Palácio Real.
Bristol, Rua Visconde de Monserrate 40 (tel. 923 3852). Close to
the Palácio Real.
Economica. One of the cheapest. Near the Palácio Real.
Sintra, Traversa dos Avelares 12, São Pedro de Sintra (tel. 923
0738). Doubles with bath from 6600$ (£27.50; $41.25).

PRIVATE ROOMS
The Tourist Office books rooms at reasonable rates. Rooms are
frequently touted by locals at the train station.

YOUTH HOSTEL
Sta. Eufémia (tel. 924 1210). 900−1100$ (£3.75−4.50; $5.50−6.75).

CAMPING
No really convenient site. The nearest options are:

Capuchos convent (Parque de Campismo dos Capuchos) (tel.
862350). Over 9.5km from Sintra. The nearest bus stop is

about 5km from the site, with most of the remaining walk
uphill.

Parque de Campismo Praia Grande (tel. 929 0581) is situated on
the coast 12km from Sintra, and 4km from Colares. Open year
round. Ask the Tourist Office for details of the bus service. The
bus stops only 50m from the site.

ROMANIA

Accommodation in Romania is seldom cheap. Moreover, the standard on offer is generally amongst the worst in Europe. Despite the 1989 revolution, the country is still desperately poor and has yet to adapt to Western-style independent tourism.

A number of Category II **hotels** in Bucharest now offer singles for around £17 ($25.50), doubles for around £25 ($37.50). Outside the capital you can look for a 20–25% reduction on these prices for similar accommodation. *All hotel bills must be settled in hard currency.* If these prices seem attractive to you, bear in mind that either you will have to be very fortunate to get one of these rooms on arrival, or you will have to book well in advance. Do not expect too much help from the National Tourist Organization (ONT) in your quest for a cheap hotel room. ONT supply hotel lists and book hotels, but old habits die hard and, especially in Bucharest, you may find they devote much of their energy to persuading you to stay in a more expensive hotel. Expect to be told that the cheaper hotels are full. If you are not pressed for time, you can try some of the hotels in person. It is a sad fact that the staff at hotel reception desks often only remember about vacant rooms on production of a bribe in hard currency. Whether you will want to make such an offer will depend on how desperate you are. Athough it is possible to make hotel reservations through various private organizations in the UK before departure, they, like ONT, are not always too receptive to enquiries regarding the cheaper hotels.

Rooms in private homes offer budget travellers a way to avoid paying over the odds in hotels, and the efforts involved in trying to book a hostel bed. Many Romanians are keen to let rooms to earn some extra money and, as the problems besetting the country deter many people from visiting Romania, there is a plentiful supply of rooms available. Private rooms can usually be booked through ONT, and occasionally through private agencies. Prices are around £6 ($9) per person in Bucharest, £3–6 ($4.50–9.00) elsewhere. Once again payment has to be made in *hard currency*. Rooms offered by locals are much cheaper: rarely will their asking price reach £3 ($4.50) p.p., and usually it will be considerably less.

Do not be immediately suspicious of anyone offering you a room for free. This is quite a common practice. Your host may well expect some favour in return, such as exchanging money at a rate favourable to all concerned; that is, above the official rate but below the black market norm (this is still illegal). If you do decide to take up an offer of private accommodation, keep an eye on your valuables, or leave them at the station.

Youth hostels are controlled by the Romanian youth and student organization CATT (Compania Autonomă de Turismpentru Tineret — the Independent Youth Tourism Company). Like other East European tourist organizations, CATT have a marked preference for dealing with groups rather than individuals. Most of the beds at the majority of youth hostels are reserved months in advance by school and youth groups. This puts the onus on you to book well ahead of your time of arrival, a major task considering the difficulties of dealing with CATT. Incredibly, when hostels have plenty of space, many simply choose to shut their doors until the next group arrives. Prices are around £5–9 ($7.50–13.50).

During the university and college summer holidays, CATT lets out **student accommodation** (*caminul de studenti*) in towns with a sizeable student population. As with youth hostels, these lodgings are frequently filled up by vacationing groups. If you do manage to get a bed, expect to pay in the region of £3.50–4.30 ($5.00–6.50). Many towns and university rectorates maintain a surplus capacity of student accommodation, specifically for the use of visiting foreign students. Prices are exceptionally low, at around £2–4 ($3–6). Such accommodation offers an excellent opportunity to meet Romanian students.

There are well over 100 **campsites**, most of which are listed on the map *Popasuri Turistice* (text in French). A solo traveller should pay no more than £2–4 ($3–6) to pitch a tent for one night. Cabins are available at most sites, with charges of around £3 ($4.50) per person being the norm though, unfortunately, these are usually full in summer. Sites are sometimes located a good distance out of town, and occasionally are none too easy to reach by public transport. Your main complaint may be the quality of the sites. Facilities are very basic, and the toilets and washrooms can be really atrocious. **Camping rough** is technically illegal, but there are few places you are likely to have any trouble once you get out into the countryside. The authorities outside the towns often ignore freelance campers, as long as you do not light fires, leave litter, or damage the natural habitat. Occasionally, you may be sent on your way, but it is very rare for the statutory fine to be imposed.

In the countryside, there are well in excess of 100 '*cabanas*', simple accommodations for hikers and walkers, many of which are in the more mountainous parts of the country. A booklet, *Invitation to the Carpathians*, shows the locations of many cabanas, plus suggested itineraries. An overnight stay costs around £4 ($6). By law, cabanas are debarred from refusing entry to any hiker or climber, but it still might be sensible to reserve ahead, either through ONT, or through the Regional Tourist Office. Overnight stays are also possible at a number of **monasteries**, but it can be very difficult to gain entrance. An approach has to be made first to ONT, who will do their utmost to convince you to stay in a hotel instead. Persistence is essential on your part, but there is still no guarantee of success.

If you cannot find a bed in town, and face a night sleeping rough, do not attempt to bed down in the town, but rather head for the **train station waiting room**. If you are disturbed by the police explain that you are taking a train early in the morning. The chances are that you will have a few Romanians for company in the waiting room as this is quite a common practice amongst people setting off on an early morning train. Try to leave your pack in the left luggage store as theft is quite common.

As there are several long overnight train journeys in Romania it is possible to spend a few **nights on the train**. Trains are usually packed so there is little chance of you getting stretched out in a compartment, but booking a couchette gives you the chance of a good night's sleep. Prices vary according to the length of the journey, but are low by Western standards. However, couchettes have to be booked four to seven days in advance, either at an ONT office, or through a CFR (Romanian Railways) office in town (not at the station). The problem with sleeping on overnight trains is that there is a high incidence of theft from travellers on such trains.

TOURIST INFORMATION
The quality of tourist information available locally is often very poor, with stocks of pamphlets etc. liable to become exhausted long before the end of the main tourist season. Similarly, the National Tourist Offices abroad are extremely poorly stocked, reflecting the dire state of the national economy. Undoubtedly the best sources of tourist information are those provided by the major travel publishers in the West.

ADDRESSES

Romanian National Tourist Office	83A Marylebone High Street, London W1M 3DE (tel. 0171 224 3692).
Hotels	Booked in the UK by: Thomas Cook, VIP Travel, 42 North Audley Street, London, W1Y 2DU (tel. 0171 499 4221) (or your local Thomas Cook agent); any branch of American Express; or through the Romanian National Tourist Office.

Youth and student   CATT, Onesti 6–8, București (tel.
 hostels   140566). CATT, Str. Mandeleev 7–15,
                        București (tel. 144200).

Brašov (tel. code 21)

TOURIST OFFICE
ONT. In the lobby of the Hotel Aro Palace on Blvd Revolucion.
Maps of the town and the surrounding area. Open daily 7.30 a.m.–
3.30 p.m. Bus 4 from the train station to Blvd Revolucion, or a
20-minute walk.

ACCOMMODATION AGENCIES
Exo, Str. Postăvrul 6 (tel. 9214 4591). Open Mon.–Fri. 10 a.m.–
    2 p.m. and 4–10 p.m.; Sat. 10 a.m.–2 p.m.
Postăvrul, Eroilor Blvd 9 (tel. 42840).
Cristianul, Str. Toamnei 1 (tel. 87110).

HOTELS
For information on hotel accommodation contact Postăvrul or Cristianul. There is a dire shortage of cheap hotels in Brašov.

Aro Sport, Str. Sfîntul Ioan 3 (tel. 143840). Doubles around £25
    ($37.50). To the rear of the Hotel Aro Palace.
Postăvrul, Str. Republicii (tel. 44330). Around £23.50 ($35). Has a
    good restaurant.
Turist, Str. Marx 32. From £23.50 ($35) for a double.

PRIVATE ROOMS
Rooms range in price from £2.75–4.25 ($4.00–6.50). Book
through Postăvrul, ONT, Cristianul or Exo.

STUDENT ACCOMMODATION
Dorm rooms available year round, with supply greatly increased
July–Sept., at about £1.25 ($2) for those with student ID. Enquire
at the Rector's Office, Blvd Eroilor 29, University of Brašov. Open
Mon.–Fri. 10 a.m.–5 p.m. Just along Blvd Revolucion from the
Hotel Aro Palace.

CAMPING
Zimbrul. On the road to the mountain resort of Poiana-Brašov.

From Parc Central bus 20. Bus 4 links the train station to Parc Central.

Dîrste. Roughly 6.5km from the town centre, close to the motorway to Bucharest. Around £4 ($6) per person. From the Parc Central, bus 17 until it leaves Calea Bucurestilor. From here a 10-minute walk parallel to the motorway, then under the train tracks and across the river. Local trains also stop here.

Bucharest (Buceresti) (tel. code 0)

TOURIST OFFICES

Gara du Nord (tel. 170578). Look for the door marked TOURIST. Staff will provide information on rooms and transport, but do not supply maps or brochures. Open Mon.–Sat. 8 a.m.–8 p.m., Sun. 8 a.m.–5 p.m.

ONT, Carpati Centru, Blvd Magheru 7 (tel. 145160). Changes money, books rooms and transportation. Open Mon.–Sat. 9 a.m.–5 p.m. Tram 87 from the station to Piaţa Romană.

ACCOMMODATION AGENCIES

The ONT office (see above) and possible the tourist office at Gara du Nord will arrange accommodation. CATT (Strada Oneşti 4–6) and ONT can arrange beds in student hostels and will inform you of the current locations of these hostels (they tend to change annually).

HOTELS

Expect to pay £11.50–15.00 ($17.25–22.50) for singles, £18–25 ($27.00–37.50) for doubles; beware of proprietors trying to overcharge you as a rich Westerner!

Near the Gara de Nord:

Bucegi, Str. Witing 2 (tel. 637 5225). Cheap and basic.
Dunărea, Calea Griviţei 140 (tel. 617 3220).
Griviţa, Calea Griviţei 130 (tel. 650 5380).
Oltenia, Calea Griviţei 90 (tel. 503642). Cheapest of the three hotels listed on this street.
Marna, Str. Buzesti (tel. 350 2675).

More centrally located:

Opera, Str. Brezoianu 37 (tel. 614 1075). Near Intercontinental bus stop.
Muntenia, Str. Academiei 21 (tel. 614 6010).
Cişmigiu, Blvd Gheorghiu-Dej 18 (tel. 147410).
Carpaţi, Str. Matei Millo 16 (tel. 615 7690). Near Hotel Opera.

Gypsy district:

Rahova, Calea Rahovei 2 (tel. 615 2617). Near metro Piaţa Umirij.
Universal, Str. Gabroveni 41. Metro: Umirij. Cross the river and turn right on Gabroveni.

Most people arrive at the Gara de Nord. Beside the ONT office in the train station there is a board listing all the hotels in the city, with their addresses and telephone numbers.

PRIVATE ROOMS
Available through ONT main office at Blvd Magheru (tel. 145160). £6–10 ($9–15) p.p. Mon.–Sat. 8 a.m.–8 p.m., Sun. 8 a.m.–2 p.m.

HOSTELS/STUDENT DORMS
Expect to pay around £8 ($12) for singles, £14.75 ($22) for doubles

CATT are at Str. Mendeleev 7–15 (tel. 144200). Open Mon.–Fri. 8 a.m.–5 p.m. Generally unwilling to help independent travellers. You might have better luck approaching hostels/dorms in person.
N. Bălescu Agronomical Institute. Close to the Coresi Pringint House (the former Casa Şcînteii), reached by bus 131. Open 1 July–31 Aug.
Institutul Politechnic. Metro: Piaţa Polytechnica. Tram 35 or bus 95 from station. Open mid-June–mid-Sept. From £2.50 ($3.75) per night, groups preferred.

Most of the Arab, African and Asian students remain at the colleges during the summer vacation. They will probably be able to tell you where to make enquiries about staying the night. They may even offer to let you share their room. At other times, Romanian students may extend the same hospitality.

CAMPING
Bănasea. Over-priced and the pitches are poor. From Gara de Nord, bus 205 or trolleybus 81 (also trolleybus 82 from Piaţa Victoriei)

to Bănasea airport. Bus 149 runs to the site (Sundays bus 348). Bus 148 lets you off about 10 minutes' walk from the site – be warned: the road is unlit at night. This has recently become an unofficial refugee camp.

Constanţa (tel. code 16)

Affordable accommodation in Constanţa is limited so you may have to stay in one of the resorts nearby. Two of the easiest to reach are Mamaia and Eforie Nord, 6km north and 10km south respectively. Trolleybus 41 from the station in Constanţa will take you to Mamaia, and trolleybus 11 runs from the Sud bus station to Eforie Nord. Ask the ONT office in Constanţa about the availability of rooms in the cheap hotels in Mamaia or Eforie Nord, or of bunga-lows at the campsites.

ACCOMMODATION AGENCIES
ONT, Blvd Tomis 46, Constanţa (tel. 614800). Open Mon.–Sat. 8 a.m.–6 p.m., Sun. 9 a.m.–1 p.m. In the past, this office has been staffed by unhelpful non-English speakers. If this is still the case, try asking the English-speaking staff in the Hotel Continen-tal (tel. 15660) at the intersection of Blvd Tomis and Blvd Repub-licii for advice on accommodation possibilities.
CATT, Blvd Tomis 20–24, Constanţa (tel. 16624).
ONT, Hotel Perla, Mamaia (tel. 31670). Also in the Bucureşti B hotel (tel. 31152/31179).
Eforie Nord Tourist Office, Blvd Republicii 13 (tel. 41351). A second office is situated next to the Hotel Europa.

HOTELS
Ask ONT about rooms in the hotels below, or at other hotels.

Expect to pay £6.25–7.50 ($9.50–11.25) for singles, £9.25–12.00 ($14–18) for doubles

Victoria, Blvd Republicii 7 (tel. 17622).
Constanţa, Blvd Tomis 46. Above the tourist office. Open for business, though you may have a hard time finding staff.

● **Mamaia Nord:**
The Tourist Office lets rooms in those hotels which have not been block-booked by travel operators. Amongst the cheapest in town

are the Favorit and the Paloma. There are a number of others which are only slightly more expensive, such as the Apollo, Select, and the Caraiman I and II. The Albatross, at Blvd Siulghiol 8 (tel. 831047), is more expensive but very comfortable.

- ● **Eforie Nord:**
Much the same system as in Mamaia. Hotel beds start at around £7.50 ($11), so state that you are looking for a bed around that price (quote the $11 figure).

PRIVATE ROOMS
Enquire about their availability at any of the tourist offices.

HOSTELS
CATT control the letting of dormitory accommodation during the summer, but are more accustomed to dealing with groups.

CAMPING
No sites in Constanţa. Just north of Mamaia is Turist, while another 5km further on is Hanul Piraţilor. There are two sites in Eforie Nord: the Şincai and the Meduza. In July and August, the sites are invariably overcrowded. All four sites have bungalows for hire and in summer these bungalows are very popular, but try to make reservations at the Tourist Offices before going to the sites and consider yourself fortunate if you are successful.

Sibiu (Sibiu/Hermannstadt)
(tel. code 24)

ACCOMMODATION AGENCIES
Prima Ardeleana, Praţa Unirii 1 (tel. 11788). Open daily 8 a.m.– 5 p.m.
CATT are located at Str. Kornhauser 4, close to the ONT office. They operate a student hotel in town, where reasonable doubles with a shower cost around £23 ($40). In summer, you can also ask them about any cheaper accommodation which might be available in student dormitories.
Exo, behind Str. Nicholae Bąkcesu 1. Private rooms around $6.50 ($10).

HOTELS
The cheapest hotel is the Impăratul Romanilor, just off Piaţa Republicii on Str. N. Balcescu. Cheaper lodgings are available at the inn

on Calea Dumbravii: from the bus station (adjacent to the train station on Piaţa Garii) take the bus to Pădurea Dumbrava and you'll find the inn located next to the campsite, on the left as you travel down Calea Dumbravii. Also recommended is the La Podul Minciunilor, Str. Azïui 1 (tel. 17259): from the station, walk up Str 9 Mai past Liar's Bridge.

STUDENT HOSTEL
Hotel Sport, Str. Octavian Goga 2, next to the sports stadium (tel. 22472). All rooms £3.50 ($5).

CAMPING
Mediocre camping at the Drumbava complex: bus no. 1 heading south-west will take you there. Over-priced and unsavoury.

Sighişoara (tel. code 950)

TOURIST OFFICE
Birolilade Turism, Str. 1 Decembrie (tel. 71072). Hotel accommodation agency and tour guide all under one roof.

HOTELS
Steaua, Str. 1 Decembrie 12 (tel. 71594). Doubles around £23.50 ($35).

PRIVATE ROOMS
Enquire at ONT on Str. 1 Decembrie 10 (tel. 71072).

CAMPING
The Dealul Gării site (tel. 71046) offers camping and bungalows to let. It's on top of the hill to the rear of the train station.
The Hula Danes site is located about 4km from town along the road to Mediaş. Hula Danes also has bungalows for hire.

Timişoara (tel. code 961)

TOURIST INFORMATION
ONT, Str. Craiului 12. West off Blvd 30 Decembrie, a little way

north of Parcul Central. This is the best office for accommodation advice. Open Mon.–Sat. 9.30 a.m.–5.30 p.m.

Cardinal Agency, Blvd Republicii 6 (tel. 90358). Open Mon.–Fri. 8 a.m.–4 p.m., Sat. 9 a.m.–12 noon.

HOTELS

FJPT, Str. Arieş 19 (tel. 62419). Around £3 ($4.50). Quite a walk (it's not served by public transport). Head east along the canal to Str. Cluj, then south past the student complex to Str. Arieş.

Banatul, Blvd Republicii 5 (tel. 37762). Around £10 ($15). East off Piaţa Libertăţii.

PRIVATE ROOMS

Enquire at ONT (see above).

CAMPING

Pădurea Verde (tel. 33925). Located in the forest of the same name. Tent spaces £3 ($4.50), with bungalows also available. Tram no. 1 from either station to Str. Kogalniceanu, then walk 100m east.

RUSSIA AND THE UKRAINE

Though Russia, the Ukraine and Byelorussia are now individual countries, each requiring a separate visa, the accommodation situation is virtually the same in all three. In the past, visitors were only able to enter under the auspices of Intourist, the notorious official travel agency for the former Soviet Union. Their prices were steep, and so for the budget traveller (with the exception of Trans-Siberian Express travellers with transit visas) a trip to Russia was too expensive to contemplate.

With the disintegration of the Soviet Union have come changes in the tourist infrastructure, but still they are not keeping pace with changes elsewhere in the Eastern Bloc. In Riga, for example, you will find a growing range of hostels and private accommodation; this is not yet the case in the CIS. Although it is now much easier to get a visa, especially for the Ukraine and Byelorussia, and independent travel in these countries has become a viable possibility, they are still not equipped for an influx of Western visitors.

Intourist continue to operate, and their prices are gradually dropping: their **hotels** in Moscow and St Petersburg now offer doubles from around £34.50 ($52). They will also book campsite accommodation, either in tents or chalets. A 2–4 berth chalet without facilities will cost around £12 ($18), while tents and caravans cost about £9 ($13.50) per person (these prices are for Moscow and St Petersburg; other centres cost £1–4 ($1.50–6.00) less). To book through Intourist, contact them at the address shown below. They may well offer you a group package which will include cheap flights – and only the flights and accommodation are compulsory in order to acquire a visa – other than that you can do what you like, tailoring your itinerary to suit your own taste, provided everything is pre-booked. Intourist will also sort out your visa for you.

This may be a safe and secure way to see Russia, but it's hardly cheap. It's no longer strictly necessary to go through Intourist, because **independent hotels** are starting to materialize which will assist with visa support if you contact them directly. At present, Russia has two Western-style hotels, one in St Petersburg and one in Moscow. Each has English-speaking staff who will assist with your enquiries. They'll arrange domestic and international train tickets, and they offer the best tourist information in Russia. Most important, they're friendly and helpful – essential in a place where you might feel completely disorientated, as if you've left the real world behind. Furthermore, the hostels won't necessarily hold you to the number of nights you've 'booked' in order to secure your visa (although they will charge a £6.70 ($10) booking fee), so theoretically you're free to look elsewhere once you arrive.

A network of **youth hostels** is now starting to take shape in Russia. At the time of writing there are hostels in St Petersburg and Moscow, with plans for more to open soon. Bookings can be made from the YHA Travel Store, 14 Southampton Street, London WC2E 7HY (tel. 0171 836 1036). Facilities and tourist information are excellent, and these two hostels could well from the backbone of your trip to the former Soviet Union, particularly as they will help arrange your visa for you.

Bear in mind that all three countries covered in this chapter are suffering the effects of immense economic turmoil and there is a tendency to assume all Westerners are extremely wealthy. Consequently, you may find hotels increase their prices dramatically (in line with Intourist prices) the moment they become aware of your nationality. For those fluent in Russian this may not be a problem, but the majority of visitors will find that negotiations depend on the mood of the hotel staff on the day, plus your skill at haggling and looking convincingly destitute. Offering hard currency may help. One way or another, it is almost impossible to recommend specific hotels because their attitude (and pricing policy) is so inconsistent. The best advice is to be thick-skinned and keep trying your luck.

Two companies, Sputnik and CCTE, specialize in foreign/youth travel. Their hotels are listed below, though Sputnik are primarily aimed at groups and may therefore refuse individuals entry. It's worth a try, though. CCTE hotels seldom charge more than £13.50 ($20) per night (possibly less if you can negotiate in Russian).

In view of the high cost of hotel accommodation, it makes sense to listen to offers of **private rooms**: some locals ask as little as £1.35 ($2) per night. The accommodation won't be palatial by any standards, but it will usually be fairly central and linked to the city centre by public transport. You have no guarantee of quality or safety, so use your discretion. On the plus side, you may gain a rare and rewarding insight into a lifestyle entirely different to your own (even if you do find yourself watching *Blake's Seven* dubbed in Russian on a flickering black-and-white TV).

In many places – hotel lobbies and stations are the prime locations – you will see an individual sitting at a desk with a pile of handwritten postcards. They're probably acting as an agent for local families or pensioners offering accommodation in their homes to subsidize their income. These private enterprise networks offer a slightly greater guarantee of safety and the promise of a more convenient location, although prices may be slightly higher than you'd expect to pay when dealing direct. Haggling and impressive body language should get you a room for around £3.50 ($5) per night.

University dorms are worth a look, especially if you speak the language. Many dorms have spare rooms, and the individuals who supervise each dorm will often take people in (even though they're not supposed to). Again, it's a question of using skilful haggling and quite possibly a little bribery to get in.

A word on bribery: the former Soviet Union is home to a barter system that would not seem out of place in a medieval town. Step out of just about any metro station at midnight and you'll see dozens of women exchanging everything from salami to Reeboks out of sturdy white shopping bags. The black market is essential to the survival of most citizens, so 'bribery' isn't quite so illicit as it might sound to a Westerner. But be discreet.

If all else fails, an overnight train is always a possibility. Distances are vast — Moscow to St Petersburg, for example, is an eight-hour train journey, with as many as eight overnight trains running in each direction — so you'll have a range of choices available to you.

USEFUL PHRASES

ENGLISH	RUSSIAN
Yes	Dah
No	Nyet
Please	Pa-zhol-sta
Thank you	Spaseebo
Good morning	Dobro oo-tram
Goodbye	Do sveda-ya
Where is/are	Gdyeh
Excuse me	Izveneetya
How much?	Skolko so-eet?
Can I have . . .	Yah hot-choo
I don't understand	Yah nyeh ponimay-oo
Do you speak English?	Voi govoreet-yeh Angleeskee yazik
My name is . . .	Men-yah za-voot . . .

ADDRESSES

Intourist	Intourist Travel Ltd, Intourist House, 219 Marsh Wall, London E14 9FJ (tel. 0171 538 5967).
Russian Youth Hostels	St Petersburg 193312, P O Box 57, Russia (tel. (812) 277 0569/329 8019; fax (812) 277 5102).

Russia

MOSCOW (tel. code 095)

TOURIST OFFICES
Central Excursion Bureau, ul. Belinstovo 4A (tel. 203 8016). Two blocks from Red Square. Open daily 9 a.m.–9 p.m. English-speaking staff, but aimed mainly at high-spending hard-currency tourists.

Moscow Excursion Bureau, ul. Rozhdestvenka 5 (tel. 923 8953). Open daily 10 a.m.–2 p.m. and 3–6 p.m. Russian-speaking. Accept payment in roubles.

Intourist's information desk, Tverskaya ulitsa 1 (tel. 203 1497). Will only help with entertainment information (or, of course, bookings for Intourist hotels). They also operate an information line (tel. 203 6962) which will supposedly answer your questions from 9 a.m.–6 p.m. daily, but their English is limited.

It's advisable to begin your stay at least at the Traveller's Guest House, which has information and maps.

BASIC DIRECTIONS
Moscow is served by an extensive and efficient metro system. This links all the major railway stations (there are eight) and any accommodation you're likely to find (including the Traveller's Guest House).

HOSTEL
The first budget accommodation run on Western lines opened last year at the Traveller's Guest House, ul. Bolshaya Pereyaslavskaya 50, floor 10 (tel. and fax. 971 4059). It's not easy to find: take the metro to Prospekt Mira, turn left and then take a right after about 400 metres. If you're heading towards four chimney stacks, you're going in the right direction. Turn left on Pereyaslavskaya and the building – which hardly advertises itself – is on your right. Rates are £6.70 ($10) per night. The hostel will help with visa support, tourist information and domestic/international train tickets (for which there is a £3.35 ($5) service charge).

426 · *Cheap Sleep Guide to Europe*

PRIVATE ROOMS

In the lobby of the Gosinitsa Centralnaya, next door to Pizza Hut on ulitsa Tverskaya, there is usually a woman with a pile of postcards who is offering private accommodation with Moscow residents. Knowledge of Russian will help you considerably, and for a few dollars a night you will find yourself enjoying a unique experience of life in the home of a Russian family or pensioner, within easy reach of the city centre.

Other sources of private accommodation are:

Russian Bear Travel Services, Andropov Avenue 35 (tel. 114 4223). Arrange dorm-style accommodation in apartments around the city for £4 ($6) upwards.

Vladimir Martof (tel. 936 3985).

Alexi (tel. 142 3097).

Kseniy (tel. 165 3995).

Ivan, Andrew (tel. 207 7204).

Alber, Maria (tel. 129 156).

HOTELS

Intourist hotels:

Moskva Hotel. Singles £49.50 ($74), doubles £56 ($84) without breakfast.

Ukraine Hotel. Singles £49.50 ($74), doubles £63.50 ($95) without breakfast.

Sevastopol Hotel. Doubles £52 ($78), breakfast included.

Mozhaiskaya Hotel. Singles £28 ($42), doubles £34.50 ($52), breakfast included.

Izmailovo Hotel. Singles £28.50 ($43), doubles £32 ($48), breakfast included.

Sputnik hotels:

Hotel Orlyonok, ul. Kosygina 15 (tel. 939 8884).

Hotel Molodzhnaya, Dimitrovskoe shosse 27 (tel. 210 9311). Bus 227 from Savyolovskaya metro.

CCTE hotels:

Hotel Druzhba, Prospekt Vernadskovo 53 (tel. 432 9631).

Tsentralny Dom Turista, Leninsky Prospekt 146 (tel. 438 5510).

Hotel Salyut, Leninsky Prospekt 158 (tel. 438 0224).

Hotel Turist, ul. Selskokhozyzystvennaya 17 (tel. 181 0158). Metro:
  Botanichesky Sad.

CAMPING
At the Hotel Solnechnaya, Varshavskoe Schosse Km 21 (tel. 119
7100). Bus 679 from Varshavskaya metro.

St Petersburg (tel. code 812)

TOURIST OFFICES
Hotel service bureaux can advise on travel and entertainment, even
if you're not a guest of that hotel. Intourist's office is at Isaakiev-
skaya ploshchad 11 (tel. 210 5046), opposite the Astoria hotel. The
same address is home to the St Petersburg Travel Company (tel.
315 5129).

Since there's no Westernized system of tourist information, your
best bet is to start at the RYH hostel. They provide a very useful
free map and the most up-to-date guide to the city: *The New
St Petersburg*.

BASIC DIRECTIONS
St Petersburg's metro system efficiently links most points of interest
in the city, including the four main stations, the RYH hostel, university dorms and the city centre.

HOSTELS
RYH (Russian Youth Hostel), 3rd Sovetskaya ul. 28 (tel. 277 0569;
  fax 7 812 277 5102). Opened in 1992, the first independent in
  the former Soviet Union, owned by an American who plans to
  follow it with similar hostels in Moscow, Yalta and elsewhere. It
  costs £9.50–10.50 ($14–16) per night, breakfast included, plus
  a £6.70 ($10) reservation fee if you use them for visa support.
  From Ploshchad Vosstaniya metro station (Moscow station), turn
  right on to Nevsky Prospekt away from the city centre, then left
  on to Suvorovski Prospekt and right on to 3rd Sovetskaya Ulitsa
  at the second traffic lights after the Phillips store. An excellent
  hostel, with showers so good they could conceivably alter your
  political beliefs.
Hostel Altus, 15–yaliniya 4–6 (tel. 213 4738). A more typically
  Russian hostel offering 11-bed B&B on the ground floor of a
  hospital. Take tram 63 from Gorkovskaya metro station.

STUDENT DORMS

Be aware that there's no guarantee you'll get in (see introduction
to this chapter). If you want to try your luck, the best-situated
dorm is at Plekanova 6, behind the Kazan cathedral on Nevsky
Prospekt; the most promising is at Grazhdansky Prospekt 28, near
the metro of the same name. It's also worth checking with the
university itself (tel. 218 2000).

PRIVATE ACCOMMODATION

*The following accommodation agencies, who you can contact in advance
and request visa support from, offer B&B from around £10 ($15):*

Elpis, 917101 Kronverskaya ul. 27 (tel. 232 9838, fax 332 2688).
Host Families Association, 193015 Tavricheskaya ul. 5—25 (tel.
  2751962, fax 552 6086).
Lingva, 7—y Lingva 36, Vasilevskiy Island (tel. 218 7339).

The following individuals offer private rooms:

Bob (tel. 553 3435).
Sergei, Irina (tel. 268 6894).
Sergei (tel. 246 2969).
Emma (tel. 314 5240).
Irina, Katia (tel. 242 1436).
Marina (tel. 272 7847).
Leonid (tel. 230 7397).
Irina (tel. 597 2666).
Tanya (tel. 298 9343).

The History, Arts and Culture Club of St Petersburg, run by Andrey
Andrienko, was said to be considering a plan to open cheap accommodation in the city. Contact Andrey on 217 0218.

HOTELS
Intourist hotels:

Karelia Hotel. Doubles £42 ($63).
Gavan Hotel. Singles £34.50 ($52), doubles £48.50 ($73).
Olgino Hotel. Singles £36 ($54), doubles £44.50 ($67).

Sputnik hotels:

Hotel Druzhba, ul. Chapygina 4 (tel. 234 1844). Metro: Petro-
  gradskaya.

Dvorets Molodyozhy, ul. Professora Popova 47 (tel. 234 3278). Bus 25 from Nevsky Prospekt.

Vyborgskaya, Torzhkovskaya ul. 3 (tel. 246 9141). Metro: Chyornaya Rechka. Reserve through the Otyabrskaya (see below).

Hotel Sputnik, Prospekt Morisa Toreza 34 (tel. 552 5632). Metro: Ploshchad Muzhestva.

Kievskaya Hotel, Dnepropetrovksaya ul. 49 (tel. 166 0456). Bus 14 from Ligovsky Prospekt Metro.

Hotel Ladoga, Prospekt Shaumyana 26 (tel. 528 5393). Metro: Krasnogvardeyskaya.

CCTE hotels:

Hotel Gavan, Sredny Prospekt 88 (tel. 356 8504). Bus 30 from Nevsky Prospekt or the Hermitage.

Hotel Morskaya, Ploshchad Morskoy Slavy 1 (tel. 355 1416). Bus 7 from Nevsky Prospekt.

Other:

Akademicheskaya, Millionaya ul. 27 (tel. 315 8986). Previously reserved for guests of the Academy of Science but now accepting tourists in exchange for roubles. A little way east of the Hermitage.

Oktyabrskaya, Ligovsky Prospekt 10 (tel. 277 6330). By Moscow station. Accepts roubles.

Plukovo, Pavlogradskiy pereulok 6. Operated by Oktyabrskaya; reserve and pay for your room (in roubles) there.

Mir, ul. Gastello 17 (tel. 108 5165). South of metro Park Pobedy.

Rossiya, pl. Chernyshevskovo 11 (tel. 296 7649). Same metro as the Hotel Mir.

Zara, Kurskaya ul. 40. Handled by the Kievskaya. Take bus 14 from Ligovsky Prospekt.

CAMPING
Motel-Camping Olgino, Primorskoe shosse 59 (tel. 238 3551). It's notoriously dangerous and there was a shoot-out there two years ago, but if you want to risk it take the metro to Chyornaya Rechka then bus 411 or 416.

The Ukraine

Kiev (Kyyiv)

HOTELS
CCTE hotel:

Druzhba, Bulvar Druzhbi Narodiv 5 (tel. 683406). Nearest metro:
  Dzerzhinskaya/Lyubanka. Charges £13.40 ($20) per night,
  though some travellers claim to have got in for £1.35 ($2).

Sputnik hotels:

Mir, Prospekt 40–Richya Zhovtnaya 70 (tel. 637063). South of the
  river, nearest metro: Dzerzhinskaya/Lyubanka.
Goloseevskaya, Prospekt 40–Richya Zhovtnaya 93 (tel. 614268).
  See Hotel Mir for directions.
Zolotoy Kolos, Prospekt 40–Richya Zhovtnaya 95 (tel. 614001). See
  Hotel Mir for directions.

Intourist hotel:

Lybrd Hotel. Singles £38.50 ($58), doubles £60 ($90), including
  breakfast.

PRIVATE ROOMS
Locals hang around in the city centre offering private accommodation for around £1.35 ($2) per night in various dingy suburban
abodes.

CAMPING
Motel-Camping Prolisok, Prospekt Peremogi 179 (tel. 444 1293).
A good Intourist campsite, 12km from town. Bus 37 from metro
Svyatoshino.

Lvov (L'viv)

TOURIST OFFICES
The Travel Bureau (tel. 72675), in the lobby of the Hotel Intourist (see below).
The Travel Agency (tel. 798 5721), in the Hotel Dnestr, by the Park Ivan Franko, across from the university.

HOTELS
CCTE hotel:

Turist, vulitsaya Engelsa 103 (tel. 351065). Tram 2 from Russkaya ul. (which forms one side of the Rynok).

Sputnik hotels:

Ukraina, Ploshchad Mitskevicha 3 (tel. 726656).
Verkhovina, Prospekt Lenina 13 (tel. 741222).
Pershotravnevaya, Prospekt Lenina 21 (tel. 742060).
Kiev, vulitsay 1—go Travna 15 (tel. 742105).
Ulyanovsk, vulitsay Marchenka 6 (tel. 728512).

Intourist hotel:

Hotel Intourist, pl. Mickiewicza 1 (tel. 799011). Singles £42.50 ($64), doubles £84.50 ($127), including breakfast.

CAMPING
Camping Lvovsky (tel. 721373). Intourist campsite, 7km out of town on the Kiev road.

Odessa

HOTELS
CCTE hotel:

Turist, Genuezskaya ul. 24A (tel. 614057). Bus 129 from the station to the 10 Aprelya stop.

Sputnik hotels:

Bolshaya Moskovskaya, Deribasovskaya ul. 29 (tel. 22549). Two blocks back from Ploshchad Potyomkintsev, near the northern shore. Some travellers have got rooms here for £3 ($4.50).

Arkadia, Genuezskaya ul. 24 (tel. 250085). Near Arkadia beach, south of town.

CAMPING

Camping Delfin, doroga Kotovskovo 299. Intourist campsite, 10km north of Odessa in Luzanovka. Take a ferry to Luzanovka pier, 500m south of the campsite, from the Morskoy Vokzal terminal in the north of the city.

Yalta

HOTEL

There is a Sputnik hotel, Krym, at Moskovskaya ul. 1–6 (tel. 326061). Travellers report getting beds here for £1.50 ($2.25). Moskovskaya ul. is the road by the bus station.

CAMPING

Camping Polyana Skazok (tel. 395249). Intourist campsite, 5km out. Buses 4 and 8 run from the station to a little way past Polyana Skazok.

Byelorussia (Belorus)

Minsk

HOTELS

Intourist operates three hotels – Yubileynaya, Planena and Minskiy – offering singles for £28 ($42) and doubles for £56 ($84).

CCTE hotel:

Turist, Partizansky Prospekt 81 (tel. 454031).

Sputnik hotels:

Belarus, Storozhevskaya ul. 15 (tel. 292610). By the river in the north-west of the city.
Minsk, Leninsky Prospekt 11 (tel. 200702). On Ploshchad Lenina.
Druzhba, ul. Tolbukhina 3 (tel. 662481). Near Park Chelyuskintsev metro.
Mezhdunarodny Turistky Tsentr Yunost (tel. 362397). Beside the Minsk Sea, 18km north-west of the city. Take bus 125 from the railway station.

Brest

HOTEL
The CCTE-run Hotel Belarus is at bulvar Schevchenko 150 (tel. 61161). From the station head left up ul. Ordzhonikdze, then right on to Schevchenko (also called Kosmonavtov).

SLOVAKIA (Slovensko)

Slovakia's emergence as a country separate from the Czech Republic has been a mixed blessing, for the traveller as well as for the nation itself. You will now require two separate visas rather than one. And although Slovakia is not yet the tourist destination that the Czech Republic has become, it still suffers from the same accommodation crises that Czechoslovakia's inclusion in the Inter-Rail scheme caused. Bratislava, for better or worse, is not Prague, but you can nevertheless expect a hard time finding a place to stay in high season. Smaller towns should not present a problem. As a rule, Slovakia is a poorer country than its neighbour and prices are therefore slightly lower.

An easy system of reservations would have alleviated the accommodation problem, but as yet no such system has materialized. Both CKM and Čedok profess to operate booking services, but the procedures are time-consuming and elaborate, and in reality there is no regulated accommodation system. If making direct contact with hotels etc. doesn't appeal, then try to avoid arriving at weekends (when Germans and Austrians flood in for weekend breaks, exacerbating the accommodation problems).

Hotels are divided into five categories; A or deluxe/five-star, A*/four-star, B/three-star, B*/two-star, and C/one-star. Čedok say that hotels rated in the C/one-star category 'truly have no frills', but from the budget traveller's point of view they are a real bargain. In most towns, doubles are available from around £10 ($15). The situation whereby hotel bills had to be settled in hard currency seems to be disappearing, but if you offer dollars rather than Slovakian Crowns you're unlikely to be turned away.

It is possible to stay in the homes of local people. Prices for **private rooms** booked through agencies are no longer officially fixed, with the result that they have risen. Expect to pay around £6 ($9) in most towns. Although alternatives are developing, Čedok remain the most prominent organization, a legacy from the days of state-ownership of the tourist industry. Some rooms in the cities can be far from the centre, but as public transport systems are cheap and efficient, distance should not deter you.

Private rooms offered by individuals will be a similar price to official ones, but standards may vary dramatically. Accessibility is important, but staying one night in the middle of nowhere need not be a disaster if it allows you to get an early start next day to look elsewhere. If you do take up a private offer, take care of your valuables.

Hostelling offers arguably the best value for money out of all the accommodation possibilities, but beds are not easy to find. Around 50 HI hostels exist in former Czechoslovakia, operated by CKM (the student travel organization). Prices range from £2.50–12.00 ($3.75–18.00). The few permanent hostels are a great bargain, and standards are high, but advance booking is advisable. In Slovakia permanent hostels are a rarity; most are converted **student dormitories** which open in July and August. If you're around then, contact CKM, who control the letting of rooms in student dormitories, often in towns not mentioned in the HI handbook. Many independent hostels are housed in converted student dormitories, and most of these are either unknown or unacknowledged by the official tourist agencies. Apart from relying on word of mouth, advertisements in train and bus stations may be your best guide to new hostels.

Most small towns have very basic dormitory hostels known as *turisticka ubytovna*, where a bunk bed costs around £1 ($1.50). Facilities seldom extend to anything more than toilets and cold showers. These hostels are meant primarily for workers living away from home, or for groups of workers on holiday, but it is most unlikely you will be turned away if there is room at the hostel. Unfortunately, many such hostels open only when they have a group booking. Nevertheless, enquire at the local Čedok or CKM offices, as they sometimes offer the only hostel accommodation available in town.

If you are travelling in summer, **camping** is a great way to see the country very cheaply (few sites remain open before May or after September). *Camping Czechoslovakia* (from Čedok) lists around 250 sites in former Czechoslovakia, graded A, AB and B, with details of opening times and facilities available, and has a map showing their locations. Prices for a solo traveller are about £1.50–2.50 ($2.25–3.75) per night, but, as Čedok warns, 'don't expect luxury'. Sites are usually clean, but at the B-class sites outside showers are the norm. At many sites it is possible to rent two-or four-bed chalets (*chata*). Standards vary, and be warned: at some sites you may be required to pay for all the beds in the chalet, even if they are not all occupied. Expect to pay between £2–4 ($3–6) per person in a fully occupied chalet.

Further off the beaten track, more primitive campsites exist, known as *tborisko*. Facilities are spartan, and consequently prices can be as low as £1 ($1.50) per night. Again, these sites may not be open outside the summer months, and even then you may find tourist offices are loath to admit their existence; try asking the locals if there is a *tborisko* in the vicinity.

Those with rail passes can solve an accommodation crisis by taking an overnight train. The Bratislava to Prague connection runs nightly (see **Czech Republic** chapter for timetable), but be warned: this journey has become notorious for the number of thieves operating.

TOURIST INFORMATION
Few cities have tourist offices run along Western lines. If the situation is bleak in the Czech Republic, it is twice as antiquated in Slovakia. In most towns you'll have to rely for information on Čedok or CKM, which specialize in accommodation and travel. For guides on what to see, it is best to buy a guide book before setting off. Čedok offices may supply a list of altered street names; euphoric as the Velvet Revolution was, it did have the side-effect of sending countless weary travellers in search of addresses which have ceased to exist in post-Communist Slovakia.

ADDRESSES
Čedok Tours & Holidays 49 Southwark Street, London SE1 1RU
(tel. 0171 378 6009).
Agencies in Slovakia Bratislava Information Service Panská 18, 814 28 Bratislava.
Karta mládeže Slovenska, Pražská 11, 816 36 Bratislava (tel. 07 498090).

Bratislava (tel. code 07)

TOURIST OFFICES
BIPS, Laurinská ul 1 (formerly Leningradská) (tel. 333715/334325/334370). Open June–Sept., Mon.–Fri. 8 a.m.–6 p.m., Sat. 8 a.m.–1 p.m.; Oct.–May, Mon.–Fri. 8 a.m.–4.30 p.m. General information, plus advice on the hostel situation. Just off Hviezdoslavovo náměstí.
Slovakotourist, Panská ul. 13 (tel. 335722/331607) advise on regional travel. Useful if you're planning to visit the mountains.

ACCOMMODATION AGENCIES
Čedok, Jesenkého 5–9 (tel. 499613/490406/499645). Open Mon.–Fri. 9 a.m.–6 p.m., Sat. 9 a.m.–12 p.m. Tram 13 from the main train station. Also at Stúrova ul 13 (tel. 52834).

CKM, Hviezdoslavovo náměstí 16 (tel. 331607). Open Mon.–Fri.
9 a.m.–12 p.m. and 1–4 p.m.
Bratislava Information Service, Panská 18, organizes cheap accommodation in Bratislava year round, but specializes in summer hostels.

ARRIVING IN BRATISLAVA
Most trains to Bratislava arrive at hlavná stanica, about 15 minutes' walk from the Old Town, or a short trip on trams 1 or 13. Head away from the station past the train terminal and on to Pražka. Turn left down Pražka and go straight ahead, on down Štefánikova until you arrive at the Trinity Church. Follow the road round to the left a short distance, then turn right heading for the old St Michael's Gate (Michalská brána). Going through the gate follow Michalsk downhill and continue straight ahead to reach Hviezdoslavovo náměstí.

Some trains from Slovakia arrive at the Bratislava Nové Mesto station. Trams 6 and 14 link Nové Mesto to the city centre. Most buses arrive at the bus station on Bajkalská. Going right from the bus station for about 100m you reach Vajnorská from which you can take any tram heading down into the city.

HOTELS
For information on hotels and reservations contact Čedok.

Ustav vzdelávania ve stavebnictve, Brodošova 33 (tel. 375212). Doubles with a bath £7 ($10.50), triples £10 ($15). From the main train station take tram 44 to the third stop on Bárodošova. Walk back a short distance, then head uphill to the three-storey building with the name of the hotel on top. From the bus station take electric bus no. 211.

Krym (B/two-star), Safarikovo náměstí 7 (tel. 554713/325471). Off Štúrová, close to the Danube. Around £43.50 ($65) for a double.

Palace, Poštová 1 (tel. 333656). Tram 14 from the train station to the fifth stop. Singles around £14 ($21); doubles £18 ($27).

Motel Zlaté Piesky, ul. Vajorská (tel. 65170/66028). On the fringes of the city, by the campsites. See the **Camping** section for directions.

CKM Juniorhotel Sputnik, ul. Drieňová 14 (tel. 234340/238000). Singles £12 ($18), doubles £20 ($30). From the main train station take tram 8 to the eighth or ninth stop, or take bus 34 from the centre. The hotel is on the opposite side of the small lake visible to your left.

Flóra, Senecká cesta (tel. 214154/214122). Doubles £14.50 ($22).

On the outskirts. From the main train station take tram no. 2 to the last stop.

PRIVATE ROOMS
Contact Čedok or Slovakotouríst.

HOSTELS
During the summer, Bratislava is well supplied with hostel beds, mostly in converted student dormitories. CKM, BIPS and Uniatour are the organizations to approach for information regarding hostels. The bus station and the main train station are favourite places for hostel operators to pin up advertisements, usually with rates and directions to the hostel.

CKM Juniorhotel Sputnik, ul. Drieňová 14 (tel. 234340/238065). Singles and doubles £4.20 ($6.25) per person for HI members and ISIC card holders. Frequently full, so try to reserve ahead. See the entry in the **Hotels** section above for directions.

CKM Youth Hostel Ružinovsk 1 (tel. 220441/220442/220052) £3.50 ($5.25) per person for HI members in singles, doubles or triples. For non-members singles cost £9 ($13.50), doubles £13 ($19.50), and triples £17 ($25.50). Well advertised at the bus and train stations. From the bus station or Hlavná Stanica take tram no. 8.

Studentský domov J. Hronca, Bernolákova 3 (tel. 42612). Open July–Aug. Student dorm converted into a temporary HI hostel controlled by CKM. £3.50 ($5.25) for HI members. See the Bernolak YH below for directions.

Bernolak Youth Hostel (BIPS), Bernolákova 1 (tel. 58019/497721). Open July–Aug. Doubles £6 ($9), triples £8 ($12). Reduced prices for ISIC card holders: £5.75 ($8.50) and £6.50 ($9.75) respectively. Adverts in the bus and train stations. From hlavná stanica or the bus station take trolleybus 210 to Račianske myto, or bus 27 or 47 to Zochova, then (in both cases) bus 39 to the terminus. From the bus stop red footprints signed 'elam' show the way to the hostel.

Mlada Garda, Račianska cesta 103 (tel. 253136). Operated by Uniatour. Open July–Aug. Around £2 ($3) per person. Small reduction for ISIC card holders.

YMCA Interpoint Bratislava, Karpatská 2 (tel. 493267/498005). Open 15 July–15 Aug. £4.50 ($6.75). From Hlavná Stanica walk down past the tram terminus on to Malinovského. Turn left and follow Malinovského until you see Karpatská on the left.

Študentský domov N. Belojanisa, Wilsonova 6 (tel. 497735). Next
   to Bernoláova.

CAMPING
Two sites at Zlaté piesky, both with bungalows. Tram 2 from town
centre, tram 4 from train station or tram 12 to the Zupka crossroads,
then bus 32 to the third stop:

Senecká cesta 10 (tel. 66028/214000). Grade AB site. Open all year
   round.
Senecká cesta 12 (tel. 65170). Grade A site, open 15 May—15 Sept.

Košice (tel. code 095)

TOURIST INFORMATION
Small maps to guide you round the city remain hard to obtain
locally, though the Hotel Slovan (Hlavná ul. 1) may be able to help.
For general information, approach Čedok or CKM. The former are
also your best bet in other east Slovakian towns.

ACCOMMODATION AGENCIES
Čedok (tel. 3121) is located by the Hotel Slovan at Rooseweltova
   1, at the foot of náměstí Slobody. Open Mon.—Fri. 9 a.m.—5 p.m.,
   Sat. 9 a.m.—12 p.m.
CKM, Hlavná Ulica 82 (tel. 27458/20248). Open Mon.—Fri. 9 a.m.—
   4.30 p.m., Sat. 9 a.m.—12 p.m.

FINDING ACCOMMODATION
Košice is a major international rail crossroads and a town where
many travellers have to (or choose to) break their journey. Many
of the visitors you see here only stay in town for a few hours before
continuing their journey. In the past, this has ensured that the
supply of accommodation has managed to meet demand. Now
more people are arriving in Košice and using the main town of east
Slovakia as a base from which to visit nearby towns, with the result
that finding cheap accommodation is becoming more difficult. This
is especially true of late June, just before CKM open up student
dormitories as temporary hostels.

HOTELS
Rooms in local hotels can be booked through Čedok.

Expect to pay £12–15 ($18.00–22.50) for a double

Europa, Protfašistických Bojovnkov 1 (tel. 23897). Singles £10 ($15), doubles £16 ($24). From the station, walk straight ahead to the small park and cross the bridge.

Club, Nerudova (tel. 20214.27678).

Centrum. Close to the Čedok office.

Strojár, Tr. Sovietskej Armady 53.

Hutník, Tyršovo nábrežie 6 (tel. 37780/37511). Near main square behind Dom Kultury. Singles £18 ($27), doubles £26.50 ($40).

Coral, Kasárenské náměstí (tel. 26095). Singles £8 ($12), doubles £10 ($15).

PRIVATE ROOMS
Enquire at CKM for private rooms in the city. Čedok are useful for places outside of Košice.

HOSTELS
CKM control the letting of beds in student dormitories converted into temporary hostels during July and August. In addition, university dorms are available at Vysok Škola Technická, ul. Vysoko Školská 4 (tel. 31731). Or try the hostel at Považska 40 (tel. 436240), but phone ahead as rooms fill quickly.

CAMPING
Auto Camping Salas Barca, Alejová (tel. 58309). Open Apr.–Sept. Bungalows available. Five kilometres from the city, just off the road to Rožňava. From the Slovan hotel take tram 1 or 4, or bus 22 or 52 as far as the flyover. From there the campsite is about 5 minutes' walk along the road to Rožňava.

SLOVENIA

The first thing to say about Slovenia is that it's safe. While the war in the rest of former Yugoslavia makes that an unviable travel destination, Slovenia's transition into an autonomous country has been relatively painless and undisputed. The state of its tourist industry in the face of the understandable concern people feel about visiting it means that the country is filled with friendly people eager to reassure you.

Slovenia now offers the full range of budget accommodation in line with Western Europe, and since prices are fixed in Deutschmarks or dollars, they're unlikely to fluctuate madly, regardless of the state of the country's economy.

Hotels are, for the most part, expensive. Prices range from £28.50–103.50 ($42.75–155; DM70–254). Except in Ljubljana, where prices are constant all year, expect to pay considerably more in July and August. Many hotels close in winter.

Motels and **guesthouses** supplement hotels at prices of £20.50–36.60 ($30.45–54.90; DM50–90) per double. Small **pensions** are typically better value, and solo travellers should opt for these as prices tend to be per person rather than per room. In addition, there is a growing supply of **private accommodation** at about £11–13 ($16.50–19.50; DM27–32); authorities prefer longer stays and may impose a surcharge of up to 30% if you only stay for one or two nights. A house bearing a sign saying *sobe* (room) is offering private accommodation. Approach the owner directly and you may get a better rate than the agencies offer.

There are also several **student hotels**, although the majority of these are open only in July and August. Many **student dormitories** are converted into hostels in summer. Expect to pay £6.10 ($9.10; DM15) per person here.

Slovenia also boasts a number of campsites at up to £4.80 ($7.30; DM12) per person. Campgrounds are spread all over the country, with sites in the mountains and by the sea.

ADDRESSES

Ljubljana Tourist Information Centre	Slovenska 35, 61000 Ljubljana Slovenia (tel. 61 224 222).
Slovenian Tourist Office	Moghul House, 57 Grosvenor Street, London W1X 9DA (tel. 0171 499 7488).

Ljubljana (tel. code 061)

TOURIST OFFICES
TIC, the Tourist Information Centre, Slovenska 35 (tel. 224222). From the station, follow Trg osvobodilne fronte to the right, then turn left on to Slovenska cesta, Ljubljana's main street. Open 8 a.m.–12 noon and 4–7 p.m.

For train information, try the station on Trg OF (tel. 315167), or Slovenijaturist on Slovenska 58 (tel. 311851).

HOTELS, MOTELS & PENSIONS
Grandovec, Dolenjska 336 (tel. 666350). £20.30 ($30.40; DM50) for a double, £12.20 ($18.30; DM30) for a single. Bus 3.

Pri Mraku, Rimska 4 (tel. 223412). From £22.80 ($34.20; DM56) for a double, £15.90 ($23.80; DM39) for a single. Bus 1, 2 or 5.

Pri Nikotu, Cesta v Zgornji log 1 (tel. 268630). £24.40 ($36.60; DM60) for a double. Bus 6.

Super Li Bellevue, Pod gozdom 12 (tel. 33404). £20.70 ($31; DM51) for a double, £12.20 ($18.30; DM30) for a single.

PRIVATE ROOMS
Book through Tourist Information Centre (see above). There is a choice of three categories with prices rising accordingly, ranging from £11–13 ($16.50–19.50; DM27–37) for a double to £6.10–6.75 ($9.10–9.75; DM15–22) for a single.

HI HOSTELS
Dijaški dom Bežigrad, Kardeljeva ploščad 28 (tel. 342867). Open July–Aug. £6.10 ($9.10; DM15) per person. Bus 6 from Titova Cesta to Stadion. Walk a short distance, then go right on to Dimičeva, then left.

Dijaški dom Tabor, Viduvdanska 7 (tel. 321060/7). Open July–Aug. Bus 5.

STUDENT HOSTELS
Around £4.90 ($7.30; DM15) per person. Open July–August

Dijaški dom Ivana Cankarja, Poljanska 26–28 (tel. 318948). Bus 11 from the train station.

Dijaški dom Tabor, Vidovdanska 7 (tel. 321067).

Dijaški dom Vič, Gerbičeva 51a (tel. 261282).

CAMPING
Autocamp Jezica, Dunajska 270 (tel. 371382). Bus 6 from the train station. Around £11−13 ($16.50−19.50; DM12) per person.
Autocamp Smlednik, 61210 Dragočajna (tel. 627002).

Bled (tel. code 064)

TOURIST OFFICE
Turistično Društvo souvenir stand, below the Park Hotel Bled. The booklet *Bled Tourist News* is recommended.

PRIVATE ROOMS
Kompas Tourist Agency, at the Hotel Krim and in the new shopping mall, rents private accommodation at £6.10−6.50 ($9.10−9.75; DM27−32) per single, (DM15−16) per double.
Emona Globtour (tel. 78385); by the bus station.

HOSTEL
Bledec Youth Hostel, Grajska cesta 17 (tel. 221352). Slovenia's only year-round hostel. Up the hill from the bus station. Around £6.70 ($10; DM16.40) per person, regardless of membership, but HI members are excused tourist tax. Supplement charged for one-night stays.

CAMPING
Zaka (tel. 77325). In a valley at the west end of Bled lake, 2km from the bus station. Around £6 ($9; DM14.80) per person.

SPAIN (España)

Although prices have risen substantially over the past decade Spain still offers the budget traveller a plentiful supply of some of the least expensive accommodation possibilities in Europe. Virtually all the various types of accommodation are inspected and categorized by the Secretaria de Estado de Turismo. If you are looking for your own room there is quite an array of officially categorized lodgings to choose from (for the sake of convenience, these are grouped together under the heading **pensions** in the city sections below). The intricacies of the rating system detailed below are intended as a rough guide. For the reasons given, do not treat them as hard and fast rules.

Least expensive of all the officially categorized accommodations are *fondas*, denoted by a white 'F' on a square blue sign. Next up the scale are *casas de huespedes* (blue sign with white CH), followed by *pensiónes* (P), graded from one up to three stars. Then come *hospedajes*, infrequently seen in the country as a whole, but common in Santiago do Compostela. At this lower end of the market there is little point expecting anything other than basic facilities, but standards of cleanliness are usually perfectly acceptable. *Hostal-residencias* (HR) and *hostales* (H), both graded from one up to three stars, are a bit more expensive, while at the pinnacle of the rating system are *hoteles* (H) and *hotel-residencias* (HR), graded from one up to five stars. The appendage *residencia* indicates that no meals, other than (perhaps) breakfast, are served at the establishment; otherwise a *hostal-residencia* or *hotel-residencia* is similar in every respect to a comparably rated hostal or hotel.

As a rule the singles in any establishment cost around 60–80% of the price of comparable doubles. By law, guests can request that an extra bed be included in a room. This should add no more than 35% to the cost of a double and no more than 60% to the cost of a single. The Secretaria de Estado de Turismo not only categorizes establishments but also sets maximum prices for their rooms, according to the facilities available. By law these prices have to be displayed on the door of the room. With certain agreed and stipulated exceptions, it is illegal for owners to charge more than the stated price. The more usual exceptions are the peak season (usually July and August) and, in Seville, during Holy Week and the April Fair, when prices can be raised quite legally. Some owners choose to offer their rooms below the official price, though this can create the impression that the whole system is a bit of a shambles; for example, you can pay more for a room in a *casa de huespedes* than for a similar room in a better category of accommodation such as a *pensión* or *hostal-residencia*. During the quieter period of the year (October to early March) there is scope for bargaining with owners who have not already voluntarily dropped their prices. Understandings can be reached fairly easily with owners who know there are plenty of rooms available just down the street.

Even in peak season there are rooms available in all the types of accommodations mentioned above which fall into the budget category. Your interest in *hoteles* and *hotel-residencias* however is likely to be confined to the bottom ranking, as prices for a basic one-star double start at around 3600–4000ptas (£18–20; $27–30). A comparable room in a three-star hostel or *hostal-residencia* is usually similar in price, though they can be considerably more expensive. In other types of accommodation singles in the price range 1000–2000ptas (£5–10; $7.50–15.00) are widely available, as are doubles for 1600–3500ptas (£8.00–17.50; $12.00–26.25). You are more likely to find rooms at the lower end of these price scales outside the main resorts and the more popular tourist towns. On average you can expect to pay around 1600ptas (£8; $12) for singles, 2400ptas (£12; $18) for doubles in the main tourist destinations. Although there are some very cheap rooms available in popular places such as Madrid, Barcelona and the Andalucian cities, these tend to fill early in the day during the peak season. Phoning ahead is difficult unless you speak Spanish as very few owners speak any other language (signs outside their establishment claiming otherwise are often just a ruse to attract your attention), and in any case, owners seldom accept reservations made by phone. At best, phoning ahead will let you ascertain whether rooms are available, but do not be surprised if they have been filled by the time you arrive in person. One consolation is that there are generally a host of other accommodation possibilities in the same street, or even in the same building.

Now and again you may also see *camas* (beds), *camas y comidas* (bed and board), or *habitaciones* (rooms) advertised in bars or private homes. These can work out the least expensive accommodation option of all, with the possible bonus of good, cheap meals thrown in. As always, have a look at the room before making a firm acceptance. Again, there is probably nothing to be lost by trying to haggle the price down a bit, except in the peak periods when owners can afford to be choosy, and may just send you packing. Last year Barcelona began a regulated system of Bed & Breakfast accommodation (see below), and other cities may follow suit.

Hostelling is not a particularly good option in Spain as a whole. There are about 150 hostels of vastly differing quality, at which HI cards are obligatory. Most of the main places of interest are covered, with several notable exceptions, such as Salamanca and Santiago de Compostela. Only about 20 hostels remain open all year round, with many operating from July to September only. This means that outside these months hostel accommodation is lacking in a number of places of considerable interest. Even during the period from July to mid-September independent travellers may not be able to get into the temporary hostels in places such as León, Segovia and Avila, as they are frequently filled by school and youth groups.

However, hostelling is not to be dismissed as a way of seeing the main cities, with the possible exception of Seville (with a very small hostel for so popular a city, which is usually full of local students). The question is whether prices, curfews, lack of security and the fact hostels are rarely centrally located make hostelling worthwhile. The normal hostel curfew of 10.30 p.m. in winter and 11.30 p.m. in summer is extended to 1–2 a.m. in Madrid, Barcelona and San Sebastian (no curfew at Madrid 'Richard Schirrmann' but the hostel is a long way from the centre if you miss the last metro). Even a 1 a.m. curfew is a bit early for anyone wanting to enjoy the nightlife of the cities, where things do not really begin to get going until around midnight. Charges for an overnight stay at hostels are around 650–1700ptas (£3.25–8.50; $5.00–12.75).

Camping is not a great option either, and probably not worth considering unless you plan to travel extensively outside the main towns. Sites are frequently situated far from the town centre, and ill served by public transport. In effect, this can impose a curfew more restrictive than at any hostel. If you are keen on camping, at least the standards at the government-regulated sites are quite high, and although rating makes little difference to price, the facilities at the Class 1 sites do tend to be better than at the lesser-rated sites. Even in the sites serving the main towns you should pay no more than 400ptas (£2; $3) per person and per tent. However, to this you can add the cost of getting to the site, and, as security is a problem, the cost of leaving your luggage at the train or bus station, usually 150ptas (£0.75; $1.25).

Camping rough outside the official campgrounds is possible, provided the consent of the landowner is obtained. However, tents must not be pitched in a town; close to roads, military bases or reservoirs; in a dry river bed which may be subject to flooding; or within 1km of any official site. Camping on publicly owned land is prohibited by some local authorities.

Throughout most of the year the weather will present few problems for those **sleeping out**, but the Guardia Civil make a habit of patrolling areas which are popular and will wake up anybody they discover. Only if you are very short of money will they charge you with vagrancy. This leaves you with the same dilemma as in Belgium or the Netherlands: namely, staying within the law makes you an attractive target for muggers. Basically, sleeping out is foolhardy, especially in the cities and coastal resorts. If you are attacked it is likely to be by an organized gang, who may well become vicious if you try to resist (and sometimes even if you do not).

In the remote mountain regions, a network of cheap **refuges** with bunk-bedded dormitories and basic cooking facilities is maintained by the Federacion Español de Montañismo. It may also be possible to stay in some **monasteries** in the more isolated areas. As the number of inhabitants have fallen, some monasteries have taken to letting vacant cells for about 1200ptas (£6; $9) per night in order to supplement monastic income. Some do not charge a set fee, preferring to suggest a donation. Many admit visitors of either sex. Some, especially in Galicia, Catalonia, and Majorca, are located in spectacular settings. It is possible simply to enquire about staying the night on arrival, but as there may be no one about it is advisable to contact the local Tourist Office first. They will arrange a time for you to show up at the monastery.

ADDRESSES

Spanish Tourist Office	57 St James's Street, London SW1A (tel. 0171 499 0901)
Spanish YHA	Red Española de Albergues Juveniles, José Ortega y Gasset 71, Madrid 28006 (tel. 91 347 7700).
Camping	Federacion Española de Empresarios de Campings, Gran Via 88, Madrid 28013 (tel. 91 242 3168).
	ANCE, Principe De Vergara 85, 2 Ocha, 28006 Madrid. Maps and information on the official campsites from the above. A map is also available on request from the Spanish Tourist Office.
Mountain refuges	Federacion Español de Montañismo, Calle Alberto Aguiler 3, Madrid 15 (tel. 91 445 1382).

Barcelona (tel. code 93)

TOURIST OFFICES
Oficina de Turismo e Información. Various locations throughout the city:

Barcelona Sants train station (tel. 250 5224). Open daily 7.30 a.m.–10.30 p.m.

Barcelona Termino train station (tel. 319 2791). Open Mon.–Sat. 8.30 a.m.–9 p.m.

Placa Sant Jaume (tel. 318 2525). Open Mon.–Fri. 9 a.m.–9 p.m., Sat. 9 a.m.–2 p.m. In the Gothic Quarter. Metro: Jaume I, then follow Jaume I.

Monumento a Colón, Porta de la Pau (tel. 302 5224). Open Mon.–Fri. 9.30 a.m.–1.30 p.m. and 4.30–8.30 p.m. Metro: Drassanes, then a short walk down to the Columbus monument on the waterfront.

Gran Via Corts Catalanes 658 (tel. 301 7443). Open Mon.–Fri. 9 a.m.–1.30 p.m. and 4–7 p.m., Sat. 9 a.m.–2 p.m. Information on all of Spain. Metro: Passeig de Gràcia.

Airport (tel. 325 5829). Open daily 8 a.m.–8 p.m., except Sun. (morning only).

Barcelona Information. Round the clock information service (tel. 010). English speakers available.
  The youth tourist office is at Carre Gravina (tel. 302 0682).

• **Street names**
Most street signs in Barcelona give the Catalan and Spanish versions of the street's name. The Catalan version is used in most of the addresses below.

TROUBLE SPOTS
The Placa Reial is best avoided after 10–11 p.m., as is the area around the docks at the foot of the Ramblas (by the Columbus monument). During the daytime the crowds which throng the Ramblas provide an attractive working environment for pickpockets and petty thieves, so be especially careful with your valuables.

PENSIONS
Expect to pay at least 2000ptas (£10; $15) for a double room – possibly much more. In summer prices can reach double the off-

peak rate. There are, however, hundreds to choose from and even if you choose to search on foot you will find many of the pensions listed below share a building with similar establishments.

Cheapest doubles around 1050ptas (£5.25; $7.90)

1. La Paz, Argentera 37 (tel. 319 4408). Metro: Jaume I. The street is left off Via Laietana heading towards the waterfront.
2. Call, Arco San Ramón del Call 4 (tel. 302 1123). Metro: Jaume I. Along Jaume I and through the square until you see Sant Domenc del Call on the right. From this street, Call on the left takes you into the square.
3. Río, Sant Pau 119 (tel. 241 0651). In the area between Av. del Paral-lel and the Ramblas. Metro: Paral-lel. Go right at the junction of Paral-lel and Ronda de Sant Pau.
4. Romea, Junta do Comercio 21 (tel. 318 0299). Metro: Jaume I, then follow Princesa.
5. Sant Pancrás, Merced 4 (tel 302 2426). Metro: Barceloneta. Head left along the main road PG de Colom towards the Columbus monument, then right at Marquet.
6. Iglesias, Nou de la Rambla (tel. 318 8534). Metro: Liceu. Right off the Ramblas, walking down towards the port.
7. Plaza, Fontanella 18 (tel. 301 0139). Doubles 3500ptas (£17.50; $26.25). Between Plaça Catalunya and Plaça del Bisbe Urquinaona. Metro: Urquinaona or Catalunya.
8. Alhambra, Jonqueres 13 (tel. 317 1924). Metro: Urquinaona. Jonqueres runs out of Urquinaona square to the right of Trafalgar.
9. Asunción, Rambla de Catalunya 42 (tel. 301 2869). Metro: Catalunya. A few blocks down the street from Plaça Catalunya.
10. El Cantón, Nou de Sant Francesc 40 (tel. 317 3019). Metro: Drassanes. Walk down towards the Columbus monument, left along J.A. Clave, then left.
11. Florinda, Montserrat 13 (tel. 302 2053). Metro: Drassanes. Off the Ramblas near the stop is Madalena, from which Montserrat runs off to the right.
12. Meridiana, Avda Meridiana 2 (tel. 309 5125). Near the Parc de la Ciutadella. Metro: Marina.
13. New York, Gignas 6 (tel. 315 0304). Metro: Barceloneta. Head away from the port, across the main road and take the street to the left of Laietana into Gignas.
14. Nilo, J Anselmo Clave 17 (tel. 317 9044). See 10. Outside the period July—Aug. the price falls by about 10%.

15. Le Parisien, Rambla de Sant Josep 114 (tel. 231 8519). Metro: Liceu. Walk towards the Plaça Catalunya.
16. Mediterráneo, Rambla de Catalunya 106 (tel. 215 0900). Around 5000ptas (£25; $37.50) for a double. Metro: Provença. A few minutes' walk along Rossello brings you to Rambla de Catalunya and the hotel.
17. Lepanto, Rauric 10 (tel. 302 0081). Metro: Liceu. Near the station Boqueria heads off the Ramblas (opposite Hospital). Rauric is right off Boqueria.
18. La Lonja, PG d'Isabel II 14 (tel. 319 3032). Metro: Barceloneta. On the main road opposite the port. From Sept.–June prices are about 20% cheaper.
19. Marmo, Gignas 25 (tel. 315 4208). Doubles 2500ptas (£12.50; $18.75). Metro: Barceloneta.
20. Noya, Rambla de Canaletas 133 (tel. 301 4831). Doubles 3200ptas (£16; $24) in winter, 6000ptas (£30; $45) in summer. Just off Plaça Catalunya. Metro: Catalunya.
21. Victoria, Comtal 9 (tel. 317 4597). Doubles 2400ptas (£12; $18). Metro: Urquinaona. Follow Laietana from the square, then right.
22. Dali, Boqueria 12 (tel. 318 5580). Doubles 2900ptas (£14.50; $21.75) in winter, 3400ptas (£17; $25.50) in summer. Metro Liceu.
23. Calella, Calella 1/Pral 2 (tel. 317 6841).
24. Layetana, Pl. Ramón Berenguer el Grand 2 (tel. 319 2012). Doubles 3500ptas (£17.50; $26.25). Off Via Laietana. Metro: Jaume I. Head up Via Laietana away from the port.
25. Santcarlo, Plaça de Urquinaona 5 (tel. 302 4125). Metro: Urquinaona. From Oct.–May rooms are about 20% cheaper.
26. Barcelona, Roser 40 (tel. 4242 5075). Metro: Paral-lel. Roser runs off Paral-lel near the station towards the hills. Doubles from 3000ptas (£15; $22.50), but almost twice as much in summer.
27. Levante, Bajada San Miguel 2 (tel. 317 9565). Doubles 3500ptas (£17.50; $26.25).
28. Sans, Antonio de Campmany 82 (tel. 331 3700). Doubles 2500ptas (£12.50; $18.75).
29. Lloret, Rambla de Canaletas 125 (tel. 317 3366). 4500ptas (£22.50; $33.75). Metro: Catalunya.
30. Palacios, Gran Via Corts Catalanes 629 Bis (tel. 301 3792). Doubles 3400ptas (£17; $25.50). Metro: Passeig de Gràcia. A short walk from the exit on Corts Catalanes.
31. Roma, Plaça Reial 11 (tel. 302 0366). Metro: Liceu. Right off the Ramblas as you head down to the Columbus monument.

32. Conde Guell, Comte d'Urgell 32–34 (tel. 240 0257). Metro: Urgell (closest) or Hospital Clinic.
33. Cervantes, Cervantes 6 (tel. 302 5168). Metro: Liceu. Near the station Boqueria heads off the Ramblas (opposite Hospital). At the end of Boqueria turn right, go straight on across Ferran and on down Avinyo into Cervantes.
34. Colón, Aragó 281 (tel. 215 4700). Metro: Passeig de Gràcia (exit on to Aragó).
35. La Hípica, General Castanos 2 (tel. 315 1392). Metro: Barceloneta. From Pas de Sota take Muralla. General Castanos is on the opposite side of Plaça del Palau. From Termino station head left on Av. del Marqués de l'Argentera then left again.
36. Nuevo Colón, Avda. Marqués de la Argentera 19 (tel. 319 5077). One street further up Plaça del Palau from General Castanos.
37. Vergara, Bergara 5 (tel. 317 3035). Off Plaça Catalunya. Metro: Catalunya.
38. La Cartuja, Tordero 43 (tel. 213 3312). Doubles from 3000ptas (£15; $22.50).
39. Hosteria Gray, Ramalleres 27 (tel. 302 3130). Doubles around 4000ptas (£20; $30).
40. Rosa, Pelayo 14, 4–1 (tel. 301 0842). Doubles from 3000ptas (£15; $22.50).
41. Nilo, J. Anselmo Clave 17 (tel. 317 9044). Doubles 2600ptas (£13; $19.50); more in summer.
42. Goya, Pau Claris 74 (tel. 302 2565). Metro; Urquinaona or Passeig de Gràcia (exit onto Via de Corts Catalanes).
43. Lider, Rambla de Catalunya 84 (tel. 215 5065). Doubles from 3200ptas (£16; $24). Metro: Passeig de Gràcia (exit onto Arag). Short walk to Rambla de Catalunya.
44. Pension 45, Tallers 45 (tel. 302 7061). Doubles from 4000ptas (£20; $30). Tallers runs out off Plaça de la Universitat to the left of Sant Antoni. Metro: Universitat.
45. Alcazar, Via Laietana 145 (tel. 215 3868). Metro: Passeig de Gràcia (exit onto Arag). Short walk to Via Laietana.
46. Fontanella, Via Laietana 71 (tel. 317 5943). Doubles 3600ptas (£18; $27). Metro: Urquinaona. Via Laietana runs out of the square.
47. Opera, Sant Pau 20 (tel. 318 8201) Metro: Liceu. Sant Pau runs off the Ramblas near the station, one street closer to the port than Hospital.
48. La Palmera, Jerusalem 30 (tel. 317 0997). By the 'La Boqueria' market, also known as the Mercat de Sant Josep, off Rambla de Sant Josep. Metro: Liceu.

49. Lleida, Corsega 201 (tel. 430 0122). Metro: Hospital Clinic. Follow Comte d'Urgell one block (ascending street numbers) then right two blocks on Corsega.
50. Cisneros, Aribau 54 (tel. 254 1800). Doubles around 3800ptas (£19; $28.50). Aribau runs from Plaça de la Universitat.
51. Felipe II, Mallorca 329 (tel. 258 7758). Metro: Provença. From Provença turn left down Girona onto Mallorca.
52. Pereira, Diputacio 346 (tel. 245 1981). Metro: Universitat. Walk up Aribau from Plaça de la Universitat, then right.

HOSTELS
Hostal de Joves, Passeig de Pujades 29 (tel. 300 3104). Midnight curfew. 825ptas (£4.15; $6.20). By the Parc de la Ciutadella. Only 300m from the Termino station. Right on leaving the station, left on PG de Picasso, then right. Metro: Arc de Triomf on Line 1. From Barcelona Sants take Line 3 to Espana to change to Line 1.

'Mare de Deu de Montserrat', Passeig de Nostra Senyora del Coll 41–51 (tel. 210 5151). Curfew 1 a.m. 850–1275ptas (£4.25–6.40; $6.40–9.60). A 25-minute trip from the centre. Bus 28 from Plaça de Catalunya (Metro: Catalunya). Although the other permanent hostels are very good, this is a particularly pleasant hostel to stay in.

Alberg Joves Sagrada Familia, Industria 81 Tda.1 (tel. 457 8471).

Alberg Palau, Palau 6 (tel. 412 5080). Bus 14 or 18.

Kabul, pl. Reial 17 (tel. 318 5190). 800ptas (£4; $6) per night. Bus 14 or 18.

'Pere Tarres', Numancia 149–151 (tel. 410 2309). Numancia runs from Barcelona Sants station in the opposite direction from Tarragona. The hostel is a 15-minute walk along the street. Two metro stops are slightly closer: Les Corts and Maria Cristina.

'Studio', Duquesa d'Orleans 58 (tel. 205 0961). Open 1 July–30 Sept. Bus 22, 34, 64 or 66.

Saint Joan de la Salle, St Joan de la Salle 37 (tel. 418 8261). Open 1 July–30 Sept. Bus 22.

PRIVATE ACCOMMODATION
Amics per Sempre, c/Valencia 304, 08009 Barcelona (tel. 488 2424; fax 498 3232). Advance bookings preferred.

CAMPING
Cala-Gogo-El Prat (tel. 379 4600). Open Mar.–Nov. 500ptas (£2.50; $3.75) per person, tent included. By the beach in Prat de Llobregat, 8km from the city. Take bus 605 from Plaça de Espanya to the terminus in Prat, then change to bus 604 to the beach.

El Toro Bravo (tel. 637 3462). Open year round. 550ptas (£2.75; $4.15) per tent and per person. In Vildecans, slightly further out than the site above. Bus L93 from Plaça de la Universitat, or bus L90 from Plaça Goya.

Filipinas (tel. 658 2895). Open year round. Same prices as the El Toro Bravo. Also in Vildecans. Buses as above.

La Ballena Alegre (tel. 658 0504). Open Apr.–Sept. The third site in Vildecans; considerably more expensive than the other two. 750ptas (£3.75; $5.65) per tent, 400ptas (£2; $6) per person.

Barcino, Laureano Miro 50 (tel. 372 8501). Open year round. 500ptas (£2.50; $3.75) per tent and per person. In Esplugues de Llobregat, the closest site to the city. Accessible by bus CO or BI from Plaça de Catalunya.

Tres Estreallas (tel. 662 1116). Open Apr.–Sept. 600ptas (£3; $4.50) per tent and per person. In Gava: bus L93 from Universital or L90 from pl. Goya.

Albatros (tel. 662 2031). Open May–Sept. Up to 800ptas (£4; $6) per person. Also in Gava; buses as above.

Córdoba (tel. code 957)

TOURIST OFFICES

Oficina de Turismo de la Junta de Andalucá, Torrijos 10 (Palacio de Congresos), 14003 Cordoba (tel. 471235). Open Mon.–Fri. 9.30 a.m.–2 p.m. and 5–7 p.m., Sat. 10 a.m.–1 p.m in summer; Mon.–Fri. 9.30 a.m.–2 p.m. and 3.30–5.30 p.m., Sat. 10 a.m.–1 p.m. in winter. Well supplied with information on the city and the region.

Oficina Municipal de Turismo, Plaza Judá Levi (tel. 472 0000). Open Mon.–Fri. 8 a.m.–3 p.m. A useful source of information on the city.

BASIC DIRECTIONS

The two Tourist Offices are close to the Mezquita, the focal point of the old city, a 20-minute walk away from the train station on Avenida de América. Take the main road (Avda. de Cervantes) running away from the train station slightly to the right across Avda. de América, and then continue on down Paseo de la Victoria. Turn left along Lope de Hoces heading towards the Trinidad Church, then right down Tejón y Marn. Go across Fernandez into Almanzor and continue straight ahead to the junction with Deanes.

Head right along Deanes (at which point Plaza Judá Levi is off to your right) and then left down Medina y Core to the Mezquita. Torrijos runs down the side of the Mezquita towards the Triunfo de San Rafael and Puerta del Puente.

FINDING ACCOMMODATION

The best area to look for cheap accommodation in Córdoba is the Juderńa, the old Jewish quarter between Plaza de las Tendillas and the River Guadalquivir. Within this district the streets to the east of the Mezquita (the opposite side of the Mezquita from Torrijos) are particularly good places to look, with Rey Heredia having the largest concentration of cheap accommodation in the city.

PENSIONS

La Milagrosa II, Rey Heredia 12 (tel. 473317). Close to the Mezquita. On the opposite side of the Mezquita from Medina y Core Encarnación leads into Rey Heredia.

Perales, Avda de los Mozrabes 15 (tel. 230325). Doubles 2400ptas (£12; $18). Head right along Avda de América from the train station and the street is off to the left after Avda de Cervantes.

Rey Heredia, Rey Heredia 26 (tel. 474182). Doubles 3000ptas (£15; $22.50). See La Milagrosa.

El Portillo, Cabezas 2 (tel. 472091). Doubles 3000ptas (£15; $22.50). Off the right-hand end of Rey Heredia if you join the latter from Encarnación (see La Milagrosa).

Mari, Pimentera 6–8 (tel. 479575). Doubles 3000ptas (£15; $22.50).

Trinidad, Corregidor Luis de la Cerda 58 (tel. 487905). The street begins at the foot of Torrijos, near the Triunfo de San Rafael and the Puerta del Puente.

El León, Céspedes 6 (tel. 473021). The street runs from the Mezquita, along the tower.

Las Tendillas, Jesús y Maria 1 (tel. 473029). Doubles 2800ptas (£14; $21). From the train station head left, then turn right and follow Avda del Gran Capitán to its end. Go left along Conde Gondomar into Plaza de las Tendillas, then right to the start of Jesús y Maria.

Alhaken, Alhaken II 10 (tel. 471593). Left off Avda de Cervantes.

Martinez Rücker, Martinez Rücker 14 (tel. 473561). Doubles 3000ptas (£15; $22.50). Off Magistral Glez Frances, the street running down the opposite side of the Mezquita from Torrijos.

Mary II, Horno de Porros 6 (tel. 486185). In the Judeńa. Doubles 2000ptas (£10; $15).

El Alcazar, San Basilio 2 (tel. 202561). From the foot of Torrijos turn right along Amador de los Rios, cross the gardens and take

Caballerizas Reales, turn left up M. Rao, then left into San Basilio.

La Paz, Moreira 7 (tel. 473780). Doubles 2650ptas (£13.25; $20).

Lucano, Lucano 1 (tel. 476098). Go left from the foot of Torrijos and follow Ronda de Isasa along the river. Turn left at Cruz Rastro. Lucano is to the right at the junction of Cruz Rastro and San Fernando.

Almanzor, Corregidor Luis de la Cerda 10 (tel. 474354). See Trinidad.

El Cisne Verde, Pintor Greco 6 (tel. 294360). Doubles from around 3000ptas (£15; $22.50).

Seneca, Conde y Luque 7 (tel. 473234). Doubles 3500ptas (£17.50; $26.25), breakfast included.

La Alegria, Menéndez Pelayo 8 (tel. 470544). Right off Avda del Gran Capitán (see Las Tendillas), opposite Gongora.

Luis de Góngora, Horno de la Trinidad 7 (tel. 295399). Double with bath 4500ptas (£22.50; $33.75). Off Plaza de la Trinidad by the Trinidad Church.

HI HOSTEL
Residencia Juvenil Cordoba, Plaza Judá Leví (tel. 290166). Around 1000ptas (£5; $7.50) per person, 1200ptas (£6; $9) for those over 25. Excellent hostel, opened as recently as 1990. Fine location, a couple of blocks from the Mezquita.

CAMPING
Campamento Municipal, Avda del Brillante 50 (tel. 472000/ 275048). Buses every 10 minutes to/from the city centre. 400ptas (£2; $3) per tent and per person. Grade I site, open year round.

Cerca de Lagartijo (tel. 250426). Situated 3km out on the Madrid-Cádiz road. 290ptas (£1.45; $2.20) per tent and per person. Grade II site, open 1 June–30 Sept.

Granada (tel. code 958)

TOURIST OFFICES
Oficina de Turismo de la Junta Andalucá, Calle Liberos 2, 18001 Granada (tel. 225990/221022). Open Mon.–Fri. 10 a.m.–1 p.m. and 4–7 p.m., Sat. 10 a.m.–1 p.m. From Gran Vía de Colón turn right down Cárcel de Baja along the north side of the cathedral, then head left along the western facade of the cathedral and straight on. Libreros runs away to the right.

Oficina de Turismo del Patronato Provincial de Turismo, Plaza Mariana Pineda 10 (tel. 226688). Open Mon.–Fri. 10 a.m.–1.30 p.m. and 4.30–7 p.m., Sat. 10 a.m.–1 p.m. From Puerta Real follow Angel Ganivet into Plaza Mariana Pineda.

BASIC DIRECTIONS

The train station is linked to the town centre by buses 4, 5, 9 or 11, but it is only 15 minutes on foot if you want to walk. From the station, go straight ahead down Avenida de Andaluces then turn right along Avenida de la Constitución. Continue straight on until you see Gran Vía de Colón running away to the right. This street leads right into the heart of old Granada, passing the cathedral before arriving at Plaza Isabel la Católica. Turning left from this square along Calle Reyes Católicos brings you to Plaza Nueva, the modern city centre.

FINDING ACCOMMODATION

As a rule you should not have much trouble finding a bed in Granada. Two streets near the station are particularly well supplied with cheap rooms: Avenida Andaluces and, a bit further away, Calle San Juan de Dios. The small streets on either side of Gran Vía de Colón are also worth investigating. In the town centre, the streets around Plaza Nueva (Cuesta de Gomérez in particular) and Plaza del Carman (especially Calle de Navas which runs off the square) have a more than adequate number of cheap establishments at most times of year, as has the area around Plaza Trinidad. The exceptions to this happy situation are the very peak of the summer season and the period immediately before and during Holy Week, as all the Andalucian cities receive a huge influx of visitors at this time.

PENSIONS

Castil, Darrillo Magdalena 1 (tel. 259507).

Savoy, Avda Dr. Olriz 4–4 (tel. 270847). Across Avda de la Constitución from Avda de Andaluces.

Yale, Santos 2 (tel. 279592). Turn right off Gran Vía de Colón down Boquerón Almona, then left.

San Jerónimo, San Jerónimo 12 (tel. 275040). The street runs from Plaza Universidad. Turn right off Gran Vía de Colón down Marqués de Falces and go straight ahead until you reach Plaza Universidad, then go left.

Mesones, Mesones 44 (tel. 263244). Doubles from 1800ptas (£9; $13.50) in winter, 2600ptas (£13; $19.50) in summer.

Gomérez, Cuesta Gomérez 10 (tel. 224437). Doubles 2000ptas (£10; $30). No curfew.

Sevioca, Avda Dr Olriz 12 (tel. 202366). See Savoy, above.

Los Montes, Arteaga 3–1 (tel. 277930). Doubles 2300ptas (£11.50; $17.25). Left off Gran Vía de Colón.

El Hidalgo, Horno de Espadero 8 (tel. 263384).

Turin, Ancha de Capuhinos 16 (tel. 200311). Follow Avda Andaluces, then go straight down Avda del Dr. Olriz into Ancha de Capuchinos.

Andalucia, Campo Verde 5–1 (tel. 261909). Near Puerta Real. Follow Mesones until you see Campo Verde on the right.

Plaza Isabel, Colcha 13 (tel. 223022).

Colonial, Joaquín Costa 5 (tel. 227673). Near the cathedral turn left off Gran Vía de Colón down Cetti Meriem then right.

La Redonda, Camino de Ronda 84 (tel. 254477). Near the main bus station.

Gran Capitan, Plaza Gran Capitan 4 (tel. 272124).

Muñoz, Mesones 53 (tel. 263819). Doubles 2400ptas (£12; $18). Near the Cathedral.

Romero, Sillerá de Mesones (tel. 266079). Off Plaza Trinidad.

San José de la Montaña, San José Baja 19 (tel. 252490).

Olimpia, Alvaro de Bazán 6 (tel. 278238). The street crosses Gran Vía de Colón.

San Antón, San Antón 51 (tel. 262365). Off Recogidas close to Puerta Real.

Veracruz, San Antón 39 (tel. 262770). See San Anton.

Mario, Cardenal Mendoza 15 (tel. 201427). Left off San Juan de Dios.

Martínez, San Pedro Mártir 34 (tel. 228793). From Puerta Real follow Acera del Casino and head straight on across Plaza del Campillo and Plaza Bitaubin to San Pedro Mártir.

Navarro Ramos, Cuesta de Gomérez 21 (tel. 250555). Clean, friendly and cheap. Doubles 1900ptas (£9.50; $14.25).

California, Cuesta de Gomérez 37 (tel. 224056). Doubles from 2500ptas (£12.50; $18.75), breakfast 300ptas (£1.50; $2.25).

Yuca, Moral de la Magdalena 38 (tel. 266735). From Alhóndiga turn right down Calle de la Gracia, left along Puentezelas then right.

San Joaquín, Mano de Hierro 14 (tel. 282879). Left off San Juan de Dios near the church.

Landazuri, Cuesta de Gomérez 24 (tel. 221406).

Nuevas Naciones, Plaza Triviño 1 (tel. 270503).

Las Cumbres, Cardenal Mendoza 4 (tel. 291222). Left off San Juan de Dios.

Gran Vía, Gran Vía de Colon 17 (tel. 279212). Close to Pl. Isabel Católica. Doubles from 2500ptas (£12.50; $18.75).

Zacatín, Ermita 11 (tel. 221155). 2400ptas (£12; $18). Near the Cathedral.

Roma, Navas 1 (tel. 226277). Off Plaza del Carmen.

Vista Nevada, Dr. Guirao Gea 6 (tel. 271506). Right off Avda del Dr. Olóriz. See Savoy.

Sevilla, Fábrica Vieja 18 (tel. 278513). Off Tablas near Plaza Trinidad. From Alhóndiga turn right down Mlaga and keep going until you see Fábrica Vieja on the left.

Viena, Hospital de Santa Ana 2 (tel. 221859). The street runs between Cuesta de Gomérez and Plaza Santa Ana.

Granadina, Párraga 7 (tel. 256714). From Alhondiga turn right down Calle de la Gracia then left. Párraga runs from Calle de la Gracia to join Recogidas near Puerta Real.

Granada-Ronda, Sócrates 12 (tel. 280099). Off Camino de Ronda by the Glorieta Arabial and the main bus station.

HI HOSTEL
Camino de Ronda 171 (tel. 272638). Not far from the station. Turn left as you leave, left under the tracks. This takes you to the start of Camino de Ronda.

HOSTEL
Albergue Juvenil de Viznar, Camino de Fuente Nueva (tel. 490307).

CAMPING
There are a number of sites in and around Granada, all of which charge 340–440ptas (£1.70–2.20; $2.55–3.30) per person and per tent:

Sierra Nevada, Avda de Madrid 107 (tel. 150954). Grade 1 site, open 15 Mar.–15 Oct. Bus 3.

El Ultimo, Camino Huetor Vega 22 (tel. 123069). Grade 2 site, open all year.

Maria Eugenia, Carretera de Malaga (tel. 200606). Grade 2 site, open all year.

Los Alamos, Carretera Jerez-Cartagena (tel. 208479). Grade 2 site, open 1 Apr.–30 Oct.

Madrid (tel. code 910)

TOURIST OFFICES
Información turistica Oficina Nacional. Various locations. The head office is in the Torre de Madrid at Plaza de España 1 (tel. 541

2325). Open Mon.–Fri. 9 a.m.–7 p.m., Sat. 9.30 a.m.–1.30 p.m. Metro: Plaza de España. Branch offices operate in the Chamartin train station (tel. 315 9976) and near the international arrivals desk at Barajas airport (tel. 305 8656).

Información turistica Oficina Nacional, Plaza Mayor 3 (tel. 266 5477). Metro: Sol. Along Calle Mayor from Puerto del Sol.

The municipal office, Calle duque de Medicanel 2 (tel. 429 4951), will provide you with tourist information about the city, the national offices with information about Madrid and the country as a whole. None of the offices will book rooms, though they will offer advice on accommodation. A private agency called Brujula will book rooms (office in the underground bus terminal at Plaza de Colon. Metro: Colon).

There is also a youth tourist information office in the underground station at Puerta del Sol.

TROUBLE SPOTS

While Fuencarral and Hortaleza are safe places to stay, you should be wary of the nearby Chuecca quarter (right of Hortaleza as you walk up from Gran Vía). This area, around Plaza de Chuecca including Reina, Utantas, San Marcos and the streets in between, is the gay and hard drugs centre of Madrid. Although there is plenty of cheap accommodation in this area (including some listed below), this part of town should be a last resort if you are looking for somewhere to stay.

FINDING ACCOMMODATION

Madrid has a more than adequate supply of cheap rooms, even in summer. The hotels section below offers numerous possibilities which you can telephone to see if they have rooms available. If you would prefer simply to head off in search of a room, some areas are particularly good to look in. Gran Vía, the main thoroughfare, has an excellent supply of rooms, but prices are generally higher than elsewhere in the city. Prices are noticeably lower in the streets leading off Gran Vía. Amongst these Hortaleza and Fuencarral (metro: Gran Vía) and San Bernardo (metro: Noviciado) are especially well supplied with cheap places to stay. The cheapest part of town to stay in is between the Atocha train station and Puerta del Sol. Some of the cheapest establishments around Puerta del Sol are used by prostitutes, which, although the hotels are usually safe enough, hardly makes for a peaceful night. Whichever way you set about looking for a room, read the section on Trouble Spots above before you begin.

PENSIONS
Cheapest doubles from 1500ptas (£7.50; $11.25)

1. Corros, Atocha 28 (tel. 239 0025). The street leading from Atocha train station towards Plaza Mayor. Metro: Atocha or Antón Martín.
2. Gravina, Gravina 4 (tel. 222 3862).
3. Mola, Principe de Vergara 8 (tel. 435 7022).
4. Muñoz, Andrés Borrego 14 (tel. 531 4249).
5. Suiza Española, Carrera de San Jerónimo 32 (tel. 429 6814). Metro: Sol or Sevilla. San Jerónimo runs out of Puerta del Sol.
6. Josefina, Gran Vía 44 (tel. 521 8131). Metro: Plaza de España.
7. Vives, Barquillo 25 (tel. 232 5263). Off Gran Vía. Metro: Banco.
8. Higueras, Toledo 46 (tel. 265 9618).
9. Imperio, Relatores 3 (tel. 227 5018).
10. Marbella, Plaza de Isabel II 5 (tel. 247 6148). Metro: Opera.
11. Commercio, Santa Barbara 2 (tel. 531 0091).
12. Canoa, Silva 26 (tel. 532 1034).

Cheapest doubles from 2000ptas (£10; $15)

13. J.B., Blasco de Gueray 36 (tel. 448 9753).
14. Puebla, Puebla 9 (tel. 232 1918).
15. Mori, Plaza de las Cortés 3 (tel. 429 7208). Metro: Banco. Walk down Marqués de Cubas, then across Carrera de San Jerónimo.

Cheapest doubles around 1800–2100ptas (£9.00–10.50; $13.50–15.75)

16. Nuestra Señora del Camino, Fuencarral 39 (tel. 522 8481). Metro: Tribunal (closest) or Gran Vía. Fuencarral is off Gran Vía.
17. Marimart, Puerta del Sol 14 (tel. 522 9815). Metro: Sol. Iserte.
18. Fuencarral 16 (tel. 231 5212). Off Gran Vía. Metro: Gran Vía.
19. Miño, Arenal 16 (tel. 531 5079). Arenal runs out of Puerta del Sol towards the opera. Metro: Sol.
20. Universal, Carrera de San Jerónimo 32 (tel. 429 6779). See 5.
21. La Montaña, Juan Alvarez Mendicibal 44 (tel. 247 1088).

Cheapest doubles from 2500ptas (£12.50; $18.75)

22. El Bao, Espada 6 (tel. 369 1816).
23. Atocho, Rondo de Atocho 3 (tel. 227 4879).
24. La Noyesa, Aduana 16 (tel. 531 3844). Aduana runs between

Montera (off Puerta del Sol) and Peligros (off Alcala). Metro: Sol or Sevilla.

25. Delfina, Gran Vía 12 (tel. 522 6423). Metro: Banco or Gran Vía.
26. Odesa, Horteleza 38 (tel. 521 0338). Off Gran Vía. Metro: Gran Vía or Chueca.
27. Faustino, Cruz 33 (tel. 532 9098). Metro: Atocha or Antón Martín.
28. Fontela, Gran Vía 11. Metro: Banco or Gran Vía.
29. Alicante, Arenal 6 (tel. 531 5178). Off Gran Vía. Metro: Gran Vía or Chueca.
30. Tineo, Victoria 6 (tel. 521 4943).
31. Canal, Huertas 4 (tel. 530 2221).
32. Rivera, Atoche 79 (tel. 429 6130).
33. Calleja, Fernando VI 8 (tel. 319 4046).
34. Valdeorresa, Fuencarral 41 (tel. 232 7897). Off Gran Vía. Metro: Gran Vía or Tribunal.
35. Las Murallas, Fuencarral 23 (tel. 232 1063). Off Gran Vía. Metro: Gran Vía or Tribunal.
36. Río Navia, Infantas 13 (tel. 532 3050).
37. Don José, Gran Vía 38 (tel. 232 1385). Metro: Plaza de España.
38. Laredo, Arenal 15 (tel. 248 2423). Arenal runs out of Puerta del Sol towards the Opera.
39. Alcoriza, Gran Vía 20 (tel. 521 3308). Metro: Gran Vía or Banco.
40. Breogán, Fuencarral 25 (tel. 522 8153). Off Gran Vía. Metro: Gran Vía.
41. Mondragón, Carrera San Jerónimo 32 (tel. 429 6816). See Suiza Española, above.
42. Quintana, Tetun 19 (tel. 531 8676). Metro: Sol. Take Carmen (near the El Corte Inglés department store) out of Puerta del Sol, then right.
43. Riosol, Mayor 5 (tel. 532 3142).
44. Acapulco, Costinalla de Los Angeles 15 (tel. 559 6226).
45. Cereo, Costinalla de Santiago 2 (tel. 241 5378).
46. Marsella, Pez 19 (tel. 531 4744).
47. Los Angeles, Artistas 18 (tel. 533 0375).
48. La Noyesa, Aduna 16 (tel. 531 3844).

Cheapest doubles from 2800ptas (£14; $21)

49. Excelsior, Gran Vía 50 (tel. 547 3400). Metro: Plaza de España.
50. Mairu, Espejo 2 (tel. 547 3088). Very good, but also very popular. Off Plaza de Isabel II, to the right of the steps leading down into Escalinata. Metro: Opera.

51. America, Hortaleza 19 (tel. 522 6448). Off Gran Vía. Metro: Gran Vía.
52. Miami, Gran Vía 44 (tel. 521 1464). Metro: Plaza de España.
53. La Perla Asturiana, Plaza de Santa Cruz 3 (tel. 266 4600). By the Church of the Holy Cross (Iglesia de Santa Cruz). Metro: Sol. Follow Mayor from Puerta del Sol, then left down Esparteros towards the church.
54. Splendid, Gran Vía 15 (tel. 522 4737). Metro: Banco or Gran Vía.
55. Alonso, Espoz y Mina 17 (tel. 531 5679). See Corros, above.
56. Conchita, Preciados 33 (tel. 522 4923). Metro: Callao or Sol (near the El Corte Inglés department store) to Plaza de Callao (off Gran Vía).
57. Cosmopólitan, Puerta del Sol 9 (tel. 522 6651). Metro: Sol.
58. Cruz Sol, Plaza Santa Cruz 6 (tel. 532 7197). Metro: Sol.

UNIVERSITY ACCOMMODATION
Available to those wishing to stay five days or more. Ask the Tourist Office for details.

HI HOSTELS
Calle Santa Cruz de Marcenado 28 (tel. 547 4532). HI card required at both hostels. Recently renovated. Beds from around 650ptas (£3.25; $5). Metro: Arguelles.

'Richard Schirrmann', Casa de Campo (tel. 463 5699). A pleasant hostel, with a well run lock-up at the reception. No curfew, but far from the centre if you miss the last metro. Set in a large park within easy walking distance of the Lago and Batan metro stops. From Lago the shortest route is to turn left on leaving the station and follow the dirt track along the side of the wire fence.

CAMPING
Osuna, Avda de Logroño (tel. 741 0510). 400ptas (£2; $3) per tent and per person. About 16km out of the city beside the Ajalvir to Vicalvaro road. Metro to Canillejas, then bus 105.

Madrid, Iglesia de los Dominicos (tel. 202 2835). Same prices as Osuna. Located just off the N-II, the main road to Barcelona. Metro to Plaza de Castilla, followed by bus 129.

Málaga (tel. code 952)

TOURIST OFFICES
Oficinas de Turismo de la Junta de Andalucá. The head office is at Pasaje de Chinitas 4, 29016 Malaga (tel. 221 3445/222 8948). Open Mon.–Fri. 9 a.m.–2 p.m., Sat. 9 a.m.–1 p.m. Pasaje de Chinitas is just off Plaza de la Constitución. Branch offices operate at Málaga airport (tel. 230488), and outside the main train station (Málaga Principal) on the Explanada de la Estación.
Oficinas Municipales de Turismo. One office is in the Area Municipal de Turismo at Cister 111 (tel. 222 7907), the other is at the bus station on Paseo de los Tilos (tel. 235 0061 ext. 260).

BASIC DIRECTIONS
The main bus and train stations are close to each other on the opposite side of the Guadalmedina river from the historic centre of the city. From Málaga Principal (the main train station) head left from the exit until you reach Paseo de los Tilos. The bus station is a short walk up this street to your left. Bus 3 links both stations to the centre. Otherwise it is a 15–20 minute walk.

FINDING ACCOMMODATION
The streets to the north of Alameda Principal (left as you come from the train station) are well supplied with cheap rooms but the quality of the establishments varies considerably, so make a point of checking rooms out before you agree to take them. As a rule, you get what you pay for, so it is probably best to go for a moderately priced room. Streets which are especially well endowed with cheap lodgings include Calle Martínez, Calle Bolsa and Calle San Augustín. Martínez runs between Puerta del Mar and Marqués de Larios. From Marqués de Larios you can turn right down J. Diaz into Bolsa, while San Augustín is reached by going round the cathedral.

TROUBLE SPOTS
Be aware that Málaga is a very large and poor city with high rates of unemployment and crime. It's one of the most dangerous in Spain, and independent travellers can stand out as an easy target. If at all possible, leave your pack in the left luggage at the railway station while you look for a hotel, or even while you visit the Tourist Office. Sleeping rough in Málaga would be sheer madness.

PENSIONS
Cheapest doubles around 2000–2200ptas (£10–11; $15.00–16.50)

Hostal Galicia, Ayala 5 (tel. 231 3842). Walk right from the train station exit then down Fortuny into Ayala.

Córdoba, Bolsa 9–11 (tel. 221 4469). From Marqués de Larios turn right down J. Diaz into Bolsa.

Hostal Lampaerez, Calle Santa Maria 6 (tel. 221 9484). Cheap and cheerful. Just off pl. Constitución.

Viena, Strachan 3 (tel. 222 4095). Right of Marqués de Larios.

Las Antillas, Heroes de Sostoa 31 (tel. 231 4388). Go right from the train station exit, then right again along Heroes de Sostoa.

Hostal Magaña, Rio 11 (tel. 354308).

Casa Vasca, Avda Dr. Galvez Cinanchero 14 (tel. 230 5794).

La Palma, Martinez 7 (tel. 222 6772). Between Puerta del Mar and Marqués de Larios.

El Ruedo, Trinidad Grund 3 (tel. 221 5820).

Olimpia, Salitre 35 (tel. 235693).

Cheapest doubles from 3000ptas (£15; $22.50)

Las Tres Rosas, Heroes de Sostao 168 (tel. 233 3266). See Las Antillas, above.

Chinitas, Pasaje de Chinitas 2 (tel. 221 4683). Off Plaza de la Constitución, beside the main Tourist Office.

Andalucia, Alarcon Lujan 8 (tel. 221 1960).

Hostal Aurora, Muro de Puerta Nueva 1 (tel. 222 4004).

Acapulco, Explanada Estación, Edif. Terminal 3 (tel. 231 8988).

El Cenachero, Barroso 5 (tel. 222 4088). Turn left off Alameda de Colón.

Buenos Aires, Bolsa 12 (tel. 221 8935). See the Córdoba above.

HI HOSTEL
Calle Piaza Pio XII 6 (tel. 230 8500). About 700m from the railway station, or bus 18.

CAMPING
Balneario del Carmen, Avda Juan Sebastian Elcano (tel. 229 0021). Open year round. 380ptas (£2; $3) for a small tent, 450ptas (£2.25; $3.50) per person. About 3km out on the road to El Palo. Bus 11.

Salamanca (tel. code 923)

TOURIST OFFICES
Oficina de Turismo de la Communidad de Castilla y Leon, Gran
Vía 39—41, 37071 Salamanca (tel. 268571). Open Mon.—Fri.
9.30 a.m.—2 p.m. and 4.30—7 p.m., Sat. 10 a.m.—2 p.m., Sun.
11 a.m.—2 p.m. Good source of information on the city, and the
region. Free plan of Salamanca and a list of local accommodation.
Oficina Municipal de Turismo, Plaza Mayor 10 (tel. 218342). Open
Mon.—Fri. 10 a.m.—1.30 p.m. and 5—7 p.m., Sat. 10 a.m.—2 p.m.,
Sun. 11 a.m.—2 p.m. A basic information service. Fine if you
have a few simple questions you want answered.

BASIC DIRECTIONS
The train station and bus station are on opposite sides of the town,
both about 15—20 minutes' walk from the centre. From both
stations you can catch a bus to Plaza del Mercado which adjoins
Plaza Mayor. To walk from the train station, head left along Paseo
de la Estación to Plaza de España and the ring road which circles
the historic centre. Almost directly opposite Paseo de la Estación
across the junction is Azafranal. Take this road and go straight
ahead till you arrive at Plaza Mayor. Just to the left of Azafranal
at the junction with the ring road is Calle de España, otherwise
known as Gran Vía. From the bus station follow Avenida Filiberto
Villalobos down to the ring road. Crossing over directly ahead is
Ramon y Cajal. At the end of this street turn left, then right up
Prior to Plaza Mayor.

FINDING ACCOMMODATION
Prices for accommodation are relatively low by Spanish standards,
but rooms disappear fast in July and August. Then, just as you
might expect things to improve, the September fiesta makes finding
a room even more difficult. At these times, you are likely to be
approached at the train station with offers of accommodation in
local houses. If you are wary of accepting such offers, ask at the
tourist offices if they have a list of rooms available in private houses
that are occupied by students during the university year (ask about
casas particulares).
    Outside these times of year you should be able to fix yourself up
with a cheap bed easily. The small streets in the area around Plaza
Mayor have a large supply of fondas, casas de huespedes and cheap

hostales, particularly Meléndez, which runs from the church at San Martín down to the seminary (La Clerca).

PENSIONS
Cheapest doubles from 1500ptas (£7.50; $11.25)

Cristo de los Milagros, Cristo de los Milagros 6 (tel. 261127). Off Azafranal near the ring road.
Africa, Tejares 5—7 (tel. 232325).
Italia, Av. Italia 46 (tel. 241335).

Cheapest doubles from 2000ptas (£10; $15)

Salamanca, Avda S. Augustín 23 (tel. 252208).
Barez, Meléndez 19 (tel. 217495).
Lisboa, Meléndez 1—2 (tel. 214333).
Barragués, Plaza de España 12 (tel. 263433).
Las Vegas, Meléndez 13—1 (tel. 218749).
Currican I, Los Hidalgos 8—12 (tel. 220159). The Currican II at Hidalgos 5—6 has the same rates and same owner.
Libano, Paseo San Vicente 16—6 (tel. 264350). Left at the end of Avda F. Villalobos as you walk from the bus station.

Cheapest doubles from 2500ptas (£12.50; $18.75)

Estefania, Jesús 3—5 (tel. 217372).
Emma, Paseo San Vicente 16 & 18—1 (tel. 264303). See the Libano for directions.
Carabela, Paseo de Canalejas 10—12 (tel. 260708). Head left from the end of Paseo de la Estación when you reach the ring road walking from the train station.
Laguna, Consuelo 19 (tel. 218706).
Torio, Maria Auxiliadora 13 (tel. 226601).
Marly, Plaza de España 12 (tel. 263432).
Alianza III, Avda Villamyor 2 (tel. 268360).
València, Paseo San Antonio 5 (tel. 269864).
Madrid, Toro 1 (tel. 214296). The street runs from the ring road (right of Azafranal as you walk from the train station) down to Plaza Mayor.
Internacional, Avda de Mirat 15 (tel. 262799). Right along the ring road from the end of Paseo de la Estación.

Cheapest doubles from 3000ptas (£15; $22.50)

Uría, Garca Moreno 1 (tel. 223054).
Los Hidalgos, Pollo Canalejas 14–16 (tel. 261036).
Oriental, Azafranal 13 (tel. 212115).
Mindanao, Paseo San Vicente 2 (tel. 263080). See the Libano, above, for directions.
Tormes, Rua Mayor 20 (tel. 219683). The street is just off Plaza Mayor, running from the church of San Martín down past the Casa de las Conchas.
Hispánico, Avda Italia 21 (tel. 226286).
Goya, Avda Alemania 58–62 (tel. 267886). Head left from the bus station from the end of Avda F. Villalobos onto Avda Alemania.

PRIVATE ROOMS
Casas particulares are the cheapest accommodation possibility, other than camping. During the university year many local people let rooms to students. Outside term-time these rooms are available to visitors. Ask about availability of casas particulares at the Tourist Offices.

CAMPING
There are several campsites a few kilometres outside the city. The Tourist Offices will inform you as to the relevant bus services.

Regio (tel. 200250/138888). Open year round. 400ptas (£2; $3) per small tent, 440ptas (£2.20; $3.30) per person. In Santa Marta de Tormes, 3km out on the road to Madrid.
Don Quijote (tel. 257504). Open 20 Jan.–10 Dec. 300ptas (£1.50; $2.25) per small tent, 350ptas (£1.75; $2.65) per person. In Cabrerizos, 3km out on the road to Aldealengua.

San Sebastian (Donostia/San Sebastián) (tel. code 943)

TOURIST OFFICES
Eusko Jaurlaritza, Kultura Eta Turismo Saila, Gipuzkoako Lurralde Ordezkaritza, Miramar, s/n. 20004 Donostia. Contact this office if you want information on the city in advance. On arrival, go to the Tourist Office the Basque government operate in the city.
Turismo Bulegoak, Hiribidea Astatasunaren (Avda de la Liberdad), on the ground floor of the Victoria Eugenia Theatre) (tel. 426282/

481166). Open Mon.–Fri. 9 a.m.–1.30 p.m. and 4–7 p.m., Sat. 9 a.m.–1 p.m. Turn right after crossing the Maria Cristina bridge and follow the River Urumea to the second bridge (Zurriola) at which point Kalea Reina Regente runs left.

BASIC DIRECTIONS

From the train station, walk towards the River Urumea, cross the Maria Cristina bridge, and head straight on into Plaza Bilbo. From Plaza Bilbo, Kalea Bergara (Vergara) and Kalea Getaria run to the right, crossing Kalea San Martin and Kalea San Martzial before arriving at Hiribidea Askatasunaren (Avda de la Libertad). Walking right a little you can then turn left down Kalea Okendo (Oquendo) which runs as far as the junction of Boulevard Zumardia (Alameda del Boulevard) and Kalea Reina Regente. Going straight across this junction you can follow Kalea Aldamar down to the coast. If on leaving the train station you turn right down the side of the station you can follow Pasealekua Frantzia (Paseo de Francia) to its junction with Kalea Iztueta. Heading right you can then turn left down Kalea Iparragirre, right along Kalea S. Esnaola, and then left down Kalea Aita J.M. Larroka to reach Plaza Katalunia (Plaza de Cataluña).

● **Street names**

In the accommodation listings below the Basque version of the street name is used. In most cases this bears sufficient resemblance to the Spanish version to be easily identified on street maps printed in Spanish. Where this is not the case, the Spanish version is bracketed.

FINDING ACCOMMODATION

Donostia is immensely popular during the summer months, so you may experience some difficulty in finding cheap accommodation. Prices are high in the peak season (June/July–Sept.) so do not expect to find a double for under 2000ptas (£10; $15) per person outside a *fonda* or *casa de huespedes*. As a rule, prices are higher in the Old Town between Boulevard Zumardia and Urgull. The area around the cathedral has a particularly good supply of (by local standards) cheap rooms. Kalea Urdaneta, Kalea San Bartolemé and Kalea Loiola are especially good streets to look in. The streets around Plaza Katalunia are also a good place to look for relatively inexpensive lodgings. If you are visiting Donostia outside the peak season you should have no trouble finding suitable accommodation at a reasonable price as the cost of rooms often falls substantially.

FONDAS

Donostia, Hondarrabia 19–3 (third floor) (tel. 422157).

Garate, Triunfo 8 (tel. 461571). The street runs from San Bartolome across San Martin.

Vicandi, Iparragirre 1 (tel. 270795).

Goi-Argi, S. Esnaola 13 (tel. 278802).

Garcia, Soraluze 6 (tel. 427236).

CASAS DE HUESPEDES

Aldazabal, San Martin 36−5 (tel. 420094).

Ezkurra, Hiribidea Ametzagaina 5 (tel. 273594). From the train station head left until you reach Pasealekua Duke de Mandas. Head right but take the left fork in the road to reach Egia. Follow the main road round until you see Ametzagaina on the left.

La Parisien, Urdaneta 6 (tel. 464312). After crossing the Maria Cristina Bridge watch out for Kalea Prim heading left to the start of Urdaneta. The street passes by the cathedral.

Ricardo, San Bartoleme 21&23−3 (tel. 461374).

Lau Aizeta, Lau Haizeta (Alza) (tel. 352445). Out from the centre in Intxaurrondo.

ONE-STAR PENSIONES

Amaiur, Abuztuaren 31 44−2 (31 de Agosto) (tel. 429654). Abuztuaren 31 is a continuation of Soraluze. Left off Aldamar.

Añorga, Easo 12−1 (tel. 467945). Singles from 2500ptas (£12.50; $18.75), doubles from 4000ptas (£20; $30). The street crosses San Bartolome.

Aralar, Easo 12−2 (tel. 470410). See Anorga.

Arouaga, Calle Narrica 3 (tel. 420681). Singles from 2000ptas (£10; $15), doubles from 3500ptas (£17.50; $26.25).

Donostia, Hondarribia 19−3 (tel. 422157). Open July−Sept. only.

Josefina, Easo 12 (tel. 461956). Open July−Sept. only. See Anorga.

Kaia, Portu 12−2 (tel. 431342). Walk left along Boulevard Zumardia, right up San Jeronimo into Konstituzio Enparantza, and then go left along Portu.

Larrea, Narrika 21−1 (tel. 422694). Walk left along Boulevard Zumardia, then right.

San Jeronimo, San Jeronimo 25 (tel. 281689). See Kaia.

San Lorenzo, San Lorenzo 2−1 (tel. 425516). Doubles with shower/bath 4500ptas (£22.50; $33.75) from late June−Sept. At other times prices fall to around 2800ptas (£14; $21). Singles 1150ptas (£5.75; $8.65) in the off-season. Walk left along Boulevard Zumardia, right up San Juan, then left.

Urgull, Esterlines 10−3 (tel. 430047). Walk left along Boulevard Zumardia, right up Narrika, then left.

TWO-STAR PENSIONES
Doubles from around 4000ptas (£20; $30), but prices fall outside peak season

Donostiarra, San Martin 6 (tel. 426167).
La Concha, San Martin 51 (tel. 450389).
La Perla, Loiola (tel. 428123).
Lorea, Boulevard Zumardia 16–1 (tel. 427258).
Maite, Hiribidea Madrid 19–1B (tel. 470715). Out from the centre, on the way to Anoeta. Take a bus dir: Amara-Anoeta from Brbieta (the street crosses San Bartolome), or a walk from the centre. Turn left down Prim at Plaza Bilbo and head straight on until you reach Plaza Pio XII, then go left down Hiribidea Madrid at the fork in the road.
Yolon, Camino Luis Pradera 60 (tel. 393217).

HOSTALES AND HOSTAL-RESIDENCIAS
Doubles from 4500ptas (£22.50; $33.75), but off-season prices may fall below 4000ptas (£20; $30)

Easo, San Bartoleme 24 (tel. 466892).
Lasa, Bergara 15 (tel. 423052).
Comercio, Urdaneta 24 (tel. 464414).
Ozcáriz, Hondarrabia 8–2&3 (tel. 425306).
Fernando, Enparantza Gipuzkoako 2 (Plaza de Guipuzcoa) (tel. 425575). From Bergara cross Hiribidea Askatasunaren into Idiakez, which leads into the square.
Isla, Pasealekeu Mirakontxa 17 (tel. 464897). Pleasant location near the Kontxa beach. Follow San Martin to its end.
Alameda, Boulevard Zumardia (Alameda del Boulevard) 23 (tel. 421687).

PRIVATE ROOMS
In the past, a list of private rooms (casas particulares) has been available from the Tourist Office. The owner of the Hostal Eder, Calle San Bartolomé 33, is also reputedly helpful in finding private lodgings.

HI HOSTELS
Albergue de Ulia Mendi, Parque Ulia, s/n (tel. 471546/293751/452970).
La Sirena, Igueldo Paseolekua 25 (tel. 310268). A new hostel close to the end of Ondaretto Beach. Bus 16 or 25. Summer: 1500ptas (£7.50; $11.25); winter 1000ptas (£5; $7.50).

CAMPING
Igueldo (tel. 214502). Open May–Sept. Located about 5km west of the town centre on the landward side of Monte Igueldo. The Barrio de Igueldo bus 16 from Boulevard Zumardia will get you there, but the service is poor. Only 13 buses per day Mon.–Sat.; 5 buses on Sun. Last bus from town 10 p.m.

SLEEPING ROUGH
Although sleeping on the beach is technically illegal the police invariably turn a blind eye during the peak season. If you are sleeping out, bed down beside other people to give you some extra security, and leave your pack and valuables at the train station.

Seville (Sevilla) (tel. code 95)

TOURIST OFFICES
Oficina de Turismo de la Junta de Andalucá, Avenida de la Constitución 21, 41004 Sevilla (tel. 422 1404). Open Mon.–Fri. 9.30 a.m.–7.30 p.m., Sat. 9.30 a.m.–2 p.m. A good source of information on the city and the region. Well-informed and helpful staff. Centrally located. A branch office operates at San Pablo airport (tel. 425 5046).

Oficina Municipal de Turismo, Edificio Costurero de la Reina, Paseo de las Delicias 9 (tel. 423 4465). Friendly staff, but the office is less well stocked with pamphlets and is on the edge of the old city. By the Guadalquivir river, a short distance from the Glorieta de los Marineros Voluntarios and the Puente del Generalsmo.

BASIC DIRECTIONS
All mainline trains stop at Estación de Santa Justa, about 30 minutes' walk from the Tourist Offices. The main bus station on Plaza de San Sebastian (just off Menéndez Pelayo) is much closer to the centre; about 10 minutes' walk from the Tourist Offices. From the bus station walk down on to Menéndez Pelayo and head left a short distance until you reach Plaza Don Juan de Austria. At this point you can head straight down to the Glorieta de los Marineros Voluntarios by following Avda del Cid and then Avda de Maria Luisa. Turning right from Plaza Don Juan de Austria you can walk down San Fernando to the Puerta de Jerez, from which the Tourist Office on Avda de la Constitución is just a minute's walk to the left. From the Santa Justa train station you can take

bus 70 to the main bus station. The airport bus EA also picks up near Santa Justa and lets you off at Puerta de Jerez, but the service is less frequent than bus 70.

FINDING ACCOMMODATION

Only during Holy Week (the week leading up to Easter) and around the time of the April Fair are you likely to have difficulty finding cheap accommodation in Seville. At these times not only do large numbers of visitors converge on the city, but room prices can be raised quite legally, sometimes by as much as 70–100%. Otherwise, even during July and August, there are enough cheap beds to go round. The area around the old Plaza de Armas station on the western fringe of the old city has a large supply of cheap lodgings, especially San Eloy, which probably has more *fondas* and *casas de huespedes* than any other street in the city. In contrast, the streets around the new Santa Justa Station are relatively bare of cheap lodgings, so it is no longer really possible to find a cheap bed within 10–15 minutes of getting off the train. The other area with a good supply of relatively cheap lodgings is the Barrio Santa Cruz, in the heart of the old city around the Giralda. Although rooms here are slightly more expensive than around the old train station, their location cannot be matched and they are now easier to reach from the main train station.

PENSIONS

Cheapest doubles around 1600ptas (£8; $12)

Estoríl, Gravina 78 (tel. 422 5095). Close to the Museo de Bellas Artes, in the area around the old Plaza de Armas station.

Cheapest doubles around 2500ptas (£12.50; $18.75)

Gravina, Gravina 46 (tel. 421 6414). See Estoríl, above.

Cheapest doubles around 3000ptas (£15; $22.50)

Casa Saez, Plaza Curtidores 6 (tel. 441 6753). Five minutes north of the centre.
Espadafor, Avda Cruz Campo 23 (tel. 457 3866).
Jerez, Rastro 2 (tel. 442 0560).
Monsalves, Monsalves 29 (tel. 421 6853).

Cheapest doubles around 3500ptas (£17.50; $26.25)

Pino Lordelo, Quintana 29 (tel. 438 7905).
La Posada, Relator 49 (tel. 437 4768).

Cheapest doubles around 4000ptas (£20; $30)

Avenida, Marques de Paradas 28 (tel. 422 0688).
Dulces Sueños, Sta Maria La Blanca (tel. 441 9393).
Lis I, Escarpin 10 (tel. 421 3088). In the very centre.
Lis II, Olavide 5 (tel. 456 0228).
Macarena, San Luis 91 (tel. 437 0141).
Rio Sol, Marques de Paradas 25 (tel. 422 9038).
Torreblanca, Pl. Corazon Maria 3 (tel. 451 5368).
Trajano, Trajano 3 (tel. 438 2421).

HI HOSTEL
Albergue Juvenil Fernando el Santo, Isaac Peral 2 (tel. 461 3150).
No curfew. Generally filled to near capacity with local students. HI
members aged under 26 pay around 800ptas (£4; $6), those aged
26 and over about 1000ptas (£5; $7.50). Roughly 2.5km from the
city centre. Bus 34. For up-to-date information contact the English-
speaking Inturjoven (tel. 422 5171).

CAMPING
Buses to the three sites below depart from the main bus station on
Plaza de San Sebastian.

Sevilla (tel. 451 4379). Grade 2 site, open all year. 400ptas (£2;
$3) per tent and per person. About 9.5km out on the road to
Madrid. The bus service to Empresa Casal runs more or less
hourly from 7 a.m.–9.30 p.m. Take the bus as far as Carmona.
Villsom (tel. 472 0828). Grade 2 site, open year round. 350ptas
(£1.75; $2.65) per tent and per person. In Dos Hermanos, 18km
out on the road to Cádiz. The Los Amarillos bus runs about every
45 minutes from 6.30 a.m.–midnight.
Club de Campo, Avda de la Liberdad 13 (tel. 472 0250). Grade 1
site, open year round. 380ptas (£1.90; $2.85) per tent and per
person. In Dos Hermanos, 16km out on the road to Dos
Hermanas. Same bus as for Villsom above.

Toledo (tel. code 925)

TOURIST OFFICES
Junta de Communidades de Castilla-La Mancha, Oficina de Turismo, Puerta de Bisagra, 45003 Toledo (tel. 220843). Open Mon.–Fri. 9 a.m.–2 p.m. and 4–6 p.m., Sat. 9 a.m.–1.30 p.m. A 15-minute walk from the train station. One of the local buses stops near the office. A basic information booth operates on the main square (Plaza Zocodover), again a 15 minute walk from the train station or bus 5 or 6 to the terminus.

BASIC DIRECTIONS
The old part of the town is a maze of small streets. Arriving at the train station, head right along the main road in front of the station. Go right where the road forks, cross the river and go straight ahead to arrive at the Puerta Bisagra. Head left along Paseo de la Rosa at the fork in the road you arrive at the Alcantara gate and bridge. Cross the river and then make your way up the steps to the left. Going straight on from the top of the steps will take you to Plaza Zocodover. Take Comercio from the square and continue straight ahead for the Cathedral and the start of Trinidad. This street leads down to the junction of Rojas, San Tome, San Salvador and Santa Ursula by the church of San Tome.

PENSIONS
Las Armas, Calle Armas 7 (tel. 221668). Doubles from 2900ptas (£14.50; $21.75). Open April–Oct.

Lumbreras, Juan Labrador 7 (tel. 221571). Singles around 1500ptas (£7.50; $11.25), doubles around 2400ptas (£12; $18). From Zocodover follow Barrio Rey to the Magdalena church. Juan Labrador is one of several streets which starts on the other side of the church.

Segovia, Recoletos 2 (tel. 211124). Doubles around 2100ptas (£10.50; $15.75). Off Silleria, which runs out of Zocodover.

Nuncio Viejo, Nuncio Viejo 19 (tel. 228178). Doubles 2600–2800ptas (£13–14; $19.50–21). Close to the cathedral. The street runs away to the right near the start of Trinidad.

Labrador, Juan Labrador 16 (tel. 222620). Singles around 2050ptas (£10.25; $14.40), doubles around 2700–3200ptas (£13.50–16; $20.25–24). See Lumbreras above for directions.

Hostal Descalzos, Descalzos 30 (tel. 222888). Singles around 2050ptas (£10.25; $14.40), doubles start around 3300ptas

(£16.50; $24.75). Jan.–mid-Mar. prices are reduced by one sixth. A short way along Santa Ursula from the end of Trinidad turn right down Taller del Moro. Go left at the end of the street and follow the street to the right of Calle San Cristobal and Paseo de San Cristobal.

Hostal Esperanza, Covarrubias 2 (tel. 227859). Doubles 4100ptas (£20.50; $30.75).

Los Guerreros, Avda Reconquista 8 (tel. 211807). Doubles start around 4350ptas (£21.75; $32.65). Mid-Oct.–mid-Apr. the price falls by about 15%. Outside the Old Town. Continue on beyond the Puerta Nueva de Bisagra then head right at the main intersection.

HI HOSTEL

'San Servando', Castillo de San Servando (tel. 224554). Midnight/ 12.30 a.m. curfew. Juniors pay slightly above the normal price for a Spanish hostel. Those aged 26 and over can expect to pay around 1200ptas (£6; $9). A 15-minute walk from the train station by the simplest route. Walk towards the Alcantara gate, then just before the gate, turn sharp left up the hill.

CAMPING

Circo Romano, Circa Romano (tel. 220442). Around 400ptas (£2; $3) per tent and per person. Not a particularly good site. On the outskirts of the old town, off Carretera de Carlos III. Carretera de Carlos III begins at the major intersection beyond the Puerta Nueva de Bisagra.

El Greco (tel. 220090). Around 450ptas (£2.25; $3.75) per tent and per person. Far superior to the Circo Romano site. Splendid view of the old town. About 1.5km out on the road to Madrid (N-401).

València (tel. code 96)

TOURIST OFFICES

Oficina de Turismo, Calle de la Paz 46 (tel. 352 2897/4000). Open Mon.–Fri. 10 a.m.–2 p.m. and 4–8 p.m., Sat. 10 a.m.–2 p.m. Free reservation of hotel rooms for personal callers when the office is open ör over the phone 9 a.m.–9 p.m. daily.

Oficina Municipal de Turismo, Plaza del Ayuntamiento 1 (tel. 351 0417). Open Mon.–Fri. 9 a.m.–1.30 p.m. and 4.30–7 p.m., Sat.

9 a.m.–1 p.m. Follow Avda Marqués de Sotelo from opposite the train station exit to Plaza del Ayuntamiento.

There are another two more basic information points, one in the Estacion del Norte railway station, the other at the airport.

PENSIONS
Cheapest doubles around 1800ptas (£9; $13.50)

Hospedera del Pilar, Mercado 19 (tel. 331 6600).
El Rincón, Carda 11 (tel. 331 6083).
Aparicio, Torao del Hospital 3 (tel. 331 5280).

Cheapest doubles around 2100ptas (£10.50; $15.75)

Hostal el Cid, Cerrajeros 13 (tel. 932 2323).
Carrasco, Buenos Aires 61 (tel. 341 5527).
España, Embasador Vich 5 (tel. 352 9342).

Cheapest doubles around 2550ptas (£12.75; $19.15)

Boluda, Bailén 10 (tel. 351 0650). July–Sept. the price rises to
    around 3300ptas (£16.50; $24.75).
San Andrés, Matemático Marzal 3 (tel. 352 8512).
Castelar, Ribera 1 (tel. 351 3199).
San Vicente, San Vicente 57 (tel. 352 7061).

Cheapest doubles around 3000ptas (£15; $22.50)

Alicante, Ribera 8 (tel. 351 2296).
Moratín, Moratín 15 (tel. 352 1220).
Univers, General San Martin 1 (tel. 352 9761).
Granero, Martinez Cubelis 4 (tel. 351 2548).
La Palmera, Julio Antonio 1 (tel. 342 3816).
Lyon, Jativa 10 (tel. 351 7247).

Cheapest doubles around 3600ptas (£18; $27)

Venecia, En Llop 5 (tel. 352 4267).
La Pepica, Avda de Neptuno 2 (tel. 371 4111). A one-star hotel-
    residencia, close to the beach. Good value for money.

HI HOSTEL
'Colegio Mayor La Paz', Avda del Puerto 69 (tel. 361 7459). Open
July–Sept. Around 800ptas (£4; $6) per person. Midnight curfew.

Bus 19 from Plaza del Ayuntamiento (follow Avda Marqués de Sotelo from opposite the train station to reach Plaza del Ayuntamiento).

CAMPING
There is no site close to the city centre, but there are two grade-one sites easily reached by bus from the Puerta del Mar by the Glorieta Park:

El Saler (tel. 367 0411). Open year round. About 10km south of the city on a pleasant beach.
El Palmar (tel. 161 0853). Open June—Sept. About 16km south of València near La Albufera, beyond El Sater.

SWEDEN (Sverige)

As with the other Scandinavian countries, the best advice to the budget traveller in Sweden is to prepare for hostelling and camping. While many **hotels** cut their prices substantially during the summer, even this, unfortunately, does not bring them into our accommodation price range, as you can still expect to pay from 250kr (£21.25; $32) in singles, and 450kr (£38.25; $57.50) in doubles. Very occasionally, you may find hotels or *pensionat* outside the main cities which charge 180–220kr (£15.25–18.75; $22.75–28.00) in singles, 220–330kr (£18.75–28.00; $28–42) in doubles all year round. If this is within your budget, enquire at the local Tourist Office about the cheapest hotels in town. Tourist Offices will also book **private rooms** for you where these are available, costing around 150kr (£12.75; $19) for singles, 250kr (£21.25; $32) in doubles or larger rooms. In villages and small towns look out for the 'Rum' sign, because approaching the owner directly will save you paying the 50kr (£4.25; $6.50) booking fee charged by the Tourist Offices.

Most towns that you are likely to visit will have an **HI hostel**. Of the 280 HI hostels (*vandrarhem*) in Sweden, about 130 stay open all year round, others open only during the main tourist season (June to late August). Most of the hostels are located in the southern and central regions of the country. Prices vary from 76–90kr (£6.50–7.50; $9.75–11.25) according to location and standard. Non-members are charged an extra 35kr (£3; $4.50), though International Guest Cards can be bought at most hostels. Outside the main towns superior-grade hostels are very popular with families, so no matter where you are heading, it makes sense to book a bed in advance. If you expect to arrive after 6 p.m. you should inform the hostel, otherwise your reservation will not be held beyond that time. In university towns, it is often possible to find a bed in a student hostel during the summer. The local tourist office will advise you about the availability of such accommodation.

Almost every town or village of any size has a **campsite**, and quite often you will have a choice of sites. There are some 750 sites officially approved and classified by the Swedish Camping Association. Approved sites are rated from one star up to five stars. A one-star site has everything you would expect, while five-star sites tend to offer a whole range of facilities you will rarely use, if at all. Most sites operate with all their facilities between June and September, while in those which are also open in April and May, certain supplementary facilities may not be available. The Tourist

Office boasts that the overnight charge for a family is one of the lowest in Europe, and this is hard to refute. But, as the fee for a tent is the relatively high 50–100kr (£4.25–8.50; $6.50–12.75), and some sites also make a nominal charge per person, this means that solo travellers do not benefit from the pricing system, whereas three or four people sharing a tent certainly do. There are very few sites at which a camping pass is not required, so unless you have an International Camping Carnet you will be obliged to buy a Swedish camping pass at the first site you visit, which costs 45kr (£4; $6) and is valid for the rest of the camping season. These can also be purchased in advance from SCR. There are also 4500 cabins for rent, spread over 350 sites. Cabins sleep between two and six people, are usually equipped with a kitchen and their overnight charges vary from 75–100kr (£6.40–8.50; $9.60–12.75) per person.

Under the ancient law of Allmannsratt it is possible to **camp for free**, with certain restrictions. It is permissible to erect a tent for a day and a night on land that is not used for farming, providing you are some distance from habitations. You must obtain the consent of the landowner before pitching your tent near any dwelling place or if you are camping in a group. Avoid setting any potentially dangerous fires, and make sure you leave no rubbish behind on your departure. In more sparsely populated areas, such as the mountains, it is perfectly acceptable to stay longer than a day and a night. As with neighbouring Norway, the two problems facing campers are the cold nights and mosquitoes, so prepare yourself accordingly.

The Swedish YHA operates two other types of accommodation in the mountains. **Mountain centres** can be expensive, with the cost of a bed ranging from 70–350kr (£6.00–29.75; $9.00–44.50). Mountain huts, however, offer relatively cheap beds for around 75kr (£6.40; $9.60), in areas where any accommodation can be hard to find. These huts are normally sited far from either roads or railways, so they are likely to appeal only to those planning on doing some hiking.

ADDRESSES

Swedish Travel & Tourism Council	73 Wellbeck Street, London W1M 8AN (tel. 0171 935 9784)
Camping	Stanfords, 12–14 Long Acre, London, WC2 (tel. 0171 236 1321) sell a comprehensive list. The Swedish Tourist Board supplies shorter lists free of charge.

Swedish Campsite Owners Association (SCR)	Box 255, S-451 17 Udevalla, Sweden
Swedish YHA	Svenska Turistföreningen (STF), Box 25, 101 20 Stockholm. Information Office, Drottninggaten 31–33, Stockholm (tel. 08 790 3100).
Mountain huts and mountain centres	Contact the Swedish YHA Information Office.

Gothenburg (Göteborg) (tel. code 031)

TOURIST OFFICES
Göteborg's Turistbyrå, Kungsportsplatsen 2, 411 Göteborg (tel. 100740). Open daily in summer, 9 a.m.–8 p.m., at other times, 10 a.m.–8 p.m. A 10-minute walk from the train station. From the Brunnsparken by Drottningtorget head left down stra Larmgatan. A branch office operates in the Nordstan Shopping Centre, about 200m from the train station of Nils Ericsonsgatan (open Mon.–Fri. 9.30 a.m.–6 p.m., Sat. 9.30 a.m.–3 p.m.)
STF, Drottninggatan 6 (tel. 150930). Open Mon.–Fri. 9 a.m.–5 p.m.

HOTELS
Cheapest doubles around 450kr (£38.25; $57.50)

City Hotell, Lorensbergsgatan 6 (tel. 180025). Behind Kungsportsa-venyn (from the station, turn left to cross the river and follow Ö Larmgatan).
Savoy, Andra Lönggatan 23 (tel. 124960). 15–20 minutes' walk from the railway station. Price applies 20 June–25 Aug. only.
Maria Erikson's Privata Rumspens, Chalmerg 27a (tel. 207030). Ten minutes south-west of the railway station.

Cheapest doubles around 500kr (£42.50; $63.75)

Royal, Drottninggatan 67 (tel. 806100). Price applies from mid-June–mid-Aug. A few minutes' walk from the train station.
Hotell Onyxen, Stenstaregatan 23 (tel. 160136). Price applies summer only.

PRIVATE ROOMS
Either of the city Tourist Offices will make bookings. Expect to pay from 200kr (£17; $25.50) in doubles and larger rooms. A

commission of 25–50kr (£2.00–4.25; $3.00–6.50) is charged for private rooms and 20kr (£1.75; $2.50) for hotels.

HI HOSTELS
Studenthemmet Ostkupan, Mejerigatan 2 (tel. 254761/401050). Open June–26 Aug. 90Skr (£7.50; $11.25). About 3km from the city centre. Tram 5 to St Sigfridsplan, then bus 62 or 64 to Gräddgatan.

Vandrarhem Partille, Landvettervägen 433, Partille (tel. 446163). 90Skr (£7.50; $11.25). About 16km from the centre. Bus 513 from Central Station to Åstebo.

Torrekulla turistation, Kållered (tel. 795 1495). 90Dkr (£7.50; $11.25) for HI members, 35kr (£3; $4.50) supplement for non-members. About 13km from the centre in a nature reserve. Bus 730 from Central Station.

HOSTELS
Nordengården, Stockholmsgatan 16 (tel. 196631). Open all year. 75kr (£6.40; $9.60) per night in dorms, 40kr (£3.50; $5) sleeping on a mattress with your own sleeping bag. More centrally located than the HI hostels. Tram 1 or 3 to Stockholmsgatan.

M/S Seaside, Packhuskajen (tel. 101035). Beds in the cabins of this ship moored about 300m from the train station cost around 180kr (£15.25; $22.75).

KFUK/KFUM (YMCA/YWCA), Garverigatan 2 (tel. 803962). Open 12 July–16 Aug. Midnight curfew. 75kr (£6.40; $9.60). A 15-minute walk from Central Station, or tram 1, 3 or 6 to Svingeln.

CAMPING
Kärralund (tel. 252761). From Brunnsparken, a few minutes' walk from the train station, take tram 5 dir: Torp to Welandergatan. Near the beach.

Gielas, Järnvägsgatan 111, Arvidsjaur (tel. 0980 13420) 80kr (£6.75; $10) for a tent and all its occupants. chalets available: twin bedded 175kr (£15; $22.50), 4-bedded 450kr (£38.25; $57.50), 5-bedded 500kr (£42.50; $63.75), 6-bedded 540kr (£46; $69). An 800m walk along Järnvägsgatan from the train station in Arvidsjaur.

Delsjö Camping (tel. 252909). A 20-minute walk from the nearest train station.

Valhalla Idrottsplats (tel. 204185).

Kiruna (tel. code 0980)

TOURIST OFFICE
Hjalmar Lundbohmsvägen 42 (tel. 18880). Open mid-June–mid-Aug., Mon.–Fri. 9 a.m.–8 p.m., weekends 10 a.m.–6 p.m.; rest of the year, Mon.–Fri. 10 a.m.–4 p.m.

HOTEL
Yellow House, Renstigen 1 (tel. 11451). 300kr (£26.50; $38.25) for a double.

PRIVATE ROOMS
Tourist Office (see above). Expect to pay 160kr (£13.50; $20.25) p.p. No commission is charged.

Gult Hus (tel. 11451). This organization lets both second homes and the houses of locals away on holiday. They will pick you up at the train station for free. Singles and doubles both cost around 160kr £13.50; $20.25) p.p., but renting a three-, four-or five-bed apartment works out at around 100kr (£8.50; $12.75) p.p. per night.

HI HOSTEL
Vilam, Skyttegatan 16A (tel. 17195). Open 13 June–31 Aug. 76kr (£6.50; $9.75) for HI members, non-members pay a 35kr (£3; $4.50) supplement.

CAMPING
Radhusbyn Ripan (tel. 13100). Just over 1.5km from the train station. 75kr (£6.40; $9.60) per tent and all occupants. Cabins sleeping four are available for around 560kr (£47.50; $71.25).

Stockholm (tel. code 08)

TOURIST OFFICES
Stockholm Information Service, Box 7542, Kungsträdgården/Hamgatan, 103 93 Stockholm (tel. 789 2000/2490). Open mid-June–late Aug., Mon.–Fri. 8.30 a.m.–6 p.m., weekends 8.30 a.m.–5 p.m.; rest of the year, Mon.–Fri. 9 a.m.–5 p.m., weekends 9 a.m.–2 p.m. In the Sverigehuset in the Kung-

strädgården on Hamngatan. T-bana (underground): Kung-strädgården.

Hotellcentralen (tel. 240880). In Stockholm Central train station on the lower floor. Open June–Aug., daily 8 a.m.–9 p.m.; May and Sept., 9 a.m.–7 p.m., at other times 9 a.m.–5 p.m.

ACCOMMODATION AGENCIES

From June to August, finding somewhere reasonably cheap to stay in Stockholm can be difficult. If you have not booked ahead con-sider using the services of the Tourist Offices for a hostel bed. The charge for this service is 12kr (£1; $1.50). The Tourist Offices will also find you a hotel room for about 25kr (£2; $3), but hopefully you will not be reduced to this option as even the cheapest hotels are outside the budget-travel category.

Hotelljänst, Vasagatan 15–17 (tel. 104437/104457/104467). Open Mon.–Fri. 9 a.m.–5 p.m. Accommodation found free of charge, provided you stay at least two days. Close to Central Station.

Allrum, Wallingatan 34 (tel. 213789/213790). Open Mon.–Fri. 9 a.m.–5 p.m. Specializes in finding private rooms and apart-ments. No commission, but a 5-day minimum stay.

Caretaker, Vasagatan 15–17 (tel. 202545).

HOTELS

Many hotels lower their prices in summer. At other times, prices can be much higher.

Cheapest doubles around 350kr (£29.75; $44.50)

Residens, Kungsgatan 50 (tel. 233540). Price applies 23 June–6 Aug. only. Good location, about 8 minutes' walk from Central Station.

Cheapest doubles around 450kr (£38.25; $57.50)

Jerum, Studentbacken 21 (tel. 663 5380). Price applies 1 June–31 Aug. only.

Gustavsvikshemmet, Vastmannagatan 15 (tel. 214450). Year round price. Ten-minute walk from Central Station. 350kr (£29.75; $44.50) for singles.

PRIVATE ROOMS

Book at either of the Tourist Offices, or through Allrum, Hotelljänst or Caretaker. Expect to pay from 150kr (£12.75; $19) for singles, and from 250kr (£21.25; $32) in doubles, plus commission if you book through either of the Tourist Offices.

HI HOSTELS
Prices 76–90kr (£6.50–7.50; $9.75–11.25) for members, plus 35kr (£3; $4.50) for non-members

Långholmen, Gamla Kronohäktet (tel. 668 0510). No curfew. On Långholmen Island. T-bana: Hornstull.

Zinken, Zinkensväg 20 (tel. 668 5786). No curfew. T-bana: Zinkensdamm, then right on to Hornsgatan. Follow the street to no. 103, then go left down the steps at the hostel sign.

Skeppsholmen, Västra Brobänken (tel. 679 5017). In the Hantverk-shuset, close to the 'Af Chapman'.

Botkyrka, Eriksbergsskolan, Tre Källors väg 8, Norsborg (tel. 0753 62105). Open 22 June–7 Aug.

Gravlingsberg, Drottningv. 15 (tel. 747 8288). Open May–mid-Oct. About 19.5km from the centre. Bus 421 from Stockholm-Slussen train station.

Hökärangens-Martinskolam, Munslychsvagen 18 (tel. 941765). Open 28 June–15 Aug.

HOSTELS
Sleep Inn (Balletalademein), Döbelnsgatan 56 (tel. 363064). Open July–Aug. 1 a.m. curfew. Mattresses on the floor 85kr (£7.25; $11). T-bana: Rådmandgatan, or bus 52 from Stockholm Central to the stop across from the Hard Rock Cafe. From the bus stop follow Surbrunnsgatan to the crossroads and head left.

Kista InterRail Points KFUM (YMCA), Jyllandsgatan 16 (tel. 752 6456). Open 20 July–16 Aug. Midnight curfew. 75kr (£6.40; $9.60). T-bana line 11 dir: Akalla to Kista. Leave the station by the Sorogatan exit.

Frescati, Professorsslingan 13–15 (tel. 159434). Student accommodation converted into a hostel from June–Aug. Doubles 350kr (£29.75; $44.50). Singles around 250kr (£21.25; $32). T-bana: Universitetet.

Columbus Hotell-Vandrarhjem, Tjarhovsgatan 11 (tel. 644 1717). No curfew and 24-hour reception. Two- to six- bedded rooms. 110kr (£9.35; $14). T-bana: Medborgarplatsen.

Bryghuset, Nortullsgatan 12N (tel. 312424). Open June–Aug. Price as HI.

Gustaf af Klint, Stadsgårdskajen 153 (tel. 640 4077). In an old navy ship. 24-hour reception. 120kr (£10.20; $15.25). T-bana: Odenplan.

Frösling Sarmens, Vandrashem, Väastberga Allé (tel. 191330). Open May—Aug.

Klubbensborg (tel. 646 1255), T-bana: Mälarhöjden.

CAMPING

Bredäng (tel. 977071). Open all year. Expensive. About 10km south on Lake Mälaren. T-bana: Bredäng (line 13 or 15). Ten-minute walk signposted from the station.

Ångby (tel. 370420). Open all year. Also on Lake Mälaren. T-bana: Angbyplan (line 17 or 18).

Flaten (tel. 773 0100). Open May—Sept. Bus 401 from Slussen.

Spånga Kings Camp (tel. 760 6230). New site 14km north-west of the city.

Uppsala (tel. code 018)

TOURIST OFFICES

Turistinformation Uppsala, Fyris Torg 8 (tel. 274800). Open June— Aug., Mon.—Fri. 9 a.m.—7 p.m., Sat. 9 a.m.—2 p.m.; May and Sept., closes 6 p.m. Mon.—Fri.; rest of the year, Mon.—Fri. 10 a.m.—6 p.m., Sat. 10 a.m.—2 p.m. From the train station, head right along Kungsgatan until you see St Persgatan on the left. Fyris Torg is across the river.

Turistinformation Uppsala, Domkyrkoplan (tel. 161880). By the cathedral, in the castle complex. This office is open Saturday afternoons and Sunday when the other office is closed.

HOTELS

Cheapest doubles around 480kr (£41; $61.50)

Hotell Årsta Gård, Jordgubbsgatan 14 (tel. 253500). From the Town Hall (Stadshuset) on Kungsgatan, just to the right from the train station, take bus 19 (day) or bus 52 (evening). The bus stops a short distance from the hotel.

Scandic Hotell, 6a Uppsalag 50 (tel. 200280). From station follow Bangårdsgatan then turn right on to Dragarbrumsgatan. After five blocks the hotel is on your left. Summer price only.

HI HOSTEL

Sunnersta herrgård, Sunnerstavägen 24 (tel. 324220). HI members pay 83kr (£7; $10.50), non-members 118kr (£10; $15). From

Dragarbrunnsgatan, not far from St Persgatan, bus 20 as far as Herrgardsvagen. After 6.20 p.m. and at weekends take bus 50 instead. Short walk from the bus stop.

HOSTEL
Uppsala KFUM-KFUK (YMCA-YWCA), Torbjörnsgatan 2 (tel. 156300/276635). Open 29 July–9 Sept. 75kr (£6.40; $9.60). Twenty minutes from the town centre at the corner of Svartbecksgatan and Torbjörnsgatan. Bus 10 from Stora Torget. After 6.20 p.m. bus 50 from Dragarbrunnsgatan.

CAMPING
Fyrishaus (tel. 232333). Down by the river. Open all year. 70kr (£6; $9) for a tent and all occupants. Four-bedded cabins are available: 545kr (£46.25; $69.50) for the superior grade.

SWITZERLAND (Helvetia)

Despite being widely regarded as one of the most expensive countries in Europe, it is quite possible both to eat well, and to sleep cheaply in Switzerland. **Hotels** are likely to be outside your budget, and probably only to be considered in emergencies. Even the very cheapest hotels cost 40–50SFr (£20–25; $30.00–37.50) in singles, 68–80SFr (£34–40; $51–60) in doubles. In country areas, **B&B**s or **private rooms** can be more reasonable but, in the main, your choice is between hostelling or camping. In some ways, this is quite fortuitous because both of these give you the opportunity of meeting other travellers, and also vastly increase your chances of meeting young Swiss holidaymakers. In a country where the cost of a night out can limit your visits to pubs and clubs, these opportunities to make friends can be invaluable.

There are about 100 **HI hostels**, the vast majority of which are open to members only. While hostels in the larger towns may admit non-members (not Lucerne), this tends to incur an extra charge of 7SFr (£3.50; $5.25). In the main towns, hostels are open all year, except perhaps for a couple of weeks around Christmas and the New Year. Elsewhere, hostels shut for differing periods, from a few weeks to several months, at no specific time of the year. In the larger cities a midnight or 1 a.m. curfew is normal in summer, but you can expect a 10 p.m. closing time at the others. Prices vary according to the grading of the hostel: the top-rated ones cost up to 21SFr (£10.50; $15.75), mid-range hostels up to 18SFr (£9; $13.50), and the lower grade up to 14SFr (£7; $10.50). Facilities in the lower-grade hostels tend to be quite basic, but are perfectly adequate. In the top-rated hostels you will have no access to kitchen facilities, though these are available in many of the lesser-rated establishments. Except in the main towns, where a three-night maximum stay operates in summer, there is no limit to how long you can stay at any hostel. During the summer it is advisable to reserve hostels in the larger towns, either by letter or by phoning ahead. If you find a hostel full, you might consider staying in one in a nearby town if you have a railcard, rather than having to pay for a room in a hotel. In summer, some **student dorms** are converted into hostel accommodation, with dorm beds going for anything from 15–29SFr (£7.50–14.50; $11.25–21.75). You don't have to be a student to use these dorms. An excellent leaflet, *Student Lodgings in University Cities*, is available from the SNTO (address below).

There is no shortage of **campsites**; around 1200 in all.

Unfortunately, there are three camping organizations, which makes advance planning slightly more complicated. Swiss campgrounds rank amongst the best Europe has to offer, being particularly clean and well run. Prices can vary quite substantially, starting at around 4SFr (£2; $3) per tent and per person, but rising to 10SFr (£4.75; $7.15) per tent and 6SFr (£3; $4.50) per person charged at one site in Interlaken. On average a solo traveller might expect to pay around 8−10SFr (£4−5; $6.00−7.50) per night. One drawback to camping is that some of the large towns have no central or easily reached site, such as Berne. In other places, however, you may have a choice between two, or more, sites. Some campsites also offer dormitory accommodation.

Tourist Offices will also have information on whether you can **camp rough** in the area. Most cantons allow freelance camping on uncultivated land, but the permission of the landowner is required on privately owned land. Camping in public places or along the roadside is expressly forbidden. Whether you camp or sleep rough a good quality sleeping bag is recommended as it gets very cold at night, even in summer, and especially in the more mountainous areas. Hikers and climbers might wish to take advantage of the chain of **mountain refuges** run by the Swiss Alpine Club.

ADDRESSES

Swiss National Tourist Office	Swiss Centre, Swiss Court, London W1V 8EE (tel. 0171 734 1921)
Hotels	Swiss Hotels Association, Montbijoustraße 130, 3001 Bern (tel. 031 370 4111).
B&Bs	Bed and Breakfast Club, Case Postale 2231, 1110 Morges 2 (tel. 021 802 3385).
Swiss YHA	Schweizerischer Bund für Jugendherbergen, Postfach, 3001 Bern (tel. 031 302 5503). List available from the Swiss National Tourist Office.
Camping	Schweizerischer Camping und Caravanning-Verband, Habsburgerstraße 35, 6000 Luzern 4 (tel. 041 234822). Guides available from the Swiss National Tourist Office. They will tell you the latest price. Expect to pay around £4.
	Touring-Club der Schweiz Division

	Camping, rue Pierre Fatio 9, 1211 Genève 3 (tel. 022 737 1212).

Camping, rue Pierre Fatio 9, 1211
Genève 3 (tel. 022 737 1212).
Verband Schweizer Campings, Seestraße
119, 3800 Interlaken (tel. 036 233523).

Mountain huts   Schweizer Alpine Club (SAC),
Helvetiaplatz 4, 3005 Bern
(tel. 031 351 3611).

Basle (Basel) (tel. code 061)

TOURIST OFFICES
Generally the accommodation on offer is outside the budget traveller's price range, but under-26s should contact the Tourist Office
for details of the youth discount scheme.

City-Information and Hotel Reservation. In Basel SBB train station
(tel. 271 3684). Open May—Sept., Mon.—Fri. 8.30 a.m.—7 p.m.,
Sat. 8.30 a.m.—12.30 p.m. and 1.30—6 p.m., Sun. 10 a.m.—2 p.m.;
Oct.—Nov. and Mar.—Apr., closed Sun.; Dec.—Feb., open only
8.30 a.m.—12.30 p.m. on Sat.

Basel Hotelreservation, Messeplatz 7, 4021 Basel (tel. 691 7700).
A short walk down Rosentalstraße from Basel Bad Bhf. Open
Mon.—Fri. 8 a.m.—12 p.m. and 1—5 p.m.

Offizielles Verkehrsbüro Basel, Blumenrain 2/Schifflande, 4001
Basel (tel. 261 5050). Open Mon.—Fri. 8.30 a.m.—6 p.m., Sat.
8.30 a.m.—1 p.m. A short walk along the Rhine from the Mittlere
Rheinbrücke. Tram 8 from Basel SBB.

HOTELS
Steinenschanze, Steinengraben 69 (tel. 272 5353). Students with
ISIC pay 38SFr (£19; $28.50) for B&B in singles or doubles for
the first three nights. Walk left on leaving Basel SBB, turn right
downhill at Steinertorberg until it joins the main road on the
right. Follow the main road to the hotel.

Cheapest doubles around 110SFr (£55; $82.50)

Hecht am Rhein, Rheingasse 8 (tel. 691 2220). Tram 8 from in
front of Basel SBB. Rheingasse is on the right, a short distance
after the tram crosses the Rhine.

Cheapest doubles around 135SFr (£68; $102)

Steinenschanze, Steinengraben 69 (tel. 272 5353). Normal price paid by non-students. See above for directions.
Klingental Garni, Klingental 20 (tel. 681 6248). Same directions as for the Hecht am Rhein, above, but look for Untere Rheingasse on the right. This street leads into Klingental.
Stadthof, Gerbergasse 84 (tel. 261 8711). Walk left from Basel SBB, then left on to Margarethenstraße, where you can catch tram 16 to Gerbergasse.
Bristol, Centralbahnstraße 15 (tel. 271 3822). The street running along the front of Basel SBB.

Those who would prefer a hotel room to hostelling or camping but cannot afford the prices quoted above should consider staying over the border in Germany or France where rooms are cheaper. Local trains run from Basel Bad Bhf (tram 2 from Basel SBB) to a number of small German towns where you should be able to find a room for DM30 (£12.70; $19) per person. Rheinfelden is a particularly pleasant place to stay. The Rhine divides the town in two, one part German, the other part Swiss. Regular trains from Bâle SNCF (adjoining Basel SBB) make the 40-minute trip to Mulhouse in France. Trains from Paris, Calais, Ostend, Luxembourg and Strasbourg stop in Mulhouse before reaching Basle. The Office du Tourisme in Mulhouse is at av. de Maréchal Foch 9 (tel. (0)89 45 68 31). From the train station, head straight across the river down av. Auguste Wicky, right at rue 17 Novembre, then left into av. Foch. Mulhouse is well worth a visit in its own right.

HI HOSTEL
St Alban Kirchrain 10 (tel. 272 0572). Dorms 20SFr (£10; $15). Singles and doubles 26SFr (£13; $19.50) per person. 1 a.m. curfew during the summer, midnight the rest of the year. Only 5 minutes' walk from the town centre, 15 minutes from Basel SBB. Take tram 1 from Centralbahnplatz to Aeschenplatz (the first stop), then tram 3 to the stop by the St Alban-Tor. Alternatively, take tram 2 to Kunstmuseum stop. Accessible to wheelchairs.

CAMPING
About 9.5km out of Basle along Highway 18 is the town of Reinach, which has the cheapest site in the area: 'Wahldort', Heideweg 16 (tel. 711 6429). Open Mar.–Oct. However, those with a railpass would probably be better making their way to the site in Muttenz.

HI HOSTELS NEARBY

Route de Bâle 185, Delemont (tel. 066 22 20 54). Regular trains, half-hour trip. 18SFr (£9; $13.50)

Steinenweg 40, Lörrach (Germany) (tel. 07621 47040). Ten-minute trip on the regular service from Basel Bad station. Trains from Basel SBB heading for Germany stop at Basel Bad. The station is about 15–20 minutes' walk across the Rhine from the town centre.

Rue de l'Illberg 37, Mulhouse (France) (tel. 89 42 63 28). Near the university, 2.5km from the train station. From the town centre, take bus 2 to Coteaux or bus 1 to Hericourt. For further information on Mulhouse see the **Hotels** section, above.

Berne (Bern) (tel. code 031)

TOURIST OFFICE

Verkehrsverein Bern, Offizielles Verkehrs- und Kongressbüro, Im Bahnhof, Postfach, 3001, Bern (tel. 22 76 76). Open in summer, Mon.–Sat. 8 a.m.–8.30 p.m., Sun. 9 a.m.–8.30 p.m.; in winter, Mon.–Sat. 8 a.m.–6.30 p.m., Sun. 10 a.m.–5 p.m. In the train station.

HOTELS

Cheapest doubles around 90SFr (£45; $67.50)

Bahnhof-Süd, Bumplizstraße 189 (tel. 56 51 11). Offers probably the cheapest singles in Berne, from 35SFr (£17.50; $26.25). Bus 13. Nearest train station Bern-Bumpliz.

Hospiz sur Heimat, Gerichtigkeitgasse 50 (tel. 22 04 36). Bus 12, or a 15-minute walk from the train station through the Old Town. From Bahnhofplatz head down Spitalgasse, Marktgasse and Kramgasse into Gerichtigkeitgasse.

National, Hirschengraben 24 (tel. 381 1988). A 5 minute walk from the train station. Head right along Bubenbergplatz, then left on to Hirschengraben.

Marthahaus Garni, Wyttenbachstraße 22a (tel. 332 4135). Bus 20, or a 15-minute walk from the train station. From Bahnhofplatz follow Bollwerk, cross the River Aare by the Lorrainebrücke, turn right down Schanzlihalde, then left.

Alpenblick, Kasernenstraße 29 (tel. 42 42 55). Tram 9.

GUESTHOUSES

More affordable than the city's hotels are guesthouses in neigh-bouring towns which you can book through the Tourist Office. Prices are normally in the range 26–40SFr (£13–20; $19.50–30.00) per person. If you have a railpass you can easily travel to any of the small towns nearby which have a train station. Otherwise you will have to take into account the cost of getting to the guesthouse.

HI HOSTEL

'Jugendhaus', Weihergasse 4 (tel. 311 6316). 16SFr (£8; $12) Mid-night curfew. A 10–15-minute walk from the train station. From Bahnhofplatz cross Bubenbergplatz then go along Schauplatzgasse until you reach Bundesplatz with the Swiss Parliament. Look for the sign near the Parliament pointing down the steps to the hostel.

CAMPING

Eichholz, Strandweg 49 (tel. 961 2602). 4SFr (£2; $3) per tent, 4.80SFr (£2.40; $3.60) p.p. Also twin-bedded rooms 12SFr (£6; $9), plus 4.80SFr (£2.40; $3.60) p.p. Tram 9 to Wabern, the end of the line.

Eymatt (tel. 901 1501). 4SFr (£2; $3) per tent, 6SFr (£3; $4.50) p.p. From the train station take the postal bus dir. Bern-Hinterkappelen to Eymatt.

HI HOSTEL NEARBY

Rue de l'Hôpital 2, Fribourg (tel. 037 23 19 16). 18SFr (£9; $13.50). From the train station follow av. de la Gare from pl. de la Gare, along rue de Ramont into pl. Georges Python from which rue de l'Hôpital runs off to the left. Take the first right off av. de la Gare for the Tourist Office on Grands Places (tel. 037 81 31 75). Fribourg is an attractive and interesting old town on the train line between Geneva and Berne. Linked to Berne by frequent Inter-city trains, a half-hour trip. Accessible for wheelchairs.

Geneva (Genève) (tel. code 022)

TOURIST OFFICES

Office du Tourisme de Genève, Casa Postale 440, 1211 Geneve 11. The administrative office. Contact this office for information or to book.

Office du Tourisme de Genève, Gare de Cornavin (tel. 738 5200). In the main train station. Open June–Sept., Mon.–Fri. 8 a.m.–8 p.m., weekends 8 a.m.–6 p.m.; at other times, Mon.–Sat. 9 a.m.–6 p.m.

ARRIVING BY TRAIN

The main train station in Geneva is the Gare de Cornavin, which receives trains from Spain, Italy, Nice and Paris, as well as from all over Switzerland. Coming from Chamonix or Annecy (via La Roche-sur-Foron) you arrive at the Gare des Eaux-Vives. There is no connecting train service between the stations, but you can easily get between them by bus. The simplest way to get from Eaux-Vives to Cornavin is to walk down av. de la Gare, turn right down Route de Chêne, then right again at av. Pictet-de-Rochemont which leads into pl. des Eaux-Vives, from which you can take bus 9 to Cornavin. Alternatively, walk left a short distance up Route de Chêne to the bus stop, then take bus 12 to pl. Bel-Air, from which you can take bus 1, 4 or 5 to Cornavin. If you fly into Cointrin Airport there are trains about every six minutes to Cornavin (railpasses valid).

BASIC DIRECTIONS

From pl. de Cornavin in front of the train station rue des Alpes runs from the left-hand end of the square down to Lake Geneva (Lac Léman). At the right-hand end of the square rue du Mont-Blanc leads to the Pont du Mont-Blanc which crosses the River Rhône just as it flows out of the lake. Going straight ahead you arrive at pl. du Port from which pl. Longmalle and then rue de la Fontaine lead into the picturesque pl. du Bourg-de-Four, in the heart of the Old Town, beneath the cathedral. The walk from Cornavin to pl. du Bourg-de-Four takes 10–15 minutes.

HOTELS

If you want a hotel room but cannot afford the prices quoted below, those with railpasses can stay in the French town of Bellegarde, a half-hour train trip from Cornavin.

Cheapest doubles around 70SFr (£35; $52.50)

1. Hôtel de la Cloche, rue de la Cloche 6 (tel. 732 9481). About 10 minutes' walk from Cornavin. Left off rue des Alpes along rue Philippe-Plantamour at place des Alpes, then right at rue Cloche.
2. Pension de la Servette, rue de la Prairie 31 (tel. 734 0230). Breakfast included. A 10-minute walk from Gare de Cornavin.

From the rear exit head left, diagonally right at rue de la Pepinière, across rue de la Servette and into rue de Lyon, then first right up rue de Jura into rue de la Prairie. Bus 6 or 26 from Cornavin run along rue Voltaire, stopping at one end of rue de la Prairie, while buses 3, 10 and 15 run along rue de la Servette passing the other end of the street.

3. Hôtel Pâquis Fleuri, rue des Pâquis 23 (tel. 731 3453). About 8 minutes' walk from Cornavin, left off rue des Alpes at place des Alpes. Bus 1 dir: Wilson from Cornavin runs along the street.

4. Hôtel Saint Victor, rue Lefort 1 (tel. 346 1718). Bus 8 from Cornavin to Florissant then a short walk, back to blvd des Tranchées, from which any of the small streets on the opposite side of the road will take you into rue Lefort.

5. Centre Saint Boniface, av. du Mail 14 (tel. 321 8844). Bus 1, 4, or 44 from Cornavin to place du Cirque, or a 15-minute walk. Right from Cornavin along bd James-Fazy to the Rhône. Cross the river and go straight on, along bd Georges-Favon to place du Cirque, then right on the other side of the square down av. du Mail.

6. Pension Rhodania, rue Paul-Bouchet 5 (tel. 731 4720). Right from Cornavin, left on rue Chantepoulet, then right again on to Paul-Bouchet. Will allow 3 or 4 in a room.

Cheapest doubles around 75SFr (£37.50; $56.25)

7. Hôtel Luserna, av. Luserna 12 (tel. 344 1600/345 4676). A 20-minute walk from Cornavin. Right down rue de la Servette (see 2), left at av. Wendt, right at av. Luserna. Buses 3, 10 and 15 from Cornavin stop at Servette Ecole, just before av. Wendt.

8. International et Terminus, 20 rue des Alpes (tel. 732 8095).

9. Hôtel Beau Site, pl. du Cirque 3 (tel. 328 1008). Triples around 95SFr (£48; $72), quads around 110SFr (£55; $82.50). A 15 minute walk from Cornavin or a direct bus (see 5).

10. Hôtel du Lac, rue des Eaux-Vives 15 (tel. 735 4580). Slightly cheaper per person in triples. Bus 9 from Cornavin to pl. des Eaux-Vives, then a short walk along rue des Eaux-Vives. A 15–20-minute walk from Cornavin. Left along Quai Général Guisan after crossing the Pont du Mont-Blanc and straight on along rue Versonnex into pl. des Eaux-Vives.

Cheapest doubles around 85SFr (£43; $64.50)

11. Rio, place Isaac Mercier 1 (tel. 732 3264). Around 90SFr (£45; $67.50) for triples. A few minutes' walk from Cornavin, right along bd James Fazy into pl. Isaac Mercier.

12. Pension Ravier, rue Argand 2 (tel. 738 3773). Five minutes from Cornavin. Right along blvd James Fazy, then left.
13. Hôtel Saint Gervais, rue des Corps-Saints 20 (tel. 732 4572). Five minutes from Cornavin. The street is a continuation of rue Cornavin.

HI HOSTEL

14. Nouvelle Auberge de Jeunesse, rue Rothschild 28–30 (tel. 732 6260). Midnight curfew in summer, 11 p.m. at other times. HI members pay 18SFr (£9; $13.50) in dorms. 70SFr (£35; $52.50) for doubles with shower and WC. Overnight price includes breakfast. About 8 minutes' walk from Cornavin, left along rue de Lausanne, then right. Or take tram 1 to Palais Wilson stop.

HOSTELS/FOYERS/STUDENT ACCOMMODATION

15. Armée du Salut, Ch. Galiffe 4 (tel. 44 91 21). 11 p.m. curfew. B&B in dorms 13SFr (£6.50; $9.75). A 10-minute walk from Cornavin. Left from the rear exit, following the tracks all the way, across rue de la Servette and along rue de Malatrex until you see ch. Galiffe on the right.
16. Armée du Salut, rue de l'Industrie 14 (tel. 733 6438). Women only. Curfew 10.30 or 11 p.m. Dorms 14–17SFr (£7.00–8.50; $10.50–12.75) without breakfast. Just over 5 minutes' walk from Cornavin. Left from the rear exit, right up rue des Grottes until you see rue de l'Industrie on the left.
17. Home St-Pierre, cour St-Pierre 4 (tel. 328 3707/310 3707). Women only. No curfew. Dorms start at around 15SFr (£7.50; $11.25), triples around 52SFr (£26; $39), doubles around 42SFr (£21; $31.50) and singles around 26SFr (£13; $19.50). Breakfast included. Excellent location by the Cathedral.
18. Cité Universitaire, av. Miremont 46 (tel. 346 2355). Curfew 10 p.m. Dorms 15SFr (£7.50; $11.25), doubles start around 56SFr (£28; $42), singles around 28SFr (£14; $21) without breakfast. From place de 22 Cantons by Cornavin station take bus 3 to the Crêts de Champel terminus.
19. Centre St-Boniface, av. du Mail 14 (tel. 321 8844). Dorms 18–27SFr (£9.00–13.50; $13.50–21.75) for B&B. See 5.
20. Maison International Etudiants, rue Daniel-Colladon 2 (tel. 29 30 34). B&B in singles 29–35SFr (£14.50–17.50; $21.75–26.25). Near the Reformation Monument. Bus 5 from Cornavin to Croix Rouge. A 15–20 minute walk from Cornavin.

From pl. du Bourg-de-Four follow rue St-Léger, first right, then first left.

21. Bureau Logements Université, rue de Candolle 4 (tel. 705 7720). Singles 29—35SFr (£14.50—17.50; $21.75—26.25) with breakfast. Three-day minimum stay. See 18.

22. Evangelische Stadtmission, rue Bergalonne 7 (tel. 321 2611). Curfew 11 p.m. B&B in dorms 22—25SFr (£11.00—12.50; $16.50—18.75). Triples 85—100SFr (£42.50—50.00; $63.50—75.00), doubles 70—80SFr (£35—40; $52.50—60.00), singles 42—50SFr (£21—25; $31.50—37.50). Bus 1, 4 or 44 from Cornavin to to Ecole-Médecine (rue Bergalonne is to the rear of the Musée d'Ethnographie), or a 15—20-minute walk. Rue Bergalonne runs right off av. du Mail (see 5).

23. Centre Masaryk, av. de la Paix 11 (tel. 733 0772). 11 p.m. curfew. B&B in dorms 27SFr (£13.50; $20.25). Triples 90SFr (£45; $67.50), doubles 65SFr (£32.50; $48.75). Singles 38SFr (£19; $28.50). Near the Palace of the United Nations. Bus 5 or 8 from Cornavin to the Nations terminus, or a 20-minute walk.

24. Foyer l'Accueil, rue Alcide-Jentzer 8 (tel. 320 9277). 58SFr (£29; $43.50) for doubles, 35SFr (£17.50; $26.25) for singles with breakfast. Bus 1 or 5 to Hôpital. Walk back onto blvd de la Cluse, head left, then left again at rue Alcide-Jentzer by the maternity clinic.

25. Foyer St-Justin, rue du Prieuré 15—17 (tel. 731 1135). Singles 30—43SFr (£15.00—21.50; $22.50—32.25) without breakfast. A 5-minute walk from Cornavin, left along rue de Lausanne, then right.

26. Centre Universitaire Zofingien, rue des Voisins 6 (tel. 29 11 40/29 51 13). With breakfast. Triples 95SFr (£47.50; $71.25), in doubles 78SFr (£39; $58.50), in singles 51SFr (£25.50; $38.25). During the university year only.

27. Hôtel le Grenil, av. Ste-Clotilde 7 (tel. 328 3055). B&B in dorms 27SFr (£13.50; $20.25) for under-25s. Prices in triples and doubles are higher than in the hotels listed above.

28. Residence Universitaire Internationale, rue des Pâquis 63 (tel. 732 5606). Singles 30—40SFr (£15—20; $22.50—30.00), doubles 42—52SFr (£21—26; $31.50—39.00). See 3.

CAMPING

Sylvabelle, Chemin de Conches 10 (tel. 347 0603). Open Apr.—Oct. 3SFr (£1.50; $2.25) per tent, 4SFr (£2; $3) per person. About 3km out, the closest site to the city centre. Bus 8 from Cornavin dir: Vernier

Pointe-à-la-Bise (tel. 752 1296). Open Apr.–Sept. 5SFr (£2.50; $3.75) per person, tents from 5SFr (£2.50; $3.75). About 8km out from the centre, close to Lake Geneva. From Cornavin take bus 9 to Rive, then change to bus E.

D'Hermance, Chemin des Glerrêts (tel. 751 1483). 6SFr (£3; $4.50) p.p. 2.50SFr (£1.25; $2) per tent. Open Apr.–Sept. About 16km from the city centre, close to Lake Geneva. Bus 9 from Cornavin to Rive, then take bus E to the terminus.

Lausanne (tel. code 021)

TOURIST OFFICES

Office du Tourisme et des Congrès, av. de Rhodania 2, Case postale 248, 1000 Lausanne 6 (tel. 617 7321, or tel. 617 1427 for general tourist information). Open Easter–mid-Oct., Mon.–Sat. 8 a.m.–7 p.m., Sun. 9 a.m.–12 p.m. and 1–6 p.m. At other times, closes Mon.–Fri. at 6 p.m., open Sat. 8.30 a.m.–12 p.m. and 1–5 p.m., closed Sunday. In Ouchy. From the train station take the metro to the end of the line. The office is about 100m from the metro stop.

Office du Tourisme et des Congrès. Branch office in the train station.

HOTELS

Cheapest doubles around 70SFr (£35; $52.50)

Hôtel du Marché, Pré-du-Marché 42 (tel. 657 9900). Near pl. de la Riponne.

Auberge de Rivaz (tel. 946 1055). In Rivaz, 13km out of Lausanne.

Cheapest doubles around 95SFr (£47.50; $71.25)

Hôtel d'Angleterre, pl. du Port 9, Ouchy (tel. 617 2111). Lakeside location. Take the metro from the train station to the last stop.

Hôtel Près-Lac, av. Général Guisan 16 (tel. 284 901).

Hôtel de la Foret, Pavement 75 (tel. 37 92 11).

Hôtel Rex, av. de Chailly 3 (tel. 652 5121), in Chailly.

Hôtel Regina, Grand St Jean 18 (tel. 320 2441).

HI HOSTEL

Chemin du Muguet 1, Lausanne-Ouchy (tel. 616 5782). 18SFr (£9; $13.50), breakfast included. Take bus 1 dir: La Maladière to the La Batelière stop, from which the hostel is signposted.

HOSTELS/DORMITORIES

Prés de Vidy, Chemin du Bois de Vaux (tel. 24 24 79). Further out of town on the same bus route as the HI hostel.
Foyer la Croisée, av. Marc Dufour 15 (tel. 20 42 31).

CAMPING

Camping de Vidy-Lausanne, Chemin du Camping 3 (tel. 24 20 31). High quality lakeside site. 4–8SFr (£2–4; $3–6) per tent, 6SFr (£3; $4.50) p.p.

Lucerne (Luzern) (tel. code 041)

TOURIST OFFICES

Tourist Information, Frankenstraße 1 (tel. 51 71 71). Open Mon.–Fri. 8 a.m.–6 p.m., Sat. and public holidays 9 a.m.–5 p.m. Leaving the train station head left down the side of the station, Frankenstraße is to the right off Zentralstraße.
Hotel Information (tel. 23 52 44). In the train station.

HOTELS

Hotel Schlüssel, Franziskanerplatz 12 (tel. 23 10 61). Bus 2, 9 or 18, or a ten minutes walk from the train station. Head left along the River Reuss, past the Jesuit Church, then left into Franziskanerplatz. Doubles from 86SFr (£43; $64.50).
SSR Touristenhotel, St Karliquai 12 (tel. 51 24 74). Bus 2, 9 or 18, or a 15-minute walk from the train station. From Kramgasse (directions see Hotel Linde, above) go left through Muhlenplatz and back towards the River Reuss and St Karliquai. Doubles from 44SFr (£22; $33), dorms for 33SFr (£16.50; $24.75).
Hotel Villa Maria, Haldenstraße 36 (tel. 31 21 19). Overlooks the lake. A 25 minute walk from the train station (follow the directions for Camping Lido, below), or take bus 2 to the stop near the Hotel Europe. Doubles around 80SFr (£40; $60).
Pension Pro Filia, Zäringerstraße 24 (tel. 22 42 80). Singles 60SFr (£30; $45), doubles from 95SFr (£47.50; $71.25). South of the river. Take bus 2, 9 or 18.

DORMS
Available at the SSR Touristenhotel, but more expensive than those of the HI hostel. See also Camping Lido.

HI HOSTEL
Am Rotsee, Sedelstraße 12 (tel. 36 88 00). 21SFr (£10.50; $15.75), breakfast included. 11.30 p.m. curfew. Not central. A 30-minute walk from the train station. Bus 18 to Goplismoos/Friedental leaves you with a couple of minutes' walk. Last bus 7.30 p.m. The more frequent bus 1 to Schloßberg leaves you a 10-minute walk down Friedentalstraße. Reception opens 4 p.m., and 1½ hour queues are not uncommon during the summer, with no guarantee of getting in.

CAMPING
Lido, Lidostraße (tel. 31 21 46). Near the beach and the lake. A 35 minute walk from the train station, over the Seebrücke, then right along the lakeside. Bus 2 to Verkehrshaus. 2.50SFr (£1.25; $2) per tent, 5SFr (£2.50; $3.75) p.p. Also dorms 14SFr (£7; $10.50). Cheapest in town. Site open Apr.–Oct.

Steinbachried (tel. 47 35 58). Bus 20 for a 20 minute trip to Horw Rank. 4SFr (£2; $3) per tent, 5SFr (£2.50; $3.75) p.p. Open Apr.–Sept.

HI HOSTEL NEARBY
Allmendstraße 8, Sportstadion 'Herti', Zug (tel. 042 21 53 54). 21SFr (£10.50; $15.75). 11.30 p.m. curfew. Frequent trains, 30-minute trip.

Zürich (tel. code 01)

TOURIST OFFICE
Offizielles Verkehrsbüro Zürich, Bahnhofplatz 15, 8023 Zürich (Hauptbahnhof) (tel. 211 1131 for hotel reservations; tel. 2114000 for general information). Right in the city centre. Open Mar.–Oct., Mon.–Fri. 8 a.m.–10 p.m., weekends 9 a.m.–6 p.m.; Nov.–Feb., closes 8 p.m. Mon.–Thurs., closed at weekends.

TROUBLE SPOTS
In recent years, the city authorities operated a controversial needle exchange in one of the city's parks. It has been claimed that this

attracted drug users from all over the country (and even from Germany) to the city. In late 1991, the authorities halted the scheme and closed the park. The result was that addicts began to gather on the city's streets, particularly around the main train station. Although there have been no reports of violence around the station at the time of writing, the sight itself is harrowing (particularly as drugs are injected quite openly), and you are likely to be pestered for money.

HOTELS

Hinterer Sternen, Freieckgasse 7 (tel. 251 3268). Doubles around 60SFr (£30; $45). A 10-minute walk from Zürich Hbf. Cross the river Limmat, right along Limmatquai, then up Ramistraße at Bellevueplatz. Or take tram 4, 5, 8 or 15 to Bellevueplatz.

Justinusheim, Freudenbergstraße 146 (tel. 361 3806). Singles around 33SFr (£16.50; $24.75), doubles from 70SF4 (£35; $52.50). Open July–Oct. and Mar.–Apr. Few vacancies. Tram 9 or 10 to the junction of Winterthurerstraße and Langensteinerstraße, then bus 39 to Freudenbergerstraße. You can also catch bus 39 from the terminus of trams 5 and 6 near the zoo, though this is a longer journey.

Regina, Hohlstraße 18 (tel. 242 6550). Doubles from 110SFr (£55; $82.50). A 10 minute walk from Zürich Hbf. Diagonally right across Bahnhofplatz, along Gessnerallee, right over the Gessnerbrücke, left along the River Sihl, then right down Zeughausstraße.

St Georges, Weberstraße 11 (tel. 21 11 44). Just over 10 minutes' walk from Zürich Hbf. Diagonally right across Bahnhofplatz, along Gessnerallee, right over Gessnerbrücke then left along the River Sihl until you see Webergasse on the right after the second bridge.

Splendid, Rosengasse 5 (tel. 252 5850). Doubles from 96SFr (£48; $72). A 5 minute walk from Zürich Hbf. Cross the River Limmat by the Bahnhofsbrücke, then right along the Limmatquai until you see Rosengasse on the left after Mühlegasse.

Seefeld, Seehofstraße 11 (tel. 252 2570). Tram 4 along Seefeldstraße until you see Seehofstraße on the right after the tram turns off Ramistraße along Theaterstraße, or a 15 minute walk from Zürich Hbf. Follow the directions for Hotel Hinterer Stern to Ramistraße, then turn right along Theaterstraße and keep going until you see Seehofstraße on the right.

Vorderer Sternen, Theodorestraße (tel. 251 4949). Doubles from 86SFr (£43; $64.50). A 10-minute walk from Zürich Hbf. See Hotel Hinterer Sternen for directions.

Hirschen, Niederdorf Straße 13 (tel. 251 4252).

HI HOSTEL
Mutschellenstraße 114, Zürich-Wollishofen (tel. 482 3544). 26SFr (£13; $19.50), breakfast included. 1 a.m. curfew. Tram 6 or 7 to Morgental, then a well-signposted 5-minute walk. There is a local train station, Zürich-Wollishofen, if you have a railpass and want to save some money on transport.

DORMITORY ACCOMMODATION
City Backpacker (Hotel Biber), Schweizerhofgasse 5 (tel. 251 9015). Dorm beds from 26SFr (£13; $19.50), private rooms from 55SFr (£27.50; $41.25). In the heart of the old town.

Hotel Martahaus, Zähringerstraße 36 (tel. 251 4550). Six-bed dorms 30SFr (£15; $22.50). Doubles around 95SFr (£47.50; $71.25). A 5-minute walk from Zürich Hbf. Cross the River Limmat by Bahnhofsbrücke. Limmatquai runs away to the right along the river. Zähringerstraße runs parallel to the Limmatquai, two streets back from the river.

Foyer Hottingen, Hottingerstraße 31 (tel. 261 9315). Dorms 30SFr (£15; $22.50). Doubles around 95SFr (£47.50; $71.25). This one-star hotel run by nuns is open to women, married couples and families only. Tram 3 to Hottingerplatz from Bahnhofplatz.

CAMPING
'Seebucht', Seestraße 559, Zürich-Wollishofen (tel. 482 1612). 5SFr (£2.50; $3.75) p.p., 8SFr (£4; $6) per tent. Open May—Sept. Excellent site on the Zürichsee. Local train to Zürich-Wollishofen, then a 10-minute walk. Alternatively, take bus 161 or 165 from Bürkliplatz.

HI HOSTELS NEARBY
Kanalstraße 7, Baden (tel. 056 21 67 96). 18SFr (£9; $13.50). Open 16 Mar.—23 Dec. Frequent trains, a 30 minute trip.

Allmendstraße 8, Sportstadion 'Herti', Zug (tel. 042 21 53 54). 21SFr (£10.50; $15.75). Frequent trains, a 45 minute trip.

Cevi-Zentrum, Stockerstraße 18, Horgen (tel. 01 725 8934/3104). Open 27 July—30 Aug. 23SFr (£11.50; $17.25). About 500m from the train station in Horgen. Trains run thrice hourly from Zürich Hbf.

Schloß Hegi, Hegifeldstraße 125, Winterhur (052 27 38 40). 10SFr (£5; $7.50). Open Mar.—Oct. Twenty minutes by train from Zürich. From Winterhur, take bus 1 to Oberwinterhur. Situated within a 15th-century castle.

TURKEY (Türkiye)

As a rule, budget travellers will seldom encounter any difficulty finding suitably priced accommodation in Turkey, with the notable exceptions of the coastal resorts and the capital at the height of the summer season. While Ankara is not really a tourist town (and is correspondingly short on budget accommodation), it seems to attract many travellers on the basis of its status as the national capital. Otherwise, it is usually quite simple to find a place to stay for about £3.35–5.35 ($5–8) per person along the Aegean coast, £2.65–4.65 ($4–7) along its Mediterranean counterpart, or from £2–4 ($3–6) per person in the very east of the country.

In any town with a reasonable tourist trade you will have the option of staying at one of the **hotels** which are registered with the Ministry of Tourism. These hotels are rated from one star up to five stars. Standards of cleanliness and comfort are rigorously enforced by the authorities, so it is highly unlikely that you will ever have cause for complaint if you stay at one of these hotels. In hotels registered with the Ministry of Tourism you can expect to pay from £10–20 ($17.50–35) for a double in a one-star hotel, rising to £12–24 ($21–42) in Istanbul. The cost of a double in a two-star hotel starts around £18 ($27), again being slightly higher in Istanbul.

The vast majority of locally licensed hotels are perfectly acceptable, with some almost on a par with one-star hotels, so you should have no trouble finding acceptable and similarly priced accommodation nearby. Locally licensed hotels are usually a good bit cheaper than those registered with the Ministry of Tourism; expect to pay in the region of £4–6 ($6–9) per person in singles or doubles.

During the peak season, it is not unusual for hotel touts to approach travellers at bus and train stations, and at ferry terminals. Where there are several touts trying to attract custom, there is a fair chance of bargaining them down from their initial asking price.

An excellent alternative to hotel accommodation is a **guesthouse**, known as a *pansiyon*, or in ski resorts as an *oberj*. Guesthouses are plentiful throughout the country, often small family-run establishments providing good-value meals. A few guesthouses are registered with the Ministry of Tourism. The standard of accommodation in these establishments is uniformly high. Doubles cost £8–20 ($14–35), depending on the facilities available. At other guesthouses you can expect to pay from £2–5.35 ($3–8) per person in singles or doubles. As with locally licensed hotels, check rooms at unregistered guesthouses before making a firm acceptance, just in case you have been unlucky enough to come across a rogue establishment where standards are less than acceptable. Another cheap accommodation option are **private rooms**, though these are much less common than guesthouses. Look out for the sign 'Oda Var' indicating rooms are available (sometimes also advertised in German: 'Zimmer frei'). Prices for private rooms are unlikely to be above £2.50 ($4.50) per person.

There are 45 **youth hostels** in Turkey, only one of which is affiliated to the HI. Some student residences also serve as hostels (mainly during the months July and August, though some operate all year round). Normally a student ID card guarantees entrance to a hostel, but it makes sense to have an HI card as, for some strange reason, even some of the non-affiliated hostels sometimes ask for an HI card. Hostel dormitories are called Yurtkur. A booklet, *Youth Tourism in Turkey*, available from Tourist Offices, lists over 100 Yurtkur dorms as well as nearly 50 youth and forest camps. Converted **student dorms** usually cost around £3.35 ($5) per person.

Camping is popular in Turkey, and the number of sites is growing annually. Campsites are generally open from April/May to October. Although facilities are still on the whole exceptionally basic, you nevertheless get reasonable value for money as prices are normally around £1 ($1.75) per person (tent included) for an overnight stay. At the network of BP mocamps, prices are around £2 ($3.50) per person per night, again including tent (a 20% surcharge is added in July and August). Some campers have cast doubt upon whether BP mocamps offer good value for money. In truth, you might wonder how BP mocamps can justify charging twice as much as most other sites in Turkey, but on a European scale it is fair to say that they do offer reasonable value for money. Unless you are going to be travelling widely outside the main towns, it may not be worth taking a tent: the sites serving the cities can be inconveniently located far out of town, and not always well served by public transport. In the cities, your best bet for finding a convenient place to pitch a tent can be to make enquiries as to any hotels which allow camping in their garden for a small charge.

Freelance camping is not illegal, but it is very rarely practised, except in the remoter areas. In the east, where official sites are few and far between, it is best to choose a location, and then ask the permission of the locals to pitch your tent. If nothing else, this is likely to prevent any possible misfortune arising out of camping in a military area. Anyone (women especially) worried about camping out in the country but who, for any reason, get stranded outside the towns, should note that petrol stations will rarely object to you pitching your tent close to the station, so affording you that little extra security. If you set up a tent in a town you can expect to be disturbed by the police. Their concern is more likely to be for your safety than anything else. Street crime and petty theft are remarkably low in Turkey, but it is inviting trouble to camp or **sleep rough** in the larger towns, Istanbul especially. It is safe to say that of those travellers who do encounter serious trouble in Turkey, the vast majority have been sleeping rough or camping rough in the cities.

ADDRESSES

Turkish Information Office	First Floor 170/173 Piccadilly, London W1V 9DB (tel. 0171 734 8681)
Gençtur	Yerebatan Caddesi 15, 3 Sultanahmet, 33410 Istanbul (tel. 01 5136150/513 6151). Information on youth and student travel and accommodation possibilities.

Ankara (tel. code 04)

TOURIST OFFICES

The administrative office is at Gazi Mustafa Kemal Bulvarı 121, Demirtepe (tel. 488 7007). Contact this office if you want information on the city in advance. The main information office (tel. 230 1911/231 7380), Gazi Mustafa Kemal Bulvarı 33 is by the Maltepe mosque. Open in peak season, Mon.–Fri. 8.30 a.m.–6.30 p.m., weekends 8.30 a.m.–5 p.m.; at other times, Mon.–Fri. 8.30 a.m.–6.30 p.m. only. Two offices operate in the city centre: one at Istanbul Caddesi 4 (tel. 311 2247/310 6818), by the Cumhriyet Museum in Ulus (same hours as the main office), the other at the Atatürk Cultural Centre off Kâzim Karabekir Caddesi. Another branch office is located at the international terminal of Esenboğa airport. There is also a free telephone information line on 90 044 7090.

BASIC DIRECTIONS

Ankara's train station is about 10 minutes' walk from Ulus Meydanı in the centre of the old town, straight down Cumhuriyet Bulvarı opposite the station. About 750m down the street is the Cumhuriyet Museum, with one of the branches of the Tourist Office nearby.

Three important streets lead out of Ulus Meydan. Left from the end of Cumhuriyet Bulvarı is Çankırı Cad. Hisarparki Cad. is across the square and to the right, while a sharp right takes you onto Atatürk Bulvarı.

The bus station is about 400m from the train station, left along Hipodrum Cad. near the junction with Kâzim Karabakir Cad. Turning right up the latter, after a short distance you will see the Atatürk Cultural Centre on your left; turning right Kâzim Karabakir Cad. leads under the rail lines to Tandoḃ Meydan, from which Gazi Mustafa Kemal Bulvarı runs off to the left.

Talat Paşa Cad. heads right from the train station, towards the Samanpazari and Dörtyol districts. About 800m along the street is the crossroads with Atatürk Bulvarı. Going right Atatürk Bulvarı leads down into the modern part of the city, passing thorugh the Kizilay district.

FINDING ACCOMMODATION

The largest concentration of cheap hotels are located in the streets off Atatürk Bulvarı between the Opera and Ulus Meydan. Hotels in this area have the advantage of being centrally located, and close to both the bus and train stations. There are also plenty of cheap hotels along this stretch of Atatürk Bulvar, but street noise is a major problem afflicting these establishments. Although less conveniently located for the centre of the old city (but still within easy walking distance), Gazi Mustafa Kemal Bulvarı and the Maltepe district contain a good supply of cheap hotels. The Kizilay district (2.5km from the centre) is also well supplied with cheap and moderately priced hotels, the standards of which generally surpass similarly priced accommodation elsewhere.

HOTELS
Locally licensed hotels. Expect to pay from £5–10 ($7.50–15.00) for doubles

Pinar, Hisar Cad. 14 (tel. 311 8951). Ulus district.

Babil, Gazi Mustafa Kemal Bulvarı 66 (tel. 231 7877).

Buhara, Sanayi Cad. 13 (tel. 324 5245/5246). Good value for money. Ulus district.

Sıpahı, Itfaiye Meydan, Kosova Sok 1 (tel. 324 0235/0236). Simple, clean rooms. Recommended. Across from the Opera, take the road leading off Atatürk Bulvarı to the junction of Derman Sok and Kosova Sok.

Hisar, Hisarparki Cad. 6 (tel. 311988/3108128). Particularly good. Ulus district.

Zümrüt Palas, Posta Cad. 16 (tel. 310 3210/3211). One of the best hotels listed here.

Çoruh, Denizciler Cad. 47 (tel. 312 4113/4114).

Suna, Çankırı Cad., Soğukkuyu Sok 6 (tel. 311 5465). Ulus district. Off Çankırı Cad. near the Olimpiyat Otel.

Avrupa, Posta Cad., Susam Sok 9 (tel. 311 4300). Ulus district.

Devran, Opera (Itfaiye) Meydanı (tel. 311 0485/0486). Small rooms, but clean and comfortable. Recommended.

Erden, Itfaiye Meydanı (tel. 324 3191/3192).

Kösk, Denizciler Cad. 56 (tel. 324 5228/5229).

Mithat, Itfaiye Meydan, Tavus Sok 2 (tel. 311 5410/5651).

Oba, Posta Cad. 9 (tel. 312 4128/4129). Ulus district.

Sahil Palas, Posta Cad. Ulus district.

Lale Palas, Hükümet Meydanı, Telegraf Sokak 5 (tel. 312 5220). Just north of Julian's Column.

Santral Palas, Denizciler Cad., Dibek Sok (tel. 312 5577/6588).

Uğur Palas, Itfaiye Meydanı Sanayi Cad. 54 (tel. 324 1296). On the east side of Opera square.

Ertan, Selanik Cad. 70 (tel. 118 4038). Kizilay district, at the junction of Atatürk Bulvarı and Gazi Mustafa Kemal Bulvar, follow the street opposite Gazi Mustafa Kemal until it is crossed by Selanik Cad.

Turan Palas, Çankırı Cad., Beşik Sok 3 (tel. 312 5225/5226). Ulus district.

Savaş, Altan Sok 3 (tel. 324 2113). Off Anafartalar Cad.

Beyrut Palas, Denizciler Cad. 11 (tel. 310 8407).

Esen Palas, Hükümet Cad. 22 (tel. 311 2747). Ulus district. Near the Column of Julian (Jülyanüs Sütunu), left off Hisarparki Cad., a short walk from Ulus Meydan.

Pamukkale, Hükümet Cad. 18 (tel. 311 7812). Ulus district. See the Esen Palas above, for directions.

Tarabya, Itfaiye Meydan, Kosova Sok 9 (tel. 311 9552). Dull, but acceptable rooms. See the Sıpahı, above, for directions.

Ucler, Itfaiye Meydan, Kosova Sok 7. See the Sıpahı, above, for directions.

Uğrak, Itfaiye Meydanı, Tauus Sokak (tel. 311 2948).

One-star hotels. Expect to pay from £12 ($18) for doubles

As, Rüzgarli Sok 4 (tel. 310 3998/3999). Singles £8.60 ($13), singles with bath £13.30 ($20), doubles £14.70 ($22), doubles with bath £16.70 ($25). Ulus district.

Safir, Denizciler Cad. 34 (tel. 311 6194). Singles and doubles £10 ($15) per person.

Paris, Denizciler Cad. 14 (tel. 324 1283/1284/1285).

Efes, Denizciler Cad. 12 (tel. 3243211). Singles with bath £12.70 ($19), doubles with bath £18.70 ($28).

Ergen, Karanfil Sok 48 (tel. 4117 5906). Singles £12 ($18), doubles £16.70 ($25). Kizilav district. At the junction of Atatürk Bulvarı and Gazi Mustafa Kemal Bulvarı follow the road opposite Gazi Mustafa Kemal, then turn right almost immediately down Karanfil Sok.

Bulduk, Sanayi Cad. 26 (tel. 310 4915). Singles £8 ($12), doubles £13.30 ($20). Ulus district.

Terminal, Hipodrum Cad. (tel. 310 4949). Singles £8 ($12), singles with bath £9.30 ($14), doubles £12 ($18), doubles with bath £14.70 ($22). Near the bus station.

Öztürk, Talat Paşa Bul. 57 (tel. 312 5186/5187). Samanpazari district.

Tac, Çankırı Cad. 35 (tel. 324 3195). Ulus district.

Olimpiyat, Rüzgarli Eşdost Sok 14 (tel. 324 3088). Ulus district.

Sembol, Sümer Sokak 28 (tel. 2318222). Singles £13.30 ($20), doubles with bath £20 ($30). Off Gazi Mustafa Kemal Bulvarı between the Maltepe Mosque and the junction with Atatürk Bulvarı.

Medine, Istanbul Cad. 14 (tel. 309 1381/1382/1383). The street runs left off Cumhuriyet Bulvarı by the Cumhuriyet Museum, crossing Kâzim Karabakir Cad. after about 500m.

Yenibahar, Çankırı Cad. 25 (tel. 310 4895). Singles £10 ($15), doubles £16.70 ($25). Ulus district.

Elhamra, Ismetpaşa Mah. Çankırı Cad. (tel. 310 4885). Ulus district.

Two-star hotels. Expect to pay from £16 ($24) for doubles

Basyazicioğlu, Çankırı Cad. 27 (tel. 310 3935). Singles £11.30 ($17), doubles £21.30 ($32). Ulus district.

Akman, Opera Meydan, Tavus Sok 6 (tel. 324 4140). Singles with bath £12 ($18), doubles with bath £18.70 ($28).

Barinak, Koç Yurdu Yani Onur Sok 25 (tel. 231 8040). Singles with bath £16.70 ($25), doubles with bath £25.30 ($38). The street runs off Gazi Mustafa Kemal Bulvarı.

Erşan, Meşrutiyet Cad. 13 (tel. 418 9875). Singles with bath £16.70 ($25), doubles with bath £25.30 ($38). Kizilay district. Off Atatürk Bulvar, about 400m beyond the junction with Gazi Mustafa Kemal Bulvarı.

Ercan, Denizciler Cad. 36 (tel. 310 4890).

YOUTH HOSTELS
Cumhuriyet Öğrenci Yurdu Cebeci, Siyasal Bilgiler Fakultesi Arkasi
(tel. 362 9750). Open 15 July–10 Sept.
Atatürk Erkek Yurdu, Plevne Cad. 5 (tel. 362 9740). Summer only.
Yildirim Beyazit, Erkek Yurdu (tel. 317 0202). Summer only.

CAMPING
Altinok (tel. 341 4406/7291). About 20km out on the road to
Istanbul.

Antalya (tel. code 31)

TOURIST OFFICE
Turizm Danisma Burosu, Cumhuriyet Cad. 91 (tel. 411747). Open
Mon.–Fri. 8 a.m.–5.30 p.m., weekends 9 a.m.–5 p.m. The office
distributes small plans of the city, and lists of local accommodation
registered with the Ministry of Tourism, but no lists of locally
licensed accommodation. As you walk along Cumhuriyet Cad. from
Kazim zalp Cad. the office is about 250m beyond the Atatürk statue,
set back a little off the right-hand side of Cumhuriyet Cad.

Note: The telephone exchange in Antalya is currently undergoing
modernization and many numbers are in the process of changing.
Contact the Tourist Office if you have difficulty dialling a number.

BASIC DIRECTIONS
Walking down Kazim Özalp Cad. (also known as Sarampol) from
the bus station you arrive at the junction with Cumhuriyet Cad.,
at which point you should turn right to reach the Tourist Office.

FINDING ACCOMMODATION
Over the past decade, many townhouses in the old town (Kaleiçi
the area roughly bounded by Cumhuriyet Cad. and Atatürk Bulvarı
have been converted into guesthouses. Hıdırlık Sok and Hesapçı
Sok are particularly well supplied with guesthouses. There is a clus-
ter of cheap hotels around the bus station, but this area is much
noisier than the old town.

GUESTHOUSES
Locally licensed guesthouses

Adler Pansiyon, Barbaros Mahalle, Cıvelek Sok 46 (tel. 117818). £5.30 ($8) in singles or doubles. Cıvelek Sok runs between (and roughly parallel to) Hıdırlık Sok and Hesapçı Sok.

Saltur Pansiyon, Hesapçı Sok 67 (tel. 176238). Singles £8.00–10.70 ($12–16). Near the Hıdırlık Tower.

Pansiyon Falez, Hıdırlık Sok 48 (tel. 227 0985) Singles £5.30 ($8), doubles £9.30 ($14). Breakfast included.

Tunay Pansiyon, 7 Mermerli Sok (tel. 124677). Singles £4.70 ($7), doubles £6.70 ($10). From the Clock Tower by the junction of Kazim Özalp Cad. and Cumhuriyet Cad. walk towards the coast, and then look for the signs leading up to the guesthouse.

Aksoy Pansiyon, Kocatepe Sok 39 (tel. 126549). Doubles £8 ($12). Just around the corner from the Adler, above.

Atelya Pansiyon, Cıvelek Sok 21 (tel. 116416). Singles with bath £9.30 ($14), doubles with bath £16 ($24). Breakfast included. See the Adler, above.

Sabah Pansiyon, Hesapçı Sok 60a (tel. 475345). Singles £6.70 ($10), doubles £10.70 ($16). Breakfast included.

The Garden, Hesapçı Sok 44 (tel. 471930). Singles £5.30 ($8), doubles £9.30–13.30 ($14–20). Most rooms have a shower. Breakfast included. Across from the Truncated Minaret (Kesik Minare).

Hadriyanus Pansiyon, Zeytin Çıkmaı 4 (tel. 112313). Singles with bath £8 ($12), doubles with bath £13.30 ($20). Breakfast included. Off Hıdırlık Sok.

Erken Pansiyon, Hıdırlık Sok 5 (tel. 176092). Singles with bath £8 ($12), doubles with bath £14.70 ($22). Breakfast included.

Dedkonak Pansiyon, Hıdırlık Sok 11 (tel. 175170). Singles with bath £8 ($12), doubles with bath £13.30 ($20). Breakfast included.

Mini Orient, Cıvelek Sok 30 (tel. 124417). Singles with bath £12 ($18), doubles with bath £16.70 ($25). Breakfast included. See the Adler above.

Guesthouses registered with the Ministry of Tourism

Ak-Asya, Yeni Kapı Fırın Sok 5 (tel. 411404).
Holland, Lara Yolu, Barinaklar 2049 Sok 17 (tel. 231389).
Altun, Iskele Cad. 7, Kaleiçi (tel. 416624).
Gözde, Kazim Özalp Cad., 106 Sok 3/C (tel. 429066).
Anadolu, Gençlik Mah. 1311 Sok 18 (tel. 425938).

Türel, Çağlayan Mah. 2055 Sok 39 (tel. 231382).
Ozkavak, Cıvelek Sok 6 (tel. 427055). See the Adler above.
Frankfurt, Hıdırlık Sok 25 (tel. 476224).
Abad, Hesapçı Sok 52 (tel. 476662). Singles £20 ($30), doubles £40
   ($60).
Alahan, Cebesay Cad. 61 (tel. 217730).
Ruki, Lara Yolu, Menekşe Cad. (tel. 490270).
Tülpe, 4156 Sokak, Konyaaltı (tel. 290046)
House, Tuzcular Mah, Kaleiçi (tel. 126630).

HOTELS
Locally licensed hotels

Sargin, 459 Sok 3 (tel. 111408). Singles £4 ($6), doubles £6.70
   ($10). Off Kazim Özalp Cad.
Kaya, 459 Sok 12 (tel. 321 1391). Singles £6 ($9), doubles £10.70
   ($16). Off Kazim Özalp Cad.
Kumluca 457 Sok 21 (tel. 321 1123). Singles £4 ($6), doubles £8
   ($12). Between Kazim Özalp Cad. and Ismet Paşa Cad.
Süngül, 459 Sok (tel. 411408).
Nas Hotel (tel. 413411).

One-star hotels

Büyük, Cumhuriyet Cad. 57 (tel. 111499).
Perge, Karaali Park Yani 1311 Sok (tel. 123600). By the coast at
   the Karaalioglu Park.
Aras, Hüsnü Karakaş Cad. (tel. 118695). Off Atatürk Bulvar, close
   to the junction with Cumhuriyet Cad.
Duru, Lara Cad. 150 Demircikara Cad. (tel. 118636).

SUMMER DORM
Akdeniz Üniversitetsi Kampusü (tel. 274650). Open July–Sept.

CAMPING
Camping Bambus, Lara Yolu (tel. 215263). By the beach at the
Bambus Motel, 3km out of town along the road to Lara. Although
the site is expensive by Turkish standards, the facilities available
are of a good standard. Freelance camping within Antalya itself is
not to be recommended.

Ephesus (Efes) (tel. code 5451)

The ruins of the city of Ephesus, one-time Roman capital of Asia Minor, are only 16km from Kuşadasi, so it is quite possible to stay there and visit Ephesus on a day trip. If you would prefer to stay closer to Ephesus, or to stay for a few days, then there are plenty of cheap places to stay in the village of Selçuk (tel. code 5451), about 1.5km from the ruins. The Tourist Office in Selçuk is at Atatürk Mah., Agora Çarşisi 35 (tel. 51945/2712/1328), across from the bus station. Open daily in the summer, 8.30 a.m.–6.30 p.m.; in winter, Mon.–Fri. 9 a.m.–5.30 p.m.

GUESTHOUSES
Locally licensed guesthouses. Expect to pay around £4 ($6) per person

New Zealand Pension, Atatürk Mah. Kubilay Cad. 18 (tel. 232 891 4892). Excellent facilities include library, pool table and laundry. £3.75 ($5) per person. Free lift to Efes.

Barim, Turgutreis Sok 34 Muze Arkasi Sok (tel. 1923). Off Turgutreis Sok, the street to the rear of the Ephesus Museum. Recommended. £4 ($6) per person.

Cedik. Directions and prices as Barim.

Kirhan, Turgutreis Sok 7 (tel. 2257). Behind the Ephesus Museum.

Star, Atatürk mah. Ova Sok 22 (tel. 3858). Rooms with baths £3.60 ($5.50) per person. Close to the Kirhan.

Australian, Zafer mah. Durak Sok 20/A (tel. 1050). Signposted from the rear of the Ephesus Museum.

Ilyada, Miltner Sok 17 (tel. 3278).

Deniz, Sefa Sok 9 (tel. 1741).

Suzan, Kallinger Cad. 46 (tel. 3471). Along the street heading towards the Isa Bey Camii.

Amazon, Serin Sok 8 (tel. 3215). About 200m from the Isa Bey Camii.

Artemis, Zafer mah. Atilla Sok 5 (tel. 1862).

Blue, Isa Bey mah. Eski Izmir Cad. (tel. 3646).

Çakiroğlu, Atatürk mah. Kubilay Sok 9 (tel. 2582).

Isa Bey, Isa Bey mah, Serin Sok 2. Close to the Isa Bey Camii.

Öztürk, Fevzipaşa Cad. 2 (tel. 1937). Close to the main square.

Galaxi, Atatürk mah. Atatürk Cad. 21. (tel. 1304).

Evin, Isa Bey mah. Meydanı Sok 37 (tel. 1261).

Taşkin, Isa Bey mah. Meydanı Sok 21 (tel. 2171).

Sevil, Atatürk mah. Turgutreis Sok (tel. 2340).

Saray, Atatürk mah. Kubilay Sok (tel. 3820).
Buket, Isa Bey mah. Atatürk Cad. 6 (tel. 2378).
Ferah, Atatürk mah. Karanfil Sok 5/A (tel. 3814).
Gezer, Ikinci Spor Sok 9 (tel. 2010).
Akbulut, Ikinci Spor Sok 4.
Mengi, Ikinci Spor Sok 8.
Önder, Ikinci Spor Sok 7.
Hasan Ağa, Atatürk mah. Koçak Sok.

HOTELS
Locally licensed hotels

Akay, Atatürk Mah. Serin Sok 3 (tel. 3009/3172). £6.70 ($10), per
  person in singles or doubles with bath. About 200m from the Isa
  Bey Camii.
Aksoy, Isa Bey Mah. Cengiz Topel Cad. (tel. 6040). £6.70 ($10),
  per person in singles or doubles with bath. By the aqueduct.
Subası, Cengiz Topel Cad. 10 (tel. 6359). £6.70 ($10) per person
  in singles or doubles with bath. Opposite the post office (PTT).
Hasan Ağa, Kocak Sok. (tel. 1317).
Ürkmez, Isa Bey Mah. Cengiz Topel Cad. (tel. 1312).
Victoria, Cengiz Topel Cad. (tel. 3203).
Artemis, Atatürk mah. 2 Pazaryeri Sok (tel. 1191).
Karahan, Atatürk Mah. 1 Okul Sok. (tel. 3294).

One-star hotels

Katibim, Atatürk Cad. Spor Sok 1 (tel. 2417).
Tusan Motel, Efes Yolu 38 (tel. 1060). Along the road to Ephesus.
Kalehin II, Atatürk Cad. 49 (tel. 1154).
Kale Han Motel.

CAMPING
Tusan Motel. Just off the road to Ephesus. See above.
Blue Moon Camping. By Pamucak beach, 9km from Selçuk.
Garden Motel and Camping (tel. 6165). West of Ayasoluk.

İstanbul (tel. code 01)

TOURIST OFFICES
The administrative office is at Beyoğlu Mesrutiyet Caddesi 57/6.
Contact this office if you want information on the city in advance.

On arrival, head for one of the several offices the Tourist Board operates in the city. Arriving by train from Europe, the most conveniently located office is at Divanyolu Cad. 3 (tel. 522 4903), in the Sultanahmet district (open daily 9 a.m.–5 p.m.). The offices at the Karaköy ferry terminal (tel. 2495776) and at Atatürk airport (tel. 573 7399/4136) keep the same hours as the Sultanahmet office. Another office operates in the Hilton Hotel Arcade, off Cumhuriyet Cad., in the Harbiye district (tel. 233 0592).

BASIC DIRECTIONS
Trains from Europe arrive at the train station in Sirkeci, a short distance from the main sights in the Sultanahmet district. Going left from the exit of the station you cross two main roads before arriving at the junction with Aşirefendi Caddesi (right) and Ebussuut Caddesi (left). Go straight across and follow the winding Ankara Caddesi into Yerebatan Caddesi. Go right and follow the street down to the magnificent Aya Sofya Church. The Tourist Office is just a short walk to the left at the start of Divan Yolu Caddesi. The walk from the train station to the Tourist Office takes about 10 minutes.

Divan Yolu Cad. runs into Yeniçeriler Cad. which subsequently becomes Ordu Caddesi. The Lâleli Mosque, about halfway along Ordu Caddesi is about 20 minutes' walk from the Tourist Office. Many of the Tourist Board registered hotels listed below are in the streets off Ordu Caddesi. around the mosque.

FINDING ACCOMMODATION
Due to its proximity to the major sights, the Sultanahmet district is a particularly popular place to stay. The area has the largest concentration of cheap rooms in the city, so outside peak season you are virtually assured a room here. Although there are few one-star hotels in the district, the standard of locally licensed accommodation is generally fine, but check thoroughly before accepting a room as there are some very poor establishments in Sultanahmet. There is quite a choice of one-star hotels in the Lâleli and Aksaray districts (a 20-minute walk from Sultanahmet), as well as a host of hotels licensed by the municipal authorities.

LOCALLY LICENSED HOTELS AND GUESTHOUSES
Sultanahmet district:

Hippodrome Pansiyon, Üçler Sok 9 (tel. 516 0902). Singles £6.70 ($10), doubles £9.30 ($14), triples £12 ($18). A short walk from the Hippodrome.
Hacıbey Pansiyon, Özbekler Sokak. Singles £3.30 ($5), doubles

£5.30 ($8). Close to the Sokullu Mehmet Paşa Mosque, about 200m from the Hippodrome.

Optimist Pansiyon. Singles £7.30 ($11), doubles £10.70 ($16). Breakfast included. Contact the Optimist Guesthouse (see below) and the staff will take you to the pansiyon.

Side Pansiyon, Utangaç Sok 20 (tel. 517 6590). Doubles from £10 ($15), triples and dorms £5.30 ($8) per person.

Hotel Park, Utangaç Sok 26 (tel. 522 3964). Singles £5.30 ($8), singles with shower £11.30 ($17), doubles £10.70 ($16), doubles with shower £14.70 ($22).

Hotel Anadolu, Salkim Söğüt Sok 3 (tel. 512 1035). £6 ($9) per person. Off Yerebatan Cad.

Optimist Guesthouse, Hippodrome (tel. 516 2398). Singles £10.70 ($16), singles with bath £17.30 ($26), doubles £14.70 ($22), doubles with bath £21.30 ($32). Spotlessly clean, with superb views from the roof. Understandably popular, so advance reservation is recommended.

Berk Guesthouse, Kutluğun Sok 27 (tel. 516 9671). Doubles with bath £21.30 ($32). The street runs from the rear of the Sultan Ahmet mosque to the walls of the Topkap Palace.

Hotel Antique, Küçük Ayasofya Cad., Oğul Sok 17 (tel. 516 4936/ 0997). Doubles with bath £18.70 ($28). Looking at the Sultan Ahmet mosque from the Hippodrome, Küçük Ayasofya Cad. runs from the rear of the mosque, to the right.

Elit Hotel, Salkim Söğüt Sok 14 (tel. 511 5179/519 0466). Doubles with bath & WC £16 ($24). Dorms £5.30 ($8). Off Yerebatan Cad.

Hotel Merih, Zeynep Sultan Camii Sok 25 (tel. 522 8522). Singles £6.70 ($10), doubles £9.30 ($14), and dorms £4 ($6). The street runs off Alemdar Cad., which is off Yerebatan Cad. by Aya Sofya.

Hotel Ema, Salkim Söğüt Sok 18. Singles £9.30 ($14), doubles with bath £16 ($24). Dorms £4.30 ($6.50). Roof space £2.30 ($3.50). Off Yerebatan Cad.

Hotel Klotfarer, Klotfarer Cad. 22 (tel 528 4850). Singles with shower £9.30 ($14), doubles with shower £14.70 ($22). Left off Divan Yolu as you walk from Aya Sofya and the Hippodrome.

Yusuf Guesthouse, Kutlugün Sokak 3 (tel. 516 5878). Singles £5.30 ($8), doubles £8 ($12).

Alp Guesthouse, Adliye Sokak 4 (tel. 517 9570). £20 ($30) for a double.

Lâleli and Aksaray districts:

Hotel Mine Pansiyon, Gençtürk Cad. 54 (tel. 511 2375). Singles £6.70 ($10), doubles £10.70 ($16). Four-bedroom flats £24 ($36).

Hotel Burak, Fethibey Cad., Ağa Yokusu 1 (tel. 511 8679/522 7904). Singles £12 ($18), doubles £6 ($9).
Hotel Neşet, Harikzadeler Sok 23 (tel. 526 7412/522 4474). Singles £10 ($15), doubles £16 ($24).
Hotel Kul, Büyük Reşit Paşa Cad., Zeynep Kamil Sok 27 (tel. 526 0127/528 2892). Singles with shower £10.70 ($16), doubles with shower £16 ($24).
Hotel La Mirajz, Fethibey Cad. 28 (tel. 511 2445). Singles £11.30 ($17), doubles £12–16 ($18–24). Another hotel of that name at the same location is considerably more expensive.

ONE-STAR HOTELS
Expect to pay from £12 ($18) in doubles

Around the Sirkeci train station:

Ağan, Saffetinpaş Sok 6 (tel. 527 8550).
Eriş, Istasyon Arkasi 9 (tel. 527 8950). The street runs down the side of the station.
Yaşmak, Ebussuut Cad. 18 (tel. 526 3155).

Lâleli and Aksaray districts:

Nobel, Aksaray Cad. 23 (tel. 522 0617).
Okey, Fethi Bey Cad. 65 (tel. 511 2162).
Uzay, Şair Fitnat Sok 30 (tel. 526 8776). Off Ordu Cad., near Koska Cad.
Selim, Koska Cad. 39 (tel. 517 5533).
Side Koska Cad. 33 (tel. 518 7924).
Ensar, Yeşiltulumba Sok 39 (tel. 520 6135).
Florida, Fevziye Cad. 38 (tel. 528 1021).
Karakaş, Gençtürk Cad. 55 (tel. 526 5343).
Karatay, Saitefendi Sok 42 (tel. 526 5692).
Oran, Harikzadeler Sok 40 (tel. 528 5813).
Babaman, Lâleli Cad. 19 (tel. 526 8238).
Geçit, Aksaray Cad. 5 (tel. 518 6765).
Tebriz, Muratpaşa Sülüklü Sok (tel. 524 4135).

HI HOSTEL
Yücelt Youth Hostel, Caferiya Sok 6/1 (tel. 513 6150). Doubles £18.70 ($28); dorms £5.30 ($8). HI membership compulsory, but cards are sold at the hostel for £8 ($12). Best reserved in advance. The street runs from the foot of Yerebatan Cad. along the side of Aya Sofya.

HOSTELS

Hotel Büyükayasofya, Caferiya Sok 5 (tel. 5222981). £6.70 ($10) per person in rooms with showers, £5.70 ($8) in rooms without. Roof space £1.70 ($2.50). Next door to the HI hostel.

Topkapı Hostel, Işakpaşa Cad., Kutluğun Sok 1 (tel. 517 6558). Doubles 14.70 ($22), dorms £6 ($9). Roof space £4.30 ($6.50). The street runs from the rear of the Sultan Ahmet mosque to the walls of the Topkap Palace.

True Blue Hostel, Akbyk Cad. 2. Doubles £10.70 ($16). Dorms £4 ($6). Akbyk Cad. runs parallel to Kutluğun Sok (see the Topkapı hostel) one block closer to the old city wall and the sea.

Orient International Youth Hostel, Akbyk Cad. 13 (tel. 516 0171/ 517 9493). Doubles £8 ($12), triples £10 ($15). Dorms £3.30 ($5). Along the street from the True Blue Hostel, above.

Sultan Tourist Hostel, Akbıyık Cad., Terbiyik Sok 3 (tel. 5169260). Doubles £6.70 ($10), dorm beds £3 ($4.50). There have been complaints about this hostel from women travelling alone.

Hanedan Hostel, Adliye Sokak.

Dorms and roof space, as well as comparably priced smaller rooms, are available at several of the locally licensed hotels and guesthouses listed above.

STUDENT ACCOMMODATION

Converted into temporary hostels during July and August:

Topkapı Atatürk Öğrenci Sitesi, Londra Asfalt, Cevizlibağ duraği (tel. 582 0455/525 5032/523 9488/525 0280). Topkapı district.

Kadrga Öğrenci Yurdu, Sahsuvar Mah. Comertler Sok (tel. 528 2480/2481). In the Kumkap district.

Ortaköy Kiz Öğrenci Yurdu, Palanga Cad. 20 (tel. 160 0184/160 1035/161 7376). In the Ortaköy district.

CAMPING
Expect to pay £5.30–6.70 ($8–10) for a tent site

Londra Mokamp, Eski Londra Asfalt, Bakrkoy (tel. 559 4200/560 4200). Very crowded site, about 1km from the airport. Linked to Aksaray by buses and dolmuses.

Ataköy Tatil Köyü, Rauf Orbay Cad., Ataköy (tel. 559 6000 – 6 lines). Just south-east of the airport, between the main road and the Marmara Sea.

Yeşilyurt (tel. 573 8408/574 4230). By the Marmara Sea, close to the village of Yeşilköy.

Kervansaray Kartaltepe Mokamp, Çobançeşme Mev., Bakırköy (tel. 575 4721).

Florya Truistik Tesisleri, Florya (tel. 574 0000). About 24km from the city centre. Local trains run from Eminönü and Ataköy to Florya station, 500m from the site. From the Topkapı bus station there is a dolmus service to Florya, while bus 73 runs from Taksim to Florya.

Izmir (tel. code 051)

TOURIST OFFICES
The main information office is at Gaziosmanpaşa Bulvarı 1/C 5(tel. 842147/199278), next to the Turkish Airlines office in the Büyük Efes Oteli. Open daily June–Oct., 8.30 a.m.–7.30 p.m.; Nov.–May, Mon.–Sat. 8.30 a.m.–5.30 p.m. If you arrive by ferry there is an office at Alsancak Harbour (tel. 631600/631263), while the administrative office is between the harbour and the Alsancak train station at Atatürk Cad. 418. A fourth office operates at the Adnan Menderes airport (tel. 512626/511950/511081). There's a good city information desk at the bus station.

BASIC DIRECTIONS
There are two main train stations in Izmir, the Alsancak station which serves the ferry terminal, and the Basmane station serving the city centre. The main Tourist Information Office is by the Büyük Efes Hotel and the THY office on the stretch of Gaziosmanpas Bulvarı between Gazi Bulvarı and Cumhuriyet Meydan.

The city's main bus station is by the Atatürk stadium, about 2.5km from the Basmane train station and the city centre. Buses 50, 51 and 52 (red-and-white) run from the bus station to Konak Meydan, but these buses are few and far between. A more frequent service to the city centre is provided by the blue-and-white minibuses marked Çankaya-Mersinli, which stop on Gazi Bulvarı about 250m from 9 Eylül Meydan.

FINDING ACCOMMODATION
With the exception of Izmir's annual fair (late August to mid-September) when you will toil to find a room in any price category, there are usually more than enough cheap beds to go round. Most of the cheaper hotels are in the Akinci area (also known as Yenigün), roughly the district bounded by Anafatraler Cad., Gaziosman-

paşa Bulvarı and Gazi Bulvarı. As a rule, hotels in the streets between Fevzipaşa Bulvarı and Gazi Bulvarı are of a better standard than those between Fevzipaşa Bulvarı and Anafartalar Cad., with only a minimal difference in price. The average standard of locally licensed accommodation is probably the lowest in the hotels lining (and just off) 1294 Sok and 1296 Sok.

GUESTHOUSES
Registered with the Ministry of Tourism

Imperial Pansiyon, 1296 Sok, 54 (tel. 149771). Turn left off Fevzi-paşa Bulvarı along 1295 Sok, then right on to 1296 Sok.

HOTELS
Locally licensed hotels

Olimpiyat, 945 Sok 2 (tel. 251269). Doubles £8.70 ($13). Off Anafartalar Cad. after the street bends sharp right.

Saray, Anafartalar Cad. 635 (tel. 836946). Singles £5.30 ($8), doubles £6.70 ($10). Within easy walking distance of Basmane train station. Very popular.

Yıldız Palas, 1296 Sok 50 (tel. 251518). Doubles £8 ($12). One of the good hotels on 1296 Sok. Turn left off Fevzipaşa Bulvarı along 1295 Sok, then right into 1296 Sok.

Bakıklı, 1296 Sok 18 (tel. 142560). Doubles £6.70 ($10). Another reasonable hotel on 1296 Sok. See the Yıldız Palas above for directions.

Özcan, 1368 Sok 3 (tel. 835052). Singles £6.70 ($10), doubles £10.70 ($16), doubles with bath £12 ($18). 1368 Sok runs right off Fevzipaşa Bulvar, a short walk from the train station. Also on this street are the Akgün, Oba and Çiçek Palas, all at similar prices.

Yeni Park, 1368 Sok 6 (tel. 135231). Doubles £12.70 ($19). See the Özcan, above.

Bilen Palas, 1369 Sok 68 (tel. 839246). Singles £5.30 ($8), doubles £9.30 ($14). Off 9 Eylül Meydan, between Anafartalar Cad. and Gazi Bulvarı.

Işık, 1364 Sok 11 (tel. 831029). Doubles with bath £12 ($18). Right off Fevzipaşa Bulvarı.

Bayburt, 1370 Sok 1 (tel. 722013). Doubles with bath £13.30 ($20). From Fevzipaşa Bulvarı turn right along 1361 Sok, then left down 1369 Sok. Almost immediately 1369 Sok is crossed by 1370 Sok: the hotel is at the junction of the two.

Efes, Gaziosmanpaşa Bulvarı 48 (tel. 147276). Doubles with shower
£10.70 ($16).

Atlas, Şair Eşref Bulvarı 1 (tel. 144265). Doubles with shower
£12.70 ($19). At the junction of Gaziosmanpaşa Bulvar, Gazi
Bulvarı and Şair Eşref Bulvarı.

Baylon, 1299 Sokak 8 (tel. 131426). Doubles £21.30 ($32).

Hikmet, 945 Sokak 26 (tel. 142672). Doubles £8.70 ($13).

Meseret, Anafartalar Cad. 66 (tel. 255533). Doubles £9.30 ($14).
Close to Konak Meydanı.

Ankara Palas (tel. 142850/137969). Doubles with bath £12 ($18).
By the elevated walkway near Konak Meydanı.

One-star hotel

Babadan, Gaziomanpaşa Bulvarı 50 (tel. 139640). Doubles with
bath £20 ($30).

YOUTH HOSTEL
Atatürk Öğrenci Yurdu, 1888 Sok 4, Inciraltı (tel. 152980/152981/
152856). Open 1 July–31 Aug.

CAMPING
Lervamsarau Inciraltı Mocamp, Balcova (tel. 154760). Closed during the winter months. About 12km from the centre.

Kuşadası (tel. code 636)

TOURIST OFFICE
Turizm Danisma Burosu, Iskele Meydanı (tel. 11103/16295). Open
July–Aug., 7.30 a.m.–8 p.m. daily; May–June and Sept.–Oct.,
8 a.m.–6 p.m. daily; Nov.–Apr., Mon.–Fri. 8.30 a.m.–5.30 p.m. The
office distributes a list of around 300 local hotels and guesthouses,
and a decent plan of the town. Across from the ferry terminal.

FINDING ACCOMMODATION
Outside the peak months of July and August, finding a cheap room
in Kuşadası is usually quite simple. Several streets within easy walking distance of the Tourist Office are particularly well supplied with
reasonably priced accommodation: Kıbrıs Cad., Yıldırım Cad.,
Aslanlar Cad., and Bezirgan Sok. Following the street leading away
from the ferry terminal (Liman Cad.), turn right at the end of the

street and then left to reach Kıbrıs Cad. Aslanlar Cad. crosses the
other end of Kıbrıs Cad. Going left at this point, Aslanlar Cad. runs
into Yıldırım Cad.; going right Bezirgan Cad. is off to the right after
a short distance.

GUESTHOUSES
Locally licensed guesthouses

Su Pansiyon, Arslanlar Cad. 13 (tel. 41453). £4 ($6) per person in
singles or doubles. Breakfast included.
Cennet Pansiyon, Yayla Sok 1. Doubles with bath £10 ($15).Break-
fast included. At the junction with Yıldırım Cad.
Dinç Pansiyon, Mercan Sok (tel. 14249). Doubles £6.70 ($10).
Breakfast included. Mercan Sok is off Bezirgan Sok.
Şanli, Bezirgan Sok 13 (tel. 13028). Doubles £10 ($15). Breakfast
included.
Isikli Pansiyon, Aslanlar Cad. 22. £4.70 ($7) per person.
Özhan, Kıbrıs Cad. (tel. 12932). Singles £4.70 ($7), doubles with
bath £9.30 ($14).
Safak (tel. 11764). £3.70 ($5.50) per person. A block further up
the hill from Su Pansiyon (see above)
Seçkin, Yıldırım Cad. 35 (tel. 14735). Doubles with bath £10 ($15).
Breakfast included.
Golden Bed, Aslanlar Cad., Uğurlu Çikmazi 4 (tel. 18708). Doubles
with bath £10 ($15). Breakfast included.

Guesthouses registered with the Ministry of Tourism

Perle, Güvenevler 8 (tel. 17723/19393).
Bahar, Cephane Sok 12 (tel. 11191).
Grup, Istiklal Cad. 3 (tel. 11230).
Özer, Istiklal Cad. 11A (tel. 11138).
Çi-Dem, Istiklal Cad. 9 (tel. 11895).
Yunus, Istiklal Cad. 7 (tel. 12268).
Nil, Ismet Inönu Bulvarı 59 (tel. 11492).
Balcilar, Kadinlar Denizi Mevkii (tel. 11410).
Diamond, Yilanbumu Mev. (tel. 13134).
Posaci, Ieylak Sok 5 (tel. 11151).
Romantic, Yilanburnu Mevkii (tel. 14632).

HOTELS
Locally licensed hotels

Rose, Aslanlar Cad., Aydnlk Sok 7 (tel. 41111). Singles £6.70 ($10), doubles £12 ($18). Beds on the roof £3 ($4.50). Right at the junction with Kıbrıs Cad.

Kalyon, Kıbrıs Cad. 7 (tel. 13346). Singles £12 ($18) doubles with bath £16.70 ($25). Breakfast included.

Panorama, Kıbrıs Cad. 14 (tel. 14671). Singles £12 ($18), doubles with bath £16.70 ($25). Breakfast included.

Dülger, Yıldırım Cad. (tel. 15769). Doubles £16 ($24). Close to the bazaar.

Konak, Yıldırım Cad. 55 (tel. 16318). Doubles £16 ($24). Breakfast included.

One-star hotels

Atadan, Ismet Inönu Bulvarı (tel. 19064).
Aram, Kaya Aldoğan Sok 2 (tel. 11075/11325).
Ekin, Kadinlar Pasaji 33 (tel. 13970).

CAMPING
Camping Önder (tel. 42413) and Camping Yat (tel. 41333) are located close by each other on Atatürk Bulvarı about 2.5km out of town on the road to Seluk (behind the yacht marina). Three-bed bungalows are available at both sites at £4 ($6) per person.

UNITED KINGDOM

If, as is probable, London is your first stop in the UK, you might well wonder just how long your budget will survive, given that hostels cost £10−21 ($15−31.50), B&B is rarely available for under £22 ($33) and the Tourist Information Centre charges a staggering £5 ($7.50) to find rooms that are well outside the budget category − the comparable service in Paris charges 15FF (£2; $3). And although you may find some comfort in the knowledge that things improve once you get outside the English capital, a trip to the UK is likely to put some strain on your budget, as there is a shortage of accommodation possibilities under £10 ($15) per night.

Bed and breakfast accommodation in guesthouses and B&Bs is available throughout the UK, with prices starting at around £11−12 ($16.50−18). In most towns, including popular destinations such as Edinburgh and York, you should be able to find a bed in the £11−13 ($16.50−19.50) price range without much difficulty, except at the height of the season or during special events. However, in some of the more popular small cities, such as Bath and Oxford, you can consider yourself lucky if you find a bed for under £15 ($22.50).

Tourist Information Centres distribute free lists of local guesthouses and B&Bs, so unless the town is very busy you can normally find a bed quite easily by trying a few telephone numbers from the brochure. However, there is not much point in doing this if the office operates a free local room-finding service. Many offices run a system whereby you pay a deposit (not a commission) at the office, which is then deducted from your final bill. A few offices do charge for finding a room, normally £1.50−2.50 ($2.25−3.75). One really useful service provided by Tourist Information Centres is the Book-a-Bed-Ahead facility, which costs £2.50 ($3.75). This service lets you make a reservation at your next destination, and can save you a great deal of time, aggravation and even money, especially if you are heading for a town where you anticipate trouble in finding cheap accommodation, such as Edinburgh during its festival, York at weekends, or London at any time.

The **HI hostel** network in the UK is extensive, although there are several important gaps: notably some of the larger English cities such as Birmingham, Leeds, Manchester and Liverpool. There are three youth hostel associations in the UK: the Youth Hostels Association of England and Wales, the Youth Hostel Association of Northern Ireland, and the Scottish Youth Hostels Association. Curfews are normally 11 p.m. in England and Wales (later in London −

some London hostels have no curfew), 11.30 p.m. in Northern Ireland and 11.45 p.m. in Scotland (2 a.m. in Glasgow, Edinburgh, Aberdeen and Inverness).

Prices vary according to the standard of facilities and the age of the user. At the Scottish and Northern Irish hostels those aged over 18 and over are referred to as 'seniors', whereas in England and Wales 'seniors' are those aged 21 and over, while visitors aged 16 to 20 are classed as 'juniors'. In the Northern Irish hostels, seniors pay around £6.75–8 ($10.15–12) during the peak season (May– Sept.), except at the Belfast hostel which charges £8.50 ($12.75). The most expensive hostels in Scotland, those in the cities and Inverness, charge around £7–9.20 ($10.50–13.80) for seniors, but normally seniors pay £5–6 ($7.50–9). Prices tend to be higher in English and Welsh hostels. Seniors normally pay £5.25–7.75 ($7.90–11.65), but there are also a fair number of hostels which charge £8–12 ($12–18) and the London hostels charge from £11.40–19.30 ($17–29) (a small peak-season supplement of around £0.50 ($0.75) is added at many English and Welsh hostels in July and August).

Advance booking of hostels in the main places of interest is advisable from May to September and around Easter, preferably in writing, with payment enclosed. Telephone reservations are accepted on the day, but you must turn up by 6 p.m. to claim your bed. A new scheme covering all seven hostels in London, as well as several other major tourist centres, has been introduced: callers can ring 0171 228 6547 and receive an instant confirmation of their booking. Hostels in 26 popular destinations in England and Wales are also part of a Book-A-Bed-Ahead scheme for which a £1 ($1.75) fee is charged (the An Oige hostels in Dublin are also included in the network). Full details are available at hostels or in the Youth Hostels Association of England and Wales handbook. A similar system operates at 20 of the most visited Scottish hostels. Beds reserved through the Book-A-Bed-Ahead system can be claimed up until 10 p.m.

There are a number of **independent hostels** in the main places of interest. Standards are generally on a par with the local HI hostels, prices are generally slightly higher. The YMCA and YWCA operate hostels in several cities in which accommodation is usually in singles or doubles. However, prices can be as high as for bed and breakfast accommodation. During the Easter and summer vacations (normally mid-March to mid-April and July to early September) many universities let rooms (mostly singles) in student residences. The universities are primarily concerned with attracting visiting groups, so to be sure of a place you will have to book well in advance. Overnight prices are generally in the £12–24 ($18–36) price range. If there are any spare beds available some universities will let rooms on the day for around £10 ($15) to students with ID. If there are a number of you travelling together, renting a furnished student flat from a university is better value. The Tourist Information Centre will inform you about individuals and organizations letting self-catering accommodation in the locality. The one hitch to renting a flat may be an insistence on a minimum stay of up to one week, although this is not always the case.

There are campsites in, or just outside most of the main places of interest (Glasgow is a notable exception). Standards, and prices, vary dramatically but, short of sleeping rough, **camping** is the best option for keeping accommodation costs low. That said, you may still be bemused by the cost of camping in the UK. In comparison to other European countries, prices are high. In popular tourist destinations it is not unusual for a solo traveller to pay £7–8 ($10.50–12) for an overnight stay. Elsewhere it is unusual for prices to rise above £5 ($7.50) for an overnight stay. In smaller towns and villages, which have a minimal tourist trade, local farmers will usually let you pitch a tent on their land if you ask permission first. In the more remote areas, there will seldom be any objection to your camping rough, provided you do not leave litter lying about, or set any potentially dangerous fires. As the nights can be very cold in the hilly parts of the country, a good-quality sleeping bag is essential, especially in the Scottish Highlands (anyone visiting the Highlands in summer would also be well advised to invest in an effective insect repellent). The one main drawback to camping is the damp climate, so be sure that your tent really is waterproof.

NB: From April 1995, telephone codes in the UK will change in most cases adding a '1' to existing codes e.g. London 0171. Call British Telecom if you experience problems.

ADDRESSES

National Tourist Boards English Tourist Board, Thames Tower, Black's Road, Hammersmith, London W6 9EL. Enquiries in writing only.
Northern Ireland Tourist Board, St Anne's Court, 59 North Street, Belfast, BT1 2DS (tel. 01232 231221).
Northern Ireland Tourist Board, 11 Berkeley Street, London W1X 5AD (tel. 0171 493 0601).

Scottish Tourist Board, 23 Ravelston
Terrace, Edinburgh EH4 3EU
(tel. 0131 930 8661).
Bwrdd Croeso Cymru (Welsh Tourist
Board), Ty Brunel, 2 Ffordd Fitzalan,
Caerdydd CF2 1UY
(tel. 01222 499909).

HI hostels

Youth Hostels Association of England
and Wales, Trevelyan House,
St Stephen's Hill, St Albans,
Hertfordshire, AL1 2DY
(tel. 01727 55215).
Youth Hostel Association of Northern
Ireland, 56 Bradbury Place, Belfast
BT7 1RU (tel. 01232 324733).
Scottish Youth Hostels Association,
7 Glebe Crescent, Stirling, FK8 2JA
(tel. 01786 51181).

Bath (tel. code 01225)

TOURIST OFFICE
Tourist Information Centre, The Colonnades, Bath Street (tel.
462831). Open June–Sept., Mon.–Sat. 9.30 a.m.–7 p.m., Sun.
10 a.m.–6 p.m.; Oct.–May, Mon.–Sat. 9.30 a.m.–5 p.m. The small
city plan sold at the office is useful for sightseeing and for finding
your way to accommodation. £0.25 ($0.40). Free local accommoda-
tion service and walking tours. You pay a 10% deposit at the office,
which is subtracted from your final bill. Book-A-Bed-Ahead service
available.

FINDING ACCOMMODATION
The popularity of the town, especially with more affluent, middle-
aged tourists, means that prices in local B&Bs are slightly higher
than normal. You can expect to pay about £14–15 ($21–22.50)
per person to share a room in one of the cheaper establishments.
  Finding a bed in one of the cheaper B&Bs can be difficult in
summer as the city attracts large numbers of visitors. At this time
of year, you are as well heading straight for the Tourist Information
Centre and asking them for the cheapest B&B available. If you
arrive early in the morning there are a few areas of the city you

can look in before the office opens, all within 15 minutes' walk of the bus and train stations. The best area to look is around Pulteney Road, as this has the highest concentration of the cheaper B&Bs. After that the area around Wells Road is probably just slightly better than that around the start of Upper Bristol Road.

GUESTHOUSES AND B&Bs
Doubles from £23 ($34.50)

Wellsway Guest House, 51 Wellsway (tel. 423434). Fifteen minutes' walk from the train station. Wellsway is a continuation of Wells Road.

16 Bloomfield Road, Bear Flat (tel. 337804). A 15-minute walk from the train station. Right off the A367.

Doubles from £25 ($37.50)

Athelney Guest House, 5 Marlborough Lane (tel. 312031). Just under 15 minutes' walk from the train station, right off the Upper Bristol Road.

Old Mill Lodge, Tollbridge Road (tel. 858476). By the River Avon, 2.5km from the city centre.

The Terrace Guest House, 3 Pulteney Terrace (tel. 316578).

Arney Guest House, 99 Wells Road (tel. 310020).

Sovereign Guest House, 38 St. James' Park (tel. 338162). Within 10–15 minutes' walk of the city centre.

The Shearns, Prior House, 3 Marlborough Lane (tel. 313587). See Athelney Guest House.

Doubles from £27 ($40.50)

Avon Guest House, 160 Newbridge Road (tel. 423866). In the Lower Weston Area of town. Bus 17 to Upper Weston from the bus station runs along the street.

2 Crescent Gardens (tel. 331186).

Membland Guest House, 7 Pulteney Terrace (tel. 336712).

Arosa Guest House, 124 Lower Oldfield Park (tel. 425778). About 15 minutes' walk from the train station. Cross the Churchill Bridge and head right along the Lower Bristol Road, then left at Lower Oldfield Park.

Abbey Rise, 97 Wells Road (tel. 312031).

Doubles from £29 ($43.50)

Cherry Tree Villa, 7 Newbridge Hill (tel. 331671). About 1.5km from the town centre, right from Upper Bristol Road. Bus 17 from the bus station.

Kinlet Guest House, 99 Wellsway (tel. 420268). See Wellsway Guest House.

Sampford, 11 Oldfield Road (tel. 310053). A 10–15-minute walk from the train station, right off Wells Road.

Mardon Guest House, 1 Pulteney Terrace (tel. 311624).

Sheridan Guest House, 95 Wellsway (tel. 429562). See Wellsway Guest House.

Astor House, 14 Oldfield Road (tel. 429134). See Sampford.

Baileys, 46 Crescent Gardens (tel. 333594).

Ashley House, 8 Pulteney Gardens (tel. 425027).

Toad Hall Guest House, 6 Lime Grove (tel. 423254/312853).

Doubles from £30 ($45)

The Albany Guest House, 24 Crescent Gardens (tel. 313339).

Abode, 7 Widcombe Crescent (tel. 422726). A 10–15-minute walk from the station. After crossing the Churchill Bridge follow Claverton Street. Widcombe Hill is on the left as the main road bends away to the right.

Elgin Villa, 6 Marlborough Lane (tel. 424557) See Athelney Guest House.

Chestnut Guest House, Henrietta Road (tel. 425845).

Doubles from £32 ($48)

Smith's, 47 Crescent Gardens (tel. 422382).

Lynwood Guest House, 6–7 Pulteney Gardens (tel. 426410).

Holly Villa Guest House, 14 Pulteney Gardens (tel. 310331).

Waltons Guest House, 17 Crescent Gardens (tel. 426528).

Mrs Guy, 14 Raby Place (tel. 465120).

The Georgian Guest House, 34 Henrietta Street (tel. 424103). From Grand Parade follow Argyle Street across the River Avon into Laura Place, then head left.

Crescent Guest House, 21 Crescent Gardens (tel. 425945).

Joanna House, 5 Pulteney Avenue (tel. 335246).

Milton House Guest House, 75 Wellsway (tel. 335632) See Wellsway Guest House.

The White Guest House, 23 Pulteney Gardens (tel. 426075).

Alderney Guest House, 3 Pulteney Road (tel. 312365).

Ashgrove Guest House, 39 Bathwick Street (tel. 421911).

HI HOSTEL
Bath Youth Hostel, Bathwick Hill (tel. 465674). Juniors £7 ($10.50), seniors £8.25 ($12.40). In July and August, a supplement of £0.50 ($0.75) is added to these prices. A 15–20-minute walk from the train station. From the roundabout on Pulteney Road by St Mary's Church turn down Raby Place, which becomes George Street and then Bathwick Hill. Badgerline bus 18 from the bus station £0.70 ($1).

HOSTEL
YMCA International House, Broad Street Place (tel. 60471). Open to men and women. No curfew. Dorms around £10.50 ($15.75), doubles around £11.75 ($17.65) per person, singles £12.75 ($19.15). Very popular, so reserve in writing well in advance. About 300m from the Tourist Office.

CAMPING
Newton Mill Touring Centre, Newton Street Loe (tel. 333909). The site charges an extortionate £6.75 ($10.15) per tent, £3.50 ($5.25) per person. About 5km from the centre. Bus 5 from the bus station to Newton Road (every 12 minutes).

HI HOSTEL NEARBY
Bristol International YHA Centre, Hayman House, 64 Prince Street, Bristol (tel. 01272 221659). Two- to six-bed rooms. Juniors £10 ($15), seniors £13 ($19.50). About 8 minutes' walk from Bristol Temple Meads train station. Bristol is 22.5km from Bath and the two towns are linked by frequent trains.

Cambridge (tel. code 01223)

TOURIST OFFICE
Tourist Information Centre, Wheeler Street (tel. 322640). Open Mar.–Oct., Mon.–Sat. 9 a.m.–6 p.m., Sun. 10.30 a.m.–3.30 p.m.; Nov.–Feb., Mon.–Fri. 9 a.m.–5.30 p.m., Sat. 9 a.m.–5 p.m. Room-finding service for £1 ($1.50) fee. The office sells a list of local accommodation for £0.30 ($0.45), a copy of which is displayed in the office window. Book-A-Bed-Ahead service available.

BASIC DIRECTIONS

The train station is just under 20 minutes' walk from the centre. Head down Station Road, turn right at the end of the street along Hills Road (A604), and keep going straight ahead until you see Downing Street running left off St Andrew's Street. Turning right off Downing Street along Corn Exchange Street takes you into Wheeler Street. Buses 1, 5 and 9 link the train station with the centre. The Drummer Street bus station is right in the heart of the city. From the bus station, the lane running down the side of Christ's College brings you out on to the main street opposite the Post Office. Cross the road, head right, and then take the lane on your left to reach Wheeler Street.

FINDING ACCOMMODATION

Cambridge has a plentiful supply of rooms, so only during the peak season (late June to the end of August) are you likely to have some difficulty finding a room, at which time it is advisable to try to reserve a bed in advance. Tenison Street, near the train station, is a good place to look for one of the cheaper B&Bs at any time of year. Outside university term-time in and around Jesus Lane, near Jesus College is another good area to look in. Many of the establishments in this part of town are only open to visitors during the university vacations (mid-June—end Sept., and possibly Easter and Christmas), because they are filled with students during the university year.

GUESTHOUSES AND B&Bs

Doubles from around £25 ($37.50)

Lyngamore Guest House, 35/37 Chesterton Road (tel. 312369).
Tenison Towers Guest House, 148 Tenison Road (tel. 63924).
Mrs C. McCann, 40 Warkworth Street (tel. 314098). University vacations only.
Mrs H. Barr, 25 Worts Causeway (tel. 245391).
Acorn Guest House, 154 Chesterton Road (tel. 353888).
Mr J. Antony, 4 Huntingdon Road (tel. 357444).
The Milton Guest House, 63 Milton Road (tel. 311625).
European Centre Guest House, 94 Milton Road (tel. 357474).
Mrs P. Droy, El Shaddai, 41 Warkworth Street (tel. 327978). University vacations only.

Doubles from around £27 ($40.50)

Lovell Lodge Guest House, 365 Milton Road (tel. 425478).

Railway Lodge, 150 Tenison Road (tel. 467688).
All Seasons Guest House, 219 Chesterton Road (tel. 353386).
Mrs M. Saunders, 145 Gwydir Street (tel. 356615).
Arbury Lodge Guest House, 82 Arbury Road (tel. 64319).
Mrs A. Bartram, 18 Covent Garden (tel. 323340).
Green End Guest House, 70 Green End Road (tel. 420433).
Mrs S. Bradshaw, Mowbray House, 153 Mowbray Road (tel. 411051).
Abbey Guest House, 588 Newmarket Road (tel. 241427).
Mr & Mrs M. Dixon, Windy Ridge, 4 Worts' Causeway (tel. 246783).
Mrs J. Norman, 27 New Square (tel. 355613).
Mrs R. Tempest-Holt, 44 Natal Road (tel. 249003).
Mrs M. Spence, St Mark's Vicarage, Barton Road (tel. 63339).
Mr S. Brown, 40 Lensfield Road (tel. 62839). University vacations only.
Mrs H. Rowell, 39 Trumpington Street (tel. 355439). University vacations only.

Doubles from around £29 ($43.50)

Mrs M.E. Lockwood, 'Alfriston', 7 Harvey Goodwin Avenue (tel. 359351).
Antwerp Guest House, 36 Brookfields, Mill Road (tel. 247690).
Mrs M. Anderson, Norman Cross, 175 Hills Road (tel. 411959).
Southampton Guest House, 7 Elizabeth Way (tel. 357780).
De Freville House, 166 Chesterton Road (tel. 354933).
Mr & Mrs Dow, Hazelwood, 58 Maids Causeway (tel. 322450).
Mrs S. Payne, 16 Eltisley Avenue (tel. 328996).
Mrs J. Diaper, 22–24 Portugal Street (tel. 357769). University vacations only.
Mr & Mrs Holmes, 6 Portugal Street (tel. 67845). University vacations only.
Benson House, 24 Huntingdon Road (tel. 311594).
Belle Vue Guest House, 33 Chesterton Road (tel. 351859).
Warkworth Guest House, Warkworth Terrace (tel. 63682).
Mrs S. Cook, 7 Brookfields, Mill Road (tel. 211259).
Bon Accord House, 20 St Margaret's Square (off Cherry Hinton Road) (tel. 246568/411188).

HI HOSTEL
Cambridge Youth Hostel, 97 Tenison Road (tel. 354601). Open year round. Mostly four- to seven-bed rooms. Described by the YHA England and Wales as one of their busiest hostels, so try to reserve

well in advance. Juniors £8.40 ($12.60), seniors £11.59 ($17.25). In July and Aug., a supplement of £0.60 ($0.90) is added to these prices. A few minutes' walk from the train station, right along Tenison Road from Station Road.

HOSTEL

Cambridge YMCA, Queen Anne House, Gonville Place (tel. 356998). Open to men and women. B&B from £15.75–19 ($23.65–28.50). Clean and bright, with a buzzing social scene. Call ahead for reservations.

CAMPING

There is no shortage of sites in the Cambridge area (16 in all). Details of these sites are contained in the list sold by the Tourist Information Centre for a nominal fee.

Camping & Caravan Club, Cabbage Moor, Cambridge Road, Great Shelford (tel. 841185). Open Apr.–Oct. Peak season (24–30 May and 21 June–29 Aug) £4.50 ($6.75) per person; at other times, £3.75 ($5.65) per person. About 5km south of town. Follow the A10 and turn left along the A1031.

Highfield Farm Camping Site, Long Road, Comberton (tel. 262308). Open Apr.–Oct. £6.25 ($9.40) for a small tent in July and August, £5.75 ($8.65) at other times. About 6.5km from town, on the B1046 (turn off the A603 at Barton). Bus 118 or 119 from the Drummer Street bus station.

Exeter (tel. code 01392)

TOURIST OFFICE

Tourist Information Centre, Civic Centre, Paris Street (tel. 265297). Open Mon.–Fri. 9 a.m.–5 p.m., Sat. 9 a.m.–1 p.m. and 2–5 p.m. Local accommodation service and Book-A-Bed-Ahead. The office provides free lists of local accommodation. A short distance northeast of the Cathedral.

GUESTHOUSES AND B&Bs
Expect to pay £12–16 ($18–24) per person

The Old Mill, Mill Lane, Alphington (tel. 59977). About 1.5km from the city centre. Enter through Brookfield Gardens.

Mr & Mrs Pearmain, 12 Devonshire Place (tel. 58147) A 10-minute walk from the city centre.

St David's Lodge, 65 St David's Hill (tel. 51613).

Mr & Mrs La Pla, 64 Collins Road (tel. 50266). Non smokers only.

Cyrnea, 73 Howell Road (tel. 438386).

Mead's Guest House, 2 St David's Hill (tel. 74886).

Janbri Guest House, 102 Alphington Road (tel. 77346).

Rhonas, 15 Blackall Road (tel. 77791). Close to the centre. Off the New North Road, near the castle.

Dunmore Hotel, 22 Blackall Road (tel. 431643. See Rhonas, immediately above.

Telstar Hotel, 77 St David's Hill (tel. 42466).

Viburnum House, 80 Topsham Road (tel. 76344).

Fort William Guest House, 75 St David's Hill (tel. 438495).

The Helliers Guest House, 37 Heavitree Road (tel. 436277). Close to the Tourist Information Centre, across the roundabout at the end of Paris Street.

Highbury, 85 St David's Hill (tel. 58288).

UNIVERSITY DORMS

University of Exeter (tel. 211500). Singles £10 ($15), doubles £17 ($25.50), breakfast included. During student vacations only.

HI HOSTEL

Exeter YH, 47–49 Countess Wear Road (tel. 873329). Juniors £6.60 ($10), seniors £8 ($12). Supplement of £0.50 ($0.75) in July and August. Closed in December. About 3km from the centre in the direction of Topsham. From the High Street, take bus K or T to Countess Wear Post Office, and then walk along Exe Vale Road.

CAMPING

Hill Pond, Sidmouth Road (tel. 32483).

The Lake District

Carlisle (tel. code 01228)

TOURIST OFFICE
The Tourist Information and Visitors' Centre in the Old Town Hall on Green Market (tel. 512444) books rooms in the city and throughout Cumbria. This service is effectively free. Although you pay a 10% deposit at the office, this is subtracted from your final bill. Book-A-Bed-Ahead service also available. The office also has a vast range of tourist literature.

B&Bs & GUESTHOUSES
Expect to pay from £12 ($18) in local B&Bs

Mrs Thompson, 19 Aglionby St. (tel. 24566). Around £13.50 ($20.25). From the train station right along Botchergate, then left along Tait St, which runs into Aglionby St.
Cornerways Guest House, 107 Warwick Road (tel. 21733). B&B £11.50 ($17.25). From the station, cross Butchergate, walk round the crescent and take a right turn on to Warwick Road.

HI HOSTEL
Carlisle Youth Hostel, Etterby House, Etterby (tel. 23934). Juniors £5.70 ($8.55), seniors £6.80 ($10.20). Bus 62 from the City Centre to the Red Fern Inn, then walk down Etterby Road.

Keswick (tel. code 017687)

Keswick is about 55km from Carlisle, and 19km from Grasmere. The Tourist Information Centre in the Moot Hall on the Market Square (tel. 72645) books local accommodation free of charge. Book-A-Bed-Ahead service available.

B&Bs
Bridgedale, 101 Main St. (tel. 73914). £10 ($15) without breakfast. By the bus station.

Mr and Mrs Nixon, Grassmoor, 10 Blencathra St. (tel. 74008). £13
   ($19.50). Price falls by around 20% in the off-season.
Mrs Walker, 15 Acorn St. (tel. 74165). £13 ($19.50).
Mrs Peill, White House, 15 Ambleside Road (tel. 73176). Around
   £13.25 ($19.90).

HI HOSTELS
Keswick YH, Station Road (tel. 72484). Off the Market Place, down
   towards the River Greta. Station Road runs from the TIC.
Derwentwater YH, Barrow House, Borrowdale (tel. 77246). About
   3km out. Hourly Borrowdale bus CMS 79 to Seatoller.

CAMPING
Castlerigg Hall (tel. 72437). About 1.5km out of town to the
   south-east.
Dalebottom Holiday Park (tel. 72176). About 3km south-east. More
   expensive than Castlerigg Hall.

Grasmere (tel. code 015395)

About 8km from Ambleside and 20km from Keswick. In summer,
a Tourist Information Centre operates on the Redbank Road (tel.
35245) providing a local accommodation service and a Book-A-
Bed-Ahead facility.

B&Bs
Prices in the village's B&B are slightly higher than is normal for
the Lake District, with few rooms available for under £14 ($21)
per person.

HI HOSTELS
Butharlyp How YH (tel. 35316). Just outside the village. A few
   minutes' walk along the road to Easedale. The hostel is on your
   right.
Thorney How YH (tel. 35591). About 1.5km out. Follow the road
   to Easedale for about 1.25km. You will see the hostel signposted.
High Close (Langdale) YH, High Close, Loughrigg (tel. 37313).
   About 3km from Grasmere, 6.5km from Ambleside.
Elterwater YH (tel. 37245). About 5.5km from Grasmere and
   Ambleside, 1.5km from High Close (Langdale) YH. Close to Lang-
   dale Pike.

Ambleside (tel. code 015394)

About 8km from Grasmere, 9.5km from Hawkshead, 6.5km from Windermere. The Tourist Information Centre in the Old Court-house on Church Street (tel. 32582) books local accommodation free of charge. You pay 10% of the bill at the office as a deposit and the remainder to the proprietor. Book-A-Bed-Ahead service also available.

B&Bs

Prices start around £12 ($18). Try Church Street or the Compston Road. The road leading out to Windermere, Lake Road, is particularly well supplied with B&Bs.

Mr and Mrs Richardson, 3 Cambridge Villas, Church St. (tel. 32307). By the Tourist Information Centre.
Raaesbec, Fair View Road (tel. 33844).
Thorneyfield, Compston Road (tel. 32464). More expensive. Prices start at around £16 ($24).

HI HOSTEL

Ambleside YH, Waterhead (tel. 32304). By Lake Windermere. Juniors £7 ($10.50), seniors £8.10 ($12.15) in July and Aug.

HOSTEL

YWCA, Old Lake Road (tel. 32340). Open to men and women. Dorms and smaller rooms from £11.50 ($17.25).

CAMPING

Low Wray (tel. 32810). About 5.5km from town, on the road to Hawkshead. The bus to Hawkshead stops nearby.

Windermere and Bowness
(tel. code 015394)

About 6.5km from Ambleside and 14.5km from Hawkshead (by ferry). Another of the major gateways to the Lake District, thanks to the town's train station. Windermere's Tourist Information Centre is in Victoria Street (tel. 46499), close to the railway station.

The office books local accommodation for free: a 10% deposit is paid at the office, the remainder to the owner. Book-A-Bed-Ahead service also available. In summer, similar services are available at the Bowness Tourist Information Centre in Glebe Road (tel. 42895).

B&Bs
Prices in local B&Bs start around £11-12 ($16.50-18)

Mr and Mrs Austin, 'Lingmore', 7 High St. (tel. 44947). One of the cheapest. £11 ($16.50).

Mrs Graham, Brendan Chase Guest House, College Road (tel. 45638). Around £13 ($19.50).

Kirkwood, Prince's Road (tel. 43907). From around £14.50 ($21.75). The owners will pick you up from the train station. Down the main road to Bowness.

HI HOSTEL
Windermere YH, High Cross, Bridge Lane, Troutbeck (tel. 43543). Juniors £5.60 ($8.40), seniors £6.80 ($10.20). Troutbeck village is 3km to the north of Windermere, off the A591. The bus to Ambleside stops in Troutbeck Bridge, about 10 minutes' walk from the hostel.

CAMPING
Park Cliffe, Birks Road (tel. 015395 31344). Open May–Oct. Off the A592 to the north of Windermere (dir. Patterdale and Penrith).

Limefitt Park (tel. 015394 32300). Mixed couples and families only. More expensive than the site above. On the A592 6.5km south of Bowness.

Kendal (tel. code 01539)

About 18km from Windermere, Kendal's train station and its proximity to the M6, mean it is likely to be on your route if you are coming from the south. The Tourist Information Centre is in the Town Hall on Highgate (tel. 725758). Local accommodation and Book-A-Bed-Ahead services available.

HI HOSTEL
Kendal YH, Highgate (tel. 724066). In the town centre, close to the bus and rail stations.

London (tel. code 0171 or 0181 – use the 0171 prefix unless otherwise indicated)

TOURIST OFFICES

London Tourist Board, 26 Grosvenor Gardens, London SW1 0DU. Write to this office for information on the city in advance. For help with making reservations, write to the Accommodation Services department at the same address, at least six weeks before you plan to arrive.

There are seven/eight Tourist Information Centres operating in Central London, according to the time of year. All these offices will book accommodation in London for a hefty £5 ($7.50) commission.

Victoria Station Forecourt (tel. 730 3488; 824 8844 for accommodation). Open Mon.–Sat. 8 a.m.–7 p.m., Sun. 8 a.m.–4 p.m. Book-A-Bed-Ahead service available.

Liverpool Street Underground station, Liverpool Street (tel. 730 3488; 824 8844 for accommodation). Open Mon. 8.15 a.m.–7 p.m., Tues.–Sat. 8.15 a.m.–6 p.m., Sun. 8.30 a.m.–4.45 p.m. Book-A-Bed-Ahead service available.

Selfridges, Oxford Street (Basement Services Arcade, Duke Street Entrance) (tel. 730 3488; 824 8844 for accommodation). Open during store hours.

British Travel Centre, 12 Regent Street, Piccadilly Circus (tel. 730 3400; 930 0572 for accommodation). Open May–Sept. Mon.–Fri. 9 a.m.–6.30 p.m., weekends 9 a.m.–5 p.m.; for the rest of the year Saturday hours are 10 a.m.–4 p.m. Book-A-Bed-Ahead service available.

Tower of London, West Gate. Open during the summer only.

Clerkenwell Heritage Centre, 33 St John's Square (tel. 250 1039). Book-A-Bed-Ahead service available.

Bloomsbury Tourist Information Centre, 35–36 Woburn Place (tel. 636 7175). Open 9.45 a.m.–7 p.m. Book-A-Bed-Ahead service available.

Heathrow Terminals 1, 2, 3 Underground Station Concourse, Heathrow Airport (tel. 730 3488; 824 8844 for accommodation). Open daily 8 a.m.–6 p.m. Book-A-Bed-Ahead service available.

FINDING ACCOMMODATION

There is a serious shortage of cheap places to stay in London throughout most of the year, but especially in the summer. If you plan to arrive during the summer months, it is advisable to book

a bed as far in advance as you possibly can as you will struggle to
find a place in a hostel, hall of residence, or one of the cheaper
guesthouses or hotels on arrival. Outside the HI hostels and a few
independent hostels it is difficult to find a bed for under £15
($22.75). You can expect to pay from £20 ($30) for a single in a
guesthouse, with doubles rarely available for under £30 ($45).
There are cheaper guesthouses, but they are invariably filled with
homeless families, temporarily boarded by the Department of Social
Security.

HOTELS & GUESTHOUSES

The cheapest singles at the establishments listed below are generally
around two thirds of the price of the cheapest doubles. All hotels
and guesthouses listed are in Central London, unless stated otherwise. For details of special offers etc, try the accommodation pages
of travel magazines such as *Australian Traveller*, distributed free at
many rail and underground stations.

Doubles from £22 ($33)

Europa Hotel, 60−62 Anson Road (tel. 607 5935). North London.
    Underground: Tufnell Park (Northern Line).
Eric House, 328 Green Lanes (tel. 0181 800 6125). North London.
    Underground: Manor House (Piccadilly line).
Sass House Hotel, 10 & 11 Craven Terrace (tel. 402 0281). Under-
    ground: Paddington (Circle, District, Bakerloo and Hammersmith
    & City lines). BR mainline station.

Doubles from £22.50 ($33.75)

Colliers Hotel, 97 Warwick Way (tel. 834 6931/828 0210). Under-
    ground: Victoria (Circle, District and Victoria lines). BR mainline
    station.
Hyde Park Rooms Hotel, 137 Sussex Gardens, Hyde Park (tel. 723
    0225/0965). Underground: Paddington (Circle, District, Bakerloo
    and Hammersmith & City lines). BR mainline station.
Ms Julie Samuel, 37 Stokenchurch Street (off New Kings Road)
    (tel. 371 0230). Underground: Fulham Broadway (District line).

Doubles from £25.50 ($38.25)

Pearl Hotel, 40 West Cromwell Road, Earl's Court (tel. 373 9610/
    835 2007). Underground: Earl's Court (District and Piccadilly
    lines).

Grangewood Lodge Hotel, 104 Clova Road, Forest Gate (tel. 0181 534 0637). East London. Close to British Rail's Forest Gate station.

Janus Hotel, 26 Hazlitt Road (tel. 603 6915/3119). Underground: Kensington (Olympia) (District line).

Rasool Court Hotel, 19–21 Penywern Road, Earl's Court (tel. 373 8900/4893). Underground: Earl's Court (District and Piccadilly lines).

Doubles from £27.50 ($41.25)

Charlotte Guest House & Restaurant, 221 West End Lane, West Hampstead (tel. 794 6476). North London. Underground: West Hampstead (Jubilee line).

Westpoint Hotel, 170–172 Sussex Gardens (tel. 402 0281). Underground: Paddington (Circle, District, Bakerloo and Hammersmith & City lines). BR mainline station.

Luna & Simone Hotels, 47 Belgrave Road (tel. 828 1563). Underground: Victoria (Circle, District and Victoria lines). BR mainline station.

Kensbridge Hotel, 31 Elvaston Place (tel. 589 6265). Underground: Gloucester Road (Circle, District and Piccadilly lines).

Nevern Hotel, 29–31 Nevern Place (tel. 244 8366/8367). Underground: Earl's Court (District and Piccadilly lines).

Abbey Court Hotel, 174 Sussex Gardens (tel. 402 0704). Underground: Paddington (Circle, District, Bakerloo and Hammersmith & City lines). BR mainline station.

Doubles from £30 ($53)

Royal Hotel, Woburn Place (tel. 636 8401). Underground: Russell Square (Piccadilly line).

Hotel Strand Continental, 143 The Strand (tel. 836 4880). Underground: Charing Cross (Jubilee, Northern and Bakerloo lines). BR mainline station.

Oxford Hotel, 11 Craven Terrace (tel. 262 9608). Underground: Lancaster Gate (Central line).

Doubles from £31 ($46.50)

James Lodge, 116 Barry Road, Dulwich (tel. 0181 693 7744). South East London. Close to Crystal Palace stadium. Nearest rail station is British Rail's East Dulwich.

Sara Hotel, 15 Eardley Crescent (tel. 244 9500). Triples from £40

($60). Underground: Earl's Court (District and Piccadilly lines).

Belgrave House Hotel, 28–32 Belgrave Road (tel. 828 1563/834 8620). Underground: Victoria (Circle, District and Victoria lines). BR mainline station.

Dillons Hotel, 21 Belsize Park, Hampstead (tel. 794 3360). North London. Underground: Belsize Park (Northern Line).

Stanley House Hotel, 19–21 Belgrave Road (tel. 834 5042/7292). Underground: Victoria (Circle, District and Victoria lines). BR mainline station.

Windsor House, 12 Penywern Road (tel. 373 9087). Underground: Earl's Court (District and Piccadilly lines).

Hyde Park House, 48 St Petersburgh Place (tel. 229 9652). Underground: Queensway (Central line).

Doubles from £33 ($49.50)

Melbourne House, 79 Belgrave Road (tel. 828 3516). Underground: Victoria (Circle, District and Victoria lines). BR mainline station.

St George's Hotel, 25 Belgrave Road (tel. 828 2961/3605). Underground: Victoria (Circle, District and Victoria lines). BR mainline station.

Romany Hotel, 35 Longmoore Street (tel. 834 5553). Underground: Victoria (Circle, District and Victoria lines). BR mainline station.

Manor Hotel, 23 Nevern Place (tel. 370 6018/4164). Underground: Earl's Court (District and Piccadilly lines).

Acton Hill Guest House, 311 Uxbridge Road (tel. 0181 992 2553). West London. Underground: Acton Town (Piccadilly and District lines).

Half Moon Hotel, 10 Earl's Court Square (tel. 373 9956/2900). Underground: Earl's Court (District and Piccadilly lines).

Astoria Hotel, 39 St George's Drive (tel. 834 1965). Underground: Victoria (Circle, District and Victoria lines). BR mainline station.

Moss Hall Hotel, 10–11 Moss Hall Crescent, Finchley (tel. 0181 445 6980). North London. Underground: West Finchley (Northern Line).

Claremont Hotel, 154 High Street, Wealdstone, Harrow (tel. 0181 427 2738). North London. Underground: Harrow & Wealdstone (Bakerloo line). The underground service operates at peak hours only. At other times you have to catch a British Rail train.

White Lodge Hotel, 1 Church Lane, Hornsey (tel. 0181 348 9765). North London. Underground: Turnpike Lane (Piccadilly line).

Brindle House Hotel, 1 Warwick Place North (tel. 828 0057). Underground: Victoria (Circle, District and Victoria lines). BR mainline station.

B&B Flatlets, 64 Holland Road (tel. 229 9233). Underground: Holland Park (Central line).

London Tourist Hotel, 15 Pennywern Road (tel. 370 4356). Underground: Earls Court (District and Piccadilly lines).

Doubles from £35 ($52.50)

Andrews Hotel, 12 Westbourne Street, Hyde Park (tel. 723 5365/4514). Underground: Lancaster Gate (Central line).

Acton Grange Guest House, 317 Uxbridge Road, Acton (tel. 0181 992 0586). West London. Underground: Acton Town (District and Piccadilly lines).

Shellbourne Hotel, 1 Lexham Gardens (tel. 373 5161). Triples £43 ($64.50). Underground: Gloucester Road (Circle, District and Piccadilly lines).

Albro House Hotel, 155 Sussex Gardens (tel. 724 2931). Underground: Paddington (Circle, District, Bakerloo and Hammersmith & City lines). BR mainline station.

Ruddimans Hotel, 160–162 Sussex Gardens (tel. 723 1026). Underground: Paddington (Circle, District, Bakerloo and Hammersmith & City lines). BR mainline station.

Norfolk Court & St David's Hotel, 16 Norfolk Square (tel. 723 4963). Underground: Paddington (Circle, District, Bakerloo and Hammersmith & City lines). BR mainline station.

Dalmacia Hotel, 71 Shepherds Bush Road, Hammersmith (tel. 603 2887). West London. Underground: Hammersmith (District, Piccadilly and Hammersmith & City lines).

Hotel Cavendish (tel. 636 9079) and Jesmond (tel. 636 3199), 75 and 63 Gower Street. Underground: Goodge Street (Northern line).

Doubles from £36 ($54)

Gower House Hotel, 57 Gower Street (tel. 636 4685). Underground: Goodge Street (Northern line).

More House, 53 Cromwell Road, South Kensington (tel. 584 2040/2039). Underground: Gloucester Road (Circle, District and Piccadilly lines).

St Athan's Hotel, 20 Tavistock Place, Russell Square (tel. 837 9140/9627). Underground: Russell Square (Piccadilly line).

York House Hotel, 27 Philbeach Gardens (tel. 373 7519/7579). Underground: Earl's Court (District and Piccadilly lines).

Melita House Hotel, 35 Charlwood Street (tel. 828 3516). Underground: Victoria (Circle, District and Victoria lines). BR mainline station.

Garden Court Hotel, 30–31 Kensington Gardens Square (tel. 229 2553). Underground: Bayswater (District and Circle lines).

Brookside Hotel, 32 Brook Avenue, Wembley Park (tel. 0181 904 0019/908 5336). Underground: Wembley Park (Metropolitan and Jubilee lines).

Doubles from £38.50 ($57.75)

Holly House Hotel, 20 Hugh Street (tel. 834 5671). Underground: Victoria (Circle, District and Victoria lines). BR mainline station.

Kirness Hotel, 29 Belgrave Road (tel. 834 0030). Underground: Victoria (Circle, District and Victoria lines). BR mainline station.

Falcon Hotel, 11 Norfolk Square (tel. 723 8603). Underground: Paddington (Circle, District, Bakerloo and Hammersmith & City lines). BR mainline station.

Chumleigh Lodge Hotel, 226–228 Nether Street, Finchley (tel. 0181 346 1614). North London. Underground: West Finchley (Northern line).

Kenwood House Hotel, 114 Gloucester Place (tel. 935 3473/935 9455/486 5007). Underground: Baker Street (Circle, Bakerloo, Jubilee, Metropolitan and Hammersmith & City lines).

Rilux House, 1 Lodge Road (tel. 0181 203 0933). North London. Underground: Hendon Central (Northern line).

Regency House Hotel, 71 Gower Street (tel. 637 1804). Underground: Euston (Northern, Piccadilly and Victoria lines). BR mainline station.

Doubles from £40 ($60)

Rhodes House Hotel, 195 Sussex Gardens (tel. 262 5617/0537). Underground: Paddington (Circle, District, Bakerloo and Hammersmith & City lines). BR mainline station.

Oxford House, 92 Cambridge St. (tel. 834 6467). Underground: Victoria (Circle, District and Victoria lines). BR mainline station.

PRIVATE ROOMS

Alma Tourist Services, 10 Fairway, West Wimbledon (tel. 0181 542 3771). Rooms available in South-West and Central London. Minimum stay of two nights. Singles from £17.50 ($26.25), doubles from £28 ($42). With breakfast.

Anglo World Travel Limited, 18 Ogle Street (tel. 436 3601). Office open Mon.–Fri. 9 a.m.–5.30 p.m. Rooms available in the suburbs of Harrow, Wembley, Streatham and Bromley. Minimum stay of 3 nights. Reservations taken in advance or on the day. Full payment required with advance bookings. Singles from £17.50 ($26.25), doubles from £26 ($39). With breakfast.

Best London Homes, 126 Lower Richmond Road (tel. 0181 780 9045). Rooms available in Central London, Chelsea, Fulham, Kensington, Bayswater and South and West London. No minimum stay, but a surcharge is added for stays of less than three nights. Reservations taken in advance or on the day. Deposit of 25% required with advance bookings. Singles from £14.50 ($21.75), doubles from £28 ($42). With breakfast.

Capital Homes, 200 Chase Side (tel. 0181 440 7535); at weekends and evenings 0181 441 7378). Rooms available in North, Northwest and South London. Minimum stay of two nights. Reservations taken in advance or on the day. Payment for the first night required with advance bookings. Singles from £16.50 ($24.75), doubles from £28 ($42). With breakfast.

Host and Guest Service, The Studio, 635 Kings Road (tel. 731 5340/ 736 5645). Office open Mon.–Fri. 9 a.m.–5.30 p.m. Rooms available in Greater London. Minimum stay of three nights. Advance and same day reservations. Full payment is required with advance bookings. Singles from £14 ($21), doubles from £24 ($36). With breakfast.

In London, London House, Suite 409, 19 Old Court Place (tel. 376 0405/1070). Office open 9.30 a.m.–6 p.m. Rooms available in Central, North-west and South-east London. Minimum stay of two nights. Singles from £17.50 ($26.25), doubles from £31 ($46.50). With breakfast.

Le Weekend London West, Ealing Broadway (tel. 0181 998 0413). Office open daily 7.30 a.m.–9.30 p.m. Rooms available in West London. Singles from £17.50 ($26.25), doubles from £34 ($51). With breakfast.

London Homestead Services, Coombe Wood Road, Kingston-Upon-Thames, Surrey (tel. 0181 949 4455). Rooms available in Central London, and in the suburbs. Minimum stay of three nights. Advance and same day reservations. Deposit of 25% required with advance bookings. Singles from £16.50 ($24.75), doubles from £28 ($42). With breakfast.

Central London Accommodations, P.O. Box 2623, London W14 0EF (tel. 602 9668). Minimum stay of three nights. B&B from £14.50 ($21.75) per person.

HI HOSTELS

London's eight HI hostels are frequently filled to capacity around Easter, and from June to September, so advance reservation is highly recommended. If the hostel you write to is full on the dates you want, they will automatically transfer your booking to any other hostel with space available, unless you state otherwise. You can book any London HI hostel at the central reservations office (tel. 0171 248 6542). Full information on London's hostels is available from: YHA London Regional Office, 8 St Stephen's Hill, St Albans, Herts AL1 2DY (tel. 01727 55215).

City of London YH, 36 Carter Lane (tel. 236 4965). Open year round. No curfew. Juniors £16 ($24), seniors £19.30 ($29). About 300m from St Paul's underground station (Central line) and Blackfriars underground (Circle and District lines) and BR station.

Earl's Court YH, 38 Bolton Gardens (tel. 373 7083). Open year round. Apr.–Sept. Juniors £14.50 ($21.75), seniors £16.10 ($24.15), including breakfast. Prices fall by £1 ($1.50) at other times of the year. 300m from Earl's Court underground station (District and Piccadilly lines), off the Earl's Court Road.

Hampstead Heath YH, 4 Wellgarth Road (tel. 0181 458 9054). Open year round. Apr.–Sept. Juniors £11.80 ($17.70), seniors £13.90 ($20.85). About 400m from the Golders Green underground station (Northern line), off North End Road.

Highgate Village YH, 84 Highgate West Hill (tel. 0181 340 1831). Open year round. Juniors £7.60 ($11.40), Seniors £11.40 ($17.10). The Archway underground station (Northern line) is about 10 minutes' walk away. Walk past the Whittington Hospital, then turn left off Highgate Hill down South Grove into Highgate West Hill.

Holland House YH/King George VI Memorial YH, Holland Walk, Kensington (tel. 937 0748). Open year round. Juniors £16 ($24), seniors £18.10 ($27.15), breakfast included. About 400m from both the Holland Park underground station (Circle and District lines) and the High Street Kensington underground station (District and Circle). Holland Walk cuts through Holland Park between Holland Park Avenue and Kensington High Street.

Oxford Street YH, 14 Noel Street (tel. 734 1618). Open year round. No curfew. Groups are not admitted to this hostel. Juniors £13.50 ($20.25), seniors £16.70 ($25.05). About 400m from both the Oxford Circus (Central, Bakerloo and Victoria lines) and Tottenham Court Road (Central and Northern lines) underground stations. From Oxford Street, turn down Poland Street or Berwick Street.

Rotherhithe YH, Island Yard, Salter Road (tel. 232 2114). Open year round. Juniors £13.80 ($20), seniors £17.10 ($25.65). 300m from Rotherhithe underground station on the East London line.

Join the East London line at Whitechapel (District and Metropolitan lines). Bus P105 from Waterloo BR station runs straight to the hostel.

HOSTELS/STUDENT RESIDENCES

Astor College, 99 Charlotte Street (tel. 580 7262/7263/7264). Singles and doubles. £15−21 ($22.50−31.50). Underground: Goodge Street (Northern Line).

Bryanston Residence, 16 Bryanston Square (tel. 402 8608/796 3889). Singles, doubles and larger rooms. B&B from £11−22 ($16.50−33) Weekly rates offer a small reduction. Underground: Marble Arch (Central line).

Carr-Saunders Hall, 18−24 Fitzroy St. (tel. 580 6338). Open Mar.−Apr. and July−Sept. Singles and doubles. B&B £17.50 ($28.25) per person. Underground: Goodge Street (Northern line), or Great Portland Street (Circle line).

Goldsmid House, 36 North Row (Oxford Street) (tel. 493 8911/629 2977). Open June−Sept. Singles and doubles. £12−20 ($18−30). Underground: Marble Arch (Central line). For advance reservations contact: Reservations Dept, EST (Goldsmid House), 34−36 South Street, Lancing, West Sussex BN15 8AG (tel. 01903 75 3555).

International Students House, 229 Great Portland Street (tel. 631 3223). Singles, doubles and larger rooms. £20 ($30) for B&B. Underground: Great Portland Street (Circle and Hammersmith & City lines).

Allen Hall Summer Hostel, Allen Hall, 28 Beaufort Street (tel. 351 1296/1297). Open July−Aug. Singles and doubles. B&B from £20 ($30). Underground: Sloane Square (Circle and District lines).

Anne Elizabeth House Hotel, 30 Collingham Place. (tel. 370 4821). Doubles and larger rooms. B&B from £9.50−21 ($14.25−31.50). Underground: Earl's Court (District and Piccadilly lines).

Museum Inn, 27 Montague Street (tel. 580 5360), opposite the British Museum. Doubles and dorms, £12.50−16 ($18.75−24). Underground: Holborn (Central and Piccadilly lines).

Crofton Hotel, 13−16 Queen's Gate (tel. 584 7201). Singles, doubles and larger rooms. £13−30 ($19.50−45). Underground: Gloucester Road (Circle, District and Piccadilly lines).

Culture Link International Student Residence, 161 Old Brompton Road (tel. 373 6061). Singles, doubles and larger rooms. Underground: West Brompton (District line).

Curzon House Hotel, 58 Courtfield Gardens (tel. 373 6745). Singles, doubles and larger rooms. £13–20 ($19.50–30) for B&B. Underground: Earl's Court (District and Piccadilly lines).

Queen Alexandra's House, Bremner Road, Kensington Gore (tel. 589 3635). Open July–Aug. Women only. Singles and doubles. B&B from £22 ($33). Underground: South Kensington (Circle, District and Piccadilly lines).

Queensberry Court, 7–11 Queensberry Place, South Kensington (tel. 589 3693). Singles, doubles and larger rooms. B&B from £17–33 ($25.50–49.50). Full board £100–200 ($150–300) per week. Underground: South Kensington (Circle, District and Piccadilly lines).

Hotel Saint Simeon, 38 Harrington Gardens (tel. 373 0505/370 4708). Doubles and larger rooms. £9–12 ($13.50–18). Full board £65–92 ($97.50–138) per week. Underground: Gloucester Road (Circle, District and Piccadilly lines).

Holland Park Independent Hostel, 41 Holland Park (tel. 229 4238). Triples and larger rooms. £7.50–12 ($11.25–18). Underground: Holland Park (Central line).

Palace Court Hotel, 12–14 Pembridge Square (tel. 727 4412). Singles, doubles and larger rooms. £8–18 ($12–27). Underground: Bayswater (Circle and District lines).

Palace Hotel, 31 Palace Court (tel. 221 5628). Dorm beds £10 ($15). Underground: Notting Hill Gate (Central, Circle and District lines).

C/E/I International Youth Hotel (Centre Française), 61 Chepstow Place, Notting Hill Gate (tel. 221 8134). Singles, doubles and larger rooms. £12.90–16.40 ($19.35–24.60) in dorms, £23 ($34.50) in singles. Underground: Bayswater (Circle and District lines).

Glendale Hotel, 8 Devonshire Terrace (tel. 262 1770). Singles, doubles and larger rooms. £11.50 ($17.25) for B&B. Underground: Paddington (Circle, District, Bakerloo and Hammersmith & City lines). BR mainline station.

Maranton House Hotel, 14 Barkston Gardens (tel. 373 5722). Some dorms at £10 ($15) per night; doubles from £28 ($42). Underground: Earl's Court (District and Piccadilly lines).

Lords Hotel, 20–22 Leinster Square (tel. 229 8877). Singles, doubles and larger rooms. B&B from £14–42 ($21–63). Underground: Bayswater (Circle and District lines).

Ifor Evans Hall/Max Rayne House, 109 Camden Road (tel. 485 9377). Open Mar.–Apr. and June–Sept. Singles and doubles. B&B from £21–34 ($31.50–51). Underground: Camden Town (Northern line).

John Adams Hall, 15–23 Endsleigh Street (tel. 387 4086/307 4796).

Open Dec.–Jan., Mar.–Apr. and June–Sept. Singles and doubles. B&B £21.40 ($32.10). Underground: Russell Square (Piccadilly line) or Euston (Northern and Victoria lines). BR mainline station.

Passfield Hall, 1 Endsleigh Place (tel. 387 7743/3584). Open Mar.–Apr. and July–Sept. Singles, doubles and larger rooms. B&B from £18–21 ($27–31.50). Underground: Euston (Northern and Victoria lines).

Regent's College, Inner Circle, Regents Park (tel. 487 7483). Open Dec.–Jan. and May–Sept. Singles, doubles and larger rooms. £20.50–33 ($30.75–49.50). Underground: Baker Street (Jubilee, Northern, Metropolitan, Bakerloo and Hammersmith & City lines).

Repton House Hotel, 31 Bedford Place (tel. 636 7045). Doubles and larger rooms. B&B from £12.50–28 ($18.75–42). Full board £75–180 ($112.50–270) per week. Underground: Russell Square (Piccadilly line).

Rosebery Avenue Hall, 90 Rosebery Avenue (tel. 278 3251). Open Mar.–Apr. and June–Sept. Singles and doubles. B&B from £19–20 ($28.50–30). Underground: Angel (Northern line).

Queen Mary & Westfield College Halls of Residence, 98–110 High Road, South Woodford (tel. 0181 504 9282). Open Mar.–Apr. and July–Sept. Singles and doubles. B&B £17.50 ($26.25). Underground: South Woodford (Central line).

Finsbury Hall, City University, Bastwick Street (tel. 251 4961). Open Mar.–Apr. and July–Sept. Singles and doubles. B&B from £20–22 ($30–33). Underground: Barbican (Circle and Metropolitan lines).

King's Campus Vacation Bureau, 552 Kings Road (tel. 351 6011). £20 ($30).

London Student Hotel, 14 Pennywern Road (tel. 244 6615). Dorms from £9 ($13.50). Underground: Earl's Court (District and Piccadilly lines).

Airton House Youth and Student Hotel, 8 Philbeach Gardens (tel. 244 7722). £9–11 ($13.50–16.50). Underground: Earl's Court (District and Piccadilly lines).

Kent House, 325 Green Lanes (tel. 0181 802 0800/9070). Singles, doubles and larger rooms. £8.50–17 ($12.75–25.50). Reduced rates in the off-season. Underground: Manor House (Piccadilly line).

Northampton Hall, City University, Bunhill Row (tel. 628 2953). Open Mar.–Apr. and July–Sept. Singles and doubles. B&B from £20–33 ($30–49.50). Underground: Old Street (Northern line).

Polytechnic of North London, James Leicester Hall, Market Road (tel. 607 3250). Open April, and July–Sept. B&B in singles from £18.50 ($27.75). Underground: Caledonian Road (Piccadilly line).

Polytechnic of North London, Tufnell Park Hall, Huddleston Road (tel. 607 3250). Open Mar.–Apr., and July–Sept. B&B in singles from £18–20 ($27–30). Underground: Tufnell Park (Northern line).

Waynefleet House, 5 Lynton Road, Kilburn (tel. 625 6839). Doubles and larger rooms. £8.50–15 ($12.75–22.50). Full board from £60–115 ($90–172.50) per week. Underground: Queens Park (Bakerloo line).

Driscoll House Hotel, 172 New Kent Road (tel. 703 4175). Full board £150 ($225) per week. Underground: Elephant & Castle (Bakerloo and Northern lines).

Westbourne International Residence, 104 Westbourne Terrace (tel. 402 0431). Dorms from £10 ($15). Underground: Paddington (Circle, District, Bakerloo and Hammersmtih & City lines). BR mainline station.

King George's House YMCA, 40–46 Stockwell Road, Stockwell (tel. 274 7861). Singles, doubles and larger rooms. B&B from £16.50 ($24.75). The hostel is primarily aimed at long-term guests. Underground: Stockwell (Piccadilly and Northern lines).

Milo Guest House, 52 Ritherdon Road, Balham (tel. 0181 671 3683/ 767 7225). Singles, doubles and larger rooms. From £7.50 ($11.25). Underground: Tooting Bec (Northern line). For advance bookings contact: Ms H. Milo, 'Kismet', Poynders Road, Clapham Park, London SW4 8PS (tel. 0181 671 3683).

Tent City, Old Oak Common Lane, East Acton (tel. 0181 743 5708). Open June–Sept. Simple accommodation under several large marquees. 448 beds. £5 ($7.50) per night. Underground: East Acton (Central line).

Imperial College of Science & Technology, 15 Princes Gardens (tel. 589 5111). Open Easter and summer. B&B £18–24 ($27–36). Underground: South Kensington (District, Circle and Piccadilly lines).

Corfu Hotel, 41 Longridge Road (tel. 370 4942). From £10 ($15) per night, standard hostel accommodation. Underground: Earl's Court (District and Piccadilly lines).

CAMPING

Lea Valley Campsite, Sewarstone Road, Chingford (tel. 0181 529 5689). Open Easter–Oct. £4.50 ($6.75) per person per night (tent included). About 19.5km from the centre. British Rail train from Liverpool Street to Chingford, then take bus 505 or 379, both of which stop about 800m from the site. Alternatively, take the underground (Victoria line) to Walthamstow Central, then bus 505 or 215 to Chingford, 800m from the site. In peak season, bus 215 runs right to the site.

Pickett's Lock Sport & Leisure Centre, Pickett's Lock Lane, Edmonton (tel. 0181 345 6666). Open year round. Minimum pitch fee of £6 ($9), so this is what solo travellers must pay. £4.50 ($6.75) per person. About 16km from the centre. British Rail train from Liverpool Street to Lower Edmonton, then bus W8. Alternatively take the underground (Victoria line) to Seven Sisters, then take a BR train to Lower Edmonton, followed by bus W8.

Tent City, Old Oak Common Lane, East Acton (tel. 0181 743 5708). Open June–Sept. About 9.5km from the centre. £5 ($7.50) per person (tent included). Similarly priced dormitory accommodation available. Underground: East Acton (Central line). Bus 12 or 52A.

Abbey Wood, Federation Road, Abbey Wood (tel. 0181 310 2233). Open year round. About 19km from the centre. Peak season (18 May–31 Aug.) £3.50 ($5.25) per person (tent included). £3 ($4.50) in the off-season. British Rail train from Charing Cross to Abbey Wood.

Crystal Palace Caravan Club Site, Crystal Palace Parade (tel. 0181 778 7155). Open year round. About 19.5km from the centre. Peak season (18 May–31 Aug.) £3.50 ($5.25) per person (tent included), £3 ($4.50) in the off-season. British Rail train from Victoria to Crystal Palace. Buses 2A, 3 and 3A stop close to the site.

Eastway Cycle Circuit and Campsite, Temple Mills Lane, Stratford (tel. 0181 534 6085). Open Mar.–Oct. £5 ($7.50) per person (tent included). About 6.5km from the centre, 1.5km from Leyton underground station (Central line).

Hackney Camping, Millfields Road (tel. 0181 985 7656). Open 18 June–25 Aug. £4 ($6) per person for those with their own tent. Bus 38 from Piccadilly stops at Clapton Pond, from which you can walk along Millfields Road to the site. Bus 22A from Liverpool Street stops in Mandeville Street, from which you can cross the canal to the site.

SLEEPING ROUGH

It is not possible to sleep in the train stations, nor is it safe to sleep in the surrounding areas. Sleeping rough is not to be advised in London as a whole, but if you must sleep rough, at least try to bed down beside other people (other travellers, preferably). The embankment at Westminster Bridge, or Hyde Park, are the most obvious places to try.

Manchester (tel. code 0161)

TOURIST OFFICE
Tourist Information Centre, Town Hall Extension, Lloyd Street (tel. 234 3157/3158). Rooms found in local accommodations for £1 ($1.50) fee. Book-A-Bed-Ahead service also available.

FINDING ACCOMMODATION
Local B&Bs start around £12–13 ($18–19.50), but it is very difficult to find a centrally located B&B at those prices. The most reasonable terms for B&B in the city centre are offered by some of the pubs along Chapel Street. Apart from these, you are going to have to base yourself outside the centre. One of the better areas to look is the Chorlton district of the city, a 15–20-minute trip from the centre by bus 85, 86, 102 or 103.

B&Bs
The Black Lion, 65 Chapel Street (tel. 834 1974). Around £15 ($22.50).
Mrs McMahon, 7 The Meade (tel. 881 2714). £14 ($21). About 6.5km out from the centre. Bus 47, 82, 86 or 87 to Beech Road. From Beech Road turn left along Claude Road, left again onto North Meads, which subsequently becomes The Meade.
Mrs Matheson, 41 Atwood Road, Didsbury (tel. 434 2268). £10 ($15). Bus 40, 42 or 45.

STUDENT RESIDENCES
University of Manchester, Wolton Hall (tel. 224 7244). Mainly singles, with only a limited number of doubles. B&B £16 ($24). Highly popular with groups. Buses 40–46 and bus 49 to Owens Park.

HOSTEL
Mr Bed's, 89 Otterburn Close, Hulme (tel. 226 3777). From £8 ($12). Tiny hostel, so reserve in advance.

Oxford (tel. code 01865)

TOURIST OFFICE
Tourist Information Centre, St Aldate's (tel. 726871). Open
Mon.–Sat. 9.30 a.m.–5 p.m., Sun. (summer only) 10 a.m.–11 p.m.
and 3–3.30 p.m. There is a huge charge of £4 ($6) for the room-
finding service. During the summer, long queues are the norm.
Any time after the office closes up until 10 p.m. you can obtain
free help with finding accommodation by phoning Mrs Downes,
Secretary of the Oxford Association of Hotels and Guesthouses (tel.
241326/250511). Book-A-Bed-Ahead service available.

FINDING ACCOMMODATION
Rooms (especially singles) can be at a premium in July and August
in Oxford, so try to book a bed in advance if possible. You may be
asked to send a deposit to confirm a booking. Local guesthouses
and B&Bs are more expensive than normal, which means you will
struggle to find a double room for under £15 ($22.50) per person.
The least expensive B&Bs are on Iffley Road (nos. 200–240), on
Cowley Road (nos. 250–350), and on Abingdon Road.

GUESTHOUSES AND B&Bs
The prices quoted below are based on two people sharing a double.
Expect to pay a further 15–20% for a single.

B&B from £14 ($21) per person

Windrush Guest House, 11 Iffley Road (tel. 247933).
Brenal Guest House, 307 Iffley Road (tel. 721561).
Pine Castle Guest House, 290 Iffley Road (tel. 241497/727230).
Hansa Guest House, 192 Iffley Road (tel. 249757).
Bronte Guest House, 282 Iffley Road (tel. 244594).
Beaumont Guest House, 234 Abingdon Road (tel. 241767).

B&B from £16 ($24) per person

Southfields, 240 Abingdon Road (tel. 244357).
Micklewood, 331 Cowley Road (tel. 247328).
Bravalla Guest House, 242 Iffley Road (tel. 241326/250511).
Acorn Guest House, 260 Iffley Road (tel. 247998).
Shannon Guest House, 329 Cowley Road (tel. 247558).
Ascot Guest House, 283 Iffley Road (tel. 240259/727669).

Newton House, 82–84 Abingdon Road (tel. 240561).
Lakeside Guest House, 118 Abingdon Road (tel. 244725).
Sportsview Guest House, 106 Abingdon Road (tel. 244268).

B&B from £17 ($30) per person

Adams Guest House, 302 Banbury Road, Summertown (tel. 56118).
Burren Guest House, 374 Banbury Road (tel. 513513).
St Michael's Guest House, 26 St Michael Street (tel. 242101).
The Whitehouse, 315 Iffley Road (tel. 244524).
Becket House, 5 Becket Street (tel. 724675).
The Ridings, 280 Abingdon Road (tel. 248364).
Greengables, 326 Abingdon Road (tel. 725870).
White House View, 9 White House Road (tel. 721626).
Conifer Lodge, 159 Eynsham Road, Botley (tel. 862280).

B&B from £18 ($27) per person

Five Mile View, 528 Banbury Road (tel. 58747).
Gables' Guest House, 6 Cumnor Hill, Botley (tel. 862153).
Westminster Guest House, 350 Iffley Road (tel. 250924).
Earlmont Guest House, 324 Cowley Road (tel. 240236).
The Athena, 253 Cowley Road (tel. 243124).

HI HOSTELS

Oxford Youth Hostel, Jack Straw's Lane (tel. 62997). Open daily 1 Feb.–28 Dec. Juniors £6.80 ($10.20), seniors £8.20 ($12.30). About 3km from the city centre. Frequent minibus service – bus 73 – runs every 15–20 minutes until 10.30 p.m. from the Job Centre (near the Tourist Information Office) or from Queen's College.
Charlbury Youth Hostel (tel. 01608 810202). A 15-minute train journey from Oxford.

HOSTEL

YMCA, Alexandra Residential Club, 133 Woodstock Road (tel. 52021). Women aged over 16 only. 2 a.m. curfew (2.30 a.m. Fri. and Sat.) Three-night maximum stay. Around £6.50 ($9.75) for one night, £12 ($18) for two nights, and £16 ($24) for three nights. About 1.5km from the centre. Bus 60 or 60A.

CAMPING

Oxford Camping International, 426 Abingdon Road (tel. 246551).

Open year round. Around £7 ($10.50) for a tent and two adults. About 2.5km from the centre, to the rear of the Texaco petrol station.

Cassington Mill Caravan Site, Eynsham Road, Cassington (tel. 881081). Open Apr.–Oct. Around £6.50 ($9.75) for a tent and two occupants. About 6.5km out of town, off the A40 to Cheltenham. Bus 90 from the bus station.

Stratford-upon-Avon (tel. code 01789)

TOURIST OFFICE

Tourist Information Centre, Bridgefoot (tel. 293127/294466). Open Apr.–Oct., Mon.–Sat. 9 a.m.–5.30 p.m.; Nov.–Mar., Mon.–Sat. 10.30 a.m.–4.30 p.m. Room-finding service. After office hours an accommodation list is displayed. Book-A-Bed-Ahead service available.

Guide Friday, Civic Hall, 14 Rother Street (tel. 294466). Limited range of information. In the past, this office has operated a room-finding service but at an extortionate £3 ($4.50) fee.

FINDING ACCOMMODATION

Even though the town has a large number of B&Bs considering its size, rooms (especially singles) are in short supply from late June to early September. At these times, try to book lodgings at least one week in advance. The best area to look for B&Bs is around Evesham Road, Evesham Place and Grove Road. To get there go down Alcester Road from the train station, then right on to Grove Road. This road runs into Evesham Place, which subsequently becomes Evesham Road. Across the river, the Shipston Road also has quite a concentration of B&Bs.

GUESTHOUSES AND B&Bs
Doubles from around £23 ($34.50)

Bradbourne Guest House, 44 Shipston Road (tel. 204178).
Amelia Linhill Guesthouse, 35 Evesham Place (tel. 292879).
Kawartha House, 39 Grove Road (tel. 204469).
Clomendy Guest House, 157 Evesham Road (tel. 266957).

Doubles from £25 ($37.50)

34 Banbury Road (tel. 269714).

Bronhill House, 260 Alcester Road (tel. 299169).
Field View, 35 Banbury Road (tel. 292694).
Compton House, 22 Shipston Road (tel. 205646).
Salamander Guest House, 40 Grove Road (tel. 205728/297843).
Barbette, 165 Evesham Road (tel. 297822).

Doubles from £27 ($40.50)

Green Gables, 47 Banbury Road (tel. 205557).
Stretton House, 38 Grove Road (tel. 268647).
Naini Tal Guest House, 63A Evesham Road (tel. 204956).
Courtland Hotel, 12 Guild Street (tel. 292401).
The Croft, 49 Shipston Road (tel. 293419).
Arden Park Hotel, 6 Arden Street (tel. 296072).

Doubles from £30 ($45)

Cherangani, 61 Maidenhead Road (tel. 292655).
Aberfoyle Guesthouse, 3 Evesham Place (tel. 295703).
Newlands, 7 Broad Walk (tel. 298449).
Parkfield, 3 Broad Walk (tel. 293313).
Woodstock Guest House, 30 Grove Road (tel. 299881).
Moonlight Bed & Breakfast, 144 Alcester Road (tel. 298213).
Brett House, 8 Broad Walk (tel. 266374).
Chadwyns, 6 Broad Walk (tel. 269077).
Winterbourne Guest House, 2 St Gregory's Road (tel. 292207).
Nando's, 18–19 Evesham Place (tel. 204907).

HI HOSTEL
Stratford-upon-Avon YH, Hemmingford House, Wellesbourne Road, Alveston (tel. 297093). Open mid-Jan.–mid-Dec. Juniors £8.40 ($12.60). Reserve well in advance. About 3km from the centre of town: walk along the B4086 to Alveston, or take the hourly 518 bus from the Travel Shop (at the junction of Guild Street and Warwick Road) or from the bus station.

CAMPING
Elms, Tiddington Road (tel. 292312). Open Apr.–Oct. £3.50 ($5.25) per tent, £2 ($3) per person. On the B4056, 1.5km north-east of the centre.
Dodwell Park, Evesham Road (tel. 204957). Open year round. Similar prices to the site above. About 3km out from the centre on the A439.

York (tel. code 01904)

TOURIST OFFICE
There are three official City of York Tourist Information Centres in the city. The main office is close to York Minster in the De Grey Rooms on Exhibition Square (opposite the Art Gallery) (tel. 621756). Branch offices operate in the train station (tel. 643700) and in the Askham Bar Visitor Centre on the Tadcaster Road (tel. 701888). From June–Sept. opening hours are Mon.–Sat. 9 a.m.– 8 p.m., Sun. 10 a.m.–1 p.m.; from Oct.–May. open Mon.–Sat. 9 a.m.–5 p.m. All the offices are well supplied with information on the city. A local room-finding service is provided which is effectively free; you pay a 10% deposit at the office, which is subtracted from your final bill at the B&B. Outside office hours an accommodation list is displayed at the office on Exhibition Square. Book-A-Bed-Ahead service available.

FINDING ACCOMMODATION
Finding a cheap place to stay in York during the summer can be very difficult. At this time, even campsites are best reserved in advance. The city is also highly popular with visitors taking weekend breaks, so try to arrive in midweek if possible. B&Bs start at around £11–12 ($16.50–18.00), but the cheapest establishments fill early in the day. If you arrive in York when the Tourist Information Centres are open there is little point in looking around on your own. This is true even in the summer when the long queues can be off putting. However, if you get into town early in the morning during the summer there are a few areas which are worth looking in if you want a B&B. The Bootham area of the city, the Haxby Road, Bishopthorpe Road and the streets off Scarcroft Road are all well stocked with B&Bs and within easy walking distance of the bus and train stations.

GUESTHOUSES AND B&Bs
The cheapest singles at the guesthouses and B&Bs listed below are normally around 50–60% of the cost of the cheapest doubles.

Doubles around £21 ($31.50)

1. South View Guest House, 114 Acomb Road (tel. 796512). Just over 10 minutes' walk from the train station. From Blossom Street turn right down Holgate Road then left at Acomb Road.

Doubles from around £21 ($31.50)

2. Dalescroft Guest House, 10 Southlands Road (tel. 626801). Right off the Bishopthorpe Road, about ten minutes' walk from the train station.
3. Southland's Guest House, 69 Nunmill Street, South Bank (tel. 631203). A 10-minute walk from the train station. From the Bishopthorpe Road turn right along Scarcroft Road then take the first left.
4. Burton Villa, 22 Haxby Road (tel. 626364). About 15 minutes' walk from the train station.

Doubles from around £22 ($33)

5. Bronte House, 22 Grosvenor Terrace, Bootham (tel. 621066). About 15 minutes' walk from the train station. Follow Bootham, then take the first right beyond the railway line.

Doubles from around £23 ($34.50)

6. Birchfield Guest House, 2 Nunthorpe Avenue (tel. 636395). About ten minutes' walk from the train statino. Turn left off Blossom Street/The Mount along Scarcroft Road, then right at Nunthorpe Avenue.
7. Clifton View Guest House, 118 Clifton (tel. 625047). About 15 minutes' walk from the train station.
8. Queen Anne's Guest House, 24 Queen Anne's Road, Bootham (tel. 629389). About 15 minutes' walk from the train station. Follow Bootham then take the second left beyond the railway line.
9. York Lodge Guest House, 64 Bootham Crescent, Bootham (tel. 654289). About 15 minutes' walk from the train station. Follow Bootham, then take the second right beyond the railway line.

Doubles from around £25 ($37.50)

10. Aaron Guest House, 42 Bootham Crescent, Bootham (tel. 625927). See 9.
11. Acorn Guest House, 1 Southlands Road (tel. 620081). See 2.
12. Bishopgarth Guest House, 3 Southlands Road (tel. 635220). See 2.
13. Staymore Guest House, 2 Southlands Road (tel. 626935). See 2.

14. Heworth Guest House, 126 East Parade, Heworth (tel. 426384).
15. Green Guest House, 31 Bewlay Street (tel. 652509). About 10 minutes' walk from the train station, left off the Bishopthorpe Road.
16. Romley Guest House, 2 Millfield Road (tel. 652822). A 10-minute walk from the train station. Right off the Scarcroft Road immediately after Nunthorpe Avenue. See 6.
17. Greenside, 124 Clifton (tel. 623631). About 15 minutes' walk from the train station.
18. Alemar Guest House, 19 Queen Anne's Road, Bootham (tel. 652367). See 8.
19. Bank House, 9 Southlands Road (tel. 627803). See 2.
20. Grange Lodge, 52 Bootham Crescent, Bootham (tel. 621137). See 9.
21. Healey Grange Guest House, Malton Road (tel. 415700).
22. Minster View Guest House, 2 Grosvenor Terrace, Bootham (tel. 655034). See 5.
23. The Limes, 135 Fulford Road (tel. 624548).

Doubles from around £26 ($39)

24. Arnot House, 17 Grosvenor Terrace, Bootham (tel. 641966). See 5.
25. Tree Tops, 21 St Mary's, Bootham (tel. 658053). A 10-minute walk from the train station, left off Bootham.
26. Ashwood Place, 19 Nunthorpe Avenue (tel. 623412). See 6.
27. Claremont Guest House, 18 Claremont Terrace, Gillygate (tel. 625158). Good location close to the centre. From Exhibition Square follow Gillygate and then turn left at Claremont Terrace.
28. Bridge House, 181 Haxby Road (tel. 636161).
29. St Raphael Guest House, 44 Queen Anne's Road, Bootham (tel. 645028). See 8.

Doubles from £27 ($40.50)

30. Brookside Guest House, 73 Huntingdon Road (tel. 633575).
31. Sycamore Guest House, Sycamore Place, Bootham (tel. 658053). About 15 minutes' walk from the train station. Follow Bootham and take the first left beyond the railway line. Follow Bootham Terrace until you see Sycamore Place on the right.
32. Hillcrest Guest House, 110 Bishopthorpe Road (tel. 653160).
33. Martin's Guest House, 5 Longfield Terrace, Bootham (634551).

A 15-minute walk from the train station. Follow Bootham and take the first left beyond the railway line. Longfield Terrace is an extension of Bootham Terrace.

34. Holmlea Guest House, 67 Southlands Road (tel. 621010). See 2.
35. Mont Clare Guest House, 32 Claremont Terrace, Gillygate (tel. 627054). Well located, close to the centre. See 27.
36. Alcuin Lodge, 15 Sycamore Place, Bootham (tel. 632222). See 31.
37. Craig-y-Don, 3 Grosvenor Terrace, Bootham (tel. 637186). See 5.
38. Gleneagles Lodge Guest House, 27 Nunthorpe Avenue (tel. 637000). See 6.
39. The Hollies, 141 Fulford Road (tel. 634279).

SELF-CATERING ACCOMMODATION

Bishophill Holidays, 5 Kyme Street. House sleeping up to six people. High season price from around £170–260 ($255–390) per week. Low season price from around £100–160 ($150–240) per week. The house is about 5 minutes' walk from the train station, off Victor Street, which runs off Nunnery Lane. For bookings contact Mrs L.A. Shimmin, 49 Moorgate, Acomb, York, Y02 4HP (tel. 796118).

Abba House, 42 Hambleton Terrace. House sleeping up to six people. High season rates from £220–260 ($330–390), low season rates from £140–210 ($210–315). Hambleton Terrace is off the Haxby Road, about 10 minutes' walk from the city centre. For bookings contact Mrs A. M. Paterson, 14 Sycamore Terrace, Bootham York, Y03 7DN (tel. 630750).

UNIVERSITY ACCOMMODATION

Fairfax House, University of York, 98 Heslington Road (tel. 432095). Open Mar.–Apr. and July–Sept. Singles from £12–16 ($18–24).

HI HOSTEL

Peter Rowntree Memorial Hostel, Haverford, Water End, Clifton (tel. 653147). Curfew 11.30 p.m. Juniors £8 ($12), seniors £9.50 ($14.25). The hostel is about 1.5km from the train station and the town centre, close to the River Ouse. Water End runs left off Clifton. From the train station head left along Station Road, turn left at Station Rise and then follow Leeman Road to the left past the National Railway Museum. At the end of Kingsland Terrace turn left and follow Salisbury Terrace and then Salisbury Road on to Water End. Turn right and cross over the Ouse to get to the hostel.

HOSTELS

York Youth Hotel, 11—13 Bishophill Senior Road (tel. 625904). Singles £13—17 ($19.50—25.50) doubles £11—15 ($16.50—22.50), dorms £9 ($13.50). About 5 minutes' walk from train station. At the end of Queen Street turn left along Micklegate, then right on to Trinity Lane which leads into Bishophill Senior.

Maxwell's Hotel, 54 Walmgate (tel. 624048). Singles and doubles £12—15 ($18—22.50) per person. From the end of Duncombe Place turn right along High Petergate and go straight ahead until you reach Walmgate.

The New Racecourse Centre. Singles, doubles and dorms. The booking office is at 5 High Petergate (tel. 636553). The accommodation is in the racing stables at Dringhouses on the outskirts of the city.

HI HOSTELS NEARBY

Malton Youth Hostel, Derwent Bank, York Road, Malton (tel. 01653 692077). In a picturesque small town about 32km from York. The hostel is just over 10 minutes' walk from the train station in Malton. Juniors £5.50 ($8.25), seniors £6.80 ($10.20).

Beverley Friary Youth Hostel, The Friary, Friars' Lane, Beverley (tel. 01482 881751). In a historic market town with a beautiful minster, 48km from York. Juniors £5.50 ($8.25), seniors £6.80 ($10.20).

CAMPING

Caravan Club Site, Terry Avenue (tel. 01203 694995). Around £4.50 ($6.75) per person. The only site within the city. In summer, the site is often filled to capacity, so reserve as far ahead as you can. A 10—15-minute walk from the train station. Follow Nunnery Lane and when the road forks go left along Price's Lane. Cross Bishopsgate Street and follow Clemnthorpe down to the River Ouse. The site is along to the right.

Bishopthorpe (tel. 704442). Open Easter—Sept. Around £4 ($6) for one person and tent. Not much more expensive for four sharing a tent as the price per person is low. By the river in Bishopthorpe, 5km out on the A64 towards Tadcaster and Leeds. Bus 14, 15 or 15A.

Post Office Site (tel. 706288). Open Apr.—Oct. Similar price for a solo traveller to the Bishopthorpe site. Also by the river, 1.5km further out on the A64 than the Bishopthorpe site. Any Acaster Malbis bus will get you to the site.

Poplar Farm (tel. 706548). Not far from the Post Office Site. Around £5 ($7.50) per person. Same buses as for the Post Office site. Also the 'Sykes' bus, which runs every two hours from Skeldergate.

Wales (Cymru)

Aberystwyth (tel. code 01970)

TOURIST OFFICE
Tourist Information Centre, Terrace Road (tel. 612125). Open year round. Local accommodation service and Book-A-Bed-Ahead.

GUESTHOUSES AND B&Bs
The greatest concentration of guesthouses and B&Bs are along South Marine Terrace and Rheidol Terrace.

Myrddin, Rheidol Terrace (tel. 612799). Singles and doubles from £12 ($18) per person.

Yr Hafod, South Marine Terrace (tel. 617579). Singles and doubles from £15 ($22.50) per person.

Marine Hotel, The Promenade, has dorm B&B accommodation for £8–18 ($12–27).

HI HOSTEL
The closest HI Hostel is 13km away in Borth, a town linked to Aberystwyth by train and bus.

Borth YH, Morlais (tel. 01970 871498). Juniors £6.20 ($9.30), seniors £7.60 ($11.40).

CAMPING
Midfield Caravan Park (tel. 612542). 1½ miles out on the A4120, high season £4.80 ($7.20).

Betws-y-Coed (tel. code 01690)

TOURIST OFFICE
Tourist Information Centre, Royal Oak Stables (tel. 710426). Open in the summer season only. Local accommodation service and Book-A-Bed-Ahead. Information on the Snowdonia National Park and nearby Swallow Falls. The National Park Information Centre is also recommended.

GUESTHOUSES AND B&Bs
Glan Llugy, Holyhead Road (tel. 710592). Singles from £13 ($19.50), doubles from £24 ($36).
Mount Pleasant, Holyhead Road (tel. 710502). Singles from £13 ($19.50), doubles from £24 ($36).
Bryn Llewely, Holyhead Road (tel. 710601). Singles and doubles from £13 ($19.50) per person.

HI HOSTELS
There is no HI hostel in Betws-y-Coed, but the Capel Curig and Lledr Valley Hostels are only 5 and 9.5km away respectively. A mountain path links these two hostels (8km walk).

Lledr Valley YH, Lledr House, Pont-y-Pant, Dolwyddelan (tel. 01286 870428). Juniors £6 ($9), seniors £7.30 ($11). The hostel is located on the main road linking Betws-y-Coed to Ffestiniog (A470).
Capel Curig YH, Plas Curig, Capel Curig (tel. 710225). Juniors £6 ($9), seniors £7.30 ($11). A supplement of £0.40 ($0.60) is added to these prices in July and August. By the garage in Capel Curig, a village on the main road (A5) between Betws-y-Coed and Bangor.

CAMPING
Riverside Caravan Park (710310). Behind the railway station, £3.50 ($4.75) per person.

Caernarfon (tel. code 01286)

TOURIST OFFICE
Tourist Information Centre, Oriel Pendeitsh, Castle Street (tel. 672232). Open year round, 10 a.m.–5.30 p.m. daily. Local accommodation service and Book-A-Bed-Ahead available.

GUESTHOUSES AND B&Bs
Mrs Hughes, Victoria Road (tel. 76229). Around £13 ($19.50) per person in singles and doubles.

Wallasea Guest House, 21 Segontium Terrace (tel. 3564). Singles from £14 ($21), doubles from £27 ($40.50).

Menai View Hotel, North Road (tel. 4602). Singles from £17 ($25.50), doubles from £27 ($40.50).

Gorffwysfa Private Hotel, St David's Road (tel. 2647). Singles around £17 ($25.50), doubles around £28 ($42).

Tal Menai, Bognor Road (tel. 2160). Singles from £16.50 ($24.75), doubles from £29 ($43.50).

HI HOSTELS
There is no HI hostel in Caernarfon. The Llanberis and Bangor youth hostels are 13 and 19.5km away respectively.

Llanberis YH, Llwyn Celyn (tel. 01286 870280). Juniors £6.40 ($9.60), seniors £7.80 ($11.70). Llanberis is on the A4086 between Caernarfon and Betws-y-Coed. Bus Gwynedd 88 from Caernarfon. The hostel is just outside the village.

Bangor YH, Tan-y-Bryn (tel. 01248 353516). Juniors £6.40 ($9.60), seniors £7.80 ($11.70). Frequent bus services run between Caernarfon and Bangor.

CAMPING
Cadnant Valley Park, Llanberis Road (tel. 3196). Around £5.75 ($8.65) for a solo traveller.

Cardiff (Caerdydd) (tel. code 0222)

TOURIST OFFICE
Tourist Information Centre, 814 Bridge Street (tel. 227281). Open year round 9 a.m.–7 p.m. daily, except in winter, when the office

is closed on Sundays. Local accommodation service and Book-A-Bed-Ahead available. Free guide to the city's sights.

GUESTHOUSES AND B&Bs
The Bed and Breakfast, 2 Shirley Road, Roath (tel. 462843). Singles and doubles from £13 ($19.50) per person.

Y Dderwen Deg, 57 Ninian Road, Roath Park (tel. 481001). Singles and doubles from around £13.50 ($20.25) per person.

Ty Gwyn, 5–7 Dyfrig Street (off Cathedral Road) (tel. 239785). Singles from £14 ($21), doubles from £26 ($39).

Plas-y-Bryn, 93 Fairwater Road, Llandaff (tel. 561717). Singles from £15 ($22.50), doubles from £27 ($40.50).

Austins Hotel, 11 Coldstream Terrace (tel. 377148). Singles from £15 ($22.50), doubles from £28 ($42). Great location, 400m from the castle.

Bon Maison, 39 Plasturron Gardens, Pontcanna (tel. 383660). Singles from £16 ($24), doubles from £28 ($42).

Albany Guest House, 191/193 Albany Road, Roath (tel. 494121). Singles from £17 ($30), doubles from £28 ($42).

HI HOSTEL
Cardiff YH, 2 Wedal Road, Roath Park (tel. 462303). Reception does not open until 3 p.m. Juniors £7.30 ($11), seniors £8.50 ($12.75). About 3km from the city centre, near the Roath Park Lake at the junction of Wedal Road and Lake Road West. Bus 80 or 82 from the centre.

HOSTELS
YWCA, Newport Road (tel. 497379). Women and married couples only. Singles £8.50 ($12.75).

YMCA, The Walk, Roath Park (tel. 489101). Men only.

St David's (Tyddewi) (tel. code 01437)

TOURIST OFFICE
Information on the town, the surrounding area and on accommodation possibilites available from the National Park Information Centre (tel. 720392).

GUESTHOUSES AND B&Bs
The Mount, 66 New Street (tel. 720276). Doubles from £24 ($36).

Ty Olaf, Mount Gardens (tel. 720885). Singles and doubles from
£13 ($19.50) per person.
Y Gorlan, 77 Nun Street (tel. 720037). Singles and doubles from
£13.50 ($20.25) per person.

HI HOSTEL
St David's YH, Llaethdy (tel. 720435). Juniors £4.80 ($8.50),
seniors £6 ($9). Open Mar.–Oct. In July and August a supplement
of £0.75 ($1.15) is added to these prices. About 3km from the town.

Scotland

Edinburgh (Dun Eid Eann)
(tel. code 0131)

TOURIST OFFICES
Edinburgh & Scotland Information Centre, 3 Princes Street (tel.
557 1700). July–Aug. open daily, 8.30 a.m.–9 p.m.; May–June
and Sept. daily, 8.30 a.m.–8 p.m.; April open Mon.–Sat. 9 a.m.–
6 p.m., Sun. 11 a.m.–6 p.m.; Oct.–Mar., Mon.–Sat. 9 a.m.–6 p.m.
Book-A-Bed-Ahead and local accommodation services. £2.50
($3.75) fee for finding rooms in local guesthouses and B&Bs; the
only town in Scotland charging for this service (see **Finding
Accommodation** below). You pay 10% of the bill at the office
as a deposit, and the remaining 90% to the proprietor. Free lists
of local guesthouses and B&Bs, and hostels. The staff will check
the availability of beds in local hostels, but cannot make bookings. Good range of information on the city. Very helpful staff.
Set back off Princes Street, by the Waverly Steps, right above the
Waverley Market shopping centre.
Tourist Information Desk, Edinburgh International Airport (tel. 333
2167). Open Apr.–Oct., Mon.–Sat. 8.30 a.m.–9.30 p.m., Sun.
9.30 a.m.–9.30 p.m.; Nov.–Mar., Mon.–Fri. 9 a.m.–6 p.m., weekends 9 a.m.–5 p.m. Opposite Gate 5 in the main hall.

BASIC DIRECTIONS
All trains to Edinburgh stop at the main Waverley station, just off
Princes Street. With the exception of express services running on

the East Coast line (through Newcastle and Berwick-upon-Tweed) all trains also pass through the Haymarket station, about 2km from the Waverley Station along Princes Street, Shandwick Place and West Maitland Street. To reach the Tourist Office from the Waverley station either go up the Waverley Steps (beginning near platforms 1 and 19) and turn left at the top, or go out of the rear exit used by taxis, turn right up Waverley Bridge towards Princes Street, then right again across the pedestrian concourse. Some long-distance coaches drop passengers on Waverley Bridge, but most use the nearby St Andrew's Square Bus Station. From the bus station, walk out on to the open space of St Andrew's Square, turn left and follow South St Andrew's Street on to Princes Street, at which point the Tourist Office is diagonally left across the street. The shuttle buses which serve the airport run from/to Waverley train station or Waverley Bridge.

FINDING ACCOMMODATION
Despite the fact that the Scottish capital has more guesthouses and B&Bs than any other city in the UK save London, plus a relatively large hostel capacity in peak season, you will toil to find a bed in a hostel or one of the cheaper guesthouses or B&Bs if you arrive without reservations during the annual Edinburgh Festival (a three-week period in August). If you are arriving from another Scottish town at this time it is a good idea to try and fix up one of the cheaper B&Bs in advance using the Book-A-Bed-Ahead service; you pay roughly the same fee as the local Tourist Office charges to find a bed, but will avoid the queues, which can be horrendous. There is a free accommodation service in the Waverley train station (by platforms 1 and 19) but they have a limited supply of rooms, while phoning around on your own during the Festival period can be both soul-destroying and expensive. If you arrive without reservations and find all the affordable accommodations gone, those with railpasses might consider staying in the surrounding counties of East Lothian, Midlothian and West Lothian for your first night, while trying to make a reservation in the city for subsequent nights. Fortunately, the accommodation situation improves dramatically outside the Festival period: even in July it is not too difficult to find one of the cheaper beds, provided you arrive reasonably early in the day. The exception is in the week leading up to one of the Five Nations' rugby internationals (played Jan.–Mar.), when hordes of visiting fans descend on the city. The situation is at its worst when the Welsh are the visitors, as they not only fill up the cheaper accommodation in the capital but in most of the towns within 50km south and east of the city. If you want to look

for guesthouses and B&Bs on your own, particularly good areas to search in are Bruntsfield, and Newington/Mayfield (between the Royal Commonwealth Pool and the Cameron Toll shopping centre). LRT buses running up Lothian Road will take you into Bruntsfield, while those heading up The Bridges will take you into Newington/Mayfield.

TROUBLE SPOTS
If you are staying in Bruntsfield, Newington or Mayfield, the tree-lined park known as the Meadows can be a useful short cut to the centre if you are on foot. The Meadows should, however, be avoided after dark. In recent years there have been a number of rapes here and numerous instances of women being subjected to severe sexual harassment. Unprovoked assaults on men by gangs of youths have also become regrettably common over the last few years.

GUESTHOUSES
Generally open all year. Expect to pay £13–20 ($19.50–30.00) more during the Festival.

Armadillo Guest House, 5 Upper Gilmore Place (tel. 229 4669).
Leamington Guest House, 53 Leamington Terrace (tel. 228 3879). By the Bromfield Hostel.
Lorne Villa Guest House, 9 East Mayfield (tel. 667 7159).
Cree Guest House, 77 Mayfield Road (tel. 667 2524).
Kingsview Guest House, 28 Gilmore Place (tel. 229 8004).
Dargil Guest House, 16 Mayfield Gardens (tel. 667 6177).
Waverley House, 75 Viewforth (tel. 229 8627).
Appleton House, 15 Leamington Terrace (tel. 229 3059). See Leamington Guest House.
Quendale Guest House, 32 Craigmillar Park (tel. 667 3171).
Sharon Guest House, 1 Kilmaurs Terrace (tel. 667 2002).
Sherwood Guest House, 42 Minto Street (tel. 667 1200).
Cafe Royal Guest House, 5 West Register Street (tel. 556 6894). Behind Princes Street.
Averon Guest House, 44 Gilmore Place (tel. 229 9932).
Ardmor Guest House, 74 Pilrig Street (tel. 554 4944). Pilrig Street is off Leith Walk, at the end of Princes Street.
Allan Lodge Guest House, 37 Queens Crescent (tel. 668 2947).
Devon House, 2 Pitville Street (tel. 669 6067).
Dunard Guest House, 16 Hartington Place (tel. 229 6848).
Edinburgh Thistle Guest House, 10 East Hermitage Place (tel. 554 8457).
Hillview Guest House, 92 Dalkeith Road (tel. 667 1523).

Torivane, 1 Morton Street (tel. 669 1648). Open Mar.–Oct.

Balmoral, 32 Pilrig Street (tel. 554 1857).

Glenburn Guest House, 22 Pilrig Street (tel. 554 9841).

Dalwin Lodge Guest House, 75 Mayfield Road (tel. 667 2294).

Glenesk Guest House, 39 Liberton Brae (tel. 664 1529).

Hopetoun Guest House, 15 Mayfield Road (tel. 667 7691).

Joppa Turrets Guest House, 1 Lower Joppa (tel. 669 5906).

Blairhaven Guest House, 5 Eyre Place (tel. 556 3025).

Bruntsfield Guest House, 55 Leamington Terrace (tel. 228 6458).

Falcon Crest, 70 South Trinity Road (tel. 552 5294).

Highfield Guest House, 83 Mayfield Road (tel. 667 8717).

Tankard Guest House, 40 East Claremont Street (tel. 556 4218).

Tiree Guest House, 26 Craigmillar Park (tel. 667 7477).

Valentine Guest House, 19 Gilmore Place (tel. 229 5622).

Arenlee, 9 Eyre Place (tel. 556 2838).

Balquidder Guest House, Pilrig Street (tel. 554 3377).

B&Bs

Most B&Bs are open from May–Sept, unless otherwise stated.
Expect to pay between £12–17 ($18–25.50) per person, more during the Festival

Mrs J. Ferguson, 20 Restalrig Gardens (tel. 661 3762).

Mrs M. Melrose, 26 Dudley Avenue (tel. 554 1915). Open June–Sept.

Sylvia Cranston, 17 McDonald Road (tel. 557 8367).

Catherine Duncan, 68 Willowbrae Avenue (tel. 661 2699). Open Aug.–Sept.

Carol Glover, 13 Lismore Crescent (tel. 661 2699).

Mrs A. Hamilton, 6 Cambridge Gardens (tel. 554 3113).

Mr and Mrs Irvine, 116 Greenbank Crescent (tel. 447 9454).

Mrs H. McKue, 1 Moat St. (tel. 443 8020).

Kathryn H. Robertson, 12 Swanston Avenue (tel. 445 1103).

Rachel G. Argo, 61 Lothian Road (tel. 229 4054).

Angela Burnett, Roxzannah, 11 Bernard Terrace (tel. 667 8933).

Mrs Monica M. Fallon, 5 Cameron Park (tel. 667 3857).

Mrs S. Sadol, Harrist, 33 Straiton Place (tel. 657 3160).

M. A. Urquhart, The Rowans, 34 Liberton Brae (tel. 658 1980).

Mr Lawrence Essien, The Hedges, 19 Hillside Crescent (tel. 558 1481).

Mr J. McConnachie, Ben Aven, 3 Shandon Road (tel. 337 8839).

E. C. Simpson, 17 Crawfurd Road (tel. 667 1191).

Mrs Mary Coutts, Meadowplace House, 1 Meadowplace Road (tel. 334 8459).

Mrs M. Fitzgerald, 10 Lauriston Gardens (tel. 229 3848).
Barbara Mallen, 33 Belgrave Road (tel. 334 5721).
Mrs M. Vance, 21 Murieston Crescent (tel. 337 7108).
J. Ruth Hutchison, 38 Hope Terrace (tel. 447 7627).
Elizabeth F. Smith, 36 Farrer Terrace (tel. 669 1262). Open
  Apr.–Sept.
Mrs R.C. Torrance, 15 Viewforth Terrace (tel. 229 1776).
A.M. Royden, Coigach, 5 Polwarth Grove (tel. 337 9866).
Mrs L. Birnie, 8 Kilmaurs Road (tel. 667 8998).
Mrs E. McTighe, 4 Coinyie House Close (tel. 556 3399).

STUDENT RESIDENCES
Prices in local student residences are expensive, although if there
are any beds which have not been pre-booked by groups, they may
be let out to students with ID for about half the normal price.

Pollock Halls of Residence (University of Edinburgh), 18 Holyrood
  Park Road (tel. 667 1971). Open for four weeks in the period
  Mar.–Apr. and July–early Sept. B&B from £16.90–24 ($25.35–
  36). By the Royal Commonwealth Pool.
Melvin House, 3 Rothesay Terrace (tel. 220 6715). Open year
  round. B&B from £20–23 ($30–34.50). Down Palmerston Place
  from West Maitland Street, then right along Rothesay Place.
Napier Polytechnic, 219 Colington Road (tel. 444 2666). Bed £12
  ($18). Open Easter and July–Sept.
Queen Margaret College, Clerwood Terrace (tel. 317 3000). B&B
  £18 ($27). Open Easter and July–Sept.
Moray House College, Newington Campus, East Suffolk Road (tel.
  668 3377). B&B £15 ($22.50). Open June–Sept.

HI HOSTELS
18 Eglinton Crescent (tel. 337 1120). Curfew 2 a.m. £9.25 ($13.90),
  breakfast included. Best reserved in advance with payment during peak period July–Sept. A 20-minute walk from the Waverley train station but only 5 minutes from the Haymarket station.
  From West Maitland Street, turn down Palmerston Place and
  watch for Eglinton Crescent on your left. Buses 3, 4, 12, 13, 22,
  26, 28, 31, 33 and 34 run along Princes St to Palmerston Place.
7 Bruntsfield Crescent (tel. 447 2994). Curfew 2 a.m. Check in
  from 11.30 a.m. (no earlier). £7 ($10.50). Again book well in
  advance during the peak season. About 30 minutes' walk from
  either train station. Buses 11, 15, 16 and 17 run down Lothian
  Road into Bruntsfield.

HOSTELS

Belford Youth Hostel, 6/8 Douglas Gardens (tel. 225 6209). Within a church, choose between sleeping in the Great Hall or a private room. A lovely new hostel with great facilities. Free bus from train or bus station. Advance booking recommended. Open 24 hours. No rules worth mentioning. £7.50 ($11.25) nightly. Breakfast £1 ($1.50). Laundry available. From Princes Street go to Queensferry Street, bear left to Belford Road. Hostel is at intersection with Douglas Gardens.

High Street Hostel, 8 Blackfriars St. (tel. 557 3984). Open to British students and foreign visitors only. £7.20 ($10.80). Advance bookings are accepted if accompanied by the cost of the first night's stay. Free luggage storage. Turn left down the High Street from the Bridges, then right down Blackfriars Street. From Waverley train station, go out the exit the taxis use, then left up Waverley Bridge. At the mini-roundabout go uphill on Cockburn Street, then turn left down the High Street to the junction with The Bridges. Go straight ahead, then turn right at Blackfriars Street.

Cowgate Tourist Hostel, 112 The Cowgate (tel. 226 2153). Open during the Edinburgh Festival. Singles from £11 ($16.50), doubles from £18 ($27). If you go right down Blackfriars Street (see the High Street Hostel) you arrive in the Cowgate.

Christian Alliance Frances Kinnaird Hostel, 14 Coates Crescent (tel. 225 3608). Open year round. Midnight curfew, extended to 1.30 a.m. at festival time. Women, married couples and children only. Singles from £18 ($27), doubles from £12 ($18) per person. Free luggage storage. A five-minute walk from Haymarket Station, left off West Maitland Street two streets after Palmerston Place. A 15-minute walk from Waverley, or bus 3, 4, 12, 13, 22, 26, 28, 31, 33 or 34 along Princes Street ot Palmerston Place. Walking from the Waverley, Coates Crescent is the right turning off Shandwick Place after Stafford Street.

CAMPING

Muirhouse Caravan Park, Marine Drive, Silverknowes (tel. 312 6874). Open Apr.–Oct. Two sharing a tent pay £6.50 ($9.75). Bus 14. Do not walk through the nearby Muirhouse or Pilton housing schemes: much of Edinburgh's reputation as the heroin and AIDS capital of Europe was built around these areas and unprovoked assaults are common.

Little France Caravan Park, 219 Old Dalkeith Road (the A68) (tel. 666 2326). Two people sharing a tent pay £7 ($10.50). LRT bus 33, 82, or 89 from The Bridges. Open Apr.–Oct.

Mortonhall Park Caravan Park, 38 Mortonhall Gate, Frogston Road

East (tel. 664 1533). Two people sharing a tent pay £8.50 ($12.75). LRT buses 11, 81 or 81B run from Princes St to Mortonhall.

Glasgow (Glas Chu) (tel. code 0141)

TOURIST OFFICES

Tourist Information Centre, 35 St Vincent Place (tel. 204 4400). Open June–Sept., Mon.–Sat. 9 a.m.–9 p.m., Sun. 10 a.m.– 6 p.m.; Easter–May, Mon.–Sat. 9 a.m.–7 p.m., Sun. 10 a.m.– 6 p.m.; Oct.–Easter, Mon.–Sat. 9 a.m.–6 p.m. Free local accommodation service. Lists of local accommodation. Book-A-Bed-Ahead service available. The office is just off George Square, a short walk from both Queen Street train station and the Buchanan Street bus station, and about 10 minutes' walk from Glasgow Central railway station.

Tourist Information Desk, Glasgow Airport (tel. 848 4440).

Free maps are available from the Travel Centre, St Enoch Square (tel. 226 5826).

FINDING ACCOMMODATION

Glasgow has become increasingly popular in recent years, partly due to a vigorous advertising campaign. Unfortunately, the supply of accommodation possibilities has failed to keep pace with the increasing demand, and you are still likely to encounter difficulties in finding a bed during the summer months (August especially). At this time of year, there is little point phoning guesthouses and B&Bs yourself, since the Tourist Information Centre provides an efficient and free room-finding service. Most of the cheaper accommodation is at least 20 minutes' walk from the centre, so you are probably going to have to use local buses or the underground to get to them. Railpass holders can save money if there is a local rail station close to their lodgings: ask the owner or the Tourist Information Centre.

TROUBLE SPOTS

Trouble in the city centre in the immediate aftermath of a football match is not uncommon, particularly at bus and train stations, and in the bars nearby, with sporadic outbreaks of trouble possible at night as well. At the time of writing there is good reason for anyone to be wary of a night out in Glasgow. Since early 1992 there has been a huge upsurge in late night violence both inside and outside the city centre, which is all the more worrying because so many of the serious assaults seem to be totally unprovoked.

GUESTHOUSES AND B&Bs

The prices quoted below are minimum and maximum prices per person for Bed & Breakfast based on two people sharing a room. In a few cases, singles are available at the same price; more commonly, you can expect to pay another £1–2 ($1.50–3). Unless stated otherwise, the establishments below are open all year round.

From £11–13 ($16.50–19.50)

Mrs M. Williamson, 15 Kintillo Drive (tel. 959 1874). Open May–Sept. Off Queen Margaret Drive, near the Botanic Gardens.

Mrs J. Freebairn-Smith, 14 Prospect Avenue (tel. 641 5055). Same price for singles. Off the Glasgow Road in Cambuslang.

Mrs C. McArdle, 171 Mount Annan Drive (tel. 632 0671). Same price for singles. Ten minutes' walk from King's Park train station. Off the Aikenhead Road towards Hampden Park (home of Queen's Park Football Club and the Scottish national team, and occasionally a concert venue).

Browns Guest House, 2 Onslow Drive (tel. 544 6797). In Dennistoun, a short walk from Duke Street.

Mrs M. Prior, 24 Jedburgh Avenue (tel. 647 7970). In Rutherglen.

From £13–15 ($19.50–22.50)

Mrs C. Allan, 25 Stamperland Avenue (tel. 544 2757). Same price for singles.

Linby Guest House, 29 Carmyle Avenue (tel. 763 0684). Same price for singles. In Carmyle.

Mrs E. Anderson, 3 King Edward Road (tel. 954 8033). Open Apr.–Sept. Same price for singles. Near the Gartnavel Royal Hospital. A short walk from Anniesland train station.

Mrs M. Coyle, 18 Arnhall Place (tel. 882 6642). Open Apr.–Sept. Off the Paisley Road West in Cardonald.

Mrs I. Campbell, 12 Regent Park Square (tel. 423 0727). Open Apr.–Sept. No singles. Close to the Pollokshaws Road and the Queen's Park. Short walk from Pollokshields (West) train station.

Mr & Mrs J. Shearer, 2 Avdie Place (tel. 632 0644). Same price for singles. Off Propecthill Road, near Hampden Park.

Symington Guest House, 26 Circus Drive (tel. 556 1431). Close to the centre. In the area to the rear of the cathedral between Duke Street and Alexandra Parade.

Mrs J. Forsyth, 3 Blairbeth Terrace (tel. 634 4399). Open Apr.–Oct. Same price for singles. A few minutes' walk from Burnside train station.

Alamo Guest House, 46 Gray Street (tel. 339 2395). By Kelvingrove Park.

Mrs J. McArthur, 62 Mill Street (tel. 550 0270). Open Apr.–Sept. £14 ($21) for B&B in the owner's one single. By the River Clyde at one end of Glasgow Green.

Mrs D. McEwen, 36 Dorchester Avenue (tel. 339 6076). Open Apr.–Sept. Off the Great Western Road beyond the Botanic Gardens.

Mrs J.T. McLeod, 4 Islay Avenue (tel. 634 4689). Open Apr.–Sept. In Rutherglen.

From £15–17 ($22.50–25.50)

Mrs J. Cunningham, 160 Wedderlea Drive (tel. 882 4384). Off the Paisley Road West in Cardonald.

White Pillars Guest House, 385 Hamilton Road (tel. 773 1170). No singles. In Uddingston.

Mrs M. Hendry, Redtops, 248 Wedderlea Drive (tel. 883 7186). Off the Paisley Road West in Cardonald.

Mr R. Bruce, 24 Greenock Avenue (tel. 637 0608). Singles similarly priced. Off the Clarkston Road.

Mrs M. McAdam, 33 Finlay Drive (tel. 556 1975). In Dennistoun, just off Duke Street.

Mr & Mrs J. Demarco, 5 Erskine Avenue (tel. 427 6205). Open Apr.–Sept. Same price for singles. In Pollokshields.

Mr G. Beattie, 18 Walmer Crescent (tel. 427 5231). Same price for singles. Off the Paisley Road, just before the junction with Emiston Drive. Close to Ibrox Park, home of Rangers, Scotland's most successful football team.

Craigielea House, 35 Westercraigs (tel. 554 3446). Singles similarly priced. Just off Duke Street in Dennistoun.

Craigpark Guest House, 33 Circus Drive (tel. 554 4160). Close to the centre. In the area to the rear of the cathedral between Duke Street and Alexandra Parade.

Mr & Mrs P. Michael, 8 Marlborough Avenue (tel. 334 5651). Open Apr.–Sept. Same price for singles. Off the Crow Road, near the Victoria Park. Just under 10 minutes' walk from Hyndland train station.

McClay's Guest House, 268 Renfrew Street (tel. 332 4796). Behind Sauciehall Street.

STUDENT RESIDENCES
Rooms in local student residences are expensive. The University of Glasgow charges £22 ($33) per person for B&B in singles and doubles, and in summer £10 ($15) per person for bed only. With a few exceptions, similar rates are charged in the University of Strathclyde halls listed below. If you have a student ID it may be worth phoning the halls on arrival to see if any spare rooms might be let at a reduction. The University of Strathclyde halls have the advantage of being located right in the city centre.

University of Strathclyde (tel. 553 4148 – central office).
Baird hall, 460 Sauciehall Street. Open year round. Usual rate for singles, around £17 ($25.50) per person in doubles.
Forbes Hall, Rottenrow East. Open June–Sept. Singles only.
Garnett Hall, Cathedral Street. Open June–Sept. Singles only.
Murray Hall, Collins Street. Open Mar.–Apr. and July–Sept. Singles only.
Clyde Hall, 318 Clyde Street. Open June–Sept. Singles from £22–29 ($33–43.50), usual rate for doubles.
University of Glasgow (tel. 330 5385 – central office). All halls open Mar.–Apr. and July–Sept.
Keith Hall, 10–13 Botanic Crescent (tel. 945 1636). Singles and doubles. By the Botanic Gardens.
Queen Margaret Hall, 55 Bellshaugh Road (tel. 334 2192). Singles and doubles. Off the Great Western Road, by the Botanic Gardens.
Horselethill House, 7 Horselethill Road (tel. 339 9943). Singles and doubles. Off the Great Western Road, near the Botanic Gardens.
Dalrymple Hall, 22 Belhaven Terrace West (tel. 339 5271). Singles and doubles. Off the Great Western Road, near the Botanic Gardens.
Wolfson Hall, Garscube Estate, Maryhill Road (tel. 946 5252). Singles and doubles.
McLay Hall, Woodlands Terrace (tel. 332 5056). Singles, doubles and triples.
Jordanhill College, 76 Southbrae Drive (tel. 950 3320). Bed only £14 ($21). Bus 44.
St Andrew's College, Duntocher Road, Bearsden (tel. 950 3320). Bed only £13 ($19.50).

HI HOSTEL
7/8 Park Terrace (tel. 332 3004). Curfew 2 a.m. Mainly two-, three- and four-bed rooms, with some six- and eight-bed dorms. Around £7.50 ($11.25). Advance reservation advised in summer. By the Kelvingrove Park. At Charing Cross, turn off Sauchiehall Street up Woodlands Terrace (site of the old hostel) then turn left along Lynedoch Street into Park Terrace. Three-night maximum stay, at least in theory.

HOSTELS
Glasgow Central Tourist Hostel, Balmanno Building, 81 Rottenrow East (tel. 552 2401). Open in summer only. Right in the centre of the city.
Brown's Hostel, 1 Woodlands Drive, flat 3/1 (tel. 332 1618). Small capacity. £9.20 ($13.80). Near the Kelvinbridge metro station.

CAMPING
Craigenmuir Caravan Park, Campsie View, Stepps (tel. 779 4159) is the closest site, with tents at £5 ($7.50). Unfortunately it's not accessible by public transport.

Inverness (Inbhir Nis) (tel. code 01463)

TOURIST OFFICE
The Inverness, Loch Ness and Nairn Tourist Board, 23 Church Street, Inverness IV1 1EZ (tel. 234353). Open in summer, Mon.–Sat. 9 a.m.–8.30 p.m., Sun. 9 a.m.–6 p.m.; at other times, the office shuts at 5.30 p.m. Mon.–Fri. and is closed at weekends. Beds in local B&Bs registered with the office are booked free of charge. Book-A-Bed-Ahead service available. Five minutes' walk from the bus and train stations.

FINDING ACCOMMODATION
Throughout most of the year you should have little trouble finding a room in one of the places listed below. The exception is the summer months when finding lodgings is not easy. At this time of year, unless you arrive before the Tourist Office opens, there is not much point in looking on your own. Not only is it difficult to find an unregistered guesthouse or B&B with space, but there is no guarantee that their rooms will be cheaper than those on the Tourist Office book. If you want to look for a room on your own, then

Kenneth Street, Argyle Street and the Old Edinburgh Road are best supplied with relatively cheap lodgings. If your train or bus is scheduled to arrive in Inverness in the late afternoon it is probably wise to have accommodation pre-booked through the Scottish Tourist Board's Book-A-Bed-Ahead scheme, as poor rail services and heavy traffic on the roads can mean your arrival will be a lot later than you planned.

GUESTHOUSES (Tourist Office registered)
Singles and doubles £12–14 ($18–21) per person

Eskdale House, 48 Greig Street (tel. 240933). A 10-minute walk from the stations.

Rozean Guest House, 44 Crown Drive (tel. 239001). A 10-minute walk from the stations. An extension of Crown Road.

Ivanhoe Guest House, 48 Lochalsh Road (tel. 223020). A 10-minute walk from the stations. From Friars Bridge turn right along Abban Street (by the junction with Huntly Place) into Lochalsh Road.

Ardnacoille Guest House, 1a Annfield Road (tel. 233451). A 15-minute walk from the stations. Left off Old Edinburgh Road near the junction with Southside Road.

Singles and doubles £14–15 ($21–22.50) per person

Glen Fruin Guest House, 50 Fairfield Road (tel. 712623). A 10–15-minute walk from the stations.

Heathfield Guest House, 2 Kenneth Street (tel. 230547).

Cedar Villa Guest House, 33 Kenneth Street (tel. 230477). A 10-minute walk from the stations.

Leinster Lodge Guest House, 27 Southside Road (tel. 233311). A 10–15-minute walk from the stations.

Crown Hotel, 19 Ardconnel Street (tel. 231135). A 5–10-minute walk from the stations.

Crownleigh Guest House, 6 Midmills Road (tel. 220316).

B&Bs (Tourist Office registered)
Singles and doubles £10–12 ($15–18) per person

Mrs A. Buchan, 1 Cuthbert Road (tel. 237924). Quite far from the centre, off the Old Perth Road beyond the golf course. For a small fee to cover the petrol the owner will provide you with transport.

Mrs C. McQueen, 80 Telford Road (tel. 240502). A 10-minute walk from the stations. From Friars Bridge turn right along Abban Street (by the junction with Huntly Place) and head straight on until you reach Telford Road.

Mrs A. MacDonald, 31 Clachnaharry Road (tel. 235954). Overlooking the Caledonian Canal, about 20 minutes' walk from the stations. At the end of Friars Bridge turn right along Telford Street and onto Clachnarry Road.

Mrs I. Fraser, 3 Ballifeary Lane (tel. 232028). Singles similarly priced. A 15–20 minute walk from the stations. Cross the Ness Bridge, turn left along the riverside and follow the Ness Walk until you see Ballifeary Lane on the right.

Mrs Zandra MacDonald, 5 Muirfield Gardens (tel. 238114). No singles. A 15–20 minute walk from the stations. Turn left off Culduthel Road at Sunnybank Road and follow the street round into Muirfield Gardens.

Mrs A. MacKinnon, 6 Broadstone Park (tel. 221506). A 10 minute walk from the stations, left off the Kingsmills Road.

Mrs Boynton, 12 Annfield Road (tel. 233188). No singles. A 15-minute walk from the stations, left off the Old Edinburgh Road by the junction with Southside Road.

Mrs MacCuish, 5 Drumblair Crescent (tel. 231104). No singles. Well out from the centre, a 20–25-minute walk from the stations. Off the B862 to Dores. From the foot of Bridge Street turn left along Castle Road, and continue straight ahead along Haugh Road and Island Bank Road until you see Drumblair Crescent to the left off Dores Road.

Mrs MacCuish, 50 Argyle Street (tel. 235150). A 10-minute walk from the stations.

Mrs M. Green, 64 Telford Street (tel. 235780). A 10–15-minute walk from the stations, left at the end of Friars Bridge.

Mr Eric MacFall, 10a Ballifeary Road (tel. 234363). About 15 minutes' walk from the stations. Cross the Ness Bridge, turn left along the riverside and follow the Ness Walk. Turn right up Bishop's Road, then left at Ballifeary Road.

Mr L. P. Cook, 9 Fairfield Road (tel. 232058). A 10-minute walk from the stations.

Mrs F. Thompson, 4 Glenurqhart Road (tel. 221660). About 15 minutes' walk from the stations. The street is a continuation of Tomnahurich Street.

Mrs M. J. Cameron, 9 Aultnaskiach Avenue (tel. 235400). Singles similarly priced. A 15-minute walk from the stations, right off Culduthel Road.

Mrs Mactaggart, 1 Ross Avenue (tel. 236356). No singles. Just over 10 minutes' walk from the stations. The street runs between the Friars Bridge end of Kenneth Street and Fairfield Road.

HI HOSTEL
1 Old Edinburgh Road (tel. 231771). Open year round except 5 Jan.–1 Feb. 2 a.m. curfew. £6.85 ($10.30). Latest check-in 11.30 p.m. Advance booking essential at Easter and during July and August. A 10-minute walk from the stations. Follow Castle Street from the High Street.

HOSTEL
Inverness Student Hotel, 8 Culduthel Road (tel. 224926). Open year round. 2.30 a.m. curfew. £7 ($10.50) per night, without breakfast. B&B £8.20 ($12.30) per night. Telephone reservations not accepted unless made by Edinburgh's High Street Hostel, but phoning ahead will allow you to check out the availability of beds. A ten minute walk from the stations. Follow Castle Street from the High Street.

CAMPING
In summer sites are frequently filled with caravans.

Bught Caravan and Camping Site (tel. 236920). Open Apr.–Oct. Cheap municipal site near the Bught Park and the Ness Islands. From around £3–5.20 ($4.50–7.80) per person. The closest site to the town centre, about 20–25 minutes' walk from the stations off the main road (A22) to Loch Ness and Fort William. Turn left off Glenurqhart road (a continuation of Tomnahurich Street) at Bught Drive. On the Craig Dunain bus route.

Torvean Caravan Park, Glenurqhart Road (tel. 220582). Open Easter–Oct. From £6.50 ($9.75). Only slightly further out than the Bught Caravan and Camping site, on the other side of the Caledonian Canal.

Scaniport Caravan and Camping Site (tel. 0146 375351). Open Easter–Sept. Around £3.50 ($5.25). A small site about 8km out from Inverness, off the B862 to Dores.

Bunchrew Caravan and Camping Park (tel. 237802). £7–8 ($10.50–12) per person. On the shores of the Beauly Firth, 5km along the A862 from Inverness.

Northern Ireland

Belfast (tel. code 01232)

TOURIST OFFICE

Northern Ireland Tourist Board, St Anne's Court, 59 North Street, Belfast BT1 1ND. Head office of the Tourist Board. Very helpful if you want information to help you plan your trip. On arrival, head for their Tourist Information Centre at the same address (tel. 246609). Open June–Sept., Mon.–Fri. 9 a.m.–5.15 p.m., Sat. 9 a.m.–2 p.m.; Oct.–May, closed on Sat. Courteous and knowledgeable staff. Room-finding service £0.50 ($0.75) fee. The office distributes a good map, complete with bus routes, and a pamphlet detailing an enjoyable walking tour of the city. From Central Railway Station go left along East Bridge Street, right at Victoria Street, left along Chichester Street into Donegall Square, then right along Donegall Place and straight on down Royal Avenue into North Street.

FINDING ACCOMMODATION

No matter when you arrive in Belfast you should be able to fix yourself up with suitable accommodation without too much difficulty. The bulk of the accommodation possibilites are about 3km south of the centre, around the Botanic Gardens and the university, along or just off the Lisburn Road and Malone Road. There is also a reasonable supply of B&Bs to the east of the River Lagan, around Belmont Road and Upper Newtonards Road.

PUBLIC TRANSPORT

Although most of the accommodation is out from the centre, regular buses run all over the city. Most buses depart from Donegall Square, or from the streets off the square. To get to the area around the Botanic Gardens and the university take bus 69, 71, 84 or 85 from the City Hall on Donegall Square. Bus 16 runs along Upper Newtonards Road, while Belmont Road is served by buses 20, 22 and 23. Those with a railpass staying around the Botanic Gardens area can save on bus fares by taking a train to the Botanic Rail Station or the City Hospital station. The Adelaide, Balmoral and Finaghy stations may be useful if you are staying around Lisburn Road and Malone Road.

TROUBLE SPOTS

Do not be deterred from visiting Northern Ireland because of fears about your safety. Tourists have nothing to worry about, either in or outside the capital, provided they are sensible. A bonus is that the incidence of petty crime is actually considerably lower than in mainland Britain. Another plus point is that there are few places in the United Kingdom where visitors are as warmly received by the local people as in Belfast. For obvious reasons, you should avoid talking about politics, religion and Irish history. Young males from mainland Britain should make sure they cannot be mistaken for off-duty soldiers if they are planning to travel around a bit (avoid really short haircuts and shave irregularly is the advice many soldiers give).

GUESTHOUSES AND B&Bs

Prices quoted below are for a double room with breakfast. Singles generally cost slightly more than half the price of a double room. Dundonald is easily reached by bus: the telephone code is 0247.

Around £25 ($37.50)

East Sheen House, 81 Eglantine Avenue (tel. 667149). Singles half the price of doubles. The street runs between the Lisburn Road and Malone Road, near the start of the latter.
Mrs J Dornan, 385 Comber Road (tel. 873240). In Dundonald.
Innisfail, 16 The Green (tel. 610044). Singles half the price of doubles.
Marine House, 30 Eglantine Avenue (tel. 666828).

Around £28 ($42)

The Eagles, 131 Upper Newtonards Road (tel. 673607). Singles half the price of doubles.
Marantha, 398 Ravenhill Road (tel. 645814). Singles half the price of doubles. Buses 78 and 79 run along Ravenhill Road.
James House, 55 Oakland Avenue (tel. 650374). East of the Lagan.
Lucy's Lodge, 72 Salisbury Avenue (tel. 776036). Singles half the price of doubles.
Aisling House, 7 Taunton Avenue (tel. 771529). Off the Antrim Road. Buses 2 and 45 run along the Antrim Road.
Mrs E. MacNamara, 7 Fortwilliam Park (tel. 779904). Off the Antrim Road, see Aisling House.

Around £30 ($45)

Dun-Roamin, 170 Upper Newtonards Road (tel. 659902).
Beaumont Lodge, 237 Stanmills Road (tel. 667965).
Eglantine Guest House, 21 Eglantine Avenue (tel. 660769).
Ben Eadan Cottage, 9 Thorburn Road (tel. 777764). Off the Antrim
    Road. See Aisling House.
Bowdens, 17 Sandford Avenue (tel. 652213). Singles half the price
    of doubles.
Drumragh, 647 Antrim Road (tel. 773063). See Aisling House.
The George, 9 Eglantine Avenue (tel. 683212). Singles half the
    price of doubles. See East Sheen House.
Harberton Lodge, 1 Harberton Avenue (tel. 666263). Singles half
    the price of doubles. University/Malone Road area.
Liserin Guest House, 17 Eglantine Avenue (tel. 660769). See East
    Sheen House.
Helga Lodge, 7 Cromwell Road (tel. 324820). Off Botanic Avenue,
    near the Botanic Rail Station. Bus 83 or 85 from Donegall Square.

Around £32 ($48)

Botanic Lodge Guest House, 87 Botanic Avenue (tel. 327682/
    247439). See Helga Lodge.
Pearl Court House, 11 Malone Road (tel. 666145). Singles half the
    price of doubles.
Crecora, 114 Upper Newtonards Road (tel. 658257). Singles half
    the price of doubles.
Somerton Guest House, 22 Lansdowne Road (tel. 370717).
The Cottage, 377 Comber Road (tel. 878189). In Dundonald.

STUDENT RESIDENCES
Queen's Elms, Queen's University, 78 Malone Road (tel. 381608).
    Open mid-June–mid-Sept. No curfew. £13.50 ($20.25) per
    person in singles or doubles. Student discount of around 20%
    on these prices. Bus 71 from Donegall Square East. The closest
    rail station is Adelaide.
Ulster People's College, 30 Adelaide Park (tel. 665161/381368).
    Open year round. £13 ($19.50) per person in singles or doubles.
    Close to the Queen's Elms residence above. Adelaide Park runs
    between Malone Road and Lisburn Road.

HI HOSTEL
Belfast International Youth Hostel, 'Ardmore', 11 Saintfield Road
(tel. 647865). Closes for a couple of weeks around the Christmas/

New Year period. Open all day during the summer. July and Aug.: £8.50 ($12.75) for seniors. Around £7.50 ($11.25) at other times. About 3km from the centre on the Newcastle road. From the City Hall on Donegall Square East take bus 38 or 84 and ask the driver to stop at the hostel. A new hostel will be operating in Belfast in 1994. Contact the Youth Hostel of Northern Ireland or the Tourist Information Centre for details, or consult the HI handbook.

HOSTELS
YWCA, Queen Mary's Hall, 70 Fitzwilliam Street (tel. 240439). Singles £13.50 ($20.25), doubles £25 ($37.50). Fitzwilliam Street runs between the Lisburn Road and University Road, joining the latter opposite the university. The hostel is just off Lisburn Road. Bus 59 runs along the Lisburn Road. The closest rail station is City Hospital, just over 5 minutes' walk away.

YWCA, Wellesley House, 3/5 Malone Road (tel. 668347). Singles £13.50 ($20.25), doubles £24 ($36). Close to the other YWCA hostel. Take bus 71 from Donegall Square East.

YMCA Interpoint, 12 Wellington Place (tel. 327231). Bus/walk to Belfast City Hall, about 500 metres further on.

CAMPING
Belvoir Forest. The closest site to the city, 5km from the centre off the A504. The site is operated by the Forest Service. A permit is required to use all Forest Service sites. A casual permit is valid for anything between two days and two weeks. Annual permits are also sold. Forest Service, Dundonald House (Room 34), Belfast BT4 3SB (tel. 650111 ext. 456).

'YUGOSLAVIA'

At the time of writing, the war in former Yugoslavia showed no sign of abating. The Foreign Office advises strongly against visiting the area at this time. This chapter does not deal with Slovenia and Croatia, discussed elsewhere, but with Serbia, Macedonia and Bosnia-Hercegovina. The information below has not been updated since peacetime, and in a sense is purely academic. Given the time it has taken neighbouring Croatia to recover from the war, it is likely to be several years before there is a suitable network of accommodation to make possible any kind of budget travel. If you do go, proceed with extreme caution. This guide is not intended to encourage travel to the region.

ADDRESSES

Yugoslav YHA	Ferijalni savez Jugoslavije, Mose Pijade 12/V, 11000 Beograd (tel. 011 339802).
International Youth Centres	Yugotours-Narom, Dure Dakoviċa 31, 11000 Beograd (tel. 011 764622).
Youth hostels, travel, and International Youth Travel	Accommodation Centre, FSJ/FSH, Trg žrtava fasizma 13, 41000 Zagreb (tel. 041 415038).
	International Information Centre, FS Srbija, Mladost-turist-Beograd, Terazije 3, Beograd (tel. 011 322131).
Camping	Maps and lists of organizations booking private rooms are available from the National Tourist Office in London or your capital city.

INDEX